INNOCENCE ABROAD

The Dutch Imagination and the New World, 1570–1670

Innocence Abroad explores the process of encounter that took place between the Netherlands and the New World in the sixteenth and seventeenth centuries. The "discovery" of America coincided with the foundation of the Dutch Republic, a correspondence of much significance for the Netherlands. From the opening of their revolt against Habsburg Spain through the climax of their Golden Age, the Dutch looked to America – in political pamphlets and patriotic histories, epic poetry and allegorical prints, landscape painting and decorative maps – for a means of articulating a new national identity. This book demonstrates how the image of America that was fashioned in the Netherlands, and especially the twin themes of "innocence" and "tyranny," became integrally associated in Dutch minds with evolving political, moral, and economic agendas. It investigates the energetic Dutch response to the New World while examining, more generally, the operation of geographic discourse and colonial ideology within the culture of the Dutch Golden Age.

Benjamin Schmidt is Assistant Professor of History at the University of Washington. He has received fellowships from the National Endowment for the Humanities and the Woodrow Wilson Foundation. His many publications on early modern European cultural history and Atlantic world history include recent articles in the *Renaissance Quarterly* and *William and Mary Quarterly*.

INNOCENCE ABROAD

THE DUTCH IMAGINATION AND
THE NEW WORLD, 1570–1670

BENJAMIN SCHMIDT

University of Washington

CAMBRIDGE
UNIVERSITY PRESS

PUBLISHED BY THE PRESS SYNDICATE OF THE UNIVERSITY OF CAMBRIDGE
The Pitt Building, Trumpington Street, Cambridge, United Kingdom

CAMBRIDGE UNIVERSITY PRESS
The Edinburgh Building, Cambridge CB2 2RU, UK
40 West 20th Street, New York, NY 10011-4211, USA
10 Stamford Road, Oakleigh, Melbourne 3207, Australia
Ruiz de Alarcón 13, 28014 Madrid, Spain
Dock House, The Waterfront, Cape Town 8001, South Africa

http://www.cambridge.org

© Benjamin Schmidt 2001

First published 2001
Reprinted 2004

Printed in the United States of America

Typeface Palatino 10/12 pt.   *System* QuarkXPress 4.04 [AG]

A catalog record for this book is available from the British Library

Library of Congress Cataloging in Publication data is available

ISBN 0 521 80408 6 hardback

For Louise with love

Contents

List of Illustrations

Acknowledgments

I T is a pleasure to acknowledge the many friends, colleagues, and institutions who have supported this project over the years. I have been, from the start, fortunate in my mentors. This book began under the tutelage of Simon Schama, who, on a brisk walk through Harvard Yard, first introduced me to the term "cultural geography" and then later encouraged me to think about and write about Dutch culture as broadly and energetically as possible. I had the good luck in Holland to fall under the expert guidance of Henk van Nierop, who served as my unofficial supervisor during a delightful research year in Amsterdam. I have taxed Professor van Nierop's immense knowledge of Dutch history more than I care to admit; he has provided – as mentor, colleague, and friend – more generosity than I can ever hope to repay. Anthony Pagden has provided plentiful ideas and support, too, throughout the course of my research. He has been a remarkably rich spring of intellectual sustenance and a steady font of assistance from the start – a stimulating graduate seminar he conducted on European ideas of the Other – to the finish. I am very grateful, also, for the encouragement and sage advice – on matters Hispanic, geographic, and otherwise – of Richard Kagan, who, with characteristic energy and good humor, reviewed the manuscript and stimulated its author in the final stages of production.

Numerous others have read the manuscript over the years of its making, either in small part or in its entirety, in chapter or in article form. For reading it *twice* – and offering excellent criticism in both instances – special thanks go to Wim Klooster. Also in line for thanks are Bernard Bailyn, Natalie Zemon Davis, Jorge Cañizares Esguerra, Margot Finn, Wayne Franits, Richard Helgerson, Hugh Honour, Olwen Hufton, Thomas Da-Costa Kaufmann, Mark Kishlansky, Craig Koslofsky, Karen Kupperman, Peter Mason, William O'Reilly, Judith Pollmann, Katrin Schultheiss, Patricia Seed, Stuart Semmel, and Scott Smith. During my many visits to the Netherlands, Dutch colleagues have given freely of their time, offering assistance on matters small and large, and I would like to take this opportunity to acknowledge the advice, references, and other courtesies tendered by Pieter Biesboer, Karel Bostoen, Rolf Bremmer, Roger Diederen, Florike Egmond, Roelof van Gelder, Paul Hoftijzer, Daniel Horst, Paul Knevel, Ger Luijten, Nicolette Mout, Gert Oostindie, Herman Roodenburg, Mieke Smits-Veldt, Marijke Spies, and Kees Zandvliet.

Library and archive staff in the Netherlands have likewise demonstrated graciousness (and patience) beyond the call of duty, and I thank the librarians and archivists at the Koninklijke Bibliotheek and the Rijksarchief in The Hague, the Gemeentearchief in Amsterdam, the Rijksprentenkabinet in Amsterdam, the Koninklijk Instituut voor Taal-Land-en Volkenkunde in Leiden, the rare book (and map) collection of the Rijksuniversiteit Leiden, and, most especially, the Rare Book Department (ZKW) of the Universiteitsbibiliotheek Amsterdam, which supported this publication both through access to its remarkable collection and through the liberality of its capable keepers (who very generously waived reproduction fees for many materials).

Many other research institutions, both at home and abroad, have facilitated my research. Thanks go to the staffs of the Widener and Houghton Libraries of Harvard University; the John Carter Brown Library of Brown University (and the library's very resourceful director, Norman Fiering); the Folger Library in Washington, D.C.; the Sir Thomas Browne Institute of the University of Leiden; the Atlantic History Seminar of Harvard University (and its energetic organizer, Bernard Bailyn); the Department of History at the Johns Hopkins University, which invited me to present my research in the context of a superb Mellon–Sawyer seminar on "National Cultures"; the Newberry Library in Chicago, where I spent a most enjoyable year revising the manuscript for final publication (with particular gratitude to Jim Grossman, Jim Ackerman, and Hjordis Halvorson); and, last but certainly not least, the Department of History, my colleagues, and my very supportive chair, Robert Stacey, at the University of Washington.

I am grateful for the financial support that I have received from the National Endowment of the Humanities, the Woodrow Wilson Foundation, the H. F. Guggenheim Foundation, and the Fulbright Cultural Exchange program. Smaller grants from the Gladys Krieble Delmas Foundation, the Mellon Foundation, the Committee on Degrees in History and Literature of Harvard University, and the Keller Fund of the University of Washington permitted me to pursue and gather source materials that proved instrumental for the publication of this book. On that note: I wish to thank the production staff at Cambridge University

Press and acknowledge the editorial support of Frank Smith and Alia Winters.

The most expert advice and editorial assistance came from a source closer to home, and I feel obligated to declare that all errors of fact, all mistakes of analysis, and all infelicitous phrasings go against the better judgment of Louise Townsend, who has read and reread this manuscript with unlimited patience and oceans of good will. It is a feat of great innocence, surely, to imagine that this book's dedication can ever repay her.

Cultural Geography in an Age of Encounter

From the vantage point of Godefridus Udemans, the New World turned out not to be so new after all. "It has been inhabited in fact since ancient times," pronounced Udemans (1580–1649), a prolific and sometimes pugnacious *predikant* who peered out onto the world from his pulpit in the Zeeland town of Zierikzee, "as is apparent from its cities, villages, splendid dwellings, manner of governance, incalculable multitude of peoples, and so forth." Socially, politically, and culturally more impressive than often allowed, America had been erroneously tagged as "new" – and Udemans took the word to have pejorative implications – owing only to the ignorance of certain geographers, who had plainly, and perhaps even willfully, misled their readers.[1]

Udemans had substantially more to say on the Indies (his preferred nomenclature) and their configuration, topics he explored in his expansive meditation on godliness and commerce in the Dutch Republic, *'t Geestelyck roer van 't coopmans schip* (The spiritual rudder of the merchant's ship). The *dominee* doubted, to begin with, America's putative "discovery" – how could one discover something so long in existence? – and he contested Castile's claims to colonial authority in the West. Would the Spanish crown have tolerated an Indian claim to Castile, he wondered, if the natives of America had landed in Iberia before the soldiers of Spain had reached the Indies? More fiercely still, Udemans challenged Castile's assertion of undertaking a "civilizing" mission in the Indies, articulating for his readers an utterly contrary conception of "civility," "savagery," and the Habsburg mission abroad. While Spanish observers briskly dismissed American culture as "barbarous," Udemans found much to admire in the orderly polities, thriving market towns, subtle craftsmanship, and "civic virtues" (*burgerlijcke deughden*) of the Indians. As for savagery, the Castilian colonizers far outstripped their American subjects. Udemans decried, in no uncertain terms, the "demonic cruelty," "gruesome depravity," "horrific perfidy," and

xvii

"cursed avarice" of the conquistadors, qualities he expected his readers to recognize – a point made repeatedly in the volume – from their experience of Spanish rule in the Netherlands. Indeed, the Dutch shared a special kinship with the Americans, both "nations" having suffered the yoke of Spanish tyranny; and Udemans encouraged all efforts to support the Americans, most particularly those of the Dutch West India Company (WIC), lately established "with the intent not to conquer [the Indies], but rather to protect the poor Indians from Spanish violence, and perhaps also to trade with them."[2]

Bourgeois virtue among Indian allies in a less-than-new world? Tempting though it may be to impute such geographic musings to the peculiarly baroque imagination of a provincial Calvinist preacher, Godefridus Udemans's notions of the Indies are not at all unique. They derive from a distinctly Dutch conception of the New World, and they indicate a broader pattern of cultural geography that flourished, as did Udemans, from the earliest years of the Republic through the pinnacle of its Golden Age. The *stadhouder*, Willem of Orange, wrote movingly in his foundational *Apologie* of the "poor Indians" of America; the architects of the WIC proposed a strategic alliance with the same; and Joost van den Vondel, the leading poet of the land, composed stinging verse against the "tyranny" of Castile, perpetrated in the New World and the Netherlands alike. The image of America and its natives, as promoted by Udemans and his compatriots, suggests the powerful purposes of geography in the Dutch Republic and, by extension, the fascinating process of assimilating new worlds in early modern Europe. The significance of America, as perceived in the Netherlands, was carefully considered, contested, and calibrated from the earliest years of the sixteenth century – well before our recent debates on "discovery," "encounter," and "impact" in the Renaissance, and predating even the Enlightenment polemics on the topic, from which our own scholarly deliberations are said to derive. Indeed, from his perch in provincial Zierikzee, Udemans demonstrated a most savvy understanding of colonial discourse.

This is a study of cultural geography in early modern Europe: of the manner in which other places and peoples were imagined, appropriated, and manipulated in a period of "encounter." It takes as its subject the Dutch representation of the New World during the formative first century of the Republic, circa 1570–1670, exploring the process of geographic assimilation in conjunction with those political, economic, and cultural developments that guided it. It examines how the idea of America first entered the Dutch imagination, how it evolved into a staple of political rhetoric, and how it ultimately came to influence an extraordinary range of concerns, both at home and abroad. From the earliest years of their revolt against the Habsburgs, the Dutch formulated an image of rapacious Spanish "tyranny" in America committed at the expense of "innocent" natives. With enormous polemical energy, the rebels exploited this image to blacken the reputation of Habsburg Spain. With still greater geographic ingenuity, their heirs extrapolated from it a projected "alliance" with the Indians – Udemans's sense of "kinship" – to create a moral basis for overseas commerce. The twin topoi of American innocence and Spanish tyranny appear time and again in Dutch discourse of the period – in rebel propaganda and colonial polemics no less than patriotic history and moralizing letters – and attest to the profound interest of the Dutch in new worlds. Indeed, the very novelty and plasticity of the New World perfectly suited the purposes and polemics of the Republic. It enabled the Dutch to fashion a version of America that matched the rhetorical imperative of the day: to produce a usable geography that addressed the evolving needs of the Republic. This book investigates the energetic Dutch response to the New World while examining, more generally, the operation of geographic discourse and colonial ideology within the culture of the Dutch Golden Age.

The broader study of early modern Europe's encounter with America has failed, in many ways, to account for the likes of Udemans. There is, most basically, a nearly complete lack of attention to the case of the Netherlands, a surprising state of affairs given the obvious economic, cultural, and political prominence of the Dutch Republic from the late sixteenth through mid-seventeenth centuries.[3] It might be easy enough to justify this lacuna by pointing to the relatively meager Dutch presence *in* America: modest settlements in New Netherland (1624–1664) and Brazil (1630–1654) were indeed quick to collapse. Yet, much as the Republic may have lost the colonial contest in the New World, it did triumph in its colonial struggles in the Old, winning independence from Habsburg Spain in the Eighty Years' War (1568–1648) and emerging from that conflict as one of the leading powers of post-Westphalia Europe. More essentially, the Dutch won the contest of *representing* a New World whose encounter was experienced, for the most part, as a textual affair. For the early modern Dutch possessed an empire of print second to none in Europe; the presses of Antwerp, Amsterdam, and Leiden produced a stream of histories, broadsides, and geographies that served as a crucial conduit between the New World and the Old. And these Dutch representations, in their many and varied and often multilingual forms, have only rarely received the notice they deserve.

Such neglect reflects the somewhat uneven shape of encounter studies, which, though admirably attentive to the consequences of Europe's "invasion" of America, have tended to diminish the effects of America's reception back in Europe.[4] The term of choice here is "impact" and the signal thesis that of John Elliott, who argued, in a pioneering and provocative essay, that the New World had an "uncertain" or at best "blunted" impact on the Old. Elliott, that is, proposed a narrative of indifference. The discovery of new worlds only marginally influenced European politics, society, and culture; works of history, geography, and theology failed to grapple with the new continents and failed to comprehend what Elliott has called "the American reality." What notions early modern observers may have contrived of a New World proved "fragile" and ultimately ineffectual, as most Europeans evinced "little interest in or concern for the new worlds overseas."[5] Yet Udemans's own engagement with America, from the relative backwater of Zierikzee, indicates far deeper inroads made by American discourse than the "minimalist" thesis allows. It also implies a more complex and nuanced process of cultural encounter, and suggests the usefulness of focusing less on *whether* Europeans responded to the New World than on how, why, and to what ends they did so. The energetic and creative pattern of Dutch reception complicates the contention of widespread European indifference, pointing rather to the active and engaged enterprise, in the Old World surely no less than the New, of constructing cultural geography. The Dutch devised an image of America that, "real" or not, proved highly effective and ultimately influential in the production of political and colonial ideology.[6]

Europe's encounter with the New World was a necessarily diverse process (far more so than the designation "Europe" can possibly convey), and it is a goal of this study to contextualize a single, and in many ways singular, chapter of a larger early modern narrative.[7] When *dominee* Udemans extolled the *burgerlijcke* manners of the Indians, and when a defiant Willem exposed the "tyranny" of their oppressors, each articulated a distinctly Dutch idea of America, expressed in the idiosyncratically Dutch vocabulary of political rhetoric. The global pronouncements of both men betrayed the provincial accent of the Republic. Neither's version of America would have enjoyed much currency outside of the Netherlands, and it is worth emphasizing that *all* early modern encounters with America would have been distinctive. Yet the Dutch case may have been especially so – or at least especially so perceived and so promoted – since the Republic uniquely shared with America the formative experience of Spanish imperial tyranny. This, of course, was an exaggeration: inhabitants of Granada and Moriscos across Spain may have had something to say on the issue, as might subject populations in Milan, Naples, and Sicily, where Spanish dominion also prevailed. Yet it was an exaggeration that worked and one that encouraged a strikingly sympathetic rendering of the Indian and an extraordinarily ambitious rhetoric of "alliance." It placed the Dutch response to the New World, moreover, on a wholly different trajectory than elsewhere in Europe. Thus, whereas Willem of Orange could console the Indians, who shared with him firsthand knowledge of the "barbarousness" of Spain, James VI of Scotland (later James I) had only haughty disdain for the "incivility" of the Americans. "Lett us abhorre the beastlie Indians whose unworthie particulars made the way patent of their miserable subjectioun and slaverie to the Spaniard," wrote the future king of England and ally of Castile, who by this time (1596) nurtured imperial ambitions of his own.[8]

The cultural geographers of the Netherlands – perhaps uniquely, certainly imaginatively, and unquestionably vigorously – fashioned themselves colonial subjects of Spain who had been made to suffer, like the natives of the New World, the unbearable yoke of Habsburg imperial rule. This would have remarkable implications both for the early reception of America and for the eventual strategy for America promoted within the Republic. For Udemans was hardly alone in anticipating a "natural" and "easy" alliance with those presumptive brothers-in-arms of the Dutch, the Indians. The original advocates of the Dutch West India Company likewise seized upon the rhetoric of "Spanish tyranny" to bolster their American project, predicating an ambitious colonial program on assumptions of an expansive colonial partnership with the put-upon American. They gazed upon the New World not as colonizers but rather as the colonized.[9]

Might the Dutch case, then, with its shifts from anti-imperial rhetoric to procommercial imperative, be understood within the context of colonial discourse? With a few adjustments to the standard conception of "colonial," there is certainly some sense in situating the early modern Dutch experience within the (post)colonial paradigm.[10] By converting the Habsburg elite (often drawn from Dutch ranks) into "Spanish overlords" and by portraying the army of Flanders (teeming with local mercenaries) as "Spanish wardogs," the rebels masterfully generated a "colonial" antagonist where only a centralizing bureaucracy had existed. Their expansion-minded successors neatly segued from anti-Spanish propaganda to a pro-American literature that appropriated the well-worn tropes of "innocence" and "tyranny" abroad. This move partly resembles what the critic Partha Chatterjee has termed a "moment of maneuver" – popular elements of an anticolonial struggle are mobilized for another, in this case, overseas enterprise ("capitalism" is largely irrelevant here) – though with significant and extenuating complications.[11] The role of the subaltern, for starters, is ambiguous. In the first instance, the "Dutch" themselves fill the role, since it is they who must endure Habsburg persecution. In the second, it is the Americans of the Dutch imagination, who would dissolve into a heap of sand no sooner did Dutch emissaries land on New World shores to present their terms of alliance (an actual scenario described in Chapter Four). Furthermore, the colonial "contact zone" construed by the Dutch – to invoke Mary Louise Pratt's critical lexicon – was wholly chimerical; no "transculturation" took place for the half century (1566–1621) between the rebels' rhetorical appeal to Indian "innocence" and the WIC's bona fide contact with Indian merchandise. The colonial discourse spun in the Netherlands was solely for domestic consumption.[12]

Here is an important distinction and one that calls attention to the subtleties – to the possibilities – of cultural geography in an age of encounter. The Dutch responded effusively to the New World, and this project focuses principally on the copious Dutch representations of "America" rather than the limited engagements *in* America or with Indians as such.[13] It charts the development of a colonial discourse, to be sure, though one that requires substantial modifications to the concept of "colonial" and the putative "orientalist" (or occidentalist, as the case may be) agenda of such a discourse. It is not that American rhetoric was without effect, and it is one of the chief contentions of this study that rhetoric in the early modern Netherlands was not merely reflective of culture, but also effective – that the brand of polemical discourse that so thrived in the Republic had a causal role in the policies of the Republic. In the case of "American" rhetoric, however, this role pertained first and foremost to domestic affairs: to debates on revolt, to topoi of resistance, and to conceptions of fatherland history, which, in the Dutch case, habitually invoked the sister narrative of America's *Conquista*. It pertained, secondly, to proposals for expansion and initiatives for partnership in the West, yet these were quick to peter out; and, in the end, Dutch constructions of the Indies played a limited role when it actually came time to "settle with the Indians."[14] The Dutch discourse on America, finally, was never one of "empire" (let alone "conquest") but always of "alliance." It projected an image not of a savage Other, but of a sympathetic partner and potential brother-in-arms, generously drawn, widely endorsed, and earnestly solicited to partake in the campaign against Habsburg's "universal monarchy." Cultural geographers in the Netherlands endeavored to domesticate, not exoticize, the natives of America.

Attention to the New World in the Netherlands, in truth, had less to do with matters overseas than matters at home. From the earliest moments of their conflict with the Habsburgs, Dutch representations of America became implicated in a project of "nation-ness" – Benedict Anderson's term, inelegant though it may be, makes better sense in the context of early modern Europe than does "nationalism"[15] – descriptions of the new and very remote world of America relating to articulations of the new and very radical character of the Revolt and subsequent foundation of the Republic. When one Dutch editor praised the love of *patria* among "Chileans" who had fought a decades-long war against Spain (he had in mind, vaguely, the Araucanians), and when another bemoaned the "forfeiture of liberties that the blameless, innocent Americans have unjustly suffered," both expressed through a New World idiom a narrative that was in fact Dutch. In the eyes of both, America's history – real or not – reflected Dutch struggles, Dutch deprivations, Dutch foundational mythologies. Imagined geographies helped in this way to establish the "imagined community" of the nascent Dutch Republic. In describing the innocent suffering and valiant resistance of the Indians, the Dutch, naturally, were describing themselves.[16]

Why America? This had to do with global contingencies of time and space – history and geography – that Udemans, once again, so keenly understood. "It should be noted that the discovery of these lands," he wrote of America, "was revealed to our nation at the very moment that God Almighty struck down the whore of Babylon." Or more prosaically: "The Reformation in Europe and the Discovery of the Indies occurred at the same time."[17] To many in the godly Republic, the arrival of Protestantism announced both spiritual renewal and political revolt; sacred and patriotic history were intimately linked. To Udemans's readers, these affiliations spanned oceans as well; the coincidence of the Revolt and the Discovery was no accident. That both events centrally involved that which Udemans branded "the empire of the Antichrist" – Habsburg Spain – only made this coincidence more compelling and further distinguished the Dutch response to the New World. For, while other Europeans, Protestant or Catholic, might have read the narrative of Discovery as a sacred text, only the Dutch could import patriotic meaning to their exegesis. The Indians and Dutch shared a mutual enemy, and, if there was an "Other" in the Republic's geography, it was the Spaniard. The Dutch used Spain – Spanish tyranny, Spanish avarice, Spanish darkness – to define America, which, in turn, became a key component in the exercise of defining the Dutch.[18]

This is a project, then, of understanding encounter and understanding Dutchness. "Just who, exactly, did the Dutch think they were?" asked Simon Schama, provocatively, in his interrogation of the culture of the Golden Age. More simply, who were "the Dutch"?[19] Discussions of the Dutch in this book refer to an early modern community that was outstandingly urban, phenomenally literate, and substantially less provincial than the word *burgerlijcke* might imply. They were the architects of the dazzling political, economic, and cultural expansion that took place in the northern provinces of the Netherlands beginning in the late sixteenth and climaxing in the mid-seventeenth century and producing what one historian has felicitously labeled "the New World of the Dutch Republic." Not all took part in this expansion, of course, just as not all followed the rebel party in a conflict – the Dutch Revolt – that is now regarded more as a civil war than an epic struggle against foreign "tyrants."[20] Those who did, however, and especially those in the wealthy cities of the powerful maritime provinces of the Republic, were exceptionally outspoken on the matter of their communal identity. The Dutch were those who articulated their Dutchness in the remarkable outpouring of histories and poetry, broadsides and ballads, atlases and almanacs, paintings and prints, produced over the course of the Golden Age. They did so, too, in a very expansive conception of geography – this is meant in the broadest sense of representations of the world – and they did so, notably, in their unhesitant, unambiguous, and enthusiastic embrace of the New World.

To discover the New World in the Netherlands, this study ranges widely, eclectically, and sometimes serendipitously across sources, genres, and decades, gathering evidence from all manner of description and representation of America. Writing at the opening of the seventeenth century, when the prospect of peace with the Habsburgs loomed ever more likely, a certain "lover of the Fatherland" published a pamphlet in Holland admonishing his countrymen never to abdicate their freedoms, for the enemy aimed "to exterminate your mother tongue" and enforce the use of Castilian, "as has been done in fact with the Indians, who are compelled to speak Spanish."[21] This, happily, never came to pass. Quite the contrary and to the delight of all freedom-loving patriots, the early modern Dutch issued a profusion of words and images and other cultural artifacts that expressed, in their own particular idiom, their opinion of Spain, its vast empire, and especially the Indies. These materials form the basis of this book. The sweep of this project is purposefully broad, covering a wide array of texts and genres, stopping to read some more closely though naturally not all alike. The story constructed from these materials, however, traces its subject along fairly direct narrative lines, progressing from the initial sightings of America in the early sixteenth century to the Republic's colonial debates in the final decades of the seventeenth century.

The original reports and chronicles of the New World available in the Netherlands comprise the sources for Chapter One, which examines the reception of early Americana under the Habsburg regime. In part an overview of sources available to the Dutch in the period preceding the Revolt (those materials that would form the building blocks of later ideas of America), this chapter also provides a case study of the process of European assimilation in the wake of the voyages of discovery. Over the first two-thirds of the sixteenth century, patterns of publication in the Low Countries reveal habits of reading that inclined, at first, indiscriminately toward a broad range of romances of conquest, and, with time, toward narratives more plainly critical of the Spanish conquerors. Rather than indifference, one detects increasing discernment in the Dutch selection of Americana for import and translation. Together with the literary sources, this chapter also considers the remarkable *West Indies Landscape* of Jan Mostaert – done in the first half of the sixteenth century, it is considered the first European painting of its kind – which is viewed from three varying perspectives: the scant testimony of Mostaert's contemporaries; the voluminous opinions of modern scholars; and the more compelling commentary of Karel van Mander, the late-sixteenth-century poet and painter who perceived in the lyrical landscape a subtle critique of the conquest of America.

By the eve of the Revolt, the Dutch had read, in fact, quite extensively on America, yet written only sparingly and circumspectly about the overseas empire of their Habsburg overlords. All of that changed abruptly in 1566, when a group of nobles challenged the Spanish king's government, citing the "abuses in the Indies" to bolster their case. Rebel pamphleteers seized upon this allusion to "tyranny in America," warning shrilly of the Habsburg intent to colonize the Netherlands as they had the New World. In the subsequent war of words against Spain, references to "cruelties in America" and "atrocities against the Indians" become ubiquitous in Dutch polemics. Chapter Two analyzes how these topoi emerged, proliferated, and became codified in Dutch rhetoric of 1570–1600. It demonstrates, on the one hand, how political events in the Netherlands shaped perceptions of "tyranny" in America; and, on the other, how the literature on America, and especially the *Brevíssima relación* of Bartolomé de Las Casas, affected representations of Habsburg "tyranny" in the Netherlands. In anatomizing the rebels' polemical corpus, this chapter also traces the origins of the Black Legend and identifies the long-overlooked contribution of the Dutch to this crucial chapter of European propaganda.

How the rebels' conception of America framed the Republic's policy *for* America forms the subject of the third and fourth chapters. In conjunction with the image of Spain's tyranny developed one of America's innocence and a contention that their mutual sufferings somehow allied the Indians and the Dutch. The earliest Dutch colonialists, and especially the indefatigable Willem Usselincx, made much of this presumed kinship and the Republic's implied responsibility to assist their American "brethren." The Dutch West India Company, traditionally viewed as the product of hard-line Calvinist politics nurtured by hard-nosed expansionist economics, had its roots in fact in the ideological soil of the late sixteenth century and the rebels' idea of America. Usselincx's campaign for an American enterprise underscored the moral obligation of the Republic to "free" the Indians and grant them their "natural liberties" – by which he meant both freedom of conscience and freedom of trade. The promotional literature for the WIC reveals a deep ambivalence among pamphleteers who appealed simultaneously to readers' moral sensibilities – the Company's mission to "save" the Indians – and to their financial self-interest – the Company's hope to *exploit* the Indians. That this incongruous rhetoric could be taken seriously is shown by a series of policy initiatives – an official solicitation to the "Lords of Peru" to billet Dutch "liberators," for example – that counted on the eager assistance of American allies. In the end, however, the idealistic view gave way to a more practical discourse of profits. The New World's gold took precedence over the Indians' souls. When Admiral Piet Heyn intercepted the Spanish silver fleet in 1628, Dutch poets celebrated his daring feat by casting it as a "romantic" intrigue. He had stolen the king of Spain's beautiful mistress (America) and "ravished her with piety." America's age of innocence had surely passed.

The middle decades of the seventeenth century, reviewed in the fifth and final chapter, witnessed the high and low points of the Dutch New World adventure. Finally ensconced *in* America, the WIC enjoyed successes in Brazil and New Netherland, where settlements prospered through the 1630s and 1640s. By the 1660s, however, Dutch Brazil had fallen to the Portuguese, New Netherland had succumbed to the English, and the WIC found itself irreparably mired in debt. "America" during this period could still symbolize for some a brave new world of innocence, incorruptibility, or even epic heroism. Yet, at the other end of the spectrum, it came to represent for many precisely the decadence and "tyranny" of appetite so central in the minds of Dutch moralizers and *predikanten*. Contemporary religious sermons and didactic poetry drew on the imagery of the New World to expound on the forever compelling themes of innocence and sin. The godly, to be sure, still cited America as a final outpost of pure and "natural" living, neither so corrupt nor so compromised as that closer to home. Yet, whereas the innocent Indian

"ally" of the late sixteenth century was meant to expose the barbaric
Spaniard for what he was, the noble savage of the mid-seventeenth century was meant to rebuke the decadent Dutch who, as the *predikanten*
would have it, had fallen into an abyss of wantonness, decadence, and
moral decrepitude. From here it was only a matter of time until the root
of this corruption would be located in America, or at least its exports:
gold, sugar, tobacco, and syphilis, to name the most poisonous. "America," in this paradigm, possessed the power to corrupt, and, to the fire
and brimstone preachers, none appeared more corrupt than those
Dutch *in* America. The pamphlet literature on Dutch activities in America (ca. 1640–1660) tells a horrific tale of Dutch tyrannies against the Portuguese in Brazil, of WIC economic warfare against competitors in New
Netherland, and of Dutch savageries against the Indians all over. This
chapter concludes with the original Dutch pirate literature and demonstrates how these narratives pit rapacious French and English "buccaneers" against native Americans and by now "innocent" Spanish settlers. (These works date from the 1660s and 1670s, when Dutch relations
with England and France had reached their nadir and those with Spain
were on the mend.) Innocence and tyranny had become finally and ironically inverted; for the Dutch, too, could now be counted among the
tyrants, and the Spanish, even, among the innocents of America.

An analysis of geography within its cultural, political, and economic
contexts, this project ends as it begins: at a watershed in the history of
the Netherlands. The starting date of circa 1570 delineates the foundation of the Dutch Republic and the creation of a new geography to serve
evolving political and ideological circumstances. The closing date of
circa 1670 marks the loss of New Netherland and the bankruptcy of the
WIC, as well as the collapse of the Dutch government itself in the face
of overwhelming pressure from English, French, and Orangist enemies.
In between these moments of transition unfolds a story of geographic
imagination set against the background of prolonged war against Spain,
naval conflict with England, and dramatic expansion and later contraction of economic might. Whether or not the Republic's Golden Age terminated abruptly in the final decades of the seventeenth century, the
perception of decline most certainly set in following the convulsions of
the 1670s, and this engendered a final, signal shift in geographic sensibilities. The twilight of the Republic's Golden Age (considered in the
Epilogue) saw a retreat in terms of Dutch polemics on America and an
abandonment of the topoi of tyranny and innocence. The geographers
of the Netherlands did not so much diminish their representations of the
New World, however, as shift to images less peculiarly "Dutch" – images, that is, less specific to the political and economic circumstances of

the Republic and more broadly accessible to a wider European audience. At the end of the seventeenth century, Dutch representations of America appeared more plainly exotic.

The theme of exoticism, it may be noticed, does not play a particularly central role in Dutch representations of America. Rather than exoticizing the New World, the Dutch expended a great deal of energy domesticating it; rather than perceiving the Indians as strange, the Dutch did their best to see them as familiar – as "brethren" and "allies." All of which is not to say that the Dutch contemplated the New World without a sense of distancing wonder. The cultural geographers of the Republic, however, managed to ground the lofty disposition of wonder in the more earthly domain of state and society. In a sense, this book affords precisely an interrogation of Dutch geographic wonder, though one that reveals the distinctly local orientation of that disposition.[22] It examines how politics were reflected in geography and how geography in the early modern Netherlands was also refracted through politics, economics, and culture. It details how the Republic projected an image of innocence onto America and how it integrated distant lands into domestic debates. Wonder and imagination were put to the service of patriotic polemics. The encounter with the New World granted the Republic a precious opportunity for self-exploration and even self-definition. America shaped Dutchness. And more broadly: geographic discourse in the early modern Netherlands, even when it related to the most exotic of locales, reflected decidedly provincial concerns.

A Note on Nomenclature

In a project concerned chiefly with language and geography, care has been taken to distinguish among peoples and places. "The Netherlands" is meant to designate the whole of the United Provinces (for the period after the Revolt), while "Holland" refers specifically to the individual province of that name. That said, it should be added that, first, many of the sources themselves speak of Holland in the same breath as "the Fatherland," "Batavia," or "the nation." Second, most of the materials for this study were in fact published in Holland, where the Republic's Golden Age was centered. Third, if indeed an author from another province wished to contribute to discussions on the New World, he (and it almost invariably was a *he*) did so on terms set by Amsterdam, Leiden, or The Hague. The "Dutch image of America" may in fact represent the vision of Holland as opposed to that of Overijssel, yet the same can be said more generally for many other aspects of Dutch culture. In discussions of the overseas colonies of the Republic, the designation "New Holland" refers specifically to the Dutch colony in Brazil, "New Netherland" refers to the primary Dutch possessions in North America, and "New Amsterdam" refers to the Dutch settlement on the lower tip of Manhattan. Note also that the term "New World" – much out of favor today, although no less Eurocentric than "America" or "Western Hemisphere" – has been used, as it appears in the sources, to refer generally to America. "Indian" and "American" refer throughout this book to what the Dutch broadly imagined to be a coherent native population in America. (Specific tribal names are employed when appropriate.) Finally, the term "America" itself refers to both the northern and southern continents, between which no fast distinction was made in the early modern period.

CHAPTER 1

The Dutch Discovery of America

To begin at *a* beginning – a speculative and retrospective, yet singular and imaginative beginning all the same, articulated in both word and powerful image: "There is . . . a landscape, essentially a West Indies landscape, with many naked people, a jagged cliff, and a strange construction of houses and huts." So wrote Karel van Mander, the doyen of sixteenth-century Netherlandish art and a leading man of letters in the Republic, upon his encounter with the impressively grand *West Indies Landscape*, the very first painting of America by a European artist. Those who wished to judge for themselves could do so by visiting the town of Haarlem, where the panel decorated the residence of the *schout* (sheriff), Nicolaes Suyker, a grandson of the artist, Jan Mostaert. The latter would have encountered the New World sometime in the early years of the century and well before the Dutch ever ventured west: perhaps during his service in Mechelen as court painter for the regent Margaretha, perhaps during his European travels as a member of the Habsburg entourage, or perhaps even in his native Haarlem, where Mostaert began and ended his illustrious career.[1]

And what did America look like from the vantage point of Haarlem in the opening decades of the sixteenth century? Jan Mostaert's remarkable *West Indies Landscape* (fig. 1) offers a vista in certain ways provocative, though in other ways not: America appears less obviously exotic or familiar than it does familiarly exotic. A vast panoramic landscape, the painting shares certain compositional conventions with the work of the Northern Mannerists of the 1520s and 1530s, yet it also exhibits elements that distinguish it from virtually all other landscapes of its day and indicate an extraordinary painterly consideration of its exceptional subject. It illustrates, as van Mander sagely observed, "essentially" a West Indies landscape. Occupying the immediate foreground of the panel is a scene of bucolic tranquillity in which familiar European farm animals – cows, sheep, hare – graze peacefully on gently rolling

1

Figure 1. Jan Mostaert, *West Indies Landscape*, ca. 1520–30 (86 × 152 cm). Haarlem, Frans Halsmuseum.

hills of russet-colored pasture. On either side of the fields, land gives way to water: to a calm blue sea on the right and a pale, meandering river on the left that snakes back into a sylvan passage of green and, further, to a slate alpine range that recedes, like the sea, into the distant horizon. A bright, if brooding, sky with billowing clouds caps this view of the natural world: sky, sea, stream, forest, meadow, and mountain as seen by a Northern European mind's eye. Despite the prevailing sense of pastoral calm that fills the panel's peripheries, however, a disturbing scene of violent confrontation lies at the heart of the painting and sets a significantly different agenda. A host of steel-clad soldiers marches into the center of the composition (from the right), met by an advancing parade of naked, and apparently agitated, men. This second group is armed with simple farm tools and crude weapons of wood and stone – a sharp contrast to the foreboding array of cannons, muskets, and pikes borne by the phalanx of soldiers. A primitive hut in the center borders on an imposing and curious configuration of cliff-dwellings – "strange" is the adjective used by van Mander – beneath which rages a battle between the naked and armored troops. Caught in the crossfire, as it were, and at the narrative focus of the panel is an isolated pair of women (also naked), one clutching an infant and child, the other gesticulating desperately as she flees the scene of imminent bloodshed (fig. 1a).

Figure 1a. Detail of figure 1.

Figure 1b. Detail of figure 1.

Closer inspection reveals further curiosities. A monkey sits on a withered stump in the foreground, oblivious to the turmoil behind it; and a parrot, the bird most widely associated with the New World, perches on a similarly wizened trunk. Together, they lend a distinctly foreign flavor to the otherwise familiar fauna. Among the corpus of "natives," two bearded men wear distinctive, fur-lined caps, headware commonly associated with Asian costume; while another figure (just behind them and in this case beardless) sports a laurel wreath of suggestively classical dimensions (fig. 1b). Two other men, running among the scattered village "huts," blow on a pair of medieval-looking horns, as they call their countrymen to arms. Behind them and trailing off in the center looms a prominent geological arch of a sort that, like the "jagged cliff," would seem utterly out of place in a Northern European landscape.

Place, however, may be beside the point. Or rather, the setting of America may be necessarily indeterminate at this early, if vivid, moment of geographic imagining, and Mostaert's construction well illustrates how disparate themes and settings comprised an as yet inchoate New World. The landscape itself, stripped of the central narrative, conveys a keen appreciation for the natural world in all its configurations and topographical variety. The prevailing mood is one of peaceful pastoralism, which, with its warm earthen tones and lyrical arcadian motifs, might have fit a Dutch burgher's notion of rural repose. The painting resembles, in this regard, the popular *Weltlandschaften* produced by the Flemish Mannerists, such as Joachim Patinir and his followers.[2] In quite another way, though, the central scene of soldiers and "naked people" would seem to allude to the meeting of Spaniards and native Americans sometime during the early course of the *Conquista*. The simplicity of the village, the rudimentary straw huts, the absence of clothing, and the very fabric of the natives' resistance – sticks and stones to chase away cannon-fortified pikesmen – recall a social state of innocence as conceived by the Renaissance, a prelapsarian golden age disturbed by men of iron. (And the lithe athleticism of the natives suggests the artist's gesture toward humanist taste for classicism.) A "world-landscape" perhaps, Mostaert's painting also conveys a worldly message of certain relevance to the Habsburg Netherlands. Finally, the curious wildlife, the fantastic rock formations, and the dash of extra-European costume lend the composition an air of exoticism. Yet, since these references seem oddly incongruous – an Asian hat, an American bird, and a more than likely African simian – the effect appears less convincing than gloriously chaotic. So, too, with the ancient wreath, the medieval horns, and the quintessentially early modern assortment of farm animals, the combination of which might seem otherwise incoherent.[3]

"All coherence gone," wrote John Donne many years later of his own encounter with America, and, in reading an earlier rendition of the same, coherence may not prove the most helpful criterion. Throughout the sixteenth and well into the seventeenth century, the New World remained just that: "new." Its very novelty, as well as its remoteness, sanctioned a certain elasticity, or even experimentation, in its representation. Rather than any single, broadly accepted picture of the New World, a number of "Americas" would compete for viewers' attention over the duration of its early reception. European authors and artists continually recast America to reflect not only the latest reports and discoveries, but also the latest tastes and trends. America could conform to literary styles or iconographic conventions; it could suit aesthetic preferences or patrons' demands; it could reflect political programs or historical traditions. America, naturally, could mean many things to many people and different things at different moments. New worlds assimilated in Renaissance Europe rarely came in tidy packages.

The Dutch, like the rest of Europe, fashioned America out of disparate fabrics and followed changing styles. In different stages and according to evolving sensibilities, the idea of America entered the literary, artistic, scholarly, and – only later – political discourse of the Netherlands, and all this well before any serious Dutch involvement *in* the New World. The Mostaert work brings together in a single panel many of the themes and conceptions of the New World prevalent in the Netherlands by the mid-sixteenth century: the marvel at the wonders of the natural world, the fascination with the exoticism of the unknown world, the predilection for the arcadianism of the ancient world, the concern with the expansionism of the Spanish world. It presents neither a fully coherent, nor an ultimately conclusive, view of "America," but something fundamentally more complex. The *West Indies Landscape* offers a pastiche of Netherlandish notions of the New World as they developed over the course of the sixteenth century, a suggestive pattern of assimilation rather than a singular paradigm of perception. It records, most particularly, a painter's process of discovery. And it testifies, more generally, to the powerful possibilities of America as they appeared in that pregnant period between the Spanish voyages of exploration and the ultimate discovery by the Dutch of the relevance those events could have to the Netherlands.

I

The New World came to the Netherlands long before the Netherlands ever went to the New World. In a dazzling variety of texts – travel accounts and historical narratives, learned cosmographies and political pamphlets, decorative maps and epic poetry, popular prints and painted landscapes – the Dutch read about, gazed upon, or otherwise contemplated the "wondrous" novelty of the *mundus novus*. In the course of doing so, they embarked upon a process of discovery that permitted them, much like Jan Mostaert, to sift through and sort out the various versions of America. Early Americana circulated widely in the Low Countries, a region in many ways superbly situated to receive reports from abroad; and the Dutch process of reception turned out to be a rich one. It was extensive as well, stretching from the late fifteenth through the later sixteenth century, when a steady stream of texts conveyed the New World to the Netherlands. During this critical time and from their privileged place, the Dutch could freely investigate and interrogate the meaning of America, though the purpose of these textual explorations would only slowly become apparent.

News of the New World arrived in the Netherlands notably quickly and in abundance. Like the rest of Europe, the Low Countries first learned of America from the carefully crafted public letters and reports issued in the wake of the discoveries, some translated into Dutch, others into French, and many in Latin, the lingua franca of scholarly circles in the North. From the start, the New World found a broad and exceptionally receptive audience among readers of the Netherlands, who avidly consumed the earliest Americana. "These islands [recently discovered] are wondrous to describe," wrote a leading Dutch humanist in the opening years of the sixteenth century, "but there are already books written on them," and, in his opinion, the plethora of print rendered further comment unnecessary.[4] Those books would have included editions of Columbus and Vespucci, which appeared in Antwerp within months of their original publication. Other works of the first generation of conquistadors and chroniclers soon followed. The letters of Hernán Cortés to Charles V, López de Gómara's chronicle of Mexico, and Cieza de León's description of Peru all came off the presses of the Low Countries virtually simultaneously with their publication in Spain. The narratives of Agustín de Zárate (Peru) and Hans Staden (Brazil) went through more editions in Dutch than any other language, including those of their original composition.[5] All these and more filled the libraries of the Netherlands in impressive proportions. Well over half of the oldest private libraries in the (in this case Northern) Netherlands included books on America within their collections. Americana, moreover, featured twice as frequently in these collections as did works on Asia – a striking contrast to the oft-cited case of France, where four times as many books focused on Asia than on America in the period 1480–1609. In the textual mix of the Netherlands, the New World did make a splash.[6]

That printed accounts of foreign discoveries fell on fertile ground in the Netherlands should come as no surprise. Antwerp, the printing center of Northern Europe and home to a highly literate community of cosmopolitan merchants and Habsburg civil servants, was ideally suited to convey the latest tidings from America. More generally, the social, economic, and cultural development of the Netherlands on the eve of the Discoveries positioned it perfectly to assimilate the latest news from abroad. America played to the cities; and, in the late fifteenth century, the northwest corner of Europe, together with the northern strip of Italy, comprised the most urban and populous region in Christendom. In some provinces of the Low Countries (Holland is a prime example), nearly half of the population lived in cities, and those who remained in the densely packed countryside found themselves at most a short distance from an urban center. Sizable cities (over ten thousand inhabitants) proliferated: more than twenty at the turn of the sixteenth century, thirty by the turn of the seventeenth.[7]

Such outstanding levels of urbanization translated into equally impressive levels of urbanity. The burghers of the Low Countries made their money through trade, and their commerce in merchandise invariably encouraged a lively commerce in ideas and information – including news of the western "enterprise." By the early sixteenth century, the Netherlands lay at the economic center of an international Habsburg empire. The traffic of imperial goods brought the Dutch into regular contact with navigators from the Iberian peninsula, their financial backers from the emperor's German-speaking lands, and now the East and West Indies. Merchants from across Europe, moreover, worked and lived in the Netherlands and particularly in Antwerp, which developed during this period into a thriving and cosmopolitan metropolis. The city's population more than doubled in the decades spanning Columbus's voyages and Pizarro's conquests.[8] By the middle of the sixteenth century, some one thousand foreign merchants resided in Antwerp, the majority of whom came from Spain, Portugal, and Italy – those countries, in other words, most intimately involved in early exploration. Antwerp emerged in these years "not only [as] the first and principal commercial city of all Europe," as the city fathers proudly put it, "but also the source, origin and storehouse of all goods, riches and merchandise, and a refuge and nurse of all arts, sciences, nations and virtues": civic boosterism, to be sure, though not entirely off the mark. The growing population, the international community of merchants, and – not least – the emporium of exotic products all contributed to the city's considerable savvy concerning matters abroad. "Antwerp was like a world," wrote one contemporary, dazzled by the city's multinationalism; "one could lie there concealed without ever going outside it."[9]

One could lie there and read of other worlds, too, since the Netherlands during this period also enjoyed prominence as a center of the book trade, a purveyor of products about, no less than from, distant lands. Movable type came relatively early to the Low Countries and spread rapidly to nearly every province. Dutch printed books date from 1473, and by 1500 over twenty presses had been in operation. During the postincunabula period, it is Antwerp, once again, that stands out. Between 1500 and 1540 – the crucial decades for early Americana – at least sixty-six printers (about half the Netherlands' total) plied their trade there and published well over two thousand titles – in Dutch no less than Latin, French, Spanish, and English. And books found readers in similarly impressive proportions. Literacy rates in sixteenth-century Antwerp ran as high as fifty percent (among men), which matches the level for Amsterdam in the early seventeenth century.[10] "They all have some smackering of their Grammer [sic], and every one, yea every husbandman can write and read," wrote the Florentine historian, Lodovico Guicciardini, of antebellum Antwerp. He and others marveled further at the "infinite number" among the Dutch who possessed fluency in French, and the many more who were capable in Spanish, Italian, English, and German. Publishers of Americana prospered easily in this culture of polyglot readers and international traders.[11]

And what did the Dutch, "husbandmen" or otherwise, read? Print culture – or what has more aptly been termed "typographic culture" in the wide-ranging context of Dutch literary, graphic, and cartographic printing – thrived in the Netherlands, and this too contributed to the warm reception of early accounts of the Indies.[12] Devotional literature, in the Low Countries as elsewhere in Europe, topped most publishers' lists – the difference being that more readers in the Netherlands, where the *Devotio Moderna* movement and its emphasis on reading and Scripture had taken strong hold, may have been able to read it. Humanist literature also did well, building on the solid foundations of Burgundian, and later Habsburg, literary patronage and the Dutch tradition of classical education at the grammar school level. The influence of Erasmus encouraged the development of belle lettres from the early sixteenth century, as did the foundation of the Collegium Trilingue (1517) in Leuven, where Dirk Martens ran one of the most admired presses of Northern Europe. (Martens would publish among the first editions of Columbus's *Epistola* in 1493.) Cornelius Aurelius, a humanist-minded monk of Gouda, collaborated on one of the earliest printed maps to feature America (1514). And Aurelius's colleague, Erasmus, also acknowledged the Columbian voyages, which he cited typically as a "foolish passion," the outcomes of which could only encourage the legions of Folly.[13]

Along with devotional and humanistic literature, the Dutch also consumed a considerable quantity of vernacular texts that often fall under the rubric of "urban" or "bourgeois" (*burgerlijk*) literature. This literature – sometimes homegrown, though just as commonly annexed from other, nonbourgeois literatures – flourished in the civic culture peculiar to the late medieval Netherlands, where it appealed to the broad and urbane middle-classes, especially of citified Flanders, Brabant, and Holland.[14] Marco Polo's description of the Great Khan's domains fits into this category, as do other medieval travel narratives, whose success adumbrates the enthusiastic reception later accorded to Renaissance narratives of new worlds. Polo's account of the East, with its valuable trade information and useful travel instructions, enjoyed particular popularity among Dutch readers, first in manuscript form and later in printed editions. It was in fact an Antwerp edition from circa 1485 that Polo's Genoese successor, Christopher Columbus, read and carefully annotated in preparation for his own historic voyage; and Polo's account continued to be read and admired in the Netherlands well into the sixteenth century. So too did a full menu of late medieval travel literature: a mid-fourteenth-century anthology of geographic writings, the *Livre des merveilles*, which conveyed readers alluringly to the East; the late fourteenth-century *Itinerarius* of Jan Voet, describing an Utrecht priest's journey to the Holy Land and the *curiositas* that lay beyond; the *Voyage* of Master Joos van Ghistele, which follows a Ghent patrician, on the very eve of the Columbian expedition, to the Levant and North Africa; and that most popular of vernacular texts – for which the *Livre des merveilles* may have served as a source and on which the *Itinerarius* and *Voyage* almost certainly were modeled – the *Travels* of John Mandeville.[15]

The spectacular success in the Netherlands of "Jan van Mandevil" suggests both the breadth of "bourgeois" literature and the limited usefulness of that category. The utterly sensational narratives of that dubious Christian knight (and suspect overseas traveler) would hardly seem the stuff of sober merchants preoccupied with commerce. The numerous surviving manuscripts of the *Travels* attest, rather, to readers' delight in the magnificent realms, fabulous landscapes, and (not least) vivid naturalism of the late medieval imagination. The still more numerous *printed* editions – sixteen by the close of the seventeenth century – indicate that, even during the age of expansion, Dutch interest in the marvelous exotica "discovered" by Mandeville scarcely flagged.[16] They highlight a predilection in the Netherlands for the transporting *ridder-roman* – roughly "romance of chivalry" (Mandeville was a knight, after all), a notably inclusive genre that counts among the most popular of the first century of Dutch printing – and the taste of traders for pleasurable, no less than practical, prose. They hint as well, though, at an inherently moralizing component of *burgerlijk* literature in general and geographic prose in particular, since, much though Mandeville would convey his readers to the most distant of wonders, he asked that they bear with his sermonizing all along the way. As would presbyter Jan and master Joos in the coming years, Sir John designed his narrative to be both delightful and didactic. He offered Dutch readers a pleasant journey with a pointed message – *lering en vermaak* in the vernacular – using the boisterous genre of travel literature to get at the discomfiting failings of Christendom: *ridendo dicere verum* (to tell the truth with a smile) in more Erasmian phrasing. That Mandeville and his fellow wayfarers became so conspicuous in the Netherlands by the turn of the sixteenth century suggests, finally, that a strong textual basis had been set for later Dutch encounters with distant worlds.[17]

Increasingly, too, sources other than Mandeville and Polo offered the pleasure of the exotic between the bounds of a book. In the Low Countries as elsewhere, the discovery of the New World coincided with the recovery of the ancient world – and the consequent expansion of Europe's intellectual world in newly published forms. From the west came the explorers' reports of exotic *naturalia* and unknown lands, while from the south – Italy – came humanists' editions of the ethnographic and geographic wisdom of antiquity. From the Netherlands itself came new editions of classical texts and fresh experimentation with rediscovered genres, such as the bucolic eclogue, a pastoral form whose development had been fostered, presumably, by the relentlessly crowded cities of the Low Countries. By the opening of the sixteenth century, in all events, Mandeville's monsters competed not only with Polo's treasures, but with Plinean races and Ovidian fables, Virgilian landscapes and Herodotean histories. Texts ancient, medieval, and now "modern" all converged to create a collage of new worlds, each more tantalizing than the next.[18]

The impending encounter with America would be, in its earliest years at least, a textual affair, and the Dutch were certainly well placed to participate in the ensuing process of textual reconnaissance. On the eve of the Columbian voyages, the Low Countries could be counted among the most urban, cosmopolitan, and literate regions of Europe. The Dutch – naturally not all, though an impressive number all the same – could obtain and read a variety of books (sometimes in multiple languages), which circulated in a vibrant typographic culture. The burghers of the Netherlands had ample reason to read energetically as well: to seek what commercial advantage, geographic knowledge, spiritual guidance, and, most basically, exotic entertainment that late medieval literature had to offer. Still, if the Dutch read perhaps more vigorously than others, there is scant indication that they would read the earliest Americana any more discriminatingly: many readers meant many audiences. And while a peculiarly Dutch pattern of description would develop later in the century, this is hardly the case at the start, when readers in the Low Countries as elsewhere delighted in the marvelous and monstrous, the pastoral and pious motifs of the late medieval imagination. Early Americana in the Netherlands joined a rich stew of texts – though a stew of yet indeterminate flavor.

II

Word of the New World reached the Netherlands promptly in 1493.[19] The electrifying *Epistola* of Columbus provided readers of the Low Countries with their first glimpse of the wondrous harbors, rivers, and hamlets, the enchanting pine groves, pastures, and mountains, and the "marvelously timorous" natives of the West Indies. To the mystically inclined Columbus and, undoubtedly, many of his readers, the New World's pastoral idyll evoked images of the elusive earthly paradise. To city-dwelling Netherlanders, the mellifluous singing of nightingales and "other birds of a thousand kinds" must have resonated with particular charm, echoing as it did the naturalism that featured so prominently in late medieval Dutch literature. Other readers had other agendas. Antwerp's merchant community followed the discovery of this Genoese rival in the employ of their Iberian clients with conspicuous concern; the city's traders hoped themselves to fulfill the Columbian enterprise, so that "all of Europe shines with silver and gold." Meanwhile, more spiritually inclined readers detected the more heavenly profits to be made in bringing the Gospel to the heathens, those miraculously unknowing and hitherto unknown souls. The marvelous mingled easily, too, with the monstrous. Despite Columbus's contention that "in these islands I have so far found no human monstrosities, as many expected," reports of man-eating Caribs would have persuaded many otherwise. Certainly some of the American novelties approximated the more familiar Asian exotica described in medieval geographies, and the fantastic landscapes of the latter could not have been far from Dutch readers' minds. One of the many Dutch editions of "Jan van Mandevil" came out in 1494, ending up presumably in some of the very libraries of readers of Columbus's account.[20]

In 1494, in truth, America may not have quite fully arrived in the Netherlands. Columbus's description of the "new" Indies – or rather the published form that description quickly took – approximated in many

ways versions of the "old" Indies widely available in late medieval letters. The *Epistola,* that is to say, fell into tropes of narration and habits of
representation that derived, quite naturally, from earlier literary models. In their earliest printed form, the Columbian texts stressed continu-
ities as much as novelties, as they insinuated themselves into preexist-
ing contexts of geographic description – which *inter alia* might be said
of many other first generation Americana. To project a more fully "new"
world required emphasizing more effectively perhaps certain aspects of
the older models, while articulating more forthrightly – in choice of language, use of rhetoric, strategy of presentation – the salient distinctions
of the discoveries. It required making the case, as Columbus only re-
luctantly did, for a new paradigm of geography: a New World.[21]

Columbus's reluctance was Vespucci's opportunity. If the *Almirante*
espied "many islands" off the coast of Cathay, the future *piloto mayor*
"discovered a continent . . . new regions and an unknown world." And
more pertinently: if Columbus's narrative left lingering doubts as to the
novelty of the Indies, the Vespuccian texts pronounced far more dramatically and certainly more emphatically the revelation of what had
now been labeled – *titled* even – a new world. In this sense, the *Mundus
novus* and *Lettera* of Vespucci marked the true literary debut of America.
Printed an astonishing sixty times between 1503 and 1529 – more than
twice per year on average over the course of a quarter century, and
nearly three times as frequently as Columbus's *Epistola* – they rank also
among the first international bestsellers of the age of printing. Translated into half a dozen languages (including Dutch, French, and Latin),
they spread the remarkable news of the discoveries from Paris to Pilsen
and from Augsburg to Amsterdam. An Antwerp edition appeared
within a year or so of the Florentine original and brought the Vespucci
phenomenon swiftly to the Low Countries.[22]

There is a conspicuous irony, of course, to the success of this Florentine merchant who so quickly supplanted Columbus as "discoverer" of
the eponymous "America." Since Vespucci's published accounts have
long been considered fraudulent and their nominal author something
of a charlatan – Amerigo arrived in Seville to tend the Medici's money;
what navigating he may have done came only as an afterthought – it has
become an article of faith to dismiss America's namesake as a usurper
(a "fortunate impostor," railed William Robertson) and denounce his account ("crammed with contradictions") as an ironic mistake. "A very
civil and plausible man was this beef contractor," pronounced C. R.
Markham contemptuously, echoing Ralph Waldo Emerson's famous
"false pickledealer" put-down.[23] Yet Amerigo's accolades are in many
ways well deserved and his discoveries no less significant than Colum-

bus's. If his nautical skills paled in comparison with those of the *Almirante,* Vespucci's rhetorical skills – his talent for articulate expression and his gift for literary self-fashioning – easily outshone his rival's. As a publicist in particular, he possessed a Machiavellian sense of opportunity and a Renaissance understanding of print. Amerigo *published* America – or rather, his Tuscan editors did when they rendered his reports into elegant Latin, framed them with humanist flourishes, and then dispersed them throughout Europe. Vespucci discovered neither America nor a new world so much as the public's appetite for discoveries and the growing market for "Americana."

Vespucci had discovered, in effect, the widespread interest in wonders, and, in the *Mundus novus,* wonders never cease. The "entirely new world" reported by Vespucci drew consistent attention to its singularity – much though it may have appeared, upon closer inspection, not altogether different from the marvelous landscapes sketched by Columbus and his medieval predecessors. What set Vespucci's texts apart was the spectacular breadth of his wonders, the very plenitude of the singular, and – most essentially – the unwavering insistence on originality. The Florentine culled from earlier literature the most compelling *mirabilia* available. These, further embellished to suit a Renaissance audience (both learned and not), presented a world of endless novelties and limitless potential; of seductive riches and gargantuan monsters; of luscious fruit and lascivious women. Vespucci's America partook of the fabulous as well as the ferocious, exotic landscapes alternating with edenic. Amazonian warriors held cannibal feasts, seduced Christian sailors, and hoarded unchristian quantities of gold, pearls, and treasure. Where Columbus insisted he had found no monstrosities, Vespucci claimed to see nothing but: "Epicurean" savages with faces like "Tartars," lion-colored skin, and grossly enlarged penises. Amerigo's world was unstintingly entertaining.[24]

It was dazzling as well, perhaps even confusingly so. The Vespuccian texts mix and match their themes, presenting traditional marvels as radically new and reporting bona fide discoveries with alternatively classical and modern tags (both Pliny and Petrarch merit mention in the masterful opening of the *Lettera*). They possess a heterogeneous quality. And if this multiplicity of images created something of a garbled picture for the reader, this would have been all the more the case in the Netherlands, where publishers chose to scramble the New World still further. The first Antwerp "Vespucius" appeared circa 1505, followed by a vernacular edition circa 1506. Jan van Doesborch, publisher of the Dutch-language version, next put out a provocatively titled *De novo mondo* (ca. 1510) that included a one page précis of Vespucci's "Letter on his Third

Voyage" (containing the word "Armenica" and a description of "Brazilians"), followed by a lengthy account of Balthasar Springer's travels to the *East* Indies under the command of Francisco d'Aleida. It concluded with a single-page abridgment of Vespucci's chapter on cosmography (intended, perhaps, to fill the final verso), extracted from the 1507 *Cosmographiae introductio* of Martin Waldseemüller. Van Doesborch reissued this hybrid work in 1522, now bearing the subtly misleading English title *Of the newe landes and of ye people found by the kynge of Portygale*. Both of these works were presumably based on the more aptly named *Flemish* work of 1508, *Die reyse van Lissabone* (The voyage from Lisbon) – yet another production of the enterprising van Doesborch. Publishers of early Americana, in the Low Countries at least, placed little stock in geographic precision.[25]

The messy publication history of Vespucci in the Netherlands exemplifies the early Dutch reception of America more generally: enthusiastic yet chaotic. The eye-catching phrases "new world," "Armenica," and "discovery" circulated in enough texts to impress upon readers the basic fact of the discoveries. Yet the packaging of America together with ancient tales of Amazons, Tartars, and the usual array of marvels placed the latest news in the more familiar context of medieval geography. In the end, Dutch readers of early Americana faced a fabulous kaleidoscope of things American, things Asian, and things imaginary, which informed descriptions of both. The pamphlets that many read included part Vespucci, part Springer, and part Ptolemy – yet all purportedly "new." Van Doesborch especially traded on America's novelty, capitalizing on the Vespucci phenomenon by splashing Amerigo's name and his "discoverer" reputation on as many title pages as possible. And the Antwerp publisher, like the *piloto mayor*, would seem to have prospered. In the earliest years of the sixteenth century, Dutch readers evinced palpable interest in exotic new worlds even as they seemed wholly unable to assimilate the New World per se. They discovered Vespucci's "America" to be very similar to the worlds they visited in Mandeville, Polo, and other late medieval geographies explored in the comfort of their libraries. The New World featured as one of many in an age of literary discovery.

III

By the second decade of the sixteenth century, the New World, if still somewhat novel and inchoately imagined, had come to occupy a recognizable site on the Dutch horizon. It had also become, in the case of van Doesborch's America, a broadly *accessible* site, "popular" in the very basic sense that it appealed to the widest possible audience. Van Does-borch, who published other travel works that fit neatly under the rubric of *burgerlijk* literature, packaged his Vespuccis to sell. The original Dutch-language edition of the *Mundus novus* was printed in inexpensive quarto. It comprised sixteen brief pages, set in traditional gothic type and illustrated with crude woodcuts. The publisher enticed his readers not only with promises of marvels "newly discovered" – Vespucci's own carnivalesque blend of curiosities – but also with images provocatively posed: a "wild" couple on the title page, unclothed and long-haired; four naked (and armed) women illustrating the temptations (and dangers) of Christian travel (fig. 2); a nautical vignette showing a man diving into the gaping mouth of a sea monster. All of this may well have appealed to all manner of reader – why would Antwerp's elites have been any less susceptible to tales both tantalizing and moralizing? – though van Doesborch's products would seem more carefully calibrated for consumers of medieval romances than humanist letters.[26]

Yet the Vespuccian texts were inherently more multivalent than van Doesborch's versions might suggest. And more generally, the New World, in its earliest representations, could play to multiple constituencies. The *Mundus novus* had erudite airs as well; it was "elite" in the sense that it engaged a learned audience attracted to other aspects of overseas discoveries. In its Latin form – published in Antwerp by Willem Vorsterman, though available in nearly identical editions from Paris, Cologne, and other printing centers of the Northern Renaissance – the reader is drawn more directly to the scholarly apparatus of the text. Gone are the racy woodcuts of "natives," here replaced by an orthogonal triangle to illustrate new data on the southern skies. Two cosmographical vignettes sketch out other novelties of the American heavens; and the latest navigational instruments – "the quadrant and the astrolabe, as everyone knows" – are briskly (if weakly) explained. In deference to humanist sensibilities, classicisms abound: in the reflexive allusions to ancient authorities, in the Arcadianism subtly invoked, and in the none too subtle contrasts drawn between classical and modern exploration.[27]

The *Mundus novus*, in its Latinate formulation, indicates how the New World initially circulated among a certain class of reader. It attests to the development of, and ready Dutch audience for, what might be called a "learned" America. Other evidence points further in this direction. Cornelius Aurelius, humanist historian of Holland and friend (some say teacher) of Erasmus, was quick to incorporate the New World into his much admired *Divisiekroniek*. His references to the "wonderful creatures" and "naked inhabitants" of the West Indies hint at a familiarity

Figure 2. Illustration from Amerigo Vespucci, *Vander nieuwer werelt oft landtscap* (Antwerp, ca. 1506). Courtesy of the John Carter Brown Library, Brown University.

with Vespucci and Columbus; though he may have gleaned his information from the Basel humanist (and friend of Erasmus), Sebastian Brant, whose satire, *Das Narrenschiff*, described "naked men, gold islands too / Of which no mortal ever knew." Then there is the case of Erasmus himself. From the evidence of his carefully managed literary persona, the illustrious son of Rotterdam would seem to have paid scant attention to events outside of Europe: no published text by Erasmus directly mentions America. Yet his voluminous correspondence does reveal a somewhat greater awareness of the New World: of missionary activity, of gold deposits (not unrelated), and of imperial expansion in the West. Yet another friend of Erasmus provides telling comment, articulating more fully the themes and sources of a humanist-inflected America. Juan Luis Vives of Bruges, a towering figure of Renaissance learning, imagined a social state of nature in the New World and wrote admiringly of the prevailing "harmony" among the Indians – this in a work otherwise dedicated to the mounting disharmony of Reformation Europe. On another occasion Vives described the native Americans as "rude," by which he meant something more akin to simple – lacking in complex civil institutions and social regulations – than savage. Finally, in his widely disseminated *Disciplinis,* Vives made a recommendation to those armchair travelers who would discover more of America: the savvy reports of his fellow humanist, Pietro Martire d'Anghiera.[28]

For those who inclined toward a more refined, more literate, more learned version of the New World, Vives had fingered the single most important source of narrative information. The Milanese scholar Peter Martyr (as his name has been anglicized) composed, in an engaging and elegant style, and disseminated, beginning in the 1510s, the first full-scale history of the discoveries: *De orbe novo,* also known as the *Decades.*[29] Martyr's account gave new shape to America. An author of an altogether different temperament, social class, and intellectual generation than either Columbus or Vespucci, Martyr refashioned America by imparting the new continent with the luster of ancient learning. His was above all a humanist's vision, one that articulated a distinct, and distinctly Renaissance, image of the Indies that spoke to similarly disposed readers across Europe – including those among the swelling ranks of humanists in the Netherlands. It was also the work of a cinquecento courtier-scholar, and this too played its part. The son of minor nobility, Martyr received an appropriately literary training, which he used ably to advance through the ranks of Renaissance patronage. His education and later role as an educator – he set up a palace school for Queen Isabella that served as a conduit for the new learning trickling into the peninsula – gave him entrée to the courts of Lombardy, Rome, and ultimately Castile, where he served the Spanish crown and later the Habsburg emperor as chronicler to the Council of the Indies. Martyr's social as well as literary sensitivities distinguished his New World from that of his predecessors. He possessed a different sense of style and narration, which produced a prose that was gracefully, if also consciously, imbued with the spirit of classical antiquity.[30] The *Decades,* composed mostly over the first quarter of the sixteenth century and circulated widely throughout the quarter century that followed, evoke a new world strikingly reminiscent of Ovid's Golden Age. Not unlike Jan Mostaert's panel, they portray a peaceful, bountiful, utopian America largely undisturbed prior to its invasion by rapacious soldiers from an age of iron.

To discover the Golden Age in America required a thoroughly classical cast of mind, which Martyr assuredly had. The author of *De orbe novo* was enamored with antiquity, and this affected the form, style, and content of his work. Martyr's *Decades* are patterned after Livy's histories: each (there are eight) contains ten parts, dedicated to a different patron, and framed by a carefully constructed theme of the *Conquista*. Though officially presented as history, the work conveys an epic sweep, part chronicle, part ethnography, part tragedy, recalling in many ways the literary products of Martyr's other models, Herodotus and Pliny the Elder. And the work abounds in classical learning and analogies to antiquity. Vasco Núñez de Balboa conjures up an image of Hercules, the Tascaltecans resemble Republicans of Rome, and the Temistitans live in a state of "Elysian repose." Martyr's classical perspective encourages him to remodel the marvels of Vespucci in terms familiar to the Renaissance: in language, topoi, and contexts that made sense to a humanist reader. Anthropophagi and Amazons appear less threatening than heartening, confirming as they do the testimony of the Greeks; mammoth fish and sea monsters recall Arion's dolphin and the Tritons rather than some vaguely hyperborean horror. Part of this, of course, is a rhetorical stance, a Renaissance author's *de rigeur* allusions to ancient authority. At times, too, Martyr takes a more skeptical line, dismissing certain less credible narrative heirlooms from antiquity. If willing to repeat tales of Caribbean "Amazons," the author ultimately decides, "I think this story is a fable." Still, a pervasive classicism sets the tone. If the wisdom of antiquity failed to explain all of the novelties of America, it provided the prose, the paradigms, and the rhetorical tools necessary to contemplate these phenomena in the first place.[31]

Antiquity failed to account for the natives of America, and to do so – and contextualize the Indians for a Renaissance readership – Martyr resorted to one of the more compelling models of the humanist imagination, the myth of the Golden Age. The *Aurea Aetas,* as described by Ovid, represented the earliest stage in human history, a period of innocence and peace that predated social conflict and predatory war. By the Renaissance, it was further understood to be an age of natural plenitude and harmony, blissfully ignorant of the greed, envy, and violence that plagued contemporary Europe.[32] Looking westward and backward, Martyr repositioned the "primitive" societies of the New World to situate them at the heart of the Golden Age. They too occupied a pastoral landscape peopled by noble, if naked, innocents, flourishing in a utopian, almost prelapsarian, state of nature.[33] This theme is central for Martyr, and he introduces it in one of the very first encounters between Europe and America – in this case, between Columbus and a native elder who "astonished" the Admiral with his "sound judgment though he went naked." This naked philosopher-cacique lived "in a state of nature." Martyr elaborates:

It is proven that amongst them the land belongs to everybody, just as does the sun or the water. They know no difference between *meum* and *tuum*, that source of all evils. It requires so little to satisfy them, that in that vast region there is always more land to cultivate than is needed. It is indeed a golden age, neither ditches, nor hedges, nor walls enclose their domains; they live in gardens open to all, without laws and without judges; their conduct is naturally equitable, and whoever injures his neighbour is considered a criminal and an outlaw.[34]

To Martyr's audience – fellow humanists who took their classical mythology seriously – all of this struck a familiar chord. America harked back not to the monsters of the Middle Ages but to the luster of the Golden Age. The western world lately discovered resembled an ancient world recently revived by imaginative scholars of Renaissance Europe.[35]

Martyr's narrative design, innocent enough on the face of it, had certain unforeseen consequences. For a golden age in the New World would have enduring repercussions back in the Old: utopianism revealed implied utopianism undone. To be sure, Martyr never intended through his descriptions to "ennoble" the American savage. The more deliberate strategy of elevating the Indians, adapted somewhat later in the century by Montaigne (among others), presupposed a critical attitude toward his fellow Europeans that Martyr did not possess. As a courtier in the service of Castile, it hardly suited his purposes to censure the conquistadors or their royal patrons, and most of the *Decades* concentrate on celebrating the Spanish mission overseas. The king and queen of Spain grace Martyr's work as pious bestowers of Christianity on the heathens, and Columbus, their servant, emerges as a visionary hero. For his efforts Martyr gained a post as spokesman for Spanish expansion (he served as chronicler of the Council of the Indies from 1518), and the author of the *Decades* has long been counted among the champions of Spain's American enterprise.[36] Be that as it may, a golden age visited upon by an army of iron inevitably creates a cast of heroes and villains. By adopting the rhetorical strategy that he does, Martyr inadvertently gave birth to a series of striking contrasts between "innocent" Americans and conquering Spaniards, contrasts that recur throughout the *Decades* and resurface in later Americana, especially those published in Northern Europe. If Martyr casts the Indians as "peaceful" and "pure," exaggerating their simplicity and gentleness, the Spaniards ineluctably assume the role of spoilers of this ancient tranquillity. The natives offer hospitality to the invaders, behave guilelessly in the face of rapacity, and share their gold "innocently" despite the Christians' greed. The Spanish, meanwhile, quash this American state of grace.

Typical of Martyr's narrative logic is his description of the fate of the Lucayas (Bahamas). When first encountered by Spain, these islands possessed all of the bounty and blessing of an unstinting Creator: "excellent" trees that never aged and could miraculously heal, women whose renowned beauty attracted suitors from neighboring isles, a benevolent ruler who, "like a queen bee," distributed the islands' treasures to all in equal proportion. The natives, Martyr observes, "enjoy[ed] a golden age. . . . In all things they [were] contented with little."[37] Then the Spaniards arrived. In pursuit of slaves for the gold mines of Hispaniola, they descended on the islands, "anxious as hunters pursuing wild beasts," and systematically depopulated it. The Indians responded at first with kindness. "But what then!" exclaims Martyr:

> The Spaniards ended by violating this hospitality. For when they had finished their exploration, they enticed numerous natives by lies and tricks to visit their ships, and when the vessels were quickly crowded with men and women, they raised anchor, set sail, and carried these despairing unfortunates into slavery. By such means they sowed hatred and warfare throughout that entire peaceful and friendly region, separating children from their parents and wives from their husbands.

The Spaniards ultimately "exterminated and exhausted" the wretched islands, bringing this New World paradise to a tragic end. They had bluntly and irreversibly terminated a golden age.[38]

The description of the Lucayas and their destruction, echoed in similar accounts of Hispaniola, Cuba, and most other landfalls of the early *Conquista,* underscores the uncomfortable position of Martyr as a courtier-chronicler in the employ of Castile. In composing the *Decades,* Martyr had to walk a fine line between the demands of his material and those of his benefactors. All rules of patronage discouraged clients from vilifying their patrons, and it would be a misreading of the *Decades* to suggest that Martyr sought deliberately to discredit his Spanish sponsors. By all indications, Martyr possessed the level-headed and *politique* temperament that characterized the itinerant scholarly community of his age and that would have prevented him from composing a purposefully impolitic work. Taken as a whole, there can be little doubt that the *Decades* aimed to extol the Spanish discovery and conquest of America.[39] Yet there can be little doubt either that Martyr's tale of a paradise found and ultimately lost casts the conquistadors, intentionally or not, in a dim light. And it was the effect of the *Decades,* rather than their purpose, that would gain them notoriety among readers outside of Spain.

Martyr's readers, in all events, obtained a grim picture of Spanish deeds in America – or, rather, *certain* Spanish deeds, since the *Decades* relate the story not only of Spain's triumph over the Indians, but the triumphs of individual conquistador factions over others in the ongoing, internecine struggles of early colonial America. This was necessarily a damning tale. If Columbus figured in Martyr's account as a pious and faithful servant to the Crown, his detractors (and there were many) inevitably played the part of villainous rebels. Of the latter, none evokes more disdain than Francisco Roldán, equerry and chief justice for the second Columbian voyage (1493–1496). Left under the command of the Admiral's brother, Bartolomé, Roldán broke off from his superior and initiated a series of treacherous raids against the natives of southern Hispaniola. Roldán and his men, writes Martyr, "gave themselves over to violence, thievery, and massacre." Upon his return to Hispaniola (1498), Columbus found an alarming state of disorder orchestrated by Roldán and his band of renegades: "They were accused of torturing, strangling, decapitating and, in divers other ways, killing people on the most trifling pretexts. They were envious, proud, and intolerable tyrants." In one of the work's more indignant passages, Martyr meticulously – and memorably – recounts the charges against Roldán's faction:

They were debauchees, profligates, thieves, seducers, ravishers, vagabonds. They respected nothing and were perjurers and liars. . . . They had formed a faction amongst themselves, given over to violence and rapine; lazy, gluttonous, caring only to sleep and to carouse. They spared nobody; and having been brought to the island of Hispaniola originally to do the work of miners or of camp servants, they now never moved a step from their houses on foot, but insisted on being carried about the island upon the shoulders of the unfortunate natives, as though they were dignitaries of State. Not to lose practice in the shedding of blood, and to exercise the strength of their arms, they invented a game in which they drew their swords, and amused themselves in cutting off the heads of innocent victims with one sole blow. Whoever succeeded in more quickly landing the head of an unfortunate islander on the ground with one stroke, was proclaimed the bravest, and as such was honoured.[40]

Powerful and mesmerizing in its awful detail, the passage is not at all unique in Martyr's opus, since Roldán's wave of terror marked only the first trickle in a coming flood of Spanish brutalities. Both of Columbus's colonial successors, Diego de Nicuesa and Alonso de Hojeda, committed feats of similar violence, though this time in the capacity of royally appointed servants. "Never satisfied with his spoils," Hojeda pillaged and burned his way through that former paradise, Hispaniola. "It is in reality the thirst for gold not less than the covetousness of new countries," Martyr must concede, "which prompted the Spaniards to court such dangers." And as Hojeda epitomizes the sin of greed, so Nicuesa personifies vanity. Of Nicuesa's insolent stratagem to seize the colony of Urabá (Colombia), Martyr notes that "it is a common thing to observe amongst men that arrogance accompanies success" – a conquistador truism if there ever was one.[41]

Disgraceful as certain Spaniards might have been, Martyr's narrative design made them seem even more so. The repeated juxtaposition of European violence and American Arcadianism, the programmatic idealization of "primitive" New World societies, the relentless classicism of Martyr's language, style, and sensibility: all contributed to the subsequent perception of Spain's American adventure. When the thuggish Balboa confronts the son of Comogre, cacique of Comogra (Panama), Martyr has the native deliver a harangue "as does an orator preparing for a serious debate, even thinking of the bodily movements likely to convince his followers." This graceful, Demosthenic performance is then contrasted with the cruder gestures of the Spanish antagonists: "The love of gain and the hope of gold fairly made our men's mouths water." A similar confrontation takes place when the eloquent cacique Abraibes suggests to his neighbor, Abibaiba, "Let us unite our forces and try to struggle against [Balboa's troops] who have maltreated [us]." This "valiant" show of unity by the Indians (which recalls Herodotus's rendering of the Greek defiance of invading Persians) serves to discredit the pathetically selfish raids of Balboa and his accomplices. In the end, the courtier in Martyr has the good sense to rehabilitate even that "egregious ruffian" Balboa, who is likened to the heroic Hercules and soldierly Hannibal. Yet the damage had been done. The very contrast between the guileless natives and greedy conquistadors had produced a Spanish protagonist simultaneously valorous and ignominious – and the effect of this infamy would endure.[42]

In the hands of Martyr, America loses some of the fantastic hues of earlier descriptions, if only to gain a different sheen, this time the glow of the Golden Age. If Martyr, the chronicler, wrote for his Spanish patrons, Martyr the scholar appealed to a far larger audience of like-minded humanists, which showed as much concern for the ancient world as for the new. In effect, Martyr was cornered by his classicism; his preoccupation with antiquity ended up inexorably tarnishing the image of the Spanish mission in America. The language of the pastoral conjured up that of the hunt, resulting in a rougher portrait of the conquest than any hitherto produced. It gained the highest acclaim from Bartolomé de las Casas and others sympathetically disposed to the natives. It also created themes and tropes of conquest – the insatiable greed, predatory violence, promiscuous plunder – that, though not unknown in European literature, had now been relocated to, and clearly associated with, the New World, the Spaniard, and the native American. Intentionally or not, Martyr had planted the seeds for the future "Black Legend" of Spanish conquest in America.

In certain ways, those seeds took root remarkably quickly and did so, notably, in the soil of the Netherlands. In its day, Martyr's version of America found a ready audience throughout Europe, especially among the ranks of the learned. Eleven editions (all but three in Latin) printed in five different countries over the course of three decades attest to the steady attention Martyr's work commanded among Renaissance readers.[43] An Antwerp edition appeared in 1536, yet evidence of interest in the Low Countries predates even that. It was in 1531 that Juan Luis Vives cited the *Decades* as his preferred manual for America, and this followed a number of earlier, Martyr-inflected references to the guileless Indians, their absence of avarice, and the marvelous "customs of the new world." Though he had ample reason to spell out a contrast, in this regard, with the customs of Castile – Vives had settled permanently in Bruges only after the Inquisition had executed his father, burned the exhumed body of his mother, and confiscated his family's property in Valencia – he never explicitly upbraids the invaders, if he does implicitly juxtapose the innocent state of American society with the declined state of his own. In all events, Vives and others established Martyr as the surest, most learned guide to the New World. Frequent references to the *Decades* demonstrate its prominent place within scholarly libraries of the Netherlands and assured its lasting influence among Dutch readers well into the seventeenth century.[44]

IV

The publication of the *Decades* marked a significant transition in the history of early Americana. It signaled, most plainly, the involvement of a recognized scholar and respected humanist in the project of describing the New World, and this led, in turn, to a wholly fresh style of description. Peter Martyr lent a sense of literary legitimacy to the developing genre of Americana – he virtually created a new *version* of America – and introduced, in the process, a new community of readers to his subject. And though this class of reader may have connoted a certain narrowing of audience, it implied too a broadening of influence obtained by Americana, now dispersed among the ranks of Renaissance Europe's elites. Other works appeared in the coming years – the 1520s through 1530s – similarly directed. Simon Grynaeus's lavish anthology of travel texts (which included selections from the *Decades*) provided a learned mélange of reports on the discoveries. The neo-Latin poem *Syphilis*, composed by the humanist physician Girolamo Fracastoro, appeared in 1530, the same year as the comparably aimed treatise, *On the French Disease*, by the renowned Paracelsus. Those with an interest in the new world of nature could now consult Gonzalo Fernández de Oviedo's *Natural History of the Indies*, published first in 1526 and later as a companion piece to the *Decades*. Martyr had instigated, in short, a wider engagement with the New World among the learned. He brought Europe's community of scholarly readers into the orbit of Spain's American expansion.[45]

Communities of readers overlapped, of course, just as narrative lines intersected, and publishers' purposes diverged. This was especially the case with early Americana. Multiple versions of Vespucci illustrate how the very same material could be otherwise packaged by enterprising editors and printers. The very same story could be otherwise told, too – as Martyr's narrative strategy suggests – and the very same author could tell wholly different stories. Gonzalo Fernández de Oviedo penned both the first natural history of America and the first romance of chivalry *from* America, *Don Claribalte* (1519), which, though not actually situated in the Indies, was drafted during Oviedo's American tour of duty and inspired (he suggested) by military feats witnessed abroad.[46] The very same readers, moreover, had variable and shifting tastes, and a Dutch peruser of Latin letters – Martyr's history of the Indies, say – might also have indulged in *burgerlijk* prose – Oviedo's romance of chivalry. Or, in time, the same reader might have turned to a romance of *American* chivalry, since the Dutch belonged to both the republic of European letters and the empire of Habsburg arms and might have followed the progress of the second as avidly as the first. Which observation brings up a final factor in the richly complex process of narrating, publishing, and assimilating America in these early years: the very same New World was encountered in stages over time, and the story of that encounter was an evolving one. The latest installment embraced "chivalric" themes – at least in its printed form – which exercised an appeal in the Netherlands utterly distinct from, though not necessarily at odds with, that of the *Decades*.

Consider the case of Cortés. By the time Oviedo had published his romance, America had acquired a real-life hero to rival even the most stalwart knights of European tales of chivalry. Hernán Cortés descended upon Mexico in the spring of 1519 and, by the following autumn, had battled his way into the Aztec capital of Tenochtitlan, which he brashly claimed for Spain. He reported his deeds in a series of vigorously composed *Cartas* [Letters] *de relación* addressed to the newly crowned "caesarean majesty," Charles V; and much has been made of the brilliant political maneuvers of the text in justifying a ruthless and originally unsanctioned *Conquista*. (Cortés commenced his offensive with a bold act of insubordination; the *Cartas* advance, against rival accusations, an innovative appeal for "legal imperialism," oxymoronic as that may sound.)[47] Less has been made, however, of the masterful literary tactics of Cortes's letters, which deftly translate a New World campaign into terms of Old World chivalry. In fact, the *Cartas* relate a spectacular saga of swashbuckling courage and martial endurance. They narrate, in the author's distinctively muscular prose, the larger-than-life exploits of Cortés, his daring defense against challengers, and his triumphant conquest of Mexico. America now provides the background for performative chivalry; the narrator offers himself as the supreme embodiment of the knightly ideal, an *hidalgo* whose fealty to the emperor (if not the colonial viceroy) was impressively unwavering. No longer the site of arcadian repose, the New World has been transformed into an arena of valorous, robust arms.[48]

Like his military strategy, Cortés's literary offensive succeeded spectacularly. The *Cartas* achieved their desired effect both in the royal courts of Castile, where Cortés won the day, and in the wider court of popular opinion, where printed versions caused a sensation. Nowhere was this excitement more immediately apparent than in the northwest corner of Charles's empire – the Netherlands – where an Antwerp edition appeared within months of the Spanish original, a second following a year later. Both came from the press of Michiel van Hoochstraten, who framed the text with a woodcut frontispiece that effectively underscored the marvelous and "romantic," as well as the political and imperial motifs of the narrative (fig. 3). In the immediate foreground stand a native couple with child, the feather-clad "husband" aiming his bow at a perched macaw. Two European vessels moor behind them, and a fancy canoe glides off to the left, languidly poled by an Indian. Mexico's "islands and landscapes" (as van Hoochstraten terms them) are certainly of the New World: fabulous and foreign. Yet the larger setting in which they exist retains an Old World charm. Northern European castles fill the background, their rounded turrets and gabled towers suggesting the chivalric context of the tale to come. In the very center of the page, abutting the very title word "*Keysere*," dangles a Habsburg coat of arms meant to remind Dutch readers that they, like all members of the emperor's domains, had a part in Castilian adventures abroad.[49]

The imperial motif emblazoned on the title page of the *Cartas* announced a new chapter in the literature of America.[50] For the first time, a major work on the Spanish conquest of the New World was written by

Figure 3. Title page illustration from Hernán Cortés, *De contreyen randen exlanden ende lantdouwen* (Antwerp, 1523). Paris, Bibliothèque National.

a Spaniard and for a Spanish, or broadly Habsburg, audience. In many ways, Cortés's Letters embodied the ideals of the *Conquista* and Spain's self-declared mission in the Indies. They focus on imperial objectives and appeal to imperial-minded readers, both high ranking and low (readers admired the acts not just of any knight errant, but one who served the "most serene, almighty, unconquerable" Charles V). The attention, accordingly, falls mainly on Spanish deeds and the Habsburg agenda, and only tangentially on native suffering and peripheral "wonders" – the narrative focus of Peter Martyr and the Italian navigators writing a quarter century earlier. Castilian heroics are displayed in their most flattering light – the active doings of knightly conquistadors – while Indian resistance recedes to the margins – the passive plight of native victims. Indeed, the *Cartas* emphasize remarkably little of the destructiveness and wretchedness that occupied much of the *Decades* and would later become standard themes in many non-Spanish accounts of the *Conquista*. Some Cortésian violence could hardly be avoided: the gruesome mutilation of local spies, for example, or the "marvelous" number of Indian casualties left in Spain's trail, both of which are cited to illustrate the vigor of Cortés's command.[51] Still, none of this approaches the moralizing and frankly anticolonial tone that would characterize future recitations of the same events, and Cortés's Indians emerge relatively unscathed when one considers their lot in the blood-splattered accounts of the later sixteenth century. Above all, the spotlight shines on Spanish knights and their warrior-leader, Hernán Cortés.

The *Cartas de relación* enjoyed their greatest popularity in Spain, becoming the first bona fide Spanish success of the literature of discovery – eminently understandable given the work's focus on Spanish feats and conquistador adventures. Yet these themes proved nearly as appealing outside of Spain, too, where the *Cartas*, in various formats, went through thirteen editions within the space of eleven years. Many of these volumes played to Habsburg audiences in the Low Countries and Germany, though there is no reason to assume that the attraction was purely political. As was the case with so many romances of chivalry, a knight's country of origin ultimately stood for less than his deeds of valor. Cortés performed valiantly, wrote forcefully, and sold fabulously. Other narratives of the unfolding *Conquista* met with similar enthusiasm – conspicuously among readers north of the Pyrenees. Cortés's loyal secretary, Francisco López de Gómara, composed an epic tribute to his patron, which, as the first full-scale history devoted to Mexico's conquest, achieved quick and broad popularity. Antwerp printers brought out an edition within a year of its initial publication (1552) and three more by 1555. Since Gómara's account was later suppressed by the Spanish

Crown, his work received more exposure outside of Spain than within. The equally dramatic tale of Peru's conquest, as told by Pedro Cieza de León, likewise received prompt attention from publishers in the Low Countries. Within a year of its appearance in Seville in 1553, three editions streamed off Antwerp presses to slake the evidently growing thirst among readers of the Netherlands for Spanish adventures in America.[52]

This distinct taste for chivalric versions of America continued unabated in the Netherlands, climaxing in the mid-sixteenth century with the extraordinary success of Agustín de Zárate's *Historia del descubrimiento y conquista del Peru* (1555). The *Historia* told a fast-paced tale of "fire and sword," of bloody combat waged by the defiant Pizarro brothers; and it told it from a proudly Spanish perspective. As in the *Letters* of Cortés, the natives suffered their fate in silence. Aside from the occasional pronouncement by a stiff Atahualpa or some other Incan figurehead, the Indians retire stoically to the background, allowing Spanish heroes the full glory of center stage. More, perhaps, than any epic of America, Zárate's *Historia* epitomizes the romance of New World chivalry, focusing on individual Spaniards, individual battles, and individual feats of valor. The two grandest battles described, Salina and Chupas, carry the reader back to the days of Roland and El Cid, now relocated in the Andean highlands. At Salinas, Don Diego de Almagro faces the "gallantly attired" Hernando de Pizarro, and, despite the stout thrusts from the lance of Don Diego's "second," Pizarro and his brother Gonzalo win the day. Don Diego is executed following the battle (1538), yet his son lives to fight again, and the scene repeats itself at the battle of Chupas (1542). After the call of the trumpets, the mounted forces of the governor, Vaca de Castro, clash with those of Diego the Younger. "Immediately," Zárate narrates heatedly,

[the two sides] encountered with . . . great courage, in such ways that they broke on both sides almost all the lances, and many more were slain and unhorsed on each side: when their lances failed, they joined with force of sword and battle ax, in such ways that they fought with many a bloody stroke till they were well nigh breathless.[53]

Once again, the clashing of swords and the thrusting of lances found an especially eager audience among the burghers of the Netherlands, where the *Historia* – in Spanish, Dutch, and Latin – became perhaps the single most popular work of the literature of discovery. Zárate, a lifetime Habsburg bureaucrat who served as *contador* (accountant-general) for the viceroyalty of Peru, spent the second half of his career in Antwerp. This explains why the original Spanish version of the *Historia* was published in Antwerp rather than Seville. Dutch enthusiasm, how-

Figure 4. Illustration from Agustín de Zárate, *De wonderlijcke ende warachtighe historie vant coninckrijck van Peru geleghen in Indien* (Antwerp, 1563). Courtesy of the John Carter Brown Library, Brown University.

ever, accounts for the subsequent Flemish edition of 1563; two further editions issued within the next decade; and two editions from an Amsterdam publisher later in the century. Two Latin editions printed in 1566 and 1567 (both in Antwerp) brought the total available editions to eight, five of those within the ten year period 1563–1573. This, in the context of sixteenth-century printing, amounted to a literary sensation.[54]

It amounted also to a literary celebration: of chivalry, of America, and of Spanish chivalry (so configured) in America. This essentially triumphant message, imparted in Zárate's history no less than in other early Spanish accounts of the *Conquista,* was plainly well-received in the Habsburg Netherlands. And why should this not have been so? In accounting for the success of these texts, it is worth emphasizing the relative "detachment" of Dutch attention to the New World through the mid-sixteenth century. For, much as Spanish exploits in Peru and Mexico included some of the darkest episodes of treachery, cruelty, and bloodshed in the Indies, Dutch editors showed little inclination to exploit this material to the disadvantage of Spain. Quite the contrary: the introduction to the first Dutch-language version of Zárate (for example) begins by stressing history's function as a teacher of moral lessons, goes on to praise Charles's role as overseer of the *Conquista,* and concludes with hope for the spread of Christianity among the Peruvian heathen. The

Dutch text, like the Spanish, emphasizes knightly deeds and heroism to the neglect of native suffering and desolation; in some cases, the translation even suppresses material deemed offensive in the original. Woodblock prints used to illustrate the volume come from standard issues of Old World romances and underscore the exultant trend of the narrative. Knights in armor battle worthy opponents without the slightest trace of an Indian (fig. 4). Netherlandish readers of Zárate, it would appear, preferred their Old World knights uncluttered by the trappings of New World responsibilities.[55]

V

With the conquest of Peru and Zárate's telling of it, a crucial phase of Spain's New World enterprise reached its triumphant culmination. Spain and those in its service had discovered, conquered, and exploited a vast stretch of land abounding with riches, crowded with strange *naturalia,* and inhabited by unfamiliar peoples. The rest of Europe – excepting the Portuguese and the odd Norman or Flemish trader – could only read about it. Though the American literature of the first few years came primarily from Italian authors, by the 1520s Spain had begun to dominate the presses as it always had the seas. And while the early reports were concerned with the exotic shapes, smells, and colors of a new world, the later ones told an increasingly familiar story of Habsburg attainment. By the middle of the sixteenth century, those texts available to Europeans interested in America read like traditional romances of Spanish heroism.

Competing narratives naturally existed: there was a less noble side to Spanish deeds in America. Yet they circulated more narrowly or focused only peripherally on those less estimable themes of the *Conquista.* Consider a contrast to Cortés. Paralleling almost exactly the early *relaciones* of Spanish America were a series of letters sent from New Spain by the Franciscan missionary, Pieter van Gent. Pieter left his native Flanders just months after learning of Cortés's conquests and labored in Mexico for the next fifty years – not as a warrior for Charles, however, but as a soldier for Christ. It was to the emperor, nonetheless, that he reported the progress of the Savior, and this was hardly a story of Habsburg success. Pieter dispatched reports, in fact, both to Charles (later Philip II) and to his Franciscan brethren in Flanders, and the two sets of letters read somewhat differently. With the emperor, the friar pulled no punches. He complained of the colonists' greed, the natives' ill treatment, and the unholy "material benefit" derived from the enslavement and taxation of Charles's Indian vassals: "I beseech Your Majesty to remember that Christ sacrificed His blood not for taxes, but for souls." To his fellow mendicants, by contrast, Pieter communicated greater optimism, focusing not on Spain's failures but the Church's future in this new and scarcely corrupted evangelical world. He encouraged his colleagues to join him in America – a potential paradise on earth! – where they might reinvigorate the Catholic faith by converting the heathen's soul. This more enthusiastic message was duly publicized in a local Dutch chronicle and later reprinted in a volume celebrating the "fruits of Christ's Church." Meanwhile, the more grim observations sent to Charles never left the Habsburg court, which worked assiduously to prevent the spread of a negative narrative of America.[56]

Pieter van Gent's Americana are instructive. The letters written to the abbey and then published for the benefit of other Franciscans in the Low Countries point to yet another community of readers drawn to the New World, one with particular religious interests in the Indies. Pieter, too, represents another type of author. He possessed not only a distinctive spiritual background, but also a Northern European and specifically Netherlandish perspective, and this cannot help but have influenced his version – his narrative – of America. His missives to Charles differ radically from the conquistador chronicles of the same period; the religious message of Pieter's relations almost inverts the political themes of Cortés. Whereas the latter's *Cartas* celebrate military advances in the West and the advantage for the Habsburg empire, Pieter's letters lament the spiritual ruination of the Indies and the dire consequences facing the Holy Roman Emperor. "I assure Your Majesty," he warned, after detailing the appalling abuse of Mexico's natives, "that another thirty or forty years of such exploitation and this land will be lost forever." While Cortés's narrative received a wide hearing across Europe, Pieter's was pondered in discreet silence by select royal advisors. In its day, Pieter van Gent's criticism of Spanish America never received much attention.[57]

The silent treatment accorded to Pieter's and other competing accounts of the Conquista makes fairly good political and polemical sense, at least over the first half of the sixteenth century. For Spain and its imperial satellites, Charles's reign coincided with a period of tightening royal control – this despite (or perhaps because of) audible rumblings of dissent. Pieter commenced his voyage to America on the very ship that bore Charles to Castile, where the emperor undertook his own campaign to crush the insurgent *Comuneros*. Two decades later, Charles returned to Ghent (of all places) to suppress a tax revolt; and, in the intervening years, he ruthlessly stamped out all sparks of religious heterodoxy, both in Spain and the Netherlands. This was not a climate that encouraged imperial critique. Outside of the empire, too, it made little sense to attack Spanish policy, though this reflected the convoluted state of continental politics more than anything else. So long as the houses of Valois and Habsburg continued to conduct their rivalry on the battlefields of Milan and Naples, Italian city-states could still prefer a Spanish alliance to a French one. English foreign policy maintained its traditional anti-France (thus pro-Spain) stance through much of the first half of the sixteenth century, culminating in the marriage of Mary Tudor to Philip of Spain. The Marian exiles, if rabidly anti-Catholic and anti-Spanish by extension, represented as yet a negligible minority. In the German states, Protestants and Catholics, preoccupied with their own wars of religion, had little venom to spare for Spanish ignominies abroad. Only France, the counterbalance to Spain in Renaissance Europe's biggest contest of hegemony, had reason to campaign against the Spanish reputation. Yet here, too, allegiances were mixed and factionalized, and France's enemies disparate and many. No polemical version of America developed through the mid-sixteenth century – no image purposefully constructed to vilify Spain – since no cause existed to support it.[58]

All of this would change by the second half of the sixteenth century, when shifting religious, political, and imperial winds altered the polemical climate of Europe and hence the literary representation of America. Two of these shifts were fundamental. First, the New World ceased to be the exclusive domain of the Iberians – the case for the previous half-century. For, though French and Flemish traders occasionally had appeared off the coast of Brazil or the salt pans of Venezuela, and though Spanish ships normally included multinational crews of sailors and pilots, virtually no sustained or large-scale expeditions to America took place without Iberian consent until the mid-sixteenth-century forays of the French.[59] Spanish dominance, to be sure, hardly diminished in this period. If anything, royal control tightened over the nascent colonial communities of New Spain, New Granada, and coastal South America, as it did over Castile, Aragon, and the Low Countries. Still, non-Spanish participation in the New World – in expeditions of discovery, colonization, and privateering – intensified over the second half of the century, posing an ever-growing challenge to Spain's hegemony in America. As rivalries emerged over control of the New World, so too did differences develop over the narrative of the New World.

Second, the tumultuous religious debates that had shaken Europe in the first half of the century began, by the middle of the century, to spill over to America. Calvin's generation of reformers, far more than Luther's, shifted theological discussions from the soul's struggle within a body of flesh to the struggle of those "elect" souls within the body politic. By providing a religious basis for resistance to ungodly political authority ("tyranny"), Calvin sanctioned the establishment of independent, godly republics by his followers. He set up his own theocracy in Geneva, inviting the pious to join his experiment of Christian life on earth. His pastors, arriving from France, England, Scotland, and the Low Countries to receive instruction, departed Geneva prepared to recast the world, Old as well as New, in Calvin's Genevan image. They and other Protestant disciples looked to the New World with reformed sensibilities and novel expectations. Their efforts to install godly republics on earth, moreover, transported many of them across the Atlantic; and their reports of religious battles waged abroad made for some of the most dramatic descriptions of America of the later sixteenth century.

The publications of the second half of the century, then, introduced readers in the Netherlands as elsewhere to a new form of literature on America, namely, works written by Northern European authors, often with a Protestant orientation, and sometimes with a strongly anti-Spanish bias. Ultimately, the image of the New World developed in conjunction with political and religious events in the Old. The new Americana reflected the increasing involvement of Valois France in various New World enterprises, the expanding impact of the Reformation, and the widening role of the Spanish monarch as master of the New World riches and guardian of Old World Catholicism. These works also indicated a growing awareness among European publicists of the value of American themes within the context of European polemics. The French led the way in challenging Iberian hegemony on both sides of the Atlantic. Many of their efforts coincided, not accidentally, with the French Wars of Religion, and hardly a piece of French Americana from the second half of the sixteenth century is without some trace of the confessional debates of the day. The Netherlands, with their Francophone nobility and long cultural ties to the House of Burgundy, could not help but be influenced by the French example. The creation of a peculiarly *Dutch* image of the New World would have to wait until the final decades of the century and the revolt against Spain. Yet the groundwork for that image lay in the French and other non-Spanish literature on America from the third quarter of the sixteenth century.

VI

The "new Americana" debuted in the Lutheran town of Marburg in 1557 in the form of Hans Staden's *Warhaftig historia* (True history), the first substantively, thematically, and categorically Northern description of the New World. A Hessian gunner in the employ of the Portuguese, Staden set out for South America in 1549, only to return five years later having spent nearly half of his sojourn as a captive of the Tupinamba of Brazil. His account of these adventures, related in a vivid, first-person narrative, became one of the most widely dispersed works on Brazil, particularly north of the Alps. Composed in his native German, Staden's *Historia* has the further distinction of being the first original report of America authored by a non-Spaniard since the initial publication of Martyr's *Decades* a half century earlier. Four German editions of the *Historia* appeared in quick succession (1557–1558), followed promptly by a Latin translation. Nowhere, though, did Staden's account draw a greater audience than in the Low Countries, where more editions were published than anywhere else in Europe – nine over the course of the next eight decades. In its printed form, Staden's *Historia* swiftly became a Dutch bestseller.[60]

The overwhelming appeal of Staden's account certainly owed much to its various "traditional" attributes. Like the popular works of Vespucci, or even of Oviedo or Gómara, the *Historia* recounts, in relentlessly lurid detail, the cannibalistic rites of the Brazilians and other "savage" mores of the Indians. Staden improved on the by now familiar native-as-cannibal motif by positioning *himself* as the object of the Tupi's anthropophagist desires. His narrative lingers teasingly on the suspense-filled period leading up to his ultimate (non)eating and on the less fortunate fate of other captives-turned-banquet. Much like modern cinematic variations on the theme, Staden adds a sexual element to the violent by describing the Tupi practice of granting the condemned man (this includes Staden himself) a temporary concubine. The effect is both mildly shocking and titillating. The author survives his ordeal through a combination of solemn perseverance and simple piety, and in many ways the narrative also reads like a traditional moralizing tale meant to inspire, as well as caution, its Christian readers.

Yet Staden innovates, too, and his emphasis on a very personal brand of Christian virtue may explain the work's singular success among readers of Northern Europe. For Staden's was not merely among the first accounts of the Indies written by a non-Catholic; it was also in certain identifiable ways a *Protestant* text. Unlike previous accounts, which also had their share of religious homilies, Staden's history can be distinguished by its Protestant emphases: on the narrator's direct relationship with his god; on the futility of religious intermediaries in place of that god; and on the special, personal significance for the narrator of the life and death of Christ. Again and again, the text accentuates the spiritual elements of Staden's American experience. The author, thus, compares his ordeal to the "mocking" of the condemned Christ and, in a particularly poignant passage, relates how his Tupi captors "poked," "jabbed," and threatened him. "I could think only of our Savior Jesus Christ," he recalls, "and of his innocent sufferings at the hands of the Jews, whereat I was comforted." He peppers his account also with prayers and "hymns," pointedly addressed "to God alone." Lest the reader miss the point, the Protestant thematics are underscored in a didactic preface to the volume by Staden's *Landsmann,* the Marburg physician Dryander, who notes with thinly veiled contempt that "some hitherto among the papists invoke this saint or that holy one, vowing pilgrimages or offerings that they may be saved from their perils." Staden, by contrast, gave "honor and praise to God alone, and in all Christian humility." Staden's survival, Dryander concludes, testifies to the superiority of the new brand of Protestant faith.[61]

Staden's *Warhaftig historia* pointed the narrative of America, once again, in new directions. While it would be naive to accept the author's assertion that he wrote purely for pious purposes – far too much attention is focused on the gruesome details of cannibalism to discount the voyeuristic, Mandevillean agenda of the text – Staden does offer a Protestant reading of America as no previous traveler had done. He casts his New World experience in terms of a personal, spiritual conquest, and he contextualizes America in a manner more obviously sensible and distinctly familiar to a Protestant reading public. The *Historia* in many ways foreshadows the Puritan captivity narrative of the coming centuries. In the meantime, it introduced the politics of the Reformation to the literature of discovery. Staden's history, furthermore, is notable for what it is not: a chronicle of the *Conquista* (this despite the fact that its author, strictly speaking, was a German conquistador). It describes the travails of a European who himself becomes "possessed" – thus reversing the formula of Cortés and others who took possession – yet Staden's vista onto America may have looked more promising to certain readers than the prevailing conquistador view. For the *Historia,* paradoxically, is a narrative of opportunity: of spiritual opportunities, to be sure, yet also opportunities suggested by a land that remained unpossessed or "wild," as Staden's Dutch editor, Christoffel Plantijn, put it. Which brings up a final shift: Staden's text also reoriented the New World in the very real, geographic sense of redirecting readers to a fresh setting for America. Rather than describing the familiar centers of Spanish power – the Caribbean, Mexico, Peru – Staden transports his readers to Brazil, a region conferred on Portugal by the Treaty of Tordesillas in 1494, though left relatively undisturbed by Europeans for the next half century. And Brazil, as Plantijn enthusiastically pointed out to his Dutch readers, remained wide open: for evangelization, for settlement, for profit.[62]

A shift to Brazil meant more than a shift in the locale of America. It signified a change in the tenor of Americana, since authority over colonial Brazil, like authority over the narrative of Brazil, was highly contested – lately by the French, traditionally by the Portuguese, and never by the Spanish. The textual struggle over Brazil was a theme also alluded to by Plantijn in the Dutch-language *Historia*, which pointed readers toward an alternative description of the region (likewise available from Plantijn's Antwerp presses): *Les singularitez de la France antarctique autrement nomée Amérique* by André Thevet. This latest American installment recorded the recent French expedition to Brazil led by Nicholas Durand, chevalier de Villegagnon (whom Thevet served as chaplain); and it provided a portrait of the natives and *naturalia* of "France's" *Amérique*, a term under which the author included the New World most generally, though Brazil more particularly. *Les singularitez* constituted the first major French contribution on America available in the Netherlands. It signaled also a bold entrée by the French into the project of describing – of *delineating* – the New World.[63]

Some background: Thevet's history followed a prolonged period of French initiatives, largely unsuccessful, to gain a foothold in the New World. As early as 1524, Giovanni da Verrazano visited the coasts of North America on behalf of the French Crown, and between 1534 and 1542 three further expeditions took place, led by Jacques Cartier and the Protestant noble, Roberval. Cartier and Roberval explored the area along the St. Lawrence, wintering twice on the inland banks of the river near the future site of Quebec. To sixteenth-century patrons and merchants, however, these Canadian expeditions elicited far less excitement than the Spanish finds to the south; the cod harvests of the northern waters compared only dimly with the precious metals, woods, and plants of the tropics. And if French traders reached the more enticing waters of Brazil only haphazardly and unofficially during the first half of the century, scattered reports of "Brazil" and its riches fired the French imagination far more than the *faux* diamonds brought back from Canada. Indeed, the most dramatic French response to the New World occurred when the town of Rouen, the center of France's brazilwood trade, staged a *fête brésilienne* to mark the royal visit of Henri II and Catherine de' Medici in 1550. In the best of Renaissance pageant traditions, the city recreated a Brazilian village replete with American fauna and flora and three hundred "Brazilians," part imported and part French sailors, forced to brave the cold October weather with only a Tupi feather dress.

The festival made a great impression on all who visited it – Catherine reportedly returned for a second viewing. It also seemed to ignite a more concerted French colonization drive, both in Brazil and later in Florida, spearheaded by the Admiral Gaspard de Coligny. In 1555, Coligny sponsored the Villegagnon expedition in which Thevet took part, and in the 1560s he oversaw three attempts to settle the coast of northeast Florida and South Carolina, none of which succeeded. Coligny was a staunch Calvinist, and many have pointed to the rising aspirations of French Huguenots as a source for this new found enthusiasm for America. While this may explain the "Florida" efforts, the Villegagnon expedition had as much to do with the international struggle of the French Valois and Spanish Habsburgs as it did with any national religious debate. Whatever the causes, French involvement in the New World took off in the 1550s, and, in the context of this invigorated interest in the Indies, Thevet undertook his description of the French *Amérique*.[64]

Although *Les singularitez* has a distinctly Gallic flavor, Thevet's text operated within the broader framework of European Americana, picking up where his predecessors' accounts left off, both substantively and stylistically. Like Vespucci or even Mandeville before him, Thevet described the many "wondrous things" of the New World, all of which he claimed to have witnessed during his brief, ten-week stay in Brazil; and he filled his *Amérique* with the same marvelous cannibals, beasts, and Amazons that inhabited much of the earlier travel literature. Like Zárate or Cortés, Thevet incorporated dramatic episodes of romance and chivalry (including the story of one "Damoiselle Marguerite," who fell in love with a French-Canadian Romeo, languished on a bear-infested island, and miraculously returned to Paris to tell the tale). And like Martyr and Oviedo, Thevet sprinkled his narrative liberally with learned references to ancient Scythians and Thebans, to Julius Caesar and Pallas Athena. He also borrowed, sometimes verbatim, from earlier works, including those of Martyr, Oviedo, and Cortés.[65]

Yet Thevet's account did more than just rework existing Americana. Embedded among the familiar themes and tropes of *Les singularitez* lay a singularly French argument for what Thevet's none too subtle title suggested should be a French-controlled *Amérique*. This argument coincided with the rise of French trade along the Brazilian coast (especially in dyewood, but also in sugar and cotton), a trade that the Crown, and Thevet as its servant, intended to bolster. Thevet made the case for France in America suggestively – in frequently drawn analogies between things "American" and things French[66] – as well as polemically, and nowhere more strongly than in his treatment of the French-Portuguese rivalry over Brazil. The future royal geographer decried the

Portuguese monopoly of the dyewood trade and what he considered the false premises upon which Portugal staked its claim. While the Lusitanians had never legitimately discovered the land (something Thevet credits to the Italian Vespucci), they dominated Brazil's trade to the exclusion of all other nations. Moreover, Thevet complained, the Portuguese misused their position to abuse the "innocent" natives of Brazil. "The wylde men of the countrey," he wrote of the dyewood harvest, "cut it [brazilwood] them selves and sometimes they bring or carie it three of foure leagues to the shippes. I leave to youre judgement the paine and travel, and al for to get some poore or course weede [garmet] and shirt."[67] The Portuguese, in other words, performed poorly as colonialists – a job for which the French, in the author's estimation, were better suited. In a way, then, Thevet reverses the formula of Martyr. Whereas Martyr inadvertently denigrates the Spaniard in his effort to elevate the innocent native, Thevet sympathetically draws the Brazilian in order to sabotage the cruel Portuguese. In the process, he localizes "America." For, in castigating the Portuguese, Thevet appropriates the battlegrounds of America for the conflicts of Europe – a lesson European propagandists from all quarters would soon enough learn. "America" could now be recast in an anti-Portuguese, anti-Spanish, or even anti-French mold, and the native Indians usefully configured as need be.

Thevet had discovered and deployed a more polemical and more plastic form of American geography, devising a literary strategy that would recur for years to come, especially in the context of France's American enterprise. The Brazilian expedition and its ultimate failure – Villegagnon departed for France in 1559 and the colony succumbed to the Portuguese shortly thereafter – remained a lively topic of debate in the decades that followed. Thevet himself returned to the episode in a larger, more controversial work of 1575, *La cosmographie universelle*, yet this time the target of his attack was the Huguenot contingent that had joined the colony in 1556 and bore, according to Thevet, primary responsibility for its collapse. A former Franciscan friar by now well connected to the powerful Catholic Guise faction at court, Thevet heaped partisan scorn on the "seditious" Calvinists and their "bloody Gospel," blaming them for the confessional disputes that had led to the colony's unraveling. Villegagnon, the leader of the colony (and a client of the Guise), is fully exonerated. Yet, in the more hostile polemical universe of France in the 1570s, Thevet's work provoked harsh and immediate response, most vociferously from Jean de Léry, a battle-scarred veteran of France's Wars of Religion. As one of those "seditious" Huguenot ministers of the Brazil adventure, Léry took issue with nearly every aspect of Thevet's narrative and shifted the blame, accordingly, onto that "per-

fidious" papist, Villegagnon. More generally, his account of the affair –
Histoire d'un voyage fait en la terre du Bresil – reassessed the colony's demise in light of contemporary religious feuds in France. Léry directs his
calumny less at the Portuguese-Spanish enemy from without than at the
French-Catholic enemy from within. In doing so, he realigns the terms
of the New World dispute yet again. Rather than international arguments of conquest, Léry co-opts America for interconfessional arguments of conversion. What Thevet had started, Léry continued with
even greater polemical rancor, sowing Old World disputes in the terrain
of the New.[68]

Léry's engagement with America was highly consequential for the
Dutch process of reception, since both author and text intersected extensively with the world of international Calvinism. Léry's career leading up to the publication of the *Histoire* was very much shaped by the
Wars of Religion (1562–1598) that raged in the France of his day. Born in
Burgundy in 1534, Léry landed by his early twenties in Calvin's Geneva,
where he received training in the new religion. In 1556, he accompanied
a group of ministers sent to Brazil – according to Léry, at Villegagnon's
request, yet the latter denied this – as a preacher of the gospel, a carpenter, or (most probably) some combination of the two.[69] Upon his return to Europe in 1558, he resumed his work in Geneva and, in that partisan setting, composed an impassioned account of the Huguenot
mission in Brazil, *La persécution des fidèles en terre d'Amérique.* This work
appeared on its own in 1561 and as part of the Huguenot martyrology
of Jean Crespin, *L'Histoire des martyrs* (Geneva, 1564), which spread
word of the affair to Protestant communities across Europe. The story
of the "martyrdom of Brazil" first reached Dutch readers in Adriaan van
Haemstede's enormously influential *Geschiedenissen der vromer martelaren* (1566), which, like Crespin's work, became something of a handbook for the Calvinist faithful, reprinted regularly throughout the early
modern period.[70]

Léry's first ministry in Lyons (1562) put him in the thick of the increasingly violent French controversies of religion. In 1572, the year of
the St. Bartholomew's Day Massacre, he managed narrowly to escape a
violent death at the hands of an angry Catholic mob. He resurfaced in
the Calvinist stronghold of Sancerre, where he suffered, along with the
town, a royalist (Catholic) siege from January to August 1573. His *Histoire memorable de la ville de Sancerre,* published in 1574, recorded this
dark chapter in Reformation Europe's wars of faith. The *Histoire d'un
voyage,* published originally in 1578, came out three years after Thevet's
Cosmographie, six years after the St. Bartholomew's Day Massacre, and
more than twenty years after Léry's actual adventure in Brazil. It is in-

formed as much by the religious combat of contemporary France as by events of a bygone American colony; and it became an instant Calvinist classic, going through seven French-language printings within Léry's lifetime (1578–1611). Its quick translation into Latin, German, Dutch, and English, and its inclusion in Theodore de Bry's widely circulated collection, *Americae*, assured its spot in the broader Protestant canon of anti-Catholic literature.[71]

It is a spot well earned. The *Histoire d'un voyage* presented a Protestant version of America not in the gentle, suggestive tones of the tyro Hans Staden, but in the shriller notes of an experienced Huguenot minister. In rebutting the "falsehoods" of Thevet, in exposing the "perfidy" of Villegagnon, and in ridiculing the "savagery" of the Catholic Mass, Léry makes an unequivocally Calvinist case for America. The assault begins with a spirited dedication to the memory of Admiral Coligny, the recently martyred leader of the Huguenot faction, and proceeds with a vituperative harangue against Thevet and his Catholic backers. Léry then recounts the events of the ill-fated expedition as he recalled them: Villegagnon's request ("pretending to burn with zeal") for Calvinist ministers, his subsequent backsliding into the old Catholic faith, and his final, treacherous murder of five of the ministers and expulsion of the rest. For Villegagnon, who later reverted fully to Catholicism and fought until his death for the Guise party, Léry spares little venom. His pompous attire, swaggering arrogance, and fits of violence earn him Léry's utmost scorn: he is an "Orlando Furioso against those of the Reformed religion." Furthermore, his "false" prayers, poisonous pride, and unholy Mass earn him eternal damnation: he is "the Cain of America." To Léry, he embodies the corruption of Rome fused with the cruelty of the Guise – the very Whore of Babylon relocated in Brazil.[72]

Léry's Calvinist sensibilities also inform the representation of the natives and *naturalia* of Brazil, which he describes in dramatically different terms than Thevet or, for that matter, most of his non-Protestant predecessors. True to his Genevan training, Léry considers the Indians within the context of mankind's general depravity. In Léry's eyes, as Calvin's, all men were fallen, and Léry declines to single out Tupi sinfulness from that of the mass of nonelect. Such sensibilities prevent Léry from formulating a fantastic or marvelous image of the Indians – as Thevet, Vespucci, and others had done. The Tupi are humans like all others, "not taller, fatter, or smaller than we Europeans are; their bodies are neither monstrous nor prodigious with respect to ours." In fact, they had fared better than most: they are "a fine example of the corrupt nature of man," he comments not without a degree of contradiction.[73]

This somewhat sympathetic judgment betrays the presence of other influences, aside from Calvin's theology, in Léry's ethnography. At times Léry can wax rhapsodic on the "natural" gentleness of the natives' lives, using an arcadian vocabulary that suggests at least some exposure to the literature of antiquity.[74] A classicist vision, not unlike that of Martyr, colors his view of nature in the New World, its idyllic landscapes, and its innocent, if fallen, inhabitants. Léry's enthusiastic description of Brazil's *naturalia* commingles a humanist admiration for a rediscovered golden age with a Protestant love of Scripture – the Renaissance with the Reformation:

Every time that the image of this new world which God has let me see presents itself before my eyes, and I consider the serenity of the air, the diversity of the animals, the variety of the birds, the beauty of the trees and the plants, the excellence of the fruits, and, in short, the riches that adorn this land of Brazil, the exclamation of the prophet in Psalm 104 [verse 24] comes to mind; Oh Lord, how manifold are thy works! In wisdom hast thou made them all; the earth is full of thy riches.

The natives reap the benefits of such clean and salubrious air. They are peaceful, with "little care or worry"; possess strong and able bodies; and live long and robust lives – always vigorous, usually virtuous. The Tupi, in short, live in a pre-Christian state of nature. If "fallen," they seem to have landed better than most.[75]

Still, fallen they were, and Léry devotes a fair amount of attention to the "sins" of Tupi society. Once again, though, his consideration of the American scene relates closely to events in France. Integrated into his discussion of Brazilian religion – "superstitions" – runs a parallel critique of French Catholicism, which Léry denounces as inexcusably backward. Tupi attire and their concern with decorative feathers of various colors, "garments, headdresses, and bracelets so laboriously wrought," is likened to the full "papal splendor" roundly condemned by the reformers. The natives' *caouinage*, or celebratory festival with the potent *caouin* drink, includes excited, dancing performers, who remind Léry "of those over here [Europe] whom we call 'morris dancers,' who during the festivals of the patron saints of each parish, go about in fool's garb, scepter in hand and bells on their legs dallying and dancing the morris in among the houses and town squares." The *caouinage* reaches its climax with a dance of shaman-figures, who communicate with the spirits through sacred rattles called *maracas*. Léry dismisses this New World rite with obvious impatience, though not without expanding his criticism into a broader assault on Old World sorcery and the Catholic Church. "You could find no better comparison," he suggests of these native shamans, "than to the bell-ringers that accompany those impostors who, exploiting the credulity of our simple folk over here, carry from place to place the reliquaries of Saint Anthony or Saint Bernard, and other such instruments of idolatry." Elsewhere he compares the shamans to the Catholic clergy – "those superstitious ones, successors of the priest of Baal" – and Tupi object-worship to the Catholic addiction to relics and church statuary.[76]

At the center of Léry's discussion of American "sin" stands the issue of anthropophagy, and here, too, the Huguenot polemicist contrives to weave into his critique of the Tupinamba a parallel strike on Catholicism. By the 1570s, when Léry composed his *Histoire*, readers of Americana had come to expect graphic descriptions of their favorite New World savagery, cannibalism. Léry does not disappoint, providing gory details of "the ceremonies for killing and eating prisoners." French readers, additionally, had become familiar with the theme of anthropophagy in two further contexts. Not only did Huguenot pamphleteers ridicule the figurative cannibalism implied by the Roman Catholic Mass, but, in the wake of the massacres of Protestants in the early 1570s, when Catholics reportedly devoured the hearts and livers of their mutilated foes, Protestant writers also attacked the very real cannibalism of the Wars of Religion.[77] Tupi rites, viewed in this context, take on a whole new meaning. The Brazilian feasts of flesh appear relatively tame when compared to the deeds of the unruly mobs of Paris, "chewing and devouring human flesh"; or the flesh-selling butchers of Lyons, offering "the fat of human bodies . . . to the highest bidder"; or even the greedy usurers of France, "sucking blood and marrow, and eating everyone alive – widows, orphans and other poor people." The discussion of Tupi rites ends on an accusatory note, yet aimed at those "cannibals" closer to home:

So let us henceforth no longer abhor so very greatly the cruelty of the anthropophagous – that is, man-eating – savages. For since there are some here in our midst even worse and more detestable than those who, as we have seen, attack only enemy nations, while the ones over here [France] have plunged into the blood of their kinsmen, neighbors, and compatriots, one need not go beyond one's own country, nor as far as America, to see such monstrous and prodigious things.[78]

This conclusion supports Léry's ultimately sympathetic view of the Tupinamba. Poisoned until now by Catholic missionaries, the Tupi had lent an attentive ear to the Protestant proselytizing efforts of Léry, and, were it not for the heresy of Villegagnon, might have been drawn to the Reformed religion. Léry departs Brazil with mixed feelings and adds – some twenty years later – that "I often regret that I am not among the savages, in whom . . . I have known more frankness than in many over here, who, for their condemnation, bear the title of 'Christian.'"[79] What begins as a condemnation of the fallen state of natural man ends not only with reserved admiration for the Tupi, but with unreserved condemnation of the so-called civilized Catholics of France. Léry brings a process begun by Thevet to its ironic, if logical, conclusion. With Thevet, "America" becomes a subtle means to condemn the Portuguese thwarting the French in Brazil. In Léry's hands, "America" is manipulated more forthrightly to condemn the French-Catholic enemy harassing the Huguenots back home. The Pandora's box of American propaganda now lay open. Readers of Thevet and Léry learned how to maneuver the "noble savage" of the New World to attack ignoble practices of the Old. Such would be the strategy of Montaigne in "Des cannibales," and of the *philosophes* in the eighteenth century. Such would be the tactic, more immediately, of those Protestant propagandists of the 1570s and 1580s, who pressed Léry's text into action in their urgent campaign for godly reform.[80]

The excitement generated in France by the Brazilian adventure lent impetus to further efforts in, and narratives on, the New World. Under the patronage of the Admiral Coligny, three expeditions left Le Havre between 1562 and 1565 with the expressed aim of establishing a French colonial foothold on the strategic Florida peninsula. Though undertaken in the name of the Crown, these voyages, once again, assumed the more specifically Protestant character of their patrons and commanders. To captain the first and third expeditions, Coligny selected the illustrious Huguenot warrior, Jean Ribault, who would later play a role in the first French War of Religion. The second expedition sailed under the command of René de Laudonnière, a protégé of Coligny. The powerful Admiral envisioned the endeavor as a means to unite the feuding French Catholics and Huguenots against a mutual Spanish enemy and, in the process, to secure a haven for the Huguenots in America. Once again, though, the French forays failed miserably, the meager colony of Fort Caroline falling to the superior fleets of Pedro Menéndez de Avilés of Spain. Ribault, who had returned to Florida in 1565 directly from fighting in La Rochelle, was foiled, first, by the tempestuous weather and, next, by the treacherous Menéndez who massacred most of Ribault's men. Ribault himself died ingloriously – stabbed in the back, according to French accounts – and was enshrined as one of the early martyrs of the Huguenot cause. Indeed, the first Florida voyage coincided with the first French War of Religion, and, like nearly all public undertakings of that time, was an event as religiously significant for the Huguenots as it was politically relevant for France. The destruction of their coreligionists at the hands of the (Spanish) Catholics would become an event of paramount importance for French Calvinists, second perhaps only to the St. Bartholomew's Day Massacre in the collective Huguenot memory.[81]

The so-called *affaire Floride* also occasioned a flood of pamphlets which, much like the literature on Brazil, exploited events overseas to score propaganda points at home. Written originally in French, the "histories" of Florida proved popular enough to merit translation, and news of the colony quickly spread through Protestant networks of Northern Europe. Laudonnière, upon his return to France in 1565, composed a record of the voyages that placed the history of the colony within the context of the international rivalry between France and Spain. His version of events met with disapproval from the royal cosmographer, André Thevet, who objected to the poor portrayal of Spain, by now an ally of the French Catholic party; and the work remained suppressed until 1586. It gained notoriety mainly in its Latin form (produced by the Flemish printer Theodore de Bry), as part of the general anti-Spanish literature of the late sixteenth century.[82]

In the meantime, more influential narratives of the *affaire* circulated, and these emphasized precisely the perfidy of Spain. A key figure in the events he described with much at stake in terms of patronage and advancement, Laudonnière showed decorous restraint in composing what is a comparatively polished account. This is not the case with the *Discours de l'histoire de la Floride* (Dieppe, 1566) by Nicolas Le Challeux, which offered everything that Laudonnière's account did not: lurid, sensationalist tales of Spanish treachery set alongside pious homilies of Calvinist suffering. A "simple carpenter" (as all the sources describe him) of obscure Huguenot background, Le Challeux witnessed the fall of Fort Caroline in 1565 and survived to tell the dramatic story. His popular pamphlet – it went through six printings in 1566 alone and five more by the end of the century – smartly combines well-tried formulae of sacred prose with spicier tropes of secular adventure. It featured numerous pious, and largely Protestant gestures (in this regard, much like Staden's account), including passages clearly meant to appeal to a Calvinist reader. The narrator pointedly attributes his own miraculous survival neither to the intercession of any saint nor to his own (feeble) abilities, but to the "special grace" of God. "Alas, O Lord," writes this enlightened layman in one of the work's conspicuous moments of Protestant solemnity, "What are we but poor worms of the earth. . . . Let us, O Lord, remain firm in mind, sure of Thy favor and good will."[83]

At the same time, the narrative trades on details of "Catholic" tyrannies, gruesome slaughter, and Spanish cruelty. In representing a Habsburg raid on a Valois fort in a tropical setting, Le Challeux renders an exceptionally vivid impression of Spain's New World violence. All of this is accomplished with surprising theatricality, too, for a "simple carpenter." There is foreshadowing from the earliest encounter: "Our men recogniz[ed] with envy the strength of the Spaniards and their evil intent." There is mood: "Heavy showers of rain fell, the noise was deafening, and the lightning made the air like fire." There is suffering: "They [the Spanish] made a horrible, tragic slaughter of our forces, so great was the anger and hatred they had for our nation. They vied with one another to see who could best cut the throats of our people – healthy and sick, women and children. It was a pitiful and grievous sight." This last passage strikes a Hispanophobic pitch that would only intensify. The Spanish kill indiscriminately, "slaughter[ing] against all the rules of warfare"; they torture and taunt with "extreme cruelty"; and they murder most cravenly, finally slaying Ribault (Le Challeux claimed) with a dagger in the back.[84]

In all of this excitement, America and its flora, fauna, and natives have receded into the background. The presence of the Indians in particular has been virtually effaced, and much of the drama could just as easily have taken place in La Rochelle as La Floride. Virtually, but not completely: for in a rude turn of plot, Le Challeux has "Americanized" the enemy by adopting language previously used to describe the New World *sauvage* to malign the now demonized Castilian. Spanish savagery calls to mind the wildest fits of native American fury. In a passage of gratuitously graphic detail, Le Challeux sensationalizes Spanish cruelties in much the same way that earlier writers, both Spanish and French, had treated Indian violence. "They plucked out the eyes from the dead bodies, stuck them on their dagger points, and, with exclamations, taunts, and mocking, threw them at the boats," he writes of the Spanish troops. The Spanish antagonist here assumes the maim-and-mock tactics traditionally ascribed to the "wild" Indian. Le Challeux's narrative thus preserves America as the home of the savage, yet recasts the Spaniard as the primary perpetrator of American barbarities.[85]

If the Spaniard had been Americanized, the New World had finally been Europeanized. The America of Le Challeux and other French writers of the third quarter of the sixteenth century had become an extension of Europe: a place for European dynasties and European orthodoxies to extend their feuds and exert their influence. The struggle of Spain and France in Florida paralleled the struggle of the houses of Habsburg and Valois back home. This, of course, was nothing new. Since as early as the Treaty of Tordesillas in 1494, Europe had exported its differences to unsuspecting territories overseas. What had changed by the mid-sixteenth century was the introduction of a distinctly literary dimension to the equation. The French had appropriated the *prose* of the New World to settle political and religious scores in the Old. Thevet exploited the image of Brazilian toil to criticize Portuguese expansion. Beleaguered French Calvinists, more avidly still, incorporated "American" themes into their expanding repertoire of religious propaganda. Léry, in his manner, Catholicized the rites of the Tupi just as Le Challeux Indianized the cruelty of Spanish. Each, in sum, demonstrated a keen understanding of the polemical possibilities of America – and their lessons would endure.

VII

To portray America as the landscape of Spanish tyranny, as Le Challeux had done, seems in retrospect hardly a stroke of originality. Yet up until the middle of the sixteenth century, few outside of French Calvinist circles showed much inclination to wage a war of words against Spain and to use, expressly, descriptions of America to do so. Even in the literature of the Huguenots, the *Catholic* menace, French or Iberian, loomed larger than a specifically Spanish foe. Much of this changed, however, by the 1560s and 1570s, when not only Le Challeux's pamphlet began to circulate, but another, more substantial and broadly accessible work first appeared: Girolamo Benzoni's *Historia del mondo nuovo* (1565), a singularly dark, despairing, antichivalric, and anti-Hispanic description of the New World. Published a stunning seventeen times before the close of the century, and translated into Dutch, French, Latin, German, and English, it became, in the words of J. H. Parry, the "most popular" history of America in its day.[86] It set a whole new standard for the representation of the New World: one that promoted, in fiercely polemical language, a harshly critical view of Castile's *Conquista;* and one that would influence, for years to come, the shape of Northern Europe's America.

The new view of the Indies derived from an author deeply ambivalent about the colonial project he described. Girolamo Benzoni, like Peter Martyr, hailed from the duchy of Milan, a territory that, by the mid-sixteenth century, had joined the New World as part of the Spanish empire. Like Martyr, again, he came into the orbit of America by way of service to Spain – perhaps as a trader, but more probably as a soldier or adventurer.[87] Both men remained keenly aware of their Italian background and both exhibit in their writing a subtle loyalty to the Italian role in the discovery of America. (Witness the favorable treatment each accords to the oft-derided Columbus.)[88] Both, too, owed their popularity to a largely non-Spanish audience, and neither was ever translated into Castilian. Unlike Martyr, though, Benzoni lacked all but the most basic education, and he sailed to the New World at the age of twenty-two aiming to make his fortune rather than write of it. By his own admission, he took part in many of the conquistador exploits he details, including slave raids in the Caribbean, and he based his account on these and other first-hand experiences. He wrote in an unadorned, matter-of-fact style, with none of the erudition, polish, or grace of Martyr's *Decades*. Benzoni's is very much a soldierly account in contrast to Martyr's scholarly opus.

Still, on many points the two men agreed. Both reached, if by slightly different paths, an ultimately sympathetic opinion of those American natives whom their patrons had conquered. Benzoni, a participant in the slave trade, had initially dismissed certain tribes outright as "savage," "monstrous," or even "brute animals or beasts." Yet precisely because he witnessed the less seemly side of Spain's American economy, he later developed a more charitable view of the Indians' plight, which he considered "unfortunate," "wretched," or even "doleful." These judgments lead him to describe the Caribbeans in terms that, if not quite as poetic as Martyr's, recall nonetheless some of the classically tinged passages used by the elder humanist to construct an American Golden Age of peace and innocence. "Some say that these people were very great thieves," writes Benzoni of the native islanders,

[B]ut what could they steal? They are neither avaricious nor rich, and what they least prized was gold and silver, since whoever wished for any could go to the mine and get as much as they liked, as people do at a spring of water. Respecting clothing, they all go naked; as to eatables everybody gives to whoever goes to his house. And whenever they assemble at their festivals, the whole tribe brings eatables, and they sing and dance till they get drunk and are tired; and so they freely pass a happy time. I cannot imagine thieving among them, unless they learned the art . . . from the Spaniards.[89]

In this and other discourses on the nature of the Indian, Benzoni deftly blends two visions of the New World. For, while he evokes all the essential ingredients of a golden age – lack of greed, absence of clothing, indiscrete property – he also suggests the possibility of an alternative scenario – intemperance, avarice, the "art" of thieving. The Indians merit praise precisely for their *absence* of sin; they are praiseworthy in their passiveness. The Spanish, by contrast, actively stimulate vice and depravity:

If the Spaniards had shown any kindness when they first entered those countries and had persevered in exercising benignity and humanity, instead of persevering in cruelty and avarice, we might have hoped that the generation of savages would have learned to cultivate reason, to acquire some degree of virtue and honor, and have been creditable to the Christian name.[90]

This juxtaposition of New World virtue with Old World sin calls to mind, once again, the *Decades* of Martyr. Yet an important distinction separates the two: Martyr's humanism drew him to the figure of the "innocent American," who might have afforded sixteenth-century humanists a chance to observe the lost Golden Age but for the intrusion of Spain. Benzoni, guided by his own experience *in* America, focuses on the ignominies of the Spaniard, while the native's "innocence" serves simply as a useful contrast to Spanish guilt.

More than Martyr, Benzoni emphasized the dark and destructive side of the *Conquista*. Neither in the pay of the Spanish Crown nor in the thrall of classical learning, Benzoni enjoyed a freedom of expression unknown to his distinguished predecessor. His account inclines less toward the Ovidian landscape of gentle and complacent Indians than to the spectacle of pitiless and brutal conquistadors. He provided, in fact, the most complete catalogue of Spanish cruelties available to the non-Spanish reader.[91] The Spanish in Benzoni's *Mondo nuovo* commit savage tyrannies and behave with beastly rapacity. They "jump out like wolves" to attack defenseless natives who, in passive innocence, fall "like so many lambs." They maraud, like "foxes" in the night, and slaughter unsuspecting natives who lie "asleep . . . without any fear of enemies." They "burn," "ambush," and "scour" their way through the countryside in their relentless search for gold, silver, and slaves. The conquistador-as-caballero image – the spectacle of "fire and sword" that Zárate and others had invoked in their epic histories of the *Conquista* – is turned on its head. Cortés, according to Benzoni, burns "by slow degrees" an unyielding secretary of Motecuçoma. Pizarro roams the countryside of Peru "killing natives in all directions, not pardoning one," while his assistant – "the monk" – urges Spanish soldiers "to kill by thrusts lest by using the sharp edge of their swords they might break them." Benzoni reserves some of his harshest criticism for the settlers of America, who had invented ever more grisly means to torment their Indian (and African) slaves:

And there being among the Spaniards some who are not only cruel, but very cruel, when a man occasionally wished to punish a slave, either for some crime that he had committed, or for not having done a good day's work, or for spite he had towards him . . . he had his hands and feet tied to a piece of wood laid across, so permitted under the rule of the Spaniards . . . then with a thong or rope he was beaten until his body streamed with blood; which done, they took a pound of pitch or a pipkin of boiling oil and threw it gradually all over the unfortunate victim; then he was washed with some of the country pepper mixed with salt and water. He was thus left on a plank covered with a cloth, until the master thought he was again able to work.[92]

In the *Mondo nuovo,* the Spanish kill cruelly and at random. They also consume everything they can get their hands on: the land, its goods, and its people. "This province," the author writes of Panama, "used to be inhabited by several tribes. . . . But the Spanish have consumed everything." They also consume, like some great Aztec, man-eating god, the populations of Hispaniola, Cuba, and the port city of Cartagena, which "was all inhabited by Indian fishermen; but now there is no symptom even of the houses that used to be there." "Wherever the Spaniards have reached," intones Benzoni gravely, "there are scarcely any miserable Indian villages remaining." The Spaniards drive the Indians either to valiant resistance, or, equally heroic within this context, solemn suicide. The theme of suicide is Benzoni's addition to the literature of America, and it occurs with unsettling frequency throughout the account. The enslaved Indians of the mines, according to Benzoni, sought every opportunity to escape to the woods where they could hang themselves, sometimes using their own hair for lack of proper rope. The natives of Cartegena and Nicaragua threw themselves into fires or starved themselves, though not before killing their babies to protect them from Spanish swords. Benzoni's catalogue of suicides continues unremittingly. The situation on Hispaniola had deteriorated, he writes, "till the natives, finding themselves intolerably oppressed and worked on every side, with no chance of regaining their liberty, with sighs and tears longed for death."

Wherefore, many went to the woods and there [hanged] themselves, after having killed their children saying it was far better to die than to live so miserably, serving such and so many ferocious tyrants and wicked thieves. The women, with the juice of a certain herb, dissipated their pregnancy, in order not to produce children, and then following the example of their husbands, [hanged] themselves. Some threw themselves from high cliffs down precipices; others jumped into the sea; others again into rivers; and others starved themselves to death. Sometimes they killed themselves with their flint knives; others pierced their bosoms or their sides with pointed stakes.[93]

This remarkable scene of despair-driven women replays itself with uncomfortable regularity, for mother and child feature most conspicuously in Benzoni's tragedy of America. The plight of the Indian woman – hunted, raped, and enslaved by the Spanish – contrasts sharply with previous portrayals of the lascivious, New World Amazon who posed a *threat* to the Spaniard. Spanish slave raids commonly rounded up victims, "the greater part women and children." If some of these could not walk, the Spaniards, "to prevent their remaining behind to make war, killed them by burying their swords in their sides or breasts." The notorious Francisco Roldán descends on St. Domingo, attending "to nothing but robbing, ravishing the women." The governor of the island Margarita, Pedro de Herrera, leads an expedition to Amaracapanna, where he rounds up the helpless women, "unfortunate mothers, with two and three children clinging around their neck, overwhelmed with tears and grief, all tied with cords or with iron chains. . . . Nor was there a girl but had been violated by the depredators." Not without a price, though: "wherefore from too much indulgence, many Spaniards entirely lost their health" – a sly authorial reference to the "Spanish" pox. All in all, the women of Benzoni's America suffer appallingly. Some induce their own abortions; others commit suicide; and some, like the women of Nicaragua, beg their tribesmen to "kill them and their little children, so that they should not remain alone in the hands of those cruel and fierce bearded men."[94]

The *Mondo nuovo* of Benzoni harbors none of the otherworldly monsters, defiant Amazons, or enticing Lucayans that inhabit earlier Americana. Rather than harking back to the myths of antiquity or the fables of the Middle Ages, Benzoni invokes the more familiar, though no less frightening, images of sixteenth-century Europe – pillage, war, and slaughter in the name of God and gain. His tropes of New World violence refer more directly to the chronicles of sixteenth-century wars – between Spaniards and Moors, Catholics and Protestants, Europeans and Ottomans – than to the romances of medieval chivalry. And if Benzoni does not glorify Spanish deeds in the New World with the grand sweep of Martyr or perhaps Zárate, his jeremiad against Spanish misdeeds is no less monumental in its scope. Tribes are decimated, lands are ravaged, and women are raped in epic numbers.

At the heart of this American tragedy resides the "Spanish nation," to which Benzoni time and again returns. The Spanish have failed in the New World as Christians, and this, Benzoni contends, owes as much to the specific shortcomings of the conquistadors as to the more general faults of the Castilians. Their "unbearable arrogance," their internecine violence, and their insatiable lust for war, wealth, and women casts a dark shadow over the reputation of good Christians everywhere. "Seeing our rabid greediness and immeasurable avarice," notes Benzoni wryly,

there are some among the [natives] who, taking a piece of gold in their hand, say, "this is the God of the Christians; for this they have come from Castile to our countries, and subjugated us, tormented us, and sold us as slaves, besides doing us many other injuries. For this they make war and kill each other; for this it is that they are never at rest; that they gamble, swear, tell lies, quarrel, rob, tear the women away from each other . . . for this they commit every sort of wickedness."

Likewise, the clerics and monks sent by the Crown to conquer the souls of the Indians had failed miserably. These "gaming and swearing" ambassadors of the Church set the worst possible example for the native Americans. The Christian mission had been betrayed, and the Indians, as a consequence, suffered spiritual and physical abuse alike under the yoke of Spain.[95]

Where earlier chroniclers had sung "numerous praises of the Spanish nation," Benzoni assaults the very Spanish "character" itself in his ceaselessly shrill critique of the conquest of America. The violence, crudeness, avarice, disloyalty, and distrust among the competing captains of the *Conquista* provide Benzoni the opportunity to blacken the Spanish character with the broadest of strokes. In a relatively lengthy anecdote intended to illustrate the "inflated vanity" of the Castilians, Benzoni diverts his reader from events in America to the "magnificent city of Sienna," where, as he relates, a "vaunting" Spanish swordsman stationed there issued a challenge to his Italian hosts, bragging "that the virtue of the Spanish nation was superior to that of every other country." A "generous and modest" reply from a young Roman prepares the way for a duel where the Spaniard is vanquished by the "valiant" challenger. The affair takes place in the Old World – more significantly, in cinquecento Tuscany, where the "great abundance" of poets could "gloriously and learnedly" sing the praise of the victor – and in this clever narrative maneuver Benzoni relocates the New World drama to the cradle of European civilization, Italy. Where previous authors had characterized Spanish deeds in America using the popular topoi of European literature – ancient virtue, medieval chivalry, Renaissance cunning – Benzoni reverses this pattern. The topoi of Spanish misdeeds committed *in America* are now resituated in Europe: a Spanish mercenary in Italy acquires the attributes of an American conquistador. By locating this particular incident in Renaissance Italy, furthermore, Benzoni juxtaposes Tuscany's recent glory, civility, and cultural refinement with Spain's present ignominy, barbarity, and culture of "vanity." Spain fails in its civilizing program, Benzoni suggests, while Italy has succeeded magnificently in its own.[96]

Benzoni's Hispanophobia is striking. It can be explained, in part, by his actual experiences in Spanish America both as a slave trader and as a hardened veteran of the *Conquista*. Yet a certain amount of the author's rancor owes something to the European context of the account and to attitudes likely formulated before Benzoni ever left Lombardy.[97] Spain's conquest of the New World coincided with a similar plan of expansion in the Old. The concomitant Habsburg plundering of the treasure houses of Italy and America during the sixteenth century make it only natural that the Italian-born Benzoni might have adopted a somewhat skeptical, if not cynical, view of Spain's "mission" overseas. It could hardly have escaped the attention of contemporaries that, just a few years after Cortés staged Motecuçoma's oath of loyalty to the Habsburg emperor (1519), the very same Charles V and his Spanish officers orchestrated the sack of Rome (1527). Lombardy fell to the Spanish, in fact, only months after Peru. Just prior to the publication of the *Mondo nuovo* appeared the tremendously popular *Istoria d'Italia* of Francesco Guicciardini, which provided vivid descriptions of the Spanish conquest of Prato (outside of Florence) in 1512 and the subsequent barbarities of Habsburg-sponsored *Landsknechten*. Guicciardini took a similarly dim view of the aims of an expansive Habsburg empire. Benzoni told a familiar tale, only this time with a transatlantic focus.[98]

Benzoni's rendition of America, while sharing certain features with earlier accounts, established a fully new standard for the genre and set a fresh course for many of the New World narratives that would follow. The *Mondo nuovo* combined all of the high-minded indignation of Martyr with the luridly "low-brow" details of Staden. It evinced, as did Léry's account, a considerable degree of sympathy for the tormented, if heathen, Indians, while avoiding the Calvinist minister's provincialism. In the preface to the 1585 edition of the *Histoire*, Léry suggestively speculates on the relationship of his work and Benzoni's and concludes that there existed something of a "conformité entre lui et moi." The New World served both authors well as a locus of Old World conflict; both situated on the battlegrounds of America wars well underway back in Europe. Léry reverted to "America" in his attack on Catholicism, while the Catholic Benzoni used America to focus on the reckless Spanish missionaries of that faith. Both, too, published within a few years of 1570, and in many ways they mark the culmination of a trend, which had started around the middle of the century, to retell the story of America in progressively less sanguine, less romantic, and certainly less Hispanophilic terms. In important ways, however, Benzoni parted company with his literary precursors, producing a work that surpassed all others in the intensity and ferocity of its attack on Spain. Like his predecessors, Benzoni still represented the New World by employing tropes, allegories, and myths familiar to his readers; yet the myths now involved the Spaniard as much as the Indian, and the myth of Spanish cruelty had come to replace the myth of native savagery (or innocence) as the foremost theme of the story. Benzoni introduced many of the elements that would feature in the subsequent assaults on the Spanish character – the so-called Black Legend – and prove so popular through the late sixteenth and seventeenth centuries.[99]

The *Mondo nuovo* was itself popular, in fact extraordinarily so. Whatever the local, or even personal, contexts of the account, Benzoni's narrative found a wide and receptive audience among readers on both sides of the Alps who, with a variety of "Americas" to choose from, responded with evident enthusiasm to the Spanish-bashing prose of this Milanese soldier. The *Historia del mondo nuovo* was first published in Venice in 1565 (twice) and reprinted in 1572. While the Spanish showed little desire to translate the work, by the late 1570s Benzoni's narrative exploded onto the rest of the European literary market as few works on the New World had ever before. In 1578, a Latin edition came off the presses of the Calvinist and Geneva-based publisher, Urbain Chauveton, and at least four further Latin editions appeared by 1600. A widely cited French version, also published in Geneva, was printed in 1579, the same year a German translation came out in Basel. The German edition was printed repeatedly in the following years, individually and as part of de Bry's *Americae* from 1594.[100] A Dutch-language edition, translated from the Italian by Karel van Mander, was published in 1610. Since van Mander died in 1606 and had been working on his monumental *Schilderboeck* during the final years of his life, there is good reason to believe that a manuscript of the translation had been available already for some time and perhaps even circulated among van Mander's literary and artistic colleagues in Haarlem in the later years of the sixteenth century.[101]

The conduit by which Benzoni's America reached the Netherlands – the very eminent poet, painter, and humanist, Karel van Mander – is significant. A figure of van Mander's stature exercised influence not only in the world of arts and letters, but also in the broader sociopolitical circles of his adoptive cities of Haarlem and Amsterdam. His association with Benzoni appears, at first glance, somewhat curious: why the engagement with America? As a young man, van Mander did travel – a pilgrimage to Rome took him through Germany, Bohemia, and the city-states of northern Italy – though never beyond Europe. It was in Italy that he would have come across the *Mondo nuovo* (reprinted the year before his arrival in 1573) and perfected his language skills sufficiently to translate into Dutch this and other Italian and Latin works of literature. Van Mander does not mention coming across any Americana in the courts of the South; yet, upon his return, he does come into contact with what is considered the earliest landscape painting of the New World.

Van Mander, as it turns out, not only served as translator of the "most popular" history of the New World, but also provided the only description – translation, as it were – of the first portrait of the New World produced in the sixteenth century: the *West Indies Landscape* of Jan Mostaert.

VIII

Though the New World received significant notice from chroniclers, cosmographers, and even humanists of the Renaissance, it only sporadically and incidentally entered the *oeuvres* of visual artists. America could only rarely be *seen* – in the Netherlands as elsewhere in Europe through the first two-thirds of the sixteenth century.[102] There existed, certainly, a minority of travelers and scholars who recognized the importance of creating a pictorial record of the New World. "It needs to be painted by the hand of a Berruguete or some other painter like him, or by Leonardo da Vinci or Andrea Mantegna, famous painters whom I knew in Italy," asserted the naturalist Gonzalo Fernández de Oviedo in 1535. This plea, however, remained largely unanswered. In the 1570s, Francisco Hernández took a team of scholars, draftsmen, and painters with him on an expedition to Mexico, yet their results remained unpublished, destroyed by a fire in 1671; and by the early nineteenth century, Alexander von Humboldt would make an appeal similar to Oviedo's to the artists of his day. In this context of visual paucity and even painterly negligence, Mostaert's ambitious composition properly stands out.[103]

To a certain degree, crude woodblock prints and, later, more sophisticated engravings filled the visual gap. These ordinarily accompanied travel accounts, and they often show similarities, in graphic terms, to the narrative styles they illustrated. Sensationalist and often lurid depictions thus adorned the earliest broadsides and pamphlets. A 1509 German issue of Vespucci typically contained one woodcut showing the seduction and murder of a "good-looking" European (fig. 5), another displaying a "Brazilian" who urinates indifferently beside a barbecue of human flesh. Staden's account also included its share of voyeuristic snapshots of native mores (with Staden usually inserted in a helpless, if pious, pose), and even Léry's sober text featured scenes of the fabulous demons, dragons, and other beasts encountered in America. In Léry's account, the reader confronts the opposite sort of print, too, namely poetically classicized depictions of the "savage," who now possessed a vaguely European physiognomy and a vocabulary of European rhetorical gestures. More classicized still are the languid figures that decorate

Figure 5. Illustration from Amerigo Vespucci, *Diss büchlin saget wie die zwen durch lüchtigsten herren her Fernandus K. zü Castilien and herr Emanuel K. zü Portugal haben das weyte mör ersüchet unnd funden vil Insulen unnd Nüwe welt . . . vormals unbekant* (Strassburg, 1509). Photo courtesy of the Edward Ayer Collection, The Newberry Library, Chicago.

Thevet's *Singularitez*. Based on drawings by the French Mannerist, Jean Cousin, Thevet's prints elevated the native American to a level of elegant nobility far above the indifferent descriptions of the text (fig. 6). Whatever Thevet's written opinions of the Indians – and the narrative presents a uniformly dismissive vision of the depraved *sauvages* of Canada and Brazil – the graphic images of powerful Renaissance bodies, modeled in graceful *contrapposto*, tell an entirely different story.[104]

This verbal-visual hodgepodge was not uncommon, and, more often than not, the earliest prints of America conflated Old World images with New World captions. The Dutch edition of Zárate illustrated the jungle wars of the Pizarros with woodblock prints lifted directly from a late medieval romance. Knights on stalwart steeds charge across a thoroughly European scene of chivalry (see fig. 4). As late as the 1590s, the great Flemish printer Theodore de Bry adopted an Old Testament scene of the Deluge to portray the shipwreck of Nicuesa off the coast of Venezuela. A cursorily added Spanish galleon in the upper right corner confirms the scene as a *New* World adventure.[105] This lack of distinction applied also to the Amerindians, who appear, seemingly haphazardly, in a number of "oriental" prints, such as the *People of Calicut* (1517–1518) after Hans Burgkmair the Elder. "Indians" of the subcontinent, wearing Brazilian feather dresses and carrying prominent stalks of maize, solemnly march behind a large-eared (that is, *African*) elephant carrying a turbaned mahout (fig. 7).[106] Burgkmair also designed the "African People" who populate the van Doesborch-produced Asian travelogue, *Of the newe landes* (1522), that included opening and closing passages referring to "Armenica." A more elaborate version of this visual indistinction occurs in the *Adoration of the Magi*, executed circa 1505 for the polyptych of the Viseu Cathedral (Portugal). In the center of a triad of wise men from "the East" stands a tawny-skinned figure carrying a Tupinamba arrow and wearing various (Brazilian?) feather accessories. He is arrayed, however, in unquestionably European britches and an elegant blouse of gauze.[107]

Nearly all images of "Americans" portray stylized, classicized "natives," for only rarely did artists draw New World figures from genuine Indian models and only more rarely still did such images circulate widely. Christopher Weiditz's sketches of bona fide Mexican jugglers at the court of Charles V (visiting with an entourage sent by Cortés in 1528) represent the exception that proves the rule, and even these drawings never reached a broader audience. Dürer, who had seen the Aztec featherwork and richly decorated gold and silver vessels of Motecuçoma, sent in 1520, "marveled at the subtle *ingenia* of men in foreign lands." He failed, however, to give expression to his admiration on wood, cop-

Figure 6. Illustration from André Thevet, *Les singularitez de la France antarctique autrement nomée Amérique* (Antwerp, 1558). Courtesy of the John Carter Brown Library, Brown University.

per, or canvas, and the cash-hungry emperor summarily sent the exhibition to be melted down for bullion. Certainly few *paintings* of the New World were ever commissioned, suggesting an apparent lack of interest on the part of sixteenth-century patrons. Charles did retain some of the artifacts sent by Cortés, which eventually made the rounds in various courts of the Habsburgs' European empire. Some ended up with Charles's aunt, Margaretha of Austria, who served as the regent in the Netherlands. These, in turn, may have inspired Jan Mostaert, among the regent's retinue of artists, to paint what van Mander would later call the "West Indies Landscape" (see fig. 1).[108]

The unique subject, impressive dimensions, and ambitious scope of Mostaert's composition render it among the outstanding samples of sixteenth-century Americana. It has attracted outstanding scholarly attention, too, ever since the painting's identification (rediscovery, in effect, since no record exists after the sixteenth century) in 1909. At that time, the panel was ascribed to Mostaert on the basis of van Mander's simple description: "a West Indies landscape." Since then, however, the precise

Figure 7. After Hans Burgkmair the Elder, *People of Calicut*, 1517–1518 (woodcut). Staatsgalerie Stuttgart, Graphische Sammlung.

location and more specific significance of the scene have been the subject of broad speculation and lively debate, underscoring the very multivalence of "America" – in Mostaert's day no less than our own. Earliest assumptions were of a Columbian encounter: Mostaert sought to depict Europe's inaugural experience of America. Yet in 1931, Edouard Michel shifted the context by suggesting a Cortésian conquest and a Mexican scene dating from the 1520s. On that basis he argued that the panel was commissioned by Margaretha circa 1523–1525, soon after Cortés's reports reached Europe and while Mostaert was presumably still in her employ.[109] Soon this argument was challenged by R. van Luttervelt, who pointed out that none of the attributes of the scene corresponded to the fabulous descriptions of Aztec wealth or Motecuçoma's colorfully clad subjects. He proposed, rather, that the details of the painting conform more closely to accounts of an expedition by Francisco Vásquez de Coronado, who explored the area of today's Southwestern United States in search of "Cibola," the Seven Cities of Gold. In a rather ingenious argument, van Luttervelt located in Mostaert's landscape the pueblo huts and stone-throwing Zuñi tribesmen described in Coronado's *relaciones*. The extraordinary rock formations in the background, van Luttervelt suggested, matched the geological structures of the Col-

cont. of Fig. 7.

orado Plateau – the Rainbow Ridge in southern Utah or the Window Arch of Arizona, for example, both of which may have been on Coronado's itinerary. Coronado's reports arrived back in Europe from 1542, and van Luttervelt dates the painting around 1542, by which time Mostaert had already left Margaretha's court and returned to his native Haarlem.[110]

Other readers have discerned other landscapes, shifting both the place and time of Mostaert's subject. The scene depicts neither the Zuñi of "Cibola" nor the Aztecs of Mexico, according to Eric Larsen, but rather the natives of Brazil. Pointing to the nudity of the central figures, Larsen reasons that Mostaert could not have intended to portray North American tribes, since these tribes always went clothed. Based on the presence of a South American macaw perched on a stump in the foreground, Larsen proposes that the scene portrays the Tupinamba of Brazil ("land of parrots") at the moment of a fatal encounter with Portuguese forces. The Spanish flag on the right of the panel, he suggests, is a later addition. By comparing details of the painting to contemporary descriptions of Brazil, especially those of Staden, Larsen situates the action of the painting more specifically in the vicinity of the Bahia de Todos os Santos, where a series of skirmishes took place in the mid-

sixteenth century; and he dates the painting among the final works of
Mostaert's oeuvre (ca. 1550–1555), coinciding with Portugal's renewed
activity in the region.[111] In the latest contribution to the debate it is argued that the scene is not of the New World at all. Charles Cuttler has
called attention to what he considers a classical column, partly hidden
on the left side of the panel, and posits that Mostaert had a manifestly
Old World theme in mind. He cites as Mostaert's model Jacopo de' Barbari's woodcut of the *Battle of Men and Satyrs* (ca. 1497–1500), which
shows an arcadian world attacked from without by an exotic invader. It
would have been at the court of the regent Margaretha in Mechelen,
where Jacopo served from 1515–1520, that Mostaert could have studied
this mythological scene. Relating the work to Joachim Patinir's landscape style of the 1520s, Cuttler dates this "Arcadian Landscape" circa
1520, about the time Mostaert's tenure with Margaretha would have
ended.[112]

Could a "West Indies landscape" lie outside of the New World? It is
a testament to the fluidity of "America" that it very well could, in its earliest years, fall both within and without the newly encountered regions
of the West. New World landscapes, from Old World perspectives, were
necessarily complicated canvases. Cuttler and his predecessors base
their arguments on a number of assumptions about Mostaert's knowledge of the Discoveries and America. They also presume, perhaps
rashly, that there existed a single, obvious, and sensible set of ideas that
described "America." Yet various "Americas" competed for readers'
and viewers' attention throughout the early sixteenth century, and to re-
construct for Mostaert a precise and *prescriptive* body of geographic
knowledge is no simple task. Jan Mostaert (ca. 1475–1555) was, like his
biographer Karel van Mander, a long-time Haarlemmer, and he almost
certainly never made the voyage to America. Slightly more cosmopolitan than the average Netherlander of his age – van Mander reports that
the artist came from a "noble and famous family"[113] – Mostaert did
travel around Europe with the court of the regent, whom he reportedly
served for eighteen years at Mechelen. At the court, too, he would have
come into contact with New World artifacts sent by Margaretha's
nephew, Charles V.[114] Both at Mechelen and back at Haarlem, he could
have read the literary descriptions of the New World available at the
time: the wondrous reports of Columbus, the monster-filled letters of
Vespucci, the knightly *Cartas* of Cortés. As a member of a more learned
circle of artists, Mostaert might also have been drawn to the classically
informed *Decades* of Peter Martyr, which described a new world of
utopian innocence and Ovidian grace. As for the *relaciones* of Coronado,

Mostaert could only have heard gossip or hearsay from friends at court. It is unlikely, though, that he was even present at the court in the 1540s when such verbal reports would have circulated, and Coronado's written account was published only after Mostaert's death in 1555.[115]

All of this does not imply that Mostaert would not have had some idea of the events of Coronado's expedition – of the Spanish exploration of uncharted lands, of their encounter with cliff-dwelling natives, of stones hurled at steel-bearing invaders, of a fruitless search for gold – though it is doubtful that he had the neat, coherent narrative that his exegetes have come to expect from him. If early literary and graphic representations of America happily mixed fact with fiction and truth with trope, Mostaert's painting of "America" can hardly be expected to show greater consistency. His *West Indies Landscape* evokes New World themes by combining the exotic, the familiar, and the familiarly exotic. If a Brazilian parrot decorates the foreground, so too do such common European fauna as hare, sheep, and cattle, all typical denizens of the pastoral landscape. The *arco naturale* that van Luttervelt associates with the landscape of Arizona represented a common enough feature of sixteenth-century landscape painting, regularly appearing in scenes of "St. Jerome in the Wilderness" and other *Weltlandschaften* by the likes of Cornelis Massys and Henri Bles (fig. 8). A similar geological structure decorates the background of another Mostaert painting, *Portrait of a Woman*, a work hardly noteworthy for its exoticism.[116] Finally, if the figures occupying the heart of the panel lack any "American" attire, this only exposes their undeniably European bodies. Those bits of "civil" dressing that Mostaert does include – the fur-lined hats crowning the three otherwise naked men in the center of the composition – refer, iconographically at least, to Asiatic "Tartars" as featured, for example, in Abraham de Bruijn's costume book, *Omnium pene Europae, Asiae, Aphricae atque Americae gentium habitus*.[117] The *West Indies Landscape*, then, brings together a variety of exotic, otherworldly motifs as perceived by a somewhat worldly, but undeniably Netherlandish, artist of the sixteenth century. Nonetheless, enough obviously American details exist – the bizarre cliff houses and straw huts; the rude, rock-throwing defenders; the European assault on a primitive society – to suggest that the work was based, at least in part, on reports of the New World. It shows, in all cases, the clash of European (whether Spanish or Portuguese) steel with an innocent age of stone. While it would be possible to *avoid* calling this scene a specifically New World landscape and place it instead within the context of Renaissance Arcadianism, it is also eminently possible to fit the work into contemporary views of the New World, influenced, as they

Figure 8. Henri Bles, *Landscape with St. Jerome* (76 × 106 cm). Namur, Musée des Arts anciens du Namurois. Collection de la Société archéologique de Namur, inv. 158.

were, by some of the very same images of antiquity and the Ovidian Golden Age. The demand of modern scholars for compositional precision in Mostaert's work misconceives the Renaissance's subtle and evolving notion of the (indeed) New World.[118]

Though establishing the subject of Mostaert's *West Indies Landscape* poses certain difficulties, tracing van Mander's opinion of the painting, perhaps an equally critical inquiry, presents fewer problems. To return, then, to the beginning: "There is also a landscape," records the *Schilderboeck*, "essentially a West Indies Landscape, with many naked people, a jagged cliff, and a strange construction of houses and huts; though it is left unfinished."[119] This last comment about the state of the panel implies that the painting was unlikely to have been commissioned. It is also noteworthy that the work remained within the Mostaert family and that van Mander saw it in the home of the artist's grandson, Nicolaes Suyker, then *schout* of Haarlem. Van Mander singles it out, at any rate, as one of Mostaert's principal works. It is one of only ten paintings by

Mostaert mentioned in the *Schilder-boeck*. If van Mander knew it, one can presume that others in his circle, which included the most important artists and scholars of late sixteenth-century Haarlem, were likely to have known it as well and perhaps shared the opinion of van Mander, the leading critic of his day. Prominent municipal officials and other visitors to the *schout*'s residence would certainly have seen it, and there is little reason to doubt that van Mander's authoritative assessment was broadly accepted among these viewers as well.

Yet – to re-pose the question from a late sixteenth-century perspective – what exactly did a "West Indies Landscape" mean to van Mander? Despite certain subsequent issues of nomenclature, in the late sixteenth century "West Indies" meant the whole of the New World, and to van Mander it would have signified a peculiarly Netherlandish perception of America, further informed by ideas that van Mander acquired during his travels in Europe. From 1573 to 1577, van Mander undertook the Renaissance artist's grand tour and visited Italy's centers of culture, where he studied not only the glories of a recently unearthed antiquity but also the contemporary productions of cinquecento culture. Van Mander's subsequent literary output attests to his broad and Italianate interests. He would famously compose a Vasari-inspired "Lives" of the ancient artists as well as a study of the "modern" Italian ones; and he would also translate several literary works from antiquity, including Homer (*Iliad*), Virgil (*Bucolics* and *Georgics*), and Ovid (*Metamorphosis*).[120] His familiarity with these texts would have helped him in his own career as an artist, while his translations contributed greatly to the spread of classical mythology and Arcadianism to the burgeoning Renaissance in the North. Van Mander demonstrated his personal predilection for the pastoral themes of Virgil in a painting of "Adam and Eve in Paradise" executed upon his return to Flanders.[121]

Van Mander's sojourn in the South put him in touch with more than just the classicism and art of the Renaissance, however. It also educated him in the political lessons of Italy's noted theorists, and it subjected him to the military vicissitudes and political havoc wreaked by Italy's most recent invaders. In the freshly issued *Istoria* of Guicciardini, he would have found the oft-cited thesis that the refined civilization of Renaissance Italy – the Italian Golden Age so to speak – had been ingloriously trampled upon by invading "barbarians" from Spain and France. The artist and future poet did not avoid becoming himself entangled in the political chaos of his day. Van Mander perhaps even fell into something of an "opposition" crowd in Italy. The recent discovery of frescoes by van Mander depicting scenes from the massacre of Saint Bartholomew's Day (in the Palazzo Spada in Terni) demonstrates knowledge of, if not necessarily sympathy for, the fate of Protestant martyrs closer to home.[122]

Much of this culture of violence and discord would pursue van Mander back to the Netherlands to which he returned in the late 1570s, in time to experience some of the worst turbulence of the Dutch times of troubles. The Van Mander family's ancestral village was overrun by a Walloon regiment, and Karel nearly lost his life to a pack of Habsburg mercenaries. In a telling anecdote, van Mander's seventeenth-century biographer relates how the future art connoisseur was captured, robbed, stripped naked, and strung up in a noose, before being saved by an Italian "knight," who, upon hearing the victim's elegant Italian, recognized Karel as a friend from their earlier days in Rome. This eleventh-hour cavalier scattered the executioners and saved the day. Van Mander soon thereafter abandoned Flanders for Haarlem, where he joined a group of educated, tolerant, and pacifist men of letters that included Hendrick Goltzius, Dirck Coornhert, and Cornelis van Haarlem.[123]

Van Mander's training, then, first in Italy and later in Flanders, instilled in him a wide range of sensibilities that would guide his future judgments as an art historian and inform, more specifically, his reading of Mostaert's *West Indies Landscape.* On the one hand, his exposure to classical learning, his translations of Virgil and Ovid, and his ultimate assimilation into Haarlem's more liberal and tolerant circles would have allowed him to see in Mostaert's work the pastoral, Arcadian, indeed Ovidian themes of Golden Age innocence invaded by violence and turmoil. On the other hand, his experience of Spanish ignominies, his knowledge of Benzoni's American exposé, and his domicile in the Netherlands during the height of its struggle against Spain would have encouraged him to see in Mostaert's work a *Spanish* incursion against New World innocents, who hopelessly try to defend *their* "houses and huts" against the invading, steel-bearing barbarians from abroad.

The literary sources complete the picture. For van Mander's scattered references to America in the *Schilder-boeck,* and especially in the sonnets that he composed for his translation of Benzoni, afford further evidence of the author's distinctive image of the New World. Thus, a celebration of the beauty of the human body in *Den grondt der edel vry schilder-const* (The foundation of the noble art of painting) leads him to consider the well formed physiques of the inhabitants of the "Indies." In America, notes van Mander, men go naked and without shame, as they did in the time of Saturn's rule, the *Aurea Aetas.* These unadorned innocents expose bodies more "wonderfully beautiful" than all the costly silks and dyed fabrics of European courts, where shame and a sense of indecency had infected social intercourse. America here basks in the glow of golden age simplicity. Later in the same work, van Mander returns to the pastoral image of the *"simpel"* – the word implies a naive lack of social institutions – people of the "West Indies," who remain ignorant of writing. Obliged to serve their conquerors, the Indians must bear the Spanish letters of command that contain the very instructions of their own demise. These guileless, unsuspecting creatures, concludes van Mander, must suffer the cruelties of the writing and warring Spanish nation. In this second instance, America groans under the dark shadow of Spanish tyranny.[124]

Not accidentally, these references convey much the same admixture of Arcadianism and anti-Hispanism that characterized so many passages of Benzoni's narrative. The poetry composed by van Mander for the occasion of his translation of the *Mondo nuovo* makes the case with less ambiguity. In four sonnets, van Mander sketches the outlines of the tale of the conquest, a tale of Spanish violences and Indian sufferings. Whence comes the furious barrage of iron that now visits the once peaceful New World? asks the poet artfully. Wooden boats brought iron weapons in search of golden treasure. The days of tranquillity have sadly passed:

> Hard iron weapons, never before seen,
> The sorrowful times that have come,
> The never bowed neck that must now bear a heavy yoke:
> Saturn's sweet age planted there for eternity
> Must be shunted by this poor nation;
> Hard and iron are the times that formerly were golden.[125]

Spanish greed and lust for gold, argues the poet, had destroyed a world that, if hitherto "golden," had known neither envy nor strife. An edenic idyll had succumbed to the wrath and wars of invading Spaniards. Indeed, the contrast drawn in the poem between the undisturbed "West Indies" enjoying "sweet" tranquillity on the one hand, and the leagues of restless, iron-clad soldiers on the other, reads like a virtual caption for the Mostaert panel.

In the three sonnets that follow, van Mander elaborates on the theme of Spanish tyrannies: on Spain's subjection of a peace-loving and gracious nation, on its pillaging of a "richly jeweled land," on its use of religion as a pretext for unprincipled pursuit of profit. All of these topoi would have undoubtedly rung familiar to Dutch readers who, after years of bitter war, knew all too well of the Spanish abuse of rights, riches, and religion. (The connection between the Indians' suffering and that of the Dutch is expressed more bluntly by the printer, who calls the history "a mirror" in which the "cunning, unfaithful, and cruel nature of the Spanish nation is exposed," and further rallies the Dutch to rise against the Spanish enemy in the Netherlands.)[126] Between the sonnets, the scattered American references, the translation of Benzoni, and, not least, the "translation" of the Mostaert panel, a vision of America begins to emerge. For the poet van Mander, steeped as he was in classical literature, the New World represented an Arcadian site of peace and prosperity, inhabited by a society that knew neither shame nor war and had survived (until recently) in a golden age of innocence. Yet for the refugee van Mander, whose adult life coincided with nothing *but* war, America appeared a landscape of destruction, a sorrowful illustration of sixteenth-century greed and aggression, and a theater of Spanish cruelty and tyranny. To be sure, van Mander's "West Indies" partook of a number of the literary motifs employed throughout the sixteenth century, and it betrayed, too, some of the imprecision and vagueness that characterized the earlier, graphic sources. Yet van Mander's representation of America ultimately combined these literary and visual traditions with a distinctly Netherlandish sense of history. America acquired its relevance for poetic as well as political imperatives.

Virtually all of van Mander's notes on America appeared in the *Schilder-boeck*, published in 1604, with the exception of the translation of Benzoni which came out posthumously in 1610. Van Mander's reference to the translation in the *Schilder-boeck* as already completed, however, implies that the manuscript lay finished already by 1603.[127] It is tempting to suppose that the work was undertaken sometime in the late 1570s or early 1580s; for this would conform with the publishing pattern in the Netherlands where, in the final decades of the sixteenth century, a veritable torrent of Americana – including translations of Staden, Léry, and José de Acosta's classic, *Historia natural y moral de las Indias* – streamed off the presses of the Low Countries. Also in the late sixteenth century the first translations – initially in Dutch, and only later in French and Latin – of Bartolomé de las Casas's catalogue of Spain's American cruelties, the *Brevíssima relación*, began to appear with remarkable regularity, first in Antwerp and later in Amsterdam.[128] The Dominican friar's account of Habsburg atrocities perpetrated against the gentle Indians had a phenomenal impact on Dutch authors. In the famous *Apologie* (1581) of Willem of Orange, in which the ranking Dutch noble defended his abjuration of Philip II, numerous passages appeal to the memory of fellow-suffering natives of America. By the turn of the century, Willem Usselincx, a tireless promoter of overseas trade and, like van Mander, a war refugee from the South Netherlands, initiated a pamphlet campaign calling for an American trading company, a company that would not only trade with the New World, but also save the "innocent Indians" from the clutches of Castile. The foundation of the Dutch West Indian Company would have to wait until the end of the truce with Spain, in 1621. Yet already by the close of the sixteenth century, a full one hundred years after the voyage of Columbus, one could say that the Dutch had finally discovered America.

CHAPTER 2

Revolutionary Geography

In early November 1565, there arrived in Brussels the long-awaited response of King Philip II to reports of social, political, and religious unrest in the Low Countries. The famous letters from Segovia Wood, named after the country estate where they were drafted, made clear the Spanish king's intention strictly to maintain the unpopular heresy laws he had confirmed a number of years earlier, and vigorously to persecute all manner of heterodoxy. The king further rebuffed the advice of the leading nobles of the Netherlands that they be granted a broader role in supervising – and moderating – the enforcement of the king's religious "placards." By the following spring, a league of some two hundred noblemen had rallied together and, in response to the stated position of the Spanish Crown, gathered in Brussels to present to Margaret of Parma, governess-general of the Netherlands and half-sister to Philip, a "Request" for the moderation of the placards and abolition of the Inquisition. These events, which took place against a backdrop of expanding religious disorder and contracting economic growth, traditionally mark the beginning of the Revolt of the Netherlands.[1] On the face of it, they had little to do with events in the New World, where the sway of Habsburg rule also happened to prevail. Yet within a matter of months, another group of Dutch nobles, this time assembled in Rotterdam, offered the case of Spanish abuses in America – "tyranny" as they termed it – to justify their own opposition to Spanish rule in the Netherlands. Resistance was necessary, the nobles maintained, for "the Spanish seek nothing but to abuse our Fatherland as they have done in the New Indies." The Revolt had thus begun, and with it commenced a revolution in Dutch representations of America.[2]

I

The nobles' complaint of Habsburg misrule in America signaled an audacious shift in the political and geographic imagination of the Dutch.

It indicated, too, a dramatic reorientation of Netherlandish notions of the New World. For, later developments notwithstanding, evidence in support of the nobles' position was, by the mid-1560s, hardly overwhelming. On the eve of the Revolt, a number of different visions of the New World coexisted in the books and pamphlets, broadsides and prints, published lately in the Low Countries. The image of "Spanish tyranny in the New World," however, was not necessarily, or even most likely, the preeminent of these. In the early reports of Columbus and Vespucci, "America" appeared simultaneously marvelous and monstrous, descriptions of edenic landscapes alternating with exotic. In the later accounts of Cortés's adventures and in the mid-century chronicles of Mexico and Peru, the New World represented a new frontier of Spanish bravery and chivalric derring-do. The Castilian role in the conquest, according to these histories, merited more praise than criticism, not least for spreading the glory of Christianity to the godless "savages" of America. Martyr's *Decades*, it is true, had portrayed the Spanish conquistadors in a number of unflattering roles; yet this learned, and undeniably influential, work lingered more happily on the natives' "ancient" state of grace than on the Spaniards' part in disrupting it. The politically (and religiously) incendiary accounts of Le Challeux, Léry, and Benzoni had not yet, or only recently, been published, and in 1565 none of these works had attracted the widespread attention it would later receive from Protestant publishers and translators. The most popular descriptions of the New World, to judge from the evidence of private Dutch book collections, were in fact the epic, Spanish-authored accounts of the *Conquista.* The histories of Cortés, Gómara, Cieza de León, and Zárate all rank among those accounts of the New World, published prior to 1565, most frequently listed in catalogues of contemporary Dutch libraries. Rather than diminishing the Spanish achievement in America, these works tended to celebrate the heroism, perseverance, and piety of Spanish discoverers and their royal patrons.[3]

Rather than simply presenting these accounts, moreover, Dutch editors assertively shaped Spanish narratives, and they did so in a manner that left little doubt of their approval – indeed promotion – of the Habsburg agenda abroad. Such was certainly the case with Agustín de Zárate's exceptionally popular *Historia* of the discovery and conquest of Peru, a work that appeared in Antwerp on three separate occasions in the decade preceding the Dutch Revolt. Such was still more emphatically the case with the prefatory material appended to the Dutch translation of Zárate, published twice on the very eve of the Revolt.[4] In a dedication to the burgomasters and aldermen of Antwerp, the printer, Willem Silvius, presents the work as "a mirror and example" of what good government can accomplish, taking special care to praise the Spanish monarch and his servants for their endeavors in the New World. "A valiant, courageous, and adventurous undertaking," the conquest of Peru reflected in the eyes of Silvius the sagacity, benignity, and excellence of its patron, "the most serene and invincible Emperor Charles V." Indeed, all had benefited from the Discovery. To the emperor and his subjects, the conquest brought glory and fortune. The town fathers of Antwerp could take pride particularly in the expansion of the Christian faith, spread by Charles V's soldiers to the heathen of America. To the merchants and governors of Antwerp, it brought "various wares and spices, very useful to society." The city's warehouses could accommodate, and naturally profit from, these valuable products. And to the ordinary reader, it brought "adventure . . . and many wonders" conveniently packaged in Silvius's small-format, Dutch-language volume. The "common folk," as Silvius referred to them, could enjoy the pleasures of foreign lands without the dangers of overseas travel. Pride, profit, pleasure: all of these Silvius promotes in order to sell America to a Dutch audience in 1563. Spain's American triumphs, not tyrannies, should guide the city fathers, Silvius suggests; Spain's example should teach Antwerp the lessons of effective government.[5]

Silvius was not alone in his admiration. Much the same perspective informs an early pamphlet, redundantly praising the "wonderful wonders" performed by Catholic missionaries in the West. And the same beaming sense of pride permeates an extensive collection of travel literature devoted to the "new world of lands and islands."[6] The latter (like Sylvius's work, published in 1563) represents the first Dutch anthology of Americana, a potpourri of popular narratives based on an earlier German collection that was itself modeled on a Latin anthology produced by the Basel humanist, Simon Grynaeus, and the eminent geographer, Sebastian Münster. The Dutch editor of the 1563 compilation, Cornelis Ablijn, rearranged and augmented these earlier works with more recent materials to produce one of the broadest ensembles of travel literature available north of the Alps. He also introduced the massive volume – it runs over eight hundred folio pages – with a new and elaborate prologue addressed to the prince of Orange, in which he outlined for his readers the advantages they might derive from his elaborate literary endeavor. In the process, Ablijn summed up succinctly how "America" appeared to antebellum Antwerp.[7]

Like Silvius, Ablijn recommended the work on the twin bases of "pleasure and profit." The prince, Ablijn suggested, would find in the work a "cheerful" and pleasing respite from the burdensome responsibilities of state. Lesser readers as well would enjoy the simple pathos of the narratives, which related the "fear and deprivation . . . hunger and thirst . . . heat and cold" suffered in the course of the *Conquista*. The histories of America, Ablijn emphasized, abounded in passages of "faith, love, and hope" that would regale readers of all social backgrounds and all levels of learning. They promised, in short, a good read. As for the practical advantages, here too the volume had much to recommend it. The prince and other noble readers would glean from these pages important political and geographic information regarding the governments of distant lands, Ablijn promised. Merchants and traders would discover new products and potential overseas markets. And the "common reader" would learn of the "obedience" and civil order of the subjects of foreign lands – of the good government in America, in other words. Above all, Christians of every station would rejoice in the "valorous" and "faithful" labors of the Spanish explorers, who had extended the word of God to the "nations" of the West.

All ranks of people can profitably read this book, everyone according to his understanding; and everyone will generally be astonished and grateful that God, in recent times, has revealed so many peoples . . . [T]hereby they [the natives] and we may greatly profit. They, because they may learn from us the true knowledge of God and godly things. . . . Yet we may henceforth gain more at their expense – from the gold, pearls, and precious stones, and also from the variety of spices and herbs [brought] into general and medicinal use.[8]

The histories of Spain in America served as a "mirror," Ablijn maintained, falling back on a trope familiar to so many of the moralizing texts of this period. The conquistadors embodied such virtues as loyalty, courage, and Christian piety (and here Ablijn cited, oddly enough, the otherwise thuggish example of Vasco Núñez de Balboa). Ultimately, Ablijn exalted the Spaniards for their role in the New World, much as Silvius had. The Habsburgs had spread the knowledge of God and gathered a harvest of gold. The records of their tenure in America could, in the early-1560s, still furnish positive exempla for God-fearing burghers of the Low Countries.

Though not for long. Ablijn's and Silvius's enthusiasm could hardly contrast more with the views expressed in the coming years, when ringing endorsements of Spain's New World adventure gave way to far shriller cries of "Spanish tyranny in America." Rather than admiration, Dutch authors now voiced disdain – shock even – at the conduct of Castile in the Indies. While no comparable anthology followed in the wake of Ablijn's, syntheses of important travel narratives surfaced in the broader, geographic compilations published around this time that later came to be known as "atlases." America did not feature especially prominently in the first and most famous of sixteenth-century atlases, Abraham Ortelius's *Theatrum orbis terrarum* (1570); yet it did play a conspicuous role in the Dutch-language "epitome" of Ortelius's work published a few years later, the *Spieghel der werelt* (Mirror of the world). With its reduced format and abbreviated text – set in verse by the Antwerp poet Peeter Heyns – the *Spieghel* represented a more broadly accessible and more self-consciously provincial work than the sumptuous, yet imposing, *Theatrum*. It also carried an extensive introduction addressed particularly to readers of the Low Countries and concerned, significantly, with affairs of the Indies.[9]

In a wittily devised prologue, "To the wayfarer," Heyns invites his fellow readers-cum-travelers to join him on a literary journey around the world, to abandon the chaos of war-ravaged Antwerp (plundered by Spanish mutineers in 1576) in search of respite and the pleasures of armchair travel. This conceit conveys the reader across the Atlantic where the irony of the plan quickly becomes apparent. For the very first land "espied" turns the whole formula on its head. "We received a great shock," reports Heyns of his imagined journey, "from [seeing] the inhuman cruelty of Spanish tyranny in the new found world named America." The author beats a hasty retreat to England, yet the specter of "Spanish tyranny" persists in rearing its discomfiting head. In London, Heyns runs into the Antwerp expatriate, Emanuel van Meteren (a cousin and close colleague of Ortelius), who tells of similar Spanish tyrannies lately committed in the Netherlands. In France he encounters yet another associate from Antwerp who reports of the Spanish-sponsored attempts on the life of the prince of Orange; and an excursion to Germany brings news much the same. The entire voyage, in fact, consists of such stopovers and glimpses into the the progress of Spanish misrule. Spanish tyranny, according to Heyns's geography, begins in America, yet ultimately winds its way back to the Netherlands whence the "pleasant journey" had started.[10]

On the face of it, the purpose of the *Spieghel der werelt* bears a striking resemblance to that of the travel literature of the early 1560s. In the spirit of Silvius and Ablijn, Heyns emphasized the "pleasure and profit" his work afforded, and he guided his readers through the rich exempla of foreign lands. Yet, whereas the subject of America had led earlier authors to praise Spanish valor, it indicated for Heyns the extent of Spanish "tyranny." While Spain's New World advances promised profits in the eyes of the 1563 editors, they boded badly for an Antwerper writing only two decades later. America's "usefulness" now derived from its ability to forewarn Dutch readers – to "mirror" for them – their potential future under Habsburg rule. Spanish tyranny in America, Heyns implied, foreshadowed the possible course of Habsburg government in the Netherlands; Spanish government in Brussels threatened to go the way of the Indies. In all three works, Dutch editors shaped their geographic literature around related concerns of politics and patronage, and pitched their products in terms of "pleasure and profit." Heyns in particular constructed his preface around the notion of a cultural geography, a tour of the world in the eyes of a late-Renaissance Antwerper. Like his predecessors, he carefully crafted the literature – and the world – that he presented to his readers. Yet within Heyns's "mirror of the world," the reflection of America had fundamentally altered from the hopeful descriptions of the mid-1560s to the more despondent pronouncements some two decades later.

II

Over the course of the 1560s and 1570s, the Dutch vision of the New World evolved from what might loosely be called a Hispanophilic attitude to one decidedly Hispanophobic. The new geographic sensibilities emerged less from any abrupt change that may have occurred in the distant climes of America than from shifting political winds in the Netherlands. As enthusiasm for the Habsburg regime in the Low Countries subsided, criticism for perceived Habsburg abuses in the Indies gathered force. The attitudes expressed by Ablijn and Silvius typify, in many ways, the geopolitical orientation of antebellum Antwerp. With good reason, both men elected to praise Spain's conquests of, and sovereignty in, America. Both published with the privileges of the Habsburg monarch; both served in quasi-official positions (Silvius as *typographus regii,* or printer to the king, and Ablijn as a public notary); and both sought patronage from public figures who, though living in or near Antwerp, served governments in Brussels and Madrid. Both too, it might be added, lived in a cosmopolitan city where men of letters looked southward to Spain with admiration and respect.[11] Moreover, each author prefaced materials written chiefly by, and primarily for, Spaniards, and, whatever their selling points for a Dutch reading public, they remained essentially Spanish works. On the eve of the Revolt, it should be emphasized, few bona fide Netherlandish descriptions of America existed outside of sporadic comments embedded in works not otherwise focused on the New World. For the first two-thirds of the sixteenth century, in fact, the Dutch relied mainly on the plentiful, translated works of non-Dutch authors for their news on America.[12]

The nobles' cry of "Spanish tyranny in America," however, signaled an about-face in terms of Dutch representations of the New World. The rebel gentry who confronted Philip II in the later 1560s with the evidence of America did so not in the preface of a conquistador's *relacíon* or in a larger body of Spanish travel literature, but in a public remonstrance to the Spanish king from his disgruntled Dutch subjects. They wrote not to accommodate but to assail the king's servants, in the Low Countries as well as the Indies. They called for a political realignment, and in the process they effected a geographical reorientation. Attitudes toward Brussels still shaped descriptions of America, yet as the political point of reference shifted, so too did the needle of the cultural geographer's compass.

The nobles' case against Spain in America indicated both a reinvigorated interest in the New World and a reformulation of its significance. It heralded the rebels' creation of a new geography – a usable geography – to accompany their new political aspirations. It also commenced a process of articulating a self-consciously "Dutch" identity partly through reference to "American" history. Between the publication of Cornelis Ablijn's anthology of early travel narratives and Peeter Heyns's compilation of cartographic literature, the Dutch fashioned an image of the New World that served the political demands of their revolt against Spain. References to "Spanish tyranny in America," cited increasingly from the late 1560s, buttressed Dutch opposition to Habsburg rule in the Netherlands. The building blocks for this geopolitical construct had been in place already from the mid-1560s in the form of Martyr's lyrical evocation of American "innocence" (freshly republished in Ablijn's collection) and Benzoni's depiction of Spanish-American violence (published originally in 1565). Dutch pamphleteers and printers, and especially those in the service of the rebel party, now joined these topoi to create an image of intolerable Spanish tyranny visited upon the innocent natives of America. "In the newly discovered lands . . . they have murdered practically all of the natives," wrote a pamphleteer in 1574 of Spain's American adventure. "Whoever wishes to see an example of their tyranny, and to know fully how they would reign," it was suggested, could observe the fate of the New World. The "innocent blood" of the Indians vividly alerted the Dutch; for the experience of America suggested what could yet transpire in the Netherlands. "Let us imagine the example of the Indians," wrote a leading figure of the rebel party in a work brazenly published by the archtypographer to the king, "and let us imagine that our descendants will be abused as are they."[13]

The creation of the rebels' "America" proceeded gradually in the years following the initial Dutch resistance to Habsburg rule. It followed approximately the shape of the campaign against the Spanish government and the progress of political events in Brussels, where the regent, Margaret of Parma, resided. It followed more closely, however, the contours of the war of words waged against "Spanish tyranny" and the progress of printers in Antwerp, where the rebel image-makers reigned. From the start – the "Request" of the nobles published in 1566 – the rebels recognized and exploited the power of print in their battle for public opinion. The "flood of publications" noted by contemporaries prompted action first from Margaret and later from her replacement, the duke of Alba, who sought to stem the flow with a sharply worded edict in 1568 against the "mutinous, wretched forgers, enemies and disturbers of the public welfare." Yet these and later Spanish governors scored little success. "The more the court issued edicts against them," wrote a supporter of Orange, "the more the number of such booklets and writings increased." Indeed, the Dutch rebels were extraordinarily prolific writers.[14]

The rebels' use of America to vilify Spain fit into the context of such pamphleteering. It emanated from the pens of those Alba branded "rabble-rousers, distributors of notorious pamphlets, publishers of booklets, seditious, malicious, turbulent, impudent people," that is, from the great rebel propagandists including Jacob van Wesembeke, Petrus Dathenus, Philip Marnix van St. Aldegonde, and above all, the prince of pamphleteers, Willem of Orange.[15] These and others adopted "America" into their repertoire of anti-Habsburg invective. The topos of "Spanish tyranny in America" developed alongside, and in conjunction with, broader attacks against the Spanish Inquisition and the abuse of local privileges; against the kings' "evil-advisors," especially the duke of Alba; against the use of religion as a "pretext" for unholy and acquisitive ends; and, ultimately, against the king himself and the inherent wickedness of the "Spanish nation." The pervasiveness of "America" also paralleled the general swell of rebel propaganda. Like much of the rebel literature, it appeared originally in the years 1566–1568 only to subside with the first round of expulsions in 1568–1569; it regained momentum in 1572 (the capture of Brill by the rebels) and 1576 (the Spanish Fury); and it reached its fullest expression around 1580–1581, conspicuous in the *Apologie* of Willem and the *Plakkaat van Verlatinge* (Act of Abjuration) of the States General – the two primary, public expressions of anti-Spanish sentiment of the Revolt. In general, it may be said that the geographic topos of "America" developed alongside the political polemic of revolt. Finally, the rebels' projection of the New World corresponded to broader efforts to articulate a "Dutch" world: to shape a distinctly Dutch identity at the very moment that such a coherent, national construct seemed most in doubt. America and Spain's tyrannical record there were promoted in print in much the same way – with much the same rhetorical strategy – as other foundational myths of the Republic. In writing America, the rebels essayed to write themselves.[16]

Opposition to Habsburg rule in the Netherlands converged originally around the issue of the Inquisition. Though a mechanism to pursue heresy had existed in the Low Countries from the earliest moments of the Reformation, public reaction remained generally muted throughout the first half of the sixteenth century and reached crisis proportions only by the mid-1560s. The reinvigorated attention paid by Philip II to the "plague" of Protestantism following the Peace of Cateau-Cambrésis (1559), and the concurrent circulation within Calvinist circles of a number of particularly inflammatory attacks on the Holy Office, help to explain the intensified campaign conducted by Dutch Reformers around this time against the Inquisition. These developments fail to clarify, however, why the predominately Catholic population of the Seventeen Provinces went along with the Reformers' agenda. Much of the explanation lies in the strategy of those Reform-minded gentry who led the attack and took care to focus less sharply on the goals of the Holy Office – to root out heresy – than on its methods – to seize, torture, and execute accused heretics without recourse to local systems of justice.[17] Those nobles who, in December of 1565, bound themselves by solemn oath "to prevent by all means the introduction of this inquisition in whatever shape, open or covert, under whatever disguise or mask it may assume," acted less to sanction Protestantism (which may well have been their unstated goal) than "to extirpate and eradicate" the Inquisition itself "as the mother and cause of all disorder and iniquity." The Inquisition, they maintained, had introduced "a great crowd of foreigners" to the Netherlands and thereby destroyed good order by "ignoring the old laws, customs, and ordinances observed from time immemorial." It had intolerably subverted the traditional mechanism of justice and abused time-honored privileges, bringing unwelcome Spanish officials into the provincial system of local government. The cure, in short, had proven worse than the disease.[18]

Attacks on the Spanish Inquisition, and especially on its abuse of local privileges, surface repeatedly in the earliest round of anti-Habsburg literature. The group of nobles who confronted Margaret in April of 1566 with a public Request petitioned the king formally to repeal the edicts of the Inquisition. Within a month of that audacity, a Protestant pamphleteer, Gilles le Clercq, penned a scathing attack on "the violent and extraordinary methods" of the Inquisition, which randomly selected its victims and subjected them to "all types of savagery, including fire, sword, water, and whip." The Holy Office, claimed le Clercq, had "employed highly uncommon procedures and punishments which accord neither with the dictates of fairness and justice, nor with the rights and privileges of these lands." Its continued presence spelled certain slavery and "the destruction and devastation of the whole land."[19]

The theme of abused privileges agitated the earliest antagonists of Spain like no other. On the heels of le Clercq's pamphlet came the provocatively titled exposé, *The Holy Spanish Inquisition, its sundry and crafty secrets, tricks, and practices discovered and brought to light*, which made a point of indicting the Inquisition not only for its assault on religious rights, but also for its attack on "rights of the naturally born princes and lords of the land." Much the same concern galvanized the former pensionary of Antwerp, Jacob van Wesembeke, who complained that Philip II's agents in Brussels had circumvented the normal, established channels of government in enacting the religious edicts. Above all, they had failed to convoke the States General "in the old way." Orange echoed the same themes in his public *Warning* published in exile in 1568. The Netherlands had always been governed "wholly in accordance with their freedoms, rights, customs, traditions and privileges" established in former times, noted the prince. Cardinal Granvelle and other henchmen of the Holy Office, however, had stealthily initiated "many strange innovations [*vreemde nieuwicheden*], cruel persecutions, bloody edicts, [and] an unbearable inquisition," thereby upsetting the normal rhythm of government. In another pamphlet published later that year, Orange exhorted his fellow nobles to "resist such manifest violent infringements of your privileges, such suppression of your liberties, such massacre of yourselves and ravishing of your possessions." Under the pretext of religion, the prince protested, the Spanish Inquisition had subtly supplanted the natural leaders of the Netherlands – Catholic and Protestant alike – with "foreign and tyrannical invaders" who trampled, with utter disrespect, upon the traditional privileges of the Low Countries.[20]

"America" originally entered the repertoire of the rebels as a parallel case of inquisitorial imperiousness. In the New World, it was proposed, the Spanish Inquisition had similarly violated indigenous rights and abused "native privileges." With striking geographic imagination, Dutch pamphleteers posited a didactic connection between Spanish actions taken in America and Habsburg rule in the Netherlands, warning that within the first example lay a lesson for the second. Already in 1566, le Clercq intimated that the Dutch should keep a wary eye on the far-flung advances of their Habsburg enemies. The Spanish Inquisition had spread around the world, and no one lay beyond its reach. A group of nobles who signed a remonstrance against the "inconveniences arising from the Inquisition and the [religious] placards" made the case much more explicitly. The Spanish, they warned, "seek nothing but to use [*bruyken*] our Fatherland as they have done in the New Indies which they have recently won." The same conceit, expressed in virtually identical language, appeared in the following year (1568) in a pamphlet by one of Willem's chaplains, Adrianus Saravia. Wary of the recent encroachments on Dutch liberties by Alba – "he will appoint in every city justices from his own people" – Saravia accused the duke of treating the Netherlands like "newly won lands," territories to be conquered and converted. A number of years later, the States General fell back on a similar trope in explaining their resolve to oppose Spanish rule. Letters intercepted in 1568, they claimed, had convinced them that the Habsburg government in Brussels "had for a long time been seeking and hoping for an opportunity to abolish all the privileges of the country and to have it tyrannically governed by Spaniards like the Indies and newly conquered countries." They claimed to fear, as did other rebel pamphleteers, that Spain would rule without consulting the natural leaders of the Netherlands, that Spain endeavored (to cite the *actual* words of Alba) "to create a New World" in the Netherlands.[21]

In suggesting that the Inquisition would alienate the Netherlands from its natural leaders, rebel pamphleteers presumably sought the support of precisely those provincial justices and councilmen slighted by the Spanish-sponsored regime. To sway opinion more widely, the pamphleteers simultaneously launched broader attacks on the "Spanish Inquisition" intended to create a villain sufficiently abhorrent to win readers of all stripes. The Inquisitors were depicted as pernicious complotters of boundless greed and expansive ambition from whom no one – neither noble nor commoner, Protestant nor Catholic – was entirely safe. Philip van Marnix considered the Inquisitors "the enemies of the Burgundian House" and speculated that it was they, not the disgruntled Protestants, who had incited the iconoclastic riots of 1566 that sparked the Revolt. In a tract popularly known as "The Legend of the Inquisition," it was purported that the Spanish Inquisition had contrived to shorten Charles V's tenure in the Netherlands and thereafter held a duped Philip II imprisoned in Spain, docilely to approve the destruction of his beloved Netherlands.[22]

Surely the wildest allegations appeared in two notorious forgeries, "The Articles of the Inquisition" and "The Advice of the Inquisition," both presented as official documents of Alba's Council of Troubles and published by the rebels in a widely circulated and frequently cited pamphlet.[23] In the form of twelve articles, the first of these documents purported to record the fantastic machinations of a diabolic Holy Office. From as early as 1550, its readers learned, the Inquisition had masterminded Charles V's abdication, Philip II's acquiescence, and even Alba's obedience. More sinister still, it had decreed the total destruction and utter desolation of the Netherlands. "We shall consider no one in all of the Netherlands, apart from our agents, worthy of living," reads the ninth article, "and in the end, all will be uprooted to make room for a new state and new nation." The second text, the "Advice," contains the pitiless death sentence ("signed" on 26 February 1568 in Madrid) passed for the entire population of the Netherlands – men and women, young and old, Catholic and Protestant – on trumped-up charges of *crimen lese majestatis.* Both of these "documents" were supported by the mysteriously and anonymously published *Sanctae Inquisiionis Hispanicae,* which vividly detailed the malevolent instruments and the barbaric tortures available to the Holy Office. For the piously indignant as well as the courageously curious, the very dungeons of the Inquisition stood brightly exposed.[24]

Within this paradigm fit, once again, the evidence of America. The "Legend of the Inquisition" contended that the Holy Office already controlled most of Europe and aspired to nothing less than a grand *rijk,* a universal monarchy patterned after the empires of antiquity. To the members of the exiled Dutch Reformed community in Emden, it seemed that the Holy Office had, by 1570, already realized most of its goal, at least on the Western flank. In that community's published appeal to the German Diet "to defend our miserable and afflicted innocence [against] the outrageous power and unbridled boldnesse of our enemies," the Inquisition assumes menacing proportions that are especially evident in the New World. In America, the Inquisitor's dominion had greedily and insatiably advanced:

Yea they not onely ranged to the uttermost Indians, and to the farre distant landes . . . but also under the pretense of orderyng religion they spoyled the poore and simple inhabitantes of those contreyes of all their goods and possessions, and of their wives, children and lives, yea and cruelly lyke butchers tearyng them with all kinde of tormentes they slew them by the heapes, and brought them to such miserie and wretched plight, that a great number of them chose rather to slay themselves, than to come under such cruell subiection of unnaturall men.

A second publication from the early 1570s sounded a similar alarm over the relentlessness of the Inquisition at home and abroad. Not only had Spain and Italy been brutally subdued, it was argued; so too had "the new found lands (named new Indies)," which had been oppressed and made to languish under the Holy Office's "power and mastery." In the meantime, the Inquisition had "sharpened its teeth" on the Netherlands, and the message was abundantly clear: to tolerate Spain's Holy Inquisition was to invite such unholy disaster as Spain had inflicted upon America – a risk the Dutch could scarcely afford.[25]

By directing their attacks on the Inquisition, both at home and abroad, the pamphleteers scrupulously avoided taking the more scandalous step of criticizing the king himself. To oppose a monarch to whom allegiance had been sworn would indeed have amounted to *crimen lese majestatis*, an offense that, in the early 1570s at least, few dared commit. This encouraged the rebels to look elsewhere in their opening assaults – beyond Madrid and the person of Philip II – and thus instigated a fair amount of creative calumny. The myth of the "Spanish Inquisition," to be sure, provided but one of the many cloaks behind which reluctant rebels could hide. A related strategy involved upbraiding the king's "evil councilors," men who, so the pamphleteers reasoned, had orchestrated the unrest in the Netherlands against the king's better judgment. Cardinal Granvelle – who did in fact advise Philip II on matters of heresy – filled just such a role in the earliest pamphlets, even though he had departed the Netherlands (1564) before the actual "troubles" arrived. The duke of Alba, a fierce and uncompromising soldier sent by Philip II to remedy the ills of the Netherlands once they did begin, filled this role even better.[26]

Alba's reputation was not entirely unearned. In August of 1567, he descended on the Low Countries with ten thousand hardened veterans, and, within a matter of months, wrested control of the government in Brussels from his more moderate predecessor, Margaret of Parma. To deal with the heretics and rebels, the "iron duke" quickly established a tribunal, the *Conseil des Troubles*, whose ruthless efficiency earned it the nickname, the Council of Blood. He also levied, against the will of the nobles, a battery of taxes including the infamous "Tenth Penny," which came to embody in the popular imagination the avarice and oppression of the Habsburg regime. Above all, Alba made his presence felt in a series of military campaigns meant to punish those towns that, in the wake of rebel victories in the spring and summer of 1572, had defected to the Orangist camp. The brutal reprisals carried out by Alba against Mechelen, Zutphen, and Naarden seemed to defy the laws of just war. Though Mechelen had opened its gates to the Spanish, Alba permitted his troops to sack and plunder the town "in order to refresh them a little." In Naarden, which put up only minimal resistance, all of the inhabitants were put to the sword – "not a mother's son escaped," reported the duke coolly – and the entire town was razed to the ground. The sieges of the following season included heartless campaigns against Haarlem, Alkmaar, and Leiden. Though only the first of these actually fell to the Spanish, the cold-blooded execution of Haarlem's two thousand-man garrison after assurances of clemency seared an indelible mark on the collective memory of the Netherlands.[27]

Whatever the actual extent of Alba's "policy of beastliness" – and historians are now more inclined to deemphasize the relative severity of Alba's fiscal and military policies[28] – the effect it had on the rebels' imagination was formidable. The deeds of the "Moorish tiger-beast," as Orange famously dubbed him, featured prominently and vividly in the plethora of print produced by Spain's enemies. It was not that the rebels ceased to target the Inquisition, the abuse of privileges, or the infringement of traditional rights. Alongside these attacks, however, arose some of the most scathing propaganda of the war, focusing on the cruelty of Alba, the tyranny of his policies, and the violence of his troops. The pamphlets, prints, and ballads of the early 1570s – coincident that is, with the so-called second revolt, 1569–1576[29] – made much of the theme of conquest, and Alba featured above all as an invading conquistador. Both were themes with obvious relevance to America.

Orange took the lead in attacking Alba, as he later would in the case of Philip II. He appealed to the nobles to renounce the "barbarian upstart" whom he denigrated, not without a degree of contradiction, as an "effeminate Sardanapalus, [a] cruel Phalaris, [a] tyrant, hated by God and mankind alike . . . possessed by insane fury and madness."[30] Other pamphleteers showed equal ingenuity in casting their aspersions. The iron duke was said to have dismissed his Dutch subjects as mere "men of butter," according to one broadside. Another asserted Alba's intention to mix Dutch blood into the mortar he used for his castles and defenses. Like the pharaohs and kings of antiquity, Alba was a tyrant of dramatic and excessive sins. His legislation also attracted abuse, as opposition to the Tenth Penny especially, became a rallying cry for the rebels. A symbol of Alba's avarice, the Tenth Penny featured on the mastheads of rebels' ships and in the refrains of scurrilous ballads. It even inspired a children's game in which a tenth child was chosen by his playmates "for the duke of Alva" and then put through a mock drubbing. "If [Alva] gets the upper hand," warned a public missive from the leading knights, nobles, and towns of Holland, "then all you can expect is eternal and ignominious slavery . . . because of your refusal to pay the Tenth Penny." The Tenth Penny and "similar menaces" demonstrated that Alba's ultimate purpose was "to ruin and raze this country to the ground."[31]

Alba's "Spanish rabble" – that is, the generally well-disciplined troops employed by the Spanish army of Flanders – likewise exercised the rebels' ire and imagination. Though composed of mercenaries from all across Europe (including the Low Countries themselves), the army was collectively dismissed as "savage war dogs of Spain" and consistently associated with Alba himself. By popular (rebel) consent, the duke's army occupied itself with nothing but

plundering, robbing and ravaging, evicting and desolating, apprehending, and intimidating, banishing, expelling and confiscating goods, burning and scorching, hanging, chopping, hacking, breaking on the wheel, and torturing and murdering with gruesome and unheard of torments the [Dutch] subjects of your Majesty, noble as well as common, poor and rich, young and old, widows and orphans, men, women and young maidens.[32]

Or, as a less prolix chronicler put it, they robbed and plundered "as if the peasants were enemies." Alba and his men came not to govern but to conquer. In Orange's estimation, the iron duke was a "rogue of rogues" who had enticed his reckless men to join him "by dangling before their eyes the hope of planting colonies in our Fatherland."[33]

It was precisely this theme of conquest and colonization that directed the rebel writers, not without a certain logic, from the Netherlands to America. "Ravaging," "banishing," "torturing": all provoked images of – and once again comparisons with – the Indies. Accordingly, those pamphleteers writing in the wake of Alba's conquest, and in particular those originating from the provinces with the most recent and least pleasant memories of Alba's army, bolstered their recriminations of Spain with reference to the New World. There too Spanish "bloodhounds" had demonstrated their addiction to plunder and their aversion to lawful government; there too Habsburg soldiery had "scorched" and "hacked" their way to conquest. With the experience of Alba's fury in Holland and Zeeland fresh in their mind, the States of these provinces penned a collegial "Admonition" to their counterparts in Brabant and Flanders in which they alerted them to both the degree and the range of Spain's brutality. "Do not expect," the Northerners warned the Southerners,

that they [the Spanish] will bring any order to the wild consumption, plundering, and other inconveniences by which they thoroughly destroy the countryside. For their greatness and the security of their dominance depends upon the desolation and impoverishment of the commonalty; all of which can be attested by the Kingdom of Naples, Sicily, Sardinia, and all other lands in which they have gained the upper hand. . . . Indeed in the new found lands, for which they praise [the Spanish king] so highly, they have murdered almost all of the native population, so that they could, with but minimal manpower . . . keep the land more easily under their control and tyranny.[34]

A similar admonition from Holland and Zeeland of that same year (1574) noted that "also in the new found lands" the natives had been made to suffer under the "yoke and tyranny" of the Spanish conquerors. Those provinces that came to terms with the Habsburgs, it was proposed, could count on much the same treatment. Even in victory the rebels kept a vigilant eye on the example of America. A song composed to commemorate the capture of a Spanish flotilla on Whitsunday, 1574, pointedly concludes with a reference to the subjection of the Indies. After exulting in the feat of the rebel pirates, the balladeer reminds his listeners of Spain's own record of conquest, of Spanish pride earned off the waters of America. The Dutch must remain prepared for the next "vaunting and boasting" Spanish admiral sailing back from the New World:

> Just as he [the Spanish admiral] has done in the Indies,
> So he intends to betray us completely;
> To put Holland and Zeeland to their death,
> To deprive them utterly of their last breath.

The conquest of the Indies, thus, served as a moralizing model, or reminder, meant to galvanize the Dutch. It demonstrated to them, in good times as well as bad, the urgency of ousting the "colonial" government of Spain.[35]

In late 1573 Alba departed the Netherlands a broken man, if we can believe the pamphleteers, having failed to suppress the rebels. His replacement, the former Spanish governor of Lombardy, Don Luís de Requesens, generally followed Alba's policies and advice. He continued to wage a war of *reconquista* against those regions that remained loyal to Orange; he resumed Alba's sieges, for example, against Leiden; and he refused, in the beginning at least, to join at the negotiating table with the "rebels." For their part, the latter had little difficulty refocusing their rhetorical campaign against the latest of the kings' "evil-advisors." They bombarded Requesens with a barrage of broadsides and pamphlets, recycling their favorite topoi of tyranny, violated privileges, and intrusive foreigners – though now including Requesens with Alba and the unholy Inquisitors as the architects of it all.[36]

If anything, the level of invective only intensified during, and in the years immediately following, the tenure of Requesens. This had less to do with Requesens himself or any outstanding antipathy felt towards him by the rebels – how could he fare worse than the much maligned "tiger-beast," Alba? – than with changes in the course of the war and in the tactics of the rebel party. For Requesens had the bad fortune of serv-

ing a Spanish paymaster during some of the most acute months of
Castile's financial crisis. As the army of Flanders required more and
more funds to maintain, the king's treasury plunged deeper and deeper
into insolvency. Taxed by a costly and prolonged war against the Turks,
and without the taxes normally exacted from the now warring Netherlands, Philip II faced an abyss that not even the silver of the Indies could
help him bridge. In September of 1574, Tunis fell to the Turks, and the
rebels rejoiced. One year later, Philip declared bankruptcy and Requesens (reportedly) wept. Meanwhile Spanish troops stationed in the
Netherlands panicked and mutinied with malicious abandon. The
king's fiscal woes explain in part the desperate attempt to levy the innovative taxes proposed first by Alba and later Requesens. The failure
of both actually to collect these taxes, though, explains the restlessness
among Spanish troops who lagged already years behind in the collection of their arrears. The soldiers' unruliness not only compounded Requesens's troubles; it also spilled over into the countryside where unsuspecting towns and villages were made to suffer the devastating
mutinies that occurred between 1573 and 1576. In the summer of 1576,
a particularly reckless band of Spanish mutineers wreaked havoc on the
loyal town of Aalst, which lay only a short march away from Brussels.
Months later the "Spanish Fury" visited Antwerp itself and with terrifying results. Thousands of florins of damage was caused and eight
thousand lives were taken in what a leading expert on Renaissance warfare has called "one of the worst atrocities of the sixteenth century."[37]

The mutinies had a profound impact on Spain's detractors in the
Netherlands. "The Spanish mutinies would be enough to make us
loathed," wrote a despondent Requesens to the king already in 1574. In
fact, the rebels needed little convincing. They responded to the "Spanish violences" with polemical vigor and obvious relish. Don Juan of
Austria, the royal governor sent to replace Requesens and also the half-
brother of Philip II, became the new target of abuse in the pamphlets
composed following the mutinies of 1576. "It is common knowledge,"
wrote Marnix, "that Don Juan intends, as he has always done, to set the
country ablaze with war; and . . . to remedy matters by fire and bloodshed."[38] Increasingly, though, the blame shifted from the king's lieutenant in Brussels to his soldiers in the field. For every missile hurled at
a besieged Dutch town, for every ransom demanded by a mutinous regiment, the rebels struck back with language and trope every bit as violent. The army of Flanders, which had otherwise gained a reputation for
discipline, featured as "Spanish bloodhounds," "Spanish rabble," "cir-
cumcised Moors," "Marranos," and "pigs" (the final curses ironically
inverting Spain's own rhetorical offensive against its *converso* popula-

tions).[39] They committed "cruel," "horrifying," "murderous," "savage," and "atrocious" deeds. The list of epithets lacked nothing for color or hyperbole. Nor did the similes. The Spanish overtook the Carthaginians in treachery and surpassed the Scythians in cruelty. Even the reputation of the Turks for tyranny and torture paled in comparison with that of Spain. Marnix catalogued in his famous *Oration* to the German Diet of 1578 the "wantonness, fury, insolence, and malice of the Spanish." Orange exposed the "natural disposition of the Spanish soldier," showing it to be "alwais cruel."[40]

Remarkably, these soldiers of ill-repute, whatever their actual country of origin, were consistently represented as "Spanish" – this despite the fact that Spanish soldiers accounted for only a minority of the army of Flanders. (Spain's army in the Low Countries comprised mainly German, Walloon, Italian, and Spanish troops, and, in the 1570s, the Spanish made up approximately fifteen to twenty percent of the total – albeit relatively more of the officer rank.) This reflected the growing willingness of the rebels to forgo the myth of the "evil-advisor" and to engage in a frontal assault on the Spanish "nation" itself. It also suggests a subtle strategy of opposition. By aiming their invective at a unified target – the "Spanish" army, "Spanish" Inquisition, "Spanish" tyranny in America – the rebels sought to unify the disparate factions of their opposition. By articulating a single and easily identifiable enemy, the pamphleteers hoped to promulgate a single and easily justifiable "Dutch" revolt.[41]

In the end, no symbol registered as more Spanish than the Crown itself, and before long, the king too became the object of the pamphleteers' wrath in what amounted to a startlingly bold, and unapologetically treasonous, step by the supporters of Orange. Marnix, who had railed tirelessly against the "cruel disposition" and "natural tyranny" of the Spanish, was among the first to present the case against Philip II in a work published pseudonymously in 1578. If the king's government in the Netherlands amounted to "tyranny," reasoned Marnix, it left the Seventeen Provinces with little alternative but to "depos[e] as unworthy [the] king from his kingship by public authority." Orange promoted Marnix's speculative incriminations to the level of official dogma in his *Apologie* of 1581, in which he defended his decision to renounce Philip as the lawful sovereign of the Netherlands. The Spanish and their leaders, maintained Willem, shared the same "cruell, covetous, and proud disposition." "Whether it were by reason of nourishement which he had in Spaine, or by the counsell of those which then did, or even to this time have possessed him, I know not, he hath alwaies fostered in his hearte, a minde to make you [the Netherlands] subject to a certaine simple and absolute bondage." Philip II came from the same "infected race" as his clients in Brussels and his mercenaries on the battlefield. It now remained for the Dutch to "purge the countrey from these pernitious and hurtful Spanishe humours," king and all.[42]

The period between the Spanish Fury in 1576 and Orange's *Apologie* in 1581, the so-called third revolt, marks the culmination in many ways of the rebels' verbal offensive against Spain – and another chapter in the development of American rhetoric. This period witnessed some of the most intense polemical violence of the Eighty Years' War, and the pamphlets from this period gave form to many of the future mythologies of Spanish tyranny. The rebels now held Philip II directly responsible for the violence in the Netherlands; they discredited his actions both public and private (Willem accused him of adultery, bigamy, incest, and murder); and they launched a broader onslaught against that which Willem termed "the cancker of Spain."[43] In this feverish state of virulence, the rebels turned once more to America as a means of illustrating the extent of Spain's malignancy. In the New World, it was argued, Spain had shown its true tyrannical colors. The enslavement of the Indies by Spain justified the abjuration of Philip II by the Netherlands. Marnix, as might be expected, took the lead in a particularly vitriolic work that appeared in 1578 and attacked the "mutinies, plundering and vexations, murders and arsons, all over the land." The Spanish, warned Marnix, sought to destroy and impoverish the land, to enslave all of the leading citizens, and to abduct all of the "wives and daughters to satisfy their unchaste desires." Philip could not be trusted as both history and the Spanish "nature" well attested – and as the case of America so well illustrated:

The Spaniard is very haughty, vengeful, and tyrannical. And do we believe that, once they have subjected the land and subdued it with arms, they will treat us with friendship and love? . . . what can we expect from those to whom haughtiness, vanity, and cruelty come more naturally than anything else? Let us imagine the example of the Indians, and let us keep in mind that our descendants will be abused as are they.[44]

A similar tenor of discourse informed a polemic printed the following year (1579), which assailed the negotiations underway in Cologne between agents of the king and the States General. Predictably, the anonymous author opposed any sort of return to "the yoke, slavery, or absolute tyranny of the Spanish" and implored the reader to recall the abuse of privileges, confiscation of goods, and violation of women and children that had taken place over the previous dozen years. Spain had treated the Dutch "like foreign enemies." They had "spilled so much blood, pitilessly killed so many people by water, sword, fire, and rope," that they could no longer be trusted and needed to be, once and for all, ousted. Had not Philip always treated his inherited lands like conquered territories? Had he ever shown them mercy?

One need only cite the examples of Naples, Milan, Granada and especially the Indies where they, according their own witnesses, have murderously killed more than twenty million souls and have utterly destroyed and completely desolated more lands than would fit between Castile and Constantinople or even Jerusalem.[45]

By the end of the decade, the example of the Indies – *"especially* the Indies" – had begun to recur with remarkable regularity.[46] It was in the *Apologie* of Willem, though, published in early 1581 and at least sixteen more times before the end of the century, that the topos became fully codified and definitively registered in the vocabulary of the patriotic party. Written in response to a royal ban and the twenty-five thousand ducat price placed on his head, the *Apologie* purports to be Willem's personal response to Philip II as well as his quasi-official abjuration of the king of Spain. It also functioned as a compilation of the rebels' grievances against Habsburg rule and an appeal to the noncommitted States to support Orange and their "natural" leaders. Toward all of these ends, Willem included a summa of anti-Spanish slander and a vicious assault on Philip II designed to convince his readers of the legality as well as necessity of the Dutch Revolt.[47] In the course of this lengthy and often acerbic work, America played a conspicuous role. Willem alluded to the New World frequently and imaginatively to convey what he called "the natural disposition of the Spaniards." In the Indies, servants of the Spanish Crown "commanded absolutely [and] yeelded to evident a proofe, of their perverse, naturall disposition, and tyrannous affection and will." America also indicated patterns of government of which the Dutch should take note. Spain's aim of "depriving you altogether of your ancient privileges and liberties that they may dispose of you, your wives, and your children," Willem informed his readers, was evident from the way "his officers have done to the poore Indians." The fate of the Indies portended a miserable future for the Netherlands; it served Willem as a sort of (failed) litmus test of Spanish ability to govern its colonies. "I have seene (my Lordes) their doings," recalled Willem of his experience as a *stadhouder* (lieutenant) to the Spanish monarch,

I have heard their words, I have bin a witnesse of their advise, by which they adjudged all you to death, making no more account of you, than of beastes, if they had had power to have murthered you, as they do in the Indies, where they have miserablie put to death, more than twentie millions of people, and have made desolate & waste, thirtie tymes as much lande in quantitie and greatnes, as the

lowe countrie is, with such horrible excesses and ryottes, that all the barbarousnesses, cruelties, and tyrannies, whiche have ever bin committed, are but
in sport, in respect of that, which hath fallen out upon the poore Indians.[48]

The New World, then, illustrated Spain's proclivity toward absolutism, its instinctive abuse of privileges, its habitual plundering of
property, and its miserable record of tyranny. America presented a pattern of history, a code of Spanish behavior, that appeared to parallel
closely events in the Netherlands. Partisan readers like Willem further
proposed that the history of the New World charted a course that the
Netherlands would follow if the troops of Spain were not turned back.
The case of America convinced the Prince that it would be good "to
cause (if we could) the Spaniards to departe out of the countrey." Only
months later (July 1581), the States General came to a similar conclusion
in their *Plakkaat van Verlatinge,* an informal declaration of independence
from the sovereignty of Philip II. Twice the States referred to Spanish
tyranny in America in their effort to legitimate the States' course of action against Spain in the Netherlands. They maintained that Philip II
sought to "conquer . . . these territories again so that he might rule them
freely and absolutely." He hoped "for an opportunity to abolish all the
privileges of the country and to have it tyrannically governed by
Spaniards like the Indies and newly conquered countries." "All of this,"
concluded the States, "has given us more than enough legitimate reasons for abandoning the king of Spain and for asking for another powerful and merciful prince to protect and defend these provinces." The
case of the Indies, once again, validated that of the Low Countries.[49]

The *Apologie* of Willem and the *Plakkaat* of the States constitute a climax of sorts in late-sixteenth century opposition to Habsburg rule in the
Netherlands. Together they represent the central public documents of
the Revolt. That both contain multiple references to "Spanish tyranny in
America" indicates just how quickly and pervasively the topos had developed and how extensively the rebels made use of it. Between its first
appearance in the late 1560s and its later prominence in the early 1580s,
"America" had become a ubiquitous component of Dutch propaganda.
Many an author singled out the "example of the Indies" to clinch the
case against Spain. The evolution of the American topos followed generally the patterns of anti-Habsburg literature that developed over the
two decades that preceded, and finally culminated with, the *Apologie* of
Willem. Throughout this period, it served authors by providing a con-
venient case of Spanish tyranny whose circumstances seemed remarkably similar to those in the Low Countries. It illustrated the abuses of

the Holy Office, the greed of the king's "evil-advisors," the "beastliness" of the Spanish nation, and ultimately the perfidy of Philip II himself. "Spanish tyranny in America," in short, developed as a metaphor of exceptional value for those who would justify the Revolt of the Netherlands.

III

The vision of America shared by the likes of Orange and Marnix denotes an abrupt and dramatic shift in the geopolitical thinking of the Dutch. The rapid success and the subsequent durability of the rebels' representation of America, however, neither implies its inevitability nor explains its incipiency. If the notion that Spain had desolated the New World seems perfectly obvious in retrospect, one need only recall the enthusiastic preface to Cornelis Ablijn's *Nieuwe weerelt* to realize just how radically images of America had evolved in the space of two decades. In the relative calm of 1563, Ablijn deemed it expedient to celebrate the glory of Spain's New World adventure and emphasize the heroism and the piety of Habsburg soldiers abroad. The prince of Orange, to whom Ablijn dedicated his work, was advised to extract from the history of the conquest the appropriate lessons of statesmanship and geography. The conclusions ultimately drawn by the prince, though, bespeak a drastically altered vision of the New World's significance. In Willem's imagination, the Spanish conquerors of America brought disgrace, rather than glory, to the "poore Indians." The history of the New World taught of the evils of tyranny rather than the triumphs of good government.

This shift in opinion is less easily explained than it might first seem. The impulse to vilify Spain resulted undoubtedly from those political events that consumed the prince's attention between Ablijn's anthology and Willem's own *Apologie.* Yet while the Revolt of the Netherlands would have served as a catalyst for the generally Hispanophobic turn of Dutch political literature, it in no way suffices to account for the shift of vision specifically regarding the New World or for the relevance Dutch authors attached to this sort of cultural geography. The fact of Orange's political and military opposition to Philip II and the Habsburg government in Brussels, in other words, fails to explain how Spain's experience *in America* became so quickly transformed from a source of pride to a gold mine of propaganda. It accounts neither for the origin of the topos of "Spanish tyranny in America" nor for the appeal of the topos among otherwise provincial rebels. It fails to resolve fully whence the idea came to relate events in the Netherlands to Spanish tyranny in

America, or why the rebels elected the metaphor of America as a prime means to sabotage the Spanish government in the Netherlands.

Where *did* "America" come from? As some rebel pamphleteers would have it, the idea sprang from the Spanish themselves: the program to govern the Netherlands as the Indies had been governed had some actual basis in Spanish policy or, at least, in Spain's expression of that policy. There was, these writers implied, some truth to the matter. This was not to say that Spain had ever announced its intention to conquer the Netherlands or to annihilate the entire native population as it purportedly had done in the Indies. It *was* to suggest, though, that Spanish governors, envious of "successes" overseas and frustrated with their own problems closer to home, referred (or were believed to have referred) with certain satisfaction to the vigorous government of the Indies as an antidote to the poisonous troubles in the Netherlands. In fact, a theory of empire predicated on the absolutist practices perfected in the Indies did circulate among the king and his leading advisors. A suggestive note, scribbled on the reverse of a letter sent in 1570 by the governor of Milan to Philip II, alludes to precisely such a strategy of control. "These Italians," wrote the governor, "although they are not Indians, have to be treated as such, so that they will understand that we are in charge of them and not they in charge of us." A brief two years earlier, Alba sent the king a similar piece of advice, insinuating that the only solution to the crisis in the north was "to create a New World " in the Netherlands. Willem, a number of years later, claimed to have witnessed meetings in his capacity as a loyal Habsburg noble (presumably before 1567) in which the Spanish governors and councilors "adjudged [the Netherlands] to death" and devised a plan to abuse the native (Dutch) population as they had the Indians in America. Likewise, the States General alleged to have intercepted letters from the Spanish ambassador in France, Francis d'Alana, which contained details of a Spanish Council policy to implement a "tyrannical government" in the Netherlands similar to that in place in the Indies and other newly conquered countries.[50]

These supposed musings of the Habsburg governing class would presumably have trickled down to the civil servants in Brussels and ultimately to the soldiers in the field. Both of these groups, indeed, harbored notoriously arrogant attitudes toward the "subject populations" that they were commanded to subdue. Most famously, a government official in Brussels imperiously dismissed the noblemen who petitioned Margaret in 1566 as "Beggars" (*Gueux* or *Geuzen*). The name stuck, yet was promptly transformed by the rebels into a badge of honor (literally), which they fashionably affixed to the brims of the hats they wore into battle. Other anecdotes suggest that Spanish troops regarded their "heretic" enemies with hardly more respect. The outrageous behavior of soldiers stationed in the Low Countries gave rise to the Spanish proverb, *Estamos aquí o en Flandes?* – Are we here or in the Netherlands? – implying that service in the Netherlands condoned conduct elsewhere unacceptable.[51] Whether such suggestive proverbs, insinuating letters, and cryptic jottings articulate an official Spanish policy seems rather unlikely. Alba, Alana, and the Spanish councilors in Brussels would not have advised literally to annihilate the Low Countries, effective though that policy might have been in America. Nonetheless, many would have supported clamping down on dissent with the same vigorous resolve that Spain had manifested in the *Conquista*. Whatever their intent, the Spanish employed an *idiom* of conquest in their notes, minutes, and conversations, and the rebels picked up on this idiom and exploited it for all it was worth.

To the extent that the Spanish Council resorted to a discourse of conquest, and to the extent that the Dutch identified the Council with such a policy, neither party would have been unique in associating the Habsburgs' European demeanor with their American record. Though the Dutch may have waged the fiercest campaign against the Spanish reputation, they did not wage the first, and it is also possible that the rebels derived their topoi of Spanish tyranny from earlier, non-Dutch sources. The Black Legend had its origins before and beyond the Revolt of the Netherlands; precedents existed upon which the Dutch could draw.[52] In sixteenth-century Italy, the *école de guerre* of successive Spanish monarchs, resentment toward Spain grew in proportion to the number of Habsburg fleets swarming the Mediterranean and Habsburg *tercios* roaming the Italian countryside. The infamous sacks of Prato (1512) and Rome (1527) occasioned especially vitriolic attacks on the invaders (many of whom were in fact German) and provoked some, like the future Cardinal Gasparo Contarini, to draw a connection between Spain's conquests *transalpino* and *transatlántico*. Contarini, who resided in Spain during the early 1520s, sent back to his Venetian compeers reports of the latest Castilian-sponsored cruelties in the Caribbean, which confirmed in his mind the barbarity native to the Spaniard.[53]

Contarini was not alone in his suspicions. Though England experienced only a brief spasm of Hispanophobia during the reign of Queen Mary and the "alien" Prince Philip, many "true naturall Englishe men" reacted, nonetheless, as if London had been sacked. The "great discomfort" caused by the Habsburg entourage revealed to some, like John Bradford, the "vile nature" of the Spanish in general and the "horrible practices of the king of Spayne" in particular. To illustrate just that, and to disabuse the English of any possible sympathy for the new Habsburg prince, one such affronted Briton, John Ponet, referred his readers to the West Indies where the Spanish program of tyranny and enslavement had brutalized the "simple and plaine" natives.

[A] great nombre of them (not used to suche paines) died, and a great nombre of them (seeing them selves brought from so quiet a life to such miserie and slaverie) of desperacion killed them selves. And many wolde not mary, bicause they wolde not have their children slaves to the Spaniardes. The women whan they felte them self with childe, wolde eat a certain herbe to destroie the childe in the wombe. So that where at the comming thider of the Spaniardes, ther were accompted to be in that countrey nine hundred thousaunt persones, ther were in short time by this meanes so fewe lefte.[54]

In France, the relatively recent experience with Spain *in* America – the infamous *affaire Floride* of the 1560s – produced a sharp outburst of anti-Habsburg rhetoric on the very eve of the Dutch Revolt. French polemics (most notably the multiple editions of Nicolas Le Challeux's *Discours*) came mainly from the Huguenots and often conflated attacks on Spain with broader assaults on the Catholic-Guise faction or the influence of Catherine de' Medici. These polemics, it is true, targeted Spanish-Catholic violences committed against French-Protestant colonialists – as opposed to tyrannies against "innocent Indians" who were largely ignored. Yet they contributed just the same to the general swell of indignation gathering against the Spanish presence in the New World and their patterns of government in the Old.[55]

For the Dutch opposition, the French connection was an important one. While the missives of Contarini may indicate a tone, or tenor, of discourse shared by various enemies of Spain, they hardly suggest a natural link with the rebels in Northern Europe. The pamphlets of the French Wars of Religion, by contrast, had a more obvious and direct connection to the Dutch Calvinists. The leaders of the French Huguenots and of the *Gueux* (many of whom were Francophone) shared ties of kinship, patronage, politics, and religion. The influential Montmorency family of the West Netherlands, for example, linked the great Huguenot leader and Protestant martyr, Admiral Coligny, with his Dutch cousins (and fellow martyrs) Montigny, Hoorn, and Egmont. Orange cemented these ties by wedding, first, Anne of Egmont and, later, Louise de Coligny. The rebels took advantage of their French relations as early as 1566 when Montigny met with his cousin, Anne de Montmorency, and the latter's nephew, Coligny, to discuss strategic cooperation between the two parties. More generally, Orange dispatched diplomats on a regular basis to the courts of France (as well as Germany) in pursuit of money, men, and moral support.[56]

These networks thrived, too, on a more modest level. Several exiled Dutch Protestants passed through France and Geneva, and sizable exile communities sprang up not only in Emden and London, but also in Orléans and Strasbourg, Heidelberg and Frankfurt, and naturally Geneva. French Calvinists, for their part, lent support to the rebels' cause in the form of advisors and skilled polemicists. François du Jon (Junius), who served as a minister in Antwerp and later a professor in Leiden, wrote an important *Discours* in 1566 advocating religious freedom and developing a case for tolerance very similar to the one later adopted by Willem of Orange. Willem's key advisors in 1570s and early 1580s (and the most likely candidates for ghostwriters of the *Apologie*) included Philippe du Plessis Mornay, a leading Huguenot and author of a discourse "sur la permission de liberté de religion, dicte Religions-vrede au Pais Bas"; Hubert Languet, the Bourgogne-born diplomat who contributed to Willem's *Justification* (1568); and Pierre L'Oyseleur de Villiers of Lille, Willem's court chaplain by way of Orléans, Paris, and Geneva.[57]

All of this added up to a network of contacts, exchanges, and cooperation between Calvinist rebels in the Netherlands and Protestant supporters primarily in France and Geneva, yet also in Germany and England. It constituted what has suggestively been described as an international Calvinist party. Among these communities flowed shared strategies, ideas, and even idioms of expression that were conveyed in the texts circulating between Emden, Geneva, and, ultimately, Antwerp. Above all, the martyrologies, composed in the 1550s and 1560s, drew upon "a common fund of experience, a common ideological commitment, [and] a common historical perspective."[58] They also introduced a broad range of Reformed readers to the tyrannies of America. Jean Crespin, a Walloon exile who settled in Geneva, included Jean de Léry's "La persécution des fidèles en terre d'Amérique" in his 1564 *Histoire les martyrs*. Adriaan van Haemstede, who preached in London and Emden, certainly knew of Crespin's (and Foxe's) work when he composed his *Geschiedenisse ende den doodt der vromer martelaren* (History and death of the devout martyrs), which appeared in 1559 and in a much expanded version in 1566. Finally, there was Nicolas Le Challeux's sensationalist account of the destruction of the Huguenot colony in Florida. The *Discours de l'histoire de la Floride*, which saw a total of five editions in 1566 alone, quickly elevated the tale of Spanish treason in America to a level of infamy matched only by the myths of the St. Bartholomew's Day Massacre spawned some half-dozen years later. These publications not only introduced a Reformed readership to "America"; they also caused the New World to be associated with martyrdom – "innocence" – and caused Spain and Catholicism to be associated with cruelty – "tyranny." They projected a distinctly Protestant vision of America. Ultimately, the literature of the Calvinist exiles filtered into the Netherlands and placed these themes in the hands of the Spain-hating, and sometimes also Catholic-baiting, rebels.[59]

The Walloon martyrologist Jean Crespin, the Venetian cardinal Gasparo Contarini, and the Marian exile John Ponet all mined the early Americana for material that could profitably be used against the Spanish (and, in the case of Crespin, the Catholic) enemy. They also readily referred their readers to the published sources of their American expertise, thereby showing themselves to be energetic readers as well as creative exegetes. Contarini and Ponet each cite the *Decades* of Peter Martyr. It made little difference to either that Martyr had composed his work to celebrate the glory of Spain or that the recent English translation of the *Decades,* to which Ponet presumably directed his readers, had been undertaken by Richard Eden expressly to *honor* Prince Philip and his Spanish forebears. Both Ponet and Contarini extracted the incriminating passages regardless of their original context and glossed them to suit their own purposes.[60] Crespin, on the other hand, collaborated with Léry whom he knew personally from their overlapping stays in Geneva.[61]

The Dutch also referred to the literature of America, which, in their estimation, substantiated their case against Spain. The nature of Spanish tyranny, the methods of Spanish conquest, and the pattern of Spanish expansion all stood plainly stated in the famous histories of the Discovery. Moreover, as the rebels were quick to point out, it was often Spanish-authored accounts that provided the most damning evidence. "For those who say that this is just talk," challenged the brilliant young orator, Willem Verheiden, apropos of Philip II's purported desire to dominate the Low Countries as he had the West Indies,

read what the Spanish themselves have written of their treatment of the Indies. In these accounts, which they have written for their own amusement or to make themselves seem more awesome, they themselves tell of having killed millions of people who never had provoked them, or done them any harm, and over which they had not the least right of sovereignty.

The histories of the Indies, according to Verheiden, lent greater insight into the nature of the Habsburgs' hegemonic aims and the Inquisition's absolutist tendencies. The narratives of the New World would help all those who wished "to understand better" the essence of Spanish tyranny.[62]

These American "accounts" and other explosive sources could, at times, be ambiguously referenced. Like Verheiden, the rebel hacks could remain tantalizingly vague in their citations, referring only to "histories" or "reports of the New Indies," as if they themselves possessed only the most general grasp of the materials they cited. Other times, however, their footnotes left a better-marked trail. In an unsigned work of 1574, a pamphleteer referred his readers to those histories "assembled and published from the minutes and decrees of the Indian Council." More than likely, the author had in mind the work of Peter Martyr, a chronicler of the Council of Indies, or perhaps López de Gómara who, though unaffiliated with the Council, wrote a best-selling chronicle of the *Conquista* based on original sources. Marnix cited Gómara's work explicitly in the marginalia of his *Byencorf*, a scathing satire of the Roman Catholic Church, and Gómara's, along with other Spanish histories, also show up in the catalogue of Marnix's personal library. The radical *predikant*, Peter Dathenus, names no specific source for his opinion that the Spanish treated the natives of America "cruelly lyke butchers, tearying them with all kind of torments." Yet the formulaic language and familiar tropes of his description indicate his indebtedness to either Martyr's *Decades* or Benzoni's *Historia*, both of which contained notably similar catalogues of Spanish "torments."[63]

One source surfaces repeatedly in Dutch texts, conspicuous particularly in the 1580s and 1590s, in materials as varied as the songs of the *Geuzen* and the testaments of Orange. "Mark what a bishop from Spain has written / Of how the Spaniards stole Indian riches," rang a ballad composed in 1594. Willem, in denouncing the "horrible excesses and ryottes" and the "barbarousnesses, cruelties, and tyrannies" committed by Spain in America, referred to things that "even by their own Bishoppes and Doctours, hath been left in writing, and to make the king without excuse before God and men, the historie thereof was dedicated unto him, by one of his own subjectes, in whom there remained, as should seeme, some final sparke of justice." The prince and the poets alluded to the same cleric: Fray Bartolomé de Las Casas, onetime bishop of Chiapas and longtime "Apostle of the Indians." That cleric's history to which both gestured was the *Brevíssima relación de la destruyción de las Indias*, dedicated to (then) Prince Philip in 1552 and destined to enjoy near canonical status among the sacred texts of the Revolt. Printed repeatedly throughout the late-sixteenth and seventeenth centuries, it ranks among the most successful descriptions of America to appear in early modern Europe. Replete with lurid tales of Spanish tyranny, it also became one of the most commonly cited texts of the Dutch patriotic party.[64]

Bartolomé de Las Casas (1484–1576), whom the rebels associated chiefly with the bishop's miter, donned in fact quite a few hats in a long and controversial career that spanned both sides of the Atlantic, the reigns of three Castilian kings, and virtually the entire duration of the *Conquista*.[65] In his youth, Las Casas sailed to the New World (1502) in time to participate in the conquest of Hispaniola. He later joined Diego Velázquez in the campaign to subdue Cuba and there gained firsthand experience of the bloody massacres and slave raids that would feature so vividly in his later writings. A brief spell as an *encomendero* (or overlord of "encommended" native serfs) followed these adventures, and Las Casas, who had in the meantime entered the ranks of the lay clergy, seemed well on his way to a profitable and comfortable career in colonial Spanish America. On the Sunday before Christmas 1511, however, he heard an arresting sermon delivered by the Dominican, Antonio Montesinos, condemning the Spanish brutalization of the Indians. Three years later he encountered a yet sterner admonition, this time in the form of a text (Eccl. 34:21–2), which caused the proverbial scales to fall from his eyes and paved the way for a dramatic conversion from a colonizing priest to a moralizing apostle.[66] The thunderstruck *clérigo* – he would later join the Dominicans – dedicated the rest of his considerable years to evangelizing the Indians, defending their "humanity," and bringing to the Crown's attention the ignominious assaults perpetrated against them. With remarkable persistence and equally remarkable patrons, Las Casas established himself as the most influential Spaniard to take up the plight of the Amerindians. He emerged as the central figure of an Indianist movement that occupied the moral periphery of the Spanish enterprise in America.

The *Brevíssima relación* represented but one of the many treatments by Las Casas of the Indian question, and it appears, at first glance, unusual that an otherwise obscure tract written for a royal Spanish audience should end up some thirty years later in the hands of Dutch rebels. Conceived as early as the 1520s, the *Brevíssima relación* was drafted (for Charles V) originally in 1542, printed (for Philip II) ultimately in 1552, and abandoned for all intents and purposes promptly thereafter to languish in the Spanish royal archives. Though Las Casas and his ideas exercised undeniable influence over certain members of the royal circle, and though Philip continued to regard the Dominican with respect and even favor, the "Indianist policy" ultimately ceded to the expediency of financial crisis, and Lascasian rhetoric gave way to the stronger pressures of the colonialist lobby. Little in the mid-sixteenth century would have indicated that Las Casas's account would endure over the next four centuries. Yet that changed dramatically and abruptly in 1578, when the Dutch discovered "the bishop's histories" and their uses. The *Brevíssima relación* fit the rebels' agenda perfectly. It catalogued vividly the "great miseries and wretched destruction" visited upon America and thereby exposed the extent of Spain's perfidy. It addressed directly the emperor Charles V and the future king Philip II and thereby implicated (indirectly) the Spanish crown, which, by 1578, had not altered a course of government that had plainly gone awry. Best of all, it flowed passionately from the pen of a reputable Spanish cleric, an eyewitness to the events described, and thereby lent greater legitimacy to the rebels' case against Spain.[67]

It also worked spectacularly. The rebels consequently not only rehabilitated Las Casas' tract; they also reprinted it tirelessly, translated it quickly, and disseminated it widely across Northern Europe. Following the cautiously produced Dutch translation in 1578, which appeared without the name of the printer or translator or the place of publication, an astonishing twenty-five more Dutch-language editions rolled off the presses of the Low Countries by the time the war with Spain had ended (1648). Over the course of the late-sixteenth and seventeenth centuries, the Dutch published altogether some thirty-three editions of Las Casas, more than did all other European countries combined. Furthermore, those editions produced outside the Netherlands originated largely from texts either translated or printed by the rebels. In 1579, the Reformed *predikant* and Orangist, Jacques de Miggerode, undertook a French translation of the *Brevíssima relación* meant "to serve as an example and warning to the Seventeen Provinces of the Netherlands."[68] Since two of those provinces, Artois and Hainault, had just come to terms with Parma (Treaty of Arras, 1579), Miggerode presumably labored also to persuade his French-speaking cousins to reconsider their *rapprochement* with Spain. Though he failed to convince the Walloon provinces, Miggerode found an immensely receptive audience elsewhere in Europe. His *Tyrannies et cruautez des Espagnols* served as the basis for multiple French-language editions in Geneva, Paris, Lyon, and Rouen, as well as an English translation that appeared in time to greet the Spanish Armada. The Liège-born and Protestant printer, Theodore de Bry, transformed Miggerode's text into Latin and German editions, which de Bry supplemented with graphic (in both senses of the word) illustrations designed by the South Netherlandish artist Joost van Wingen (Ioducus á Winghe). De Bry's illustrated volume, perhaps more than any other, spread the word and image of Spanish tyranny in America.[69]

As the history of its publication makes apparent, the *Brevíssima relación* had an extraordinary impact on the Dutch. It was cited by such pamphleteers as Marnix and the ghostwriters of Orange; it was listed by such prominent geographers as Ortelius and Mercator; and it was consulted by such patriotic historians as Emanuel van Meteren and P. C. Hooft. Lascasian language, style, and metaphors appear in texts as varied as Justus Lipsius's humanist *De constantia* and Adriaan Valerius's musical *Nederlandsche gedank-clank*. Lascasian imagery colored the Dutch perception of their Spanish governors and invariably encouraged speculation on the relation between Spanish tyranny at home and abroad.[70]

Nonetheless – and this point is crucial – the preponderant presence of the *Brevíssima relación* within Dutch letters still does not satisfactorily explain the *origins* of the rebels' geographic turn to America. First, the phenomenal pace of publication of Las Casas, though begun already in 1578, took off in earnest only in the seventeenth century. The overwhelming majority of issues, in Dutch as well as Latin and German, appeared in the quarter century, 1596–1621: in a period that coincided largely with the "cold war" of Philip III's reign, and in a period that *followed* the politically incendiary years between 1568 and 1581. Second, numerous references to the New World preceded the original publication of Las Casas in the Netherlands. The States of Holland's *Admonition* of 1574 refers to Spain in America, and the petition presented by the exile community of Emden to the German Diet made mention already in 1570 of Spanish cruelties committed in the "uttermost Indi[e]s." As early as 1568, a gathering of nobles warned that Spain intended to abuse the Netherlands "as they have done in the New Indies"; and in 1569, a sensationalist satire suggested that Philip was plotting to shackle and ship to America all those of the Reformed faith. By 1578, then, the Netherlands provided already fecund ground in which to plant the seeds of Lascasian discourse.[71]

To credit Las Casas with the Dutch formulation of the Black Legend of Spanish tyranny, or the creation of the topos of Spanish cruelties in America, is to confuse the messenger with the message. Whatever its later influence, the *Brevíssima relación* did not introduce the Netherlands to Spain's abysmal reputation in America. Though Las Casas added much to the rebels' stock of Hispanophobic invective, he did not suggest to them, in the first place, the usefulness America might have in their struggle against Spain. Those geographically adventurous Netherlanders who first published and later cited, the "bishop's histories" did so only after sailing substantial reconnaissance missions to explore the shoals of anti-Spanish polemic. By the time the Dutch discovered Las Casas, Spain's New World reputation had already become old news. "The tyranny of the conquistadors had been too widely bruited in both the Old and New Worlds," wrote the eighteenth century French Dominican, Antoine Touron, in defense of Las Casas. "Men of good will had complained too loudly for the past forty or thirty years for the Dutch to be unaware of facts so generally known throughout Europe."[72] The rebel publicists incorporated Las Casas into an already growing repertoire of anti-Spanish propaganda, in which the New World occupied a position of honor. From the earlier histories of America – especially that of Benzoni, published in 1565, 1573, and 1578, and that of Martyr, published in 1555, 1574, and 1577 – from the references to Spanish tyrannies circulating among the various stations of the international Protestant community, and from the scattered comments of the Spanish governors themselves, the Dutch formulated an image of Spanish tyranny in America that was meant to serve "as an example" for readers in the Habsburg-controlled Low Countries. Las Casas added grist to a propaganda mill already well in motion. Recognizing the obvious use that the *Brevíssima relación* might have in their program, the rebels adopted and popularized what turned out to be one of the most compelling pieces of colonial literature to emerge from the *Conquista*, a work that might otherwise have faded into obscurity. The colonial critique by the bishop of Chiapas filled a need for all those who sought to discredit Spain and its leaders, yet that need predated the Dutch discovery of Las Casas. By 1578, those opponents of Philip II who published the *Brevíssima relación* were merely stoking fires already strongly burning.

IV

Wherever they came from, descriptions of the conquest of the Indies, and particularly those that cast Spain in an unfavorable light, well suited the rebels' program. The theme of "America" expanded geographic horizons at a moment of acute political contraction. The turn of events in the late 1560s and 1570s had effectively isolated the Dutch opponents of Habsburg government. Many of the leading members of the rebel party fled the Netherlands in 1567 at the onset of Alba's regime. For his part, Alba arrested and executed countless others, condemning *in absentia* all those who dared not appear before his dreaded "Council of Blood." Within the space of a few years, and with the support of more than a few thousands troops, Alba had transformed the Low Countries, politically speaking, from a cosmopolitan collection of cities and towns associated with a hitherto accommodating Habsburg sovereign to a small band of isolated "rebels" confronted by an immense and resolute Spanish empire. Under such circumstances, the rebels perceived themselves, not without an element of truth, threatened by a formidable Spanish monarch with extensive resources and superior forces. To rally support and convince potential allies of the severity of their situation, the rebels portrayed themselves, not without a degree of hyperbole, as threatened by an omnipotent, "universal" monarch with limitless resources and equally infinite ambitions. Spain had embarked, already from the late fifteenth century, on a program of world-wide expansion, contended Marnix in his apocalyptically titled, *Faithful exhortation to the conquered provinces of the Netherlands on the general aim and plan of Spain to establish a projected fifth monarchy.* Castile's imperialist designs, charged Marnix, had already engulfed the whole of the Iberian peninsula, Italy and the Mediterranean islands, and the New World. The Netherlands represented a final and crucial bulwark between Philip II and his villainous ambitions.[73]

To an extent, accusations of universal monarchism developed from a frank recognition, in the Netherlands as elsewhere, of the spectacular expansion of the Habsburg sphere of influence over the course of the sixteenth century. Under Philip II's father, Charles V, the House of Habsburg added the Spanish kingdoms, most of the Burgundian Netherlands, and large parts of Italy to its traditional possessions in Germany and Austria. Philip's reign witnessed still further expansions. In 1554 Philip positioned himself to control the crown of England; in 1580 he maneuvered to secure the Portuguese throne (and the vast Lusitanian colonies in Asia and Brazil); and, by the mid-1580s, it was generally believed, he had gained a hold on France through his influence on the Catholic League. Add to this vast lands of the New World and colonies in the East (including the "Philippines"), and it is easy to understand the concern of contemporaries.[74]

Still, little hard evidence exists for the sort of ambitious and calculated "universalist" policies that Marnix and his associates had in mind. The topos of "universal monarchy," it would seem, derived more from patterns of rhetoric than reality.[75] From the earliest moments of opposition, thus, the rebel minority accused its enemies of harboring designs of the grandest and most sinister magnitude. The contention that the Holy Office sought to establish a "great empire" to rival those of antiquity found expression in an oft-cited tract published originally in 1566 and popularly known as the "Legend of the Inquisition." (It was republished in 1580 with the more provocative title, *The book of the three popes,* a reference to its claim that the popes of Rome, the Netherlands [Cardinal

Granvelle] and France [Cardinal Lorraine] had conspired to establish, and then to divide among themselves, a European empire.) A pamphlet appearing two years later similarly alleged that the Spanish Inquisition sought to use the Netherlands as a springboard for further conquests across the whole of Europe. Meanwhile, Reformed pamphleteers regularly insinuated that Madrid and Rome were cooperating to establish a Catholic empire with which they would roll back the recent gains of their mutual Protestant enemies.[76]

These arguments took on a more plainly political shape in the late 1570s, as the rebels began to accuse Spain directly (and Philip II indirectly) of the expansionist designs previously imputed to the Holy Office. By the time Marnix delivered his *Oratio legatorum* to the German Diet in 1578, the emphasis had shifted from the sacred to the secular ambitions of the Spanish Crown and its "machinations" to conquer not only the Netherlands, but also Germany, England, France, the Balkans, Asia Minor, "and the whole Empire of the Orient." Like the other great bogeyman of the European imagination, the Ottoman sultan, the Spanish king desired "to dominate the whole world; for Europe [alone] is too small for [his] pride." Hoping to check Spain's relentless progress, Marnix made a precocious case for a system of balance of power in which the weaker states – in this case, the Netherlands and German estates – would align themselves against the Spanish menace.[77]

This argument quickly spread among the patriotic party. A pamphleteer writing on behalf of Johan Casimir, the count of the Palatinate who had led twelve thousand mercenaries into Brabant and Flanders in 1578, stressed in much the same way the urgency of joining forces against an expansionist Spanish monarch. Orange's supporters spoke of Philip II's "good fortune" (and the rest of Europe's bad luck) to have inherited control not only over Germany (and most pamphleteers assumed the close cooperation between the Castilian and Austrian lines of the Habsburg family), "but also over all of the provinces in Europe, as well as large regions in Africa and also the Indies and the fourth part of the world [America]." Marnix, as ever the most eloquent and emphatic voice among the rebel wordsmiths, codified the case against Spain's universal monarchism in a series of polemics published between 1583 and 1586 – after Philip II had been jettisoned, that is, and could be attacked with impunity – and addressed "to all Christian Kings, Princes, and Potentates." Marnix exhorted his audience to unite against the king of Spain's long coveted goal of universal monarchy, "an empire extending into Asia, Africa, Europe, and America, even to the East and West Indies." The Spanish "naturally" inclined toward arrogance and imperiousness, contended Marnix. Unless the nations of the world acted quickly to thwart Philip II's designs, he would proceed impiously toward a fifth monarchy. (And since Marnix and his readers identified the fourth monarchy as the Roman Empire, which was destined to last till the end of history, they condemned any latter-day world empire as a heretical usurpation).[78]

Such accusations of universal monarchism partook of the broader rebel strategy of expanding the base of Dutch support. Many of Marnix's publications, along with other key pamphlets commissioned by the States of Holland and Orange, appeared simultaneously in Latin, Dutch, French, German, and English, which gives some indication of the scope of their intended audiences. These pamphlets normally preceded or accompanied direct appeals to the leaders of France, Germany, and England for aid, mainly in the form of money and men. Eventually, the wish-list came to include "monarchy," too: ultimately, that is, the rebels solicited the leading princes of Europe to accept the sovereignty of the Netherlands in place of the now spurned king of Spain. The *Oratio legatorum* implored the German Diet to intervene on the Dutch behalf, and Johan Casimir, who came to the Netherlands in 1578, did so at the behest of the prince of Orange and queen of England. Elizabeth, in fact, financed the troops that accompanied Casimir as a gesture of support. The most serious Dutch solicitations went to Francis, duke of Anjou and Alençon, brother and heir to the king of France (Henri III). The rebels approached Anjou intermittently from 1576 and finally convinced him to become "prince and lord of the Netherlands" in 1581. Though Anjou's reign turned out disastrously for all parties concerned, this did not dissuade the States from appealing to Henri III upon Anjou's death in 1584 to assume sovereignty of the Netherlands. Once again, however, this tactic failed, and, with the loss of Orange to an assassin's bullet (1584), the rebels were left more desperate than ever. The following year, rebel envoys arrived in England to plead their case with the Protestant Queen Elizabeth. This resulted in the ill-starred lieutenantship of the earl of Leicester, whose government proved no more successful than Anjou's before him.[79]

Without a sovereign or *stadhouder*, without adequate troops or funds to pay for them, and without hope of signing an acceptable peace with Spain, the rebels faced a future more clouded than ever. They had solicited aid from all quarters of Europe yet with only limited success. A mood of despair hung over the rebel camp, an anxiety whose urgency is well captured by the advice of the secretary of Jan van Nassau (brother of Willem) to the Orangist leadership. Under the circumstances, assistance from any source would be acceptable, asserted the secretary. Anyone who might come to the rebels' aid, he wrote Nassau, must be encouraged,

even if he were a Tartar, a Samaritan, or a Muscovite – indeed even a Turk. As long as he could help us in our time of need and would maintain our privileges, rights, and freedoms of religion; then we must accept [his help] as a gift from God. To do otherwise would be to act rebelliously and defiantly against God.[80]

Indeed even a Turk: That the Dutch so much as entertained the idea of allying with the Ottomans speaks as much to the desperation of their political leaders as to the daring of their pamphlet writers. It suggests, too, an expansive geopolitical imagination unimpeded by the usual boundaries. There was certainly some precedent for an Ottoman initiative.[81] The more radically inclined Calvinist elements of the rebel party would not have shrunk from the possibility, at least, of enlisting the aid of the Sultan in their holy war against the Most Catholic King. Orange, no radical himself, had more material motives for dispatching the occasional ambassador to the Porte. An agent of the prince visited Constantinople in search of succor already in 1566, and it is speculated that Orange's diplomacy may have prompted the Sultan to send his navy in full force to Tunis in September 1574, a moment that found Spanish resources particularly overextended. More generally, the Dutch followed with great interest the vicissitudes of the Ottoman-Habsburg confrontation in the Mediterranean. Baron Hendrik van Brederode, a nobleman of Holland, "rubbed his hands gleefully," as one historian put it, upon hearing that the Turks were off Malta in the spring of 1565. Orange wrote his brother around the same time: "The Turks are very threatening, which will mean, we believe, that the king will not come to the Netherlands this year."[82] The fall of Tunis in 1572 was recorded in ironic verse that demonstrates both a keen awareness of events abroad and a sophisticated understanding of the relevance these events had closer to home:

> that Fortune can move in mysterious ways
> Is also apparent: For the bloodied sword of Zelimus [Selim II]
> Has driven the Christians out again
> At the moment when we [Dutch] were pitifully disinherited:
> Plunder generally leads to further plunder.

These and other vaguely pro-Ottoman comments earned the rebels the opprobrium of Habsburg friends and good Catholics across Europe, like the two English exiles who coined the phrase *Calvino-Turcismus* as a term of abuse for the Dutch.[83]

The rebels might have answered their antagonists with one of the more curious refrains of the Revolt: "Liever Turxs dan Paus" (Better a Turk than a Papist).[84] For, whatever the extent of the relations between the Calvinists and Constantinople – and little evidence exists to suggest that Orange's initiatives ever progressed beyond the realm of the hypothetical – the Dutch made much of the *possibility* of such an association. If an alliance or support never actually materialized, that is to say, this did not prevent the rebel publicists from speculating on what an association with the Sultan might entail. In one of the more remarkable rhetorical turns of the Revolt, then, the rebels posed the possibility of living under the Ottoman sultan as a preferable alternative to the king of Spain. In this vein, the Flemish noble D'Esquerdes issued a letter to protest the religious persecutions, claiming that he "would rather become a tributary to the Turks than live against his conscience and be treated according to those [anti-heresy] edicts" promulgated in Brussels. The same idea found expression in the rebels' pamphlets. The Turk would make a more suitable sovereign than the Spanish; for while the latter would not tolerate even Protestant dissent, the former famously protected Jews and Christians who lived peacefully within his empire. "The Turks tyrannize over the body and leave the conscience free," wrote a "True Patriot" of the Dutch dilemma. "The champions of the one and only Catholic religion [Spain] want to tyrannize over both body and mind." Those *Geuzen* who liberated Leiden from a Spanish siege in 1574 made this point more stylishly when they fastened onto their caps crescent-shaped badges bearing the slogan "Better a Turk than a Papist."[85]

The Turkish topos went only so far, however. If famous for their tolerance, the Ottomans were equally infamous for their reputed cruelty and despotism. The prospect of a Turkish alliance implied both help and hindrance. Just as a discussion of religious freedom could lead to the subject of Ottoman tolerance, a review of mutinous Spanish soldiers could elicit comparisons with Ottoman "barbarism." When discussing the brutalities of Alba's troops, then, the rebels evoked the image of "Turkish, heathen fury." When considering a future under Habsburg rule, the polemicists raised the specter of "Turkish slavery" – a reference to the political absolutism that would accompany any form of "Asiatic" government. Ultimately, the Turks were infidels, and the heresy of Islam alone disqualified them from assuming a more central (or consistent) role in the rebels' program of propaganda. One of the Revolt's most steadfast champions of tolerance, as well as the instigator of the missions to the Porte, Orange could still describe Alba as "one who hath willingly bathed him selfe in our blood, and in the blood of all Christians, carrying closely a Turkish hearte." Of Philip II's religious edicts,

Orange prophesied that they would bring "a more than Turkish igno-raunce to the Netherlands."[86]

Calvinoturcism, for what it was worth, represented an extreme, yet by no means exceptional, case of polemical posturing that matched a pattern of rhetoric otherwise pervasive from the earliest years of the Revolt. While it might seem unusual for Calvinists in the northwest corner of Europe to contemplate an association with the Ottoman Turks, it was not uncommon for the rebel publicists to look abroad – in their pamphlets, at least – for succor or sympathy. As Orangist agents lobbied princes across Northern Europe, rebel pamphleteers ranged even more widely in projecting such alliances with the nations of the world. Guided by the assumption that "my enemy's enemy is my friend," they drafted brothers-in-arms or, at the very least, cousins-in-suffering from among those who actively opposed Habsburg expansion (such as the English queen and the Ottoman sultan) or those who had experienced Habsburg expansion in the past (such as the Italians and the Moors). Fellow travelers from "the Kingdom of Naples, Sicily, Sardinia, and all other lands in which they [the Spanish] have gained the upper hand" could not only bear witness to Habsburg tyranny; they could also spare sympathy, it was hoped, for the latest of its victims. Granada, the conquest of which finally established the Castilians as unrivaled masters of Spain, had gained more recent attention among the rebels for its revolt against Spain in 1568–70. The fierce suppression of the Moriscos by Don Juan of Austria – who would later arrive in Antwerp to accomplish a similar task in the Netherlands – served Marnix as an example of what "the most wretched nation that ever existed" was capable. Like Marnix, Orange lamented the misfortunes of the Granadans together with the "poore people of Sicilia, Calabria, Lombardie, Arragon, and Castile," who had all suffered the iniquities of Spanish rule. The prince further insinuated that these nations might rise up in unison and, following the Dutch model, throw off the yoke of Habsburg tyranny. After its annexation by Castile in 1580, Portugal too joined the ranks of potential allies, as did Aragon following its revolt in 1590–1591. As Orange's comments make clear, *all* subjects of the Habsburg empire, and even those living in Castile, yearned to follow the Dutch in rejecting the unbearable tyranny of Philip II. Indeed, half of Europe represented potential allies.[87]

Not all potential allies made for comfortable bedfellows, however, and a number of factors would have tempered Dutch enthusiasm for the likes of Moors, Italians, and Aragonese. The Granadans, like the Turks, were perceived to be Muslims or, at best, fresh converts to Catholicism. Neither situation would have sat very well with the more radical *Geuzen*, for whom "Mohammedanism" registered just one notch above papism. The Aragonese, Italians, and Sicilians belonged indisputably to the Church of Rome and, as a popular Protestant proverb put it (with reference to the Italians), "The closer to Rome the worse the Christian." Equally damning, the Italians served as mercenaries in the army of Flanders and would have committed much the same battlefield atrocities as their Castilian cohorts. The Protestant community of Antwerp pointedly blamed "the Spaniards, Italians, and Albanoosen" for the havoc wreaked on their city in 1576. In a similar vein, a certain "Watchman of Dutch Liberties" called on all "lovers of the fatherland . . . to chase our enemy back over the Italian mountains." Italians played a useful role as allies, it seems, only insofar as they stayed away from Rome and outside of the Netherlands – an exceedingly tall order, practically speaking.[88]

One "nation" presented credentials that perfectly matched the rebels' needs. Neither Catholics nor soldiers, Moors nor mercenaries, the Americans appeared the ultimate ally to the Dutch geopolitical imagination. More dramatically than any other "nation," they had suffered from Spanish tyranny; less problematically than any other nation, they came unencumbered by the usual religio-cultural baggage. The Dutch, accordingly, singled out the American example from all others, as did, for example, the author who cites Spanish cruelties "in Naples, Milan, Granada, and *especially* the Indies."[89] Furthermore, they reserved a position of prominence for the "innocent" Indian in their gallery of Habsburgian victims. The *Spanish and Aragonese Mirror* (1599), an anonymous, book-length treatment of the "unparalleled savagery and tyranny" perpetrated by Philip II across Europe and around the world, does exactly that in an extraordinary engraving that decorates the title page (fig. 9). Gathered together to wag their collective finger at the Spanish – personified by a sword-yielding, mustachioed figure reflected in a "mirror" above making short work of a woman and child – stand the "nations of the world" wearing various costumes that identify their country of origin. In the very center stand two tall "Americans" wearing nothing but feather headdresses and pointing dolefully at the violence depicted in the "mirror" vignette. Beside them poses an elegantly clad European with a crescent shaped badge affixed to his broad-rimmed hat – a Dutch *Geus*, in other words. The *Geus* gestures disdainfully to the enemy above while simultaneously casting a fatherly glance at his naked brethren on center stage.[90] The rebels' perception of their own situation, their sense of isolation, and their chosen idiom of propaganda all gravitated toward this sort of gallery of "allies," real or imagined, who join together to indict the scourge that was Spain. The Dutch imagination of the Indians' situation, the very distance of the New World, and the presumed "innocence" of the natives (represented here without any of the dressings,

Figure 9. Title page illustration from *Den Spaenschen ende Arragoenschen Spiegel* (1599). Universiteitsbibiliotheek Amsterdam.

literally, of religion or state) led to the central positioning of America within that gallery. America was exceptionally useful. Its very novelty and plasticity allowed it to be molded according to the rebels' specifications. And the Dutch were exceptionally resourceful. Their very isolation and the novelty of *their* situation forced them to create the myths that justified their actions. The Dutch crafted a usable geography, and "America" lent itself to be positioned most prominently within the Dutch world view.

V

America's plasticity permitted it to be readily shaped according to circumstance and audience. The cultural geographers of the rebel party were quick to recognize and take advantage of these qualities and therefore featured the New World centrally within their anti-Spanish polemics. The experience of America, they maintained, closely paralleled that of the Netherlands, as both "nations" had tasted first-hand the bitterness of Habsburg misgovernment. Both had suffered the abuse of rights, privileges, and liberties by unlawful Habsburg civil servants; both had endured the destruction of properties, cities, and provinces by mutinous foreign mercenaries; both had sacrificed lives, wives, and children to rapacious Spanish wardogs. In both cases, the invading legions had cloaked their greed with the banner of religion and branded their enemies "heretics" or "heathen." In both instances, the lands invaded had chosen heroic resistance rather than slavish servitude to Habsburg tyrants.

Or so, at least, the Dutch would have it. To a large degree, though, the rebels' argument spun elegantly in circles. Spanish tyranny in the Netherlands, they claimed, mirrored that in the New World. Yet their perception of events in America in the first place came refracted through the lens of recent developments in the Netherlands. The Dutch, in other words, contemplated the New World through the spectacles of their own political situation. Dutch circumstances could be said to parallel those of America because the representation of American history was patterned after the Dutch Revolt. In the mind's eye of a late sixteenth-century Dutch publicist, the image of America bore a striking resemblance indeed to that of the Low Countries.

To project that peculiarly Dutch image of the Indies, rebel geographers drew on their recent political, economic, and social experience, and especially on the stock of "abuses" that filled their otherwise provincial complaints. Spanish tyranny in the New World, proposed the rebels, began most basically with the abuse of the Indians' traditional privileges and "legal" rights. Rarely did Dutch authors bring up the fact of the discovery of America itself, or question Spain's right to establish a colonial government.[91] Rather, the Dutch contended that, once the Spaniards had erected a government overseas, they promptly fell into a familiar pattern of misrule, or "tyranny." In the New World, as in the Low Countries, Spain violated the rights, riches, and religious freedoms of its subjects. "They called [it] perfect and absolute obedience: but we may better call it Tyrannie," wrote Willem Verheiden of Spain's philosophy of power. "That is, a violent doing government, which resisteth and opposeth our good lawes and customes; with the which many years agoe they have overwhelmed and distressed them of India." Legal infringements rather than military maneuvers, Verheiden posited, undid the Indies.[92] A similar contention informs the nobles' remonstrances of 1568, which introduce the history of America apropos of Habsburg encroachments on local (Dutch) privileges. Spanish governors, the discontented nobles protested, had ignored traditional rights in the Low Countries just as they had ignored rights in the New World. Spain threatened to govern the Netherlands as they had the "New Indies": without proper recourse to laws or privileges. Neither in America nor in the Netherlands had the Spaniards "kept any covenants," stated Marnix with unusual succinctness. A patriotic balladeer speaks of Indians "tyrannized against all laws," and compares the viceroys in America to as many "Jugurthas" – a reference to the second century (B.C.E.) tyrant – "who lorded over the Kingdom of Numidia so unlawfully." The Council of the Indies placed themselves above the law and ruled tyranically, the rebels protested. They demanded that legal infringements similarly promulgated by the Council in Brussels be reversed, before the Low Countries went the way of America.[93]

After the abuse of privileges followed the plunder of property. In the Dutch imagination, Spain had stripped the Indians of their rights in order to denude them of their riches. "The magnificent kingdoms of the Indies they destroyed / . . . only to gain its gold," rang a verse composed by a Holland Chamber of Rhetoric. Spanish greed, of course, was nothing new, and, on the face of it, the rebels' indictment of Spain's economic motives in America would have struck an already familiar chord. What gave the rebels' position such resonance, though, was the emphasis placed on "possessions" and "ownership" – as if the Indians' loss of property, in the larger scheme of things, merited central attention. To the rebels, however, many of whom had endured substantial material losses during the exiled, winter years of Alba's regime, property mattered. The Indians' "losses" deserved to be denounced; Spain's acquisitiveness in America needed to be exposed. If Philip II regained full authority in the Netherlands, exhorted Verheiden, neither life nor property would escape his clutches. Witness the case of the "poor Indians" in America: "There no one is permitted to own anything. Indeed a man cannot even protect his wife and children from their [Spain's] lustful greed." The exile community of Emden also expressed concern for the losses incurred by the Americans. "Under the pretense of orderyng religion," they wrote of Spain's New World mission, "they spoyled the poor and simple inhabitants of those countreys of all their goods and possessions and of their wives, children and lives."[94]

The presumption that the New World had been desolated "under the pretense of religion" was a common one, and it reflects, once again, the peculiarly Dutch version of American history promoted by the rebels. The assertion that Spain conducted its foreign policy under the guise of maintaining Catholic orthodoxy quickly became an article of faith within rebel circles and was used especially by Calvinist polemicists who hoped thereby to convince their Catholic cousins of Habsburg hypocrisy. Spain, according to the Emden petitioners, had devised the

Inquisition – had fabricated the imperative of heresy – in order to justify its illegal government, confiscations, and oppressions. "Coloring
hys owne malitious affections with the glorious pretense of zele to re-
store the Romishe religion," Alba had invaded the Low Countries and
committed "outragious crueltie[s]." Under the same "cloak of Catholicism," they asserted, the conquistadors had plundered and laid waste
the New World. "The good maisters and byshops of the Spanish inquisition," continued the Emden document, "have most furiously executed
their tyranny in . . . new India." In America as in *Belgica* – as even the
most "blockish" man could perceive – "the color of defending the
Pope's religion" gave license to

oppresse the hole libertie of the citizens . . . take away theyr magistrates au-
thoritie, and violate the hole power of theyr lawes . . . that they themselves might
without law or order at their pleasure commaund what they wyll, take what
they ly[k]e, kyll whatsoever should offend them, empty the rich mens coffers
and make themselves lordes and governors of all thinges.[95]

Less dramatically yet no less emphatically, the same point is made by "a
nobleman, lover of the Fatherland and of public peace":

We know that the only reason this war was started was to ensure that the liberties of the country would be respected so that no one might, in violation of law
and justice, be oppressed on the pretext of religion. Undoubtedly, to invoke the
pretext of religion is the best way to go about abolishing all a country's liberties,
rights, and privileges. The example of the Kingdom of Naples, the Indies, and
Spain itself bears this out.[96]

The Indians, like the Dutch, had fallen victim to Spanish stratagems.
Nothing they did deserved the degree of devastation brought upon
them by the Habsburg invaders. The rebels refer to their American alter
egos varyingly as "innocent," "blameless," "wretched," and "poor."
The Spanish had extinguished the souls of "many millions . . . who never
had caused offense or done harm, and over whom they [Spain] never
had any right of sovereignty."[97] Spain had shed "innocent blood" in
America:

> guiltless and innocent [souls] have been smothered;
> Of more terrible and inhuman cruelty who has ever heard?[98]

The rebel versemakers answered their own question with reference to
the cruelties committed by Spain in the Netherlands – the tyrannies that
had occasioned the consideration of America in the first place. Events in
the New World, reasoned the rebels, closely paralleled those in the
Netherlands, and the case of America compared instructively with that
of the Low Countries. In the Indies as in the Low Countries, Spain had

violated the political, economic, and religious rights of its subjects. The natives of America had done nothing to deserve these abuses – they were "innocent" – and when they acted in defense of their liberties, they were, like their Batavian brethren later would be, branded "rebels."[99]

The American experience, so carefully reconstructed by the rebels, was meant to provide valuable *exempla* for Dutch readers. It showed what freedom-loving enemies of Spain could expect. Spanish rule, clamored the supporters of Orange, led invariably to tyranny; and a failure to resist the government of Brussels would result in a tragedy of "American" proportions. Or still worse, as one pamphleteer warned, for the natives of America were mere "heathen" and involuntary subjects of the invading Spaniards. The Dutch, in contrast, were Calvinists who had disavowed a hereditary and piously Catholic Philip II. "Rebellious subjects, heretics, and repudiators. . . . What can *we* expect from them?" asked the patriots with alarm. *Haereticis non est servanda fides* – heretics need not be treated with fidelity – ran the adage. As brutally as Spain had handled the heathen Indian, the heretic Protestant could anticipate even worse.[100]

VI

The rebels' road to America ran both ways. If the political events in the Netherlands colored Dutch perceptions of the New World, it is also the case that descriptions of the New World, and especially those derived from Las Casas and other popular historians of the *Conquista*, worked their way back into Dutch representations of the Revolt. Rebel publicists borrowed and reborrowed their topoi of tyranny energetically and eclectically, showing themselves to be remarkably adept at the intricacies of intertextuality. America, for its part, proved exceptionally adaptable and amenable to such a process. If the natives of America could appear in Dutch writings as would-be "rebels," stripped of their rights and plundered of their property, the Spaniards stationed in the Netherlands could feature as would-be colonizers, addicted to *conquistadora* violence and committed to the wholesale enslavement of the Netherlands. The Dutch created America in their own image, yet in the process, and by dint of their exposure to certain Americana, they came to reinvent that image based on "America." Increasingly, the language of conquest and the polemic of revolt converged to form a single vocabulary of tyranny used to discredit Spanish behavior at home and abroad. In trope, topos, and metaphor, the rebels allied the Indian with the Orangist and Alba with Cortés.

What might be called the Americanization of the Revolt appears from the earliest years of written opposition to Spain, when descriptions of developments in the Netherlands began to take on many of the features associated with descriptions of the *Conquista*. Foremost among these borrowings was the idiom of conquest itself, used by the rebels to characterize Spain's malevolent intentions toward the Low Countries. A conflict that had all the makings of a limited, domestic contest – a debate over the distribution of patronage, collection of taxes, and policing of religion – took on the shape of a full blown war of conquest. From the rebels' perspective, Spain intended not simply to regain its leverage in Brussels, but fully to reconquer and colonize the "subject" population of the Netherlands. The notorious "Legend of the Inquisition" circulated the notion that the Holy Office had devised a plan to starve the Netherlands, exterminate its leading nobles, and subject its defenseless population to a yoke of intolerable tyranny. The *Articles and Resolutions of the Spanish Inquisition to Invade and Impede the Netherlands*, a scandalous forgery concocted by the rebels, imputed to Spain the goal of annihilating, literally, the entire native Dutch population. "We shall consider no one in all of the Netherlands, apart from our agents, worthy of living," read the ninth article. "In the end, all will be uprooted, to make room for a new state [*rijk*] and a new nation [*volk*]." Adrianus Saravia, among Orange's stable of propagandists in the late 1560s, insinuated that the recent arrival of Alba bespoke a similar plan of colonization. The iron duke allegedly planned to destroy the entire Netherlands and resettle it with his own men. For his effort, Alba the Conqueror, like any great conquistador, would see the lands renamed in his honor, "The Duke of Alva's Converted, Conquered New Christian Lands." Some dozen years later, Orange employed a nearly identical idiom to portray the king of Spain, whom he dubbed "Devourer of the People." Left unchallenged, Philip II would brutalize the entire native population, "noble men and the Lords of the countrey, as well as the common people." The king had forgotten the difference between lands inherited and those achieved by conquest, Orange asserted. Philip II governed the Low Countries according to the rules of the latter and with disastrous effects. The same metaphor of conquest featured in the pamphlets of Marnix. In an early publication he decried Granvelle's design to turn the land "*en pays de conquest*"; in another he proposed that Philip II would convert the Netherlands into "a second colonie of Castile." The *first* colony, Marnix added knowingly, was that of the Indies.[101]

Once conquered, soon enslaved, went the rebels' logic; and, in much the same polemical spirit, the conquering Castilians were attacked for their plots (purportedly) to "yoke" the Netherlands. Drawing once again on motifs of Lascasian rhetoric, the Dutch projected onto their

Figure 10. *The Throne of the Duke of Alba,* 1569 (engraving). Amsterdam, Rijksprentenkabinet.

Habsburg governors a master plan to reduce the Low Countries to a state of "eternal servitude." One particularly imaginative rendition of this theme saw the Catholic King placing all of the land's Calvinists in iron fetters and banishing them to, of all locations, the New World.[102] Other versions imagined domestic bondage, and this sort of invective arose most naturally around the person of Alba, who appeared in allegorical prints as a Pharaonic master lording over the shackled figures of the Seventeen Provinces (fig. 10).[103] A strongly worded pamphlet of 1582 claimed that Alba "intended to treat the [Dutch] not as subjects of a fatherly sovereign, but as a conquered nation and as slaves." Don Juan, who had violated the Pacification of Ghent by calling for the expulsion of all Protestants, fared hardly better. Typically, Marnix inveighed against the treachery of a governor who had "set these lands ablaze in order to reduce them to extreme penury and desolation and to enslave the population under the mastery [*heerschapij*] of Spain." The numerous published letters and "advices" that the rebels ascribed to the Spanish conveyed much the same message. After subjugation would come slavery. Spain hoped to place on Dutch shoulders the most heavy of yokes of "perpetual" servitude.[104]

Of course, neither the rebel publicists nor Las Casas introduced the themes of "conquest" and "enslavement" to the annals of war. Like much of the rhetoric employed by the rebels, these topoi had antecedents in a larger body of literature compiled over the course of the late Middle Ages and Renaissance. Certainly Dutch pamphleteers could have constructed their portrait of Spanish tyrannies without recourse to the histories of America. What prompts one to associate the motifs of Spanish cruelties, as depicted by the Dutch, with descriptions of America, however, is the connection drawn by the rebels themselves between their *projection* of their own predicament – potential conquest and enslavement by Spain – and their *perception* of the predicament of America. Whether by subtle use of language and metaphor, or by direct reference, the rebels related their situation very specifically to that in the New World. To endure further Spanish rule in the Netherlands would invite conquest and slavery, the rebels reasoned, since that was the course events had followed in the New World. "Since the death of the Prince of Orange the States have lost many important cities," explained the pensionary of Dordrecht in his appeal to Elizabeth for assistance.

And now, for the preservation of their existence, they have need of a prince and sovereign to defend them against the tyranny and iniquitous oppression of the Spaniards and their adherents, who are more determined utterly to destroy their country, and reduce the poor people to a perpetual slavery worse than that of the Indians.

The expectation that Spain would oppress, "utterly . . . destroy," and "reduce the poor people" of the Netherlands "to a perpetual slavery" followed logically from the assumption that Spain had done all that and more in the New World. The fear of further "abominations" in Flanders, as one Antwerper put it, gained urgency from the conviction that similar cruelties had already occurred in Peru. The specter of America's fate, in short, helped the rebels anticipate their own future.[105]

Prophesy quickly metamorphosed into memory. From the rebel doctrine that Spain sought to pursue an "American" strategy in the Low Countries, it was only a small leap of polemical faith to propose that Spain had already executed a conquistador program of violence in those towns and provinces visited by Alba's army. The image of "Spanish tyranny in America," so indelibly engraved in the Dutch mind, came to shape some of the earliest historical representations of "Spanish tyranny in the Netherlands." In both general terms and specific topoi, in word and in image, Spanish offenses purportedly committed in the Netherlands recalled those reported in the New World. "Innocent" patriots of the Netherlands, meanwhile, appeared to suffer indignities not unlike those of the innocent Indians of America.

Comparisons and juxtapositions took all forms. They could be startlingly vivid and direct: a chilling passage from one of the earliest histories of Orange's life (1586) utterly conflates the two narratives, describing how Alva, as he girded for battle, "hopes that the Indians [read Dutch] once again will be slaughtered in a bloodbath [and] that new kingdoms will be founded across an unknown sea." Or they could be more subtle and richly insinuating, alluding to graphic language and visual phrases that neatly crisscrossed Dutch and American histories. A grisly portrayal of "Spanish tyrannies" decorating the title page of a chronicle of the Revolt, for example, matches a strikingly vivid passage from the *Brevíssima relación* describing the Caribbean (see fig. 9, top center). The Dutch illustration shows a Spanish soldier skewering a Northern European-looking woman and child with a single drive of his sword. Writing of the conquistadors that landed on Hispaniola, Las Casas employs a conspicuously similar image: "They slaughtered anyone and every one in their path, on occasion running through a mother and her baby with a single thrust of their swords."[106] In another illustration from a patriotic history of the Revolt, this time depicting the "Abominations at Oudewater" (where a massacre took place in 1575), the enemy is shown ripping an unborn baby from the womb of its suspended mother (fig. 11 and compare fig. 12, showing an "American" scene). Again, the scene evokes an oft-cited passage from Las Casas: "They [the Spanish] forced their way into the native settlements, slaughtering everyone they found there, including small children, old men, pregnant women, and even women who had just given birth. They hacked them to pieces, slicing open their bellies with their swords." The verse description of the Oudewater massacre that accompanied the print resembles the Lascasian vignette remarkably:

> No one from there was spared
> No matter how young or how old
> Mothers without mercy
> They hanged by their arms
> They cut out their frail fetuses
> With angry and sharp cries
> They killed the young sprigs
> And hanged the maidens by their tresses.[107]

Such parallel passages are hardly unique. In countless instances, the story of the "conquest" of the Netherlands seemed to resonate with the

Figure 11. Illustration ("Moort tot Oudewater") from *Spaensche tirannye in Nederlandt* (1620). Universiteitsbibiliotheek Amsterdam.

rhythms of the history of America. In the Low Countries as in the West Indies, the Spanish waged a "war of fire and blood" – *guerra a fuego y sangre* as Zárate immortalized the *Conquista,* or "oorlogen door branden en bloedstorting," in the words of Marnix – or, alternatively, a crusade "by fire and sword."[108] In Antwerp as in the Antilles, they pounced upon natives like "wolves" or "lions," and they slaughtered innocent women and children "like so many sheep." The Habsburgs treated the Batavians and the Indians alike as "cattle" or "dogs," and their soldiers ruthlessly dashed new-born babies against boulders or stone walls.[109] Both landscapes were strewn with hacked and mutilated limbs, and blighted by heaps of naked, ravaged bodies (figs. 13 and 14). In one of the ruder turns of plot, the rebels associated their enemies with a perverse disrespect for human flesh that has a peculiarly American ring to it. Just as Las Casas spoke of the "human abattoir," or flesh markets, set up by the conquistadors to feed their dogs (fig. 15), the *Geuzen* accused the "wardogs of Spain" of desecrating the corpses of their Dutch subjects:

Figure 12: Illustration ("Mother and Child") from Bartolomé de Las Casas, *Den Spiegel der Spaensche tyrannye gheschiet in West Indien* (Amsterdam, 1620). Universiteitsbibiliotheek Amsterdam.

> The bodies . . .
> Of your honorable [Dutch] soldiers
> They offered to the ravens;
> The flesh of your good soldiers
> They haughtily threw
> To the animals in the fields.[110]

Tales of tyranny, in the Old World as in the New, would make the readers' "hair stand on end," claimed the pamphleteers together with Las Casas. Other Spanish misdeeds defied even description – though when described, they seemed to echo the identical tenor of tyranny.

Las Casas, in fact, qualified his remarkable catalogue of cruelties by claiming that he could not express adequately the excesses committed in America. If words failed him, though, numbers more than made up for it. For Las Casas, as one critic has astutely noted, had "his gaze forever fixed upon atrocities that could be rendered arithmetically."[111] Cal-

Figure 13. Illustration ("Antwerpen") from *Spaensche tirannye in Nederlandt* (1620). Universiteitsbibiliotheek Amsterdam.

culations of casualties, or what might anachronistically be called "body counts," recur obsessively throughout his account. During his three-month stay in Cuba, Las Casas claimed to have witnessed the death of "seven thousand children from hunger," and on another occasion he saw "some three thousand souls" perish in a single moment of Spanish frenzy. A massacre in Cholula (Mexico) took the lives of "five to six thousand . . . poor wretches" within the space of two hours. On the island of Hispaniola, Las Casas asserted, slightly under three million natives died following the arrival of the Spanish. The Bahamas lost five hundred thousand, and, in Venezuela, Las Casas estimated that "over four or five million of these poor souls have been despatched to the depths of Hell by these [Spanish] fiends." All told, Las Casas placed the death toll for the first forty years of the *Conquista* conservatively at twelve million yet believed his "own estimate of more than fifteen million to be nearer the mark." The Dominican never quite clarified how he arrived at these

Figure 14. Illustration ("Pit of Horrors") from Bartolomé de Las Casas, *Den Spiegel der Spaensche tyrannye gheschiet in West Indien* (Amsterdam, 1620). Universiteitsbibiliotheek Amsterdam.

sturdy figures, and, added all together, the sum total of casualties from the individual islands and provinces he assessed actually tops twenty million. The relative difference between these figures – twelve, fifteen, and twenty million – apparently made very little difference to readers. Any or even all of the numbers recur virtually axiomatically in later (Dutch) recitations of American tyrannies.[112]

More to the point, Las Casas's predilection for numbers caught on, as did his other rhetorical techniques, with patriotic historians of the Netherlands. Almost as obsessively, the Dutch quantified the atrocities they charged to Spain; almost as regularly, the histories of the Revolt registered the same mathematics of conquest. Orange reckoned that the Inquisition had claimed the round number of fifty thousand victims, while Marnix and others submitted the even more solid figure of one hundred thousand. Alba's six-year reign resulted in 18,000 (civilian) deaths, purported Orange in the *Apologie* (based on an overheard boast

Figure 15. Illustration ("Human Abattoir") from Bartolomé de Las Casas, *Den Spiegel der Spaensche tyrannye gheschiet in West Indien* (Amsterdam, 1620). Universiteitsbibiliotheek Amsterdam.

from Alba himself). Marnix went with the number 18,600, and generally every condemnation of Alba's Blood Council includes mention of one of these two figures.[113] (In a curious confusion of these numbers, one pamphlet speaks of "eighteen million deaths in America" – seeming, thereby, to adapt the number for Alba's tyrannies to the figure for American casualties.)[114] Similarly, for every massacre or mutiny, the rebels attached a recognizable (and repeatable) number, such that Naarden was said to have lost five hundred leading citizens, Antwerp five thousand, Haarlem twelve thousand, and so forth. During the course of the Revolt, it was said, one hundred thousand people had left the Low Countries, and Marnix estimated – roundly – that a resumption of Spanish authority in the Netherlands would mean the certain exile of one million of the Reformed religion.[115]

The correspondingly numbing numbers recited by both Las Casas and the Dutch rebels do not by themselves make the case for literary borrowing. Again, it needs to be emphasized that these rhetorical devices had antecedents, both ancient and modern. Previous chroniclers of the New World had delivered equally fabulous estimates of the number of natives encountered or the quantity of gold espied. Cortés, like Las Casas, sent the Spanish king numerical summaries of his conquests rounded up to easily citable, if barely credible, figures. Both men, albeit for vastly different reasons, intended their figures to convince the Crown of the importance of their petition and, more generally, to arouse wonder in their readers. The Roman historian, Flavius Josephus, whom Las Casas cited prominently in his massive *Historia de las Indias,* inflated the figures he gave in rehearsing the conquest and destruction of Jerusalem by Titus. In that case, as in others of ancient and Renaissance historiography, fantastic figures were meant to impress upon the reader the magnitude – and the marvel – of the events described. Late medieval chroniclers of the Low Countries recorded fatality numbers for the plague that regularly reached "thousands per town" – and this for towns and villages whose populations themselves barely reached the thousands. By the same token, other topoi of tyranny traded between Las Casas and the rebels might have derived from independent sources. Babies, no doubt, suffered woeful abominations in the literature of the Middle Ages (renditions of the Massacre of the Innocents come to mind), and maidens, too, may have succumbed to "unheard of violences" in the accounts of the Schmalkaldic War or the French Wars of Religion (and here the myths surrounding the St. Bartholemew's Day Massacre seem relevant.)[116]

Certainly, all of these sources and more influenced the myth-makers of the Dutch Revolt. Yet the role of America within the Dutch imagination still deserves to be singled out, if only because the rebels did so themselves. Time and again, they compared their own situation *specifically* with that of the Amerindians. Insistently and incessantly they juxtaposed the image of Spanish tyrannies perpetrated in the New World with those committed in the Netherlands. And with good reason: America had been victimized primarily by Spain, and not simply by a Catholic or Imperial enemy; the Americans did not yet possess any incurably damning religious or political beliefs that might have made them inappropriate models of suffering; and, not least important, reports of American atrocities did, in fact, stand out from much of the literature of conquest available at the time. Nothing matched the *Brevíssima relación* for blood and gore.

Above all, the New World, still novel and forever distant, lent itself to refashioning. The Dutch discovered America in every sense of the word. Shortly after the protests against the Habsburg government in Brussels commenced, patriotic pamphleteers recognized the role America could play in their campaign against Spain, and they quickly seized upon the image of *conquistadora* violence to blacken the Spanish reputation. Once revealed, America and the American predicament quickly took on the shape of the rebels' own situation. Innocent natives, proposed the Dutch, faced an invasive, foreign monarch who had ignored traditional privileges and pillaged private property under the pretense of religion. Yet while the Dutch fashioned their own style of America, the actual Americana that reached the Low Countries, and especially the *Brevíssima relación* of Las Casas, worked its way back into the very texture of patriotic histories. Lascasian language and metaphor colored the history of the Revolt and led to wonderfully exaggerated notions of the Spanish enemy. The invading army of Flanders, it was said, had sought to conquer and enslave the entire Netherlands, commit barbaric feats of butchery, and murder epic numbers of women and children. If the rebels had invented the New World, within time America would help to reinvent the world of the Dutch. By the end of the sixteenth century, "America" not only symbolized the extent of Spanish tyranny abroad, but also provided the model for Spanish behavior in the Netherlands. It had become a shaping force in Dutch political propaganda, coloring countless readers' vision of Spain and its empire.

CHAPTER 3

Innocence and Commerce Abroad

I

"AMERICA . . . first discovered in the year of Our Lord 1491, exhibits endless sunny provinces and very fertile realms. . . . The earth bears no metal except gold." So declares the Latin caption beneath the striking image of a woman, languidly handsome and artlessly naked, seated under a broad tree and above a peaceful landscape of mountains and gentle streams (fig. 16).[1] This quiet American moment – captured by the engraver Jan Sadeler after a design by Dirck Barendsz – represents the first of a flurry of conceptually similar, if thematically distinct, Dutch allegories of the continents executed toward the close of the sixteenth century, in this case 1581. That year, it is worth recalling, witnessed also the publication of Orange's pugnacious *Apologie* as well as numerous other polemical works that joined in bitterly denouncing the pervasive "tyranny" of Spain in America. Yet the stormy vituperations of the prince and his associates would hardly seem to match the far brighter forecast that derived from the drafting table of Barendsz. The positively serene "America" of the artist's imagination does not easily correlate to the rebels' somber vision of a plundered New World, a vision codified in scores of pamphlets and verbal assaults launched during the heady years of revolt.

Barendsz's allegorical study of "America" does correlate, though, to an expansion of images and broadening of themes pertaining to the Dutch New World. It announced the appearance not just of geographic allegories and other visual sources that endeavored to articulate a new pictorial language for the newest of continents. It signaled also a more general exploration, in disparate genres and innovative forms, of the topical theme of "America." More broadly still: it indicated a subtle shift in tone that took place in Dutch Americana, increasingly evident as both the century and the Revolt came to a close. The turn of the seventeenth century was a decidedly fertile moment for the new Republic; political

123

Figure 16. Jan Sadeler after Dirk Barendsz, *America,* 1581 (engraving). Amsterdam, Rijksprentenkabinet.

and economic circumstances dramatically altered the landscape of the Low Countries, both in the North and South. So too did the landscape of the New World undergo a significant transformation – at least from the Dutch perspective. Familiar landmarks naturally remained – the indelible image of "Spanish tyranny," which the rebels had so assiduously promoted – though fresh vistas also began to appear, and this suggested fresh opportunities to the imaginative geographers of the Netherlands. After years of relentlessly gloomy press, America, by the eve of the seventeenth century, began to look distinctly more attractive.

America cut a striking figure. The Dutch allegories of the 1580s and 1590s, much like the singular *West Indies Landscape* painted by Jan Mostaert a half-century earlier, mark an important juncture in the iconography of the New World. Produced by some of the leading Mannerist draftsmen of Antwerp and Amsterdam, these second-generation depictions of the newest continent revisited the landscape of America, the narrative of its discovery, and the question of its visual representation. They did so, moreover, using pictorial (and in some cases textual) strategies at once innovative and derivative, incorporating motifs both familiar and provocative to audiences in the Netherlands. A few of the designs, to be sure, glanced back to the poetic pastoralism of the Mostaert panorama, conveying in similarly Ovidian strokes a sense of golden age innocence. Like that earlier painting (by this time hanging in Haarlem), they implicitly censured those who had desecrated America's "virginal" grace. Yet the allegories could look forward as well, beyond the message of "Spanish tyranny," to explore the wildness and "savagery" of the youngest continent and to contemplate the wonder and desire it increasingly provoked. Some reveal a fascination with the rich natural products of America, others a lively interest in the abundant gold of America. The New World could thus appear simultaneously innocent and wild, apparently rich if also despoiled. Together with the political and poetic components of the earlier sources, the prints of the later sixteenth century added an economic factor to the equation. They testify to a growing awareness in the Netherlands of the *value* of America that is largely absent in the Mostaert landscape. The New World might have enjoyed a golden age, it was implied, yet those who traded with America might also enjoy the harvest of its gold.

The late sixteenth-century allegorical endeavors of the Netherlands put the continents on the map, so to speak, as relatively few precedents for such studies had existed.[2] Only rarely did the traditional land masses of the Old World – Ovid's *triplex mundus* – appear in the visual arts of the late Middle Ages and Renaissance, and seldom did these representations follow any fixed pattern or visual formula. Occasional depictions of the Epiphany might portray the Magi as delegates of the tripartite Christian world – descendants of the three Noachides, Shem, Ham, and Japheth – yet these types never became codified. The discovery of America, in any event, hardly fit this configuration, upsetting as it did whatever aesthetic symmetry Christian geographers had invented for themselves. The continents also played a part in Renaissance pageants and civic processions, where they figured in designs for triumphal arches and popular *tableaux vivants.* When Prince Philip visited Antwerp in 1549, the traditional three continents paid homage to the future Habsburg monarch from the heights of just such a tableau. By 1564, a full set of four continents – representing the four "empresses" of the world – graced Antwerp's Procession of the Holy Circumcision and solemnly honored the town's relic of Our Lord's foreskin.[3]

Representations of the continents also surfaced sporadically in cartographic materials, and here the evidence points more directly to the Netherlands. Increasingly complex designs for the borders of Renaissance maps had come to include, by the early sixteenth century, brief sketches of regional attributes, if not allegorical representations per se.

Figure 17. Decorative vignette ("Canibali") from Sebastian Münster, *Typus cosmographicus universalis*. Woodcut map in Simon Grynaeus, *Novus orbis* (Basel, 1537). American Geographical Society Collection, University of Milwaukee Library.

A world map printed in 1537 and attributed to Sebastian Münster contains a vignette in each of its four corners meant to illustrate the nature and natives of the earth's distinct "quarters," as they were now called. In the lower left corner of the map, corresponding to South America (though confusingly labeled "Aphricq"), a group of American "canibali" are shown preparing a barbecue of human flesh outside their crude hut (fig. 17). Less allegory than decorative anecdote, the Münster vignette nevertheless associates the New World with an identifiable set of attributes. The heirs to this tradition of emblematic geography were the early Flemish atlas-makers, who incorporated personifications of the continents into the designs for their title pages. The first and most famous of the atlases, the *Theatrum orbis terrarum* (1570) of Abraham Ortelius, displayed the *five* maidens of the world – Europa, Asia, Africa, America, and the only partially discovered "Magellanica" – on its much admired and much imitated title page (fig. 18). This established for the first time a firm foundation for future allegories of the continents, a foundation on which mapmakers and printmakers, together with poets and polemicists, would soon enough build.[4]

Construction began in earnest with Barendsz and his Dutch colleagues, who assembled and rearranged, augmented and replaced,

Figure 18. Title page from Abraham Ortelius, *Theatrum orbis terrarum* (Antwerp, 1570). Universiteitsbibiliotheek Amsterdam.

many of these continental motifs. Dirck Barendsz (1534–92) provides an interesting link between the worlds of geographic learning, visual representation, and political debate. A well-respected painter and draftsman, Barendsz enjoyed a high reputation in his day for his refinement and erudition, as well. He was exceptionally "well read, a Latinist, and well taught," according to Karel van Mander, who noted further the "superior intelligence" and "noble spirit" of his Dutch colleague. Barendsz gained this esteem after spending seven years as a young man in Italy training under the watchful eye of Titian, who reportedly treated Dirck "like a child in his house." Upon returning to his native Amsterdam in 1562, he quickly established himself as a noted painter and man of letters in his own right. He associated chiefly "with honorable and influential people" – the regents and provincial power-brokers – and counted among his friends many of the leading humanists of the Netherlands. He had contacts, too, with prominent political figures – notably Marnix van St. Aldegonde, with whom Barendsz "had become well and intimately acquainted," by van Mander's estimation.[5]

Despite this friendship, Barendsz's *America* was less polemical than it was painterly, more Mostaert in the end than Marnix. His allegory displays many of the same literary sensibilities as the earlier, humanist-inflected accounts of the New World and especially the Ovidian panorama of Mostaert himself. Like the Haarlem master, Barendsz perceived America as an Arcadian landscape of meandering rivers and dramatic peaks, a lyrical passage of hamlets and sloping countryside. "A hilly land, well-watered" and thickly wooded, America was imagined to be a region where "the temperate climate, the light dew, and the almost untroubled air are delightful." The well-formed natives who occupy the background of Barendsz's landscape exist in a presocial state of innocence, "naked except for a long cloak of parrot feathers." They live in unadorned dwellings of straw and, if the allegorical figure of "America" herself is any indication, pass much of their time in a languid state of repose. Two parrots perched on a tree recall a similarly placed bird in Mostaert's composition and remind the viewer of America's distance and exoticism. Otherwise, however, the allegorical New World recalls an ancient one readily familiar to Renaissance humanists as the Golden Age.[6]

If the setting and tone of the Barendsz landscape resemble that of Mostaert, the actual subject of the composition essentially does not. Unlike the earlier painting, which centers on a battle scene and depicts the conquest of America, the Barendsz print draws attention to the peaceful figure of "America" and the quiet scene of native industry behind her. A tall, well-proportioned and graceful woman, nude but for a feather headdress and a swath of drapery, and with a long arrow resting in the crook of her arm, "America" does possess something of an Amazonian quality. Her weapon may owe something to the bellicose "America" on the Ortelius title page. The latter figure holds a variation of a ceremonial Brazilian club, the *Iwera Pemma*, in much the same manner as the Barendsz figure (between the index and middle finger, and leaning against the right arm), and beneath the right leg of the Ortelius model lies a set of arrows similar to the one held by Barendsz's figure.[7] Yet while the Ortelius America appears (intentionally) martial, Barendsz's maiden makes a decidedly pacific impression. *All* of the allegorical figures in the Barendsz series of continents are associated with some sort of emblematic weapon, and, of these, America's seems the least threatening. Gazing dreamily at the flora and fauna that surround her, Barendsz's "America" strikes a pose more beatific than belligerent.

The background scene of the print also differs substantially from the Mostaert panel. Nothing in the Barendsz allegory would indicate that America had been, or soon would be, invaded by Spain or any other European power. In the imagination of a Dutch draftsman, circa 1581, the Indians could still go about their business quietly, seemingly unconcerned with their putative discovery, "in the year of Our Lord 1491." That business, in the meantime, has undergone a significant change. For no longer do the natives of America lead the pastoral, agrarian life of Mostaert's imagination; but they now dredge gold (so Barendsz surmises), as do the three figures in the stream behind "America" who pan in a peaceful mountain stream. If "the earth bears no metal except gold," happily "this occurs in quantity." The natural world can otherwise produce treasures, and quite generously, too: "They have many pearls," reports the text, noting the multiple varieties and their richness. The mountains yield numerous precious stones, and the temperate air of the valleys brings forth "the gold wood *guaiacum*" in addition to other exotic and valuable species. Barendsz, like Mostaert, has thus situated America in a golden age. Yet by 1581, the focus has shifted from the waning moments of the New World's idyll to the waxing opportunities of its gilded bounty.

American opportunities presented themselves in other forms as well. The allegorical *America* designed by Jan van der Straet (Stradanus) in the later 1580s makes no reference to gold or the Golden Age of antiquity, but focuses rather on the very *novelty* of the recently discovered continent (fig. 19). Engraved in Antwerp by the prolific Galle atelier, the Stradanus *America* belonged to a larger series of prints collectively titled *Nova reperta* (New discoveries), meant to herald the epochal "inventions" of the Renaissance.[8] Born in Bruges, trained in Antwerp, and em-

AMERICA.

Americen Americus retexit , & Semel vocauit inde femper excitam .

Figure 19. Theodor Galle after Jan van der Straet, *America,* ca. 1589 (engraving).
Amsterdam, Rijksprentenkabinet.

ployed in Florence for much of his career, Stradanus (ca. 1523–1605) fashioned his allegory around the person of Vespucci – fellow Florentine and
first to pronounce forthrightly the discovery of a new world – and
around the concept of discovery and all that implied. *Americen Americus
retexit* – Amerigo discovers America – puns the caption beneath the
grave figure of Vespucci as he arouses the sleeping, virginal America. He
clutches a banner emblazoned with the stars of the freshly discovered
Southern Cross in his right hand and a mariner's astrolabe in his left. She
glances drowsily from her native hammock, naked, though not noticeably alarmed, by the momentous fact of her discovery.[9]

Apart from the centrality of the episode of encounter – a wide-eyed
Vespucci confronting a groggy America with the superiority of European technology – the Stradanus print bears only vague comparison
with the Mostaert scene of conquest. Other elements of Stradanus's essentially composite image, however, recall features from earlier cartographic materials and especially the *Theatrum orbis terrarum.* For the attire of America, Stradanus may have drawn his inspiration from the
Ortelius title page. Both Stradanus's and Ortelius's figures wear close-
fitting, feathered caps that crown their long manes of (European)

tresses; both have unusual bracelets of bells fastened around their calves; and both sit surrounded by their native attributes – notably, the hammock and the Brazilian club.[10] Stradanus's *America*, still sluggish with sleep, lacks the grisly severed head that Ortelius's model holds. In the background and just above the gesturing hand of the Stradanus figure, though, is a fairly typical description of America's anthropophagous appetite. This scene, showing a group of cannibals gathered around a native *boucan* (barbecue) roasting a human thigh, closely resembles a vignette included on a Mercator *mappa mundi* of 1569 and, before that, on the Münster map of 1537.

The principle distinction of the Stradanus image consists of the attention given to the exotic natural world of America. Whereas earlier representations of imaginary New World landscapes contain essentially familiar components of the European natural world, Stradanus makes every effort to stock his American shores with wondrous species, which creep and crawl around the peripheries of the composition. And if the manuscript text – in the artist's own hand, on the verso of the original drawing – is any indication, Stradanus preferred to work precisely around the edges, such that his interest lay less in Vespucci's elegant and impressive *artificialia* (the *reperta* of European maritime technology) than in America's curious and marvelous *naturalia* (the harvest of the natural, New World). To the left of America and rambling brazenly toward Vespucci scavenges an anteater, labeled *tamandoa* by Stradanus. This creature, notes the text on the verso, grows "as large as a sheep. It has broad feet with which it scratches ants together . . . a large slit instead of a mouth, a long tongue to lick up ants, and a round stern." A horse-like beast trots behind America (above the inscription *anta*, or tapir); and a porcine *cerigon* – presumably an opossum – waddles by with "two bags at its stomach in which it carries its young, who hold on by sucking." The tree that holds America's hammock also furnishes shade for a cluster of pineapples (*ananaze*) and gives refuge to a pudgy, ursine sloth (*pigritia*). "Because of its big belly," remarks Stradanus of the latter, "it walks in fifteen days not further than one can throw a stone."[11]

The menagerie of marvels that inhabited Stradanus's allegory celebrates that which is new in America: that which had been foreign, strange, and unknown before it could be counted among the *nova reperta*. The image demonstrates, as does a contemporaneous print designed by Marcus Gheeraerts the Elder and also engraved in the Galle atelier, the evident interest in the *wonders* of America (fig. 20). Gheeraerts's purely decorative allegory – unlike the others, it lacks any textual apparatus to explain the elaborately Mannerist combination of New

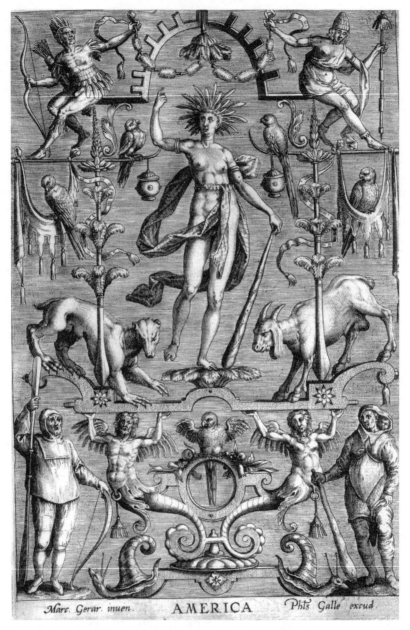

Figure 20. Philips Galle after Marcus Gheeraerts, *America,* ca. 1590 (engraving). The Metropolitan Museum of Art, Gift of the Estate of James Hazen Hyde, New York, 1959 (59.654.55).

World artifacts, animals, and peoples – virtually bursts at the borders with long-eared goats and long-nailed opossums, hide-covered Eskimos and feather-decked Incas, all of which surround a lithe "America." Like the Stradanus print, the Gheeraerts pastiche indicates the growing taste for the unfamiliar; unlike the Mostaert painting, it entices the viewer with configurations more curious than classical. (More curious still is a fabulous, llama-like marsupial that represents "America" on the allegorical title page of Cornelis de Jode's *Speculum orbis terrae,* a 1593 atlas published to compete with Ortelius's *Theatrum orbis terrarum.*) Indeed both Stradanus and Gheeraerts invite their viewers to explore, as does Vespucci, the teeming richness of the American landscape and to imagine the brimming potential of the fantastic New World.[12]

Yet another allegory of America appeared within a year or two of the Stradanus and Gheeraerts prints, this one engraved by Adriaen Collaert (a son-in-law of Philips Galle) after a design by Maarten de Vos.[13] An accomplished Mannerist draftsman who had trained in Rome, Florence, and Venice (reportedly with Tintoretto) before settling in Antwerp in 1558, de Vos (1532–1603) ranked among the leading Flemish artists of his day, and the *America* he designed quickly emerged as the most influential of the lot (fig. 21). It succeeded on two levels. By synthesizing motifs from earlier works, it produced, on the one hand, a happily composite image, broad in its appeal and recognizable in its components. By presenting a particularly elegant, imaginative, and attractive figure for "America" herself, it created, on the other hand, a model that would eventually become the definitive representation of the New World. The Collaert engraving reappeared a few of years later (ca. 1595) with a German text, and again in the mid-seventeenth century (slightly reworked) with a more elaborate Dutch text. The central figure of America was redrawn by de Vos in 1594 and subsequently used for a ceremonial architectural fixture built to celebrate the entry of the archduke Ernst of Austria into Antwerp that year. This image of a graceful, ostentatiously outfitted America astride a ferocious armadillo disseminated the iconography of the newest continent – in a variety of printed, painted, and sculpted media – as did no other. Cesare Ripa adopted a variation of the de Vos design for his *Iconologia,* first printed with woodcuts in 1603, and this established a standard reference for artists seeking to represent abstract ideas in a recognizable iconographic language. The de Vos-inspired, Ripa-produced figure endured well into the eighteenth century.[14]

At the center of the de Vos allegory sits the majestic figure of America herself whose striking pose would leave such a lasting impression on the European imagination. Tall, typically nude, and classically hand-

Figure 21. Adriaen Collaert after Maarten de Vos, *America,* ca. 1589 (engraving). Amsterdam, Rijksprentenkabinet.

some, America rides an imposing armadillo, side-saddle, across the foreground of the composition. She wears only a modest cut of drapery that folds over her lap much like the dress of the Barendsz "America." A single pearl dangles from her ear (again, like the Barendsz model); an intricate bracelet clasps her biceps; and a stylish band of feathers embellishes her already extravagant coiffure. In both hands she holds the by now standard accouterments of "war-like" America: a tasseled club, which resembles the weapon held by the Ortelius figure only vaguely; and a large bow similar to, if more decorative than, the weapons on the Ortelius title page. The most impressive innovation of the de Vos allegory is the imposing beast that serves as America's carriage. As comical as it is curious, this preposterously scaly and gargantuan creature would undoubtedly have felt at home among the wildlife that wander through Stradanus's print. Its monstrous grin could hardly contrast more with America's delicate profile. The combined effect of the pair suggests the beautiful and the beastly in the New World, America's wonders and its wonderful riches.[15]

Behind America lies a panoramic landscape that corresponds remarkably to the Mostaert panel in both form and content. To the right, in a broad, stream-filled valley, a band of naked Indians clashes with a phalanx of European soldiers. The battle takes place under a brooding sky and the ominous shadow of a geological construct – the latter with a dramatic *arco naturale* not unlike that in the *West Indies Landscape*. Armed with simple spears and clubs or inadequate bows and arrows, the overmatched Indians make little headway against the European firepower. As in the Mostaert painting, the natives appear to have the worst of it. To the left, de Vos depicts a scene of everyday life that shows the (surmised) state of America before its invasion. Nestled on a precipitous crag are a pair of straw huts and a cave into which two natives flee the chaos below – they mirror almost precisely the pair of figures running across the lower left plane of the Mostaert composition. On the sloping hills around them graze domestic animals. In the de Vos composition, though, fat-tailed sheep and long-eared goats replace Mostaert's tamer, European variants. An armadillo saunters casually through the flock where the earlier painting sufficed with a hare; and both representations contain parrots perched symbolically above the fray (in the right foreground in de Vos's work). The actual scene of native *oeconomia* deviates sharply from the Mostaert version. De Vos represents both hunters and herdsmen where Mostaert hints only at a pastoral life; and de Vos includes an unmistakable scene of anthropophagy that would suggest how the natives might supplement their diet with the chopped and roasted limbs shown outside their huts.[16] Despite all these contrasts, though, the point of the print and the earlier panel seems essentially the same: a bucolic slice of native life is juxtaposed with an episode of foreign invasion. America's pastoral, if not quite idyllic, ways have encountered the long conquering arm of Europa.

Whatever the subtleties of the de Vos image, the text that accompanied the engraving in many of its states imparts fewer ambiguities:

> Europa has discovered me and introduced me to God
> Gold, that otherwise leads to nobility, has enslaved me
> With riches I have become impoverished in my own land
> Since my natural endowments have been taken to other regions.[17]

The poet conveys a sense of indignation similar to that expressed in the Mostaert panel, implicating "Europa" for her aggression against the unknowing America. (And, in a series of the four continents, blame shifts to "Europa" rather than to any single nation, though the allusion to Spain would have been obvious.) The discovery of America has caused her enslavement. Rapacious Europeans took a booty of gold where they should have delivered the glory of God. They have impoverished the innocent maiden where they might have enriched her with the blessings of Christianity.

While word and image would appear to follow the contours of the Mostaert landscape, the de Vos print also makes adjustments and additions to the earlier image of America. Into the fabric of the political and moral indictment, the poet of the de Vos print weaves a thread of economic logic similar to that found in the other contemporary allegories. Gold, of which Barendsz noted America's abundance, now plays a more central role in the unraveling of America. Gold draws the greedy Europeans to America and distracts them from their loftier (presumably religious) mission. The same gold that engenders America's impoverishment, moreover, might easily have led to her "nobility," as it so clearly had for Europa. The richly jeweled figure of America, luxuriantly poised on her exotic carriage and splendidly surrounded by the flora and fauna that fill her well-watered valleys, has not yet resigned her fortunes completely, however. Plundered yet not depleted, her natural endowments promise future aggrandizement. De Vos and the anonymous poet condemn America's invaders less for their violence than for their greed, less for their untimely destruction of America's Golden Age than for their rapid exhaustion of her gold.

A final allegory of America (dated circa 1600 and now in Ann Arbor) brings the late sixteenth-century evolution of Netherlandish visions of the New World to its logical conclusion (fig. 22). Though inscribed on the verso with the name of Maarten de Vos, this decorative pastiche bears little resemblance either to the previous studies of de Vos or to the earlier Dutch allegories more generally.[18] Nor, for that matter, does it share much with Mostaert's landscape. Designed, presumably, for an ornamental plaque, this small, circular drawing lacks any hint of America's discovery (as emphasized in the Stradanus allegory) or conquest (as in the Mostaert and de Vos images), and it gives no indication of America's earlier age of pastoral innocence (as in the Mostaert, Barendsz, and, to a lesser degree, de Vos compositions). It gathers, instead, a motley selection of objects and creatures associated with the New World – a ceremonial Brazilian club, a severed human head, a feathered headdress and skirt, a decorative pineapple, a parrot, and other curious species, including a bizarre feline and bizarrely out-of-place rhinoceros – and it scatters them, indiscriminately, around the figure of America. America herself glitters with wealth. Bracelets adorn her ankles and arms, strings of pearls wrap around her waist and wrist, and a sash of shells drapes over her shoulder. In her left hand she bears a plate of precious gems and gold.

Figure 22. Maarten de Vos (attrib.), *America,* ca. 1600 (pen and black ink on paper; 12.5 cm. diameter). University of Michigan Museum of Art, 1960/2.24.

The eclectic exoticism of her surrounding and the resplendent richness of her costume emphasize the native wealth of America. Appropriately, a ship appears in the distance directly above the treasure-laden, outstretched arm of America. This ship does in fact have a parallel in a number of the earlier compositions, yet with a difference. The smaller vessels that dock in the distant horizon of the Mostaert painting have recently transported a cargo of conquistadors to subdue America; and the galleon that moors, partly concealed, in the Stradanus engraving has just delivered Vespucci to discover America. In contrast, the centrally situated ship of the Ann Arbor drawing conveys, one assumes, merchants to barter with America or perhaps simply to collect the largesse that she appears to offer them.[19]

The Ann Arbor allegory of America suggests the subtle changes undergone and the increasing complexities developed in the Dutch image of the New World. Though many of the motifs of the Mostaert landscape resurface in later representations, certain of the earlier foci have shifted, and altogether new themes have evolved by the close of the sixteenth century. In several ways, the Dutch continued to envision the New World blissfully preserved in a golden age of innocence. Pastoral landscapes and lyrical passages persist, especially in the prints of Barendsz and de Vos. Europe, in this configuration, has rudely invaded America; Spanish tyranny, in this context, still provokes moral indignation. By the twilight of the century, however, "tyranny" is perceived in economic as well as political terms, and the Spanish plunder of America's unprotected riches would seem to anger the poet of the de Vos (ca. 1595) allegory more than the Spanish murder of defenseless natives. The Golden Age, ultimately, attracts less of the artists' and poets' attention than the gold it supposedly preserves. If simple huts and unadorned bodies fill the background of these compositions, the foregrounds display the ornate figure of "America," lavishly bedecked, exquisitely bejeweled, and alluringly beckoning with an outstretched pot of gold.

II

At the turn of the seventeenth century, the Netherlandish view of the New World had reached a state of transition as had, too, the state of the Netherlands. The allegorical prints and drawings produced in the closing years of the sixteenth century express developing notions of America at the precise moment when the Dutch themselves had arrived at a crossroads. The iconographic exploration of the American theme coincided with the adolescence of the Republic: a period of spectacular growth and considerable national introspection. Indeed, the case of the Low Countries affords one of the rare instances when the turn of the century truly heralded substantive change, when the artificial designation, "circa 1600," actually demarcated appreciable transformation.[20]

By the beginning of the seventeenth century, the war against Spain had noticeably altered its course. With some fifty years still left to go, the Eighty Years' War had entered a new, "cooler" stage by 1600, as Spanish resources failed to keep pace with either the Crown's zeal or the army's arrears. Already in the 1580s, the king's commitment to the French Catholic League, combined with his near catastrophic engagement with the English in 1588, had severely aggravated the Habsburg financial crisis. A string of poor harvests throughout the 1590s and an equally ruinous run of mutinies in the early 1600s – culminating in a full-blown fiasco at Diest in late 1606 that involved over four thousand soldiers and more than one million florins – brought matters to their disastrous, yet inevitable, conclusion. Philip II issued his third Decree of Bankruptcy in 1596, while his son and heir broke with Habsburg creditors once again in 1607. These perilous financial straits forced the new monarch, Philip III, to reduce drastically the resources allocated to the Netherlands and restrict his troops to defensive operations. It also obliged the Most Catholic King to confront the inevitability of negotiations with the rebel "heretics." Dialogue between the two parties had begun, if hesitantly, in the late 1590s, with formal talks taking place in 1598 and 1600. In 1606 and 1607 the king dispatched agents to the North to sue for peace, which resulted in a temporary ceasefire. Following further, largely unsatisfactory negotiations, the two sides agreed to the Twelve-Year Truce, signed in April 1609. After forty years of uninterrupted hostilities, then, the States General – or, rather, their High Mightinesses, as they now presented themselves – had attained de facto recognition from their former masters and a hard-won, if temporary, peace.

Political advances were matched by social and economic ones. *Cleyne glorie en grote schade* – little glory at great expense – quipped the advocate of Holland, Johan van Oldenbarnevelt with reference to the conflict's final years of cheerless, essentially trench, warfare. As the senior statesman of the mightiest province of the recently elevated Republic, though, Oldenbarnevelt would have known better than to begrudge the outcome of the war's final stages. If the costly struggle with Spain had achieved only minimal glory, it had paid dividends in countless other ways. The United Provinces, and particularly Holland, had grown, developed, and prospered dramatically in precisely those years leading up to the Truce.[21] The Republic, to start with, was now considerably larger. Already from the fall of Antwerp in 1585, a flood of refugees had streamed across the great rivers that divided the war-ravaged South from the still defiant North. The Truce lent further impetus to this migratory pattern by recognizing the hardening line that now partitioned the officially Catholic, Habsburg domains of the South and the presumably tolerant, Republican provinces of the North. Holland's population soared in this period by as much as forty percent. Amsterdam grew most sensationally, more than tripling its population between 1585 (30,000) and the end of the Truce (over 100,000). More people required more land, and during this period the very size of Holland increased. Vast tracts of land, earlier considered *pro derelicto* – low-lying areas habitually drenched with flood waters, swept by sand dunes, or covered by peat bogs – now came under cultivation to feed the province's growing towns. Over the whole of Holland, the amount of land annually reclaimed multiplied from 128 acres on average in the 1580s to 580 acres on average between 1590 and 1614. By the end of the war with Spain, Holland had drained and reclaimed some forty percent more arable land than it possessed at the conflict's outset.[22]

The Republic had also grown richer. Economic no less than religious motives accounted for the massive, demographic shift that brought energetic and enterprising refugees from the depressed South to the burgeoning North. Battered cloth towns and blockaded ports – most particularly Antwerp, which had been sacked by Spanish mutineers in the 1570s and stifled by Zeeland privateers throughout the 1590s – surrendered their craftsmen, capital, and commercial expertise to the vigorous economies of Holland and Zeeland. In the textile towns of Haarlem and Leiden (the latter of whose population more than quadrupled over the course of the war), skilled Flemish weavers helped to triple annual cloth production between the 1580s and 1620s. In Middelburg, Flushing, and Amsterdam, wealthy (especially) Walloon merchants fueled the spectacular rise of Dutch shipping. By the early 1600s, larger and more frequent fleets plied the traditional Dutch trade in the Baltic and off the coasts of France and Iberia. Riskier, yet potentially more profitable, expeditions, meanwhile, introduced the Dutch flag to the waters of the Mediterranean, the Indian Ocean, and even the Caribbean. The émigrés also underwrote much of the Republic's financial growth. More than half of the 320 largest depositors in the Amsterdam Exchange Bank (founded in 1611) came from the South, as did over a quarter of the original subscribers to the Dutch East India Company (chartered in 1602). Walloon and Flemish exiles accounted for three of the largest shareholders of the Company, and, combined, the newcomers contributed forty percent of its startup capital. Much the same pattern would have characterized the funding of a Dutch West India Company – proposed in the early years of the seventeenth century – had the signing of the Truce not forced investors temporarily to shelve their plans.[23]

Finally, the Republic was now more cultured, or, at least, more inclined and better situated to be so following the influx of painters and printers, poets and teachers, who had been forced to abandon the desolation of Flanders and Brabant for the opportunities available in the North. Though numbers, in this case, hardly tell the full story, they do give an indication of the parameters of the Republic's stunning gains around the turn of the century. With the fall of Antwerp, bookmen – publishers, printers, and sellers of literary materials – migrated en masse to the North, primarily to Holland and Zeeland, though some reached Utrecht and even the Frisian town of Franeker. More than two-thirds of the known publishers and booksellers in the North Netherlands at this time (1570–1630) had southern origins. They included among them the most prominent and prolific publishers of the period. Christoffel Plantijn, the greatest printer of his age, stayed only briefly in Leiden; yet during his two-year sojourn, he helped to establish Loys Elsevier and François van Raphelingen. The former went on to head the most important publishing firm in Leiden, while the latter – a noted Orientalist – took over Plantijn's Leiden office while simultaneously serving as a professor of Hebrew. Willem Silvius, a *typographus regii* in his Antwerp days, assumed the position of Printer to the States of Holland in 1577. He was followed in this capacity by his son, Karel, who published the *Plakkaat van Verlatinge* in 1581. Cornelis Claesz and Jodocus Hondius brought expertise in navigation and geography with them to Amsterdam, which quickly replaced Antwerp as the leading producer of maps, atlases, and travel literature.[24]

This pattern is duplicated in other fields. Two-thirds of the school teachers and university professors accounted for in Leiden between 1570 and 1630 hailed from the South, as did a remarkable number of scholars more generally and, of course, Protestant theologians. The famous Brabant Chamber of Rhetoric, "'Twit Lavendel" (The White Lavender), opened its doors in Amsterdam in 1593, one year after the Flemish Chamber, "De Witte Angieren" (The White Carnations), set up shop in Haarlem. Poets belonging to these and other chambers with southern roots collaborated to produce *Den Nederduytschen helicon*, a celebrated volume of vernacular verse compiled in the early years of the seventeenth century and edited by Karel van Mander. A member of the "new" – that is, refugee – chambers in both Amsterdam and Haarlem, van Mander represented but one of the many rising literary stars from the South. He also led the way for a whole generation of Flemish painters, draftsmen, and engravers that migrated to the Republic and helped nourish the phenomenal blossoming of the visual arts. The Dutch Golden Age of painting, van Mander's Haarlem loyalties notwithstanding, began in the southern provinces and might not have occurred at all had the likes of van Mander, Frans Hals, Adriaen Brouwer, and scores of other leading painters not brought their talents northward around the turn of the century.[25]

Circa 1600, then, the young Republic of the United Provinces stood at the threshold of its Golden Age. The Dutch had reached a point of dramatic transition that offered a glimpse of things to come, yet not without sight of things just past. Though not yet officially ended, the war with Spain had now entered a decidedly muted period, which boded well for the North. The Truce and the promise of a future, lasting peace reduced, for some at least, the desire to blacken the Spanish reputation.

Though not yet fully ripened, the Republic's economy had quickly burgeoned and received further support from the influx of refugees from the South. The presence in the North of wealthy Walloon and Flemish merchants with command of vast trading networks suggested to many the possibility of further expanding Amsterdam's already impressive emporium of wares. Though not yet fully in place, the elements of a Dutch cultural expansion had arrived, so that some, like van Mander, could begin to contemplate a leading school of painting and a renaissance of Dutch letters in the new Republic. The literary and artistic energy of fin de siècle Holland – the experimentation with new forms, promotion of vernacular letters, organization of learned activities – pointed to a cultural moment, a Dutch self-fashioning of sorts, that lay just ahead. At the opening of the seventeenth century, the United Provinces confronted a new political future with the confidence born of economic strength and intellectual innovation. The Netherlands faced opportunities and challenges that made them adjust their attitudes toward the war, toward the Spanish, and toward the New World.

III

The din of transition did not altogether quiet traditional cries of "Spanish tyranny in America." The America of the rebels' propaganda still echoed through plenty of pamphlets, broadsides, and *geuzenliederen* (Beggars' songs) printed at the turn of the century – in more forms, if anything, than ever before. It resounded, however, less boldly than it had in earlier years and chiefly within the polemics of the war party, which, by the first years of the seventeenth century, had declined somewhat in size and importance. No longer the incessant drone it had been in the tireless attacks on Spain of the 1570s and 1580s, the topos of "America" now featured as an occasional and more rhythmic refrain that followed the political beat of the States General and their strategy toward Spain. It tended, thus, to coincide neatly with moments of negotiation: lulls in the fighting, during which the war party sought to drum up support, to revitalize the flagging stamina of the Dutch patriot by reference to the cautionary tale of America. It could be heard most articulately in 1598 and 1600 when the States General sent delegations to Brussels to confer with the archduke Albrecht of Austria, the new Habsburg sovereign in the Netherlands. In both the North and the South, Albrecht and his new bride, the Infanta Isabella, made a more conciliatory impression than had any of their predecessors – or, for that matter, the forever intransigent, and now deceased, Philip II (d. 1598). Initially, then, the States General of the United Provinces showed greater willingness to entertain Albrecht's friendly overtures.[26] The opponents of peace, however – orthodox Calvinists, exiled southerners, and ambitious soldiers – would suffer neither negotiations nor consideration, even, of reconciliation with the Habsburg "arch enemy," and they turned to America to make their case. Spain could not be trusted, they contended, as the fate of the Indies most fiercely demonstrated. "Many unsuspecting men call for peace," exhorted one (poetically) belligerent Hollander,

> hoping quickly to rejoice,
> But whosoever contemplates the bitter tyrannies,
> That the Spaniards perpetrated here and in the Indies,
> Will rather choose just war to thus preserve himself
> Than by a most false peace forfeit life and properties.

The Spanish government in America had not merely slaughtered "many times a hundred thousand souls," protested the tyranny-obsessed poets. They had also breached their promises and failed to honor their oaths:

> Behold the proffered peace, how Spaniards keep their word,
> Read all about Trinidad where they let loose their knaves:
> Although they'd reached with them a most friendly accord,
> Town and folk were burned, many [natives] captured as slaves![27]

America, thus reconfigured, represented the fullest range of Spanish treachery: heartless at war and faithless in peace. Faced with the prospect of an armistice, the war party wheeled out the double-barreled, newly refurbished guns of "America," which were now made to serve twin purposes. Not only would the New World illustrate the sins of Spain on the battlefield; it would also expose Castilian perfidy at the negotiating table. The evidence of America would reveal the very essence of Spanish tyranny in its many guises. "The disposition (and the nature) of the Spanish nation," begins the author of the *Spaenschen ende Arragoenschen Spiegel,* is reflected "in the many examples [of tyranny] perpetrated in the Netherlands, France, and the new Indian lands." A lengthy recitation of these concludes with an "admonition . . . against the great naïveté of trusting the deceitful words of the Spanish," and a warning against the sort of "fine, lubricious words" Spain had employed to ensnare, and enslave, the innocent Americans.[28] An enormously popular broadside published around this time, *Aerdt ende eygenschappen van Seignor van Spangien* (Nature and character of Seignior of Spain), strikes a similar balance between attacking Spain's thuggishness at war and slipperiness at peace. The caricatured "Seignior," as vicious as he is mendacious, not only mutilates his enemies ruthlessly and slaughters "mother with child" mercilessly; he also deceives willfully and breaks oaths habitually to Catholics and Protestants alike. As usual, the case of America provides the most damning evidence.[29]

With the thoroughly risible figure of the "Seignior of Spain" in mind, one might be tempted to conclude that the topos of America played primarily to a popular audience. A stock type derived from the moralizing tradition of Northern Europe, the Seignior had an essentially carnivalesque appeal. (The print reviews the Seignior's *nine* cardinal failings, making him – and the Spanish – a full two measures more venal than the worst of late-medieval sinners.)[30] The lyrical Hollander who cited the tyrannies in Trinidad did so in the context of a 1596 *rederijker-feest:* a provincial poetry contest sponsored by the civic Chambers of Rhetoric for the amusement of bourgeois revelers, in this case of Leiden. Though *rederijker* poetry hits a slightly different pitch than slanderous broadsides, here too the attraction was broadly festive, surely accessible, and essentially patriotic.[31] Then there was the *Antwoordt op het tweede refereyn* (Answer to the second refrain), a sharply caustic, once again "poetic," and above all legible form of propaganda that attacked the peace negotiations with pointed reference to "American tyranny." In this case, the cleverly effective format – an illustrated verse dialogue that pitted the "deceived Netherlandish provinces" (the South, in other words) against the province of Holland – plainly evoked the anticlerical prints employed by allies of the Protestant Reformers.[32] An elaborate visual allegory on the title page depicts "Peace" in the form of a small skiff, laboring to escape the clutches of an imposing galley (fig. 23). The latter is governed by a triple-headed monster – the Catholic pope, the Spanish king, and the archduke in Brussels – rowed by monks of various orders, and steered by the unmistakable figure of a Jesuit at the helm. This hostile, ostensibly "Spanish" ship advertises its duplicitous mission with an assortment of flags and banners. One bears the message, "He who cannot dissimulate cannot govern"; another commands, "One shall not keep faith with a heretic." Standing ashore within the emblematic "Garden of Holland" and the protective company of a bellowing lion, the Dutch patriot endeavors to haul in the craft of peace while fending off the ship of chicanery. Beneath the patriot reads the single caption, "I desire peace although not deceit." The pamphlet itself comprises the dueling doggerel of the Hollander and his southern cousin. To the South's heartfelt plea,

> Come Hollandia, let the peace overflow:
> In permanent peace is our mutual salvation;

Figure 23. Title page illustration from *Antwoordt op het tweede refereyn* (1598). Universiteitsbibiliotheek Amsterdam.

the Hollander responds with reminders of Philip II's universal tyranny:

> Across the whole globe, as all can plainly see,
> He plagues the savage, East, West Indies, and me.

This exchange occurs already in the "Antwoordt's" first stanza. The bulk of the poem consists of a diatribe against Habsburg *trouwloosheid* (perfidy), culminating with a crescendo of well-rehearsed motifs culled from histories of Granada, the Netherlands, and naturally the Indies. The American passages rework material from Las Casas – reports of eighteen million innocent souls slaughtered, of heinous deeds never before committed, of infants seized from their mothers' breasts and dashed against cliffs – to conclude that "the thought of such deeds would wound a heart of stone." Ironically, the memory of Spain's wars in America militates against peace in the Netherlands. Or, as the Hollander neatly sums up,

> That it's better to wage on against the enemy
> Than to be thus deceived by a false serenity.[33]

The pamphlet's pitch, once again, is popular – polemical, political, and aggressively patriotic – though references to "America" by this time need not be. Not all, that is to say, marched to a beat quite so martial, and, by the turn of the century, the war party's topoi of tyranny had begun to be incorporated into other discourses that related only vaguely to any originally Hispanophobic agenda. America's appeal was expanding. In many regards, the slogan remained the same – Spain had committed astonishing acts of cruelty, all agreed, in the Indies – yet the range of genres and the breadth of contexts in which it was broached had discernibly distended. A neo-Latin epic from the hand of Georgius Benedicti Wertelo commented on the American misdeeds of Spain in a work otherwise dedicated to the "illustrious deeds" of Orange. Wertelo, among the young humanists drawn to the new university of Leiden, added American material to his elaborate poem perhaps to lend a global context to the prince's *fama* – colonial tyranny would seem to be beside the point. Justus Lipsius, surely no ally of the war-mongering and polemic-writing Calvinist agitators, referred, in his austere *De constantia*, to the "marvellous and miserable spectacle" of the New World and Spain's tyrannical government there. "O good god, what exceeding great slaughters have they wrought? what wonderful desolations?" wrote the most influential philosopher of his generation, advocating not patriotic revolt but disciplined stoicism.[34] In Jan van der Noot's Horatian *Ode Teghen d'onwetende vyanden der Poëteryen* (Ode Against the ignorant enemies of Poetry), America was the site of horrible "strife / where gold is rife." In the poet's grand (and pointedly self-aggrandizing) itinerary, though, the New World's sorrow ultimately counted for less than van der Noot's glory – which had spread, he asserted, even among the innocent Indians.[35]

The imagery of America had spread too, attracting an ever broader audience and assuming an ever increasing number of roles. The "wonderful desolations" that so moved Lipsius did resemble the "outrageous cruelties" that agitated the rebels. Yet the effect of the wonder had transformed. The New World, furthermore, offered more than "tyranny" for those who cared to look for it – a group whose ranks were swelling. By the turn of the seventeenth century, the war party had in fact diminished; and, for the rest of the Republic, the growing prospect of peace had reduced the impetus to vilify Spain and the urge to use America to do so. To those inclined to terminate the exhausting war with the Habsburgs, America need no longer symbolize *merely* Habsburg hypocrisy. Spain's tyrannies in the New World might now excite less interest than the very distant, exotic landscape within which they took place. Increasingly, readers and writers looked beyond the patriotic rhetoric and considered the riches, wonders, and products of the West. The New World encompassed far too many curiosities – familiar to readers of the earliest Americana, published throughout the first two-thirds of the sixteenth century – to remain fixed as a monotonous landscape of tyrannies. Many began to wonder, as did a leading character in a 1596 play by Jan van Hout, what actually occurred in America besides the Spanish atrocities made famous by the rebel pamphleteers. "In *Far-and-Back* [Pernambuco]," asks Bouwen-the-Farmer, "Almighty! / Where is that?!" Steven-the-Sailor, fresh from his adventures abroad, takes the opportunity to enthrall Bouwen and the no-doubt curious audience with tales of distant Brazil and the marvelous possessions he acquired there.[36]

The "marvellous and miserable spectacle" of America, in short, now attracted many more beyond the philosopher Lipsius and the sailor Steven. The wonder of the New World had by this time enticed a whole array of visitors, some literary, some philosophical – and all well-received upon reporting back to the Netherlands. They included, for example, Christoffel Wagenaer, the accomplished alchemist and trusty disciple of the notorious Doctor Johannes Faustus. Wagenaer journeyed westward in the course of his restless pursuit of pleasure and wisdom, and brought back to Europe the latest tidings of America and its riches. He alighted from his magical rooster in Toledo in the final years of the sixteenth century in time to compose a racy, and deservedly popular, account of his adventures, which enjoyed at least four Dutch printings between 1597 and 1614. Part morality tale, part travelogue, and part magic lesson, Wagenaer's lengthy American discourse easily blends scenes of Spanish tyrannies with descriptions of American novelties. Thus, in each of his New World excursions – to the Caribbean, Mexico, Peru, and the "Island of Florida" – the author dutifully relates the deeds of those he introduces as "the Bloody Spaniards." The pitiless slaughter of innocent natives, the cruel enslavement of entire islands, the ceaseless torture of women and children: all receive their due. Yet these darker episodes of Spanish cruelties never overshadow the relatively longer (and certainly more engaging) descriptions of native customs and natural wealth. The Indians' strange manners and mores, the exotic flora and fauna, and the bounty of minerals and pearls occupy the majority of Wagenaer's, and presumably the readers', attention. On this American stage, the alchemist Wagenaer conjures up scene after glittering scene of treasure, as he transforms the natives' wealth into his own. For those curious readers who suspended their imaginations long enough to follow him, he converted the New World into a vast and inviting landscape of wonders and gold.[37]

Soon enough, *actual* travelers to America joined imaginary ones and contributed, in only slightly less sensational terms, to the impression of a marvelous New World. After a fallow period of nearly two decades – dating back to the 1570s, when Antwerp publishers last brought out editions of Zárate and Las Casas – publishers in the Republic, and especially the Amsterdam-based émigré Cornelis Claesz, began once again to produce copious American travel narratives. These consisted in some cases simply of reissues of earlier accounts: the histories of Brazil by Hans Staden and Jean de Léry came out in 1595 and 1597 respectively. Yet new narratives also appeared, and these introduced Dutch readers, in still another form, to the latest riches from the West. As they had with earlier rounds of Americana, Dutch publishers took the editorial initiative by deftly (and often swiftly) appropriating these texts and aggressively promoting them to a local readership. Francis Petty's description of Thomas Cavendish's exploits in American waters – published first in Dutch by Claesz and only later in English – presents a classic tale of pirate's progress. The English "privateers," it is true, slash and burn at the expense of the Spanish, and in this sense the account serves a certain political function. (That the earliest version of the voyage appeared in 1588 is hardly a coincidence.) Yet the details of *Santa Ana*'s capture – "one of the richest vessels that ever sailed on the seas" – could entice Dutch readers on a far more basic level.[38] So too could the magisterial *Historia natural y moral de las Indias* by the Spanish Jesuit, José de Acosta. Rather than recounting the conquest of Mexico and Peru by his Spanish patrons, Acosta addresses the "natural and moral history [in the sense of mores, or *mos*]" of those now living under Habsburg control. In fabulous detail, the *Historia* related the "domestic economy, native customs, civil laws, religions, and wars" of the great Incan and Aztec empires. It introduced Dutch readers to "the marvelousness of the world," as Jan van Linschoten emphasized in his 1598 translation. It revealed the New World's "quality, richness, and beauty [*cierlijckheyt*]," which, as an anonymous Dutch sonneteer assured, would fire both the merchant's ardor and the scholar's imagination.[39]

Nowhere did the New World sparkle more radiantly than in the reports of "the large, rich, and beautiful empire of Guiana," composed by Walter Ralegh and his lieutenant, Lawrence Kemys. Issued originally in 1596 (apparently to quiet Ralegh's critics at court), these glittering portraits of the "gold-rich kingdoms" on the Orinoco dazzled the Dutch, who promptly translated them in 1598, reissued them regularly over the subsequent two decades, and revived them once again in the 1640s. The less stylish though no less spectacular of the two narratives, Kemys' *Second voyage* proved in fact more popular in Dutch than in any other language, including that of its original composition.[40] And with good reason: if the travels of Kemys and Ralegh claimed to be more authentic than those of Christoffel Wagenaer, they left an impression no less fantastic in their exposition of America's wealth of wonders. Never had the New World's riches seemed so alluring; nowhere did the New World's *naturalia* appear so astonishing. In Ralegh's *Discoverie of Guiana*, centenarian men jostled with Amazonian women for the readers' attention. Savages had no heads, though the country itself – to quote Ralegh's most virile conclusion – "hath yet her Madenheade," left (presumably) undamaged by the English. The region possessed, moreover, "hills with stones of the cullor of Gold and Silver," behind which lay "*Manoa* the emperiall Citie of *Guiana*, which the *Spanyardes* cal *el Dorado*, that for the greatnes, for the riches, and for the excellent seate, it far exceedeth any of the world."[41]

Before the *Discoverie of Guiana*, the New World had never seemed so beckoning, either. For the narratives of Ralegh and Kemys did not rest at revealing the riches of Guiana; they strove further to demonstrate that the prizes of the Orinoco were there for the taking. With energetic prose and patriotic encouragement, the authors sought both to entice their audience with the kingdom of Guiana and to entreat them "to possess it" forthwith. Two factors recommended colonial success. First was the abusive behavior of earlier, Spanish interlopers who had alienated the native Indians. The latter, as Ralegh breezily assured, "will all die even to the last man against the Spanyardes, in hope of our succoure and returne." Kemys concurred and concluded his narrative with a call to imperial arms, "since such a plan would be for the protection of the innocent natives, who are tormented [by the Spanish] with all sorts of expulsions and oppressions, and who therefore aspire to place themselves under Her Majesty's protection."[42] Second was the natives' desperate desire particularly for Queen Elizabeth's protection, as Kemys's comments broadly hint. The Guianese, it was implied, would gladly barter their ample gold for the queen's good government. Speaking through an interpreter, Ralegh makes the natives of Trinidad understand that he came as the servant of a Queene who was the great *Casique* of the north, and a virgin, and had more *Casiqui* under her then there were trees in their i[s]land: that she was an enemy to *Castellani* in respect of their tyrannie and oppression, and that she delivered all such nations about her, as were by them oppressed, and having freed all the coast of the northern world from their servitude had sent me to free them also, and withal to defend the countrey of *Guiana* from their invasion and conquest.

When Ralegh displayed a picture of the queen, the natives "so admired and honored [it], as it had beene easie to have brought them idolatrous thereof." All along the Orinoco, in fact, Elizabeth's torch burned brightly, "so as in that part of the world her majesty is very famous and admirable, whom they now call *Ezrabeta Cassipuna Aquerewana*, which is as much as *Elizabeth*, the great princesse or greatest commaunder." Kemys's experience corroborated Ralegh's. He received much the same reaction when he discoursed to the attentive nobles of Carapana on Elizabeth's "good virtues and moderation, at which they were greatly astonished, such that their hearts became wholly estranged from the Spaniards, and favorably disposed, with true love and trust, towards us." So moved were the Carapana chieftains that they "presented their service" to Kemys and "promised to furnish all victuals, and all that their land produced," asking only for "good government" in return.[43]

Of course, it was precisely at the good governors of England and especially the Virgin Queen that Kemys and Ralegh directed their rhetoric. Theirs was an implicitly English argument, elaborately fashioned to win patronage in London, not Orinoco. The consummate courtier, Ralegh flatters Elizabeth extravagantly, promising by his deeds to enrich both the glory of the queen and the coffers of her realm. Just as he vows "to deliver [the Indians of Arromaia] from the tyrannie of the Spaniards," he takes careful – and politic – pause to "dilat[e] . . . her Majesties greatness, her justice, her charitie to all oppressed nations, [and] as many of the rest of her beauties and vertues, as either I could expresse, or they conceive." Among the female warriors of Amazonia he cleverly insinuates a natural alliance with the Virgin Queen of England: "Where the south border of Guiana reacheth to the Dominion and Empire of the *Amazones*, those women shall heerby heare the name of a virgin, which is not onely able to defend her own territories and her neighbors, but also to invade and conquere so great Empyres and so far removed."[44]

Yet such enthusiasm, as it turns out, fell on deaf ears among the flattered, but skeptical, governors of Albion. More importantly, Ralegh's rhetorical pyrotechnics failed to light up the imperial imagination of Elizabeth, out of whose favor he had famously fallen. Not so in the

Netherlands. In striking contrast to the mild response in London, the Dutch Republic granted the texts of the English courtiers a warmly receptive audience.[45] The narratives of Ralegh and Kemys not only riveted Dutch readers (for whom no less than six editions appeared within the space of two decades). They also inspired mapmakers, like Jodocus Hondius, who issued a "new map of the wonderful and gold-filled land of Guiana" in 1599 based on Ralegh's narrative; they encouraged merchants, like the burgomaster of Middelburg, who outfitted a three hundred ton ship "to visit the river called Dorado"; and they stirred colonialists, like the resourceful Willem Usselincx, who lighted upon the idea of sending Dutch settlers to join permanently those Guianese whom Kemys had reported "very eagerly desirous" of a savior from the torments of Spain.[46]

The English narratives appealed so broadly in the Netherlands because they expressed so clearly what the Dutch wished to hear. Whatever the local – English – purpose of the narratives, Ralegh's and Kemys's descriptions of Guiana met Dutch expectations of America perfectly. For the armchair traveler, they satisfied an appetite for marvels and monsters, whetted only recently by the imaginative journey of Wagenaer. For the energetic merchant, they suggested possibilities for lucrative trade in regions not yet conquered by their European rivals. And for the patriotic pamphleteer, they testified to the presence of "innocent" Indians – would-be allies – eager to conclude a "treaty of friendship" with a European nation that shared their antipathy toward Spain. The natives of Guiana, as Kemys had confirmed, anxiously sought assistance "to revenge the murderous cruelty which they have endured from the Spanish [and] to raze the poor cities inland whose foundations have been laid in the blood of their Indian ancestors."[47] Nothing could have better matched the rhetoric of the Dutch ancestors – the rebel pamphleteers of the 1570s and 1580s – and nothing could have better suited their descendants – the war party of the early seventeenth century. The potential alliance that earlier pamphleteers had so airily projected had now, in the accounts of Ralegh and Kemys, been more solidly documented. The "America" configured in the new world of Guiana beckoned the Dutch with marvels and treasures. On its shores waited friendly and obedient allies, eager to throw off their yoke of tyranny and befriend the enemies of Spain.

IV

The New World tempted, and, within time, the Dutch succumbed. The literature and prints of the late sixteenth century, with their alluring im-

ages of America's wealth and welcoming natives, ultimately spurred
the Dutch imagination to the point of action. By the turn of the century,
readers gave free rein to their lust and began to wander – or, at least, to
hire others to travel and traffic at their behest. To be sure, Dutch vessels
had ventured sporadically into Western waters from as early as the
1570s. Evidence exists for scattered, sixteenth-century contacts between
Dutch sailors and Iberian settlers in Brazil and the West Indies and, by
the 1590s, expeditions to the salt pans of Punta de Araya (off the
Venezuelan coast). Now, however, more frequent and more ambitious
fleets crossed the Atlantic; and, for the first time, enterprising merchants
launched a sustained effort to gain an independent Dutch foothold in
the New World. In 1598 alone – the year that saw Dutch publication of
accounts by Ralegh, Kemys, and Acosta – three major Dutch fleets reconnoitered the coasts of South America (led by Hendrik Ottsen, Simon
de Cordes, and Olivier van Noort). During the following years and for
the duration of the Twelve Year Truce (1609–1621), ships flying the colors of the United Provinces explored the waters off North America
(Henry Hudson); the icy islands of the Arctic (Jan van Linschoten and
Willem Barentsz); and the Cape lately called "Hoorn," after the home
port of its discoverers (Willem Cornelisz Schouten and Jacques le
Maire). More pertinently, only from this period did returning voyagers
record their travels and entrepreneuring printers publish them. By circa
1600, the Republic inaugurated a new age of travel and a new chapter
of travel literature that afforded the first genuinely Dutch glimpse of the
New World.[48]

That glimpse, of course, was hardly unobstructed. First hand accounts from on-site observers generated, it is true, the most immediate –
most immediately *Dutch* – picture of America to date. No longer did the
New World come filtered through the lenses of imported, second-hand
sources. Yet the reports came filtered all the same: most basically,
through those American frames of reference traditionally available in
the Netherlands; and further, through the complex refractions imposed
by the production of travel literature. The image of America could not
help but have a prior textual basis, and the *variety* of texts lately circulating in the Republic complicated matters even more. Still further complicating matters, though, was the very process of manufacturing travel
narratives – of reporting, transcribing, representing, and finally publishing descriptions of new worlds. What voyagers observed and
recorded publishers shaped and fashioned, with subtly differing purposes and sometimes strikingly divergent effects. The resulting corpus
of texts reveals both the continuing appeal of older models of America
as a site of "Spanish tyrannies," yet the growing attraction of newer par-

adigms, too, reflecting the evolving agenda of the Republic on the eve of its colonial debut.

The luminary of this Dutch Golden Age of travel and travel writing would, appropriately enough, read voraciously before roaming precociously across the globe. Jan Huygen van Linschoten (1563–1611), whose monumental *Itinerario* ushered in the spectacular overseas expansion of the United Provinces, took to travel only after a self-admittedly bookish youth. Reared in Haarlem, van Linschoten left that city with his family sometime around the Spanish siege of 1573 and moved to the port city of Enkhuizen where his father kept an inn. Rather than tales of passing sailors, however, he recalled the texts of distant travelers which he read throughout his childhood. "When I was young and living in my Fatherland," he confessed, "I was inclined to read of foreign lands and curious histories, wherein I took particular delight and pleasure. With the hope of satisfying my desires to see these exotic and unknown lands, or to experience some adventures . . . I resolved to leave my Fatherland for a period of time." Thus inspired, van Linschoten set off at age sixteen, determined to join two half-brothers established in Seville and desirous to improve his Spanish. Eight months after his arrival (1580), he accompanied his brothers into Portugal, where they traveled in the wake of Philip II's conquering army and in the hope of anticipated plunder. He remained in Habsburg-controlled Portugal for three more years in a commercial capacity, continuing to hone his language skills. Perseverance paid off when he finally secured a position as a clerk for the newly appointed archbishop of Goa, with whom he set sail for India on Good Friday, 1583. Five years of loyal service as an officer of the clergy came to an end with the death of van Linschoten's patron. He departed India in early 1589, and, after two years as "Factor for the King's Pepper" in the (by now also Spanish-controlled) Azores, he arrived back in Enkhuizen in September 1592.[49]

Van Linschoten's experiences in *Asia Portuguesa*, the Azores, and, not least, the Iberian peninsula, formed the basis for his *Itinerario* (1596), a behind-the-scenes account of the Habsburg world empire. Less a feckless traveler, it turns out, than a tireless compiler and intelligent annotator, van Linschoten amassed during each of his sojourns manuscript materials that furnished invaluable data on Hispanic-Portuguese traffic. In Spain he obtained a list of the King's Revenues, which detailed "all of the rents, tolls, . . . imposts and tributes" due the king of Spain. In Goa he copied the masterful *roteiros* (rutters, or sailing directions), which summarized a century's experience of Portuguese pilots. And in the Azores he assembled notes on the Iberian pepper trade, which elucidated the workings of that notoriously secretive monopoly. These he

augmented with published materials culled from Spanish and Portuguese sources otherwise inaccessible in the Netherlands and with his
own, rather keen observations of colonial life, especially in Goa. The
combined effect of these "discoveries" vastly expanded the world of
Dutch readers, sailors, and merchants alike. Van Linschoten revealed
the wonders of the world while also charting the ways to reach them. In
the process, he exposed the weaknesses of a rotting Habsburg empire in
detail never before available outside of the Iberian peninsula. Finally, he
provided his readers with "natural" and "moral" histories of the peoples of the Near and Far East, Africa, and America, and eyewitness reports of India. These descriptive passages delighted in the very sort of
exotica that had so excited van Linschoten in his youth. They also contained the most substantial accounts of the extra-European world available in the Netherlands. Van Linschoten's sections on America represented the most complete description of its kind compiled by a Dutch
author.[50]

The impact of the *Itinerario* was immediate and dramatic. It instantly
launched Dutch trade to the East, and it rapidly vaulted its author to the
heights of patriotic prominence. Van Linschoten's navigational directions, above all else, excited the Republic's merchants and regents, who
were quick to recognize their economic and political worth and anxious
to see them in print. With their publication in 1595 as the *Reysgheschrift*,
van Linschoten set in motion a process of colonial metamorphosis that
would ultimately lead to the decline of Iberian hegemony in the East
and the rise of Dutch (and, to a lesser extent, English) power in its stead.
Cornelis de Houtman led the first major Dutch fleet to the Indian Ocean
already in 1595, carrying a freshly minted *Reysgheschrift* on board. A second expedition, under the command of Jacob Cornelisz van Neck, departed Texel in 1598 to establish the first Dutch factories in the Moluc-
cas. Others soon followed, and the foundation of a Dutch East India
Company came quickly in 1602. Though efforts to form a similar company to trade in the West would temporarily stall – efforts for which the
assistance of van Linschoten had been drafted – the momentum of
Dutch expansion would otherwise only increase. The global assault on
Spanish trade – "tyranny" as some would have it – had begun and Jan
Huygen received lavish praise for firing the first shot. In the coming
years, poets and pamphleteers would celebrate the pioneering
Enkhuizener for his "heroic" service of patria.[51]

Such accolades as van Linschoten received came not without a certain
irony. Though publicists and would-be colonialists celebrated the *Itinerario* for its role in the unmaking of the enemy, van Linschoten himself
made for a rather unconvincing saboteur of Spain. To a large degree, the

effect of the work – to undermine Habsburg trade and colonial "tyranny" – distracted attention from its author's original intentions: "to visit unknown lands," as van Linschoten once put it, and to advance within the ranks of the Iberian colonial world. Curiosity and careerism, it would seem, more surely guided Jan Huygen's early adventures than did politics and patriotism. To wit: as a young man of fighting age, he departed Holland in the heat of battle (1579) in order to travel in the pay of the enemy. Once abroad, he did virtually everything in his power to advance his cause in the eyes of his Spanish and Portuguese patrons. The Catholic-born van Linschoten signed on gladly with the archbishop of Goa, whom he loyally served for as long as he could. Securely in the employ of the Church, he cast his nets even wider. He dedicated his extravagant map, *Goa metropolitana da Indiae partes orientais*, to the archbishop of Toledo, Albrecht of Austria, then governor of Portugal and future governor of the Habsburg Netherlands. (The appropriately effusive dedication, probably composed in Goa, remained on versions of the map later printed in the United Provinces.) On Terceira (the Azores), van Linschoten charted the port of Angra for the benefit of Philip II who, at that moment (1591) as in the previous decade, embodied the supreme sovereign for the expatriated Enkhuizener. Very little in these works would indicate that van Linschoten bore any ill will toward the Most Catholic King.[52]

Van Linschoten sought more than just honor and advancement, though, which he might easily have attained without ever leaving Seville. By his own admission, he traveled in search of wonders, which he had craved from the earliest moments of his youth. Unable, as an adolescent in Enkhuizen, "to quench [his] desire for strange things," Jan Huygen headed south for Spain where he experienced "at once an exceptional desire to carry on" to distant lands. Upon arrival in Goa, he declined the opportunity to return with his brother to the Portuguese court in Lisbon, choosing instead "to investigate the manners, nature, and form of the lands, people, fruits, wares, products, and other things." This became for him, as for Christoffel Wagenaer, an all-consuming passion. "Night and day my heart craves for nothing more than to see exotic lands," he wrote his family in a letter of 1584. The *Itinerario* evinces the results of such round-the-clock cravings. It reports of trees in Mozambique that bloom overnight and of elephants in Pegu (Myanmar) that rage all winter. The kings of Hormuz (Qeshm), van Linschoten discovers, blind their brothers; while the widows of India burn on their husbands' funeral pyres. Not all of this rich detail could possibly have derived from personal experience – this despite the author's frequent (and for the genre typical) claims of authenticity. Van Linschoten's prose ranges too widely for any single, early modern traveler. Yet it does not range too broadly for a voracious reader, and Jan Huygen apparently consumed travel literature even more avidly in India than he did in Enkhuizen, now reading works in Portuguese and Spanish, as well. In this way, he described what he could and collected descriptions of what he could not, producing a work that testifies more to his love of wonders than his enmity toward the Habsburgs.[53]

Wonders fascinated van Linschoten for their extraordinary ability to reveal the omnipotence of the Lord. "In all places," he wrote to the States General in defense of his career of travel, "there are remarkable and diverse reasons to be found to admire, and justly so, the manifold wonders that occur in nature." Exotica – cultural and natural "strangeness" (*vreemdheid*) – represented for van Linschoten the handiwork of the Creator; and, though an oak tree back home in Holland could also reveal the Almighty's craftsmanship, diversity and rarity enhanced an observer's ability to recognize the impressive range of that handiwork. Van Linschoten therefore searched out those objects and histories that "differed . . . and expressed novelty" in order best to illustrate "the marvelousness of the world" and the majesty of its Creator. "The further we consider the concealed power and properties with which the Almighty Creator has endowed nature," he contended, the sooner "we shall . . . confess completely that His wisdom (in that especially) has given us much to admire."[54]

The natural world so impressed van Linschoten – and here "nature" includes human nature as well as *naturalia* – that he packed up as much of it as he could and shipped it back to Holland. Hindu religious artifacts, Goan botanical specimens, Cochin mineral wealth, and other *memento mirabilia* made the trip back to the Netherlands, where they found a home in the cabinet of curiosities of van Linschoten's friend, Bernardus Paludanus, the Enkhuizen town physician. These Indian objects joined Paludanus's already extensive collection – "*celebris in tota Europa & orbe terrarum*" – that boasted rarities from Asia, Africa, and the New World. The Americana, according to visitors' accounts, included clubs, rattles, and feathered headgear from Brazil; three women's loincloths from northern Mexico; and two flutes crafted "from bones gnawed by American cannibals." Those unable to travel around the globe and witness directly "the rich treasury" of the world's wonders could experience a scaled-down version in Enkhuizen. And those unable to make the trip to Paludanus's *Wunderkammer* and tour his collection of artifacts (or, for that matter, to see other collections scattered across the Netherlands) could open the literary "cabinet" composed by van Linschoten and admire the author's disparate array of maps and figures and detailed descriptions of foreign *artificialia.* The *Itinerario* made the world, in all of its variety, accessible to Dutch readers. Van Linschoten sought to satisfy his readers' desire for marvels just as he had his own; and he aspired to invoke in them a greater admiration for the infinite wisdom of the Creator.[55]

Jan Huyghen van Linschoten, after all is said and done, valiantly strove and ultimately succeeded in opening up new worlds for the Dutch. And whether or not he raised his readers' level of piety, he did inspire other travelers, who followed in his wake and shared in his taste for marvels. The "strangeness of foreign lands" impressed the first generation of Dutch travelers – or better, travel writers – so much so that they stocked their reports and their baggage with as many *curiosa* as they could bear. They advertised their travel narratives, moreover, with reference particularly to the wonders within. Pieter de Marees, who visited the western coast of Africa in 1600–1602 and composed a racy description of the "gold kingdom" of Guinea, enlisted his readers to join in a literary tour of "the character of the people of such lands and the goods and riches found there." De Marees cheerfully regaled his audience with reports of the "large Male member" possessed by the coastal natives ("surpassing our Dutch nation in this respect") and the blue-tinted dragons that lived inland ("great enemies of the elephant"). Joris van Spilbergen, who also visited Guinea around this time, sailed the Straits of Magellan a few years later,

> In honor of the Lord, to view Earth's marvels all,
> To see the landscapes fair that rose up at his call,
> Adorned with fruits so sweet, with many kinds of creatures,
> With mountains, woods, and dales, and all such varied features
> As nature with her arts makes differently appear.

Van Spilbergen and his dauntless crew braved "Barbaric giants, [who] sprang up from their lair, / Human in shape, but of human feelings bare," in order to save their readers the "risk of life in the investigation of such rarities." The coasts of South America also lured Dierick Ruiters, a seasoned sailor from Zeeland who, refreshingly, "could handle a pen with the same skill as a rudder." Ruiters's engaging *Toortse der zeevaert* (Torch of navigation) combined sober navigational instruction with spicier travel narrative. "[H]erein," promised Ruiters, "one could observe the marvelous works of the Lord: how in all quarters of the world man is created of various natures and shapes and in multitudinous conditions."[56]

These diverse shapes and conditions sometimes defied description and classification, and this encouraged travelers to retrieve what they could for the sake of collectors, engravers, and other admirers back in the Netherlands. In the course of three voyages to the Arctic (1594–1596), Willem Barentsz and his shipmates induced a number of friendly and unsuspecting Samoyeds to join their exploration party. The Dutch hoped, first, to use the natives as guides in the northern seas that would later bear Barentsz's name; and, later, to present these exotic specimens in Holland for public display. The Arctic explorers had less success in their attempts to haul an obstinate walrus ("larger than an ox") on board, or to lasso a testy polar bear, much as they desired "to have carried her alive in the ship and to have showed her for a strange wonder in Holland." More cooperative species and less cumbersome artifacts did make the journey back to the Netherlands (though Barentsz ultimately did not), where many ended up in collections such as that of Paludanus. Others toured the Dutch countryside, exhibited for the benefit of lesser-known aficionados – such as Adriaen Coenen, a Holland beachcomber and ardent naturalist who described in his sketch pads the sundry sea monsters and other strange species that passed through his home town of Scheveningen. Finally, marvelous objects and curious breeds formed the basis for decorative maps and continental allegories lately engraved – and energetically circulated – in the Netherlands. Marcus Gheeraerts' Mannerist *America*, executed around the time of Barentsz's voyages (ca. 1590–1600), illustrates a pair of Eskimos recently abducted and brought back from America by Martin Frobisher (see fig. 20). The transplanted couple join a crowded assortment of New World figures and exotic bric-a-brac that includes much the same class of curiosities searched out by the overseas adventurers. Wonders, in all of their forms, captivated the Dutch imagination. Described in travelogues, displayed in *kunstkamers,* or depicted in allegories, they testified to the unbridled curiosity of the first generation of Dutch travelers and their armchair companions.[57]

Publishers present a different picture. Though they too indulged in wonders and printed early travel literature with remarkable alacrity, they frequently presented these materials on somewhat different terms than the traveler-authors themselves. Curiosity commonly ceded to politics in the packaging of Dutch travel literature. Publishers, that is, habitually framed their products and even advertised them with subtly different motives than the voyagers who composed them. In contrast to the seemingly naïve confession of wonder with which travelers themselves approached their subject, editors back in the Republic imparted to the same materials more sophisticated concerns of state and war. This applied especially to accounts of America, the promotion of which fell into predictable patterns of patriotic propaganda. Dutch publishers – those in the business of assembling, editing, embellishing, and ultimately printing manuscripts – shaped the initial reports from America in a manner that adavanced their agenda; Batavian adventurers were made to have voyaged less to discover new worlds than to destroy farflung Habsburg ones. Together with reports of curious exotica, publishers mixed in more familiar images of the struggle against Spain, only now set in distant locales. Travel, in this context, meant war rather than wonder. Travel literature, in this form, diluted pleasure with propaganda.

Travel literature, to be sure, had long been manipulated for one purpose or another, in the Netherlands as elsewhere. What makes the earliest Dutch-American texts notable, however, is the higher volume and higher profile of narratives appearing in the opening years of the century. Newly established publishers in the North made much of the freshly charted sea-lanes in the West as reported by heroic captains of the young Republic. A sense of occasion encouraged a habit of hyperbole, which, in the climate of the day, meant patriotic extravagance.

This accounts, in part, for the politically charged reaction upon the return of the first Dutch fleet to pass through the Straits of Magellan. The feat of Olivier van Noort, the Rotterdam innkeeper who became in 1601 the fourth navigator to circle the globe, did indeed give cause for national celebration. Still, as momentous as this accomplishment may have been for the Dutch, it hardly amounted to any great setback for Spain. This, though, was how the printer, Jan II van Waesberghe, chose to broadcast the voyage in two separate accounts published in its aftermath. Less than a month after the navigator's homecoming, an *Extract* of van Noort's journal appeared from van Waesberghe's press purporting to tell a story of Batavian exploits and Spanish devastation. On the title page, a woodblock print of a (presumably) Dutch fleet pillaging a (presumably) Spanish harbor enticed its readers with the promise of patriotic tales of conquest. The title page of the full-length account published the following year (once again by van Waesberghe, a recent immigrant from Antwerp and, by this time, municipal printer of Rotterdam) shows a cityscape of Rotterdam, with the four ships of van Noort's fleet proudly anchored in the roadstead. A pair of sonnets composed in the navigator's honor introduced "the valiant sea-knight" as one who "had challenged the Spanish where none had hitherto dared." In truth, van Noort's feckless attempts to harass Spanish shipping, first on the western coast of South America and later in the bay of Manila, had barely caused a ripple in the vast oceanic imperium of the Habsburgs. The wholly irrelevant vignette on the title page of the *Extract* –

borrowed, it turns out, from an earlier narrative of an expedition to the Canaries, where the Dutch did inflict damage on Spain – correlated not in the least to the more modest assertions of van Noort. Little in the prefatory material would indicate that only one of the four outbound ships, the *Mauritius,* actually completed the journey. Van Noort's own preface remained reticent about the single incidence of Habsburg "treachery" – an ill-fated encounter with the Portuguese on Principe. In contrast to the proud pronouncements of the printer/editor, the bulk of the author's narrative consists of the admiral's prosaic recitation of wind, weather, and waves. Hardly a whisper of the warmongering, as promised by van Waesberghe, is to be heard.[58]

This pattern of patriotic publishing – of recasting relatively demure travel writing with political purpose – repeats itself in any number of turn-of-the-century narratives, including some of the more prominent voyages undertaken by the Republic. Witness the first printed account of a Dutch voyage to South America, Hendrik Ottsen's *Journael van de Voyagie na Rio de Plata,* published by Cornelis Claesz in 1603. In wooden prose charitably called "sailorly" by a modern editor, Ottsen recorded the singularly unspectacular results of a naval voyage sent between 1598 and 1601 to explore the coasts of West Africa and South America. Under the command of Laurens Bicker and with the backing of Amsterdam merchants, the expedition confidently weighed anchor within weeks of van Noort's Rotterdam-financed fleet and followed the latter by twelve days back into Texel. The results of the Amsterdammers, however, in no way approached those of the Rotterdammers. Ottsen and his companions discovered no new sea-lanes, settled no unknown lands, and made no significant inroads into the Spanish-American empire. Their efforts, in fact, nearly led to disaster. Over the course of their journey, the Spanish and Portuguese captured both of the fleet's ships and took hostages. The Dutch escaped with their lives thanks only to the fortuitous arrival of a Dutch privateer and the kindness of a Portuguese governor.[59]

None of this deterred the Amsterdam publisher, Cornelis Claesz, or muted the grandiose claims made for the voyage. What amounted to an ill-planned adventure of incompetence Claesz heralded as a historic moment of navigation and a "valuable lesson" of Habsburg duplicity. He offered the journal as a "mirror and example" for Dutch mariners and a warning to Spanish governors of the imminent unraveling of their American empire. The narrative would prove "very valuable to read," promised a publisher's blurb on the title page, and would demonstrate "the remarkably abominable cruelty of the Spanish, their scandalous abuse of trust, honor, and faith [in their efforts] to keep all other nations out of the New World (whether by force or craftiness)." Beneath this runs another caption, boldly pronounced, in capital italics:

NITIMUR IN VETITUM SEMPER CUPIMUS QUE NEGATA[60]

The reference is to Ovid, and, since Ottsen lacked a Latin education, this display of learning would have come most likely from the publisher, Claesz. It implied the sinful covetousness of Spain's monopoly abroad, while it suggestively emboldened the Dutch to hasten its fall. The author's own sober text was notably less encouraging. Ottsen omits altogether the story of the capture of the fleet's admiral ship off São Vicente (near São Paulo); though, in relating his own imprisonment by the governor of Bahia, he admits to the fairness of his Portuguese captors. The Portuguese governor treats his Dutch prisoner with exceptional respect. He mends Ottsen's broken arm and provides him with an attendant ("a woman to help me until I recuperated"). He further pardons his subject's fruitless effort to escape and ultimately shows mercy and releases him. Far from the chronicle of "Spanish" tyrannies that Claesz had advertised, the Ottsen journal ends up reading like a testament to the kindness of Habsburg governors abroad.[61]

Claesz also had a role in the promotion of van Linschoten's *Itinerario,* a work in which the publisher's hand is particularly visible. In more ways than one, the *Itinerario,* and particularly its section on the New World, reveal the combined efforts of author, publisher, and editor. The traveler-author, van Linschoten, had initially resisted the idea of publishing the notes and charts he had compiled overseas. The resourceful publisher, Claesz, recognized the value of these materials, however, and urged van Linschoten to prepare a manuscript as quickly as possible. Claesz pressured van Linschoten "very insistently," apparently, and rushed the *Rheysgheschrift* into print by 1595 (it comprised exclusively *roteiros*). The complete *Itinerario* came out a year later, following a pre-publication period of "relentless" encouragement, as the author put it. "Daily, without letting up," recalled van Linschoten, "they exhorted me to publish the memories and thoughts of my journey." Monetary incentives, of course, might account for such unusual haste. A 1594 notary record indicates that Claesz had entered into a contract with van Linschoten to their mutual profit; and it is not hard to imagine the publisher hurrying his author to realize that profit. Yet Claesz, who also published a large number of works pertaining to politics, history, and Calvinist theology, may have taken other factors into consideration in publishing what would become a landmark of patriotic geography.[62]

To expedite the publication of the American section of the *Itinerario,* Claesz enlisted the Enkhuizen physician, Bernardus Paludanus. Van

Linschoten, it should be emphasized, despite his role in creating the first
and in many ways most influential Dutch description of the New World,
never actually visited America. He undertook the *Beschryvinghe*, as the
separately titled American segment was known, chiefly at Claesz's behest. "The author together with the printer," van Linschoten announced
in a prefatory note, "have found it expedient to place here a small description of these lands [in America]."[63] The author, however, neglected
to mention that his description took form both collaboratively and derivatively: collaboratively, since Paludanus contributed liberally to the
writing of the *Beschryvinghe*; and derivatively, since both men based
their descriptions on earlier, printed accounts, many of which were
available from Claesz's own inventory. The sections on the Caribbean,
then, derived from the works of Martyr and Benzoni, both of which the
Padua-trained Paludanus would have reworked from the original Latin
or Italian. The description of Peru came directly from of Acosta's *Historia* – translated by van Linschoten and published by Claesz in 1598 – and
that of Mexico relied in part on Oviedo. For information on Brazil, the
authors turned to the accounts of Léry and Staden, which appeared in
1596 and 1598, respectively, in Claesz-published editions. Finally, for a
general overview of the *Conquista* in all its stages, the authors had at
their disposal the *Brevíssima relación* of Las Casas, freshly reissued in
1596 and, like the *Itinerario*, available from the prolific publishing house
of Claesz.[64]

Disparate sources and multiple authors produced a somewhat uneven account, and the *Beschryvinghe* lacks cohesion. What shape the
work does assume depends precisely on those sources cited and those
passages selected. Editorial decisions are evident throughout; and, in
general, the narrative varies according to the voice of the original narrator more than that of its nominal author, van Linschoten. Thus, the section on Brazil excels in describing the native Tupinamba, just as Léry's
original work had; and the exceptional attention paid to the *naturalia* of
Peru reflects Acosta's scholarly orientation. In recounting the conquest
of the West Indies and Central America, the narrative adopts a plainly
more polemical tone – anti-Spanish, that is – and here one detects the
voices of Martyr and Benzoni. The lords of the Lucayan Islands compare
to "kings of Bees, stewards and distributors of the common goods of the
country" – just as Martyr imagined them – and the island societies more
generally, enjoyed "a golden time . . . where neither this is mine, nor this
is thine, was even heard among them." Things take a dramatic turn for
the worse with the arrival of the Spaniards, as the case of Cartagena
vividly bears out. "When the Spaniards first came into that country," we
have on the authority of Benzoni (cited explicitly),

they found it full of fishermen, where at this time they can hardly find any remnant, which is not to be wondered at, for that not only in this province, but in all the other islands wherein the Spaniards have been, there are hardly any Indians left . . . because of their tyranny.

This passage and others concerned with the early *Conquista* betray the rhetorical mark of Las Casas. In its own way, that Dominican's brooding vision of America as an innocent paradise destroyed by Spanish tyrants casts its dark shadow over the whole of the work, and this Lascasian bent, in the end, lends the narrative what coherence it has.[65]

Bound and published together with the *Itinerario*, the *Beschryvinghe van de West Indien* presented itself as an authentic Dutch account of America. In truth, it consisted of an amalgam of earlier reports, more the product of its editors, Claesz and Paludanus, than its titular author, van Linschoten – more Americana than America. The New World issued from old texts: amassed and available from Claesz, translated and truncated by Paludanus, presented and authenticated by van Linschoten. The final product retained less of the freshness of van Linschoten's reports from the East and more of the familiarity of largely Lascasian accounts of the West. The *Beschryvinghe* in this sense stands out from the rest of the *Itinerario*; for it demonstrates little of its author's original engagement with wonder and youthful restlessness. Herein lies an irony. Texts incited Jan Huygen to travel, to explore the wonders of which he read, and to compose his own, marvel-filled description of the world. The text he constructed for America, however, relied not on his experience of travel and wonder, but on the texts of Claesz's inventory. His *Beschryvinghe*, in a sense, brought his itinerary full circle. The texts of his youth had engendered the seminal text of seventeenth-century Dutch geography.

Van Linschoten's case, together with the other first-generation travel authors, well illustrate the complexities of early Dutch geography. Much went into these first travel narratives, not all of it consistent. The pioneer travel writers of the Netherlands followed the routes of literary explorers before them in their anticipation of the wonders of foreign lands. Yet they – and more often their editors – followed earlier political literature, too, in their projection of Habsburg tyranny abroad. Even as Dutch travelers read and roamed in the spirit of the earliest discoverers from Genoa and Florence, their publishers plotted and printed in the manner of the rebel geographers of Antwerp and Amsterdam. Discrepancies riddle the earliest descriptions of America, suggesting the tensions between travelers and travelogues, authors and publishers, wonders and politics. On the one hand are the travelers, their interest in novelties, curiosity in nature, and contacts with often hostile natives. On the other hand are the publishers, their belief in foreign profits, imagination of Dutch successes, and presumption of sympathetic allies. Contrasts abound between that which voyagers chose to emphasize and that which publishers chose to advertise. In the end, though, perhaps little of this ambivalence mattered to the reader. The earliest Dutch reports from America promised a new world of wonders and riches, safeguarded by friendly, Habsburg-eschewing natives. They invited the reader to test those American waters so ably explored by the navigators of the Netherlands – whether for pleasure, profit, or patriotic politics.

V

If the revelation of Spanish tyranny did not overwhelm the earliest Dutch travelers to America, it continued to captivate the imagination of the diligent armchair travelers back home. Whatever the ambivalence of actual voyagers to the New World, the cultural geographers at work in the Netherlands show nothing but resolve in decrying the sins of Spain abroad. However "innocent" the reaction overseas, the reception of America back in the Republic remained pronouncedly polemical. This pertains both to those who beat the drum of anti-Habsburg invective in political pamphlets, patriotic histories, and didactic poems, which continued to flow unabated off Dutch presses in the early years of the century. And it applies to those who composed *actual* geographies: the architects of atlases, maps, and other fundamental works of geography, which likewise appeared in these years in ever-increasing numbers. The packaging of these materials, once again, is revealing. Works with a broader, often international audience tended to be milder in their assessment of the Spanish colonial record; works pitched more provincially, by contrast, attacked with polemical abandon the "tyranny" of Spain in America. Indeed, the most parochial of these texts made the most strenuous of cases against the Habsburg enemy. They reveal the steady progress of Lascasian rhetoric in the Republic despite uneventful reports from abroad – despite eyewitness accounts that gave scant evidence of suffering Indians and tyrannical Spaniards in America.

By the turn of the century, armchair travel had become assuredly more agreeable in the Netherlands. The Golden Age of Dutch geography had been well underway in fact by 1600, its origins lying in the flourishing community of scholars, printers, and engravers of antebellum Antwerp. In many ways, that community survived the Revolt intact. Abraham Ortelius, the leading mapmaker of his day, remained in the South, as did the eminent printer (and Ortelius's sometime partner), Christopher Plantijn. Yet the tide of events ultimately caught up with the cartographic trade, as shifting political and religious winds induced many to migrate to the North (including, for a brief period, Plantijn).[66] Changes underway were qualitative as well as quantitative, and here too early signs appeared in Antwerp. Following Ortelius's *Theatrum orbis terrarum* by only a few years came the poetic "epitome" of Peeter Heyns, a smaller-format work more cheaply priced and broadly pitched than the princely *Theatrum*. The immense popularity of Heyns's *Spieghel der werelt* (Mirror of the world) spawned multiple imitators: "pocket" atlases, which appealed to readers of modest means, while conveying a message somewhat differently calibrated than that found in the more extravagant folio atlases.[67]

The distinctions between the two genres had partly to do with the business of publishing, though political factors also played a role, and here the contrast between the practice of geography in the North and the South is suggestive. Compare the *Theatrum*, pride of Antwerp publishing, and a lesser known, reduced-size atlas printed in Middelburg in 1598, the *Caert-thresoor* (Map treasury) of Barent Langenes. From the moment it debuted in 1570, Ortelius's majestic "theater of the globe" played to admiring audiences across the Continent. By the year of its author's death (1598) the *Theatrum* had gone through some two dozen editions in four languages, with ten more editions and two more languages to appear by 1612. A large, learned, and in many instances lavish volume – it could be ordered on heavy paper, hand-colored, and luxuriously bound – the *Theatrum* gained quick entry into the leading staterooms and studies of Renaissance Europe. And with good reason: Ortelius's project began as a collaborative endeavor, with data collected from correspondents scattered throughout Europe's republic of letters. The end product, while adequately scholarly, is cautiously composed all the same and notably leery of engaging matters of potential controversy. It appealed to a cosmopolitan class of humanists and their patrons; it reached the desks of French and Spanish princes alike (the first edition is dedicated to Philip II). Ortelius, moreover, was most accommodating – most *politique* – when it came to revisions, taking care in these tumultuous years not to offend. (When Philip's close advisor, Cardinal Espinosa, noted the absence of his hometown hamlet, Martinmuñoz, Ortelius promptly engraved it into the next edition.) Work on the *Theatrum* predated the Revolt, and Ortelius survived the time of troubles largely unscathed. Alba himself promoted the new "Geographer of his Majesty" just before the iron duke retreated to Castile in 1573.[68]

The *Caert-thresoor* fell on the other side of the Revolt's shadow, and

Barent Langenes, the volume's otherwise obscure editor, compiled a text of an altogether different order. To start with, Langenes's geography was of a smaller order. Like Heyns' *Spieghel*, the *Caert-thresoor* was an *atlas minor*. It offered a tour of the world that could fit in one's pocket – and that would not drain one's pocket. "For but a rather modest price / Shall the buyer be made wise," pledged the introductory ode. It delivered on this promise with a lively combination of prose and poetry (here again following the *Spieghel*), intended not simply to inform but also "for the delight of the reader." The latter, as the printer proudly noted, came from "our small Holland," and the *Caert-thresoor* may differ most sharply from the *Theatrum* in that it was conceived and composed in the vernacular. It targeted not those European princes and scholars addressed by Ortelius, but those Dutch readers whom the preface unabashedly calls "the *volck*," a group that, though recent participants in the central events of European history, preferred a provincially formatted recitation of the same. If the *Theatrum* emphasized its worldliness, the *Caert-thresoor* accentuated its parochial perspective. It made the vast globe comprehensible to the new Republic.[69]

The *Caert-thresoor* offered a local geography of the world, which, *inter alia*, presented the version of the New World favored by "our small Holland." It rendered a provincial image derived from a familiar rhetoric – the old-fashioned specter of "Spanish tyranny in America" – and here Langenes distanced himself from the resolutely *politique* Ortelius. It was not that the Middelburg-based Langenes produced a somehow insular atlas. Modestly out-of-the way need not imply cartographically out-of-date, and the *Caert-thresoor*'s elegant maps in many cases improved on those of the *Theatrum*. The text, too, updated the history of geographic expansion – "all that was new," as the title page boasted – and in most respects it skillfully revised the narrative of both the *Theatrum* and the *Spieghel*.[70] The American materials, however, told a broadly traditional, and by this time knowingly familiar, tale of Spain's assault on the New World's "innocence." Before the arrival of the Habsburgs, Langenes observed, the Indians enjoyed "poetic" tranquillity, their ancient freedoms still intact "as in the first Golden World." Then came the Spanish conquistadors, "who descended on the . . . lands with singularly insatiable ambition and greed." Despite the uncommonly stubborn resistance with which the natives defended their liberties, the Spaniards prevailed and brought to a close America's Golden Age. The once thickly populated island of Cuba had been utterly destroyed, Langenes lamented; "it is now inhabited by the Spanish."[71]

Once again, Spain's colonial tyranny is deplored in the Netherlands – in this case, in the very prominent and very popular format of the *atlas minor.* The *Caert-thresoor* set a tone, in fact, that was echoed in other geographic texts of the early seventeenth century, most of them unabashedly patriotic. Jacobus Viverius, a physician by training and fiery pamphleteer by preference, practiced a brand of cartography every bit as partisan as that of Langenes. He also administered to his readers an immoderate dose of moral didacticism, conspicuously when it came to American geography. Viverius amassed his *Hand-boek, of Cort begrijp der caerten* (Handbook or short compendium of maps), as he pronounced in its opening pages, "so that the youth of the Netherlands can spend their spare time reading the fruits of wisdom."[72] That wisdom reduced the history of America to a simple lesson of good and evil: the wicked Spaniard had tyrannized, and the innocent Indian had suffered. In Yucatan, the invaders swept down on their prey "just like a wolf raids a herd of sheep," Viverius wrote. "The innocent natives were frozen from fright and fear." In Peru, the Pizarros "unrighteously" slaughtered millions, "so that [they] could reap the profit so dearly purchased in human blood." Such profit came not without a price, though, and Viverius ended his Peru section by alluding to the moral consequences that would follow from the misdeeds of Spain:

> The thirst for human blood and will to rage on cruelly
> Continues for a spell, and like a wolf fights fiercely
> Yet in the end he must stain the land with his own blood
> He who offends innocent blood, spills his own blood.[73]

Viverius also addressed the fate of the New World in an extensive poem, *Den spieghel van de Spaensche tyrannie* (The mirror of Spanish tyranny), published in 1601. In this plainly partisan work, American geography serves as the handmaid of patriotic history. The dark "mirror" of Spanish deeds in the New World reflects those committed in the Low Countries, and both instances of "tyranny" demonstrate patterns of Habsburg greed and godlessness. Both cases, too, are meant to instruct "freedom loving citizens [*burghers*]" of these supposedly allied nations. The poem comprises forty-seven stanzas of twelve-line couplets in which Viverius mourns Spanish violence, first, in America, and, second, in the Netherlands. As in his atlas, he emphasizes Spain's lupine expansionism (and though Viverius composed otherwise decent verse, his relentless wolf-metaphors wear quickly) and contrasts this with the "innocence" of their conquered subjects.

> So strong in the Spaniard burns the fire of greed,
> That he was not contented to sheer from the sheep
> The wool off the limb: he coveted flesh, blood, and fleece:
> And thus went to the Indies to continue his chase.

The chase led to gold, and Viverius describes how the Spanish hack, hang, beat, and burn the "poor" Americans into submission, forcing them to pay enormous ransoms of gold. Greed – what the poet calls "gold-worship," punning ceaselessly with the words *Goud* (gold) and *God* – raised Viverius's moralizing temper especially high.

> It is not for faith that these natives were murdered:
> But for the gold that rightly belongs to them.

Gold was the spice that flavored Viverius's anti-Spanish brew. To Lascasian formulae of Spanish violence, Viverius adds tales of conquistador avarice, and this permits him to shift his focus doubly quick from America to the Netherlands, where the Habsburgs had likewise pursued gold in the name of God. By the early 1600s, as Viverius reminded his readers, the forty-year-old war against Spain had drained the Republic of considerable wealth.[74]

Viverius's poetic arguments harked back directly to the political pamphleteering of the 1570s and 1580s, yet with a subtle twist. As had the rebels, Viverius made a moral argument against Spain's conquest of America. He revived the image of the rapacious, wolfish conquistador and of the guileless, sheep-like Indian. Unlike the rebels, though, he introduced an economic component into the argument by emphasizing the gold that fueled the *Conquista*. The natives of America lived in a golden age and simultaneously possessed great stores of gold – which they themselves innocently eschewed. Their gold, however, attracted the Spaniards and led to America's demise:

> The poor and naked natives have shown him such respect
> Brought gold in great abundance and fruit at his behest:
> But this barbaric Wolf would not be satisfied:
> He forced the poor folk with great pains for gold to mine.
> Oh for precious gold, men like beasts must suffer!
> Money-thirst and vain honor violates the innocent natives.

Blinded by gold and blind to God, the Spanish conquered, first, America and, next, the Netherlands. Viverius's poetic recitation of these events reaffirmed the moral vision of Spanish tyranny in America, while also suggesting an economic explanation of its causes.[75]

Most of Viverius's information on the New World derived from the by now best-selling work of Bartolomé de las Casas. "Las Casas," announced Viverius in his first stanza, "is the one whom we shall try to follow." This would not have proven terribly difficult, as the Dominican's traces were all too discernible in the Republic. The *Brevíssima relación* appeared in an astonishing twelve Dutch editions between 1596 and 1612, most of these under the title, "Mirror of Spanish Tyranny." (Eight editions were from the workshop of Cornelis Claesz, two from the cartographer Barent Langenes.) It also came in a variety of forms, pitched to a diverse and wide-ranging audience. The editions of 1596 and 1607 carried on their title-pages learned citations from Cicero's *Philippics* and the Book of Numbers. The 1609 edition, on the other hand, consisted of seventeen woodcuts, each accompanied by a simple, brief, and racy synopsis of an episode of Spanish tyranny. The 1611 edition, composed entirely in doggerel, included a panegyric to a local nobleman and a "Ballad" in praise of Dutch verse.[76]

Whether in poetry, prose, or pictures, the various editions of the *Mirror of Spanish Tyranny* made the same fundamental points regarding Spain, the Netherlands, and the New World. All versions expressed what the 1596 editor called "the murderous, scandalous and abominable facts" of the Spanish conquest of America. They all conveyed, too, "sympathy for our [American] neighbors," as one translator put it; and they portrayed the Indians as typically guileless and defenseless in the face of Spanish tyrannies. In these two respects, Dutch editors followed the themes set out in Las Casas's original narrative. (And Dutch translators did, too: Dutch prose translations match the original Spanish relatively faithfully.)[77] Yet they also improvised on, and reworked, the material to their own advantage. Dutch editors pointedly drew a connection between earlier tyrannies in America and recent events in the Low Countries, suggesting the lessons the former had for the latter. The author of the verse edition of 1611 confessed that reading of Habsburg barbarities in America reminded him of identical savageries suffered in the Netherlands. He resolved to set Las Casas's history into verse in order to teach his readers a lesson in patriotic history: "that it was preferable to love the Fatherland and patriotic liberties . . . than to suffer the sort of national ruination, eternal decline, and forfeiture of liberties that the blameless, innocent Americans have unjustly suffered."[78]

Finally, Dutch editors of Las Casas invariably emphasized the divine vengeance that would visit the Spanish tyrants in America. Fortune would change swiftly and justly in the New World, enabling the oppressed to throw off the yoke of their oppressors. "The furious frenzy perpetrated by the Spaniards in the West Indies is here illustrated," reads the opening caption of a 1609 Lascasian picture book. After describing a grisly selection of examples, the caption notes that "the day of judgment will demonstrate how much these cruelties displease our Savior."[79] The excerpt from Numbers cited on the title page of many editions warned that those who had spilled blood impiously would inevitably suffer bloodshed of their own. Cicero is cited to a similar effect:

"My opinion is that those who take pleasure in discord, the murder of citizens, and civil war deserve to be dispelled from the community of mankind and driven from the face of the earth." Whether this refers to civil wars and discord in the Netherlands or to events in the New World is not altogether clear. Nor does the citation establish just who would serve as God's instrument to oust the tyrants, be it from the New World or the Netherlands. The verse edition of 1611, published just after the rebels successfully exacted a truce from Spain, suggested that the Dutch patriots, the most "stouthearted and brave" of all Castile's enemies, had proven their mettle against tyrants. If God had employed the Dutch to expel the Habsburgs from the Netherlands, the reader might well wonder, might He not use the same instrument in America?[80]

VI

PIETER: Good day friend. What's up with all these pamphlets? What do they have to say?

PAUL: They're all sorts of published Remonstrances, Discourses, Dialogues, Dreams, and Riddles about the peace negotiations. . . .

PIETER: Pray, tell us something of their contents.

PAUL: Gladly. Reread the histories of the Indies and there you will see how the king of Spain befriended the natives (or so it seemed) with sweet promises. . . .[81]

The topic of America burst back into Dutch political discourse in the wake of truce negotiations with Spain in 1607–1609. Those who opposed settling with the enemy – the so-called war party – exploited the image of Spanish tyranny in America in order to discourage the prospect of a Spanish peace in the Netherlands. In the New World, so the argument ran, Spain had made unfaithful pledges of peace with the Indians only to disarm, entrap, and enslave them in the years that followed. A naïve peace with the Habsburgs promised an all too predictable future of slavery, and the pamphleteers appealed to the tragedy of the *Conquista* to dramatize their point. This time around, as opposed to earlier configurations of an innocent, victimized America, the publicists also resorted to the image of a wealthy, profitable America to make their case. The New World constituted "the sinews of Habsburg power," they proposed; to deprive Spain of its American strengths would substantially weaken its European operations. Spanish tyranny in America provided Spanish subsidies *from* America – monies that underwrote its despotic government in the Netherlands. The patriotic pamphleteers of

1607–1609 artfully weaved moral and economic images of the New World, accordingly, to create a seamless fabric in which to dress their opposition to Spain. Habsburg conquests in America demonstrated the extent of Spanish tyranny and argued against peace with the enemy. Habsburg profits *from* America exposed the source of Spanish power and argued for a new strategy of war. The Dutch must embark on a Western campaign, argued the patriots, both to save the Indians and to trade with the Indians. "America," thus formulated, represented both the sins and the sources of empire. Moral and economic factors both warranted a West Indian enterprise.

Attacks against Spanish tyranny heated up at precisely the moment in 1607 when the war in the Netherlands started to cool down. From the opening of that year, a cash-strapped Philip III began to reduce the resources allocated to Brussels and consider a more honorable – and cheaper – solution to the crisis of the Netherlands. By March 1607, the warring parties agreed to an eight-month cease fire. Signs of imminent peace, however, only alarmed certain quarters in the Republic – hardline Calvinists and certain merchant coteries – who stepped up their attacks on the already famous tyranny of the Castilian Crown. Tyranny came as naturally to Philip as laughter to a man, according to a proverb popular in these circles. The empire of his tyranny, it was submitted, stretched across the globe, from the East to the West Indies. So, too, did the king's dark reputation for cruelty, and a Dutch traveler to Muscovy around this time reported the nervous laughter among remote Tartars upon learning of the "implacable tyranny of the Spaniards."[82]

No one laughed in the Netherlands or West Indies where, as every schoolboy and schoolgirl knew, Spanish savageries had reached tragic proportions. "What trade do they practice?" the character in a popular *Dialogue* wonders of the servants of the king of Spain.

ANSWER: They are butchers.
QUESTION: Of what?
ANSWER: Of innocent souls. . . .[83]

This exchange refers to Spanish Jesuits ("hyenas") stationed in Antwerp, yet it could just as easily have applied to the West Indies. As in the earlier literature, authors conflated Lascasian language with patriotic rhetoric in a manner that transformed the dilemma of the Republic in the early 1600s to that facing the New World in the early sixteenth century. "The tears of widows and orphans" – here the publicists combined Las Casas's evocation of the "tears of the Indians" with his endless train of women and children – implored the States General to defy the king of Spain. Philip III swore falsely when he offered peace.

Had his Habsburg ancestors not made "sweet promises" to the caciques of the Caribbean, only to lure them to the gallows? Had the Spaniards not deceived certain native tribes under the pretense of religion, only to slaughter others in the name of the pope? A "cruel Phalaris" just like his father – here the publicists recycled epithets from Orange's *Apologie* – Philip III would "convert our fatherland into another Hispaniola," as one patriot put it, if the Republic's negotiators in Brussels "innocently" succumbed to his false assurances.[84]

Whether on the battlefield or at the negotiating table, Spanish tyrannies in the New World not only paralleled tyrannies in the Netherlands, but also bankrolled them in the important sense that the riches of the Indies supported the expansion of Spain. America, as the Dutch had claimed for years, held the key to understanding the character of Spain. America, as the pamphleteers began to stress by the early 1600s, also held the key to financing the empire of Spain. And whatever helped the Habsburg empire hindered the Dutch Republic. Spain's New World fortune, accordingly, became the object of attack, identified as the source of Habsburg expansion and the conflict in the Netherlands. "What intentions do they have, now that they have discovered the New World?" asks the set-up man in a *Dialogue concerning the peace negotiations.* "That they will subdue the Old, as well," retorts the clever answer-man. Others drew a connection more directly. "According to the judgment of all knowledgeable people," wrote one of those in the know,

it is considered certain that the war in this land will neither cease nor be ended as long as the king of Spain remains peaceably in possession of the kingdom of Portugal and that kingdom's East Indian dependencies; and of the West Indies, which have made him powerful and rich such that he can afford to continue the war here in the [Netherlands].[85]

The West Indies featured as the cornerstone of the Habsburg empire, the economic basis upon which Spanish tyrannies were built.[86] In this context, pamphleteers once again raised the specter of "universal monarchy," now identifying the West Indies as its financial capital – "from where [the king of Spain] receives an enormous yearly treasure of gold and silver." Some estimated the millions shipped to the coffers of Castile. Others projected the speed with which the American gold reached the Spanish paymaster in Brussels, who dispatched it directly to his henchmen in the field. "Will he ever have his full of war," asks a certain Lover of Patriotic Liberties, "or will he continually spend all of his West Indian treasure" to perpetuate the miseries of the Netherlands?[87]

In the wake of truce negotiations with a teetering Spanish monarchy – Philip III issued another decree of bankruptcy in November 1607 – the war party focused ever greater polemical attention on the New World, which now appeared as the golden crutch on which the king so dearly depended. In an uncharacteristically charming piece of propaganda, *An Old Man from Monnickendam*, America took the form, literally, of a magical golden staff over which a Spanish seignior and a Dutch sailor do battle. Discovered originally at the close of the fifteenth century, this golden staff had conferred upon the seignior "wonderful powers," with which he had managed "to mow down all the inhabitants of the Old and New World as if he were harvesting corn." The enchanting properties of this staff had further allowed the seignior to plunder the Netherlands and hoodwink its burghers into entering specious peace negotiations. The hero of this parable, a courageous and valiant sailor of the Netherlands, could alone resist the seignior's powers and duplicities. The sailor had recently gained a firm grip on the eastern end of the staff (the East Indies) and sent the seignior reeling from the shock. "*Basta Trahidor, al fuego Lutherano*," cried the flustered Spaniard, yet to no avail. All protestations, "sweet words," and poisonous bribes notwithstanding, the sailor still held tight, all the while inching his way towards the staff's western end. Though the narrator of this tale did not yet know the outcome of the struggle, he advised the sailors of the Netherlands to take heed and stand fast. The seignior, after all, had no "sea-feet." In due time, he would lose his balance and forfeit his golden staff completely.[88]

Indeed, persistence favored the intrepid Dutch sailors for two reasons. First, there was growing confidence in the imminent possibilities of a West Indies trade. Despite recent setbacks in the American waters experienced by Ottsen, van Noort, and others, the pamphleteers assumed that profits would soon come quickly from the West Indies, since they had poured in so quickly from the East. "The East Indian trade has already brought the United Provinces great profit and honor and caused the enemy great perdition," wrote a proponent of war. "Similar results can be expected from the West Indies as well."[89] Second, it was believed that Dutch actions in America would destabilize Habsburg efforts in the Netherlands. It was believed, as the *Monnickendam* parable insinuated, that the Dutch might easily knock the Spanish Crown off balance by attacking its western perimeters. The mere *news* of Dutch plans for the West Indies "touched [the King's] soul," according to a *Vision* recorded by Jacobus Willem Migoen. "Oh holy father, what worse news can there be!" exclaimed Philip III to the pope, according to Migoen's revelation. "I believe it is as if all the devils from Hell were released to assist them and ruin us." What unnerved the king alarmed his subjects, who feared a loss of shipping revenues should the Dutch enter American waters. "They fear that we would accomplish in the West Indies as much as we already have [in the East]," suggested a patriotic participant in a *Conversation concerning the peace negotiations.*

QUESTION: Would it [the West Indian trade] be important, and of great
                    consequence for them?
ANSWER: Indeed, enough to make the Spanish merchants sing the
                    Requiem Mass.[90]

For a variety of reasons, then, Dutch action in the New World appeared to serve the Republic's best interests. The riches of the Indies represented what one publicist termed "the sinews" of Spanish power. "If he [the king of Spain] were cut off from these, he would most surely collapse." Such a collapse would reduce Spanish power abroad, hasten its decline at home, and terminate its tyrannies in the Netherlands. "If you touche him in the Indies," observed the queen of England regarding her Spanish nemesis,

you touche the apple of his eye, for take away his treasure which is *nervus belli,* and which he hath almoste [all] oute of his west Indies, his olde bandes of souldiers will soone be dissolved, his purposes defeated, his power and stregthe diminished, his pride abated, and his tyranie utterly suppressed.[91]

If the West Indian trade was construed as the sinews of the Spanish empire, trade more generally was touted as the sinews of the Dutch Republic, "without which the land could not exist."[92] Establishing a Dutch foothold in the New World would simultaneously beat back the enemy and bolster the economy. For, as pamphleteers optimistically suggested, the Dutch might help themselves to the very riches of America of which they deprived Spain. The Republic would benefit two-fold:

> The West Indies can be
> The Netherlands' great score
> Reduce the enemy's strength
> And bring silver galore.

The war party therefore endorsed an American initiative for the "patriotic" advantages it promised. They campaigned vociferously for a protraction of the war against Spain with the belief that a New World strategy would bring the Dutch conflict to an advantageous conclusion. A good war beat a bad peace, claimed a popular slogan. It remained only to establish a West Indian trading company to achieve the most "patriotic" and profitable resolution possible to the already forty-year-old Revolt.[93]

The Dutch American enterprise was initially broached in the climate of such belligerent idealism. Not surprisingly, the same advocates of war with Spain were among the first to propose a Dutch West India Company (WIC), and they did so mindful of the polemical tropes of the day. Despite the obvious political and economic attraction of a colonial policy, that is to say, the earliest proponents of a WIC emphasized precisely the *moral* imperative of an American initiative: the Dutch responsibility to avenge Spanish tyrannies and liberate American "allies." Appeals to the fate of the "innocent Indians," which recalled earlier representations of America from the 1570s and 1580s, by no means displaced appeals to the political and economic advantages of a WIC. Yet idealistic arguments often prefaced more self-serving ones, as traditional images of New World "innocence" introduced hopeful plans for New World commerce. In the initial discussions of the WIC, the moral blends almost imperceptibly into the economic, as older representations of America give way to newer ones. "The establishment of a company for the West Indies," asserted one enthusiastic proponent in 1608, "[would] greatly benefit us and our allies." The natives of America, moreover, would forever be grateful

should we deliver them from their slavery and the tyranny of Spain and emancipate them. . . . And by this means we would not only deliver the whole of Christendom from the fear of insatiable Spanish ambition and [universal] monarchy, but also rescue the Indians and others from their [Spain's] tyranny.

The author hastened to note, meanwhile, the "mutual profits" the Indians and the Dutch would earn, and the great blow the empire of Spain would suffer. Another champion of the WIC pointedly dismissed suggestions of the Company's mercenary motives. An American initiative would be undertaken not to line investors' pockets but to save "the poor Indians' throat" from the ever-sharp knife of the Spanish king.[94]

Indeed, in the imagination of the WIC's supporters, the natives of America positively implored the Dutch to come. Calls for a Dutch West India Company sounded, as it were, from the Indians themselves, who solicited a Dutch-American alliance for the benefit of both parties. "The Spanish, by their horrible tyranny, have extirpated most of the natives from the [American] lands they have settled," observed the author of a treatise exploring "how necessary, beneficial, and profitable it is for the United Netherlands to maintain the freedom to trade with the West Indies." "They [the Indians] would undoubtedly gain more advantage from our presence than they now do [under the Spanish]," he assured. So oppressed were the natives "that they would sooner die than live under [Spanish] tyranny" and, presumably, they would happily exchange their present condition for "an alliance and friendship" with their Dutch saviors. In the Dutch, the native Americans "perceived a good opportunity to unburden themselves of the Spanish yoke," the author posited. The Indians also recognized a good opportunity for trade; and it was estimated that "within three to four years" the Dutch-American alliance could turn a hefty profit to the mutual satisfaction of both "nations."A Dutch West India Company, in short, promised piety with profits. The Company would avenge the tyranny of Spain – deliver, as one poet put it,

> God's dreadful wrath
> And righteous judgment, which He has sworn
> For the innocent blood unjustly spilled.

And the Company would challenge the hegemony of Spain – trade where none had profitably traded before. Moral and economic goals, conflated into a single, all-embracing argument, justified the foundation of a company to traffic in the New World. The Dutch West India Company would serve God, *patria,* and the innocent American.[95]

VII

The campaign for an American trading company found its most vigorous and eloquent advocate in Willem Usselincx, who, perhaps more than any other individual, left his mark on the early seventeenth-century Dutch image of America. A precocious merchant capitalist, Usselincx (1567–1647) pursued a West India Company from as early as 1600, and labored indefatigably for other New World ventures throughout his lengthy career as a trader, speculator, and polemicist.[96] To this end, he produced a steady stream of pamphlets that appeared in the period both before and after the Twelve Year Truce (1609–1621) and that articulated a vision at once lofty and lucrative for the Dutch in America. The Dutch WIC, as he conceived it, would redeem the native Americans from their yoke of servitude and unite with them against the tyranny of universal monarchism. At the same time, the Company would introduce the Indians to the fruits of free trade and circumvent with them the "tyranny" of Spanish monopolism. It would establish with the Indians a "natural alliance," as Usselincx termed it, based on the twin goals shared by the Indians and Dutch alike: freedom of conscience and unfettered commerce. So, at least, Usselincx imagined, and in so doing he brilliantly bridged the gap between the moral indignation of sixteenth-century rebels, for whom America represented innocence betrayed, and the economic anticipation of seventeenth-century merchants, for whom America promised the profits of trade. To Usselincx, the two went hand-in-hand, since the free traffic of both goods and beliefs depended on the grace of God rather than the will of Spain.

Such political and religious perspectives developed from a background often construed as typically Calvinist and patriotic.[97] Born in Antwerp in 1567 – the very year that Alba descended on the Netherlands – Usselincx grew up in a merchant family of middling means and very likely of the Reformed faith. As was the fashion among sons of his class and profession, he spent his apprenticed years in Spain (as had van Linschoten), where he observed first-hand the harvests of American trade. (Years later he would recall seeing the rich cargoes annually unloaded in Seville.) By 1591, Usselincx returned to the Low Countries, yet, like many Reformed Antwerpers, he opted for the newly won freedom of the northern provinces, settling in the town of Middelburg. There he quickly established himself as a relatively prosperous merchant, while gaining, too, a reputation as a "hot Gospeller" – particularly inflammatory on the subject of Spain and papistry. He also fell in with a crowd of like-minded merchants, many of them emigrants from the South, and of geographers, including the leading authority on navigation (and himself a fiery *predikant*), Petrus Plancius.[98]

During the heady years of economic expansion at the turn of the century, investment opportunities and investors' money came and went quickly, and Usselincx lost more than his share. The Beemster land reclamation project (in Holland) famously drained him of 130,000 florins, yet Usselincx also speculated in a variety of overseas ventures that cost him almost as dearly. Of all these projects, none occupied his attention more than the proposed West India Company, in which he invested enormous amounts of time and energy (though surprisingly little money). From the earliest years of the seventeenth century, Usselincx lobbied tirelessly, in pamphlets as well as official requests, for a company that would traffic, colonize, and wage war in America. The ultimate establishment of the Dutch WIC in 1621 ended up as one of Usselincx's most bitter and ironic defeats; for the Company ignored almost completely the proposals and strategies he had set forth and took a final form utterly to his disliking. To make matters worse, the WIC offered Usselincx very little by way of compensation for his efforts, which left him, by the early 1620s, out of money and patrons.[99] Disappointed, he left the Netherlands in 1623 and journeyed for the next two decades among the courts of Northern Europe – Denmark, Sweden, Prussia, the Baltics – in an effort to promote his ideas for an American company. He met with little success: either in his sojourns abroad or in his regular attempts to solicit money from the States General for his "rightful share" in the profits by now enjoyed by the Dutch WIC. In a number of his appeals to The Hague, Usselincx made telling (and touching) reference to the fate of the older, forlorn Christopher Columbus, with whom he implied a parallel might be drawn. The States disagreed. Usselincx died in 1647 at the age of eighty, less than a year before the Republic concluded its war with Spain. His long and difficult life, as it turned out, had spanned the entire Eighty Years' War.[100]

The checkered career of Usselincx and single-minded fervor of his pursuits have tended to guide historians' assessment of his writings and his contribution to the genesis of the WIC. "A South Netherlander," intoned Catharina Ligtenberg, vaguely dismissively, in her early twentieth-century biography that remains the standard. By this, the Holland-born historian meant to ascribe to the Antwerp-born merchant the Calvinist "chauvinism" and zealous anti-Hispanism she associated with the emigrant generation of 1585–1610. In Usselincx's plans for a WIC she construed a "war instrument" designed to battle Spain in America while generating monies for the reconquest of the (South) Netherlands. The nineteenth-century American historian, J. Franklin Jameson, emphasized, much as did Motley, Usselincx's "intense hatred of Spaniards and Catholics"; and, like Ligtenberg, he saw the WIC as a primarily political (and thus religious) venture. (Designs for colonization, Ligtenberg and Jameson understood, were meant to benefit Usselincx's southern coreligionists, who required a safe haven until their provinces might be won back from the Habsburgs.)[101] More recently, historians have inclined to focus less on Usselincx's political point of departure in the South than on his economic point of termination in the North: bankruptcy. Grave financial problems forced Usselincx to devise a means to recoup his losses. The WIC, according to this view, was conceived chiefly as a profit-seeking operation to which political and religious goals took a back seat.[102]

Whether for profit or politics, Usselincx sought, by all measures, to promote *patria* or at least those patriotic shareholders, colonists and coreligionists who supported his project. Yet he also strove, or at least claimed to strive, for those most-favored allies of *patria*, the natives of America, to whose innocent cries for succor he purported to respond. It is difficult to determine just how seriously Usselincx took the rhetoric of "America" and what priority he gave to the moral obligations of a West India Company. It is all too apparent, however, just how well such rhetoric served his purpose and how effectively he enlisted the not quite exhausted topos of the innocent American ally. Images of marauding conquistadors and suffering natives retained all their vitality in Usselincx's portrait of the New World. A child of the rebel party, he couched his arguments, both political and economic, in terms of moral missions and ideological imperatives. His program for the West Indies emphasized those responsibilities, inherited by the liberated provinces of the North, toward their brethren in the South and distant West. When all was said and done – when all the military and monetary benefits of West Indian traffic had been accounted for – Usselincx adds the fate of the innocent Indians into his calculus of a Dutch West India Company.

Usselincx broached the topic of the West Indies originally in the context of the peace negotiations and as part of the broader political debate on the war with Spain.[103] A West India Company provided, most practically, an additional means by which to attack Spain. A successful Dutch campaign in the Atlantic and Caribbean – and Usselincx's contemporaries had every confidence in the naval ability of their heroic *Geuzen* – would deprive the king of his most valuable resources, the riches of America. Usselincx likened the gold of the Indies to the mortar that bonded the Spanish empire. If the Dutch could divest the king of his imperial cement, the structure of his universal monarchy "would come tumbling down like the walls of Jericho." By striking the enemy on its most western flank, moreover, the Dutch could deflect troops away from the Netherlands and force the Spanish to wage a battle within their own domain. "With minimal expense and danger," predicted Usselincx, "[and] with God's help, we will be able to divert the war from these lands." The WIC would transfer the "torch of battle" and the fire of destruction "into the very house of the enemy," Usselincx promised. The Company might thus spare the Netherlands any further hardships of war.[104]

As the Spanish empire burned to the ground none would warm their hands by its flames more gleefully than the natives of America.[105] While Usselincx hardly needed to remind his readers of the fate of the Indies, he did, and he did so often, sermonizing also on the Dutch responsibility to protect their American allies. "The pitiless slaughter of over twenty million innocent Indians who did [Spain] no harm," quotes Usselincx directly from Las Casas, demanded "God's righteous judgment." The fellow-suffering Dutch represented the most sensible choice, and a WIC embodied the most perfect instrument, to carry out the Lord's holy vengeance. This was less an opportunity than an obligation, Usselincx insisted, born of the pledges of fidelity made by the rebels to their American brothers-in-arms. "Our friends and our allies will lose all faith in us, if they see that we, but for the sake of a specious title [the Truce] abandon our own inhabitants and the allied Indians who have been so faithful and done us such good service." The Dutch could not afford to forsake their American allies; for "the Indians would be cruelly exterminated by the [king of Spain], and become our arch-enemies, since we will have handed them over (our alliance with them notwithstanding) to the butcher's block." The damage caused by inaction, concluded Usselincx, would be "irreparable." It would dishonor the Dutch and it would disoblige the Indians.[106]

Usselincx also worried about the faith of the Indians in God and their exposure to the impieties of papistry. In his earliest published proposal for a WIC, he urged his countrymen to assume their evangelical duties in America before it became too late. Though the Indians had started off innocently enough, many had fallen precipitously, after years of Spanish-Catholic government, into the abyss of sin. A Dutch West India Company could – *should* – reverse that trend and save the souls of the Indians from the tyrannies of Spain and Rome. "Everyone can well imagine also what great advantage these lands will have if we might plant colonies in the West Indies," Usselincx concluded in a work of 1608. "[T]he holy Gospel might be spread among the blind heathen and the Church of God" – by which Usselincx meant the Reformed Church – "might be propagated, . . . which is a fine opportunity we dare not pass up."[107] The Dutch needed otherwise to rise to their responsibilities and "enlighten" the Indians, as Usselincx delicately put it. With the assistance of a WIC, he proposed, the Americans might become "somewhat more civil [*wat borghelijcker*]." Usselincx's blueprints for the WIC outline a program of assistance that includes a steady supply of clothing for the naked Indians and an offering of other fine products of (Dutch) civilization. Such was the duty of the Dutch, preached Usselincx. Such, too, was the desire of the Indians, projected Usselincx, noting the great yearning among the natives for a company that might deliver the freedom, Calvinism, and civilization they so desperately desired.[108]

The Indians and the Indies would recompense the Dutch handsomely for all this, and Usselincx did not neglect to describe the economic benefits a Dutch WIC would bring. Trade with the New World promised a rich assortment of natural products for export: vast quantities of gold and silver, precious stones and pearls, costly spices such as pepper and ginger (Usselincx made much of the latter), exotic brazilwoods and hides, tobacco and cotton, sugar and salt. The Indians, for their part, would avidly consume Dutch manufactured products – especially the cloths now produced in Holland – and in this way American trade would nurture expanding Dutch industries. The rise of trans-Atlantic commerce would also lend a boost to Dutch maritime industries. Usselincx anticipated a boom in shipbuilding and an expansion of employment opportunities in ancillary economic sectors. Shipwrights, ship chandlers, and dock workers stood to gain, no less than merchants,

Figure 24. Claes Jansz Visscher and Pieter Bast, *Profile of Amsterdam from the IJ (Allegory on the Prosperity of Amsterdam)*, 1611 (engraving). Amsterdam, Rijksprentenkabinet (see note 109).

manufacturers, and investors. Finally, the Company would establish overseas colonies that would provide further employment opportunities, expanding markets for Dutch goods, and a steady supply of American-produced commodities. A committed colonialist, Usselincx envisioned a mutually profitable relationship between overseas settlements and Dutch metropolises, with raw materials and manufactured goods, jobs and labor, exchanged to the benefit of all (fig. 24).[109]

Concern with profits as such, however, did not principally fuel the drive for a Dutch West India Company. The very *freedom* to trade was, in and of itself, a fundamental and sacred right for which Usselincx piously campaigned, and he was at pains in his early writings to articulate a godly rationale for the ostensibly economic components of his agenda. Trade, like all other liberties for which the Dutch had struggled, demanded staunch defenders. The West India Company, as Usselincx perceived it, could fulfill a patriotic role by both safeguarding the Republic's rights of commerce and challenging the Habsburgs' claims of hegemony. Spain's stated plans to restrict access to the Indies, wrote Usselincx in a fiery attack on the peace negotiations, "was an absurdity and injustice," a *moral* affront to patriotic liberties. By obstructing Dutch traffic in the Indies, Philip III "seeks in effect to bring us under the utmost slavery." Usselincx would have it otherwise, and he cited "God, Nature, and the Law of Nations [*Iure gentium*]" to make his point. "By the law of man and the law of nations," wrote Usselincx in anticipation of Grotius's *Mare liberum* (1609), "trade is free for all; and no one in the world has dominion over any particular region." The Dutch had every right – nay, obligation – to defend their natural privileges to the death, and trade was no exception. As the Netherlands had struggled for forty years to maintain their religious and political liberties, Usselincx goaded them to continue for forty more if their economic liberties were threatened. "Together with religion and traditional privileges for which it has been necessary to sacrifice," Usselincx wrote, "trade, shipping, commerce, and industry likewise require every available means for their maintenance." A Dutch West Indian Company would stand firmly on the principled ground of free trade, and Usselincx rallied his countrymen to its support.[110]

Free trade, and especially trade between the Netherlands and the West Indies, would benefit the various allies of the Dutch, as well. A displaced Antwerper, Usselincx harbored particular sympathy for those compatriots left under Habsburg rule in the South. In the WIC, he foresaw a means of providing assistance and haven for the impoverished victims of war; of funneling profits into the economies of the devastated towns and countryside; and of ultimately liberating the South from the yoke of Spanish tyranny. "Some of us have seen the pitiful tragedies of the Netherlands in the time of the duke of Alva . . . the sea full of miseries caused by the enemies' arms," reflected Usselincx in a promotional pamphlet. "We are sincerely moved by the oppressed state of the conquered Netherlands, our dear brethren, who will be treated not a jot better than the natives of the West Indies were."[111] The WIC would ameliorate this suffering in a number of specific ways. It would create job opportunities in the Republic, which the poor and unemployed of the South might fill. It would provide a colonial haven in the New World, to which the religiously persecuted might immigrate. (The first arrivals in New Netherland consisted in fact of Walloon settlers.) And it would subsidize ships and troops, which could then be deployed for the eventual reconquest of the South. A West India Company, in this way, had an important humanitarian role to play in the emancipation of the South. For the sake of his oppressed brethren in the Habsburg Netherlands, Usselincx called for an American trading company.

Finally, the West India Company would improve the welfare of that other notable Dutch ally, the native American. The Indians, no less than the Dutch, deserved the freedom to trade without restriction; they too, in Usselincx's estimation, would flourish under free-market conditions. The introduction of Dutch traffic in the West Indies would provide them not only with political and religious alternatives to the tyranny of Spain. It would also offer them better merchandise, better value, and better incentives to work, earn, and consume. The Dutch would give the Americans a better deal, contended Usselincx in perfect earnestness, "because we can price all manner of manufactured goods, cent for cent, better than the Spanish." The Indians, he assured, preferred Dutch merchandise and Dutch prices, and they therefore sought out Dutch ships in the region. It was incumbent upon the Republic to meet the natives' needs and to ensure that their cries did not go unanswered. Free trade, naturally, promised the Dutch advantages no less than it did the Americans, yet this came down to an issue of prerogatives as much as price. By depriving the natives of free trade, the Habsburgs had deprived the Indians of their God-given right to commerce. As he had in the Netherlands, the king of Spain had tyrannized the inhabitants of America economically no less than politically. The Dutch allies of the Indians assumed an obligation, then, to emancipate the economically abused, "innocent" Indians. The creation of a Dutch West India Company, Usselincx argued, would liberate the commercially constrained Americans. The New World compelled the Republic, for moral reasons no less than economic, to come to the aid of its oppressed allies.[112]

Moral and religious exigencies, every bit as much as political and economic expediencies, impressed upon Usselincx the urgency of a Dutch WIC. He conveyed this forcefully to the States General in the years 1607–1608 and again in the early 1620s with the feverish energy and fiery rhetoric of the Old Testament prophets that he so readily quoted. The patriotic battle against Spain was linked with the establishment of the WIC, and the States were exhorted to maintain their stamina and forgo a dubious truce. Had the rebels waged a pious battle against the Tenth Penny, only so their descendants might forfeit two-thirds of the world? demanded Usselincx of the States, with reference to proposed Spanish restrictions on the Indies. "Our forefathers have undertaken grievous struggles and wars in the past to maintain shipping and traffic of far less significance," he reminded his readers. "Would we now subject ourselves to an injunction so tyrannical as to bar us from traffic with all other nations?" The struggle for freedom, in the Netherlands as in the New World, had cost too much blood to be abandoned for the sake of a restrictive peace. Better a good war than the moral laxity of a flawed peace – *"an evil deceitful peace"* – he thundered in a pamphlet that the States wisely tried to ban. The pursuit of an American program of war, trade, and colonization became for Usselincx nothing less than a crusade, a program "that God has blessed with especial prosperity." The States could ill-afford to ignore such an opportunity, "in the general interest of Christendom." A Dutch West India Company was a right, a duty, a blessing – in short, a manifest destiny that could brook no delay.[113]

The writings of Willem Usselincx, together with other contemporary reflections on the WIC, mark a crucial shift in the Dutch perception of the New World. America now assumed a more pronounced economic presence within the imagination of the political pamphleteers – as it did among the printers, engravers, geographers, and travel writers active at the turn of the seventeenth century. This change came gradually and gracefully, and the new sensibilities by no means supplanted earlier notions of America as a paradigm of Spanish tyranny. Usselincx, better than anyone else, demonstrated how older topoi of America might coexist with newer themes, how images of New World pastoralism and conquistador violence might help usher in a campaign for Dutch commerce. Allusions to "tyranny" and "innocence" still in fact permeated discussions of the New World. Now, however, economic tyranny – the restriction of free trade – loomed as largely as the more familiar menace of political tyranny – the restriction of privileges and religion. Spain, in this role, still deprived the innocent Indians of their rights; yet it was the right to free trade, as much as anything else, that now excited the passion of the Dutch merchant-warrior. On the other hand, representations of America's riches never appeared wholly mercenary. Trade with the Indians, it was hoped, would simultaneously liberate the Indians. It would grant the natives an alternative to the Habsburg yoke, the Romish church, and the Spanish monopoly. It would save souls no less than *reales*. The older image of America, formulated by the rebels to meet the imperatives of political and confessional freedoms, evolved in this way into a newer image, constructed by merchants with their eye on markets and colonial expansion. The political, thus, ceded graciously to the economic. In all cases, the fascination with America still retained its remarkable grip on the imagination of the Dutch.

CHAPTER 4

A Loss of Innocence

Of all the wonderful things that have been done in our age by these United Provinces – for the support of the True Religion, for the defense of our Freedoms, for the resistance to the king of Spain – I have found the most remarkable to be the foundation of the Dutch West India Company. For the Company has implemented its plans and executed its programs so successfully, and with so few forces and so little burden to the Commonwealth, and with the combined resources of so few subjects of this land, that the whole world has marveled at its success; and the pride of the Spanish has been made to yield. One can now plainly see how to harm this powerful enemy with his own resources, and how to relieve him of his American treasures, with which he has for so many years plagued and disturbed the whole of Christendom. I thought therefore that these wonderful deeds of the West India Company deserved to be recorded. . . .

Joannes de Laet, *Historie, ofte Iaerlyck verhael van de verrichtinghen der Geoctroyeerde West-Indische Compagnie* (Leien, 1644), 3

I

THE second half of the Eighty Years' War began, paradoxically, with a period of peace. After four decades of relentless hostilities and exhausting campaigns, the Spanish Crown and Dutch Republic agreed to what would become the Twelve Year Truce, signed on 9 April 1609. This brought to a standstill a struggle already perceived by contemporaries in epic dimensions. The loss of thousands of lives, no less than millions of ducats, had convinced the warring parties to come to terms, which they finally did by recognizing the status quo. Spain remained in control of the South, the Republic won its rights to the North, and each side retained its possessions in the Indies – *uti possidetis*. All things considered, the Republic fared rather well. Though it had been nowhere stated explicitly, the king had effectively conceded the political and religious independence of the rebels. By acknowledging their rights in matters of faith and law, Philip III and his principal minister, the duke of Lerma, had granted the United Provinces de facto sovereignty – no mean feat for upstart "heretics." In return, the States General under the guidance of the advocate of Holland, Johan van Oldenbarnevelt, had acquiesced to those borders that now separated the United Provinces from their "Hispanicized" cousins to the south and thus yielded to the all but certain cleavage of the Netherlands. The Republic also agreed to halt its assault on the Habsburg empire abroad, and this dealt a severe blow to growing colonial interests – in particular, plans for a Dutch West India Company. These concessions, though, seemed acceptable to the majority, who welcomed the promise of reduced taxes and increased security. The Truce, it was believed, would grant relief from the debilitating Spanish embargoes and respite from the perennial battle. Above all, the Twelve Year Truce signaled a victorious conclusion to the Dutch Revolt, as the first half of the Eighty Years' War could now properly be called, and this was cause for national thanksgiving.[1]

Celebrations turned out to be short-lived, however. After forty years of conflict with an external enemy (whether that enemy was the king of Spain, as the rebels had always insinuated, or the Habsburg-appointed officials in Brussels, as more disinterested observers had suggested), there now followed twelve tumultuous years (1609–1621) of internal discord, a situation that dangerously imploded in the final years of the Truce. In 1609, opponents of the settlement had represented a minority: the *stadhouder* Maurits and his military entourage, militantly orthodox Calvinists, and select merchant circles, especially in Zeeland and Amsterdam, with a vested interest in a protracted war. Over the course of the Truce, however, the *contra-Trevisten* rallied opposition around a series of volatile religious, political, and economic issues that ultimately convinced the majority of factions to return to arms. At the eye of this domestic storm swirled an arcane debate over the doctrine of predestination carried on by two professors of theology at Leiden, one of whom, Franciscus Gomarus, took a severely orthodox view of Calvin's concept of grace, while the other, Jacobus Arminius, allowed for a more flexible interpretation. Following a series of contentious confrontations between the divines, matters escalated in 1610 when supporters of the heterodox position lodged a formal remonstrance with the States of Holland to elaborate their position and request protection from their increasingly hostile opponents. The "Remonstrants," as Arminius's followers came to be called, thus invited the state to resolve a matter of the church. Such Erastianism naturally appealed to the regents and other moderates among the urban (and especially Holland) patriciate. It incensed the Gomarists, though, who responded with a sharply worded "contra-remonstrance" against the "free thinkers," and a demand that questions of doctrine be left exclusively to the discretion of the church. Olden-barnevelt disagreed. Mindful of the radical, strong-willed behavior of *predikanten* of earlier years, the advocate of Holland took the precautionary step in 1614 of prohibiting "that those lofty disputations, which give rise . . . to preposterous deductions and extremities, should be brought into the open, or into the pulpit, or otherwise before the commonalty." The state, in other words, would legislate the church's doctrinal obedience.[2]

What had begun as an academic debate over theology had now transformed into an awkward affair of state. The regents' involvement in the controversy not only provoked the fulminations of the Gomarists – by now in command of a majority of the Reformed clergy and a growing portion of the burghers. It also functioned as a magnet for a variety of other grievances – provincial jealousies directed at Holland, economic frustrations generated by the Truce, social tensions ignored since the Revolt – and had the effect of polarizing public opinion on issues of faith, government, and war. The "meddlesome" politics of the regents antagonized the church and galvanized opposition to the States of Holland in general and Oldenbarnevelt in particular. Maurits, reluctant at first to join the fray (he claimed not to know "whether predestination looked green or blue"), now seized the opportunity to thwart his rival Oldenbarnevelt and entered into an unholy alliance with the militant Calvinists. Against the bleak backdrop of economic recession, under the populist banner of *"Spanje of Oranje!"* (Spain or the House of Orange!), and with the solid support of the army, the *stadhouder* staged a coup. Beginning in January of 1618, Maurits purged the municipal councils of the inland provinces (notably Utrecht) of their Remonstrant magistrates in favor of their Contra-Remonstrant rivals. He simultaneously lent support to the latter's calls for a national synod that would resolve the burning religious questions of the day – to the satisfaction of the orthodox. In August, the *stadhouder* arrested the advocate and his chief political allies in Holland. He then toured that province's "recalcitrant" towns, ejecting all magistrates that had sided with Oldenbarnevelt. By November, a national synod finally convened in Dordrecht, predictably dominated by the firmly entrenched Contra-Remonstrants. The party of the orthodox voted to oust their enemies from the Dutch Reformed Church and banish any political patrons of Remonstrantism. Most dramatically, the synod condemned Oldenbarnevelt to death and sentenced his protégé, the brilliant young jurist Hugo Grotius, to life imprisonment.[3]

All of this spelled a clear triumph for the war party. The dramatic success of Maurits indicates just how far sentiment had shifted over the course of the Truce. The inflammatory sloganeering of the *stadhouder*, though, also suggests just how dangerously tensions had risen as the Truce was set to expire. The fear of Spain and the threat of internal dissent cast a doubly chilling shadow over public deliberations of the period 1618–1621. Such anxieties were easily exploited by the *contra-Trevisten* in collaboration with their Gomarist allies (the two factions overlapped considerably), who castigated Oldenbarnevelt and his supporters as *Spaansgezind* – partial toward Spain. The religious discord, it was alleged, had resulted from a sinister plot by Philip III and his "Machiavellian" ministers. Spain had devised the Truce to lull the Republic into complacency, and the advocate had allowed himself to be manipulated as a "tool" of Habsburg machinations. The party of Oldenbarnevelt was also blamed for the Republic's economic grievances, something the *contra-Trevisten* had no trouble impressing upon the riotous crowds of artisans that cheered Maurits's entourage in Haarlem, Gouda, and Leiden. As Usselincx had predicted, the industrial towns of Holland and commercial ports of Zeeland now languished from the competition of a resuscitated Brabant and Flanders. Merchants in Zeeland and above all Amsterdam renewed their calls for an expansion of overseas traffic, a demand Oldenbarnevelt had consistently managed to frustrate. The *stadhouder's* purges, however, had now installed a majority of magistrates in favor of trade and war. When the Truce expired in April of 1621, the States General promptly reinstated economic measures meant to pressure Spain, its overseas colonies, and the Spanish Netherlands. The Republic returned to arms by the following August.[4]

II

The resumption of war breathed new life into plans for a Dutch West India Company (WIC). Peace with the Habsburgs had always boded badly for engagement in America, and the cease-fire brokered in the early seventeenth century virtually stifled the original clamoring of the colonialists. The terms of the Truce had, in fact, explicitly forbidden Dutch interference with Spanish trade in the West Indies; and the cautious States of Holland went so far, in a decree of 27 August 1608, as to silence the pamphlet campaign waged by Usselincx and his colonialist allies.[5] These measures effectively shelved all prior proposals for, and even consideration of, a WIC. Indeed, very little public discussion of America took place during the first two-thirds of the Truce when Oldenbarnevelt and the *Trevisten* retained control of policy. Over the course of this period, references to Indian "allies" and Spanish "tyrannies" largely disappeared from Dutch political discourse, since the Republic, presumably, was neither at war with Spain nor in search of allies. (Merchants of Zeeland and Amsterdam did carry out small-scale expeditions to the Wild Coast and Manhattan Island – where the Spanish presence was negligible – in the early years of the Truce; yet they took care to minimize the publicity surrounding these voyages.)[6] The change of political climate around 1618–1619, though, revivified the moribund programs of the Atlantic colonialists. The *contra-Treviste* magistrates looked favorably on all opportunities to escalate the war against Spain and especially those that promised profits. With the call to arms, then, came the call for an expanded program of assault against Spain's world-wide empire, including America. The rising rhetoric of the war party resounded with the cry for battle in, traffic to, and alliance with America.

Almost as if by instinct, publishers and pamphleteers reverted to familiar declamations of Spanish "tyranny" in America. This meant, first of all, the republication of Las Casas after a nearly decade-long hiatus. Copies of the *Spiegel der Spaensche tyrannye* (Mirror of Spanish tyranny) flooded the market around the expiration of the Truce – an astonishing five editions appeared in 1620 alone – and reminded Dutch readers of Spain's horrendous record abroad. The publishers of these editions drew an unambiguous connection between events in the New World and events in the Netherlands. One offered his work to "all those who must risk their lives and property to such a blood-thirsty enemy," and warned his readers that they could expect still worse in years to come should the Republic falter in its conflict against Spain. For "if [the Spanish] have done all this to the poor, wretched, unarmed people [of America]," he reasoned, "what will they do to us, whom they have already condemned for *crimen laesea majestatis* and as heretics with whom they need not keep faith?" Beginning in 1620, moreover, editions of the *Spiegel* commonly combined Las Casas's history of the *Conquista* with a popular history of the Revolt – the latter appropriately retitled, in Lascasian fashion, *Spiegel der Spaensche tyrannye gheschiet in Nederland* (Mirror of Spanish tyranny committed in the Netherlands). This double-mirror of Spanish tyranny, as it were, carried a title page of twin atrocities that displayed matching vignettes of Habsburg despots (figs. 25 and 26). On the right side of the page stands the duke of Alba, decorated with assorted Dutch coats of arms and commanding scenes of execution and slaughter. On the left, wearing escutcheons emblazoned with the names of New World empires, stands Don Juan of Austria amidst images of conquistadors and brutalized Indians. In the center, above it all, lords the king of Spain, who peers out severely at his Dutch enemies, challenging them, one imagines, to contemplate his manifold tyrannies.[7]

The pamphlets composed in the aftermath of the Truce (1621–1624)

Figure 25. Title page from *Den Spiegel der Spaensche tyranny geschiet in West-Indien* (Amsterdam, 1620). Universiteitsbibiliotheek Amsterdam.

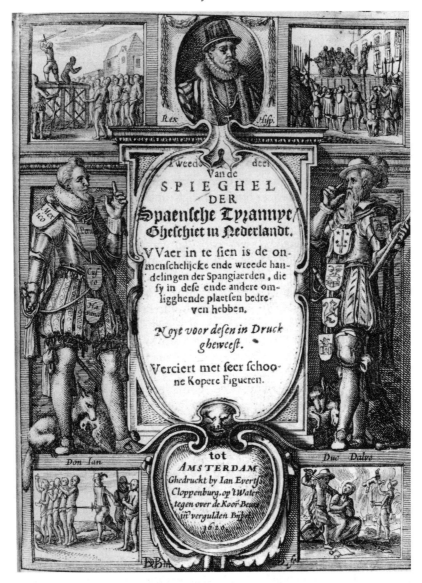

Figure 26. Title page from *Den Spieghel der Spaensche tyrannye gheschiet in Nederlandt* (Amsterdam, 1620). Universiteitsbibiliotheek Amsterdam.

utilized the image of America to goad the Republic into battle: to remind readers of the urgency of war, yet also to impress upon them the potential benefits of war. The vermilion blood "of the innocent Indians," no less theatrical in the early 1620s than it had been in the late sixteenth century, once again admonished the Dutch to turn back the "tyrannical and murderous" legions of Philip. The horrific histories of the *Conquista*, no less poignant forty years after their original (Dutch) publication, now alerted the "free" Netherlands to distrust all offers of peace tendered by the perfidious Spaniard. Thus, the author of a *Trumpet of war, or Warning to the United Netherlands* "blasted" the Dutch from their peacetime reverie with vivid recollections of Spanish atrocities in the New World. If the Republic relented to Spain, the "trumpeter" averred, Philip III would "send thousands of souls into misery, exile, and his [Peruvian] silver mines," where the Dutch would forever toil as the Indians now did. And if peace was to be eschewed, war was to be embraced. Only in battle, argued the belligerents, could the Republic escape the fate of the Indies. Or more optimistically: only in battle would the foundations of the young Republic, still wobbly from the repercussions of the Truce, be strengthened. Under the pressure of war, the Reformed religion would flourish, the revived economy would expand, and the true patriot would thrive, "in readiness, good watch and ward." "War," concluded one particularly zealous minister of the Gospel, "is a blessing."[8]

Only in battle could the Dutch *attain* the Indies, and that too registered among the patriots as a divine benefaction. In war the Dutch would win the Indies, and the Indies would ultimately win the war, reasoned the pamphleteers with elegant sophistry. America offered simultaneously the long-awaited salvation of the Dutch and the much-prayed-for destruction of the Spanish. So, at least, proposed the confidently titled *Fin de la guerre*, one of the ubiquitous "mirrors" published in the early 1620s:

> The West Indian enterprise is the only and best means not only to drive the Spaniards from the Netherlands, to put an end to this long war, to pacify the whole of Christendom, and to suppress and wound the pride of the presumptuous Spanish monarchy: But there is also a good chance to gain the West Indies. *Fortune favors the bold; the timid she repels.*[9]

The *Trumpet of war* echoed this colonialist argument in similarly clarion tones, daring the Dutch to engage the Spanish king in American waters in order to rob him of his American gold. A New World initiative represented the single most effective means to defeat the Habsburgs, fill Dutch coffers, and maintain the liberties of the Republic. It would hasten a Dutch triumph in an all-too-long war, the pamphleteers suggested.

As such, hope for a West Indies venture extended to "all good and true patriots," to their cousins in the South, and to their "allies" in America.[10]

Such attitudes greatly favored the formation of a Dutch West India Company, which did get off to a seemingly auspicious start. In contrast to the solicitations of Usselincx, sidetracked throughout the early 1600s, the proposals for a WIC now met with evident enthusiasm from the post-Oldenbarnevelt regime. A mere three weeks followed the advocate's arrest before the proposed American venture came up in the States General (September 1618). And upon the resumption of war in April of 1621, it took the States General just two months of "pregnant considerations" and "ripe deliberation" to incorporate the WIC. By early June, the Company received its official charter for "the navigation, trade, and commerce in the West Indies and Africa," and the terms were most favorable. The States agreed to furnish the Company with "troops for field and garrison duty as shall be necessary," and further to refrain from conscripting WIC ships and munitions without Company approval. On top of that, the government generously exempted the WIC from the usual tolls, convoy charges, and license fees; and it granted broad political privileges to eventual colonial regimes. In a brief two months, thus, the Company had attained much of that for which Usselincx had lobbied ceaselessly over the previous two decades.[11]

Or so at least it seemed. For the form of the new company did not much resemble the project originally submitted and persistently promoted by Usselincx and his circle. The WIC's foundation, that is to say, did not at all accord with its spiritual founder's design. Gone was the economic emphasis on settlement and agricultural production; gone was the evangelical drive and inducement of Protestant emigration; gone was the (relatively) democratic governing structure that granted nominal participation to the investors. Rather, the WIC charter established a company dedicated to trade and war: "To conserve the trade and welfare of the inhabitants of this country," as the preamble announced; and to engage the enemies of the Republic, to which end the States General allotted the Company both access to troops and the privilege to command them in battle. (The States expected the WIC to foot the bill, though; and it would appear that their High Mightinesses hoped to encourage the merchants to wage the Republic's war at bargain prices.) War and trade, of course, had constituted a significant part of Usselincx's program as well. Yet the WIC charter deviated from Usselincx's earlier proposals in its virtually *exclusive* emphasis on belligerence and commerce. Little discussion took place of the Republic's "freedoms" or "moral" rights to unrestricted navigation. No effort was made to justify the enterprise with the usual language of patriotic liberty, national security, or Calvinist sanctity. Nowhere, indeed, did the charter mention the plight of those needful allies against Spanish oppression, the "innocent Indians." If the second clause did provide the Company with the power "to make contracts, agreements, and alliances with the princes and natives of the lands," this was only to the degree "that the service of this country and the profit and increase of trade shall require." The States plainly preferred to make profits than make friends.[12]

Yet the States' preferences were not so easily satisfied, and the Company's proposals not so warmly embraced by the broader investing public. Despite the quick support from the regents, the WIC stumbled at the outset, a result of the increasingly awkward disjunction between competing notions of America. On the face of it, Usselincx's hopes for the New World did not match those of the Company's more recent promoters; original proposals for strategic alliances and long-term colonies did not sit comfortably with the latest demands for hit-and-run privateering and quick profits. A discernible contrast also emerged between the older rhetoric of "tyranny" and the newer reality of trade, and this affected the WIC's initial efforts to galvanize backers. There were confusions too about the very nature of the trade: the products, places, and profitability of American commerce. Indeed, whatever the States' desires and whatever the promoters' expectations, the WIC failed initially to excite the investors' ardor.

The ease with which the WIC acquired its charter belies the considerable difficulties, frustrations, and delays the Company experienced getting off the ground during the years immediately following its foundation. For one reason or another, America did not initially sell. A first sticking point was the matter of salt. As the charter stood in 1621, the WIC monopoly of trade excluded the thriving salt trade from the pans of Punta de Araya (off the coast of Venezuela). This represented a major concession to the towns of North Holland – in particular Hoorn and Enkhuizen – which relied heavily on salt for the local herring industry. Wartime embargoes of Spain had cut these towns off from the Portuguese pans of Setúbal, and, until now, they had successfully lobbied against all efforts to restrict the crucial supply of Caribbean salt. Other voices objected, though, and insisted that the valuable salt trade – a prime money-maker, it was believed – be included among the WIC's potential assets. After nearly a year of wrangling, the directors finally overrode the opposition of North Holland in the hope of making the Company more attractive to the general investor. An "Amplification" to the charter, published in June 1622, stipulated that the salt pans of Punta de Araya now came under the WIC monopoly.[13]

The Company's gesture satisfied some, though clearly not enough, potential investors. As of June 1622, the WIC still had not raised adequate funds to begin operations, and the Amplification extended the deadline for subscriptions to the following year. Problems persisted, however, the next pressing issue pertaining to the governing structure of the Company and the relative decision-making powers of the directors (*bewindhebberen*) and chief shareholders (*hoofdparticipanten*). Once again, debate ensued and concessions followed, producing yet further adjustments to the charter and fresh appeals to investors. Once again, too, the States General postponed the cutoff date for subscription in a desperate attempt to raise the required cash.[14] Money trickled in only hesitantly – this in sharp contrast to the brisk flow of funds into the coffers of the United East India Company (VOC) upon its formation in 1602. (And the VOC, by now profitably established in Batavia, would itself have lured investment guilders away.) This prompted yet another round of publicity campaigns and the seventeenth-century equivalent of local fund drives. In by now well-rehearsed language and format, the Company's boosters extolled the anticipated windfall that the WIC would bring to state and church, commerce and industry. Only late in 1623 did the Company finally reach its goal of seven million guilders, and it accepted an additional half million into the spring of 1624. In the end, it had taken nearly three years for the WIC to become operable, five times longer – and far less gracefully – than had been originally anticipated.[15]

The false starts and frustrations that plagued the WIC in its earliest years were, in part, to be expected. The problems the Company met raising capital pointed to the larger problem it had clarifying its agenda. It was one thing to praise the bounty of America, to fire the zeal of the patriot, or to invoke the innocence of the Indian. It was another thing entirely to expect that this menu of promises and propaganda would whet the appetite of the investing public. The image of America at this moment still lacked definition; and the Company demonstrated, at first at least, little skill in bringing their projection of the New World into focus. The campaign for a West India Company had its roots in the rhetorical soil of late sixteenth-century pamphleteering. Usselincx had cultivated the image of Spanish tyranny in America in the hope of developing a program for a political and economic alliance with the Indians. Yet when his program came under the care of the *contra-Trevisten*, they tried to graft the image of America onto a more plainly military program – the attack of Spain abroad and the advance of the war at home. The charter drafted by the WIC in 1621 reworked these earlier initiatives and made the case for trade and conquest abroad, yet apparently without sufficient clarity. Potential investors still questioned the motives of the WIC and not without reason. Some suspected the particularistic tendencies of a merchant company that originally excluded from its monopoly the traffic of salt. Others objected to the Company's autocratic structure that favored a small clique of directors to the exclusion of the investors themselves. Still others might have legitimately wondered about the political program of a company originally conceived as an antidote to Habsburg tyranny abroad. In all cases, signs of reluctance set off rounds of revisions, as the WIC scrambled to find a formula that would yield the necessary funding.[16]

Between 1621 and 1624, disarray prevailed. Lacking sufficient support, the WIC grappled with the problem of how to represent its enterprise in the most efficacious way – how best to market America. From the commotion of pamphlets and cacophony of advice, a voice of reason emerged from an unlikely source: Willem Usselincx. By this time excluded from the inner circle of directors, Usselincx had retained nonetheless a steady interest in the Company's welfare. And while he had complained early on that his beloved project had fallen under the spell of mendacious merchants – "those who use profit as their North Star and greed as their compass" – he came around quickly to believe in the power of profits to win over an audience. "It is obvious that if one wants to get money," the experienced polemicist counseled the flagging *bewindhebberen*,

something has to be proposed to the people that will move them to invest. To this end, the glory of God will help with some, harm to Spain with others, [and] with some the welfare of the Fatherland. But the principal and most powerful inducement will be the profit that each can make for himself. . . . [I] have found no one who has not agreed with me in the matter of profits. That harm can be done to the king of Spain they admit readily; but there is all too much difference between harming another and making one's own profit.[17]

Usselincx reasonably surmised that the solution to the WIC's problem consisted in identifying the perfect pitch to please investors. What he might have added, though, was that the *cause* of the Company's crisis may have been precisely the wide range of polemical pitches available to the WIC in the first place (and often from the pen of Usselincx himself). The WIC failed to articulate a believable program, and investors cautiously kept their distance. The Company, moreover, appeared to promise too much. Ultimately, the directors followed Usselincx's advice and adjusted their charter to emphasize the Company's unwavering focus on the bottom line. The Amplifications of 1622–1623 make this clear. It was the salt of the Caribbean, rather than the soul of the Indian, that the WIC promised to pursue; it was the needs of the stockholders, not the whims of the state, by which it would abide. The pursuit of profit would henceforth become the mainstay of the WIC's program and shape its discussion of America in the years to come. Appeals to the welfare of the Fatherland, the glory of God, and the fate of the Indian would largely be abandoned in WIC literature – much as these themes would endure in the context of other New World programs and in the imagination of other Dutch observers of America.[18]

III

Whatever the strategy of the WIC, half a century of rhetoric had not been without its effect. As the Republic embarked on its first major public expeditions to the New World, the perception of the Indian-as-ally still retained considerable currency within the Dutch imagination. The poetics of America – the sense of the New World as a landscape of rapacious Spanish tyrants preying upon guileless American innocents – still resonated within the politics of the Republic. There lingered in the minds of magistrates no less than publicists the hopeful belief in the natural affinity of the Netherlands and America, in the brotherhood of "innocence" between two nations united by their antipathy to Spain. Despite the more mercenary direction now taken by the WIC, there persisted within other circles the more idealistic notion that the Indians patiently awaited their "liberators" from the north, and that a Dutch-American alliance would swiftly undo a century of Habsburg hegemony. This would have remarkable ramifications. For, as the Dutch returned to arms against Spain, they acted on their beliefs regarding America: on their perceived responsibilities to the natives and their anticipated assistance from the natives. Three extraordinary New World initiatives demonstrate the resilience of the image of "innocence abroad" by illustrating the genuine faith of the Dutch in an American ally. Two of these count among the very first official, public investments in America – "official" and "public" since they originated with the States General and the *stadhouder* rather than the WIC. The third initiative came from the WIC and slightly later than the other two, yet it shares with the earlier efforts all the trappings of a public undertaking. Like the other two, it yielded only disappointment for its backers and well illustrates the inevitable tensions that arose when Dutch rhetoric of the New World encountered the hard realities of Spanish America.

The first major Dutch offensive against Spain's western empire set sail from Holland on 29 April 1623. An awesome assemblage of eleven heavy warships outfitted with nearly three hundred guns and staffed by over sixteen hundred men, the Nassau Fleet made a princely impression, as befitted its principal patron, Prince Maurits of Nassau.[19] Preparations for the voyage had begun at least six years prior during the pivotal year of 1617, when Maurits threw his support behind a proposed assault on Spanish shipping in America. The *stadhouder* drew inspiration from the voyage of Joris Spilbergen (1614–1617), which had exposed the weakness of Spanish defenses off the coasts of Chile and Peru.[20] The Nassau Fleet, as Maurits conceived it, would confound the king within his own backyard and, at the same time, "divert the war from the Netherlands."[21] Planning remained necessarily provisional while the Truce remained in effect, yet already by 1619 the States General had pledged five ships in anticipation. By 1622, the States upped their offer to six (including the navy's two heaviest vessels, the *Amsterdam* and the *Delft*); and by the following April, the prince inspected, with great pomp and parade, the fully outfitted fleet.[22]

"The greatest force ever sent to the South Seas" pushed off from Texel with grand aspirations. The optimistic reports of Spilbergen excited Maurits as much as his allies in the States General, who envisioned in the enterprise the beginning of the end of the Habsburg empire. First, the Nassau Fleet would effect a quick end to the war. A Dutch armada in the Pacific would strangle the silver convoy in America, thus crippling the royal treasury in Spain and weakening the enemy siege in the Netherlands. The fleet would "reduce the Spaniard to his ancient poverty," as a contemporary account put it, and "deprive him of that with which he has hitherto fought his war in Christendom."[23] Second, the fleet would topple the Habsburg empire *beyond* Christendom – in America, namely – and here Dutch ambitions soared their highest. For its backers expected the Nassau Fleet to ignite nothing short of a full-scale revolt in the Americas, an *alteratie* in which a Dutch-Indian alliance would oust the Spanish decisively from the New World. The prince adopted this strategy in absolute earnestness and with great expectations. From the start, he and the other organizers assumed that they might swiftly "resume communication begun by Spilbergen" and "solidify" the alliance he had broached with the natives (varyingly called "Chileans," "Peruvians," or simply "Indians").[24] Toward this end, the fleet would convey official "letters of alliance" (*brieven van alliantie*) addressed from the States General to the Indians. According to the explicit "Instructions" of the prince, these letters were to be distributed "all over the West Indies, as deemed necessary," and were to be followed up "with promises of freedoms, offices, dignities, land [*encomienden*], and other benevolences and advantages." How, precisely, the Dutch might grant "freedoms," or whose land, exactly, they would parcel out to whom, the "Instructions" fail to clarify. They propose, rather, a rhetorical strategy devised to convince the natives "to rise up against the king of Spain." One can only imagine the outlines of the Dutch oration or the contents of the "letter of alliance" – of which, unhappily, no copy survives. A Spanish report compiled from the testimony of two deserters of the Dutch fleet, though, confirms the presence on board of chests filled with *"cartas de livertad,"* apparently left undelivered.[25]

Prince Maurits would not witness the return of his fleet (he died in April 1625), but this was just as well. The expedition failed miserably, from inauspicious start to inglorious finish. Within twenty-four hours of departure, a leak developed in the hull of the two-hundred last *Eagle,* which forced the fleet to anchor off the Isle of Wight and forfeit any element of speed or stealth. By mid-October off the Cabo Lopez Gonsalvo (Gabon, West Africa), the fleet suffered another round of setbacks, first from contrary winds and then from a deranged barber-surgeon. The surgeon proved the more dangerous, murdering seven men by poison before he could be sedated, tried, and executed.[26] Further delays rounding Cape Horn prevented the Dutch from overtaking the Spanish silver-fleet as it departed Arica (Chile). The Dutch headed straight for Callao (Peru) in pursuit, yet, as luck would have it, missed the "exceptionally rich" silver-fleet by five days. Disappointed, the fleet's council decided to remain off Callao and blockade the waters around Lima. This lasted from early May until late August 1624, during which time the Fleet's admiral, Jacques l'Hermite, succumbed "to sorrow because the silver had eluded him" – or, more prosaically, died from gout. The Dutch managed to destroy over thirty enemy ships yet took hardly anything of value. Dwindling supplies and a hostile coast forced a retreat, and the fleet turned west to cross the Pacific before the end of the year. After brief service in the East Indies, a skeletal fleet returned to the fatherland in the summer of 1626, with rather little to show for its efforts.

As went the military and economic course of the expedition, so went the political and diplomatic as well. The anticipated alliance with the Indians never materialized, and the revolt of the Americas never transpired. Hope, nonetheless, remained unusually high. Published accounts of the voyage emphasized the steady stream of opportunities only barely missed, owing either to the fleet's misfortunes or to other "unavoidable" circumstances. Off the coast of Chile, according to the most complete journal of the expedition, the bedridden Admiral l'Hermite expressed his sorrow that time prevented him from landing and liberating the natives. Earlier Dutch explorers had observed "the great affection" exhibited by the Indians and their evident desire for Dutch assistance. L'Hermite regretted that duty pressed him on, "since he had greater hope that we might accomplish something good there [Chile], where the natives were stalwart enemies of Spain, than in our upcoming destination." When the fleet reached its target of Callao, enthusiasms turned to the natives of Peru, who, on good authority, "would not hesitate to rise up against their masters." "In these lands," noted the narrator of the same journal,

we also expected to make use of the good services of certain Indians who visited us the day before yesterday in their small barque. They displayed great zeal to help us and assured us of the assistance of the Indians and revolt of the Negroes, should we secure a beachhead.

Once again, though, circumstances intervened. Forewarned of the Dutch arrival at Lima, the Spanish viceroy employed two additional companies of troops to prevent an enemy landing and formed a regiment of black mercenaries (*gegagieerde Negros*) to keep the indigenous and African populations in check. By the autumn, the Dutch gave up waiting and moved north to the waters off Mexico, near the port of Acapulco. It is more than slightly ironic that the Dutch suffered at this point the costly desertion of a native American gunner "who had served us faithfully in all of our missions." The fleet's vice admiral followed this supposedly dependable "Indiaen" into a carefully laid Spanish ambush, which took the lives of six men. The printed accounts passed over this event in embarrassed silence.[27]

Indeed, whatever the reversals in America, the narration of events published back in Europe left the impression that the Nassau Fleet had scored a resounding success. Spain had suffered irreparable damage – so it was alleged – and the natives had moved one step closer to their Dutch-assisted revolt. The praise could be elaborate:

An eleven-keeled fleet was outfitted in Holland
Which sailed to the South Sea and Peruvian shore
Led by l'Hermite, [against] the Spanish and Moors
It bullied by water, by fire, and sword.[28]

A certain amount of poetic license might have construed as "bullying" the pestering of Spanish sea-lanes by the sickly l'Hermite. Only willful fantasy though – or propaganda – could have touted the voyage as a run of "notable successes," as did the *True Relation of the Success of the Fleet under the Command of Admiral Jacques l'Hermite.*[29] This pamphlet appeared already in 1625, based on early reports sent back before the fleet had abandoned the coast of Peru. It formed the basis, nonetheless, for much of the public-relations campaign that followed. A French pamphlet of the same year described *La furieuse defaite des Espagnols, et la sanglante bataille donnee au Perou* (The furious defeat of the Spanish and the bloody battle in Peru); and the English editor Samuel Purchas announced nothing less than the fall of Spanish Peru:

> There is also Newes of great preparations in Spaine to recover this losse, as also, of another famous Act of the Hollanders commanded by L'Hermit, which are said to have taken Lirma the chiefe Citie in Peru, and other places on the Peruan Coast: the old Enemy of the Spaniard, viz. the people of Chili being joyned with the Dutch. If this bee true, it is likely to prove a Costly warre to the Spaniard, and Honourable to the Dutch.[30]

The complete journal of the voyage came out in 1626 and in five subsequent editions by the middle of the century. In only slightly less sensational terms, it kept alive the image of the imminent Dutch ascendancy in the New World and the all but certain union of the young Republic with its American allies.[31]

Shortly after the return of the Nassau Fleet, the States General lent its support to a second American initiative, predicated, like the first, on the presumed affinity between the Dutch and the Indians. In 1627, the Flemish-born merchant and self-styled evangelist, Joan Aventroot, wrote an epistle to the natives of Peru urging them to rise up against the king of Spain. Addressing himself to his "Peruvian brethren" (living, as he supposed, in Buenos Aires), Aventroot detailed the manifold tyrannies and heresies of the Habsburg regime and incited his readers to armed revolt. He further advised the Peruvians to avail themselves of the assistance of the Dutch Republic, sworn enemies of Spain; and it was perhaps for this reason that the States General first took notice of, and eventually saw fit to sponsor, Aventroot's project. At the States' expense, eight thousand copies of Aventroot's epistle were printed, together with the Heidelberg catechism. The magistrates also commissioned Aventroot to draft an official "Alliance" between their High Mightinesses and the "Serene Lords of Peru" that would explain (ostensibly to both parties) the practical and spiritual advantages of a Dutch-American union. Finally, the States published a Dutch edition of the "Alliance" and the *Epistola á los Peruleras* – written by Aventroot originally in Spanish, which he assumed would be the lingua franca of the two nations – introduced by an extensive dedicatory letter from the author, dated June 1630.[32]

The similarities between Aventroot's program and that envisioned by the organizers of the Nassau Fleet – each soliciting the friendship of the "Peruvians," each including a letter of alliance, each receiving the blessings of the States – are hardly accidental. Aventroot initially approached the Dutch governors while the Truce was still in effect, and he later had a hand in devising part of the "Instructions" for the Nassau Fleet. A flamboyantly zealous warrior for the reformed religion, Aventroot began to attract notice in the early 1610s when he penned a series of remarkable letters to Philip III directing the Most Catholic King to switch over to Protestantism and to convert his entire empire in the process. The published version of this letter campaign already mentioned the plight of the Peruvians – "poor souls" drudging in the mines of America – and urgently petitioned the king to improve both the bodily and spiritual condition of his American subjects.[33] By now living in Amsterdam, Aventroot published Dutch (1613) and Latin (1615) translations of his epistle with a dedication to the States General, whose favor he hoped to win. Apparently, he succeeded; for when the States needed assistance devising a plan to convert those Peruvian natives l'Hermite would encounter, they turned to Aventroot for advice. The "Instruction" of 1623 asked the admiral to "pay particular attention to the instructions of Jan Aventroot" – a reference to a separate set of directives from the hand of Aventroot, which counseled on proselytizing the natives. With retrospective wisdom, Aventroot would judge these earlier (1623) attempts premature. The Nassau Fleet "had been embraced by the fleshy arm" of profanity, he wrote to the States General a number of years later. It had sailed without its evangelical orders – "the Christian Catechism of the Reformed Church" – and plainly before its time.[34]

By 1628, that time had arrived – precisely arrived, according to the apocalyptic visions and prognostications reported by Aventroot to the States General in support of a second American mission. The writing on the wall, as read by Aventroot, presaged a cataclysmic uprising in America: a political revolt and religious reformation, ignited by the Peruvians and fueled by the soldiers of the Dutch Reformed Church. Three times over the course of 1622, "signs and wonders" appeared to Aventroot that foretold an imminent Dutch-American alliance against Spain. Three times Aventroot brought these supernatural sightings to the attention of the magistrates until he convinced them, finally, of their portent. Only *after* the departure of the Nassau Fleet, however, did he realize that he had misread his own earlier visions. Complex numerological calculations clarified his mistakes and demonstrated that l'Hermite had departed a few years too early – a few years before the end of the third generation of conquistadors, the third reign of Spanish Habsburgs (Charles V, Philip II, Philip III), and the third cycle of tyrannies, all of which somehow terminated in the *annus miribalis* of 1628. By this year, predicted Aventroot in his epistle of 1627, the whore of Babylon would fall, bringing down her deceitful minions in Rome (the pope) and Spain (Philip IV). Aventroot called on his Peruvian brethren to destroy all vestiges of papacy in America, to purify, as the Maccabees had, the idols from their temples. "You are *obligated* to revolt," he informed them. At the same time, he appealed to the Dutch magistrates to introduce the Indians to the Reformed Church, "which must be defended not only in your own lands, but must also be planted in other lands to the best of your ability, and especially in the new lands of the West Indies."[35]

The dedicatory letter to the States General and the epistle to the Peruvians both operated on the level of such religious signs and sensibilities. The alliance itself, however, proposed a partnership on the more material bases of free labor, economic liberty, and commercial opportunity. Aventroot, who knew something of Peruvian silver production from his experience as a merchant of precious metals, deplored the harsh conditions of the Potosí mines. To feed his "insatiable greed," the Spanish king tyrannized the Peruvians' bodies no less than their souls, sending the natives ever deeper into the earth to mine its treasures. "And as he tyrannized the Indians' bodies, so too he tyrannized their goods," added Aventroot. By this he meant not merely the Spaniards' seizure of Indian lands and exploitation of their silver mines, but also the low wages they payed, the high taxes they demanded, and the burdensome tolls they collected – fiscal abuses, in other words, that might make more sense to a Dutch readership than a Peruvian one. "And finally," noted Aventroot turning to a sin "completely unheard of," the king of Spain suffocated trade: "On top of all these intolerable impositions, [he] burdens commerce with high prices," railed Aventroot in the same moral-economic tone that Usselincx had struck twenty years earlier.

The conscience of the King of Spain is verily steeped in avarice. . . . [He] does not allow that you [Indians] might traffic with other lands and enjoy the ready purchase of goods as do other nations; but that you, like slaves, must receive only that which is offered from the closed hand of Spain.[36]

The alliance proposed by Aventroot and published by the States General would rectify all that. "Because God has freed these United Provinces from the tyranny of the king of Spain," began the document's final, rather contractual sounding paragraph, "their High Mightinesses are duty bound . . . to carry out this righteous sentence." For their part, the Lords of Peru would agree to renounce the king of Spain and appoint a native king in his stead, "one who will, first and foremost, cleanse the Churches of the forbidden idols, by which the Pope has dishonored the Lord." By the terms of the alliance, the Dutch would then provide whatever support – moral, military, commercial – they could. "And to this king of yours," Aventroot informed the Peruvians, their High Mightinesses, Lords of the States, pledge their assistance, and grant by this Alliance their sworn word, to assist him to the best of their abilities, by water and land, until God shall have granted you your Christian freedoms. And likewise shall they promise you eternal relations of trade, offering you, from both the East Indies and these Provinces, basic products of better quality and lower price than those you now purchase from Spain.[37]

Military succor, Christian freedom, competitive pricing: the terms of the alliance favored the Peruvians indeed, and there would have been little reason to suspect a rejection of the States' offer – had it ever arrived. As in the case of the Nassau Fleet's "letters of alliance," though, the Dutch proposition more than likely never reached its intended destination: there is no evidence of a voyage or shipment of documents from the Netherlands to South America around this time. And if Aventroot's *Epistola á los Peruleras* did make the journey to America, it would not appear to have elicited the desired result. No large-scale revolt ever took place in or about the year 1628; the "lords of Peru" remained under Spanish control well through that and following generations. The States, nonetheless, pinned great hopes on the project, lent their full cooperation, and underwrote the unusually large printing of eight thousand copies of Aventroot's alliance. The costs must have seemed well worth it.

A number of years would pass before the Dutch undertook another mission of friendship to the New World. The third, and in many ways most decisive, attempt to forge a formal alliance with the Americans proved to be the most ambitious, however; and it produced results at once more encouraging and more disappointing than the previous two. It began in early 1643, when the veteran commander Hendrick Brouwer led a fleet of five ships and several hundred men into the Pacific to solicit, once again, a treaty of cooperation from the local Indians, in this case the "Chileans." Between the voyage of the Nassau Fleet and that of Brouwer, few Dutch ships had ventured near the southwestern corner of South America. After launching its first naval operation in 1624, the WIC concentrated its efforts on the Atlantic coasts of America and Africa and steered clear of all attempts to engage Chile and Peru. Yet Brouwer came to the Company from the ranks of the VOC, for whom he had served as a *bewindhebber* in Amsterdam and governor-general in Batavia; and perhaps it was his Pacific perspective that won over the WIC. The prince of Orange also played a part in the fleet's preparation, furnishing Brouwer with "letters of credentials" (*brieven van credentie*) and ceremonial gifts for the native caciques. So invested, Brouwer foresaw little trouble concluding an alliance of friendship with the Chileans. The Peruvians, he hoped, would join ranks, too; and this confederacy of

Batavian-American arms would rout the Spanish, reconquer America, and displace the world hegemony of the Habsburgs. It never got this far, of course, though the Dutch did present their credentials, gifts, and terms to a gathering of Chileans who indulged, then finally ignored, their fair-skinned saviors. This final fiasco, off the coast of distant Chile, forced the Dutch to confront the cumulative failure of their three-quarter century pursuit of an alliance with America.

The selection of Chile was a fitting starting point for this final appeal in America. Chile exerted a "peculiar fascination" for the Dutch, who, since the early seventeenth century, had imagined a special affinity for its natives.[38] Renowned for the beauty of its landscape, the fairness of its climate, and the richness of its products, Chile had also acquired a reputation for the fierceness of its natives, who had stoutly resisted Spanish rule from the mid-sixteenth century. By common (Dutch) consensus, the Chileans represented the best hope for an American ally. Early descriptions of the land came from Olivier van Noort, among the first Dutch sailors to reach the South Sea. In the early 1600s, van Noort sent back reports of an uprising in 1599 by the "valiant warriors" of Chile (Mapuches), who had successfully attacked Spanish positions in Valdivia and Imperial. After their "glorious victories," wrote van Noort with approval, the native braves had raised their cups "to avenging the tyranny and slavery under which Spain would have them suffer." The Chileans had also razed Spanish churches and cloisters, and piously destroyed all "popish idols . . . saying, 'Now we have put an end to the Spanish gods.'" Van Noort considered the landscape south of Santiago "the most fertile under the sun; for all that is planted, grows in great abundance . . . the gold mines and earth are indescribably [rich]."[39] The Walloon merchant Isaac le Maire concurred, and he petitioned Oldenbarnevelt "to infest the whole coast of Peru" (by which he meant western South America) with Dutch vessels and to establish there a league against Spain.[40] Spilbergen, who reconnoitered the coast of Chile during his 1614–1617 circumnavigation, paid particularly high compliments to the natives of La Mocha. "These Chileans were well bred, very polite, and friendly," he reported. "They ate and drank with manners nearly the equal of a good Christian's." They also received Spilbergen's men "with all affection," and "showed great friendship and good intentions" in their dealings. When the admiral showed them the great guns of his ships "and made signs to the effect that [the Dutch] had come also to fight the Spanish, the natives conveyed how much this pleased them, as they were enemies of the same."[41] Friendly and fierce, the Chileans were rebels to boot, as more than one Dutch chronicler noted. They had fought courageously for their freedom and swore to struggle to the last man against Spain. "The natives of this land will not suffer the foreign Spaniards and will not bear the yoke of Spain," wrote a highly regarded Dutch authority on America. "After diverse secret and conspiratorial gatherings, they commonly resolved to use every means possible to rid their country of these tiresome guests."[42]

The high reputation of the Chileans rested in part on Alonso de Ercilla's *La Araucana*, published in Dutch in 1619.[43] An epic poem in three parts, *La Araucana* narrates the valorous struggle, in the Andean highlands, between the native Araucanians and Spanish conquistadors. It distinguishes itself from virtually all other literature of the *Conquista* by its unusually high-minded and evenhanded treatment of the natives – this despite the author's impeccable credentials as a Spanish aristocrat and veteran of the early Chilean campaign. For reasons both artistic and historical, Ercilla's account ennobled the Araucanians and endowed them with traits that a Dutch audience in particular found especially admirable. The invincible spirit of the Chilean warriors, their stalwart endurance, their ancient bravery – even the tidiness of their homes – had obvious appeal to a patriotic Netherlander. Above all, the poet celebrated the Araucanian's love of freedom and pious resistance to the invaders from Spain.

> Never has a king subjected
> Such fierce people proud of freedom,
> Nor has alien nation boasted
> E'er of having trod their borders.

The Araucanians reviled the "bearded villains" from Spain with their "puffed ambition" and insolent demands for tribute. Rather than submit, they fought a heroic and protracted war against the Habsburg enemy. "Blood or life is a paltry payment," cried their chieftain, Caupolicano, in a climactic, prebattle oration:

> Let our ancient laws dishonored
> Be restored by free men's power!
> Let them be inviolate, holy
> Stretching through far distant kingdoms![44]

This rang particularly true in the Republic. The Dutch editor praised the love of *patria* among the Chileans and the valor of sons so zealous to avenge the death of their fathers in carrying on a by now (1619) seventy years' war with Spain.[45]

It was with these freedom-loving and Spanish-loathing warriors that Brouwer hoped to ally.[46] Toward this end, he directed his fleet in the spring of 1643 around Cape Horn and along the Chilean coast as far as the Isla de Chiloé, where he hoped to link up with the natives. This occurred in a series of curious encounters that reads like a bizarre comedy of diplomatic manners. Anchored in the newly christened *Brouwershaven,* the Dutch first caught sight of the "ally" in early May 1643. A white flag, a knife, and a string of coral were left for the natives, who inspected the Dutch offerings before they dumped them, unceremoniously, in a nearby river. A few days later the natives approached on horseback and reproached their visitors – first in a native tongue and then in Spanish – for their ill-intentions. This irked the Dutch, who exchanged their white flag for a red one and fired their cannons. Brouwer's men then marched on the country and took prisoners, including "an old Chilean woman with two children." Relations quickly worsened. Over the coming weeks, the natives remained aloof in the hills above the coastline, and the "alliance" degenerated into a "flee and feast" pattern: the natives fled whenever the Dutch touched shore, and the Dutch feasted on the abandoned cattle and sheep.[47]

Only by mid-July did Brouwer finally make a breakthrough. In a moment of clemency, the admiral released a captive family of natives on the condition that they convey to their countrymen, "that we [Dutch] were their friends and enemies of Castile," and that their release had been delayed only so that the Dutch could enumerate for them "the numerous tyrannies and ill-treatments suffered by the Hollanders." This, for whatever reason, encouraged the Chileans, who sent a party of dignitaries to board the admiral's ship and ascertain the Dutch intentions. Brouwer discoursed to this audience on the natural affinity of their two nations, their shared antipathy toward Spain, and the "manifold reasons" to conclude an alliance. Intrigued, perhaps, the native ambassadors listened patiently. (The Dutch reported the Chileans' "especial happiness" with Brouwer's lecture.) They positively warmed to the idea, though, when Brouwer displayed for them the cache of arms they would receive as their part of the bargain. "They were especially gratified," concluded the published Dutch journal of the expedition. At this point, however, the negotiations took a turn for the bizarre. Upon learning that the Dutch intended to sail for Valdivia (the site of a former Spanish fort, now in Chilean hands), the ambassadors volunteered their tribes' assistance and asked if they might possibly hitch a ride up the coast aboard Brouwer's fleet. (They claimed that swollen rivers and Spanish soldiers would prevent their timely arrival in Valdivia and that a Dutch ferry would serve both parties' interests.) Brouwer agreed and further rewarded his visitors with swords and pikes to prove his honorable intentions. Nine days later, two more caciques visited the ship bearing with them, as a sign of their good faith and zeal, the fourteen-day-old head of a slain Spaniard. Brouwer diplomatically accepted their gift and agreed to arm and transport them, together with their cohorts, to Valdivia. "What a pleasant odor this head emitted one can easily guess," the Dutch report dryly commented. One month later (21 August) the Dutch departed the Isla de Chiloé for Valdivia to continue their quest to liberate America. Along for the three-day, nearly two-hundred-mile ride came 470 Chilean men, women, and children who had pledged their allegiance to the Dutch, "so as to be delivered from the intolerable tyranny of Spain."[48]

This ferry of friendship reached Valdivia with little incident. Their passengers safely delivered, the Dutch promptly initiated consultations with the local caciques and resumed their Chilean diplomacy. The Valdivians called on the Dutch ships often and enthusiastically enough, yet not always for the desired purpose. While the Europeans discussed strategy for a future assault against Spain, the natives concentrated on matters closer to hand.

[They] were very impressed with the size of the ships, yet also very thievish [of their contents] and desirous of iron. Everything they saw was to their liking, including the compasses which they removed from the binnacles.[49]

The merchants deemed it expedient, accordingly, to bolt down, lock up, or hide everything of value. The ranking commander – Elias Herckmans, who had replaced the recently deceased Brouwer – decided to circumvent the self-appointed native middlemen and present his case directly to the Chilean people. On 29 August, Herckmans landed with two companies of troops and delivered "an excellent harangue and oration" to a crowd of about three hundred. The general expanded on the Dutch purpose in the South Pacific, presented the "Letters of Credentials" from the prince of Orange, and distributed (also in the name of the prince) gifts to the ranking Valdivian cacique. And, "after many discourses of the fidelity that would be shown to [the Valdivians] in the struggle against Spain," the Dutch "politely" took their leave.

Five days later, Herckmans returned in full force and, "under blue skies and before approximately 1,200 Chileans," delivered a second oration. This speech was grand, dramatic, and ultimately decisive – though not quite as Herckmans had hoped. It began by extolling the renown of the Chileans, their devotion to freedom, and their martial endurance. Herckmans reminded his audience "that the Netherlanders had likewise engaged the Spanish for nearly eighty years to maintain their freedom" and, on this basis, proposed an alliance of friendship. The Dutch would provide the Chileans with arms and other (unspecified) "merchandise," while the native would furnish the Dutch with "provisions" and other (unspecified) products. In this way, the two nations would bolster one another's efforts against Spain. To emphasize the solemnity of his offer, Herckmans issued each cacique an authorized letter from His Majesty, the prince of Orange. Perhaps to dramatize their curiosity in the offer, each cacique "kissed" the prince's letter and marveled at the distance it had traveled. In any case, the Chileans agreed to an exchange of livestock for muskets, and, from the Dutch perspective, all would seem to have gone well up to this point.[50]

It did not take long for the alliance, however limited, to unravel. "After these and other discourses," reports the fullest account of the encounter, "the Netherlanders finally and gingerly [*met soete redenen*] made mention of the ends and designs for which they had also brought their weapons thither, that is to trade them principally for gold." The mere mention of gold, coyly and somewhat digressively broached, had the effect of thunder in the cloudless sky. It arrested the caciques' indulgent attention and turned the whole negotiation process abruptly on its head. Confronted with the all too familiar European demand for gold, the caciques "thereupon uniformly denied all knowledge of the gold mines." Instead and much to the chagrin of their visitors, they now lectured the Dutch and recalled for them their *own* memories of the Spanish tributes and tyrannies imposed upon them in pursuit of gold. Herckmans tried to soothe the ruffled feathers of the Indians by mentioning the Dutch willingness to offer fair prices and good merchandise – yet to no avail. "At this moment the caciques glanced at one another and gave no further reply." The assembly soon dissolved without any further exchange of arms, foodstuffs, or good will. A few weeks later, the caciques rescinded their offer of provisions and aid. Though the Dutch would linger along the coast until mid-October, this effectively terminated their visit and pursuit of a Chilean alliance. When Herckmans bid his farewell on 19 October, the caciques expressed their regret at the fleet's departure and submitted that, had the Europeans announced their visit two years prior, the Chilean farmers would surely have sown enough to feed them. The Dutch left it at that; though in concluding their account of the journey, they wistfully noted the abundance of livestock, grain, and fruit of the Chilean countryside, the caciques' protestations notwithstanding.[51]

In its aftermath, the Dutch tried to put the best face possible on an expedition that would appear to have signaled an end to their attempts at an alliance with Chile. An early broadsheet circulated news of the Republic's success in the South Pacific in penetrating Spanish strongholds, in confederating with the natives, and – most farfetched – "in liberating 470 Chilean men, women, and children." By this account, the Chileans heartily "welcomed" the Dutch, showed great interest in the proposed alliance, and, despite their bad harvests, "prayed for us [Dutch] to stay, pledging their utmost industry in sowing more crops . . . and hoping that we free them from slavery of Spain."[52] A report of the voyage written a number of years later – after the signing of the Peace of Münster with Spain (1648) – repeats the assertion that the Dutch "liberated" the Chileans, yet takes a more frank view of the failure of the mission and the Dutch Chilean policy more generally. Of Herckmans's attempt to enlist the natives' assistance, it notes:

This all pleased them well enough, yet as soon as [the Dutch] began to say that they had come to barter for gold (which was the only motive of the West India Company) their caciques or chieftains began to excuse themselves, [saying] that for many years they neither had had nor sought any gold.

The author concludes with the notably candid – and surprisingly bleak – admission of defeat: "Thus did this voyage, which General Brouwer considered of such great consequence, come to a fully fruitless and ineffective close."[53]

The same might ultimately be said of the futile, if earnest, pursuit by the Dutch of their elusive alliance with America. The three major initiatives to solicit the partnership of the Indians ended with little result. In all three instances – collectively spanning a quarter-century – genuine anticipation of American collaboration motivated large-scale public undertakings by the Republic. In each case, though, considerable expenditure produced negligible return – a fact that dampened not the least enthusiasm for, and claims of, "successes," "liberations," and "alliances" with the natives. Taken together, the Nassau Fleet, the Aventroot *Epistola,* and the Brouwer expedition demonstrate the remarkable staying power of the image of eager, innocent Americans waiting to ally with the Dutch. They likewise indicate the seriousness with which the Dutch took the rhetoric of America and the willingness of the Republic to act upon its rhetorical projections. Yet these efforts also suggest how far into the background the Indian ally had receded. No longer did the Dutch pursue alliances simply with "Americans" or, for that matter, with the natives of recently settled Dutch Brazil or New Netherland. Innocence, rather, was sought on the peripheries in distant "Chile" or "Peru," lands that otherwise remained safely beyond the range of Dutch ships and thus secure in the realm of the Republic's imagination.[54]

IV

The earliest Dutch undertakings in the New World well illustrate the tensions that developed between expectations and outcomes, a pattern that would repeat itself in other enterprises as well. Whether or not

Dutch entrepreneurs actively sought alliances in America, they invariably anticipated an easy time of it once there: ready assistance from the Indians, quick profits from trade, favorable conditions for settlement. The directors of the WIC wisely passed on opportunities to join the Nassau Fleet or back the Aventroot campaigns. Yet, not uncommonly in their own American ventures, they operated under similar assumptions of tailor-made alliances, timely native uprisings, and craven enemy retreats. Nothing of the sort took place, and the early initiatives pursued by the Company – and in the case of Brouwer, a later initiative as well – reflect the same combination of hopeful ambition and hopeless confusion that characterized those projects they avoided. Inevitably, discrepancies arose in discussions of America during the early years of colonization, from the mid-1620s through the mid-1630s, when optimistic rhetoric ran well ahead of disappointing returns, when projections of alliances confronted the realities of encounter, and when conventions of discourse *about* the Indians yielded to necessities of discourse *with* the Indians.

The WIC launched its first American offensive in 1624, targeting Brazil and its principal port of Bahia (Salvador).[55] While the Nassau Fleet sailed for Peru with the lofty plan of liberating the Peruvians and rolling back the Spanish enemy, the Company set its sights on prospects closer to hand and plainly more material. With its hopes pinned on profits, the WIC adopted an Atlantic strategy that concentrated on plundering the sugar plantations of Brazil, harassing traffic along the coast, and gaining a foothold in the South Atlantic – preferably in Brazil or the Spanish Main, but conceivably also in West Africa. Toward these ends, a fleet of twenty-six ships led by Jacob Willekens sailed in the spring of 1624, quickly reached the Bahia de Todos os Santos, and captured the Portuguese fort there with little difficulty. Significantly, the Company had chosen as its first objective a Portuguese colony settled largely by New Christians, mestizos, and African slaves – not, thus, by Spanish overlords or innocent Indians. (In the WIC's other opening move, it sent Walloon settlers to the then peripheral island of Manhattan, which, in 1624, was as distant from Spanish America as one could imagine.) Spanish tyranny, for now at least, was left undisturbed.[56]

Expectations for Brazil ran high, particularly after reports of Willekens's early success reached the Netherlands. "Like a paradise on earth," Brazil sparkled in the pamphlet literature of the mid-1620s, enticing Dutch readers with the promise of spectacular profits. It enjoyed a warm climate, tempered by abundant rain; it overflowed with sugar, tobacco, and dyewoods; and it lay relatively close to the Netherlands – the nearest New World landfall, in fact, for outgoing ships. In Brazil, moreover, the Dutch expected to confederate with allies of two sorts:

first, the native "savages . . . who incline somewhat toward us [*eenichsins tot ons inclineren*]," as a WIC position paper put it; and, second, the Portuguese New Christians (or *conversos*, often referred to simply as Jews in Dutch accounts), who "would rather see two Orange flags than one Inquisitor."[57] News of Willekens's progress electrified the Republic and further encouraged this sort of optimism. Less than four months after the fall of Bahia, a broadsheet advertised "the latest good news" from America, including an account of the scandalous flight of the Portuguese militia from their fortifications. Another report, also printed in 1624, predicted the imminent collapse of the remainder of Brazil. "The Portuguese who would offer the most resistance and opposition are primarily of the Jewish faith and, moreover, sworn and born enemies of Spain," the author reasoned somewhat paradoxically. "They would at once submit themselves to the authority of your High Mightinesses," he confidently assured the Dutch magistrates.[58]

Yet the flush of success faded quickly. It was no small irony – from the Dutch perspective at least – that an alliance of Indian auxiliaries and Portuguese troops combined to restrict the WIC garrison to the town of Bahia and block any further Dutch advances into the Brazilian countryside. On Easter day 1625, an imposing armada of over fifty ships and 12,500 men – Spaniards and Portuguese – entered the Bahia de Todos os Santos and easily overwhelmed the isolated Dutch. Neither New Christians nor friendly Indians could save the day, and the Bahia victory evaporated as quickly as it had materialized. Other Company efforts met with similarly mixed results. Piet Heyn, who had served as Willekens's vice-admiral, returned to the Caribbean twice in the following years (1626–1628) hoping to raid Spanish shipping in the Caribbean and incite native revolts in the hinterland. While he scored spectacularly in the first instance, he suffered consistent, if less famous, setbacks in the second. A month before Heyn captured the Spanish silver fleet in the Bay of Matanzas (Cuba) in September 1628, two ships from his fleet landed on Grenada in search of friendly allies and much-needed provisions. The natives of the island greeted the Dutch "rudely," killing around thirty-four men and chasing the rest off the island. One chronicler, partisan to the WIC, attributed the attack to a prior visit by hostile French ships. Had the "savages" known the true identity of their visitors, they would surely have greeted them more cheerfully, he believed.[59] Others affected a less rosy, or at best ambivalent, perspective. Nicolaes van Wassenaer, who had heralded Willekens's feats as "the first signs of the fall of Spain," warned that the Indians of the Wild Coast (the much ballyhooed "Guianese" of Usselincx's imagination) could behave with extraordinary savagery toward outsiders – with "*groote tyran-*

nie," he wrote with no trace of irony. He recounted in his chronicle an incident in which a Dutch landing party watched the natives torture, execute, and finally cannibalize their unfortunate captives. By contrast, though, van Wassenaer drew attention just a few pages earlier to a separate tribe of "innocent" Indians, which prayed daily for the Dutch to deliver them from Spain.[60]

The WIC resumed its Brazilian campaign in 1630 with a major offensive on Pernambuco, the rich sugar-producing captaincy in the north. Once again, however, the "grand design" progressed only haltingly, with expectations well outpacing results. No sooner did the ramshackle fortifications at Olinda and Recife fall to the Dutch than the Portuguese retreated to the safety of the interior to conduct a guerrilla war against the invaders. With the help of native auxiliaries, the *moradores* (settlers) hemmed the Dutch in on three sides and harassed their foraging parties, causing them soon to quit Olinda. Where the WIC had envisaged in its instructions the quick occupation of northeast Brazil followed by the conquest of Bahia and an eventual advance on Rio de Janeiro, the directors had to suffice with "two heaps of sand and stone," as one of them put it, rapidly reduced to one. When the Dutch finally did establish a rapport with the nomadic Tarairiu, it produced little tangible effect. The bands of natives who joined Dutch troops showed themselves willing to raid Portuguese settlements, yet only in their own "wild way" and only when the prospects for booty looked good. Early reports from Brazil already expressed signs of disillusion with these less-than-innocent allies. "They asked to be allowed to kill women and children," a perplexed, uneasy, and disapproving member of the Recife political council wrote back to the *bewindhebberen*.[61] The Tarairiu were "beastly and improvident," naked and nomadic, and hopelessly enthralled by the devil – in a word, uncivilized. "They are not a people who can be encouraged to civility, to live in a country side by side with other peoples, to settle down and earn a livelihood from their work," wrote Joannes de Laet, a director of the WIC. "They do not like work, preferring to live from other people's industry and ruin what others have cultivated." "Genuine savages," opined a disenchanted missionary, who complained of the "fabulous" and shamelessly misleading accounts that had lured him to Brazil in the first place.[62]

New Netherland attracted far less attention than did Brazil in these early years, though it too provoked a certain degree of disappointment, as Dutch expectations appeared to go unfulfilled. In settling those lands that bordered the "North" (Hudson) and "South" (Delaware) Rivers of what they originally called "Virginia," the WIC could hardly sustain an argument for combating Spanish tyranny or liberating American allies. Spain had never reached this far north, and in a sense the directors' choice of New Netherland represented an obvious shirking of their "moral" responsibilities to the Indians. Nonetheless, the prevailing opinion of the region imagined a hospitable landscape peopled by well-disposed natives, inclined to be disenchanted with the Spanish and thus receptive to the Dutch. The Indians of Manhattan were expected to welcome and cooperate with the Dutch and somehow assist their American enterprise. Joannes de Laet, a director of the WIC as well as its point man on matters of geography, regarded the natives of this region as "friendly" and "very good people," who would be "well disposed, if they are only well treated." "They are, besides, very serviceable," averred de Laet, writing in the very early years of contact. "And [they] allow themselves to be employed in many things for a small compensation . . . in which they show greater fidelity than could be expected of such people." De Laet was especially encouraged by the possibilities for trade with the natives, whom he considered relatively amenable to "the habits of civilized life." Based on travelers' reports and geographic deduction, he also predicted favorable climatic conditions. (New Amsterdam was on the same latitude as Madrid and was expected to be equally mild.) The chronicler Nicolaes van Wassenaer, in his annual report for 1624, contended that near the South River, "there is no winter save in January and then but a few days."[63]

It took but a few dreary winters to revise these and other sanguine assumptions about New Netherland. Visitors quickly observed that the region's climate, if anything, seemed colder and harsher than many Northern European countries. The natives, too, gave a much cooler impression than expected. In what are considered the earliest extant letters written from Manhattan, the *predikant,* Jonas Michaëlius, complained bitterly of the "entirely savage" and all but incorrigible ways of the natives. In no uncertain terms, Michaëlius decried the "treachery," "wickedness" and "barbarity" of the colonists' aboriginal neighbors, and he all but despaired of their grace before God. "As to the natives of this country," he wrote to his patron, Joannes van Foreest, a magistrate of Hoorn,

I find them entirely savage and wild, strangers to all decency, yea, uncivil and stupid as garden stakes, proficient in all wickedness and ungodliness, devilish men, who serve nobody but the Devil. . . . They have so much witchcraft, divination, sorcery, and wicked acts, that they can hardly be held in by any bands or locks. They are as thievish and treacherous as they are tall, and in cruelty they are altogether inhuman, more than barbarous.

A Calvinist minister convinced of the general depravity of all mankind, Michaëlius maintained faith despite it all in the natives' ultimate reformation. (He was among the first Protestant ministers to recommend teaching the Indians in their native language.) His disappointment is striking nonetheless, as is his expression of amazement and consternation that he had ever anticipated anything easier.

> I cannot myself wonder enough who it is that has imposed so much upon your Reverence [he wrote to Adrianus Smoutius, a fiery Gomarist] and many others in the Fatherland, concerning the docility of this people and their good nature, the proper *principia religionis* and *vestigia legis naturae*, which are said to be among [the Indians], in whom I have as yet been able to discover hardly a single good point.

Like his missionary colleague in Brazil, Michaëlius denounced the "false reports and counsels" that had misguided opinion in the Netherlands, promoting an overly optimistic perception of America and fostering an image of the natives as amenable allies and cooperative coreligionists. The Indians, apparently, were less innocent than had been previously assumed. Much the same could now be said for those Dutch publicists who had assiduously – and some might now say, disingenuously – cultivated that image of innocence abroad.[64]

V

As the Dutch expansion in the West got underway, one can speak of a fundamental shift in the rhetoric of America. By the late 1620s and early 1630s, as the Dutch became more substantially and permanently involved in the New World – as the Dutch began to acquire Indians of their own, so to speak – the topos of native innocence was largely abandoned as a viable means to describe America. It had become increasingly improbable to sound a moral appeal for Dutch "allies" in America when plainly no such alliance was forthcoming. "America," as such, ceased to work. Those investors who contemplated the New World in the early 1620s responded to the WIC only after the Company clarified its economic goals; those colonists who visited the New World by the early 1630s reported on the Indians chiefly to express their frustration and disillusion. Talk of alliances – of the *moral* purpose of America – had lost much of its credibility. In the meantime, America became increasingly associated with concerns of commerce and conquest. Ministers, it is true, still rallied around the cause of evangelization and Dutch religious obligations in America. Yet they perceived the problem in terms of Spanish Catholicism rather than native heathenism. The Spanish enemy still remained of central interest; the American "ally" only insofar as he participated in trade. Dutch polemicists of the second quarter of the century depicted America as a holy battleground, where the church of God would be served, the tyranny of Spain would be foiled, and the profits of the Republic would be made.

Profits, above all, possessed the imagination of those reporting on America in these years. Piet Heyn's fabulous seizure of the Spanish silver-fleet in 1628 – *the* signal event of its day – captivated a Dutch public more and more enthralled by American wealth. "A treasure chamber of gold and silver," promised one author to an audience hardly in need of convincing. In the popular romance, *The wonderful adventure of two lovers,* the West Indies played the part of the pot of gold at the end of the rainbow (fig. 27). When all else fails the young couple, the suitor sails to the West Indies to amass "an excellent treasure of gold and pearls," and returns to live happily ever after with his beloved. (The title page illustrates their marital bliss literally as a heap of American treasure spilling out from a cornucopia.)[65] To those with a less romantic bent, America featured more prosaically as a market for export, a source of employment, and a target for investment. Rarely did the fate of the Indians come up in debates circa 1630 – this in marked contrast to the discussions earlier in the century on the widespread tyranny of Spain. When the subject of peace negotiations revived in 1629–1630, America once again figured centrally in the public's deliberations. Yet unlike their predecessors who had opposed the Truce in 1606–1609, polemicists now resolutely emphasized the importance of the Indies for the Dutch economy and blithely ignored the fate of the "tyrannized" Indian. Peace would halt the advance of the WIC, contended the new generation of *contra-Trevisten,* many of whom would seem to have been on the Company's payroll. And what hurt the WIC hurt the Republic by taking away jobs, trade, and markets. Peace would also disappoint Dutch "allies," though by this pamphleteers alluded to the besieged Protestants of Germany and Bohemia who depended on the States' assistance in their struggle against the long arm of the Habsburgs. The fate of *Indian* allies seemed a matter barely worth mentioning.[66]

Pamphleteers imparted an urgent sense of militancy to discussions of America. They called on the Dutch to think not defensively about the New World – protecting the Indians and preserving native liberties – but rather offensively – attacking Spain and possessing its colonies. The WIC clarified its purpose now as never before in brashly martial terms: a mission of Dutch expansion and conquest. They used fighting words to discuss their subject, and they paid scant attention to the plainly pe-

Wonderlicke Avontuer/

Van twee Goelieven, de eene ghenaemt

S^r. UUaterbrandt/

ende de ander

Joufvrouw Wintergroen.

Nu onlanghs ghebeurt aen een Jongman die men meende verflaghen te
zijn , ende een Jonckvrou, de welcke men meende verdroncken te zijn,
maer na duyfent avonturen wederom in vreughden zijn te famen
ghekomen, mede brengende eenen uyt-nemenden fchat
van Gout ende Paerlen uyt *Weft-Indien.*

Tot Leyden voor NICOLAES GEELKERCK. 1624.

Figure 27. Title page from *Wonderlicke avontuer van twee goelieven* (Leiden, 1624).
The Hague, Koninklijke Bibliotheek, 300 F 21.

ripheral task of redeeming the Indians. Like the conquistadors of old, the WIC sought to infest America "by fire and sword" and "drive a sword through the king of Spain's heart." Self-designated "lovers of the Fatherland" encouraged the WIC to "conquer" America and did so with language remarkable for its belligerence. They pressed Company soldiers to repay the Spaniards with violence every bit equal to that of Charles's original *Landsknechten.* Wreak havoc and war, they directed the Dutch conquistadors,

go ravage and plunder . . . and lay waste the population by scorching and blazing . . . and make from the West Indies a theater of miseries. For the Spaniards have well earned it by the great tyrannies they have committed both here [in the Netherlands] and abroad.[67]

The Reformed minister of Haarlem, Samuel Ampzing, rallied his Batavian brethren to take "righteous revenge" and well-deserved booty in the New World. This meant, first, inflicting maximum torment on the enemy – "to cause only suffering" – and, second, extracting maximum gain from the land. "Just war makes fair booty," declared Ampzing approvingly in reference to the enormous prize of silver lately stolen by Heyn.[68]

Lost in all this Batavian bravado was the fact that the riches of America belonged to Spain only by the sweat of the Indian's brow. Yet just as attitudes toward America had shifted, so too had the consensus on its natives. Early experiences in the New World had rattled Dutch assumptions about the Indians and disappointed expectations of forming a quick "alliance." As a consequence, the Dutch now spoke less of their responsibilities to serve the Americans and more of their opportunities to bring the natives into the service of the WIC (including as soldiers). Here too rhetoric had been modified and priorities reshuffled. Writing from Olinda in 1630, the field commander Dirck van Waerdenburgh commented revealingly to the States General when he reported on the progress of his troops, the prospects for Brazil, and the *problems* with the natives. Since the local tribes had thus far not joined his efforts, he recommended that reinforcements be sent promptly so that he might enlarge on his conquests. "This," he remarked in his widely published letter, "is the only means to take away the trade of the enemy and to reduce the natives to a mutual friendship and alliance." This unusual and somewhat baffling turn of phrase – to *reduce* the natives to friendship – is repeated verbatim in the chronicle of Nicolaes van Wassenaer and picked up a few years later in a poem by Elias Herckmans. (In an epic celebration of navigation, Herckmans sings of Dutch labors "to coerce" America into obedience.)[69] Prints engraved around this time convey a

Figure 28. Title page (detail) from Johannes de Laet, *Nieuwe Wereldt* (Leiden, 1630). Universiteitsbibibliotheek Amsterdam.

similar image, in starkly visual terms, of a Dutch-Indian alliance of un-equals. On the title-page of Joannes de Laet's *Nieuwe Wereldt* (1630 and 1633 editions), a vignette shows a trio of natives paying homage to a fe-male personification of the Republic (fig. 28). She sits regally on a throne, a regimental drum and an array of weapons scattered around her. The Indians approach respectfully, bearing plates of pearls and gold, their leader astride an armadillo. Although it is they who approach her, the banner above refers to her – the Dutch – arrival: *Venisti tandem* (You have come at last). In another allegory (sometimes ascribed to François van den Hoeye), a party of natives delivers sacks of merchandise (gold ore?) to supervising Dutch sailors (fig. 29). The latter inspect, then wheel off their cargo toward war vessels moored off shore. Both images endeavor to portray a relationship of deferential service rather than "mutual friendship and alliance." The Indians assist the Dutch expansion; the Dutch accept the natives' largesse.[70]

In return, or at least in theory, the Dutch would bestow upon the Americans the gift of the gospel, yet in this instance, too, circumstances had appreciably altered. For when the Dutch justified their New World initiatives in religious terms, they focused more often on the blight of Catholicism than on the inscrutable, and in certain ways less relevant, habit of heathenism. They crusaded principally against the Spaniards' transgressions, while relegating to the sidelines the natives' salvation. There was, to be sure, talk of evangelization – if surprisingly little men-tion of the Indians. Dutch *predikanten*, as a course of habit, denounced the presumption of Pope Alexander VI, who had granted by bull the

Figure 29. Pieter Serwouters after Pieter Sibrantsz [?], *Allegory of America* (engraving). Courtesy of Hugh Honour.

New World to Spain; and they railed ceaselessly against the hypocrisy of the Most Catholic King, who had exploited the Indies "under the pretext of religion." The WIC, by contrast, pledged to introduce the New World to "the true Christian reformed religion, for the salvation of thousands of souls . . . and to wipe out Papistry and Heathenism." In this light, any sign of Dutch success was interpreted as a triumph of the Reformed faith over the heresy of Rome. The quick collapse of Bahia in 1625, for example, indicated "that the course of the Reformation cannot be hindered." By its impieties, Spain "had driven itself by force from its own home," contended a Calvinist minister, who somewhat overzealously construed America as the house of Spain. Since the Habsburgs "had neglected to take seriously the propagation of the Bible, which should have been their primary purpose," God had delivered the Dutch to America in their stead. The capture of the Spanish silver-fleet in 1628 suggested to a *predikant* of Delft the favor of God and a heavenly windfall for the Reformed Church. Taking his cue from the great, church-building monarchs of Catholic Christendom, the minister called on the WIC to endow with its lucre a Calvinist seminary, *Beth Berachah* (House of Blessing), for the training of soldiers of the righteous church. These would fan out across the globe and convert thousands of souls to the Reformed faith. Thus would the Company's profits endure eternally.[71]

In truth, the Indians had a limited role to play in all this. The New World registered as a stronghold of Spanish Catholicism, and most Calvinist pamphleteering took aim at the sins of Rome rather than the omissions of America. When a *predikant* accompanying Dirck van Waerdenburgh described his commander as Joshua before the walls of Jericho (Olinda), he intended the Portuguese defenders, not the native Brazilians, to stand in the role of Canaanites. With pious solemnity, the minister recounted the ouster of the Jesuits from Olinda, the destruction of their cloisters, and the purification of their churches – yet made no mention whatsoever of the fate of the natives. The Dutch, within this configuration, extended the battle of the Reformation to foreign soil – church militants stationed abroad – while the heart of the war raged on in Europe. The WIC, according to one pamphleteer, represented "the best means . . . to pacify Christendom," and by this he meant the defeat of Catholicism and redemption of Protestants across Europe, "starved for the gospel" and desperate for support in their ongoing campaign against the Habsburgs. More than one polemicist tied the advance of the WIC to the fate of besieged coreligionists in Central Europe and especially in the Palatinate and Bohemia. The Dutch enterprise in America would provide employment opportunities for refugees and establish a haven for them, while diverting Spanish troops from German soil. More often than not, discussions of "innocent allies" in the political literature of circa 1630 referred to the Bohemians: "our friends and partners" and the most recent victims of papist oppression. A WIC position paper, reprinted five times in 1629, concluded with a fiery "Remonstrance" from the Bohemians to the States General for assistance. In the name of the exiled Winter King (Frederick) and his oppressed nation, the WIC urged the States vigorously to pursue their war with Spain. The exiled Bohemian had quietly displaced the native American as the model of forsaken innocence.[72]

With or without the Indians, the Lord's work in America remained to be done, and the Dutch aspired to do their part. In an age of religious enthusiasms, the New World could not help but assume a heightened spiritual significance – the Indies, even *sans* Indians, had a role in the divine plan for the cosmos – and it comes as no surprise to find such considerable sermonizing and prognostication on the Indies as took place in the mid-seventeenth-century Republic. Against the backdrop of America, Dutch *predikanten* staged the religious dramas of their day: the clash of Catholicism and reformed Christianity, and the search for divine corroboration of grace. From the vantage point of the Republic's pulpits, the New World appeared as the very battleground of God and devout Dutch sailors as the Lord's elected host. Ewout Teellinck, a onetime burgomaster of Zierikzee and an early advocate of Zeeland pietism, perceived in the West Indies a holy struggle of sin and salvation. Habsburg impiety had aroused the Lord's wrath and summoned the Dutch to America. Conversely, confessional feuding within the Republic had provoked the Lord's disappointment, resulting (Teellinck believed) in Dutch setbacks overseas. In the imagination of the Haarlem Contra-Remonstrant, Samuel Ampzing, the battle in the New World pitted "them of the Devil against God's holy warriors." America had long since fallen captive to the whore of Rome (the pope) and her bastard son in Spain (the king), who had transformed Brazil into a latter-day Babylon. The blood-stained soil of America cried out for vengeance, and, at the bidding of the Lord, the Dutch Calvinists would now answer that call.[73]

The theme of divine retribution shaped many of the responses to Dutch colonial advances of the 1620s and 1630s.[74] Conquests in Brazil and privateering in the Caribbean were interpreted as "*Lex talionis,* that is, the righteous punishment of God to tyrants," as the *predikant* Jacobus Focanus termed it in his colorful survey of crime and divine punishment. Dutch windfall was Spain's downfall was divine vengeance for tyrannies past. Just as the conquistadors had met with poetic justice – death by starvation, deprivation, cannibalism, betrayal – so would the Spanish empire in America, in Focanus' view, suffer the belated, though certainly deserved, punishment of the Lord. "God's punitive arm," declared Focanus, stretched around the globe and even to America. The "righteous judgment" of God on Bahia, manifested by the Dutch capture of the colony's governor and humiliation of his Jesuit principal, betokened the cataclysmic collapse of Brazil and apocalyptic end to Spain:

> The violence and excess that Spain has committed
> On the Indies and us, has been much depicted,
> That they shall be so sternly castigated
> In ways unheard of, yea, utterly extirpated,
> And they shall be exposed to God's vengeance replete,
> The fire of which shall blacken the world complete.

Had the merciful Creator forgotten the crimes committed in America? asked one *predikant.* Would Spain go uncastigated for its "unheard of" tyrannies? "Without a doubt, God shall seek out and avenge the murderous and inhuman deeds of the Spaniards through the agency of one nation or another."[75]

More and more the Republic presumed to be that nation, appointed to carry out that vengeance. "The Spaniards shall be punished by God through us," asserted the self-righteous Focanus. This self-election had the effect of sanctioning a specifically Dutch – and by extension, WIC – role in the colonization of America, while at the same time imparting a righteous sheen to the trophies of conquest brought back to the fatherland. "He has selected us to be His instrument," claimed a partisan of the American enterprise, "to punish the great multitude of tyrannies committed by the Spaniards both here in the Netherlands and in the West Indies." The WIC was described as the *roede* (literally, rod) or scourge of God created to mete out the full measure of divine discipline on the Habsburgs. "That land [of America] still overflows with that blood which cries out for vengeance," protested a poet. Thus was the Company

> Chartered to mop up the blood of the land once again
> . . . .
> This blood cries out now for vengeance, and helps us in battle,
> It will not rest till you [Spain] have forfeited your treasure.

In another, only slightly less macabre conceit, a poet envisioned the souls of Motecuçoma, Atahualpa, and other American warriors reincarnated in the bodies of van Waerdenburgh, Heyn, and other Dutch admirals charged to avenge the impieties of Spain in the Indies.[76]

By sanctifying the Dutch West India Company, the poets and pamphleteers sanctified whatever ends, holy or not, the Company might pursue. The conquest of defenseless Portuguese settlements became the extirpation of sinful Canaanites, necessary for the purification of the land. The seizure of rich Spanish cargoes became the dispossession of unjust profits, righteously reallocated to the Netherlands. Heyn and his band of privateers, according to the poet Daniel Souterius, had "relieved" the Spanish king of his American silver as just compensation for tyrannies previously committed in the Netherlands. Like the ancient Israelites who had despoiled their Egyptian task-masters en route from Goshen, the Dutch now raided the Spanish silver of the Indies by divine injunction, as "reparation for damages these Provinces have been made to suffer after many years of tyranny from Spain."[77] Ampzing glorified the pirate "Saint Piet," as he dubbed him, and extolled the rich booty retrieved by the WIC from the Indies. "Your noble Company," he gushed to the directors, "was appointed and established at the precise moment – in the ripeness of the Lord's sentence against Spain – to throw your sickle into the harvest of Spanish gold and treasure and, with right-eousness, to reap and gather Spain's plunder into your own shed." Am-pzing considered the booty stolen from Spain – to which some critics, so he contended, had dared to object – a "wonder," a "blessing" and a "gift from God" bestowed onto the Netherlands,

> because the Marrano [an abusive term for Spaniard] has
> Maliciously raped this land by sword and violence and plunder
> And murderously slaughtered there people so very great in number:
> Will God not avenge the looting and murdering by Spain
> And recompense the innocent blood of the [Indian] . . . ?

Thus, by some wonderfully rich irony, the sins of Spain in the Indies had profited the godly Batavians in the Netherlands.[78]

Inevitably, the pious posturing of the WIC and its supporters in-volved a certain amount of rhetorical risk. When all went favorably in the New World, the Company might well represent the *roede van God*, sent to thrash the iniquitous Spaniard. When expeditions failed, on the other hand, the Dutch might appear to be on the wrong end of the stick. To link the Company's progress in America with the moral virtue of the Republic, in other words, was to invite the association of any failure in the New World with the moral deficiency of the Republic. Something on this order took place, in fact, following the rapid rise and then brisk de-cline of Dutch fortunes in Bahia in 1624–1625. Ewout Teellinck, the Zee-land pietist who had welcomed the quick victory over the Portuguese as a sign of divine favor, interpreted the following year's news of Bahia's reconquest as proof of the Republic's transgressions. Just as the Lord had sent the men of Äi to chasten those Israelites who had broken faith in the aftermath of Jericho, so He now dispatched a fleet of Spaniards to castigate the Republic for its spiritual lapses following the conquest of Bahia. To Teellinck, an avowed irenicist and, with his brother Willem, a leading figure of the *Nadere Reformatie* (Further Reformation), the "ve-hemence of disputation" within the Calvinist church had provoked the Lord's displeasure – and hence the reversal of fortunes in Bahia. Now it was Spain's turn to serve as "the scourge [*roede*] of the Lord's wrath and the rod of His fury, which the Lord uses against a false people, however many of them might be of the Reformed Church." The New World re-mained, then, the battleground of God, though in this instance the Dutch found themselves fighting on the losing side.[79]

Considerations of America and the WIC could easily transform in this way into polemics on religion and orthodoxy. Discussions of expedi-tions to, profits from, or even investment in the New World could read-ily devolve into the religio-political debate of the day. Indeed, as the Republic matured, "America" became only more supple. (And as the Republic tamped down its external crises, internal discord more freely flourished.) In the later 1620s and early 1630s, it was generally the party of the orthodox that appropriated the discourse of America for their polemical arsenal. Yet, as the example of Teellinck makes clear, that need not always have been the case. Joost van den Vondel, the leading Dutch poet of his age and a prominent critic of Calvinist orthodoxy, used the occasion of Heyn's West Indies triumph to criticize the *Geuzen* – his term of abuse for the (perhaps) Contra-Remonstrant crew members of Heyn's fleet. Of the mob of sailors gathered outside of the West-India House in Amsterdam, demanding a larger share of the booty, Vondel mocked,

> I thought, those *Geuzen* were of Spain
> Or is Saint Piet Arminian.

The WIC-employed rabble, Vondel insinuated, terrorized public order, as had the Contra-Remonstrants and the Spaniards before them, under the guise of orthodoxy. The poet conflates the Gomarists with the American enterprise – and tars them both with the brush of "Spanish" tyranny.[80]

The WIC had more than its share of defenders, though, and many from the ranks of the orthodox. Willem Usselincx reserved judgment following the fall of Bahia in the mid-1620s, yet regained his voice at the end of a decade that witnessed the jubilant return of Heyn from the Caribbean (1628) and the stunning conquest of Olinda. Writing in opposition to the peace negotiations in 1630, Usselincx extolled the company for its good works in America and railed against its detractors in the Netherlands as a gang of "libertines, freethinkers, David Jorist's [a radical Anabaptist], Remonstrants, apostates of the Reformed religion . . . heretics, sworn enemies of the state and the Reformed religion." Johan van den Sande, a professor in Franeker and a justice at the Synod of Dordrecht, considered the conquest of Brazil the hope of the Reformed – by which he meant orthodox – religion. In the path of the WIC, van den Sande asserted, stood only the obstructionist Arminians who tolerated free-thinking within the Church and free trade within Brazil, both to the detriment of the Republic. No orthodox Contra-Remonstrant himself, Nicolaes van Wassenaer alluded only vaguely and without naming names to the "malevolent enemies of the Fatherland" who thwarted Dutch progress in America. Another chronicler and, like van den Sande, a veteran of the Synod of Dordrecht, Festus Hommius had fewer qualms placing the blame for the Company's setbacks squarely on the shoulders of the "many malicious Papists and Remonstrants who not only excused themselves from subscribing [to the Company] but also discouraged others from doing so." One of those who did subscribe, Arend van Buchell, likewise noted the hesitant support of most Catholics and Arminians of his native Utrecht. Since van Buchell himself came from a Catholic background, his observation carries with it perhaps more weight than the rancorous comments of the *predikant*, Hommius. In any case, the orthodox Calvinists tended to adopt the struggle of the WIC as their own; and, with reason or without, they vilified opponents of the WIC's American project as papist backsliders and enemies of the fatherland. In the self-confident, expansionist, and martial mood of the late 1620s, the minister Samuel Ampzing could preach to an audience, largely converted, and demand that his countrymen fall piously in line with the Company:

> From whom in the land do I hear murmurs of dissent
> Or who would deny here the Lord's hand, heaven sent?[81]

The Lord's majestic hand to which Ampzing referred revealed itself on no occasion so dramatically as in the person of Piet Heyn, champion of the WIC and savior of the Republic. Never before had a Dutch admiral managed to capture the rich Spanish silver-fleet, as Heyn did off the coast of Cuba in September 1628. Never had the Company's prospects sparkled so brightly. With a modest armada of twenty ships and the favor of "Protestant" winds, Heyn realized the WIC's most ambitious dream of striking the Spanish within their own harbors. "The Lord has granted us a Man who has sailed . . . to the other world and conquered," wrote Dionysius Spranckhuysen, a *predikant* from Heyn's hometown of Delft. He also granted the WIC and its shareholders a godsend exceeding eleven million guilders, and for this the Republic feted Heyn with bells and bonfires, fireworks and parades. "In every city and joyful street," exuberant celebrations took place:

> Trumpets' voices ringing
> Clocks a' clanging-clinging . . .
> And dancing and singing.

Heyn became a national hero, and the WIC, once again, the hope of the Netherlands.[82]

Heyn's feat was sensational. It occasioned an outpouring of pomp and poetry, song and celebration; and it momentarily riveted the Republic's attention on America. The published response, too, was immense, ranging from the refined, neo-Latin verse of Daniel Heinsius, to common street-ballads, to children's doggerel:

> Even the young children playing in the street,
> Worked into their games, chatter of the fleet.[83]

And though a popular song contended that the noble general had no rival in bravery from times past or present, this did not discourage the poets and *predikanten* from comparing Heyn precisely to heroes mythological, biblical, and historical.[84] The "son of the Maas" and favorite of Neptune was lionized as a wise Ulysses and steadfast Aeneas, a champion of epic stature. His good sense and good fortune reminded some of Joshua (one *predikant* likened the planks of the Spanish galleons to the stones of Jericho's walls); others of Gideon, slayer of the Midianites and enemy of Baal; and still others of the great warrior-king, David. For his military ability, poets likened him to Alexander the Great; for his discipline, they compared him to the renowned generals of Republican Rome. In whatever guise they dressed him, all declared Heyn the *roede* of God, sent to punish Spain for its past sins. Heyn's "glorious" deeds – privateering off the coast of Cuba and taking for booty the silver mined by slaves – came by the grace of the Lord. Heyn was the preachers' favorite. "He is (to be brief) our Salvation and Spain's downfall," concluded Spranckhuysen.[85]

Still, the religious pitch never rose quite as high as the economic, as the poets never forgot the bottom line. Much as he might have served as an agent of divine vengeance, Heyn also produced a spectacular fortune for the Republic, including a 3,500,000 guilder profit for the shareholders of the WIC. (The prince of Orange, as titular admiral of the United Provinces, received 700,000 guilders; the directors 70,000 guilders; and Heyn himself 7,000 guilders. The price of the Company's stock on the Amsterdam exchange doubled on news of the fleet's return.) Heyn's reputation as a pious seaman never outshone the brilliance of his catch: a treasure of silver, silk, indigo, and cochineal, brazenly plundered from the king of Spain. The poets celebrated the very spoils themselves and the admiral's daring abduction of them, which they construed as a drama of romantic intrigue. The West Indies prize represented the king's beautifully clad mistress, "the rich royal bride" courted by the bold Heyn and his men. "The apple of my eye," protests the king on learning of Heyn's affair:

> And that these young fellows with their pitch-covered breeches:
> My wife, my true wife [they] have sullied her linens;
> Her hair, her gold-yellow hair, they nimbly unbraid
> Her silver-white visage, they shamefully besmirch,
> First they abducted my old concubine [the East Indies],
> Now they would master the true wife of mine.[86]

The Dutch entered the king's Caribbean mansion stoutly. They came as suitors, "fresh young men / In the bloom of their youth," and Heyn was their "manly [*manhaftig*]" leader, of "virile courage," "dapper," and most attractive.[87] Spranckhuysen depicted Heyn as the handsome King David to whom all the young women of Israel flocked with sighs of love and song. This Batavian David wooed a Spanish bride, however, and "zealously" seized her as his own. The language of the poets is most forthright. Heyn had managed to possess "Spain's lovely bride [and] to rape her with piety [*met vroomheydt te verkrachten*]," declared one poet. Others wrote slightly more demurely of "seduction" or "conquest," yet their meaning was abundantly clear, their language unabashedly gendered:

> In order to seduce this wealthy bride with honor
> Our clever general secured her with his weapon.[88]

Ultimately and decisively, Heyn's stratagem succeeded and signaled a strategic breakthrough for the Dutch in the West Indies. The victory of Piet Heyn – the "rape" of Spain's American bride – meant that the New World had now become an "embraced" mistress, as the poets delicately put it, open to the advances of other amorous Dutch conquerors. A new era had thus begun in the history of the Republic's western expansion. America's age of innocence had now surely passed.

VI

The rhetoric of America that accompanied Heyn's victory demonstrates the marvelous litheness of the Dutch geographic imagination, which now projected the New World not in terms of innocence, but in the language of revenue, plunder, and violation. Yet if the Dutch image of America showed a fair degree of mutability, certain elements, too, demonstrated remarkable durability. By the 1630s, the WIC's boosters and their *contra-Treviste* allies had all but abandoned their appeals on behalf of the Indian. The New World held out the far more compelling, and in a sense more realistic, promise of profit, and the pamphleteers reshaped their rhetoric accordingly to emphasize the glory of conquest and potential for gain. Still, as the topos of American innocence lost much of its resonance within the polemical literature of the second quarter of the century, it gained new relevance elsewhere within Dutch letters: namely, in the composition of patriotic history. The story of the Republic's heroic foundation, solemnly recited throughout the final, and relatively less vigorous, half of the Eighty Years' War, revived the traditional theme of tyranny in America to memorialize, as it were, the epic iniquity of Spain. Far from disappearing, the topos of American innocence passed from one genre to another – from pamphlet literature to patriotic chronicle – and from the discursive context of polemical ephemera to the more permanent repository of historical memory. As the Republic entered more conspicuously into the state of nationhood – as the war receded to the peripheries and the trading companies, including the WIC, began to pay their dividends – it glanced purposefully back to the circumstances of its own foundation. Chroniclers returned to the memory of Spanish tyrannies past, which revived the memory of Spanish tyrannies distant – in America. The topos of American innocence reemerged in this way to play yet another role, this time in the drama of patriotic historiography.

"Patriotic scripture," as Simon Schama has termed it, played an enormously vital role within the Republic. The commemoration of the history of the Revolt – in chronicle, drama, verse, doggerel, print, painting, sculpture, performance, and civic ceremony – allowed the founding generation of the United Provinces to impress upon its heirs the struggles it had heroically endured. To recollect and recite the saga of the sixteenth century was to rally the younger generation to arms and rejuvenate its flagging piety. When the religious feuds of the 1620s threatened to tear the Republic asunder, and the economic prosperity of the 1630s threatened to lull it into complacency, the lessons of patriotic scripture sounded the "alarm bell of the Independent Netherlands" and summoned the nation to persevere in its ongoing struggle for freedom.[89] The memory of Granvelle and Alba, of the executions of Egmond and Hoorn, of the sieges of Haarlem and Leiden, of the massacres of Naarden and Oudewater: all would trigger, it was hoped, the reverent recollection of, and collective allegiance to, acts of revolt and abjuration. By evoking tribulations past, history also provided the materials to forge a common identity among the present, sometimes factious, parties of the Netherlands. Patriotic scripture established retrospectively a loyalty to the fatherland by perpetuating the memory of Spanish tyrannies – whether or not, in fact, these atrocities had ever mutually affected the "united" provinces of the North, to whom these histories now appealed in the first place. The very fragility of the young Republic and tenuousness of its bonds suggested the usefulness of patriotic nostalgia. Indeed, the Republic's successes no less than its failures prompted the recourse to history and the appeal to the memory of its patriarchs' deeds. On the occasion of Heyn's victory, the participants in one dialogue, "Freemate" and "Memory," celebrated the Republic's good fortunes by recalling earlier hardships endured. On the occasion of Heyn's tragic death the following year (1629) at the hands of Dunkirk privateers, Spranckhuysen mourned the nation's loss, enjoining the Republic to reflect on both the admiral's tragedy and the sacrifices of his Batavian forebears. "Thus we say to you people," Spranckhuysen preached, "remember what the Spaniards have done to you and your Fathers when we, from the darkness of popery, passed into the light of the holy Gospel."[90]

With a variety of means and toward a variety of ends, the seventeenth-century Dutch attended to the memory of their forefathers. The historiography of the Revolt commenced already by the turn of the century with Emanuel van Meteren's massive and learned *Belgische ofte Nederlantsche historie* (1599, with expanded editions in 1608 and 1614), followed by the exceedingly popular and plainly populist *Morghenwecker der vrye Nederlantsche provintien* (1610), published promptly after the conclusion of the Twelve Year Truce.[91] These set off an avalanche of publications, some in lavish folio and others in octavo, some with learned citations and others with doggerel verse, some set to musical scores and others accompanied by illustrations – and virtually all presented "for the love of the fatherland." According to their authors, these histories represented "treasuries of time," repositories "of all sorts of feats of war . . . properties of wisdom, art, prudence, courage, strength, bravery, trust, steadfastness." Many opted for the metaphor of theater and staged the Dutch Revolt as a baroque drama of suffering and redemption. History offered the lessons of life on an "elevated stage," wrote the dean of the Veere rhetoricians, Adriaen Valerius:

[It] presents and sets forth to the heedful and clever reader much rich material, inducing *wisdom*, through the remembrance of that which has occurred; *devoutness*, through the consideration of that which should have occurred; and *circumspection*, through the observation of that which could yet occur.[92]

Dutch historiography of the first half of the seventeenth century was intended to prompt patriotism and its close relative, piety. A zealous preacher of patriotic scripture, Joannes Gijsius typically lumped the two together when he dedicated his *Oorsprong en voortgang der Nederlandtscher beroerten ende ellendicheden* (Origin and progress of the Netherland's troubles and miseries) "to all pious and upright Netherlanders who cherish the welfare and freedom of the beloved Fatherland." Gijsius submitted his narrative – "a small sampling of Spanish tyrannies and atrocities committed in the Netherlands" – to impress upon the younger generation their elders' sacrifice and to arouse (*opwekken*) in them a desire "to praise and thank the Lord ever more fervently, since He has redeemed us from such great miseries here in these free and united Netherlands." Dutch histories, like all good theater, sought to *move* their audience and incite in them strong feelings toward God, country, and the Spanish enemy. The tales of tyranny that flowed from the pen of one chronicler had the stated purpose of "refreshing" the Republic's font of Hispanophobia and refilling the wells of patriotic spirit.[93] Injunctions "to remember daily" the miseries of our forebears or "to recite solemnly" the blasphemies of Spain had an unmistakably ceremonial, Haggadah-like quality to them, a resemblance not lost on their authors. The elder generation was instructed to teach the younger of the tyrannies of Spain, lest the children forget the price of their freedom. "My dear son," begins a didactic dialogue composed as a school text, "as a faithful father it is incumbent upon me to rear you in the fear of God." This consists chiefly of rehearsing the story of Spanish oppression, of God's favor toward the rebels, and of their ultimate emancipation. "Honored father," asks the obedient son, "is it really such a blessing that the king of Spain recognizes our freedom? My youth precludes me from knowing this horrible saga." All too gladly, the parent catalogues, illustrates, and explicates the tyrannies of Spain "as a good patriot and a faithful father must do," and narrates the story of the Revolt, "just as the children of Israel were obligated . . . to narrate for *their* children the miraculous deliverance from Egypt."[94]

Patriotic scripture sermonized. It sought to educate a younger generation – by which was meant the magistrates and burghers of the post-Truce era – in the lessons of the past and to guide them toward vigilance in the future. "It can justly be said of truthful and well-postulated histories," remarked Adriaen Valerius in the opening to his own contribution, the *Nederlandtsche gedenck-clank* (Netherlands anthem of commemoration), "that they give testimony from the past, exhortation for the present, and warning to the future." To Valerius and most of his fellow historians, the emphasis lay on the future – and hence the cautionary, sometimes shrill, and always didactic tone of their work. Diligent study of the Revolt, Valerius contended in his dedication to the States General, would reward their High Mightinesses with exempla of virtue and courage worthy of emulation, and with models of ambition and greed wisely avoided. "What is more," added Valerius, "familiarity with Dutch history will be useful for our security; for . . . all pious supporters [of the Fatherland] and all good patriots will now be alerted . . . to be mindful of the menacing, perfidious, perjurious, irreconcilable, implacable, cruel, and murderous nature of our enemy."[95] The ever-present threat from Spain demanded the ever-constant vigilance of the Republic. History – the recollection of tyrannies past – would keep the Dutch on their guard. "Some, indeed quite a few, have been lulled to sleep," fretted the minister-turned-historian, Willem Baudartius. He submitted his own compilation to their High Mightinesses as a "morning-waker," or alarm bell, to arouse the magistrates from the slumber of complacency, "that our beloved Fatherland shall be preserved, that it shall never again fall into the hands of our arch-enemies, the Spanish." A vignette on the title-page showed a crane at rest, a stone clasped in one foot to prevent the bird from falling too deeply into sleep. Just as the crane kept constantly on its guard, always aware of potential dangers afield, reasoned Baudartius, so too must the Republic remain always alert to repel the perpetual attacks of Spain and reject the unceasing offers of (false) peace. Patriotic scripture was the stone in the grasp of an ever-watchful Republic.[96]

While Baudartius and Valerius appealed to the governing class, others took their case more directly to the true future of the Republic: the youth. It was "to the youth of Holland" that Johan van Heemskerk addressed his *Batavische arcadia* (1637), a combination prose and verse account of "our forefathers' wars against the Romans and the Spaniards . . . for the maintenance of patriotic freedom." Since the children of the seventeenth century had no recollection, naturally, of the events of the Revolt, it was incumbent upon the founding generation to "engrave unto their hearts" the painful memory of Spanish perfidy and to "inculcate" in them hatred of that nation. Gijsius asked of his elder readers that they "earnestly impress upon the children" – *inscherpen*, in the sense of stamping or cutting in – the history of the Revolt and the ordeal of the Dutch. To that end, an Amsterdam sexton reworked Baudartius's *Morghenwecker* for a younger audience, simplifying the prose and marginalia and deleting the difficult Latin citations (though leaving intact the pedagogically instructive examples of the enemy's incorrect Latin). Addressed "to the schoolmasters of these free Netherlands," the *Spieghel der jeught* (Mirror of youth) provided the basis "for the education of the young, very suitable for use in the schools of the free Netherlands." Very suitable, indeed: The *Spieghel der jeught* went through some twenty editions in less than half a century, including a French translation, devised, presumably, for the lycée. It allowed parents and teachers "to instill in [their] children from a young age and drill into their hearts the hatred of the imperious Spaniards." It introduced generations of Dutch students to the lessons of the Revolt. And finally, it perpetuated, "for eternal remembrance," a vivid memory of the unparalleled tyrannies of Spain.[97]

Patriotic scripture also had the effect of perpetuating the memory of Spanish misdeeds in America, a motif that would likewise become indelibly engraved onto the heart and mind of every freedom-loving Netherlander. For the seventeenth-century histories of the Revolt invariably included references, often quite extensive and central, to the purportedly related struggle that had taken place in the Indies. The two stories neatly paralleled one another, as every Dutch schoolgirl and schoolboy dutifully learned, and as Dutch historians never tired of pointing out. "Is it not strange" wonders the wide-eyed child who participates in one such lesson of patriotic history, "that all other nations are quite satisfied with Spain and we alone complain about their inhuman cruelty?" "Your wisdom is yet limited," replies his parent, who goes on patiently to elucidate "how the Spanish barbarians have dealt with the innocent Indians, . . . [and] what great atrocities, barbaric and inhuman deeds they have committed there." In this dialogue, as in so many others concerning the Revolt, the recollection of atrocities committed in the Netherlands inevitably leads to references to cruelties committed in America. The story of the Dutch ineluctably embraces that of America.[98]

By this stage, of course, there would have been little surprise in such comparisons. The highly formulaic depictions of Habsburg tyrannies owed a great deal to the literature of America – principally Las Casas – in the first place; and the Dutch had alluded to analogous outrages in the West Indies since the earliest years of the Revolt. Now, however, the Dutch were asked not simply to *recognize* events in the New World and to juxtapose these with subsequent developments in the Netherlands, but further to *recall* events in America in order to commit them to memory. Patriotic historians entreated their audience to incorporate the narrative of Spanish tyrannies in America, that is to say, into the larger body of patriotic scripture and to commemorate the history of the *Conquista*, piously and ceremoniously, just as they would memorialize instances of Habsburg abuse closer to home. The chronicler Pieter Jansz Twisck capped his extensive review of the tyrannies of Spain in America by elaborating on this didactic program and the need, more generally, to embrace the history of the West Indies within that of the Netherlands. The first, he maintained, elucidated the second and therefore deserved a special place within the Dutch national saga. "Although, dear reader, I prefer not to digress too far from my chronicle or unnecessarily to prolong or obfuscate my history," he remarks,

nonetheless I cannot desist from narrating these affairs, which may serve as a warning and [thus] merit attention. To wit: that in the events of the years 1492 through 1542 discussed above, you may detect, as in a mirror, the character, nature, cunning, deceit, falseness, faithlessness, ambition, cruelty, tyranny, and dominion of the Spaniards . . . committed in the New World. It behooves us always to remember, to recollect in lively and plain terms, and never to permit to lapse into the house of forgetfulness these memories; but rather to remain assiduously alert, diligently prepared, and always on our guard . . . that we never again fall under the dominion, tyranny, and violence of Spain.[99]

Rather than in the "house of forgetfulness," the history of America belonged in the palace of memory, preserved there in a prominent wing of
the Dutch historical consciousness, to endure forever as a locus of patriotic allegiance.

It would be difficult to exaggerate the pervasiveness of Dutch patriotic historiography and the American chapter within it. The story of
Spanish tyranny appealed to an exceptionally broad audience in the Republic. It bridged differences of taste and education, faith and faction;
and it spanned a variety of genres and circumstances. On the most basic level, it flourished in the popular texts, printed in smaller formats,
decorated with crude woodcuts and engravings, and further animated
by simple verse. Here blood-splattered vignettes of violence predominated. Descriptions inclined toward the baroque, such that no single adjective would suffice where a dozen might fit. The prototype of this
genre was Baudartius's *Morghen-wecker* (1610), itself a distillation of the
raciest pamphlet literature of the late sixteenth century, now presented
as sober history. Baudartius's seminal text – singled out by bibliogra-
phers as the "folk" text *par excellence* of the seventeenth century – served
as the basis for the *Spieghel der jeught* (1614), two works attributed to
Joannes Gijsius, and an anonymously published picture-book depicting
the "more than inhuman and barbaric tyrannies of Spain."[100] One of Gijsius's works was published as the "Second Part" of the Las Casas-in-
spired *Spiegel der Spaensche tyrannye* (1620). It carried a set of exceptionally graphic illustrations of Spanish atrocities glossed by a series of
equally expressive "sonnets" of didactic doggerel. This account, together with the slightly more literate *Oorsprong en voortgang* (1616), appeared in some dozen editions before the Peace of Münster was signed
in 1648. As in so many other patriotic histories, Gijsius's narrative began with, concluded with, and referred throughout to the tyrannies of
Spain in America. "One reads from a variety of authors of the insatiable
ambition, intolerable haughtiness, and unspeakable cruelty of the Spanish nation," Gijsius opened his history of the Dutch troubles. "First, the
Spaniards revealed their blood-thirsty nature to the innocent Indians. . . ." Only later in his account did Gijsius turn to their perfidy in the
Netherlands.[101]

At the other end of the market were the grander, more learned, and
lavishly produced volumes meant to appeal to a more prosperous, if not
more refined, audience. These tended to be folio works, illustrated with
superior engravings, and embellished by many of the devices of humanist scholarship. To be sure, a clear-cut division does not always separate the upscale histories from the more "popular" variants. Gijsius's
Oorsprong en voortgang twice appeared in a Latin translation and in this

form attracted, one assumes, an erudite readership (or at least an international one, since the Latin version included a "Tragic history of the
wars in France" attributed to François Hotman).[102] Yet Gijsius's pun-
gent volume, in Latin or not, hardly compares in scale, grandeur, and
refinement to the offerings of a P. C. Hooft or even Pieter Bor. These authors took pains to distance themselves precisely from the sort of sensationalist style otherwise on the market. Nonetheless, despite the elevated claims of many "learned" histories, beginning with van
Meteren's, of *onpartijdigheid* (impartiality), not even the most respected
texts bear out this boast. Like the popular histories, the learned ones narrate an extravagant epic of Spanish tyrannies in the Netherlands, making appropriate allusions to the memory of atrocities abroad. Van Meteren, who kept abreast of the Atlantic world from his exile in London,
scattered throughout his chronicle references to both the tyranny and
trade in America. In recording the death of Philip II, he took the opportunity to revive the memory of that monarch's far-flung abominations
and particularly of "the millions of souls murdered" in the New World.
Hooft's high drama of the Revolt, the most celebrated of all seventeenth-
century compositions, stayed aloof from the mundane concerns of commerce in favor of political intrigues of state and wrenching descriptions
of suffering. For Hooft, it was the departure of Alba from the Low Countries that triggered the sharpest memory of the Republic's anguish and,
not unrelated, the wretchedness of the Indies.[103]

Patriotic historiography – or at least its practitioners – also spanned a
broad spectrum of religious beliefs within the Republic. The popular
histories, it is true, derived most commonly from the ranks of orthodox
Calvinism. Willem Baudartius, Joannes Gijsius, and Herman Allertsz
(the Amsterdam sexton who published and very likely wrote the
Spieghel der jeught) all brought impeccable Contra-Remonstrant credentials to their tasks.[104] So too did certain historians of more accomplished
works. Festus Hommius, who chronicled the Republic's civil discord of
the 1610s and 1620s, championed the cause of orthodoxy, as did Johan
van den Sande, who was responsible for completing Everhard van
Reyd's massive history of the Revolt. (Both Hommius and van den
Sande participated in the Synod of Dordrecht, as did that tireless chronicler, geographer, and Calvinist controversialist, Joannes de Laet.) Yet
patriotic scriptures came from other pulpits as well. Van Meteren, who
lived most of his life as a Protestant refugee in London, belonged to a
circle of merchants and men of letters known for their irenicist and allegedly "libertine" views. Hooft, like Pieter Bor, came from a liberal, Remonstrant background that drew inspiration from Coornhert and the
Christian-humanist traditions of the late sixteenth century. Another op-

ponent of dogmatism was Pieter Jansz Twisck, a prominent member of
the Mennonite community of Hoorn and the author of a two-thousand-
page *Chronijk van den onderganc der tijrannen* (Chronicle of the decline of
tyrants). Twisck prefaced that work with an impassioned plea for freedom of (Christian) conscience, the suppression of which he believed led
to the sort of transatlantic tyrannies perpetrated by the Spanish – and
now laboriously catalogued by the author.[105]

Finally, patriotic history came in an extraordinary variety of forms
and contexts. For the Dutch were asked not simply to recollect, but also
to recite and to experience as nearly as possible the story of their passage from tyranny to freedom, and they were given the widest range of
means to do so. Valerius's *Gedenck-clanck* combined prose, print, verse,
and song – complete with music notes and even dance instructions – to
recount the drama of the Revolt. Valerius did not merely tell a tale of
Spanish tyrannies, but asked his readers (or listeners, as the case must
have been) to sing along as well. Here, then, was patriotic scripture with
lute and zither accompaniment, memories of Habsburg oppression set
to memorable tunes. The Zeeland poet and gardener, Petrus Hondius,
worked the history of Spanish tyrannies into his country-house poem,
Dapes inemptae, of de Moufe-schans, one of the earliest Dutch examples of
the genre. The contemplation of "the sweetness of rural life" conjures
up the bitter memory of Spain's infestation of the countryside in the second half of the sixteenth century. Set in a former battlefield that was now
part of the estate of Hondius's patron, the poem moves back and forth
between classically pastoral meditations on nature and typically Dutch
recollections of tyranny. A lengthy diversion on the subject of history
permits the poet to consider Spain's unwelcome presence in the Netherlands and America, in order finally to conclude that it is preferable to
contemplate the calmer pleasures of the garden – though in the Republic rather than in the ravaged New World. Patriotic history also features
in van Heemskerk's *Batavische arcadia,* another exercise in Dutch pastoralism that blends national history with a day in the country. Van
Heemskerk depicts an excursion taken between The Hague and Katwijk
by "some youth of Holland" during which the party consider "Batavian
freedom . . . and other earnest matters." Discussions embrace the recollections by the group's older chaperone of past ordeals, remembrances
"that make [one's] hair stand on end," and stories of how the Spaniards
"intended to desolate and annihilate our dear Fatherland as they have
the West Indies."[106]

Those who stayed in the city could visit the memorials to Spanish
tyranny that occupied the urban squares and gardens, town halls and
other public spaces frequented by Dutch burghers. Certainly among the

most curious of these was the "Oranje pot," a *doolhof* – literally, a "labyrinth," yet perhaps more accurately described as the seventeenth-century equivalent of an amusement park – popular in Amsterdam in the 1630s (fig. 30). Located in the newly constructed, relatively modest neighborhood of the Jordaan, the "Oranje pot" assembled a collection of "leisure-time diversions" ostensibly dedicated to "the pleasure and instruction of the free Netherlands" and vaguely associated with the House of Orange – a patriotic theme park, thus, with a number of fun side shows. Attractions included, on the one hand, a theatrical procession of "singing papists," a model of Christ at the well of Samaria, and a grandiose "Fountain of the Seven Provinces" (the work of Jonas Bargois, fountain-maker to the prince); and, on the other hand, a band of pipers and drummers, a menagerie of exotic fauna, and a rare elephant's skull, tusks intact. Between a carrousel-like "Fountain of Orpheus" (somewhat incongruously emblazoned with a *"Vive Orange"*) and an exhibition of "The Land's Welfare" (an armada of toy ships in a festive pool of water) stood a *tableau vivant* illustrating the "Duke of Alba's Spanish Tyranny perpetrated in the Netherlands and in the Indies": a pair of soldiers overwhelming a defenseless maiden.[107] Vividly, palpably, tangibly, during a recreational stroll in the park, the Dutch encountered yet another reminder of their circumstances of foundation and their sympathetic kinship with America. At the "Oranje pot," citizens of the Republic could study at their leisure the lessons of patriotic scripture and refresh themselves, literally, at the fountain of *patria*. The urban memorials, like the literary ones, provided every opportunity to revive the memory of Spanish tyranny and all that implied. They called on the Dutch "to bring the infamies of Spain out from the corners of forgetfulness to the attention of the good patriots and inhabitants of our Fatherland." And they guided them, all along the way, to include the image of America and Spain's tyranny there in their conception of a national memory.[108]

How centrally, in fact, did the topos of America figure in patriotic historiography? How much space, in the end, did it occupy in the memory palace of the Republic? In one manner or another, America featured fairly prominently in the construction of Dutch history, visible in some of the most crucial passages of patriotic scripture. The very placement of America and its amplitude in Dutch texts was attentively plotted out. It could, for example, conspicuously frame the narrative of the Revolt, introducing and concluding the story of Spain's oppression of the Netherlands. Gijsius opens the *Oorsprong en voortgang* with a dedication that at once sets the tone for the volume by evoking Spain's tyranny in America:

Figure 30. Hessel Gerritsz, *Int Nuwe doolhoff inde Orange pot tot Lubbert Janssen Root,* ca. 1632 (engraving). Gemeentearchief Amsterdam.

The insatiable ambition, the intolerable haughtiness, and the inhuman cruelty of the Spaniards has become all too well known over these last one hundred years, since they have begun to gain power throughout the world. The innocent Indians from among the heathen races were the first to have experienced it, and after them came the pious Netherlanders from the ranks of the Christians.[109]

Some four hundred pages of Spanish atrocities later, Gijsius closes his account by alluding to the "hundreds of thousands of Indians" that the Spanish had slaughtered in America, the memory of which should serve notice to all who would contemplate peace with the enemy. A similarly formulated pronouncement launches the *Spiegel der Spaensche tyrannye;* and indeed most of the other popular histories contain comparable remarks, strategically placed in prefatory or concluding passages. On the penultimate page of the anonymously published *Warachtighe beschrijvinghe* (1621), the author ponders Spain's barbaric treatment of the Araucanians by way of poignant conclusion. The memory of America is once again drafted for the campaign of the Dutch.[110]

In certain instances, American materials might balance Dutch ones, so that the two histories ran parallel and complemented one another. Gijsius's abridged version of the Revolt, the so-called *Tweede deel van de Spiegel der Spaensche tyrannye gheschiet in Nederlandt* (Second part of the Mirror of Spanish tyranny committed in the Netherlands), appeared in a single volume, bound together with that other famous "mirror," Las Casas's *Spiegel der Spaensche tyrannye geschiet in West-Indien.* Two mutually reflecting mirrors in this way formed a single, blinding image of the enemy's perfidy. Petrus Hondius neatly divided the "Spanish tyranny" section of his *Moufe-schans* into a pair of equally apportioned segments, the one on the Netherlands preceding the one on America. In the leisurely paced world of Hondius's country retreat, apparently, care for historical chronology could be cast to the wind.[111]

In still other cases, the image of America had a small, though pivotal, role within the scope of the narrative. None of the more prominent figures of Dutch historiography – van Meteren, van Reyd, Bor, Grotius, Hooft – devoted quite as much space to the New World as did the popular historians. Yet they did make careful and strategic reference to America, often at critical junctures in their narratives and always to great effect. The New World could appear with wonderfully thespian timing. Witness the *Neederlandsche historien* (1642) of P. C. Hooft. Hooft's history of the Dutch uprising, elaborately constructed and elegantly composed, reads rather more like drama than chronicle. As in his earlier work of theater, *Baeto,* Hooft's *Histoorien* focus on the actions of great men performed on the stage of human history and the often tragic turns of human fate that ensue. The dramatis personae of Hooft's Revolt feature the heroic prince of Orange in the leading role – "Father of the Fatherland" – and his chief antagonists, the king of Spain and duke of Alba, the latter assuming a Haman role to Philip II's Ahasuerus. Alba's departure from the Netherlands after six bloody, costly, yet inconclusive, years of war marks a climactic turning point in the narrative. It comes in the middle of the work and prompts a masterful overview of the duke's career, his rise and fall from grace, and his ignominious tenure in the Netherlands. Hooft marshals all of his considerable imaginative and descriptive powers to convey the by-now-legendary tyranny of Alba with renewed vigor and urgency: the cowardly execution of nobles, the greedy confiscation of property, the scandalous desecration of maidens, the unholy slaughter of innocents, the barbaric mutilation of corpses. As if overpowered by his own prose, Hooft steps back from the carnage and refers his reader, simply, to the literature of America. "Abominations, surely, incomprehensible even to the most impartial observer," he concludes, "are the likes of which one can find described in [Spain's] own books of the tyrannies committed on the innocent natives of the West Indies." Thus falls the curtain on this closing allusion to the histories of America.[112]

Most typically, references to America were scattered throughout the histories of the Revolt, strewn, as it were, all along the byways of patriotic memory. Discussions of cruelties committed in the Low Countries were easily elided into discussions of tyrannies perpetrated in America; the memory of the one invariably evoked that of the other. "Just as the blood-thirsty Spaniards dealt earlier with the Americans, Brazilians, Peruvians and other Indian tribes," contended Baudartius, so they had dealt with the Batavians of the sixteenth century. Baudartius and his fellow patriotic historians regularly took this topical shortcut to convey to their readers the full horror of their ancestors' ordeal. The recollection of the reign of Alba, especially, evoked the dark memory of the *Conquista*, such that the memory of the two became rhetorically – almost mnemonically – intertwined. The iron duke's policies seemed so consistently "like those in America" that one author suggested, willfully anachronistic, that it was Alba, in fact, who had orchestrated the conquest of the New World and served as one of "the principal architects of the great suffering and piteous destruction of the great land and people of America." Conversely, the legacy of Alba to the Netherlands included an army so expert in torture that "they must have been descendants of those who subjected Nova Hispania, Peru, and all the Western lands with so many kinds of torments."[113]

In truth, references to the New World did not always need to be so explicitly made; for by the early seventeenth century, writers could simply imply comparisons and expect their readers to make the obvious connections. Patriotic historians, much like the rebel pamphleteers before them, recast the history of the Revolt in so many respects that it resembled the history of the *Conquista* anyway. Shades of Americana and especially of Lascasian discourse colored the very fabric of Dutch historical memory. Body counts of the dead, obsession with mutilations of the living, lurid descriptions of tortured women, children and elderly: these patterns of description more than vaguely resembled the topoi used in the histories of America. The specific recollections of atrocities in the Netherlands, too, seem inspired by, if not actually modeled on, popular descriptions of incidents in the Indies. The fetuses ripped out of wombs in Oudewater, the infants dashed against stone walls in Naarden, and the corpses mutilated in the squares of Rotterdam all had their antecedents in the histories, and especially the historical engravings, of Cuba, Hispaniola, and the Yucatan. In calling upon their readers to preserve the sacred memory of the first, Dutch historians simultaneously enshrined the memory of the second. Through their efforts, the two experiences became intimately connected and the image of Spanish tyranny in America forever imprinted upon the historical memory of the Netherlands.[114]

As it had for the rebels a generation prior, so the image of America now served their seventeenth-century heirs by solidifying historians' sometimes airy recollections of tyrannies past and by strengthening the nation's moral suit against Spain. The memory of the conquest of the Indies allowed the Dutch, first, to heighten the drama of their own ordeal through a deliberate process of historical analogy. Motifs of tyranny shifted back and forth between the two narratives, the Dutch borrowing liberally from the American histories to embellish their own with yet taller tales of Habsburg violence and grislier vignettes of gore. The memory of America helped bloody that of the Revolt with uncommonly rich hues of crimson. Second, it permitted the Dutch to place their history in a broader, global context. "The Netherlands have become a theater of the world's bloody tragedies," wrote van Meteren in the Preface to his *Historien*. The title-page of that work, appropriately enough, showed kings and emperors from around the world – allies and enemies of the Republic – and allegories of the four continents where Spain and the Netherlands had waged their battles (fig. 31). America lent an international facade to what might otherwise have appeared a plain civil war. Third, the image of the New World encouraged the Dutch to associate the birth of their nation with the epochal events of the sixteenth century: the Reformation and the Protestant struggle against papist

Figure 31. Title page from Emanuel van Meteren, *Historien der Nederlanden en haar naburen oorlogen* (Amsterdam, 1647). Universiteitsbibiliotheek Amsterdam.

heresy, and the Discovery and the Indians' struggle against Habsburg tyranny. By placing the story of the Republic's foundation in such prominent company, patriotic historians enhanced the prestige of their past. The analogy of America dignified the Revolt of the Netherlands.[115]

Finally, the history of America, like the biblical, classical, and mythological allusions so liberally scattered throughout Golden Age historiography, helped to legitimize the Revolt. And here the parallel with the sixteenth century is most revealing. Just as the rebels, in their moment of isolation, turned to the example of the Indies in order to justify their abjuration of Philip II, so the patriotic historians, in a later moment of consolidation, revived the memory of American tyranny to sustain their project of national renewal. The remembrance of Spanish tyrannies in the New World was meant to impress upon the Dutch the validity, solemnity, and urgency of recalling the Spanish oppression of the Netherlands. The one reinforced the other, and the two combined galvanized the Dutch to remain alert and ever-watchful for signs of impiety at home and tyranny abroad. Whatever the actual circumstances by that time *in* the New World – in Dutch Brazil and New Netherland – the traditional image of American innocence remained in this way forever preserved in patriotic scripture and enshrined in historical memory. The history of America endured, thus, in the collective memory of the Dutch as part of the very fabric of the commemorative tapestry of the Republic's foundation.

CHAPTER 5

The Rise and Fall of America, or Tyranny Abroad

I

GODEFRIDUS Udemans was ambivalent about America. The subject of the New World, its "unfathomable" riches, its untapped markets, and its unconverted heathen clearly intrigued the Zeeland *predikant*, who composed a hefty volume on the topic of commerce and godliness in the Indies, *'t Geestelyck roer van 't coopmans schip* (The spiritual rudder of the merchant's ship).[1] Yet after six hundred pages of reflection, Udemans quit his topic not altogether certain of the delicate role of the Christian merchant abroad and not fully reconciled with the worldly commercialism of overseas trade. On the face of it, the Zeelander championed the merchants' cause. Dedicated to the Lord Directors of the East and West India Companies, the *Geestelyck roer* defended the practices of "righteous Christian commerce" – oxymoronic though that may sound – as necessary for the welfare of the Republic and conducive to the expansion of the Church. Udemans embraced the enterprise of the *bewindhebberen* (directors) and afforded them advice on such issues as the acquisition of "lawful" credit, the accumulation of "honorable" profit, and the stipulation of fair pricing among the infidels. He paid special attention to traffic in the Indies, a matter he considered "of the utmost importance, which, according to all judicious and righteous lovers of the true religion and our beloved Fatherland, serves not only the commonwealth, but also the propagation of the kingdom of Christ." He offered a Calvinist perspective on the Dutch enterprise abroad and a "Geestelyck roer" (together with a companion volume, the *Geestelyck compas* [spirtual compass]) to steer the pious merchant through the shoals and squalls that threatened the vessel of godly commerce.[2]

Yet herein lay the difficulty. The merchants' mission, as the Zeeland *predikant* well knew, was fraught with moral dangers and spiritual entrapments; godly commerce was devilishly difficult. A pietist, polemi-

244

cist, and fiery champion of orthodoxy, Udemans acknowledged the "great afterthoughts and doubts of tender consciences" that many harbored concerning the Republic's overseas expansion, and he expressed his own reservations regarding those perils that could divert all but the most righteous merchant from the straight and narrow path. The immoderate speculation and risk-taking of Dutch traders came dangerously close to prodigality or dissipation; and the high returns and potential profits could encourage extravagance or pride. Monopolies promoted cupidity or the covetous hoarding of profits among the few; while competition could easily foster envy among those lesser merchants tempted by the success of their more prosperous peers. Most of all, Udemans warned of the seduction of foreign riches – "the riches and goods of this world" – that could easily distract the merchant from his godly mission; and it was here that his apprehensions concerning America were most pronounced. For the America of Udemans's imagination overflowed with temptation: with gold and silver and pearls, all readily and plentifully available. Now that the Dutch had finally reached the New World and begun to reap its bounty, Udemans feared for the moral timber of the Dutch enterprise abroad and, by extension, for the very soul of the Republic. "Let a merchant hold fast to this precious maxim," he quoted sternly, "honor before gold."[3]

Udemans's image of America only compounded his anxieties. In the New World, the *dominee* averred, gold coexisted uneasily with God; indeed the two seemed related in inverse proportions. As much as the land possessed a superabundance of the first, its natives exhibited not the barest vestige of the second. Much to their credit, the Indians appeared as "innocent" to the lure of gold as they did ignorant to the ways of God. (And Udemans, like so many of his moralizing contemporaries, punned ceaselessly on the words *goud* – gold – and *God*.) The same could not be claimed for the Spaniards, however, who had conquered the New World under the pretext of religion, yet abandoned all virtue under the influence of its riches. Now, as the Dutch set out to accumulate the treasures of America, Udemans admonished his readers to retain the Lord's favor. Like so many of his colleagues who witnessed the rapid expansion of the Republic's economy, Udemans feared the corruptive power of wealth and the consequences of a nation too covetous of gold and inadequately immune to its allure. "Honor before gold," cautioned Udemans, must prevail *especially* in America.

To many in the godly Republic, Udemans had a point – though it was one that stuck like a thorn in the side of many other of his colonial-minded associates. Dutch fortunes rose remarkably – "miraculously" – in the middle decades of the seventeenth century.[4] The expansion of commerce and culture, coupled with the attainment of a now permanent peace with Spain, announced the apogee of the Dutch Golden Age. With its "grand design" for the New World, the WIC aspired to contribute to the Republic's successes by acquiring yet another source of Dutch gold; and the early efforts of the Company did meet with a fair degree of enthusiasm. Yet hopeful optimism quickly gave way to almost dire pessimism, as the New World turned out to be less a source of wealth and triumph for the Republic than of reversal and "ruination." America produced neither gold nor honor – or so, at least, was the perception among observers at mid-century. Opinions of the New World naturally shifted over this period of heightened Dutch activity abroad, though, in a certain rhetorical sense, "America" remained largely unchanged as a locus of innocence and tyranny. The doubts of Udemans raised the question of whether the same might ultimately be said for the Dutch.

II

Dutch fortunes in America rose swiftly in the second quarter of the seventeenth century. In the two decades between Heyn's capture of the silver-fleet (1628) and the conclusion of the Eighty Years' War (1648), the Dutch finally established themselves in the New World, colonizing in both North and South America. Beginning around 1630, WIC-sponsored troops conquered and consolidated most of the northeast portion of Portuguese Brazil (rechristened "New Holland"); while hopeful settlers and fur traders carved out "New Netherland" along the eastern shores of North America, squeezed between English dominions in New England and Virginia. By the late 1630s, both Dutch colonies had attracted a fair number of settlers and merchants and both had shown signs of early profit. Each received around this time, too, a governor of relative prominence: Count Johan Maurits of Nassau-Siegen in Brazil, and the patrician Willem Kieft in New Netherland. Further expansion followed in the early 1640s, by which time the Dutch began to enjoy the first fruits of their colonial investments, with every reason to expect more in the years to come. The WIC's "American enterprise" was off and running.[5]

Of the two colonies, New Netherland got off to a quicker start, though it stalled somewhat in the early stages before taking off definitively in the 1640s during the tenure of Governor Kieft.[6] In contrast to the situation in Brazil, land and conquest posed few initial difficulties for the colonists of New Netherland. No Spanish or Portuguese enemy challenged the earliest settlers; and what political protest the English ambassador made, the WIC chose to ignore.[7] Nor did the early Walloon settlers, deposited strategically along the "South" (Delaware) and "North" (Hudson) Rivers in the spring of 1624, encounter much resistance from the Algonquian tribes who inhabited the region. For their part, the Dutch behaved relatively scrupulously with respect to the natives and their property – or at least sincerely and programmatically intended to do so. An early directive of 1625 called upon the colony's then governor, Willem Verhulst, to treat the Indians with "honesty, faithfulness, and sincerity in all contracts, dealings, and intercourse." Verhulst and his successors were instructed to pursue a policy of appeasement with the natives, "faithfully to fulfill their promises to the Indians . . . and not to give them any offense without cause as regards their persons, wives, or property." Land was to be "righteously" acquired, without "craft or fraud." "In case any Indians should be living on the aforesaid [High] island," the directors charged,

> or make any claim upon it [*daerop pretenderen*], or upon any other places that are of use to us, they must not be driven away by force or threats, but by good words be persuaded to leave, or be given something therefor to their satisfaction, or else be allowed to live among us, a contract being made thereof and signed by them in their manner.[8]

Verhulst's successor, Pieter Minuit, famously purchased another island – Manhattan – for sixty guilders: certainly a bargain price in retrospect, though still considerably more than the English had paid for Jamestown or the Spanish for Hispaniola. For those who elected to venture into the majestic countryside beyond the confines of the lower Hudson, the Company stipulated simply that they "must satisfy the Indians of that place for the land."[9]

Whatever access to land it had, New Netherland initially lacked the people to settle it, a problem that dogged the colony's early development.[10] To a large degree, the difficulty derived from the restrictions imposed on the settlers by a company jealous of its monopoly. The WIC controlled all land purchases and export traffic, and this greatly discouraged potential colonists from committing to the enterprise. More than anything, colonists and their financial backers objected to the strict regulation of the fur trade, an issue they energetically contested from the late 1620s. Led by the resourceful jewel merchant, Kiliaen van Rensselaer, a faction of principal shareholders (*hoofdparticipanten*) challenged the directors in 1628 (immediately following the silver-fleet coup, when the spirit of generosity ran high) by proposing policy revisions that would relax the terms of the monopoly. This resulted in a compromise reached in the spring of 1629, which granted limited "Freedoms and Exemptions" from the WIC monopoly and free land to any investor willing to settle fifty persons over three years. This established the so-called patroon system: principal shareholders gained limited freedoms in New Netherland and access to the fur trade in exchange for their assistance in populating the colony and managing a manorial estate. Within their "domain," the patroons presided over political and juridical affairs and controlled taxes and the traffic of goods – just as the WIC would continue to do on Manhattan and other outposts outside the patroons' domain.[11]

The patroonships met with mixed results. Of those who participated in the various projects – Samuel Goldijn and Samuel Blommaert, the two Amsterdam merchants who filed for land on the Delaware and Connecticut Rivers; Johannes de Laet, a Leiden-based polymath who founded De Laetsburg deep up the Hudson; Michiel Pauw, lord of Achttienhoven, who established Pavonia on prime real estate across the river from Manhattan – none aside from van Rensselaer endured very long. Pressures mounted from both within and without the Company. Among the *bewindhebberen,* there quickly emerged a "monopolist" faction opposed to van Rensselaer's rude infringement on their hard-earned (and now less profitable) privileges. Almost at once following the granting of the 1629 *Vryheden* (Freedoms), this pro-WIC faction campaigned to reverse those concessions hastily granted and to hinder the patroons wherever possible. Meanwhile, from an altogether different perspective issued the complaints of the *coloniers* (free colonists), who contended that the *Vryheden* unfairly favored the most privileged shareholders at the expense of the merchants and colonists of middling means. Only those who could afford to transport fifty settlers, finance their farm equipment, and provide them with livestock could take full advantage of the WIC's offer. Moreover, the critics contended, since the patroons invested in one another's efforts, shared in the costs of shipping, and collaborated on pricing and wages, a new cartel had merely displaced an old monopoly. So long as trade in New Netherland remained effectively restricted, potential investors and colonists would keep their distance. Indeed, population growth faltered throughout much of the 1630s, as did nearly all of the patroonships.

By the end of the decade, the *bewindhebberen* took two steps to improve the colony's prospects. First, they drafted a set of "Articles and Conditions" (submitted in 1640 as a revised "Freedoms and Exemptions") meant to dispel the widespread reluctance to commit to New Netherland. Predictably, the amendments addressed chiefly the issues of land and commerce. Yielding to overwhelming demands for free trade, the directors finally forfeited their monopoly and opened New

Netherland's markets to all citizens of the United Provinces. (At first, the WIC proposed limiting trade to settlers actually domiciled *in* America, yet the States General prevailed upon them to include Dutch-based merchants as well. The directors held out, however, on the issue of non-Dutch traders.) To boost the number of settlers in the colony, the WIC also offered two hundred acres of land outright to anyone willing to cultivate it. New Netherland now opened its arms to all who would farm or trade there.[12] Second, the directors attended to the government of the colony and complaints concerning the competence of their agent abroad, Wouter van Twiller. Van Twiller, an inconsequential clerk promoted to an ineffectual governor, developed a yet more damning reputation as a meek alcoholic. It did not help, either, that he was the nephew of van Rensselaer and believed to be in the pay of the patroon. In 1637, the *bewindhebberen* finally recalled van Twiller and appointed in his place Willem Kieft, who arrived the following year. Kieft contrasted sharply with his predecessor. A merchant of proven ability, considerable means, and undisguised ambition, he governed New Netherland energetically and held on to his position through most of the 1640s. A figure of much greater stature than van Twiller – Kieft came from a family of Amsterdam magistrates and nurtured certain aristocratic pretensions – the new governor also lent the colony a measure of prestige and "decorum." During his tenure, New Netherland finally came into its own. Population grew, trade expanded, and profits multiplied. When Peter Stuyvesant arrived to assume command in 1647, New Netherland's prospects appeared brighter than ever and the WIC's North American experiment a colonial success.

In Brazil, the Dutch encountered greater initial difficulty establishing a land base, though fewer obstacles thereafter developing the social and economic infrastructure they inherited from the Portuguese.[13] Following its unsuccessful foray into Bahia in 1624–1625, the WIC concentrated its efforts on the northeastern region of Brazil and particularly the rich captaincy of Pernambuco, where the country's sugar industry flourished. Letters intercepted during the Bahia campaign indicated the extraordinary value of the region's plantations – 137 sugar-mills, producing over one hundred thousand pounds of sugar and generating one million guilders per annum in tithes – as well as the exceptional vulnerability of its defenses – fewer than four hundred reliable militiamen, stationed in ramshackle fortifications scattered along the coast. Though the local governor, Mathias de Albuquerque, managed to raise on short notice a standing army of two thousand local *moradores* (settlers), this proved no match for the sixty-seven-sail fleet of the Dutch that landed in early 1630 and easily captured Olinda and Recife. There the Dutch stayed, however, confined to their coastal positions, while Albuquerque's men retreated inland to wage a guerrilla campaign from strategically positioned camps in the bush. A stalemate ensued. The Dutch retained control of the harbors and supply lines from the sea, yet the Portuguese otherwise limited the invaders' land mobility and frustrated their attempts to expand on their conquests.

At first, this standoff favored the local Portuguese, yet time played into the hands of the better-positioned Dutch. From the outset, both sides suffered from dwindling supplies and meager reinforcements. The better-acclimated *moradores,* it is true, could draw on the produce of their own farms; yet stocks of essential equipment, including munitions, soon ran out. On the other side, the Dutch promptly succumbed to the tropical conditions, rampant dysentery, and malnutrition (one report tells of a desperate diet of cats and rats), though provisions did reach them more regularly from overseas. In 1631, both sides received substantial reinforcements, and an Iberian armada took this occasion to challenge the enemy; but the encounter ended inconclusively. The following spring, a mulatto deserted to the Dutch fort at Recife and provided the Netherlanders with invaluable local intelligence. Led by their new guide, the Dutch now embarked on a series of well-planned campaigns that culminated in the capture of Paraíba (north of Pernambuco) in late 1634. A successful raid against Porto Calvo in early 1635 made conditions even less tenable for the Portuguese, and, with the successful completion of further sieges later that summer, the region finally fell to the Dutch. A major Habsburg offensive was turned back in early 1636, by which time it appeared that the Dutch had convincingly established "New Holland," as they called it, on the soil of Portuguese Brazil.[14]

It was at this point that the *bewindhebberen* made what would be the signal decision in their stewardship of Dutch Brazil by appointing Count Johan Maurits of Nassau-Siegen to assume political and military command of the colony. A distinguished scion of the prince's family, an experienced commander on the battlefield, and a cultured patron of the arts, Johan Maurits turned out to be a first-rate colonial administrator as well and a gifted governor-general. He set to work at once, first consolidating, then expanding the positions he inherited upon his arrival in Recife in 1637. Within a month, he had routed the enemy at Porto Calvo, sacked the recalcitrant towns of the region, and founded a "Fort Maurits" on the bank of the Rio São Francisco, which now served as the southern border of the Dutch colony. Back in Recife, he turned to the Herculean labor of cleansing "the Augean stables" of colonial government, as the humanist poet, Caspar Barlaeus, referred to the state of administrative disrepair. The new governor dismissed and replaced corrupt officials; restored the land and rights of those *moradores* who had submitted in good faith to the conquerors; and raised two million desperately needed guilders through the sale of derelict sugar mills. He then directed his soldiers on a campaign of expansion. By the end of his first year in office, the Dutch occupied the captaincies of Sergipe to the south and Ceará to the north and thus controlled virtually all of northeast Brazil. From across the Atlantic, the prince's fleet could report the successful conquest of Elmina on the Gold Coast and assure the Brazilian colony a regular supply of African labor.[15]

In the years ahead, Johan Maurits applied his enormous energies to the adornment of Recife and its surroundings and the restoration of the colony's prosperity. Like the ancient Roman conquerors on whom he modeled himself, the Dutch governor loved to build. In Recife, he undertook the construction of roads, bridges, and canals (in the latter instance he resembled perhaps an ancient conqueror from water-minded Holland); and on the centrally situated island of Antonio Vaz, he laid out the city of "Mauritsstad." He also erected two impressive estates, the Dutch-named "Vrijburg", and the Portuguese-titled "Boa Vista." (And Johan Maurits showed a remarkable flair for multicultural gestures.) He presided over these "country-seats" in a style extraordinary for the New World and perhaps even for the Old: geometrical gardens, long-alleyed orchards, well-stocked aviaries, exotic menageries. "In short, there was not a curious thing in Brazil which he did not have," observed a sympathetic Portuguese visitor.[16] The humanist prince also assembled an impressive entourage of gifted courtiers that included natural scientists, cartographers, astronomers (who manned the first observatory in the Western Hemisphere), draftsmen, and painters. All of them, upon their return to Europe, proudly advertised the glories of Dutch Brazil and its cultivated governor.[17]

Johan Maurits also labored for the welfare of the colony more generally, in ways that benefited Dutch merchant and Portuguese planter alike. On the vigorously debated question of a WIC monopoly, the governor weighed in on the side of free trade and encouraged the directors to do for Brazil what they had already done for New Netherland. His opinion, apparently, prevailed; for in 1638 the WIC promulgated an edict that opened the Brazil trade to Dutch shareholders of the WIC and to local *moradores,* reserving for the Company only the traffic of slaves, dyewoods, and munitions.[18] This and the consistent courtesies of Johan Maurits to the Portuguese planters greatly rehabilitated the sugar industry after years of war and neglect. The *senhores de engenho* now received higher prices for their goods and greater access to imports from

Europe. Dutch merchants, meanwhile, reaped improved opportunities to transport sugar and excellent incentives to develop refining factories back in the Netherlands. Over the governor's seven-year term, sugar profits recovered nicely from their wartime lows. Exports between 1637 and 1644 totaled twenty-eight million guilders, more than a quarter of which were handled by the WIC. (The sugar exported by private traders earned the WIC an additional twenty percent in export duties.) When, at the end of 1641, the WIC decided to recall their accomplished governor – he cost too much to maintain, they contended – the Dutch colony in Brazil seemed well on its way to prosperity.[19]

So, too, did Dutch endeavors in America more generally. By the early 1640s, the WIC had strategically installed itself along the coasts of North and South America. New Netherland, under the guidance of Governor Kieft, had begun to swell with settlers and merchant ships, drawn to the prospects of free land and plentiful pelts. Dutch Brazil, after the conquest of Maranhão in 1641, encompassed half of the fourteen original Portuguese captaincies and boasted a flourishing sugar trade managed by a humanist prince. Around this time, too, fleets under Johan Maurits's command took the city of Luanda on the coast of Angola, and the islands of São Thomé and Anobom off the coast of Guinea. "The West India Company's Atlantic empire had now reached its zenith," wrote one of its leading historians with the advantage of hindsight.[20] Yet at the time, there was full reason to expect even more. Following its dramatic revolt against Spain (1640), Portugal signed a ten-year truce with the States General in 1641 that preserved the Dutch conquests in Brazil and West Africa. A Dutch peace with the battered Spanish monarch was believed to be imminent, and this would free Dutch ships and resources for the overseas empire. The Netherlands' American fortunes, it seemed, could only soar higher.

III

Steady advances in the New World encouraged giddy optimism back in the Old. The progress of the Dutch abroad and especially the conquests of Johan Maurits induced in certain circles a self-confident, expansionist mood that expressed itself in celebratory prose, heroic simile, and epic imagination. For those in the profession of literary exultation – balladeers, epicists, patriotic historians, and the ubiquitous composers of occasional verse – the triumphant news from America in the 1630s and 1640s was good for business. America, or rather the perception and configuration of Dutch attainments in America, transformed in this period into a source of pride for the Republic, which merited frequent and ostentatious mention. Successes abroad reflected brilliantly back home as yet another sign of favor in this Golden Age. The prowess of Dutch soldiers in Brazil and the bravery of Dutch settlers in New Netherland fit well into the broader context of Batavian glory and were lauded accordingly.

Batavian glory, which had been made to span the vast expanse of Dutch history, could now be shown to traverse the vast expanse of global geography as well. Both in the distant past and in the distant world of America, the Dutch burgher had prevailed. A "Friesland Triton" was how one provincially born, if imperially minded, poet praised Admiral Hendrik Cornelisz Loncq, a naval hero of recent Brazilian fame. In a grandiloquent *Zee-vaert lof* (Praise of Navigation), Elias Herckmans happily conflated his allusions in hailing the early exploits off the shores of Pernambuco as deeds of "ancient glory." Following the more significant breakthroughs of the late 1630s appeared congratulatory *Epigrammata Americana* from the pen of Johan Bodecher Banning and dedicated to the honor of Johan Maurits; and a few years later, Petrus de Lange's *Batavise Romeyn* narrated the triumphs of Dutch warriors, who "had conquered in America a great part of the land, where Spain" – read the Spanish empire, including Portugal – "alone had dared to rule." Upon his return to Europe in 1644, Johan Maurits commissioned a monumental wall map to commemorate the "glorious" expansion of Batavia into the tropics of Brazil. Recent American deeds spoke brashly of the Republic's recent ascendance.[21]

Nassau himself served as the object of many a panegyrist's praise, hailed as a civilizer of foreign lands and glorified as a conqueror to rival the ancients. Vondel, in the elaborate preface to his translation of Virgil, compared the governor-general to Aeneas and likened his noble influence in America to a golden ray of sun that had pierced the dark clouds of savagery. Johan Maurits had created a brilliant rainbow of civilization, the poet pronounced. The Dutch had brought "enlightenment" to the benighted antipodes:

> there in Brazil Prince Maurits
> Plants the flag of the lion and imparts a
> Civilized manner to a coast where other stars shine,
> [Where] cannibals roam in forests and wilderness.[22]

Though Vondel would never play Virgil to Johan Maurits's Aeneas, this was precisely the tack taken by Franciscus Plante, who composed a neo-Latin epic, the *Mauritias* (1647), to commemorate Nassau's accomplishments in America. Over the course of twelve books and 6,430 hexameters, Plante recounted the valiant conquest of Brazil by the Dutch (Books

1–6), and the heroic deeds of Nassau that followed (Books 7–12). The structure of the poem, together with its triumphant tone and patriotic rhetoric, self-consciously imitate the *Aeneid* (though the poetry itself is hardly Virgilian). Like the Augustan epicist, Plante recited the martial valor of his subject and the epochal significance of his conquests. The *Mauritias* opens with a passage strikingly similar to the first lines of the *Aeneid* and thus announces the ambitions of the poet and his project:

> I sing of war and a captain, who from his earliest years victoriously
> Challenged the might of Spain and, with his blood-stained sword,
> Shook the belligerent power of the Iberian scepter;
> A commander for whom a vast land, a world within a world opens up
> And whose victory ascends brilliantly in the Brazilian empire.[23]

The gods now favored the conquerors of New Holland just as they had the founders of Rome; Jupiter, Neptune, and Minerva dote especially on Johan Maurits. (Pluto, the god of the underworld, conspires with the enemy, the king of Spain.) In Plante's estimation, the Batavians' valor in the tropics well matched that of the Trojans on the Tiber: both yielded the stuff of *fama*. Published in lavish editions, introduced by exultant poetry, and decorated with handsome engravings, the *Mauritias* proclaimed, in form as well as content, the illustrious deeds of Nassau in Brazil. The waters of American coasts and forests of America's interiors now served, in Plante's neo-epic formulations, as magnificent backdrops against which to recount the heroism of Batavians abroad.[24]

The grand, garish, epic bombast of the *Mauritias* made a statement. It lavished extravagant attention on the doings of the Dutch abroad, and it pronounced these doings eminently worthy of national celebration. It placed the New World project, moreover, squarely before a certain class of reader – literary, learned, powerful – that was now more inclined than ever to cast an imperial glance toward, and take patriotic pride in, the Dutch engagement with America. Such pride came at an opportune moment for the Republic – the final, triumphant years of the Eighty Years' War – and it encouraged a discernible generosity of praise. Such pride, too, came from an opportunistic brand of panegyrist – prominent poets, chroniclers, and men of neo-Latin letters from the circle of Nassau, meaning in this case both Johan Maurits and the *stadhouder*, Frederik Hendrik – who hymned the princes and their armies for glories achieved on scattered battlefields. Just as the courts of the Republic had expanded, so did the poet-courtier's efforts, which now spanned both sides of the Atlantic.[25]

Perhaps no figure lent more prestige to the literary project of America than the esteemed humanist, Caspar Barlaeus, and certainly no work did more to celebrate the tropical feats of Johan Maurits than Barlaeus's *Rerum per octennium in Brasilia* (1647). The *Rerum* is a monumental work: unquestionably the most impressive description of Dutch Brazil and possibly the outstanding work overall of seventeenth-century Dutch geography. A princely volume in every sense, it included sumptuous pullout maps, designed to form a wall map of the entire domain of New Holland; dozens of original engravings, based on the on-site drawings of the landscapist, Frans Post; and lengthy disquisitions on the history, nature, and populations of Brazil, which Barlaeus drafted from the extensive manuscript sources placed at his disposal by Johan Maurits. All of this was published in folio by Joan Blaeu, the preeminent printer of his day. It appeared in three separate Latin, and two German, editions (the latter published in Cleves, where Nassau retired after his return to Europe), many of these richly bound and individually presented to princes and statesmen across Europe. "As an ensemble, it is perhaps the most splendid work ever to come from the Dutch presses," concluded a modern editor, with only slight exaggeration. As an affirmation of Dutch confidence in their American enterprise, issued at the very zenith of the Republic's Golden Age, it speaks volumes.[26]

It speaks also literately, gracefully, and imaginatively, articulating a powerful image of the Dutch New World as construed by one of the most eloquent voices in the Republic. The *Rerum per octennium in Brasilia* came from the hand of a leading Latinist of the Dutch Golden Age, a professor of philosophy at Amsterdam's Athenaeum Illustre, and a member of the fashionable literary salon, the Muiderkring. Caspar Barlaeus, as such, contemplated America from a position of exceptional prominence within Dutch letters and his perspective is revealing. In a certain sense, his perspective is also rhetorical, since, unlike Franciscus Plante, who had served as Nassau's court chaplain in Brazil, Barlaeus never visited America. He arrived at his project by way of Constantijn Huygens, the powerful secretary of Frederik Hendrik and arbiter of Dutch culture, who greatly admired Barlaeus's erudite verse. Johan Maurits did too, and he encouraged Barlaeus's efforts. (Upon his return from America, Nassau received a taste of that verse in Barlaeus's admiring poem *Mauritius redux*.) The account of Brazil was ultimately constructed from the personal papers of the prince, from previously published histories of Brazil, and from the author's own humanist sensibilities.[27]

It is this last category in particular that lends the work its character; for, as Peter Martyr had over a century before, Barlaeus made of the New World a showcase for his classical learning. He wrote of Dutch feats in Brazil with the texts of the ancients spread out in front of him: Xenophon on the Persian expedition, Arrian on Alexander's campaigns,

Livy and Tacitus on the Roman conquests. It did not suffice, however, merely to allude to the ancients or to make comparison to classical antecedents. Barlaeus wished, rather, to demonstrate how Johan Maurits ultimately *outrivaled* the ancients and how Dutch achievements in New Holland signaled the ascent of a new Golden Age, in the Netherlands and its empire abroad. The Dutch and Johan Maurits explored, conquered, and "civilized" (a word to which Barlaeus frequently returned) better than had the ancients or any of the recent claimants to the mantle of Rome. "Indeed we have surpassed the Ancients in the immense distances that we have traveled and in the inhumanity and barbarity against which we have battled," he pronounced with lofty solemnity.[28]

How had the seventeenth-century Dutch managed such epochal exploits? Barlaeus pointed to factors personal and geographical in his analysis, emphasizing both the role of the prince and the place of America. Naturally, the *Rerum*'s author commended the wisdom, courage, and piety of his patron, Johan Maurits, whose government had crowned all prior Dutch attainments in Brazil. In his triumphs over Portuguese armies and Spanish fleets, "Nassau demonstrated that valor had not expired with Scipio, Regulus, Cimon, Duilius, and Pompey." As in war, so in peace; and, while he had voyaged to America to do the labor of Mars, the prince had not neglected the work of the Lord, winning heathen souls as easily as he repulsed enemy soldiers. Barlaeus, who began his career as a *predikant*, in fact paid relatively scant attention to the missionary progress of the Reformed Church, choosing instead to focus on the governor-general's role as a "civilizer" in the broadest sense (*civitas*) of that word. The prince founded cities. Just as Alexander had established his Alexandrias and Constantine his Constantinople, so Johan Maurits now settled "Mauritsstad" and numerous other forts that bore his name. Like the great conquerors of ancient Rome, he also built roads, bridges, and palaces. Barlaeus provided extensive descriptions of Vrijburg and Boa Vista and their stunning botanical and zoological gardens ("eternal monuments to Nassau's magnanimity in America"); and made much of the bridges built, at the prince's own expense, between Recife, Antonio Vaz, and the mainland. These quintessentially colonial structures, in Barlaeus's baroque imagination, "bridged" the cultural, political, and religious differences between the various races that populated Dutch Brazil. Johan Maurits, in this regard, equaled Alexander in his ability to create a unified empire from the disparate nations native to, and drawn to, America.[29]

That Johan Maurits won his fame *in America* only enhanced his prestige, since Barlaeus, his humanism notwithstanding, presumed that the challenges of the New World exceeded those of antiquity. While the

Greeks and Romans had faced enemies in the environs of Athens or Sparta or, at the very furthest, Britannia or Persia, Johan Maurits traveled to lands enormously distant from one another, across a vast *oceanus,* and beneath the dreaded equator. Instead of the Rhine, Danube, and Indus Rivers, Nassau's soldiers traversed (or at least tried to traverse) the great Rios Amazonas, São Francisco, and de la Plata. (When Herckmans ventured, in 1641, into the Brazilian jungle, Barlaeus rendered the desperate return journey an epic anabasis.) While the ancients contended with foes from Macedon, Latium, Persia, and Carthage, the Dutch encountered wholly new enemies (or allies) such as the Caribs, Tarairiu, Tupinamba, and Araucanians – "naked soldiers armed with bows and arrows and clubs," ferocious cannibals wholly unknown to ancient geography. The "rudeness" of the native Americans made Johan Maurits's civilizing feat that much more extraordinary. "Your virtue is all the more worthy," proclaimed Barlaeus in his dedication, "to the degree that you have ventured from the seat and center of civility" – by which was meant Europe. America, however, had readily embraced the prince's "humanity." "That land [Brazil] joyfully allowed our hands to harvest its sugar and happily welcomes Chatti and Sugambri [Teutonic tribes and forebears of the Batavians] where before only savages lived." The ancient spirit of the Batavi, thus, thrived anew. "The name of Bato's progeny," wrote Barlaeus with reference to Nassau, "has struck terror on the islands of America." It also announced the renaissance of a Batavian – read Dutch – Golden Age, which now spanned powerful rivers, boundless oceans, and uncharted continents.[30]

The literary celebration of New Netherland in these years did not quite match that of Brazil, though the North American settlement did elicit its share of plaudits. None of the governors of the WIC's smaller colony enjoyed the prestige – or facilities for patronage – of the count of Nassau-Siegen, nor did any of their military campaigns rival Dutch efforts in Brazil against the combined force of the Habsburgs. Stuyvesant claimed a major victory in 1655 when he captured New Sweden, an upstart Scandinavian settlement founded by the renegade Dutch governor, Pieter Minuit. Yet the surrender of a motley group of Swedish farmers and sailors in the calms of the lower Delaware hardly excited the bards back in the Netherlands. As wrathful a soldier as Stuyvesant may have been, no Swedish Hector stood up to his cranky Achilles. Petrus de Lange recorded the event in his *Batavise Romeyn* ("all of the principal deeds of heroism, acts of chivalry, and cunning military inventions, achieved on the battlefield and at sea . . . by the Hollanders and Zeelanders in the years 1492–1661"). Yet Stuyvesant's glory went otherwise unsung.[31]

The majestic landscapes of New Netherland, on the other hand, inspired great enthusiasm among the promoters and self-declared poets of the colony. "New Netherland is an undeniably glorious land," reported one observer, who exuberantly ranked the region "the most beautiful, fertile, and wholesome of the known world." Another considered the Delaware "one of the most beautiful rivers in the world," "compared by its admirers with the Amazon, that is, by such of them as have seen them both." Perhaps with an eye on Swedish encroachments, one author likened the Delaware Valley to "a precious jewel" that ought not be squandered.[32] The Dutch showed no less ardor for the cliff-lined Hudson River. The spectacular waterfalls of its tributaries and the "monstrous" fish of its depths (which included whales by some sightings) provoked awe among the colonists and, in the opinion of Adriaen van der Donck, would have impressed the ancients as well. Van der Donck, who composed the most influential description of the colony, believed that the "grand and sublime" Hudson River and its surrounding valley begged to be painted. "Here our attention is arrested by the beautiful landscape around us; here the painter can find rare and beautiful subjects for the employment of his brush," he declared, with remarkable prescience.[33]

The land, its flora, and its fauna commended themselves to prospective farmers and traders as well. "[The] location, goodness, and fruitfulness of these provinces," van der Donck alleged, "need yield to no province in Europe." Indeed, nature in New Netherland surpassed that found most everywhere else. Large, thick oaks measured up to those of the Rhine or Weser valleys; abundant pines matched those in Norwegian forests; and the acorns "grow as large as our persimmons." All who described them – van der Donck, Dominie Megapolensis, and most other dazzled chroniclers of the early colony – raved about the fruits and wild berries that flourished and especially the grapes, "which grow very large, each grape as big as . . . an ordinary plum."[34] "The whole land is mostly covered with vineyards" contended one booster, who cheerfully believed the wines of New Netherland would soon excel those of France and Germany. The conditions for agriculture, in short, were exceptional. Everything cultivated in New Netherland turned out "sweeter, tastier, and more pleasant" than it did elsewhere. Visitors also marveled at the wild turkey, abundant deer, and graceful eagles (of which there were still "great numbers"). In an observation surely intended to raise Dutch eyebrows, van der Donck contended that cows produced better milk in New Netherland; that otherwise venomous animals proved quite harmless there; and that snakes in New Netherland, with few exceptions, "flee before men if they possibly can."[35] The land, in short, was an Eden:

New Netherland's the flow'r, the noblest of all lands;
With richest blessings crowned, where Milk and Honey flow;
By the most High of all, with doubly liberal hands
Endowed: yea, filled up full, with what may thrive and grow.[36]

In the eyes of some, New Netherland appeared a promised land. If descriptions of Brazil could assume a classical, epic tone, those of the Hudson Valley colony adapted a manner more accurately characterized as scriptural. Representations of the colony emphasized the generously blessed landscape and the natural bounty the earth would produce. The Dutch need not so much conquer and subdue, it was suggested, as occupy and reap the fruits of a land to which they had been divinely led. New Netherland's fragrant air floated like the "sweetest perfumes, . . . like an Eden's garden." Its water flooded "from the Fountain of all Good, / Overwhelm[ing] weak mortal man with royal food," streaming "as clear as crystal and as fresh as milk." (The typical Hollander, it would seem, entertained a somewhat idiosyncratic vision of paradise.) The earth – "O fruitful Land!" – had "perfection attained"; "its bosom bears / Abundant harvest."

> Air, water, soil, of greatest purity;
> And all, combined in sweetest harmony,
> . . . the masterpiece of Nature's hand.[37]

Descriptions fell easily into patterns of biblical rhetoric and simile. "It goes here after the manner of the Old Testament," wrote one visitor. "Wealth consists in oxen and horses to plow with, and in cows, sheep, and goats."[38] The curious Dutch attentiveness to grapes and their ample size finds its parallel in the story of the Israelite spies, sent on reconnaissance to Canaan, who retrieve grapes so heavy that they must be borne by two men (Num. 13:21–4). And the lyrical descriptions of the landscape evoke – and even cite – the paradise in Eden. The first "poet laureate" of the colony, as the second-rate rhymester Jacob Steendam was known, celebrated New Netherland as the "noblest spot on earth." His nearly three-hundred-line *Lof van Nuw-Nederland* (Praise of New Netherland) waxes positively rhapsodic:

> It is the land where milk and honey flow;
> Were plants distilling perfume grow;
> Where Aaron's rod with budding blossoms blow
>   A veritable Eden.
> Oh fortunate land! While envy you invite,
> You soar far over all you thus excite.
> And conquer whom by chance you meet in flight
>   God grants you peace.

Through poetic slight of hand, Canaan had become Eden had become the Dutch possessions in America.[39]

Steendam's New Netherland trilogy – he also composed a "Complaint of New Netherland" and "Spurring Verses," both meant to excite interest in the colony – thus joined Plante's *Mauritias* and Barlaeus's *Rerum per octennium in Brasilia* in extolling Dutch achievements in America. Each conveyed in its own way the optimism some cherished for the Republic's prospects in the New World. America was represented as a blessed land, the Dutch conquests there as heroic deeds. The authors of these works, along with the poets and chroniclers who extolled the WIC and its servants, all linked the progress in America with the ascension of the Netherlands. Conquests and settlements in the New World, they contended, hindered the Habsburgs, expanded the church, and profited the state. The success of New Netherland and New Holland confirmed the glory of the Republic and the arrival of a Golden Age.

IV

Not all marveled at the gold from abroad. Not all greeted the news from Dutch America, that is, with quite the same measure of jubilant optimism. Other voices within the Republic, beholden neither to the WIC nor to its patrons, dissented from the chorus of praise to sound, instead, a note of caution concerning the acquisitive spirit of the American enterprise. Certain critics – *predikanten*, moralists, world-weary merchants – joined Godefridus Udemans in reproaching the vigorous pursuit of wealth in America, the corruptive power of imports, and the compromising temptations of colonialism. The "blinding dazzle of gold" posed a threat to the godly Republic; and the very success of the Dutch overseas expansion – the accumulation of gold – provoked concern among the guardians of godliness. To be sure, material *overvloed* (abundance) from any source could imperil a Republic founded on the ideals of piety and (for many, at least) Calvinist propriety. Dutch ministers of the seventeenth century inveighed ceaselessly against "money hounds" and vilified those "acts of cunning, dodges, deceits and deviltry" that (in the words of one Calvinist writer) were the mainstay of their trade. Yet the sins inherent to the Indies trade – financing on borrowed capital, banking on enormous profits, organizing on monopolistic principles – loomed particularly largely on the moralists' horizon. It was not, either, that its critics wanted fully to proscribe the American trade and the undeniable benefits it provided, so much as they hoped to circumscribe its most damnable practices and alert the godly Republic when fine intentions went awry – hence Udemans's ambivalence. Barlaeus, in an oration delivered a decade and a half before undertaking his magnum opus on Brazil, called on Dutch merchants to mind that matters material never took precedence over those more spiritual. As an example of the former, Barlaeus cited explicitly the riches of the New World (Heyn had only recently disembarked with his cargo of silver). He exhorted the *mercator sapiens* to study the foreign peoples and places he visited and to take seriously his Christian obligations abroad. In time, the Dutch humanist would portray his patron, Johan Maurits, as the princely embodiment of this merchant ideal. Yet not all merchants shared the prince's nobility of purpose, and Barlaeus harangued the profit-minded among them.[40]

In the case of America, however, the issue of profits alone could hardly have incited such rebuke. It would have made little sense, in the boom years of the mid-seventeenth century, to single out the West Indies trade as exceptionally lucrative or perniciously enriching. If the WIC's colonies had begun to show promise, they still cost more to maintain than they managed to earn. They lagged, in his regard, well behind the Dutch East India Company (VOC). The problem, rather, lay in America itself, the particular type of trade it entailed, and the singular image it evoked. The New World – so it was widely assumed – *was* rich and spectacularly so. It had yielded its conquerors no mere *snood geld* (sordid money), but genuine gold that had proven its corruptive powers many times over. America had become veritably synonymous with gold, and gold had long been a byword for turpitude. It tempted, seduced, then perverted. Those who believed in a lasting accord with Spain had their judgment "clouded by Peruvian gold," wrote a patriotic pamphleteer of the Münster peace negotiations. Barlaeus's otherwise encomiastic history of Brazil criticizes only when it considers the malady of "gold-lust." Writing of Brouwer's disastrous expedition to Chile, the humanist lectures on the foolish pursuit, to such extreme lengths, of "barbaric gold." "The idle hope for the gold of the Chileans," he writes with uncharacteristic severity, "has contributed to the notorious poverty of the Company and that of Brouwer personally."[41] Others, too, censured the feverish hunt for gold in the jungles of Brazil and mountains of New Netherland. (Van der Donck was not alone in suggesting that the Catskills had a yellow tinge to them.) The lustful pursuit, mainly by Zeelanders, of a Guianan El Dorado was dismissed as an "alchemical" folly and roundly condemned by the pamphleteers.[42]

Juxtaposed to this European obsession with gold was the seeming lack of interest on the part of the indigenous Americans, and this perceived disparity made the New World's dangers stand out all the more prominently. The commercial encounter in America provided a vivid

lesson in vice and virtue, a sharp contrast between the covetousness of
the European, lured overseas by lucre, and the "innocence" of the Indians, tyrannized for their native wealth. No less a moral authority than
Jacob Cats – grand pensionary of Holland, prolific author of didactic
verse, and indefatigable guardian of Calvinist family values – noted this
clash of commercial cultures taking place in America. With an eye to the
failings of the Dutch, Cats described, in one of his typically sermonizing poems, the Indians' simplicity in matters of barter.

> A tiny feather from a parrot
> Is for them a wondrous present

The Dutch, by comparison, seek gold, pearls, dyewoods – "All that
makes for them a profit." And, though Dutch traders may think themselves the more clever for their exchange, "Father" Cats expressed his
doubts.

> Oh my dear God, what a folly!
> All and one are fit for mocking
> . . . .
> Pledge not yourself to things at hand
> For heaven is your Fatherland.[43]

Precisely these sorts of contrasts and contradictions rendered the efforts
in America so morally dubious. Since the natives' commercial instincts
made them so vulnerable, the *mercator sapiens* had to tread more cautiously in America. Since the Spanish precedent had been so abysmal,
the WIC had to operate more piously in America. And since the New
World's wealth appeared so plentiful, the *predikanten* had to sermonize
more shrilly on America.

Godefridus Udemans took all these contradictions to heart in his assessment of Dutch fortunes in America. The New World possessed great
stores of gold, he agreed, and its "inexpressible riches" could be har-
vested by cooperative Indian allies. Yet the gold that coaxed the Dutch
overseas could easily compromise the pious merchant once arrived.
Udemans never explicitly stated the benefits of gold – presumably he
believed it would bolster the war efforts against Catholic Spain and
serve the greater glory of the Calvinist Republic. He did lecture amply,
however, on the dangers of material wealth and on the uncomfortable
coexistence of gold and godliness. "The riches and goods of this world,"
he submitted, "are generally possessed in the largest quantities by such
people who know not God or who serve Him contrary to His will." The
Indians provided testimony of the first instance, and the papists – "who
adorn their religious ceremonies with gold and silver" – illustrated the

truth of the second. The godly must steer well clear of gold. "The poor Christian is the pious," reads one of Udemans's inspirational marginalia. Yet the almost magical properties of gold could compromise even the upright. For, although the natives of America "were strangers to covetousness," this could never be claimed for the Europeans. "Indeed it has been observed of the Americans that they hardly value gold, silver, and pearls, and that they regard feathers much more highly," Udemans opined, echoing here Cats's take on Indian barter. "What an evil it is that Christians storm and rage for the sake of gold and silver, as if their very welfare, body and soul, depended on it!"[44]

The Americans, in so many other respects, too, made the Dutch look bad, and Udemans's inquiry into the Indians' customs contrasts the instinctive virtue of the Americans with the consistent failings of the Dutch. The exercise reveals the author's superior skills as a *predikant*, if rather suspect abilities as a crosscultural ethnographer. The Americans had a "natural understanding" of political order, Udemans asserted; they organized themselves around the principles of obedience and discipline. This observation provokes a charge against the "Libertines and other lukewarm [*lauwe*] Christians" – a thinly veiled allusion to the Remonstrants and their political allies – "who always praised their own natural understanding," yet consistently failed to toe the orthodox line. The Indians cherished their fatherland, from which "they have never moved" and with which they have always been satisfied. To Udemans, this artless allegiance to one's birthplace measured up well not only to the expansionist appetites of European princes, but also to the "voluptuous" manners of Dutch youth, "who spend so much time in their peregrinations, or travels abroad, that they . . . forget their own Fatherland or begin to disdain it." Particularly galling were those heirs of rich merchants, who gallivanted "five or six years abroad and [return], claiming to be great experts or even Doctors of Philosophy." More modest and restrained in their customs, the Indians practiced a sobriety of habit that the author admired and catalogued for his Dutch readers: simplicity of demeanor, obedience to authority, respect for compatriots, contentment with one's portion. All of this reflected badly on habits lately developed in the United Provinces. Udemans heaped great scorn on the "profligate" merchants and their luxury-loving, white-bread eating, long-haired sons, whom the *predikant* considered the ruination of the Republic. (Udemans would later engage in a public debate over the appropriate length of a gentleman's hair and other "worldly vanities" of the well-to-do.)[45] He also inveighed against the "wild" dress, unrestrained appetite, and dissolute manner of young Holland dandies; and contrasted it with what he perceived as the unpretentious, industrious,

and well-disciplined decorum of American youth. "It might be worth-
while for some [Christians] to be sent to the School of the Heathens,"
mused Udemans, tongue only partly in cheek, "and not just to that of
the learned Greeks and Romans, but even to that of the blind Indians
and Americans, who, in many respects . . . put to shame various bastard
Christians." Here, then, was the noble savage *avant la lettre:* a dignified
and sober heathen brought to the service of a voluptuous and foppish,
grand-touring and grandstanding Dutch youth, the progeny of the
fallen state of Calvinist *burgerlijk* decorum. To Udemans and those of his
ilk, the most appallingly "wild" and nomadic race of his day could be
found, alas, in the Netherlands.[46]

The spoiled youth of the Netherlands craved luxury imports from
America, and these invariably incited censure from the Republic's elders. The products in question – gold, silver, pearls, sugar, tobacco – did
not necessarily come originally, or even exclusively, from America, yet
they had become by now largely associated with the opulent New
World. Sugar, for example, had been produced in Europe since antiquity. Barlaeus, always the humanist, studiously compared the ancient,
less-refined product with its modern, Brazilian variant, finding the first
superior for treating the liver and intestine, the second for baking cook-
ies and pies. Already by the late sixteenth century, sugar imported from
the West occupied a common spot in Dutch pantries, enough so to
arouse the attention of moralists and children alike. America "has so
filled our country with sugar," wrote Ortelius, "that it is now in all
kitchens and ravenously devoured in great quantities." The young child
depicted in a mid-seventeenth-century woodcut of a Brazilian sugar-
mill gestures excitedly at a sack of sweets, as his father surveys the work
(fig. 32). Beneath the print, a Jacob Cats rhyme quips:

> There is no sugar-reed that in our valley's grow,
> And yet the children here have sugar overflow.

The popular medical writer and Dordrecht physician, Johan van Beverwijck, counseled against the excessive consumption of American sugar,
though not so much for the cavities it might cause as for the damage it
would do to the local honey industry. A great patriot and promoter of
native goods, van Beverwijck lobbied for the cultivation of "Holland
medicines" – he, like the ancients, still valued sugar for its medicinal
properties – and against the corruptive importation of foreign products.
To buy *Hollands* was to support the fatherland and to fortify the godly
Republic. American sweets, as it turns out, were opposed by the Dutch
doctor more for their promotion of moral decay than dental.[47]

Figure 32. Illustration from Johan van Beverwijck, *Schat der gesontheyt* (Dordrecht, 1636). Universiteitsbibiliotheek Amsterdam.

Other American imports were likewise denounced. Though much of the gold reaching the Netherlands at this time came in fact from WIC traders in Guinea, both gold and silver continued to be identified with the conquest of Mexico and Peru (from where much of Europe's silver bullion did originate) and with the tyranny of Spain. Surplus of specie had introduced indulgence to the Netherlands, it was postulated. It bought its owners sumptuous imports, and it generated immoderate extravagance. With admirable consistency, van Beverwijck proposed doing away with gold altogether, foreign as it was to the bogs of Holland. "Indeed, hay is often better," he declared, citing the crisis faced by Alexander the Great when his army had nothing but gold to feed its horses. Gold from the New World, which the ancient Batavians had done without, had yet to cure any endemic Dutch diseases, reasoned Doctor van Beverwijck. On the contrary: it had contributed to the gold fever now rampant in the Republic and the related maladies of greed, envy, and pride. Vondel, by temperament more baroque than bourgeois, grieved over the tragedies brought on by Europe's rush on gold: "Oh avarice! Oh sorrow!" Those in pursuit of precious metals had forded "A flood / And sea of tears and spilled human blood." Pearls, another luxury import associated with America, also suffered notoriety for the harsh circumstances of their procurement. Van Beverwijck describes with great sympathy the conditions of the West Indian pearl-divers:

These pearl oysters are fished by the Indians with tremendous labor, requiring that the divers go down six, nine, sometimes even twelve fathoms, where the water is excessively cold. The divers are further exhausted from shortness of breath; for they must stay underwater a quarter, or half hour, and tear the oysters off rocks on the sea bed.[48]

Finally, there was tobacco, a commodity emphatically American despite its domestication in the Netherlands during the first half of the seventeenth century. Tobacco, in fact, came slowly to the Low Countries, though it quickly made itself at home once arrived. As late as 1598, Emanuel van Meteren had to explain to his readers the proper way to "drink" a pipe of tobacco and warned of the "sweet head" it would effect. *Nicotiana tabacum* had gained an early following for its purported medicinal qualities, and van Meteren, in deference to the humanist physicians in London and Antwerp, commended tobacco for the nourishment and energy it imparted. Patients in the Netherlands took note. The importation of American tobacco, first from Brazil and Venezuela and later from Virginia, increased rapidly over the next quarter-century. A profitable processing industry – drying, cutting, and spinning raw leaves – soon thrived in Amsterdam, and in 1623 the States of Holland imposed the first tobacco tax. Business continued to boom, both for the home market and for reexport, and this prompted a step as innovative as it was logical: the cultivation of a domestic crop within the Republic. First around Amersfoort (Utrecht) and eventually in the Veluwe (Gelderland), Dutch farmers raised a coarser-leafed tobacco, which spinners in Amsterdam blended with the superior American variety. Over the course of the 1630s and 1640s, the States of Utrecht and Gelderland abolished all duties on tobacco in an effort to support the local industry. By the mid-seventeenth century, the importation, cultivation, and processing of tobacco had firmly established the crop as a staple of the Dutch economy.[49]

Also established was the habit of smoking tobacco, which, then as today, provoked considerable controversy. The "divine" weed, not surprisingly, always had its champions. Giles Everard, the Brabanter who authored the first tract devoted exclusively to tobacco, considered his subject *"de herba panacea"* and lavished praise on the marvelous "medicinal recipes" this cure-all had introduced into Europe. Tobacco, he believed, worked well against toothaches, ulcers, warts, coughs (!), and even poison. Above all, it had a "wonderful effect" against drowsiness. The natives of America used *nicotia* as a potent pick-me-up; Everard observed that it made the tired "joyful" and the solemn "cheery," or even "drunk." For those not fatigued, he assured, it "comforted the brain." In the *Hymnus tabaci,* the Leiden-educated physician Raphael Thorius glorified the "healthful fumes" and "wondrous smoke" of tobacco for their life-prolonging properties.

> I sing the potent Herb, and sweet repast;
> Friend to the thought and grateful to the taste;
> With all the wonders of its cheering fumes;
> Whilst, lengthening life, the leaf, in brittle tubes, consumes.

Tobacco healed, nourished, energized. It lent stamina to the warriors of America and was therefore recommended to the frailer sex of Europe – *especially* during pregnancy. Like sugar, it healed ailments of the stomach; like wine, it cleared murkiness of the mind. Van Beverwijck enthusiastically endorsed tobacco (perhaps because it now grew in the Republic), though, in a note of caution, he discouraged excessive smoking among children.[50]

Tobacco's adversaries made relatively little fuss over issues of health. Even Udemans conceded that the "devil's weed" might serve a beneficial role for the weak of body. The problem rested, rather, in matters more spiritual. Tobacco was assailed as an indulgent *ijdelheid* (vanity), a dissipative luxury that would while away good time and scarce money in ephemeral clouds of smoke. Van Meteren noted early on the addictive power of nicotine. "These people become enslaved by it," he wrote of the committed aficionados, "just as drunkards do to wine and beer." Udemans chose a slightly more ministerial analogy but made essentially the same point. "There are thousands of people, who would call themselves Christians, who are just as besotted with this foul smoke as children are with sugar."[51] Whether as intoxicated drunkards or candy-craving children, smokers followed their habit down the dusky road of addiction and onward to the path of idleness, atrophy, and – inevitably – sin. In the moralizing emblemata of Roemer Visscher and Cats, the "tobacco blowers" appear slouched in their seats, solitary and slightly dazed (figs. 33 and 34). Visscher, one of the Republic's elder merchant-poets, condemned what he perceived as the trendy frivolousness of smoking (though his gruff-looking subject looks anything but stylish); and Cats made a mockery of the deceptive smoke screen behind which idlers hid, puffing away their time and money.[52]

This image of nicotine-induced stupor or smoke-hazed prodigality

Figure 35. Adriaen Brouwer, *The Smoker* (29.5 × 21 cm). Amsterdam, Rijksmuseum.

Figure 33. (*facing page top*) Emblem from Roemer Visscher, *Sinnepoppen* (Amsterdam, 1614). Universiteitsbibiliotheek Amsterdam.

Figure 34. (*facing page bottom*) Emblem from Jacob Cats, *Emblemata, ofte minnelycke, zedlycke, ende stichtelycke sinnebeelden* (ca. 1622). Universiteitsbibiliotheek Amsterdam.

Figure 36. Adriaen Brouwer, *Peasants Smoking and Drinking* (19.5 × 26.5 cm). The Hague, Mauritshuis.

exercised notable appeal in the visual arts, though here the moralizing tended to be more subtle. The rustic, or "lowlife," scenes painted by Adriaen Brouwer and his followers frequently illustrate the smokers' pastime by showing subjects inhaling deeply and meditatively on their own, or with great conviviality in a raucous tavern scene (figs. 35 and 36). Willem Buytewech's "merry company" scenes depict an upper-class variation on the theme – that is, the profligate, long-haired heirs of the regent class who so incensed Udemans, now smoking and drinking away their fortunes (fig. 37). Buytewech's compositions demonstrate the particular folly of what Cats referred to as *ydele vermaeckelijckheden* (vain diversions). Tobacco, snuff boxes, clay pipes and other smoking-related paraphernalia all show up ubiquitously in *vanitas* still lives – as, for example, in the oeuvre of Harmen Steenwijck (fig. 38) – where they underscore the ephemeral character of temporal life: "Man's life passes even as smoke."[53]

The painters and the poets did not always relate tobacco and the van-

Figure 37. Willem Buytewech, *Merry Company,* ca. 1617–1620 (49.3×68 cm). Rotterdam, Museum Boijmans Van Beuningen.

ities it signified directly to the New World. When they did, however, the implication could hardly have been more clear. America represented the land from which these follies emanated; "worldliness" had led to vanity and ultimately to sin. Perhaps the most acerbic attack against tobacco came from Dirck Pers, a poet and printer of Amsterdam and a friend of Vondel. Pers's *Bacchus wonder-wercken* (Bacchus's miracles) satirized the evils primarily of the vine, yet it also included a lengthy dissertation on the diableries of the weed, tobacco, recently imported from America.

> This miraculous herb, sent from overseas
> In isolation grown, by apes first perceived.[54]

With his allusion to apes, Pers meant not to deride the native Americans – the next lines of the poem describe how the Indians cleverly cultivated the plant after its discovery. In seventeenth-century Dutch iconography, the ape (or monkey) stood for licentiousness and imprisonment to vice. More generally, it was a symbol of appetite and folly. Pers decried this most recent infiltration of folly into the Republic and

Figure 40. Jan Miense Molenaer, *Woman at Her Toilet (Lady World)*, 1633 (102 × 127 cm). The Toledo Museum of Art.

Figure 38. (*facing page top*) Harmen Steenwijck, *Vanitas Still Life* (37.7 × 38.2 cm). Leiden, Stedelijk Museum De Lakenhal.

Figure 39. (*facing page bottom*) Gillis van Scheyndel, *Tobacco* (engraving), in Dirck Pietersz Pers, *Bacchus wonder-wercken* (Amsterdam, 1628). Universiteitsbibiliotheek Amsterdam.

Figure 41. Edwaert Collier, *Vanitas* (50.5 × 60 cm). Leiden, Stedelijk Museum De Lakenhal.

attacked "those apes of our day" enslaved to sensuality and, more particularly, tobacco. The engraving that accompanied his verse shows a prancing ape, orchestrating a bacchanal banquet of smokers (fig. 39).[55] An ape also stares out at the viewer from Jan Molenaer's painting known as *Vrouw Wereld* (Lady World), an artful meditation on the emptiness of worldliness (fig. 40). Within this elaborate catalogue of *vanitas* symbols – a prominent skull under the mistress's foot, a tell-tale mirror on her lap, costly jewelry and gold on the tables, whimsical bubbles (*homo bulla:* man is like a bubble) from the gleeful boy – a large wall map fills the background, its two discernible orbs mimicking the shape of the women's heads. Though half of the map is obscured, the visible part, which suggestively frames Vrouw Wereld's face, shows the clear outline of the American continents. The vacant gaze of the young woman reflects the hollow vanity of the New World. Similarly, a *vanitas* still life by Edwaert Collier features a terrestrial globe, carefully positioned to show the viewer an image of America (fig. 41). Affixed to the base of the globe and serving, as it were, as its didactic legend, is a slip of paper with the classic text, *Vanitas vanitatum et omnis vanitas* (Eccl. 1:2 and 12:8). The *vanitas* theme has thus attached itself, here quite literally, to the representation of America.[56] Likewise had such New World imports as tobacco, gold, and sugar become identified with the vices of folly, avarice, and corruption. And likewise had wealthy Atlantic traders, with their overly cosmopolitan sons, acquired by now a reputation for covetousness in the first instance and prodigality in the second. America had come to symbolize the vanities of the world. Or worse: America, to a growing number of moralists, represented a breeding ground of sin.[57]

V

The moral outcry against things American gained in volume during the late 1630s and the 1640s, reaching a shrill pitch by the mid-seventeenth century. This was no coincidence. The swell of discontent in the Netherlands corresponded to the broadening Dutch presence in America. More precisely, the backlash against corrupting exports and excessive wealth from the New World correlated to the widespread dissent, both in the colonies and in the Republic, against the policies of the WIC, their governors in America, and the course of the Western enterprise more generally. Following the successful installation of the WIC's colonies, it took little time for disenchantment to set in. Both settlers and investors grew quickly frustrated with the colonies' development (or lack thereof) and with the Company's mismanagement. A feeling prevailed that something had rapidly gone amiss in America. In the closing years of the war with Spain and the decade or so that followed – the final years, it would turn out, for both Dutch Brazil and New Netherland – critics stepped up their attacks on the *bewindhebberen*, their unpopular governing policies, and, most particularly, their appointed servants abroad (with the notable exception of Johan Maurits). Over these years, the New World record of the Dutch would become branded by the stigmata of incompetence, corruption, and ultimately, that most loathsome of marks, tyranny. Over the same period, America's image would perceptibly pale.

"Extravagance," "licentiousness," "covetousness," "unfaithfulness": Kiliaen van Rensselaer's barrage of epithets hurled at New Netherland bears easy comparison with judgments otherwise issued by Cats and Udemans. Yet despite its proximity to the tobacco fields of Virginia and the (purportedly) mineral-bearing hills of the Catskills, New Netherland never suffered from a reputation for nicotine addiction or gold fever. The colony provoked censure, instead, for its perceived "perversions" and deviations from righteousness, which seemed to be endemic to the land and to worsen only with time. New Netherland was declared "ungodly." To an extent, such rhetoric was not entirely unusual nor even unpredictable within the context of colonial letters. Certain standard themes of reproof, leveled at New Netherland no less than Spanish, English, or Portuguese settlements abroad, denounced the moral laxity of the colonial world, where Europe's "riffraff" predominated – where immigrants of lower economic standing and presumed lower moral standards had been summarily exported. The first *predikant* of New Netherland, Jonas Michaëlius, spoke of the common colonists as "useless ballast," prone to idleness and its cognate vices. The patrician Willem Kieft, when he arrived in New Amsterdam in 1638, expressed indignation at the disorder, lewdness, and (again) idleness that he encountered. He admonished the "turbulent and seditious" community "to abstain from fighting; from carnal intercourse with heathens, blacks, or other persons; from rebellion, theft, false swearing, calumny, and all other immoralities." Never having journeyed to the New World himself, van Rensselaer witnessed none of the transgressions he deplored in a series of pamphlets published in 1643. Yet he did not have to, it would seem, since his litany of imagined impieties reads like a set list of the seven deadly sins of colonial life: cupidity (in trade), gluttony (in drink) faithlessness (with the patroon), wantonness (with the natives), and so forth. Still others reproached the pervasive "sinfulness" of New Netherland and the settlers' "great abuse" of their political guardians.[58]

More often than not, though, fault was found in the governors themselves, the local officials who served them, and the Company that had appointed them. If the "common people" could hardly help themselves, the governors had no such excuse. Michaëlius, whose stay in New Amsterdam overlapped with that of Director-General Minuit, launched the first of many attacks against the colony's leadership. In exceptionally acrimonious language, the *predikant* set the tenor for the campaign that would ensue. "We have a governor who is most unworthy of his office," fulminated Michaëlius,

a slippery man, who under the treacherous mask of honesty is a compound of all iniquity and wickedness. For he is accustomed to the lies, of which he is full, and to the imprecations and most awful execrations; he is not free from fornication, the most cruel oppressor of the innocent. . . . He has a council at his disposition that obeys with the same iniquity as he commands, which you might call not wrongly a kind of mixture of the most pestilent kind of people. For besides cheating our Company, whose servants they are, in unworthy ways to their own profit, and having an eye only to their own interest, they also oppress the innocent, and they live so outrageously that they seem not only to be wicked, but even to propagate wickedness.

Much of this rhetoric was already commonplace in Dutch propaganda – the pretext of justice, for example, or the oppression of innocents – while other themes would become increasingly so as they reappeared in description after description of New Netherland. Warning signs, too, had appeared from the earliest years of the colony: Minuit's predecessor, Willem Verhulst, was sternly cautioned to conduct his affairs honorably, "lest we call down the wrath of God upon our unrighteous beginnings." Very quickly indeed was the wrath of God presumed to have visited New Netherland and chiefly on account of its iniquitous leadership. The colony's government and the WIC by extension were portrayed as prideful, self-seeking, treacherous, unrighteous, unchristian – in a word, tyrannical. The denunciations did much to undermine the credibility of the Company and to recast sharply the Dutch image of America.[59]

Critics of New Netherland launched their broadsides liberally and tactically, attacking their subject from every conceivable angle. In a most basic sense, they assailed the character of the director-generals, their personal behavior and public decorum. The man who succeeded Minuit and managed the colony through the 1630s, Wouter van Twiller, was widely derided as a bungler and a drunkard, "a clerk . . . who was the sport of the people." David de Vries, who twice visited New Netherland in this period, made famous the pathetic "Dutch courage" of van Twiller, who bribed his officers with wine to get them to face the English. Van Twiller's ploy failed, and de Vries dismissed it as the act of a laughable "fool . . . who knew nothing but to drink."[60] Willem Kieft, who followed as governor, earned hardly more respect. Kieft came from a well-to-do family of magistrates, yet had managed to lose his fortune through his own incompetence. (It was said that, following custom, his portrait was hung from the gallows of Amsterdam upon his scandalous declaration of bankruptcy.) He ruled New Netherland by "duplicity and craft," according to van der Donck, and much to his personal advantage. "A rascal and a bankrupt" opined one of his many detractors. During his decade-long tenure (1638–1647), he established a reputation for perverse, almost sadistic, cruelty. Allegedly, he congratulated his soldiers after they slaughtered scores of Indian women and children in Pavonia (New Jersey); and he applauded "right heartily" upon witnessing the torture of two Indians, "rubbing his right arm and laughing out loud, such delight had he in the work."[61] The imperious Peter Stuyvesant (1647–1664) gained notoriety for his vulgarity and vanity. Stuyvesant, it was said, would rail at an audience with the "ugly words" of a fishmonger (he was actually a minister's son) and would "curse and storm and rage . . . so violently that froth hung from his beard." Such unseemly manners notwithstanding, he had the arrogance of "the Grand Duke of Muscovy." When Stuyvesant first arrived in the colony, "it was like the crowning of Rehoboam," noted van der Donck severely. The feisty governor had the "puffed up pride" of a "peacock," and the ravenous greed of a "vulture." "How did this Company know where to look up all these rascals?" wonders a character from a popular dialogue, of the low-life leaders of New Netherland. "I believe that they must have magazines full of them."[62]

These crude, cruel, and incompetent managers conducted themselves as petty tyrants – or so they were represented – setting themselves above the Company and even the law. The director-generals carried on "as if they were sovereigns of the country." Kieft, it was reported, fancied himself a bona fide prince, claiming "he was sovereign in [New Netherland], or the same as the Prince in the Netherlands." Likewise did Stuyvesant allot princely powers to himself and then boldly assert the maxim, "the Prince is above the law." Collectively, the governors of New Netherland made the most of that credo. They ignored Company regulations, mocked their harassed subjects, and ruled according to greed and caprice. Van der Donck complained that the directors stuck "close by their profits," which they accumulated "under the pretext of public business." During the late 1640s, when the colony sought desperately to attract merchants, Stuyvesant made a habit of confiscating cargo at his whim, so "that not a ship dare[d] come hither." Stuyvesant also assumed for himself the exclusive right to deal arms with the Indians – a myopic policy that ultimately backfired. All of the directors taxed indiscriminately, burdening the natives and Europeans alike. De Vries recorded the complaints of the Tappan, who considered staging a minor "revolt" against the demands of Kieft. The language they used (as quoted by de Vries) echoes the famous response of the Incan leader, Atahualpa, to the mandates of Pizarro:

They said . . . that they were very much surprised that the Sachem who was now at the Fort [namely, Kieft at New Amsterdam] dare exact it; and he must be a very mean fellow to come to live in this country without being invited by them, and now wish to compel them to give him their corn for nothing.

In place of graciousness, Kieft displayed covetousness. Instead of justice, he and the governors of New Netherland offered tyranny – just as had the conquistadors of old.[63]

For their inattention to their pastoral duties the governors were also rebuked. Unlike its neighbor to the north, New Amsterdam never sought to be a city on a hill. More famous for its taverns, the Dutch colony erected an adequate church only in 1642. In that year, de Vries (by his own account) impressed upon Kieft the need to replace the "mean barn" in which services were held with a proper edifice. Though it was built with the congregation's funds, Kieft (according to van der Donck) later took credit for the project. He rarely visited "his" church, however. The director (reportedly) went nearly three and a half years, "never wish[ing] to hear God's word, nor to partake of the Christian sacraments." Engaged in a long-running feud with the minister, Everhardus Bogardus, Kieft also did his resolute best to keep others from services, encouraging the "rolling [of] ninepins, bowling, dancing, singing, leaping, and other profane exercises . . . so that a miserable villainy against God's church was perpetrated in order to disturb the congregation."[64] Van Rensselaer also grumbled about poor church attendance and joined the many who complained of the distracting presence (and the directors' tolerance) of Lutherans, Quakers, and Jews. Van Twiller, Kieft, and Stuyvesant all tolerated the impious mischief of Cornelis van Tienhoven, who occupies a special place as the most objectionable figure in the annals of New Netherland. A long-time resident of the colony who rose in favor with each successive governor, van Tienhoven gained infamy for behavior several notches below "libertine." He "ran" (as all the reports put it) nearly naked with the Indians, apparently for the purpose of sleeping with them. And he shared the frequent company of prostitutes, ultimately contriving to marry one. He also cheated, robbed, and deceived the colonists, and he reputedly instigated the disastrous wars with the Indians. "What worse can be said than murderer, thief, cheat, whoremonger, and villain?" asked one indignant pamphleteer. It was said that this "man of no religion" committed all these acts with the tacit approval of the ungodly governors of New Netherland.[65]

Van Tienhoven's run-ins with the natives demonstrate yet another facet of the colony's failed leadership, namely its appalling record with the Indians, severely criticized as "tyranny" in the literature of the period. Secretary van Tienhoven, of course, did not single-handedly bring about the bloody clashes between the Dutch and their indigenous neighbors known as Governor Kieft's Wars. The expansion of the colony from the late 1630s, its encroachment on native lands, and Kieft's injudicious policy of taxing the Indians (ostensibly to pay for their "protection") all contributed to the rapidly deteriorating circumstances of the early 1640s. It was van Tienhoven, however, under Kieft's commission, who led the bloody attack against the Raritans in the summer of 1640, which left several dead on both sides. The secretary of the governor permitted his troops, additionally, to kidnap the sachem's brother, whom they "tortured . . . in his private parts with a piece of split wood." Kieft himself behaved hardly better. In a later incident, the governor watched approvingly as his men savagely flayed an Indian prisoner. "Such acts of tyranny," observed de Vries, choosing his words carefully, led only to worse. Governor Kieft, who once expressed his intention "to wipe the mouths of the savages," acted on this impulse on a wintry night in 1643, when he authorized a surprise raid against a band of exhausted Wiechquaeskecks and Hackensacks camped across the Hudson. The infamous Battle of Pavonia, in which some eighty natives were killed, encouraged further massacres and envenomed Dutch-Indian relations for years to come. It also provided grist for the propaganda mills of those who would vilify Kieft, his supporters, and his patrons in the Netherlands. The anonymous pamphlet that reported the event (and on which all later accounts were based) resorted to language and imagery as lurid as any used by the rebels to portray the tyrannies of Spain. Indeed, the central passage describing the slaughter evoked, both implicitly and explicitly, the memory of the bloody reign of Alba in the Netherlands. It is a powerful, if terrifying, piece of prose:

Young children were snatched from their mothers' breasts, and cut to pieces in sight of the parents, and the pieces thrown into the fire and into the water; other sucklings were bound to wooden boards, and cut, stuck, or bored through and miserably massacred, so that a heart of stone would have been softened. Some were thrown into the river, and when the fathers and mothers endeavored to rescue them, the soldiers would not let them come ashore again, but caused both old and young to be drowned. Children, five or six years old, and also some old, decrepit people, as many of them as had escaped this fury and secreted themselves in the bushes and reeds, when they came forth in the morning to beg a piece of bread and to warm themselves against the cold, were murdered in cold blood, and pushed into the water or into the fire. Some came running past our people living on the farms, with their hands cut off; others had their legs cut off. Some carried their bowels in their arms; others had such horrible cuts, hacks, and wounds, that the like can never have happened elsewhere. . . .

Has the Duke of Alva done more evil in the Netherlands?

Certainly you have such Dutch governors or directors, to whom the Duke of Alva might yield in reputation.[66]

Tyranny had come full circle, for it was now the WIC that played the part of tyrants and terrorized America. Dutch soldiers, like the Spaniards before them, snatched innocent babes from their mother's breasts, dispatched young and old into freezing rivers, and dismembered, with little provocation, the innocent Indians. Dutch director-generals lorded over the settlers in New Netherland as had the Habsburgs

in the Netherlands. They enslaved the colony with unfair taxes and restrictive trade laws, and they flouted their positions as caretakers of the
Church. They and their sponsors in the Netherlands governed "under
the pretext" of the colony's common welfare, yet acted for their own personal gain. And they perverted justice. To those who challenged their
highhandedness, the director-generals responded in perfect Alba-like
fashion. Stuyvesant, very early in his service, arrested a leading colonist
on the specious charge of *crimen lesae magestatis,* an audacity that set off
all sorts of polemical alarms in the Netherlands. "It may, during my ad-
ministration, be contemplated to appeal," Stuyvesant was quoted as
saying, "but if any one should do it, I will make him a foot shorter and
send the pieces to Holland." These, it was noted, were the deeds and
pronouncements of a tyrant, a role the Dutch had lately assumed in
North America.[67]

VI

In 1643, apropos of the iniquity on the banks of the Hudson, Kiliaen van
Rensselaer warned of "injurious and destructive floods" and other divine "visitations" that would seriously imperil the colony should it refuse to repent. New Netherland, in fact, lasted until 1664, when the
Lord's wrath finally arrived in the Dutch harbor in the form of an English fleet, to which Stuyvesant stoically surrendered.[68] In Brazil, where
moral matters had similarly deteriorated, disaster struck as early as
1644, when a revolt of Portuguese planters challenged Dutch authority
and threw the country into turmoil. This, many assumed, came as divine retribution for transgressions and "tyrannies"; for, in New Holland
no less than New Netherland, the Dutch reputation had suffered
gravely. Critics lambasted the WIC for its policies in Brazil and for those
it had sent to implement them. Unlike the case of New Netherland,
though, the governor himself attracted little rebuke – at least not from
the planters, the Indians, the soldiers, and the pamphleteers, who began
their denunciations only by the mid-1640s, after Johan Maurits had already departed. Even the colony's severest critics took care to distinguish between Johan Maurits, widely admired as a conciliatory and able
administrator, and the councilors of the WIC, scorned as greedy and
godless servants of a corrupt company. The prince of Nassau had made
the best of his circumstances, kept the peace during his seven-year stay,
and occasioned great banquets and regret upon his departure. (A throng
of native Brazilians, it was reported, bore him on their shoulders and
through the crashing Atlantic surf to his waiting boat.) The WIC, by contrast, set unbearably high taxes, restricted access to trade, and played

the various European and indigenous peoples of Dutch Brazil against
one another. Upon Johan Maurits's departure, all hell broke loose. Religious tensions and economic crises – particularly the enormous level of
debt, among both Dutch settlers and Portuguese *moradores* – spilled onto
the battlefield. Meanwhile, critics in the Republic assailed the colony's
Hooghen Raad (High Council) as a corrupt clique of "evil-advisors," and
represented the *bewindhebberen* in Amsterdam as a malevolent sort of
Blood Council. Great "desperation and doubt" descended on the colony,
as one of its longtime residents put it, while a mood of resignation prevailed in the Netherlands. By the mid-seventeenth century, the WIC's
foremost effort to settle the New World seemed destined to fail. From
the pulpits of the Republic and the vantage point of the polemicists, it
appeared that God had elected the Portuguese rebels to punish what
many now perceived as Dutch tyrannies in America.[69]

New Holland's reputation suffered in stages. Established by the great
force of Republican arms and inaugurated with the high expectations of
the small investor, the Dutch colony in Brazil soon suffered the harsh assaults of its many critics, who discerned, first, unfair economic strictures
that strangulated free trade; next, judicial venality that afflicted good
governance; and, finally, obnoxious "tyranny" that victimized Portuguese and Indian inhabitants especially. Nagging frustrations in the
early years, generally related to matters mercantile, transformed in the
absence of Johan Maurits into broader denunciations of the *Hooghen
Raad* that became, by the final, dire years of the colony, all-out attacks
on the very project of Dutch Brazil. The very rapid shift in the colony's
reputation is striking. The image of Dutch Brazil underwent tremendous adjustments since its sparkling debut in the promotional literature
of the 1620s and 1630s; the luster that had originally enticed the Dutch
was quick to fade. "Brazil, in and of itself," wrote a pamphleteer in the
year of Johan Maurits's departure (1644), "is a desolate and undevel-
oped land, without demonstrable mineral wealth, without readily available natural resources, [and] without inhabitants, save a few naked savages."[70] What it did possess was a substantial population of Portuguese
settlers, nomadic and semi-urbanized Indians, and imported African
slaves, which could produce sugar for export and consume European
imports shipped via the Netherlands. As with their other commercial
operations, Dutch merchants saw their profits in the carrying trade –
and not necessarily in the working of sugar mills, the harvesting of dyewoods, indigo, and tobacco, or the mining of hypothetical gold. Any restriction or taxation of that trade (which was after all the raison d'être
of the WIC monopoly) provoked protest from those merchants who believed their profits had been curtailed. For their part, the Company, al-

ready eighteen million guilders in debt *before* the arrival of their princely governor, covetously guarded their monopoly.

The free-trade debate persisted, with surprising intensity, through virtually the entire duration of Dutch Brazil. And though it concerned issues typical to other economic disputes of the day, its setting – the New World – sharpened the exchange considerably. To the antimonopolists, the freedom of commerce now denied them resembled the freedoms of conscience and religion, for which their ancestors had strenuously struggled. The defenders of monopoly disagreed and justified their prerogatives with reference to the tremendous energies already expended in conquering Brazil, for which the WIC deserved compensation.[71] In principle, this debate barely differed from similar seventeenth-century discussions of the relative merits of unrestricted commerce. In fact, though, the pamphleteers had recourse to the discourse of America – the tropes, metaphors, and analogies employed in earlier discussions of the New World – and this made the points of conflict all the more harsh. What should have been a fairly mild discussion of trade, therefore, assumed with time an exceptionally acerbic flavor. America upped the polemical ante. The WIC, it was claimed, "enslaved" the innocent inhabitants of Brazil with its own brand of (commercial) tyranny. Under the terms of the monopoly, Dutch *vrijluijden* (free-settlers) paid artificially high prices for goods and Portuguese *moradores* sold their sugar at unnecessarily low rates. The Company's policy victimized further the "poor widows and children" of the Republic – by which was meant those in municipal orphanages and homes for the elderly that had invested in WIC stock, or those indigents who might have been the beneficiaries of WIC charity, had its stock ever paid dividends. (It was not unusual for joint-stock companies in the seventeenth century to raise capital from commonly held, in this case charitable, institutions.) The WIC "oppressed" all who would exercise their "natural liberties" and treated their opponents "as in the time of Alba." "Would a free-born Netherlander ever choose to leave his Fatherland to be a slave in the Indies?" asked one pamphleteer. "What kind of person would choose to go to Brazil, where he could prosper no more than the Lord Directors [of the WIC] permitted."[72]

Those who *could* prosper included first and foremost the Lord Directors' agents in Brazil. These were the corrupt, arrogant, luxury-loving members of the High Council, who contributed more than anyone else to the colony's declining reputation. Like the directors-general of New Amsterdam, the *Hooghen Raad* of Recife featured centrally in the assault on America; they were held up as the very model of knavery. Once again, however, the language used to denounce them far surpassed, it might seem, that normally reserved for unscrupulousness. Once again, the American dimensions of their crimes made them that much more sinful. Left to their own devices, the *Hooghen Raad* transformed into a pack of "rogues [*guyten*]" and "vagabonds," "a government of scoundrels [*rabbauwen*]," chronically corrupt and self-serving. Like indolent pashas, they indulged in banquets "and pleasurable living." "These commissaries," asserted the scurrilous *Brasilsche gelt-sack* (Brazilian money-bag), "[behaved] like minor nobility, living, eating, drinking, dressing, and holding forth like great lords." Such was the unbridled luxury of these men, contended their enemies in heated prose, that they changed their silken clothing on a daily basis. To support their lifestyle, the Council lined their pockets with illicit profits, derived through venality, bribery, and double-dealing. "Like devouring lions," they preyed on the debt-plagued settlers, their mortgaged properties, and their meager profits. They seized taxes and tolls, it was averred, "as in the days of Alba." And they abused their unfortunate soldiers "like lackeys and stall-boys." "If you only knew what a miserable life a soldier leads in Brazil!" exclaims an overseas veteran in the popular dialogue, *Brasyls schuyt-praetjen* (Brazilian barge-chatter). "I've heard many soldiers sigh, 'Oh, if only [we] could sit in a Holland *Rasphuis* [house of correction] with bread and water!'" Readers would not have missed the irony here: those incarcerated in the famous Amsterdam *Rasphuis* were made to rasp hardwoods imported precisely from Brazil.[73]

As matters in Brazil went from bad to worse, polemical assaults went from merely harsh to positively scathing. A Portuguese siege of Recife all but cornered the colony and curbed any control the Dutch may have exercised on the surrounding countryside. Efforts to relieve the siege ended disastrously, with five hundred men lost in 1648 and twice that number in an engagement the following year. In the wake of these devastating setbacks came the most vicious attacks on Dutch Brazil, which appeared around 1649. By this time, too, despite the directors' continued efforts to lobby for support, a vocal opposition began to make the case that investors – including the States General – would be wise to cut their losses and abandon the Company. The WIC was depicted as an insatiable monster that sapped more and more of the Republic's resources for its Brazilian debacle. While the "debauched" *Hooghen Raad* caroused and whored and filled their "beastly bellies" with profits, Company soldiers and capital were sacrificed to a hopeless war against the Portuguese. One broadside likened Brazil to a lion's den into which Dutch soldiers and investors' income were cast and then promptly devoured. "I shall spare you the details of all the blood that they or their servants have spilled," wrote the author, after a lengthy recitation of exactly that, "[and] of all the thousands of people that have been mauled, as if by a lion. Their Brazil . . . might rightly be called a murderer's lair or lion's den."[74]

The manifold abuses and corruptions of New Holland added up to what the pamphleteers finally and familiarly called "tyranny," showing here a fine grasp of polemical traditions in the Republic. The WIC and their High Council in Recife lorded over their Brazilian domains without recourse to law or religion, victimizing Dutch, Portuguese, and (it would later be claimed) Indian inhabitants alike. In the end, the "unbearable yoke of the Hollanders" incited revolt and caused the collapse of the colony. The "godless tyrants" who governed New Holland placed the Portuguese under "a yoke as heavy as any ever placed on us by the Spanish," wrote one historically minded pamphleteer. They enslaved the mill owners with debt, so as to extort from them sugar; they used the *moradores'* wives and daughters freely for their pleasure; and they falsely accused the planters of treason, in order to plunder their property. They tormented the Portuguese no less than "Pharaoh did the children of Israel." Such abuse weighed heavily on the Lusitanians, who finally took to arms, "just as we [Dutch] had done in the time of Alba." Under these circumstances, the planters' revolt was deemed a "just" one. Had not the Hollanders risen up under similar conditions of tyranny? reasoned one pamphleteer. The subsequent war between the WIC and the Portuguese "rebels" (as they were called) produced deeds of treachery no less black than those committed during the revolt of the Netherlands. The *Hooghen Raad* had, "in cold blood, indeed with careful deliberation, caused the massacre of many Portuguese." The details of these "wicked acts" were recounted vividly by the pamphleteers and not without a certain Lascasian flair. One popular dialogue of 1649 tells of a Dutch soldier who, with the complicity of the authorities, suspended his enemy prisoners upside down and burned the soles of their feet with hot irons. Another officer allegedly assembled the Portuguese citizens in the village square of Cunhau only to "fall upon them, when they had no weapons at all, and massacre them."[75] In the captaincy of Rio Grande, "a public resolution was taken by the heads of the government . . . to massacre twelve prisoners and the sixty inhabitants, who, being unarmed, could do no harm." The description is eerily evocative:

It happened in this massacre that a certain little girl, from eight to ten years of age, was not willing to be separated from her father, who was brought out to be massacred, and when her father was killed, went and sat upon his dead body, crying "O! matta mi tambem" – *O! kill me also with my father* – which did not happen according to her wish; but, nevertheless, that lamb was robbed of all her clothing, in the same manner as after that all the widows and orphans, who were

left by those who were killed, were despoiled, and as afterwards the Portuguese
who revolted were sent away.

The Dutch treated the Portuguese in America no less severely than
Spain had the rebels in the time of Alba. Just as the army of Philip II had
done, proclaimed the *Brasyls schuyt-praetjen*, "so we now tyrannize the
Portuguese of Brazil. We entered their land by force of arms, plundered
their cities and churches, and killed many thousands of their people, until the Portuguese were forced to bow to our regime."[76]

Relations with the natives had by now also deteriorated, pointing to
yet one more category of Dutch misdeeds in America. In many instances, it was true, the Indian partners of the Dutch served as accomplices to the colony's tyrannies. Tarairiu allies from the captaincy of
Maranhão murdered two dozen *moradores* who washed up on their
shores after the Dutch set them adrift from Recife in an ill-equipped
boat. Another band of Tarairiu, this time led by their Company-em-
ployed "supervisor," Jacob Rabe, slaughtered virtually the entire population of Cunhau, which they had cornered during a Sunday Mass in
1645. In other cases and with other tribes, however, the Dutch treatment
of the natives, and especially the Tupinamba, appeared more problem-
atic – less a matter of poor oversight than outright exploitation. Pieter
Potty, a Tupi convert to Calvinism who served as a go-between for the
Dutch, wrote an indignant letter to a Catholic kinsman in which he defended his Dutch coreligionists against charges of enslaving and murdering the Tupi. That this letter was translated from the original Tupi
into Dutch and ostentatiously published in the Netherlands strongly
suggests that many harbored doubts. The Dutch, some contended, routinely treated the Tupi as they did the Portuguese – that is to say, with
low regard and with great cruelty. They had neglected, with both the
Tupi and the Tarairiu, their obligations to convert the heathen and redeem them from the tyranny of the Iberians. Here the WIC had twice
failed; for, in the eyes of their critics, the Dutch had further "perverted"
those natives with whom they had dealt. They had "mixed" sinfully,
"even with the wives of the Brazilians [Tupi] and Tapoyers [Tarairiu],"
and had set a demonstrably poor example for their husbands. The Lord
had led the Dutch to a new promised land, wrote one author, yet the
New Hollanders had adopted the ways of the Canaanites.[77]

For their tyrannies and abominations, the Dutch earned the opprobrium of the Lord, who now afflicted New Holland with a costly and
ultimately fatal revolt. It is one of the more ironic turns of the Dutch literature on America that the Portuguese, longtime "tyrants" in the Indies and partners of Spain, could now be represented as the scourge

(*roede*) of God sent to chastise the sinful Dutch in Brazil. Yet this, precisely, was the strategy adopted by the virulently anti-WIC faction in the Netherlands. In their polemical imagination, the WIC and its servants now assumed the role of tyrants, the *moradores* and their allies that of divine avengers. "The true cause and origin of the many bizarre and pitiful miseries experienced in [Brazil], where so many people have been disastrously killed and where brutal tyrannies have become so notorious," contended one disillusioned veteran of the Dutch colony, "is the righteous punishment of Heaven."[78] The Lord had beckoned the Dutch to America to punish the Portuguese for "the great luxury and sins" in which they lived and for their negligence of the Indians. The establishment of New Holland, proposed one polemicist, had been "divine will." Yet so, too, was the uprising of the Portuguese against a Dutch regime that had itself succumbed to iniquity. "After we possessed the land for a brief period of time," wrote one distressed observer,

we far exceeded the Portuguese in sinfulness. And instead of converting the heathen by our good example, our government preferred riches to godliness; and the great multitude led a heathen, instead of, Christian life, living according to the lusts of their heart and knowing not how to satisfy themselves, so that it grieved the Lord. . . .
In good time has the chastiser been chastised by God.[79]

The Dutch had gone from being saviors in Brazil to being sinners. They had become "tyrants," an irony so rich, the pamphleteers could hardly contain themselves. In the *Brasyls schuyt-praetjen*, two moralizing poems on the shifting favor of the Lord frame a dialogue on the vicissitudes of Brazil and the decline of the Dutch. The opening poem likens the Netherlanders to the ancient Israelites, who had been redeemed from Egypt, shepherded to Canaan, and then sternly warned to shun "the daughters and gods of the land." By the end of the pamphlet, though, it has been demonstrated how quickly the Dutch in Brazil forgot their instructions and yielded to temptation. In the poem that concludes the work, the mantle of the Israelites rests on the shoulders of the Lusitanians, who (it is hoped) will soon be redeemed from their Egyptian captivity. The WIC now plays the part of the Pharaonic overlord. "Justly may the Portuguese in Brazil say," declares the poet,

God shall now redeem us from Holland's heavy yoke,
Which has for five and twenty years oppressed us with its choke.
Just as did the Lord the Jews from Egypt show,
So has He on us our former rights bestowed.
Because the Hollanders honored riches as their god,
The Lord reduced their efforts to absolutely naught.

The polemical tide had thus shifted. The Dutch were now the tyrants of America.[80]

In the face of these vilifications, the WIC waged its own counterattack, though without a great deal of success. Their apologia for Dutch Brazil and the costly wars there fell into surprisingly predictable patterns – surprising, since the WIC's detractors had conducted such a dramatic and apparently effective campaign against the Company's good name.[81] A response to the *Brasyls schuyt-praetjen* tried to align the WIC with the patriotic interest by substituting Portugal for Spain in the traditional role of the "arch enemy." The Portuguese, it was asserted, could never be trusted. They had committed ample atrocities of their own and spilled just as much "innocent blood" in their war against the fatherland. An appeal was also made for the "poor and innocent Indians" – this as late as 1655! – who could never be abandoned to the "cruel and bloodthirsty Portuguese" or to the crafty and heretical Jesuits. By withdrawing support from the WIC, as both private investors and the States General had in fact done by the 1650s, the Dutch had forsaken their Indian allies, who had only barely "tasted" – as one pamphleteer put it – "the true knowledge of Jesus Christ." Finally, the WIC appealed to the welfare of "so many innocent widows and orphans," who relied heavily on the Company for their income and charity. The Company's antagonists, of course, had made similar appeals on behalf of the poor. Yet WIC supporters now asserted that it served everyone's best interests to bolster, not undermine, the teetering Brazilian enterprise.[82]

Most of this fell on skeptical ears. The WIC had sunken especially low in the public's esteem, and few considered it prudent, at this stage anyway, to throw good money after bad. By now the WIC was the frequent butt of polemicists' jokes. "Uncle-Farmer," the naïf country bumpkin featured in the *Amsterdams dam-praetjen* (Amsterdam's dam-chatter), refers to the *bewindhebberen* of the Company as the *Wind-breakers:* "Lord Farters," as it were, or flatulents ("wind-breakers") more literally. These farters/directors were mocked as self-interested as well as self-bloated, greedy and "godless" in their management of the Company's affairs. Two housewives overheard in another pamphlet dismiss the directors as voluptuous layabouts and thievish embezzlers, and scoff at the Company more generally as a wasteful money-pit.[83] "They made the participants poor and then deserted them," wrote one surely less jocular critic. To investors, stock in the WIC was the cruelest of jokes. Share prices on the Amsterdam exchange fell precipitously throughout the 1640s and became an absolute losing proposition once the departure of Johan Maurits from Brazil was made public. By early 1650, market quotations had dropped to fourteen percent of their original value and the chief participants petitioned the States General to assume duties as overseer of the semibankrupt company. By 1655, shares dipped as low as ten percent, as creditors tried to seize the Company's property – something the States ultimately prevented for reasons more political than economic.[84]

By this time, too, the larger mechanism of overseas trading companies – chartered syndicates, privileged with exclusive monopolies and lucrative rights of taxation – came under intense scrutiny, with the WIC held up as paradigmatic of the system's worst ills. The once-promising American company, now hopelessly mismanaged and mired in debt, had squandered its fortunes and opportunities and those of the Republic, as well. Following the loss of Brazil and with the depression of the Caribbean trade, many lobbied for a new, preferably state-managed program of overseas trade. The author of the polemic, *Verheerlickte Nederland* (Glorified Netherlands), struck an oddly melancholic tone (the hopeful title notwithstanding) to describe the decline of Dutch trade and the failure of the American enterprise. Brazil had drained the WIC's funds and strained the Republic's patience. The best hope for the future, suggested the author, lay in a "free" settlement (he recommended Guiana) under the States' control. Pieter de la Court's classic defense of republicanism, the *Interest of Holland,* also made a vigorous case against monopolies. To de la Court, the chartered companies were institutes born of privilege and sustained by corruption. They smacked of favoritism and flourished under kings, which, to de la Court's sensibilities, was most repugnant. "Monarchies promote monopolies," he quoted briskly. The WIC was cited as a prime illustration of everything gone wrong with monopolies. Over time, it had enriched only its directors; in the meanwhile, it had depleted the States' resources, impoverished its investors, and restricted "the natural liberties of others" – by which the author meant the merchant class. De la Court wished for the Company's early demise, which in fact occurred, with little fanfare, when its charter expired in 1674.[85]

Along with the reputation of the WIC, its iniquitous officers, and its failing colonies went the reputation of America itself. By the middle of the seventeenth century, the Dutch had come to associate the New World with the corruption and incompetence of all those affiliated with it. The once-beckoning New World was now a metaphor for tyranny rather than innocence, for decadence rather than opportunity. Or rather, America had transmogrified into a locus of oddly distorted "innocence" and all but inevitable "tyranny." In the final hours of the Brazil colony, confidence men known as "soul-merchants" (*zielkopers*) operated in the ports of Holland and Zeeland, trying to induce young men to make the

Figure 42. Frans Post, *Brazilian Landscape,* 1665 (55.9 × 83.2 cm). Detroit Institute of Arts, Founders Society Purchase, General Membership Fund. Photograph © 1996 Detroit Institute of Arts.

journey to America that none but the foolhardy would willingly undertake. Few could be tricked into going, and those who went were thought to "degenerate" once there, owing to the insalubrious conditions and corrupting habits of the colonies. Well over a century before Cornelius de Pauw and the Enlightenment *philosophes* would denounce America, the Dutch identified the New World, and especially Brazil, with dissipation and decline. A poem by Jan Six van Chandelier employed the image of the ceaseless Brazilian rain as a metaphor for sin, loss, and postdiluvian punishment – this at the first hints of the twilight of the Republic's Golden Age. The Brazilian landscapes of Frans Post, which became popular in the 1650s and 1660s, show the now lost colony in a palpably melancholic setting (fig. 42). Partially decayed buildings (often churches) and mostly desolate farms occupy the peripheries and backgrounds of the compositions under immense, tropical skies. Lush, overgrown flora and exotic fauna fill the dark foregrounds, which seem ready to reclaim the ruins behind them. In a number of these studies, cobras and other reptiles prey on tamer creatures, such as hare – perhaps Post's macabre reference to the political events recently played out by the European colonialists. The Dutch, in any event, had already succumbed to the Portuguese by 1654. Exactly one decade later, New Netherland fell to the English, and there ceased to be any Dutch-American colonies to speak of.[86]

VII

TOWNSMAN: But our Nation, it is said, is too merciful [for such tyrannies].
SKIPPER: Nonsense![87]

By the second half of the seventeenth century, the New World, traditionally identified with the tyranny of Spain, had become affiliated with the sins of the Netherlands. Far from redeeming their innocent "allies" in America, the Dutch, in the estimation of the pamphleteers, had perpetrated against the Indians the very sort of abuses they had earlier reviled in their Habsburg antagonists. They had also tormented the Portuguese (by now themselves enemies of Spain) and had victimized even those settlers and traders from the Netherlands. In the space of two or three decades of colonial experience, the Dutch had developed a reputation as expert "tyrants" – as the skipper in the above dialogue could easily attest, with reference (in this case) to Brazil. This reputation, moreover, extended beyond the borders of the Netherlands, where others joined in to denounce the imperial ambitions and villainous methods of the Republic. For the tables had radically turned on the Dutch: whereas the rebels had led the chorus of righteous rebuke against Spain, their descendants had become themselves the objects of widespread disdain. The Portuguese, naturally, complained of Dutch "tyrannies" in America, and some of the sharpest broadsides against the WIC can be traced to the circle of Francisco de Sousa Coutinho, the Portuguese envoy at The Hague.[88] The highly defamatory *Klare beschryvinge van Brazil* (Plain description of Brazil) came from the hand of the French adventurer, Pierre Moreau. The Spanish, too, raised the alarm, if less vociferously, against the Republic's increasingly infamous cruelties abroad. The archbishop of Quito reports, with thick indignation, of a hapless friar who had fallen into Dutch hands – "[they] split his head with a cutlass and opened his stomach, removing his entrails whilst he was still alive" – though his unpublished missive, like so many others from Spanish America, remained confined to the councils in Castile.[89]

The mean reputation of the Netherlands made perhaps its deepest in-

roads in England, where, in contrast to Castile, a lively print culture in-
sured a liberal airing of all polemical charges. And quite a few of these
charges took aim, in outstandingly acrimonious and harsh language, at
the Republic's policies and purported offenses overseas. Why the onslaught from England and why the colonial habits of the Dutch? The
English availed themselves of the topos of Dutch "tyrannies abroad" because the Dutch themselves made this rhetoric so prominently available. The strenuous campaign against the bad government, bad trade
policy, and bad treatment of those in Dutch America had been superbly
effective. Word had gotten out that the WIC, and the Republic by extension, had poorly managed their colonies and those placed under
their care – that the Dutch, to use the propagandists' well-worn idiom,
were "tyrants." The effectiveness of this campaign followed, of course,
from the effectiveness of earlier ones waged against Habsburg Spain,
and, to a certain extent, Dutch propagandists fell victim to their own
success. Having assiduously codified the topos of "tyranny in America" – and editions of Las Casas continued to appear well into the middle of the seventeenth century, some "refreshed" even with details from
the Thirty Years' War – the self-same rhetoric, now cunningly reoriented, was employed at their own expense. English polemicists followed a rhetorical trail already well trodden.[90]

The English also availed themselves of an anti-Dutch discourse, since
they had strategic cause to do so: *casus belli*, more precisely, having entered by the early 1650s a period of hostilities with the Republic that
would endure for the next quarter-century. Rhetoric followed politics,
as relations between the leading Protestant nations deteriorated rapidly
following the outbreak of the English civil war. Though both parties to
that conflict had originally found sympathizers within the Republic –
the House of Orange threw its support behind the Stuarts, to whom they
were related by marriage, while orthodox Calvinists generally backed
their Puritan brethren – the execution of Charles I fully horrified the
Dutch, who found it difficult to champion the cause of regicides, republicans though they might be. The States General did try, for as long
as they could, to maintain a position of neutrality, while Cromwell made
fraternal appeals for a united Protestant front. Yet economic friction between the two maritime powers ultimately compelled a more hostile
course of action that led to war. Resentful of Dutch commercial pre-
dominance, of their expanding colonial trade, and of their unneighborly
exploitation of the North Sea fisheries, England passed the first of their
restrictive Navigation Acts in 1651. This plainly anti-Dutch legislation
prohibited all imports into England from vessels neither English nor
from the country of origin, and it suppressed all exports drawn from
"British Seas," which, in this context, meant the fish extracted by North

Holland herring busses off the coasts of England and Scotland. Envoys from The Hague, meanwhile, arrived in London to protest the "tyranny" of English privateers, whose harassment of Dutch shipping had only escalated under the Commonwealth. Finally, though perhaps not quite as crucially, mounting tensions in Asia and North America (particularly in the Connecticut and Delaware River valleys and on Long Island) added pressures to an already volatile situation.[91]

As much as the cautious government of Johan de Witt wished to avoid it, hostile English and Dutch warships clashed in the summer of 1652 and thus initiated a succession of Anglo-Dutch wars. The first of what would eventually be four wars (three over the next quarter-century) lasted from 1652 to 1654 and failed to resolve the crisis. The English dealt severe blows to Dutch shipping in and around the Channel, yet suffered substantial losses themselves in Asia, America, and the Mediterranean. To obtain peace, Cromwell had to abandon some of Parliament's original demands, though he kept in place the most aggressive components of the earlier legislation. The bite of the Navigation Act stayed just as sharp throughout the 1650s; and by 1658 the English had confiscated over three hundred Dutch vessels. Nor did the belligerent mood of Albion abate when the Restoration (1660) instated a no less determined Charles II. Despite the great banquets in The Hague that saw the prince off, the new English monarch favored his most virulently anti-Dutch advisors and was quick to decree a second and more sophisticated Navigation Act in 1660. In that year Charles II also established the Royal Africa Company (under the directorship of his brother James, the duke of York); and three years later, he permitted Sir Robert Holmes to contest the WIC in West Africa. The English sent another fleet to America to attack New Netherland, which was promptly conquered (1664) and renamed New York. These colonial showdowns precipitated a second Anglo-Dutch war, which lasted from 1665 to 1667. Like the first, it began well for England, though it ended with a string of Dutch victories – notably Michiel de Ruyter's spectacular raid on the Medway in June 1667 – that forced the king to come to the negotiating table. The Treaty of Breda (1667) recast the Navigation Acts to the partial satisfaction of Dutch merchants and settled certain colonial scores: the Republic exchanged New Netherland for Suriname and consolidated their position in the East Indies. Yet the ink was barely dry on de Witt's optimistically engineered Triple Alliance (1668) before James and his coterie began conspiring with Louis XIV to invade the Netherlands. The third Anglo-Dutch war (1672–1674) took place as the armies of France marched on the Republic, and it proved the most devastating of the three for the Dutch. The government of de Witt collapsed, paving the way for the newly elevated *stadhouder* (and nephew of Charles II), Willem III. The landward provinces fell to the French, who sacked the town of Utrecht and held a dramatic "Holy Sacrament" in its main church. And the overseas trade suffered irreversible setbacks that, if not ultimately fatal to the Republic's economy, did genuinely mark a change in the course of its expansion. Though New Netherland returned briefly to Dutch hands in 1673, it reverted permanently back to the English according to the terms of the Treaty of Westminster, signed in 1675. In the meantime, the States General decided finally to dissolve the West India Company.[92]

Throughout this period, the English waged a war of words, every bit as vicious as their naval campaign, against the "upstart" Republic. "Protestant brotherhood" notwithstanding, English propagandists, both of the Commonwealth and Royalist sort, denigrated their Dutch enemy ruthlessly and relentlessly. With every wave of British warships came a salvo of broadsides, ballads, sermons, caricatures, and other polemical devices, intended to blacken what Andrew Marvell so contemptuously dismissed as "the character of Holland." "Degenerate race!" railed one hack poet, summing up the Hollandophobic temper of Britain. "Boars," "butter-boxes," "fat, two-legged cheese-worms," "frog . . . croaking people," ran the benign, bestiary version of English taunts. To the more rabid imagination of Owen Felltham, Holland was "the buttock of the world, full of veines and bloud, but no bones in 't." A no less scatological theory posited a "monstrous horse shit" as the Netherlands' lowly pedigree, "out of which dung within nine days space sprung forth men, women, and children; the Off-spring whereof are yet alive to this day, and now commonly known by the name of Dutchmen." The natural "baseness" of the *Low* Countries kept the inhabitants of that "universal quagmire" overly close to hellishness and heresy. "If they [die] in perdition," reasoned Felltham, "they are so low, that they have a shorter cut to Hell than the rest of their neighbors. And for this cause, perhaps all strange Religions throng thither, as naturally inclining toward their center."[93] With far more wit and mercifully less muddle, Marvell made essentially the same point regarding the heterodoxy that thrived in the Republic, cleverly connecting this religious tolerance to the commercial success that had so excited English hostility in the first place:

> Hence Amsterdam, Turk-Christian-Pagan-Jew
> Staple of sects and mint of schism grew,
> That bank of conscience, where not one so strange
> Opinion but finds credit, and exchange.[94]

In a state of war, to be sure, the threat of tolerant, croaking cheese-worms with an unpleasant whiff of manure might not quite have curdled the blood of a stout Englishman. To galvanize the Britons and alert them fully to the infamy of the Dutch, pamphleteers resorted to topoi of "tyranny" and to an arsenal of epithets that might just as well have come from the Republic's own store. Recognizing the very efficacy of their enemy's own polemical tradition, the English lifted language and forms from the book of Dutch propaganda. "O Tigers breed!" vented Felltham of the Dutch perpetrators of "unnoble tyranny." English polemicists painted the enemy as cruel and despotic, imperial and expansive, tyrants well schooled in the ways of Mars and all manners of conquest. "War is their heaven," Felltham averred (echoing here earlier tropes of the Dutch war party), "Peace is their hell." "Do not wonder that the Dutch have acted so Hellishly like Devils as they have," advised an ardent enemy of the Republic, in the heat of the first Dutch war:

Do not wonder at their strategems . . . dissembling . . . their wicked traiterous and unjust wringings of all Trade out of other men's hands: Nay do not wonder at their barbarous and inhumane cruelties, since from Hell they came, and thither without doubt they must return again.[95]

Between their comings and goings from hell, the Dutch plied their heinous trade on earth, and nowhere were their misdeeds in greater evidence than their imperial adventures overseas. Here again the English followed a discursive strategy all too familiar to the Dutch, tarring their antagonists with the brush of tyrannies abroad. Within this context, the Moluccan island of Amboina, where Dutch agents had "massacred" rival English factors in 1623, became a byword for Dutch treachery, a shibboleth among devoted Hollandophobes. The Amboina affair did indeed cause the Dutch great embarrassment in Asia – ten Englishman (and ten often overlooked Japanese) were executed for treason – though never of the sort of "universal" proportions claimed by the English. On their own, the details are unspectacular. The incident took place within the confines of the Dutch Castle Victoria and under the auspices of a single governor unduly wary of conspiracy. In 1624, when the fallout first reached Europe, both the Dutch and English agreed that it had been an "unjust" mistake, carried out by an administrator overzealous in his charge and a company (the VOC) perhaps overjealous of its monopoly.[96] Yet by the time Cromwell's polemicists revived the story in the early 1650s, the memory of those "villainous" crimes bespoke the "most Horrid, Cruel [and] Barbarous" inhumanity of the Republic, and "the unsatiable covetousness of the Hollanders." Scores of anti-Dutch broadsides, ballads, and engravings recounted the gruesome detail of Batavian torture and "tyranny" in the East. Manifold iniquities abroad made the case for sustained hostilities back home. The gothically ornate rendering of the Amboina affair utterly and effectively demonized the

Dutch – as in this fairly typical sonnet, which asserted, with reference to Lucifer's horde, that "The Dutch are found more merciless than they":

> Both fire and water taught by them begin
> To swell the Body, and to scorch the Skin;
> And both seem busie, rather than relent,
> T' out-wit each other, who should most Torment:
> No malice wants, No Part is free; die Cord
> Comes in to Help, and acteth with the Sword;
> Whiles All, to aid the Innocent Blood, Comply
> To cry more loud for Vengeance to the Sky.[97]

All of this climaxed with the Restoration drama of John Dryden, *Amboyna: A Tragedy*, performed to partisan and reportedly packed crowds in London in 1673. Dryden embellished the by now famous story with the more refined vituperation of a poet and – not insignificant – with a highly baroque subplot of sex, violence, and intrigue. To explain the motives of the VOC governor, Dryden imagined the governor's son entangled in a suitor's rivalry with an English captain, each man competing for the love of a beautiful native "heiress." The younger Dutchman blunders, blusters, and then, in frustration and malice, rapes the Asian maiden – and thus, the continent, according to the didactic vision of the dramatist. Unable to accept the blame for, or consequences of, his action, he conspires with his father to torture the captain (to whom the woman was betrothed) and to extract a confession of "treason" and hence an excuse for execution. Dryden makes plain that such duplicity and cruelty represented no mere aberration, but a pattern of perfidy symptomatic of the Dutch character. He presents the drama as a "map" of Dutch morality: "No Map shews Holland truer than our Play," pronounces the Prologue. The playwright suggests that the violence, or "tyranny," displayed in colonial Amboina came naturally to the Dutch, that it ran "hotly" through their veins, and that it could never be cooled. The drama and its language of tyranny evoke, in many places, the identical rhetoric employed by the rebels against Spain. It is a resemblance on which Dryden gladly – *knowingly* – elaborates. "Are you men or Devils!" the English captain cries out as he endures the notorious "Beverage," or water torture, managing to muster strength, nonetheless, to sermonize on Dutch history:

> D'Alva, whom you
> Condemn for cruelty did ne're the like;
> He knew original Villany was in your Blood:
> Your Fathers all are damn'd for their Rebellion;
> When they Rebell'd, they were well us'd to this:

These Tortures ne're were hatch'd in Humane Breasts,
But as your Countrey lies confin'd on Hell,
Just on its Marches, your black Neighbors taught ye,
And just such Pains as you invent on earth,
Hell has reserv'd for you.[98]

Dryden touched here on an irony that well served the English cause and cleverly frustrated that of the Dutch. By describing the Dutch as tyrants, the English also made them into hypocrites and turned decades of Dutch rhetoric on its head. The rebels' topoi of tyranny now worked against them; the current of "innocent blood" now flowed in the opposite direction. In yet another recitation of the "barbarous cruelties" of Amboina, *A memento for Holland*, the anonymous pamphleteer intensified his invective by comparing Dutch tyrannies in the East Indies to Spain's infamies in the West Indies – the very deeds, in other words, formerly catalogued by the Dutch. The sadistic punishment of English prisoners in the Castle Victoria represented "the perfect Embleme of the Spaniard's cruelty to the poor Indians; for they [Spain] used not them [the Indians] with more cruelty, then the Dutch did our poor English Merchants." The aptly named *Second part of the Tragedy of Amboyna* took this polemical logic one step further by forgoing the analogy with Spain and focusing directly on *Dutch* tyrannies in America. The "second act" of the Amboina tragedy – and the dramatic idiom here suited the pamphleteers' purpose just as the polemical cant well served Dryden – presented "a true relation of a most bloody, treacherous, and cruel design of the Dutch in New Netherlands [*sic*] in America." The author purports to discover a dark Dutch plot "for the total ruining and murthering of the English colonies in New England," and narrates a number of "perfidious, bloody, and cruel" deeds attributed to the Dutch and vaguely related to English hostilities with the Pequot Indians in Connecticut. Yet the details mattered less than the larger "design." The tyrannies lately revealed in America, it was boldly asserted, mirrored tyrannies previously displayed in Asia. "Amboyna's treacherous cruelty," pronounced the pamphleteer, "extend[ed] itself from the East to the West Indiaes."[99]

English propaganda, too, passed fluently from Amboina to America. Since the Eastern "massacre" had taken place on the eve of the Western expansion of the Netherlands, pamphleteers had an easy time conflating the two. The foundation of New Netherland, wedged awkwardly between Virginia and New England, thus came at the expense of "innocent" English settlers (it was proposed) and in the wake of "violences" committed in the Far East. "Hearing that year [1624] how their East India Company had thrived with their violence upon the English at Amboyna," wrote one "angry" Englishman, the Dutch turned their

greedy gaze to the Hudson, where they usurped what "an English gentleman," after all, had rightly discovered. In Brazil, the Dutch bullied
the Portuguese (lately allied with the Stuarts) and ruthlessly suppressed
the planters, who finally rose in revolt. Here, again, a comparison was
made with Spain to discredit the Republic.

The Portugalls who suffered under the Spaniards for the space of 60 Years were
not soe much oppressed by them in the East- and West-Indies as they were by
the Hollanders who have more regard to their own profitt and advantages, than
they have to the orriginall rights or civell interests of other men.[100]

This lack of "civell interests" galled the English and nowhere more so
than in America. Up and down the coasts of the New World, the Dutch
subjected the Indians to what the English termed "insolencies" and "oppressions." The well-named publicist, William de Britaine, believed that
Dutch cruelties to the natives far *exceeded* anything done by the Habsburgs, as native opinion itself attested: "The Indians, though they have
no kindness for the Spaniard, . . . look upon him as a Gentleman, but the
Hollanders they abhor for their sordid acts and unjust practices." Dutch
tyrannies abroad convinced de Britaine to doubt the Republic's intentions
closer to home. America reflected, as it had for the Dutch rebels in an altogether different context, the true nature of the enemy. It provided the
English a "theater" in which to observe the expansionist, imperialist, and
"tyrannous" ways of the Republic. "As *America* was the Theatre where
they Acted these Tragedies, and unparallel'd Insolencies," wrote de
Britaine, "so they have not spared to manifest their Ingratitude, Affronts,
and highest Injuries against the Kings of *Great Britain,* and the English Nation here in Europe." As the "mirror" of Spanish cruelties had functioned
decades earlier, so the "theater" of Dutch insolences served in the 1670s.
The original metaphor however, was cleverly domesticated for a stage-
loving "Restoration" audience, to impugn a polemical adversary.[101]

The topos of "Dutch tyranny in America" became in this way fairly
well established in English propaganda. It featured repeatedly and often ironically in the works of Britain's leading Hollandophobes. Owen
Felltham, who provided many of the ur-epithets in his *Brief character*
(which circulated as early as 1648); George Downing, who wrote vitriolic reports to Parliament and the king from his diplomatic post in The
Hague; Henry Stubbes, whose shrill polemics managed to please patrons of both the Cromwellian and Caroline regimes: each made reference to the Republic's purported "insolencies" abroad and each used
the image of America, in conjunction with other carefully contrived
topoi, to subvert traditional themes of Dutch propaganda. Felltham, for
example, slyly decried Dutch savageries committed against the Span-

ish. He recounted the story of a rebel soldier in the 1570s who, "with a barbarous hand," had ripped the yet living heart of an enemy Spaniard and, "with his teeth, rent it still warme with blood into gobbets, which he spitted over the battlements, in defiance." Downing, who included this same anecdote in one of his many anti-Dutch polemics, made much of the "insufferable impudence" of the enemy, their "High Mightinesses," and their "Mushroom States [General]." In America, where Downing spent much of his youth (he was a nephew of Governor John Winthrop and the second graduate of Harvard College), the Dutch had displayed "the bladder of their pride blown up with violence." They denied the English their "liberties" in Suriname, complained Downing in 1672, just as they had earlier presumed hegemony in "so called" New Netherland. They were tyrants of trade, who "stretched their power to the East and West Indies." Downing implored Charles II "to appease our incensed God for the innocent blood of ours, which was plentifully spilt by them, as well in other parts, as both the Indies." Excessive pride, innocent blood, divine wrath: Downing's rhetoric can only have rung familiar to Dutch ears. Usselincx, a half-century prior, could hardly have put it better.[102]

Downing's identification of a vast empire of Dutch trade and his innuendo regarding presumptions of far-flung hegemony suggest the elements of yet another rhetorical standby of the Dutch, namely the heresy of universal monarchism. Just as the rebels had related Spain's American expansion to a grander, global plan, so the English now refashioned the argument to assail the Republic's presumably imperial ambitions. Dutch pretensions in Amboina and New Netherland indicated to Downing tyrannies stretching from the Far East to the expanded West. To John Darell, the Netherlands "hope[d] to command from North to South," and the WIC itself "endeavored" – this in 1665 – "to carry on and propagate the said old war and design into Europe and America (the other half of the whole Universe)." Never one to do things in halves, Stubbes accused the Republic of aspiring to a full "universal monarchy." "The ambition and treachery of the Hollanders," argued Stubbes in one of his *Justifications* of the third Anglo-Dutch war, proved "that they did design to monopolize the Trade of the Universe unto themselves." Very much like the overweening political ambitions of the Habsburgs, the perfidious economic designs of the Dutch crossed national borders and imperial seas – a point Stubbes practically shouted onto the printed page:

The Dutch had of a long time formed a Design to ensure themselves of the Universal Empire of the Seas, and to give Laws thereon to all Princes and States in point of Traffick, HOW AND WHETHER THEY SHOULD TRADE.... Their action in the East and West Indies, Russia, and the Baltick Sea, were evident Arguments of such Intentions.

Stubbes and company effectively inverted the Republic's polemical self-identity. As the English saw it, the Dutch had committed cruelties against Spain, perpetrated tyrannies in America, and pursued an empire across the universe. In a crowning blow of irony, Stubbes even inveighed against the Republic's "specious" protests of innocence – protests that the "innocent blood" of Amboina so dramatically subverted. In these and other dexterous rhetorical maneuvers, Stubbes joined his colleagues in appropriating Dutch strategies, then turning them against their original authors. The English Hollandophobes had pulled the rhetorical rug out from under their opponents.[103]

For the most part, the Dutch response to the English was relatively flaccid and defensive. During the first war, Republican pamphleteers sought to discredit the Commonwealth men as regicides, "murderers and tyrants" in the eyes of God. They also assailed Cromwell for his "faithless" dealings with the Royalists and his truculent war against the Irish. English atrocities in Drogheda (1649) became infamous enough for one Dutch author to warn that Cromwell planned to treat the conquered Netherlands as he had the piteous Irish. Yet this theme never quite caught on.[104] By the second Anglo-Dutch war, polemical focus shifted from Ireland to Africa, where Holmes and his men had assaulted Dutch positions in 1664. In a much publicized (and thrice published) report of the attacks, the WIC's director-general of Guinea described in grisly detail the mutilations ("noses and ears lopped off") and executions ("throats slit slowly, as with swine") of Dutch sailors by English and English-sponsored African troops. The atrocities in Guinea served as the Dutch rebuttal to Amboina; details were luridly embellished and tirelessly reprinted. As for Amboina itself, some publicists tried feebly to recast the incident so as to inculpate the English agents, justly executed for their failed conspiracy. Few found this scenario plausible, though, and, like the Irish analogy, it was largely ignored in the literature. By the third Anglo-Dutch war, in any event, the threat of invading French armies loomed larger than that of the English navy. After 1672, Dutch fury turned primarily on the Sun King, who, in this regard as in everything else, attracted most of his contemporaries' attention.[105]

Cases of "English tyranny in America" did occasionally circulate, yet these lacked the polemical punch of the earlier, anti-Habsburg propaganda. The directors of the WIC filed two remonstrances with the States

General in 1663 and 1664 to complain of "several instances of tyranny and violence committed by the English in New Netherland." These consisted of encroachments on Dutch villages on Long Island, border disputes in Connecticut, and other mild incidents of "cruelty." Stuyvesant, in his official report of his colony's surrender, wrote indignantly of the plunder carried out by "dissolute English soldiery" and of the subsequent suffering of Dutch settlers in New Amstel (Delaware) "who, notwithstanding they had offered no resistance, but requested good terms, could not obtain them, but were invaded, stripped, utterly plundered and many of them sold as slaves to Virginia." This terrifying, if somewhat colorful, spectacle of naked Dutch slaves sold to grim English plantation owners captivated at least the popular imagination. The tremendously successful satire, *Hollands venezoen in Engelandt gebakken* (Holland's venison fried in England), cautioned against England's intentions to do just that upon Charles II's conquest of the innocent, cervine Hollanders:

> [Holland] shall soon be to England delivered,
> Then will the king with violence command us;
> And transport our poor, as slaves from this land,
> To plant the Tobacco of the Englishman.

More commonly, though, pamphleteers complained of aggressive English corsairs, who wreaked havoc on Dutch shipping in American waters and plundered neutral Spanish and native American settlers.[106]

The reemergence in this literature of the Spaniard gives pause. With both sides of the Anglo-Dutch conflict busy traducing each other's reputation, the image of Spain, interestingly enough, underwent a subtle transformation. Relative to the dismal abuses of which the Protestant powers now stood accused, the long-reviled Habsburg record in America began to look better – at least from the Dutch perspective of the final half of the seventeenth century. Such agile polemical maneuvers could occur, of course, only after the Peace of Münster (1648) and the diplomatic shifts that ensued. Spain's rehabilitation was never universal, either; the province of Zeeland vehemently opposed the Peace, even long after the fact. Yet after eighty years of war, the rapid shift in language and political posture is impressive all the same. Already in 1648, supporters of the settlement with Spain questioned the incessant attacks against the Habsburgs and suggested that the Republic might reconsider its alliances. "He speaks of Spanish tyranny, as if there had never been a tyrant besides from this nation," wrote a pamphleteer to an unreformed hawk: "What is a tyrant?" With an eye toward Cardinal Mazarin's recent interventions in Dutch politics, the author proposed the model of France, for "the French government consists of so many rogues and barbarians."[107] Developments in Brazil likewise prompted thoughts of strategic realignment. Since the Portuguese rebels there had declared their independence from both the Spanish king and the Dutch regents, it was only logical for the Republic to consider its mutual interests with Castile. As New Holland's situation rapidly deteriorated, certain critics of the WIC even offered grudging praise for the "satisfactory example" of Spain's Council of the Indies and its successes in administering the Crown's American affairs. Whatever its mistakes and abuses, contended one disillusioned colonialist, Spain had managed to turn a profit.[108]

Spain had also managed to undergo, by the twilight of the Golden Age, a reversal of polemical fortunes. As Dutch antagonisms with England, and then France, intensified, the faint praise of Spain grew into a veritable chorus of adulation. Three Anglo-Dutch conflicts and an illusory alliance with France impressed upon the Republic its need for good friends. Habsburg Spain, as the natural rival of Bourbon France and the traditional foe of Stuart England, became the obvious choice. And geography, used so effectively by the rebels exactly one century prior, became once again a weapon of Dutch propaganda. Discussions of America now recast England and France as the tyrants and rehabilitated Spain as a model of colonial propriety. Witness the influential "news" series, *Maandags relaes* (Monday's report), which appeared regularly through the early 1670s. A running commentary on political events of the day, the "Reports" routinely condemned England for its "plundering and destruction" in the Caribbean; meanwhile, they generously commended Spain for its orderly and civil colonization. The "Eighth Report" (1674) complains of English privateers that menace the Spanish Main, "on the look out for nothing but booty and amusement." The "Ninth Report" (1674) implicates the king of England for his "evil intentions" in America and contrasts the Stuarts' colonial policy with that of their Habsburg predecessors. The English are seen as greedy and aggressive, the Spanish as responsible and lawful. The "Report" concludes by rallying "His Catholic Majesty" of Spain to declare war against his English counterpart, in order to recover his "legitimate" colonies in America. In these waning years of Castilian preeminence, it should be granted, such diatribes reveal more wishful thinking than realistic diplomacy. (His Catholic Majesty of Spain, in 1674, took the enfeebled form of Charles II; the United Provinces by this time were desperate.) Nevertheless, it is striking to hear, in a still later work, of a Dutch West Indies veteran who praises the ancient valor of Spain in America, lately supplanted by "effeminate timidity." And it is ironic to read, in a history of the Spanish empire, of widespread admiration for the courage and wisdom of the original Castilian conquerors of America.[109]

VIII

The original Castilian conquerors of America – those darkly cruel, fiercely rapacious inhabitants of earlier Dutch narratives – had journeyed an unimaginably long distance to reach respectability. Yet by the late seventeenth century, they had arrived: the Spaniard no longer featured as the primary target of Dutch propaganda and, sensibly enough, no longer loomed as the tyrant of America. The older models of New World violence and "tyranny" had not altogether disappeared, however. They underwent instead a process of inversion and substitution, which demonstrates both the flexibility of the Republic's geographic imagination and the suppleness and endurance of its American topoi. For, a full century after their appearance in the rebels' original attacks on Spain, conquistadors of a different stripe reemerged in Dutch discourse, once again the object of moral reprobation and once again associated with the ineradicable innocence and tyranny of America. This time around, though, they derived from the ranks of the Republic's latest nemeses, England and France, and took the form of the New World's latest scourge: the Atlantic pirate or privateer (little distinction existed at this time), lately known by the stylish neologism, "buccaneer."

The buccaneers of America disembarked in the Netherlands. Or rather, with the debut of pirate literature in the final decades of the seventeenth century, a refashioned manner of conquistador returned to European letters, and the Dutch played a central role in his recasting. Costume and accent may have changed, but deeds and morals remained uncannily familiar. Exploits of cunning and courage, tragedies of cruelty and conquest, the main components of pirate literature grew out of the popular Dutch naval narrative, itself a successful combination of travel adventure and pietistic homily. The pirates' tales told of epic endurance and "heroic" undertakings, as one editor charitably put it, yet also of the "inhuman cruelties" and ever-engaging "tyrannies" of the West Indies buccaneers (so named for the *boucan* – Tupi *mukém* – or barbecue, on which the pirates roasted their enormous, post-plunder feasts). The genre emerged first in Holland around mid-century – Willem Bontekoe's high-sea adventure might count as a forerunner, yet the first example, properly speaking, is the saga of the "most famous *zeerover* [sea rover or pirate]," Claes Compaen – and it became all the rage by the end of the century. The signal publication and astonishingly popular progenitor of the genre was Alexander Exquemelin's *De Ameri-*

caensche zee-roovers, widely known as "The Buccaneers of America" and first printed in Amsterdam in 1678. "Perhaps no book in any language was ever the parent of so many imitations and the source of so many fictions," wrote the esteemed, nineteenth-century bibliographer, Joseph Sabin, who was certainly in the position to judge. The Dutch original spawned translations into French, English, German, and Spanish within the next decade, over a dozen editions by the end of the century, and scores more after that. It paved the way for Daniel Defoe's enormously successful *History of the pyrates* (1724), as well as the corsair and captivity narratives of the eighteenth century. The original Dutch preface allows that areas of America remained "almost a new world," and promises that Exquemelin's account would guide the reader along the pirates' path of conquest and discovery. Indeed, no work had led so many readers through the terrain of America since the history of the "first" *Conquista* by Bartolomé de Las Casas, published precisely one century earlier, also in the Netherlands.[110]

Las Casas's *Brevíssima relación* provides a useful starting point from which to consider Exquemelin's narrative, as the resemblance between the two works goes well beyond their extraordinary sales figures. Exquemelin – or more probably his Amsterdam publisher, Jan ten Hoorn, who played a vital part in the preparation, presentation, and even composition of the volume[111] – rendered an unapologetically grim picture of early piracy, which he observed with none of the romance of nineteenth-century fiction. The *Americaensche zee-roovers* describes the exceptionally vicious raids carried out by English and French buccaneers against poorly defended settlements in the Caribbean and Spanish Main. Small bands of rogues inflict devastating losses in pursuit of fabulous booty. Like Las Casas, Exquemelin depicted the relentless hunt for gold by greedy renegades; like Las Casas, he provided extravagant detail of rapine and bloodshed; and like Las Casas, he denounced the protagonists' ferocity and commiserates with the victims' distress. In the crucial century that separated the pirates from the conquistadors, however, the configuration of protagonists and victims had radically changed. Very much unlike Las Casas, Exquemelin cast the Spanish-American (creole) settlers as wretched "martyrs" and the English and French buccaneers as brutish invaders. The *Americaensche zee-roovers* inverts the formula of the *Brevíssima relación* by representing the Spaniards as victims, rather than perpetrators, of American tyrannies.[112]

Both the similarities and distinctions between the two works are compelling. They reflect corresponding strategies and devices of representation – common language, imagery, rhetoric – yet they indicate also revised goals and polemical orientation. Compare, in this regard, the original Dutch frontispiece of Exquemelin's work and the much-copied title page of the Lascasian *Spiegel der Spaensche tyranny* (1620 edition) (figs. 43 and 44). The two engraved prints share virtually the same format to convey remarkably similar themes: what both titles identify, identically, as "the inhuman savageries" committed in America. In each composition, a series of vignettes and a pair of full-length portraits circumscribe a cartouche that holds the volumes' respective titles. In the niches that flank the *Spiegel's* cartouche, Alba (right) and Don John of Austria (left) stand amidst the evidence of their combined tyrannies, the first surrounded by scenes of the Revolt, the second by images of the *Conquista*. In the *Zee-roovers* print, the portraits represent an English and French buccaneer – so the title itself implies – who are encompassed by scenes of tyrannies against Spaniards and Indians. Each of the pirates tramples a victim. The dexter figure threatens a feather-clad Indian, who supplicates with a fist full of pearls; while the sinister figure taunts a Spaniard, who begs for his life. The actual vignettes of "tyranny" in the two compositions also bear comparison. The left-hand images of the 1678 print show the pirates hacking and spearing defenseless natives in much the same manner that the conquistadors, in the 1620 print, massacre the Indians. On the right-hand side, pirates roast and torment (presumably) Spaniards, just as Alba's men, as depicted on the *Spiegel's* title-page, torture innocent Netherlanders. Once again, roles are reversed. Though the Indians suffer both times around, by 1678 the English and French have replaced the Spaniards as the tyrants of America, and the Spanish-Americans have supplanted the Dutch as the hapless victims.[113]

The text itself follows in much the same vein. The *Americaensche zee-roovers* tells a story of pirates as reincarnated conquistadors, of spectacular greed and bone-chilling violence in the New World. The buccaneers, as Exquemelin portrays them, possess superhuman fortitude and enterprise, yet also the capacity for "inhuman" appetite and brutality. As do the conquistadors, they storm the American coast "by fire and sword," granting no mercy to the natives or native-born Spaniards who cross their paths. The pirates come from harsh backgrounds (again, like the conquistadors), and the author is at pains to connect their miserable origins with their despotic careers. Exquemelin himself began as an *engagé*, or indentured servant, of the French *Compagnie des Isles de L'Amérique*, which, as he puts it, "traded in human flesh."[114] Redeemed, or more often escaped, servants become pirates, though often in the employ of disenchanted planters – their former masters, thus. Exquemelin conveys well the ethos of violence that prevailed and hardened the pirates. One particularly harrowing passage early in the narrative describes the corporal punishment doled out on Tortuga, the pirate strong-

Figure 43. Title page from *Den Spiegel der Spaensche tyranny geschiet in West-Indien* (Amsterdam, 1620). Universiteitsbibiliotheek Amsterdam.

Figure 44. Title page from Alexander Olivier Exquemelin, *De Americaensche zee-roovers* (Amsterdam, 1678). Universiteitsbibiliotheek Amsterdam.

hold off the coast of Hispaniola. The account is exceedingly gruesome, though hardly uniquely so, bearing as it does so strong a resemblance to Girolamo Benzoni's description, written a full century before, of Spanish discipline on Hispaniola. Upon recapturing an unfortunate runaway, the reader of 1678 learns,

his master tied him to a tree and lashed him until blood trickled down his back. Next, he had him smeared with a mixture of lemon juice, Spanish pepper, and salt, and left him tied up like that for twenty-four hours. Thereupon he beat him anew until he died. The last words he [the servant] spoke were, "May God grant that the Devil torment you before your death just as you have tormented me."[115]

The remainder of Exquemelin's narrative catalogues in a similar tone – and, for that matter, in much the same tenor as the histories of Benzoni, Las Casas, and Martyr – the grisly tyrannies that now plagued late seventeenth-century America. It traces the histories of the different "nests" of buccaneers and the lives of their most notorious leaders, François L'Olonnais (the *nom de guerre* of Jean-David Nau) and Henry Morgan. The more ferocious of the two, L'Olonnais made a reputation for himself by inventing endlessly macabre variations of torment. He was known to lick his victims' blood before their terrified eyes so as to hasten confessions of hidden treasure. "Possessed of a devil's fury," he once wrenched the heart from a captive's chest, gnashed it with his teeth, and threw it at a disbelieving Spaniard as a warning. He met his own death in a fittingly Herodotean fashion when he fell into the hands of a hostile Indian tribe that ritually hacked, roasted, then feasted on his "infernal" body. Less sadistically, if no less ruthlessly, Sir Henry Morgan followed in L'Olonnais's wake, carrying out "pitiless tyrannies" against settlements along the coasts of Venezuela and the Isthmus of Panama. Morgan tyrannized more efficiently and purposefully than his predecessor and apparently with greater success – hence his elevation to knighthood by Charles II. In one instance, he used local monks and women as a human shield with which to storm a Spanish castle. "Many innocent people were made into martyrs," Exquemelin remarks dryly. In raids near Maracaibo, he tortured a village idiot, left behind in a deserted town, and a sixty-year-old tavern keeper – "bound by his thumbs and toes to four stakes . . . so that his body began to convulse and his nerves even started to stretch."[116]

Morgan's numerous misdeeds, perverse though they were, would have rung familiar to Dutch readers of the genre. They took place in an American landscape readily recognizable from the same "inhuman cruelties," the same "ingenious torments," and the same "unprecedented tyrannies" that Las Casas, decades earlier, could likewise only inadequately describe. It was a New World similarly strewn with bodies parts, left behind by well-known "devils," who persecuted their victims, in 1678 no less than 1578, just for sport. In the later narrative as in the earlier, marauding thugs alighted from their vessels to burn, flay, rape, slash, gouge, garrote, and most basically hunt down the natives like (and, according to both accounts, with) dogs. The buccaneers' America remained a locus of atrocities: noses and ears sliced off, hands and feet burned slowly, virgins violated in churches, elders suspended by their genitals – atrocities, in other words, that might have come directly from the traditional "mirrors" of Spanish cruelties popular in the Netherlands.

If modeled on the ancient Spanish conquerors, though, the perpetrators of these latest New World tyrannies came from Europe's newest seats of power, England and France. Exquemelin (or more likely ten Hoorn) announces this fact directly on the title-page, and this would appear to be by design. For, though the *Americaensche zee-roovers* is no plodding piece of propaganda – the narrative reads far too briskly for that to be the case – it does paint a rather black picture of the English and French abroad. This history of "the inhuman savageries of the English and French pirates" appeared, not accidentally, in the very year (1678) that the Republic finally repulsed the combined onslaught of Louis XIV and Charles II. The pirates in America engaged in the very activities that the enemy soldiers had pursued in the Netherlands: conquest and plunder. The author includes, to be sure, a colorful sketch of the Groningen-born pirate, "Rock the Brazilian," a refugee of New Holland and a renegade who took his pleasure lopping the limbs off his prey. Yet he focuses predominantly on the English and French buccaneers: François, the French corsair, and Sir Henry, England's knight-errant. These are the latest tyrants of America.[117]

The victims of the pirates are the "Americans," a designation that by now included both Indians and American-born Spaniards. Since the Indians, in fact, generally stayed inland, the wrath of the buccaneers fell most heavily on the Spanish, who occupied the coasts and filled the sea-lanes. This need not have been the case. Other vessels – of the Dutch, the Portuguese, or even the English and French – plied the Caribbean and might have enticed indiscriminately greedy buccaneers.[118] Yet the pirates of the *Americaensche zee-roovers* take special delight in tormenting the subjects of Spain. L'Olonnais, it was claimed, "dedicated himself to pillaging the Spaniards . . . against whom he committed unspeakable cruelties." Morgan, meanwhile, proclaimed his acute disdain of the "Spanish nation . . . as if they were open and declared enemies (as he termed it) of the King of England." Even "Rock" showed his predilection for Castilian blood, saving his "greatest" and most sadistic tortures for any wretched Spaniard that fell into his hands.[119] The irony of all this did not elude the author. Exquemelin notes on a number of occasions the cruelties committed by Spain in the previous century, and he implies, at least once, that Spain was now receiving its just deserts. Yet he also expresses pity for the Spaniards. He describes with great pathos the sack of Panama by Morgan's men and includes sincere and moving vignettes of Spanish anguish. The pains of a "poor helpless man," brutally mutilated by the pirates, and the tribulations of a "young and very beautiful woman," who must suffer Morgan's crude advances, seem designed to elicit sympathy for the now humbled Spaniards. Perhaps most poignant is the description of the plunder's aftermath, when the tired and hungry survivors are made to march as hostages with their conquerors. "It was pitiful to behold so many innocent women, who could not nourish the young babes at their breast." Once again, thus, innocent women and children in America must agonize – though now they are Spaniards. Innocence has been finally and ironically inverted. By the late seventeenth century, the Dutch New World had been turned upside-down.[120]

The Dutch and their New Worlds

Once again, a West Indies landscape. A lush profusion of tropical growth spills onto a sloping (in this case) Brazilian panorama through which a broad river winds gently toward the horizon (fig. 45). In certain ways, the seventeenth-century painting of Frans Post recalls the sixteenth-century one of Jan Mostaert (see fig. 1): conspicuous descriptions of flora and fauna fill both foregrounds, ample American skies yawn across both backgrounds, and relatively slender scenes of "native" activity lie in between. Yet differences also abound. In place of the wizened stumps and odd monkey of Mostaert's composition, a teeming tropical world of high palms and bright pineapples draws the viewer into Post's verdant landscape. The New World, by the second half of the seventeenth century, has become enticingly exotic. Colorful birds perch upon spindly cactuses, while giant anteaters and banded armadillos scavenge among the thick Brazilian foliage – this in contrast to the plain brown cows and mild sheep that occupy the pastoral meadows of Mostaert's West Indies. Behind the idyll of the sixteenth-century setting, to be sure, unfolds a dramatic scene of encounter between armed Europeans and frail natives of America. Beyond the botanical brilliance of Post's America, meanwhile, a far more tranquil meeting takes place – Africans gather convivially, work-baskets and babies in tow – as a lone Portuguese horseman, relegated to the periphery, disappears into the ocher *várzea*. The two paintings reverse, in fact, the placement of narrative and pictorial drama. Where the earlier panel emphasizes the invasion taking place at the center of the composition, the later one highlights the unusual *naturalia* of the expansive *repoussoir*. Post's painting, surely the more exotic of the two, is also the more calming and quiet. It offers, in all events, another rendering of the New World from another artist of the Netherlands (as it happens, also from the town of Haarlem), though a century later, the message has changed.[1]

Over the course of the sixteenth and seventeenth centuries, though

Figure 45. Frans Post, *Serinhaém* (112 × 145 cm). Paris, Musée du Louvre. Réunion des Musées Nationaux / Art Resource, NY.

the medium in many cases stayed the same, the Dutch image of America underwent a remarkable transformation. The themes of "innocence" and "tyranny" remained integral to the Dutch perception of the New World throughout this period. Yet for reasons varyingly political, economic, and cultural, the function and relative prominence of these motifs shifted markedly over time. America first appeared on Dutch horizons in the later sixteenth century, when opponents of Habsburg rule popularized the image of a rapacious *Conquista* as a means to blacken the reputation of Spain. With polemical intensity to match their geographical ingenuity, the rebels allied the Indians' suffering with their own and projected a brotherhood between the two mutually oppressed "nations." At the turn of the seventeenth century, Usselincx gave the rebels' political topoi an economic and evangelical twist by declaring the moral incumbency of the new Republic to liberate its American allies with the best weapons at its disposal: free trade and reformed religion. The Dutch West India Company, founded in 1621, exploited the rhetoric of "innocence" in its earliest years, and the Republic even pursued a number of initiatives predicated on the anticipated allegiance of Indian "brethren." Yet the Company itself lapsed quickly into a more hard-nosed pattern of conquest and commerce that its opponents assailed as "tyrannical." The WIC guarded its monopoly zealously and suppressed its "savages" ruthlessly. For their high-handed rule, the Dutch gained a reputation for iniquity, an image that only worsened during the Anglo-Dutch wars, when England led the way in vilifying the Republic's "tyranny" overseas. As political winds shifted, however, so, too, did rhetorical currents; and by the final decades of the century, it was the English and French buccaneers who were branded for their violence, and the Indians and by now pitiable Spaniards who were consoled for their anguish in America.

Such shifts and reconfigurations notwithstanding, the Dutch construction of America demonstrated an uncommon degree of resilience, and even sturdiness over time. The twin topoi of "innocence" and "tyranny" persisted for a full century following the Revolt, rhetorical pillars on which the image of America could be time and again erected. The tropes of the Republic's American geography, like the Solomonic columns so common to baroque painting, showed an ability to withstand an impressive amount of twisting and inversion; however much they may have swayed under the weight of improbable plots and far-flung rhetoric, they managed to sustain nonetheless those polemical positions balanced upon them. The defense of revolt, the urgency of expansion, the perils of consumption, the ills of colonialism, the sanctity of history: all inspired reference to the case of America. A century of Dutch observers, over the duration of the Dutch Golden Age, found compelling reason to invoke the "innocence" and "tyranny" of a New World whose novelty, it would seem, only slowly wore off.

The causes of this American discourse – of its original popularity and enduring relevance, of its patriotic tenor and moralizing timbre – are at once broadly transparent and idiosyncratically local. The cultural geography of the Republic grew out of the political, social, and economic circumstances of its authors. The rebels identified America as a locus of Spanish tyrannies because they were, at that moment, looking for them. Similarly, Usselincx and his circle discerned "innocence" abroad in a manner that suited their colonial purposes; and opponents of the WIC, in much the same vein, saw nothing but "tyrannies" when they cast a critical eye toward the Dutch New World. That world, quite naturally, reflected the world of its makers – which might be said *inter alia* of many other geographies fashioned in early modern Europe. What might further be said of the Republic's idea of America is that it came into being under peculiar historical circumstances and according to particularly Dutch sensibilities. America entered the Netherlands at a most vital moment in Dutch history. It was implicated at once in a highly charged political discourse and functioned to convey both what America seemed to be and what the Dutch hoped to overcome. America's struggle was the Republic's struggle was a patriotic narrative of innocence and tyranny. And though the contexts of American thematics shifted over time, they remained always rooted in a moralizing vocabulary that had powerful resonance within the Republic. From Orange's solicitations for the "poor Indians," to the WIC's consternation over "unrighteous beginnings," to Udemans's fulminations against "ungodly commerce," cadences of this moralizing geography run throughout Dutch Americana. Cadences can be heard, moreover, from all corners of the Republic. A Calvinist controversialist detected in America's rich cargo the ruinous seeds of heterodoxy; while a Catholic poet – Vondel – perceived in America the "tyrannical" habits of those magistrates who abused the Arminians "like Indian slaves / Pecked not by Spanish crows, but Gomarus's cruel ravens." Both men looked toward a New World painted in the broadest of strokes – good and evil, sin and salvation, innocence and tyranny – and both related these patterns to the landscape of the Netherlands.[2]

By the late seventeenth century, the landscape of the Dutch Golden Age would alter yet again, this time perhaps irrevocably, following the calamitous assault on the Republic by England and France. Once more, too, would the image of the Indies adjust, featured lately in the context of pirate literature, a genre steeped in tales of Anglo-French cruelties visited upon "innocent Americans" – though in this case Americans of both the native and Spanish-colonial sort. This final representation brought full circle a topos that had been associated with the New World from the earliest years of the Revolt through the twilight of the Golden Age. In doing so, it demonstrates the full range of that extraordinarily plastic idea of "America," which could be fashioned according to the rhetorical demands of the day. America, throughout this period, never lost its suppleness for the cultural geographers of the Netherlands, who shaped and reshaped perpetually new worlds for an ever-engaged audience. The Dutch, for their part, never lost their resourcefulness in turning geography to the service of a perpetually changing domestic agenda. Taken as a whole, the Dutch discovery, dissemination, and later reinvention of "America" well illustrate the cultural dynamics of early modern geography. They reveal geographic imagination as a cultural construct that relies heavily on the substance of politics, economics, and society. The ubiquitous topos of America served patriotic polemics, expansionist ambitions, and moralizing letters. The centrality of America within Dutch discourse adds a new dimension to the study of the Revolt and Eighty Years' War, and enriches our understanding of Dutch culture in the Golden Age. It suggests also a fresh approach to the history of early modern geography, which might be studied not simply to gauge the advances in mathematical or scientific representation, but also to locate the cultural buoys and signposts strewn across the channels and highways that lead from the land of description to the land described.

Though geography did not, by any means, disappear from the Netherlands, the closing decades of the seventeenth century do indicate a new chapter in the history of Dutch representations of America. In more than one respect, the 1670s constitute a turning point in the Republic's history. The *Rampjaar* (Year of Calamities) of 1672 witnessed the coordinated assault on the Netherlands by England and France, the collapse of financial markets, and the massacre (literally and figuratively) of the government of de Witt. Two years and substantial losses later, the colony of New Netherland fell permanently to the English, and the original Dutch West India Company closed its books indefinitely. For much of the decade, in fact, the Dutch state and the Dutch economy suffered irreparable setbacks, as Louis XIV's troops overran the countryside and an Anglo-French armada stifled overseas commerce. Not until 1678 did the Republic finally extricate itself from its costly wars and turn to the substantial task of rebuilding its much damaged and diminished trade. Colonial losses were more permanent, however, and the 1670s mark the end of the "heroic age" of the Dutch-American enterprise.[3]

In these and the coming years, Dutch writings on America did not, of course, come to an abrupt halt. Quite the contrary: in certain ways, Dutch Americana flourished in the final decades of the century as never before – though with a notable twist. For, in the changed political climate of late seventeenth-century Europe, the Dutch perceived themselves and the New World in a wholly different manner. No longer did pamphleteers write about innocence or tyranny in the New World, and no longer did America excite the polemical passion it once had. No longer, indeed, does the topos of American "innocence" feature prominently in the Republic's propaganda. The old tropes, so overly stretched and worn, had finally been exhausted. Yet, as the Dutch quit their traditional rhetoric on America, they began to produce in these years Americana of another sort: exceptionally well-regarded atlases, natural histories, promotional literature, and other descriptions of the New World that soon became the standards throughout Europe. And herein lies a paradox. At the very moment of their retreat from colonies in, and debates over, America, the Dutch, curiously enough, assumed a leading role as European purveyors of Americana – of books, prints, maps, globes, paintings, and artifacts from America. In their commercialization of Americana, furthermore, they adopted a strategy of exoticism in order to market an America that, rather than peculiarly Dutch, was more widely acceptable to the whole of Europe.[4]

The Dutch marketed America in a variety of packages of often voluminous proportions. The promotional literature on New Netherland, which came out relatively late – in the 1650s and 1660s – attempted to sell the Dutch New World with rhapsodic descriptions of the Hudson Valley and enthusiastic invitations to immigrants from across Europe. The most extravagant of these works sketched a utopian vision of American life, enticing readers with promises of free land and loans to all who would join. The much touted Dutch "scientific" literature – written under the patronage of Johan Maurits, though published well after the Brazilian colony's demise – also tried to sell a product, or in this case the natural products of American soil, water, and sky. Like the large and lavishly illustrated Brazilian history of Barlaeus, these folio volumes furnished readers across Europe with an attractive, sometimes even scholarly, guide to the newest natural world. Unlike Barlaeus's work, though, they highlighted the marvelous *naturalia* of the Indies rather than the military triumphs of the Dutch; they assiduously generalized, rather than localized, their American observations. Also from the tenure of Johan Maurits came the monumental wall maps of Brazil, coveted throughout Europe. These, along with the sumptuous atlases and globes from the ateliers of Blaeu, Janssonius, de Wit, van Keulen, and the other esteemed cartographers of the Netherlands, gave European rulers and merchants handsome visual records of the voyages to, and settlement of, exotic lands. From the hands of Dutch painters came the first landscapes of America and portraits of American peoples and products. Increasingly popular in the 1670s and 1680s – in 1679, for example, Louis XIV acquired a spectacular trove of Americana that included twenty-seven canvases by Frans Post – these images provided models of American subjects for other European painters, engravers, and tapestry weavers. The actual artifacts in these compositions could be purchased from Dutch cabinets of shells, fossils, minerals, and other curiosities; and the *naturalia* could be inspected in the famous botanical and zoological gardens of Leiden and Amsterdam. Finally, the Dutch composed some of the grandest literary *kunstkamers* in all of Europe: the immense, and immensely popular, geographical works of (for example) Arnoldus Montanus, Lambert van den Bosch, and the indefatigable Simon de Vries. These veritable catalogues of wonders listed the seemingly limitless cultures, customs, and curiosities of distant lands, easily mixing exotic Americana with odd bits of Asiana and Africana.[5]

The marvelous eclecticism of these works, their stunning breadth and formidable vastness, suggest a whole new order of cultural geography in the Netherlands. The New World had lately assumed an altered form and refashioned purpose. Dutch Americana, most strikingly, were now gargantuan projects, sprawling compendia of colorful "curiosities." They teemed, like the exuberantly cluttered foregrounds of Post's landscapes, with lush descriptions and verdant details of the late seventeenth-century world. Rather than restricting their attention to Dutch deeds and settlements abroad, they explored, with encyclopedic interest, "all" of the savage creatures, unusual inhabitants, and unknown landscapes of the Indies. Rather than following the familiar tropes of earlier Dutch narratives, they celebrated precisely the unfamiliar and indeterminate "strangeness" of the Indies. Montanus's massive volume, *America*, acknowledges as much on its title-page when it announces its subject as "The New and Unknown World" (this in 1671!). The engraved frontispiece blithely blends long-necked llamas with sharp-toothed beavers, thick-muscled Indians and a multinational assemblage of Europeans who gather to receive the gems and coins and tobacco of the land (fig. 46). In other Dutch projects, America is subsumed in a still wider whirlwind of wonders – as in Petrus de Lange's kinetic *Wonderen des Werelds* (Wonders of the World), a geography that incorporates the Indies into the growing globe of God's glories.[6]

Relative to earlier models, the new Dutch Americana are oddly decontextualized and decentered works. They offer sundry geographic bric-a-brac – *admirabilia mundi*, as de Lange puts it – intended for a vast and resolutely cluttered cabinet of curiosities. Most expressly do not develop the sort of polemical themes of the earlier literature – Spanish, French, and English cruelties in America; Dutch alliances with the natives of America; morally elusive "innocence" abroad – highlighting instead the collectively admired, if indistinctly located, rarities of the New World. De Lange states his strategy as one of purposeful discursiveness. He confesses to offering no more than quick "morsels" of exotica, since variety was (surely) the spice of the armchair traveler's life. Spain's colonial record is briefly considered and mildly commended, even, for the manner in which God had been miraculously delivered to the tropics. For Simon de Vries, Spain's greatest sin in America may have been its lack of curiosity in America – an appalling lapse for this author of tens of thousands of pages of "curious observations" of the Indies. Rarity is *de rigueur* in de Vries's *Great Cabinet of Curiosities* (1682); the reader is invited to rummage the strangeness, the "otherness," and the oddities of

Figure 46. Frontispiece from Arnoldus Montanus, *De nieuwe en onbekende weereld* (Amsterdam, 1671). Courtesy of the John Carter Brown Library, Brown University.

Figure 47. Frontispiece from Simon de Vries, *Curieuse aenmerckingen der byson-derste Oost en West Indische verwonderens-waerdige dingen* (Utrecht, 1682). Universiteitsbibibiliotheek Amsterdam.

new worlds. This amounts to a two-thousand-page tour de force of description, which skims nimbly over events and habits, objects and creatures, scattered across the Americas. Wampum in New Netherland, wantonness in Brazil, conquest in New Spain, diabolism in Virginia, dragons in New France, pearls in the Caribbean: the New World is converted into a fabulous "warehouse of wonders" (the title of another de Vries vehicle) from which readers can pick and choose among the *curiosa* of their choice (fig. 47).[7]

No longer rooted in the soil of Dutch rhetoric, America obtained in these years a new-found fluidity of form and meaning. It was transformed into a series of images, marvels, and information that could circulate easily across contexts, cultures, and media of late seventeenth-century Europe. Indeed, Dutch Americana circulated widely in these years – and not just in the thick geographies and literary compilations translated for an international readership. Paintings passed among European princes; artifacts traded among European collectors; and cartographic materials dispersed among European scholars as effortlessly as ubiquitous Dutch-made globes spun in staterooms and studies across the Continent. The movements could be dizzying. Illustrations for a Simon de Vries literary "cabinet" (in this case, by the leading Dutch engraver Romeyn de Hooghe) served as decorative models for an *actual* collector's cabinet (of richly lacquered wood painted with gold), which stored the very curiosities that de Vries so alluringly described. And Dutch cabinets of this period – circa 1700 – never sold more briskly.[8]

America, in all of these forms and contexts, was in fact a marketable commodity. The Dutch, in producing so many of these works, played a disproportionately large role in the peddling of Americana: disproportionate not only in relation to the size of the Netherlands, but also to the diminished colonial activity of the Republic at this time. It was overwhelmingly Dutch maps, Dutch books, and Dutch pictures that disseminated images of America throughout Europe in the closing years of the seventeenth century. To succeed in the European market, the Dutch had to offer an America that made sense to a broad audience; and the image of America necessarily lost much of its specificity within a Dutch national context as it gained acceptance in a wider European one. This reflected changes in the political climate back home – neither the Bourbons nor the Habsburgs loomed so ominously anymore – as well as economic changes abroad. With no sizable colonies of their own, the Dutch now plied a carrying trade in America in the service of other European powers. Battles in America and over America had quieted. By the late seventeenth century, America had become simply exotic.

Notes

Sources cited in the notes are given mostly in a condensed form, while the Bibliography provides full citations. Certain frequently used works are abbreviated as follows:

EA	John Alden and Dennis Landis, eds., *European Americana: A Chronological Guide to Works Printed in Europe Relating to the Americas, 1493–1750*, 6 vols. (New York, 1980–1997)
NV	W. Voorbeijtel Cannenburg, ed., *De reis om de wereld van de Nassausche Vloot 1623–1626*, Werken Uitgegeven door de Linschoten-Vereeniging, vol. 65 (The Hague, 1964)
"Representation"	"Representation of New Netherland," in J. Franklin Jameson, ed., *Narratives of New Netherland 1609–1664* (New York, 1909)
VRBM	A. J. F. van Laer, trans. and ed., *Van Rensselaer Bowier Manuscripts* (Albany, 1908)

Preface

1. Udemans, *Geestelyck roer,* 97, and see Chapter Five below for a more detailed discussion of the author and his work. Udemans, to be sure, was not alone in his skepticism of America's novelty. The philosopher Justus Lipsius took the long-term view, in this as in so many other matters, when he wrote of the "commonly called *new world*": *De constantia,* trans. *Two bookes of constancie* (London, 1594), 40. And of course Shakespeare has Miranda admire, "O brave new world." "'Tis new to thee," comes Prospero's worldly reply, suggesting perhaps a more subtle English response to America than is generally allowed (*The Tempest,* act 5, sc. 1, lines 183–4).
2. Udemans, *Geestelyck roer,* 170, and see also 113–14, 122 ("burgerlijcke deughden"), 174, 197, 220, and 235.
3. More generally, the field of Dutch colonial studies, while superb on matters

Asian, has paid relatively scant attention to the Dutch experience in America. See den Heijer, *Geschiedenis van de WIC,* which describes the Dutch West India Company as the neglected "stepchild" of colonial historiography (9). What recent scholarship there has been on the Dutch encounter with America dates largely from the Columbian Quincentenary: Lechner and Vogel, *Nieuwe Wereld;* van den Doel, Emmer, and Vogel, *Nieuwe Wereld;* and Klooster, *Dutch in the Americas.* The subject of America's *reception* in the Netherlands, in all events, has gone virtually unnoticed. A possible exception: Zandvliet's study of cartographic assimilation in *Mapping for Money,* 164–209.

4. See the classic studies of Jennings, *Invasion of America,* and Axtell, *Invasion Within.* Recent examples of this sort of colonialist approach—finely attuned to repercussions in the New World, if less so in the Old—include MacCormack, *Religion in the Andes;* Gruzinski, *Conquest of Mexico;* and Andrien and Adorno, *Transatlantic Encounters,* all of which contemplate the "encounter," focusing resolutely, however, on events in the West. The relative neglect of studies dedicated to the *European* perspective is pointed out by Nader, "End of the Old World"; cf. also Grafton, "Rest vs. the West."

5. Elliott, *The Old World and the New,* and see also two follow-up essays that nuance, though generally sustain, Elliott's original argument: idem, "Renaissance Europe and America," and "Final Reflections." Elliott's revisionist essay built on a number of important studies immediately preceding it: Gerbi, *Dispute of the New World,* which analyzes Enlightenment debates on the subject; Echeverria, *Mirage in the West,* which surveys the French case; O'Gorman, *Invention of America;* and Scammell, "New World and Europe." The "Elliott thesis," in turn, has been widely endorsed, most visibly in two essay collections that consider head-on the question of "impact" (or lack thereof): Chiappelli, *First Images;* and Kupperman, *America in European Consciousness.* See also Ryan, "Assimilating New Worlds" (from which the "little interest" quotation comes); and Burke, "Rewriting of World History," which makes a broad case for the so-called minimalist camp. Most of the publications of the Quincentenary, and especially the higher-profile review essays, have followed the Elliott line: see, for example, Axtell, "Columbian Encounters"; Nader, "End of the Old World"; Larner, "Foreword"; and McNeill, "Legacy of Columbus."

6. A subtly revisionist line—smartly reoriented from the project of measuring levels of "impact" to understanding *processes* of reception—is adopted by Greenblatt, *Marvelous Possessions;* Grafton, *New Worlds;* Pagden, *European Encounters;* and many of the essayists in Greenblatt, *New World Encounters.* Cf. also Liebersohn, *Aristocratic Encounters,* which also examines the operation of reception, albeit from a later perspective. Elliott, to his credit, draws attention to his own neglect of "the process of 'assimilation'" in the Preface to the 1992 edition of *The Old World and the New,* xii.

7. The rather simple, if surprisingly overlooked, thesis of divergent European strategies for assimilating new worlds is developed, for slightly different purposes, by Seed, *Ceremonies of Possession.* See also Sayre, *Sauvages Améri-*

cains; Williamson, "Scots, Indians and Empire"; and Simmons, "Americana in British books," which distinguish the French, Scottish, and British cases, respectively. Scholars of English literature especially have recently made the case for America's role in shaping ideas and letters: see Scanlan's finely argued *Colonial Writing;* Matar's comparative *Age of Discovery;* and Hadfield, *English Renaissance.*

8. David Calderwood, *History of the Kirk of Scotland,* ed. Thomas Thomson, 8 vols. (Edinburgh, 1842–1849), 5:391 (cited in Williamson, "Scots, Indians and Empire," 63). James, of course, had provincial concerns of his own—the looming "savagery" of Scotland's Highlanders, whom he imagined resembling the "beastlie" Americans. The political situation in the Netherlands, by contrast, allowed Willem to valorize the Indians at the expense of the Spaniards. Note too that James would soon come to terms with Philip III by signing the Treaty of London (1604), and that James's son, Prince Charles, would famously (and disastrously) visit Castile a few years later in search of a bride.

9. They looked to America, in this sense, from a perspective wholly different from their fellow Protestants in England, who launched their American enterprise in the wake of the subjugation of Ireland; and from their "arch enemies" in Castile, who had been seasoned by colonial experiences both on the peninsula and in the Canaries. Cf. Elliott, *Britain and Spain in America,* which emphasizes precisely the prior imperial experience that led England and Spain to America. On the English case more particularly, see Canny, *Elizabethan Conquest of Ireland;* and on Spain, see Fernández-Armesto, *Before Columbus.*

10. The debate on applying to the early modern period the methods of postcolonial studies—a field that, for the two or so decades following the publication of Edward Said's *Orientalism* (New York, 1978), has been closely associated with subaltern studies—is conducted almost exclusively in the context of Latin American studies, leaving Europe (not generally thought of as having internal "colonies") out of the picture. See Seed, "Colonial and Postcolonial Discourse"; and Adorno, "Reconsidering Colonial Discourse," where Adorno sensibly points to the need for "historical responsibility" in reading early modern texts. Colonialism in early modern Europe is broached in a provocative essay by Dandelet, "Spanish Conquest and Colonization"; and see also Armitage, "Making the Empire British," which considers the nascent British empire. On subaltern studies (and their pertinence beyond the borders of the Indian subcontinent), see Prakash, "Subaltern Studies"; and Spivak, "Subaltern Studies."

11. Chatterjee, *Nationalist Thought,* 50–1 and 85–130.

12. Pratt, *Imperial Eyes.* Of course, all colonial discourse is meant for domestic consumption. In the Dutch case, however, the *goals* of the colonial discourse—of the "production" of America—were also determinedly domestic, namely the articulation of a Dutch identity (see the following discussion).

13. It parts company, thus, with Mignolo's project of "plurioptic hermeneutics" (admirable though Mignolo's goals may be): *Darker Side of the Renaissance.* It

comes closer, meanwhile, to Hartog's methodological designs for understanding "Herodotus's Scythians. . . . that is to say, the Scythians as imagined by the Greeks": *Mirror of Herodotus*, 6, 10–11. Cf. also Schwartz, *Implicit
Understanding*, which seeks to present multiple perspectives of the encounter—though the individual essays of the volume, in practice, tend to
examine one or another side of a narrative.

14. Cf. Kupperman, *Settling with the Indians.*
15. Anderson, *Imagined Communities*, 4.
16. Anderson addresses "imagined space" more thoughtfully in the revised
    and expanded edition of *Imagined Communities*, 170–8. See also Winichakul,
    Siam Mapped; Kagan, *Urban Images;* and Smail, *Imaginary Cartographies.* On
    "Chilean" patriotism, see the "Voor reden" in Ercilla, *Historiale beschrijv-
    inghe,* sig. A; on American "liberties," see [van der Clyte], *Cort verhael,* sig.
    [aiij]r.
17. Udemans, *Geestelyck roer*, 105.
18. Cf. Hillgarth, *Mirror of Spain,* which considers the process, in a broader con-
    text, from the Spanish perspective.
19. Schama, *Embarrassment of Riches,* 51. Schama received a fair amount of crit-
    icism for his attempt to describe "the Dutch"; yet he does in fact lay out, rea-
    sonably carefully, of whom he speaks in this regard, and how culture oper-
    ated among the *brede middenstand* ("middling sort") of the Republic: see
    ibid., 4–8.
20. See Rowen, "Dutch Revolt"; and van Nierop, *Verraad van het Noorderkwartier,*
    which offers an important case study of local conflict during the war, shat-
    tering the historiographic myth of a unified "Dutch" opposition to Habs-
    burg rule. On the "New World" of the Republic, see Swart, *Miracle of the
    Dutch Republic,* 3.
21. Van den Sande [Ammonius], *Trouhertighe vermaninghe,* sig. [ciij]r. Van den
    Sande, as it turns out, was not entirely paranoid. His comments on Spain
    and the Netherlands appeared nearly simultaneously with Bernardo José de
    Aldrete's study of language and state, *Origenes de la lengua castellana* (1606),
    which contended, as one of its chapter titles so vigorously put it, that "the
    vanquished [should] receive the language of the vanquishers, surrendering
    their own [language] with their land and people." Aldrete's comments (and
    perhaps van den Sande's as well) would also have echoed Nebrija's famous
    dictum that "language is the perfect instrument of empire": that the con-
    quest of "arms and letters" together make the empire. See Mignolo, *Darker
    Side of the Renaissance,* 29–67, which explores the Spanish-American case.
22. See, on this point, Scanlan's critique of Greenblatt's *Marvelous Possessions*
    and Scanlan's sensible call "to historicize 'wonder,' and transform it into a
    term with historical and cultural depth": *Colonial Writing,* 191.

Chapter One

1. Van Mander, *Het leven,* 229v, which details much of what is known of
   Mostaert's career. The imposing (86 × 152 cm.) *West Indies Landscape* is dated
   varyingly between 1520 and 1550. The painting, its history, and its iconogra-

phy are discussed at greater length in the following. By certain criteria, of course, other paintings of America may be said to have been produced in the early sixteenth century: paintings containing depictions of native peoples, plants, animals, or artifacts from the New World. Mostaert's is the only landscape, though, and the only painting devoted *primarily* to an American scene.

2. See Gibson, *Mirror of the Earth*, which surveys *Weltlandschaften;* and Falkenburg, *Joachim Patinir.* Also suggestive is Falkenburg's *Natuur en landschap.*

3. The "glorious chaos" of sixteenth-century Americana is identified, albeit in a French context, by Lestringant, *Atelier du cosmographe*, 110, where Lestringant considers a series of eclectic engravings by Etienne Delaune that achieve a *beau désordre* in their mixing of Tupi (in this case) and classical motifs. Cf. also Mason, *Infelicities*, 39, which speaks of "a certain degree of contamination" that takes place in the Old World-New World conflations of early Americana.

4. Aurelius, *Cronycke van Hollandt*, 279. Aurelius, who composed this passage between 1507 and 1514, refers presumably to recently issued editions of Vespucci or perhaps the edition of Vespucci included in Waldseemüller's *Cosmographiae* (St. Dié, 1507). See Tilmans, *Historiography and Humanism*, 190.

5. Zárate's *Historia del descubrimiento* appeared six times in Dutch and only once in Spanish, while Staden's *Warhaftig historia* enjoyed ten Dutch (compared to six German) editions by the year 1650. For a complete bibliography, as well as the virtually definitive research tool for early printed works on America, see Alden and Landis, *European Americana* (hereafter *EA*), vol. 1.

6. For the presence of early Americana in Dutch libraries (as measured, it should be noted, by the evidence of printed catalogues), see Lechner, "Dutch Humanists," and, more generally, van Selm, *Menighte treffelijcke boecken.* The French case was examined by Atkinson, *Nouveaux horizons,* following an earlier study by Chinard, *Exotisme Américain.* Both are referenced reflexively in most "encounter" studies to demonstrate a pervasive lack of *European* attention to America: see, for example, Elliott, *The Old World and the New*, 12.

7. The British Isles, by comparison, could claim a measly six in 1600, a year when the province of Holland alone boasted twice that number. See Visser, "Dichtheid van de bevolking"; van der Woude, "Demografische ontwikkeling"; and Israel, *Dutch Republic* (1995), 113–16. Cf. more generally de Vries, *European Urbanization.* Growth extended beyond the city walls as well: the overall population of the Netherlands, North and South, grew by some fifty percent over the first six decades of the sixteenth century.

8. From around 40,000 in 1496 to 84,000 in 1542–43, as detailed in van Roey, "Bevolking." On matters of commerce, see the fundamental studies of van der Wee: "Handel in de Zuidelijke Nederlanden," and *Growth of the Antwerp Market.* Antwerp's urbanism and culture are surveyed more generally in van der Stock, *Antwerp;* and for the Flemish background, see Nicholas, *Medieval Flanders.* The correlation between commercial expansion and overseas exploration, vividly united in the sixteenth-century entrepot of Antwerp, is a central theme in Jardine, *Worldly Goods.*

9. Antoon Verdickt quoted by Adriaan van Haemstede, *Historie der Martelaren*

(Dordrecht, 1659), fol. 320, which is cited in a slightly different form in Marnef, *Antwerp*, 3; and see ibid. for the city fathers' (unattributed) boast. In reviewing the figures for Antwerp's foreign-born population, Marnef points out that the number of "transient" merchants—"foreign merchants daily coming and going," as the census of 1568 put it—amounted to *ten times* the number of permanent foreign residents (ibid., 4–6). This produced a remarkable degree of multiculturalism, which placed the entire Renaissance world (as one observer noted) within an Antwerper's reach: "Voyages to distant foreign countries are completely unnecessary for one who wants to study the customs and characteristics of one or another people: he finds them all together in this one city" (Lodovico Guicciardini cited in Stock, *Antwerp*, 8). "As one of the great centers of world trade, where merchants from all parts of Europe congregated," asserts Marnef in his study of Antwerp's Reformation, "Antwerp was exceptionally open to new ideas" (Marnef, *Antwerp*, 23). Much the same can be said, it will be argued, for the city's remarkable receptivity to early Americana.

10. On early printing, see Obbema and Derolez, "Verspreiding van het boek." Antwerp's publishing industry is surveyed by Voet, "Typografische bedrijvigheid"; and see also Voet's masterful study of Antwerp's premiere printing house, *Golden Compasses*. Literacy figures come from van der Woude, "Alphabetisering." For seventeenth-century Amsterdam, see van Selm, *Inzichten en vergezichten;* and Lankhorst and Hoftijzer, *Drukkers, boekverkopers en lezers.* Pleij, "Literatuur en drukpers," surveys literary developments in the early years of printing.

11. Guicciardini, *Description of the Low Countreys,* sig. 14r-v (and see sig. 1v, where the author heads his list of Dutch achievements with "Printing, first invented at *Mentz,* or as some write in *Harlem* in *Holland"*). Guicciardini elsewhere marvels at the French language instruction available in Antwerp schools (both boys' and girls') and at the availability even of Spanish and Italian teachers (see Marnef, *Antwerp,* 33). Scaliger, upon a visit to the Republic in 1593, was similarly struck by the widespread literacy of the Dutch, expressing his amazement that in Holland even servant girls could read. He exaggerated only slightly: half of Amsterdam grooms could sign their names (in 1630) compared to 32% of brides—both low estimates for literacy, since writing skills were taught only after reading (cf. Israel, *Dutch Republic* [1995], 686).

12. On typographic culture as it pertains to early Americana, see Lowood, "Catalogue of Nature," 306.

13. Erasmus, *Opera Omnia,* 9: 805DE. The Aurelius map, dated 1514 and initialed by the woodcutter ("C. H."), was based in all likelihood on the 1507 *mappa mundi* of Martin Waldseemüller. It was published in Aurelius's *Divisiekroniek* (see note 4) and is reproduced in Tilmans, *Historiography and Humanism,* 103. For Martens's edition of Columbus's *Epistola,* see the subsequent discussion.

14. Dutch literature of the late Middle Ages, and especially the concept of an

"urban" literature—separate from, though in no way inferior to, "courtly" literature—has been superbly studied by Pleij: see his *Sneeuwpoppen van 1511*, and *Nederlandse literatuur*, which contains excellent bibliographies. A useful survey of trends in the field can be found in idem, "Rise of Urban Literature," where Pleij considers the process of adaptation, or "annexation," of chivalric romances within an urban Dutch context; and see also the classic study of popular Dutch literature in this period: Debaene, *Nederlandse volksboeken*. A discussion of early *printed* works can be found in Vermeulen, *Profijt en genoegen*. Both Pleij and Vermeulen note the easy integration of multilingual literatures in the Dutch context—a factor that helps to explain the exceptional success of multilingual early Americana.

15. Polo's eastern *Travels* were conflated with the western voyages of the Renaissance by the publisher of the first Dutch anthology of Americana, *Die nieuwe weerelt der landtschappen ende eylanden* (Antwerp, 1563), an editorial imprecision that would not seem to have confounded many readers. See more generally Watanabe, *Polo Bibliography*. On the *Itinerarius* of Jan Voet (aka Johannes Witte de Hese), which appeared in ten manuscript and eleven printed editions (the latter dating from ca. 1490 to 1565), see Westrem, "Witte de Hese's *Itinerarius*." Master Joos's narrative appeared in at least three manuscripts before it was printed (three times in the sixteenth century), originally as *Tvoyage van Mher Joos van Ghistele, oft anders, Texcellent, groot, zeldsaem ende vremd voyage ghedaen by wylent Edelen ende weerden Heere Mher Joos van Ghistele* (Ghent, 1557).

16. Bennett, *Rediscovery of Sir John Mandeville*. For the enthusiastic Dutch response to the naturalistic "paradijs op aarde" topoi of Mandeville, see Pleij, "Literatuur en natuurgenoot."

17. The theme of moralized travel is examined in a specifically medieval Dutch context by Bejczy, "Between Mandeville and Columbus." On tropes of medieval travel literature more generally, see Campbell, *Witness and the Other World*; and cf. Vermeulen, *Profijt en genoegen.*

18. On the confluence of ancient texts and early Americana, see Grafton, *New Worlds*. For medieval traces, see Mason, *Deconstructing America*. Efforts to rectify the bucolic eclogue by Dutch humanists (including Erasmus and Petrus Pontanus van Brugge) are discussed by IJsewijn, "Wereldlijke literatuur"; and see also idem, "Humanism in the Low Countries," which surveys the reception of classical literature in the Netherlands.

19. Columbus, *Epistola* (Antwerp, 1493). Other Latin editions printed in Paris, Basel, and Rome would have circulated in the Low Countries as well. For a complete bibliography, see *EA*, vol. 1.

20. Columbus, *Four Voyages*, 14, 6; and see Bennett, *Rediscovery*, 372. On the literary imagination of Columbus, see (among the flood of Quincentenary titles) Greenblatt, *Marvelous Possessions*; Flint, *Imaginative Landscape*; and Zamora, *Reading Columbus*, which considers the Columbian texts, quite sensibly, from the perspective of both reader and author. Pleij ("Literatuur en natuurgenoot") discusses Dutch readers' predilection for literary natural-

ism; and see more generally Gerbi, *Nature in the New World*, 12–22. The "Columbian enterprise" of Antwerp's merchants—to be the prime dispensers of America's wealth—is celebrated by *Moyses' Doorn* in the 1561 *Landjuweel* of Antwerp, *Spelen van sinne* (cited by Pleij, "Antwerp Described," 82).

21. See especially Flint, *Imaginative Landscape*; and Zamora, *Reading Columbus*. Note that, while the content of Columbus's *Epistola* may make a "traditional" impression, the genre in which it appeared—a brief, breathless, epistolary report of events overseas—seems more strikingly original in the context of late-medieval travel literature.

22. The *Mundus novus* first appeared in print ca. 1503, while the more extensive *Lettera* (also known as the *Quatuor navigationes*) was published ca. 1505. The earliest Antwerp edition came from the press of Willem Vorsterman, ca. 1505: *EA* provides a complete bibliography. See also the critical edition of Vespucci, *Lettere di Viaggio*, available in an abridged, English version, *Letters from a New World* (and see ibid., 45–6, for the author's declaration of "discovery"). On the earliest printed Americana: Hirsch, "Printed Reports." The concept of "Vespuccian texts"—of a body of work historically associated with Amerigo Vespucci, even while issues of authorship remain disputed— borrows from Zamora's useful discussion of "Columbian writings": *Reading Columbus*, 6–7.

23. Magnaghi, *Amerigo Vespucci*, made the definitive case against the pseudo-Vespucci, though attacks on the Florentine's reputation began as early as Las Casas, who denounced Columbus's rival as a "usurper," a purveyor of "falsehoods," and, worst of all, a merchant. See Robertson's *History of America*, 1:150, for an indignant denunciation of Vespucci the "imposter." These and other sources pertaining to the "Vespucci question" are discussed in Formisano, *Letters*, xxviii–xxx; and see also Gerbi, *Nature*, 35–49. Markham's critique appears in his Introduction to *Letters of Amerigo Vespucci*, vi; and see Emerson, *English Traits*, 98. While Vespucci may have won the battle of Renaissance public relations, he lost the war of modern biographies to Columbus. Formisano's *Amerigo Vespucci* surveys the field while also detailing the *piloto mayor*'s original career in Seville as a provisioner of overseas voyages.

24. See Whitney, "Naming of America," for a discussion of the popularly entertaining, "carnivalesque" qualities of the Vespuccian texts.

25. The Vespuccian texts especially lent themselves to publishers' interventions, and van Doesborch was a publisher especially amenable to tricks of the travel literature trade. His list included numerous titles claiming to offer novelties, wonders, and landscapes "nieuwelicx ghevonden": a partly fictionalized account of Da Gama's second voyage (*Calcoen*, ca. 1504), an imaginative description of Prester John's domains (*Van die wonderlicheden ende costelicheden van Papa Ians landen*, ca. 1506), and the various "American" texts (for which *EA* provides bibliographic details). Vermeulen offers a fine discussion of the publisher and his methods: *Profijt en genoegen*, 100–12. Note that Waldseemüller was the geographer responsible for naming the western continents, in 1507, after Vespucci.

26. Vespucci, *Vander nieuwer werelt* (and on van Doesborch's other stock, see above). There are altogether six woodcuts, two of which are repeated and all of which may have originated in other publications. The nautical vignette derives very likely from a version of the "Jonah" story, while the "wild" couple may be a reworking of "Adam and Eve in Paradise." A final image shows a group of "wild" men with bows and arrows. Van Doesborch also inserted subtle changes to the text to make it as parochially Dutch—as *burgerlijk*—as possible, adding, for example, an announcement that Vespucci "would undertake a fourth voyage with two ships *built here in Holland*, if God spares him" (ibid., sig. [B3]v, emphasis added).

27. Vespucci, *Mundus novus*. The scholarly apparatus is believed to be the work not of Vespucci but of his presumed editor, the Veronese humanist Fra Giovanni del Giocondo. It is, in all events, an unimpressive display, especially when it comes to classical name-dropping. While Pliny and Ptolemy are reasonably cited, "Polycletus" is invoked for his skills as a painter—though he labored in the field of sculpture. In a certain sense, however, the level of learning was less important than the *look* of learning, a quality that only added to the text's multivalence.

28. Aurelius, *Cronycke van Hollandt*, 279; Brant, *Narrenschiff*, sig. liiij–v; Vives, *Concordia* (Lyons, 1529; orig. Antwerp), sig. O7; idem, *Europe dissidiis*, sig. lxx–v ("Mos novi orbis"); and idem, *Disciplinis* (Lyons, 1551; orig. Antwerp, 1531), 359. Erasmus's scattered references to the Indies are just that: scattered. For a sampling, see Erasmus, *Correspondence*, 4:95–6 (to Pieter Gillis, 1516), which refers to an ecclesiastical preferment in the West Indies; and 11: 299 (to Pierre Barbier, 1525), which contains a witty reference to "mountains of gold from Paria." Erasmus very nearly gets around to the New World in the opening passage of his *Utilissima consultatio de bello turcis inferendo* (Antwerp, 1530), where he describes the horrors of syphilis; yet the greatest humanist of his day does not actually make much of the connection between the new disease and new direction of European expansion.

There is, to be sure, a degree of truth to Jozef IJsewijn's contention that "the humanists of the Netherlands do not seem to have paid much attention to the New World in the early sixteenth century" ("Humanism in the Low Countries," 194). Yet IJsewijn bases this contention on a somewhat narrow definition of both humanism and the New World. He does not consider, for example, humanistic literature composed in the vernacular (cf. Aurelius) or indirect allusions to America (cf. Vives). He is also disinclined to measure the process of Dutch assimilation in works by other (non-Dutch) humanists, which were in fact well received in the Netherlands (the obvious example being Martyr's *Decades*, which I discussed in this chapter).

29. *De rebus oceanis et orbe novo decades tres* appeared originally in Alcalá de Henares in 1516. It was printed under the direction of the esteemed Spanish humanist, Antonio de Nebrija, which virtually guaranteed its success. Unauthorized, misattributed, and incomplete versions did appear earlier (from 1504), though with none of the fanfare of the Nebrija edition. See the detailed "Bibliography" in Anghiera, *Eight Decades*, 1:49–52.

30. Wagner takes Martyr to task, in fact, for his prose style, arguing that the author of the *Decades* faced particular difficulties, never quite surmounted, in rendering into Latin the novelties of America. As a consequence, "Martyr's [Latin style] bears little resemblance to the polished style of Cicero. He almost created a new dialect" ("Martyr and his Works," 284). Nebrija himself had a hand in the final product, though, which was certainly the most "polished" description of the *Conquista* yet available. Martyr's indisputable role in the dissemination of Renaissance humanism is discussed by Burke, "Spread of Italian Humanism."

31. Anghiera, *Eight Decades*, 1:301, 2:77, 93, 18 (on the "Amazons"). Martyr could certainly play the part of the skeptic when it came to ancient mythology—more Valla than Vespucci. In dismissing certain stories of a fountain of youth, he expressed his reservations that "any such power exists in creative nature" (ibid., 1:274). His classicism, in all events, earned him a reputation as "the Livy of American historiography," yet see Gerbi (*Nature*, 50) for a more tempered view.

32. See Ovid, *Metamorphosis* 1.89–112, and Levin's classic study, *Myth of the Golden Age*. The Golden Age topos, particularly as it related to the discovery of America, is a central theme in Honour, *New Golden Land;* and see also Baudet, *Paradise on Earth.*

33. For further examples of utopianism in the West, sixteenth-century readers could consult More's *Utopia*, which appeared, not entirely accidentally one suspects, in the very year Martyr published his original *Decades* (1516). The Renaissance engagement with utopianism and especially the case of More is studied by Skinner, "More's 'Utopia.'" The treatment of utopian themes in early (English) Americana is explored by Knapp, *Empire Nowhere.*

34. Anghiera, *Eight Decades*, 1:103–4, and note how the image of an elderly, naked man of wisdom recalls the gymnosophists whom Alexander encounters in Europe's original conquest of the Indies.

35. And when the analogy does not quite fit, Martyr adjusts it accordingly—even if this means revising his Ovid. Although the Hispaniolans "know neither weights nor measures, nor that source of all misfortunes, money," and enjoy "a golden age, without laws, without lying judges, without books, satisfied with their life," they do tolerate factionalism and ongoing squabbles. "Ambition and the desire to rule trouble even them, and they fight amongst themselves," Martyr must concede, "so that even in the Golden Age there is never a moment without war; the maxim *Cede, non cedam*, has always prevailed amongst mortal men" (*Eight Decades*, 1:79). Thus, not only has America been refashioned to fit the Golden Age; the Golden Age has been made to conform to the social patterns of America.

36. See, most recently, Lawrance, "Humanism in the Iberian Peninsula": "[Martyr] idealized the Indians because he wished to glorify the Spanish achievement in discovering and conquering 'our New World' as he called it" (256). Lawrance surely exaggerates, however, when he claims that Martyr's loyalty to his patrons induced him "to omit *all* account of Spanish atrocities" (emphasis added), a judgment that bespeaks the selective reading of Lawrance

rather than the biased reporting of Martyr, as will be demonstrated. Closer to the truth is Gerbi, who suggests that Martyr was "an unbiased and contented observer, lukewarm in his defense of Spanish interests" (*Nature,* 51). He was deemed fit, in any event, to join the Council of the Indies and was later named its secretary. Charles appointed him historiographer in 1520, a position that earned eighty thousand maravedis per annum (Anghiera, *Eight Decades,* 1:39).

37. Anghiera, *Eight Decades,* 2:252. The image of the ruler as queen (sometimes "king") bee has classical antecedents, including Pliny, *Natural History* 3.5–24 and 4.339–45, and Virgil, *Georgics* 4.149–218. It is more than slightly ironic that the English, a full century later, resorted to a similar entomological simile to describe the ideal *colonial* government: see Kupperman, "Beehive as a Model."

38. Anghiera, *Eight Decades,* 2:256.

39. Martyr's capacity to compose indisputably ingratiating prose is displayed, for example, in the closing section of the first Decade, where Spain is granted the "highest praise" for its role in the New World; and in the opening sentences of that same Decade, where Martyr "admires" and "praises" the discoverers' achievements: ibid., 1:180 and 1:57.

40. Ibid., 128, 141–2.

41. Ibid., 193, 214. One detects in these and other passages a class issue at play as well: the indignation of a refined, Milanese noble at the pretensions of the plebeian, Castilian (or Extremaduran) conquistadors.

42. Ibid., 222–3, 231–2, 301, 314.

43. For a complete bibliography, see *EA*. A second round of editions came out in the 1570s and 1580s (in Latin, English, and German), yet in this instance Protestant publishers made clear their intent to use Martyr's text to vilify Catholic Spain. The contrast between the Prefaces of the 1530s and those of the 1580s—the latter from the likes of Richard Hakluyt and Sebastian Henricpetri—demonstrates well how early Americana could be exploited long after their original publication and with little regard for their original intentions. A rather more ambiguous text is that of Richard Eden, which falls between the first and second generation editions. Published during Mary's brief reign, Eden's volume is dedicated to the consort, Prince Philip (soon to be Philip II), and praises the Spanish Crown profusely for bringing the riches of Christ to America and waging "mercyfull wares ageynst naked people": Anghiera, *Decades of the new worlde,* sig. aii–v ("To the Reader"). Eden obtained a place in the treasury under Philip, yet was accused of heresy just a year later. His worked was discovered and adapted, for very different purposes, by the Marian exiles, who paid more attention to the body of the text than to its Preface (see Chapter Two).

44. The *Novis insulis nuber repertis . . . per Petrum Martyr* was published in Antwerp in 1536, based on the Basel edition of 1521 (*De nuper sub D. Carolo repertis insulis . . . enchiridion*), which itself derived from the 1516 edition issued in Alcalá de Henares under Nebrija's direction. Other Latin editions also appeared in Paris (1532) and Basel (1533); see *EA* for full details. Mar-

tyr's name surfaces in most of the major Dutch atlases, travel accounts, and cosmographies of the sixteenth century, including works by Grynaeus, Ortelius, Mercator, and van Linschoten. Volumes of Martyr's *Decades,* furthermore, turn up more frequently in late sixteenth- and early seventeenth-century Dutch libraries than do any other of the earliest (pre-1550) Americana. Approximately ten percent of the 114 auction catalogues studied by Lechner list an edition of Martyr ("Dutch Humanists"). For Vives's Americana, see note 28.

45. Grynaeus, *Novus Orbis;* Fracastoro, *Syphilis;* Paracelsus, *Frantzösischen Kranckheit;* Oviedo, *Natural hystoria.* Both of the Latin works came out in multiple editions over the coming decades. A Dutch translation of Paracelsus appeared in 1557: *Excellent tractaet.* Oviedo, perhaps the most peripheral of these otherwise prominent authors, corresponded with Fracastoro on American flora. Fracastoro, in turn, was good friends with Giovanni Battista Ramusio, who dedicated to the Veronese humanist his impressive anthology of travel literature, *Terzo volume delle navigatione et viaggi* (Venice, 1556). This phenomenon of expanding literary genres and widening circles of readers dedicated to the new geography is studied, in a parallel context (though very similar time frame), by Lach, *Asia in the Making of Europe.*

46. Oviedo's otherwise unremarkable romance has been dubbed the "first American novel": Turner, "Oviedo's 'Claribalte.'" Note that, if the *Claribalte* had nothing overtly "American" about it, Oviedo's genuinely American scholarship did possess chivalric elements. Edmundo O'Gorman slyly observed that Oviedo's major opus, the *Historia general de las Indias,* contained episodes "[featuring] Amadis and Claribalte in the guise of conquistadors in the Indies" (cited in Gerbi, *Nature,* 203, where Gerbi does voice his skepticism).

47. See Elliott's classic essay, "Cortés, Velázquez and Charles V," which lays out the legal and political program of the *Cartas.*

48. Cortés, *Letters,* and note that the so-called First Letter was not from the hand of Cortés, if most likely dictated by him. Pagden points out that Cortés was himself steeped in the ballads and romances exceedingly popular in the Spain of his day, and he very likely believed them, too: "Translator's Introduction," in ibid., xlviii-xlix. In any case, much as Cortés's rhetorical tactics may have worked in the short term—he gained approval for his *Conquista* and a share in its profits—they failed in the longer term, since, by insisting on his faithful service to the emperor, the author of the *Cartas* gave Charles better reason to claim imperial prerogative in Mexico.

49. Cortés, *Contreyen vanden eylanden,* which is based on the French-language edition of the previous year, *Marches ysles.* The Dutch version is the first known to have a frontispiece, though it is not impossible that van Hoochstraten's French edition (of which only two copies are known) originally bore the same image.

50. Note that other editions of the Letters also made a "caesarean" impression. Latin versions printed in Nuremberg (twice in 1524) and Cologne (1532) bore a combination of imperial arms and/or royal portraits of Charles V,

while the original Spanish editions (1522–1525) showed an enthroned "sacred majesty" (with indistinct features) and/or Habsburg coats of arms. The famous fold-out map of Tenochtitlan, printed in various editions of the *Letters*, had a prominent Habsburg flag at the top-center. See Cortés, *Letters*, 33, 49, 163, and 285, which reproduce a selection of these images.

51. Cortés, *Letters*, 60–1 and passim. Cf. the curious note appended by the printer, Jacobo Cromberger, to the original edition of the *Letters* (1522), sympathetically comparing the fall of Tenochtitlan to that of ancient Jerusalem and thus converting the Indians into exiled, miserable Jews (ibid., 159). The note could hardly have been approved by Cortés.

52. In 1554, the rival Antwerp publishers Martin Nuyts, Jean Bellère, and Jan Steels each printed their own editions of the chronicles of Cieza de León (*Chronica del Peru*) and Gómara (*Istoria de las Indias*): see *EA* for details. Publication of Gómara's work in Spain ceased in 1553 following a ban by Charles V, similar to an earlier prohibition in 1527 on Spanish editions of Cortés. In both cases, censorship was intended to proscribe the spread of a conquistador mythology based on Cortés's successes and to maintain the integrity of Spain's reputation in light of Cortés's exploits.

53. Zárate, *Strange and delectable history*, 210 (spelling and punctuation modernized), and see also 97–100 and 208–12.

54. For bibliographic details, see *EA*. The appetite of Netherlandic readers for romances of chivalry, and especially Spanish variants of the genre, extended naturally beyond Americana. See Debaene, "Nederlandse prozaromans"; Robben, "Brandstichters en boekenkopers"; Pleij, *Thomas van der Noot*, 13, 31; and Peeters-Fontainas, *Bibliographie des impressions espagnoles*.

55. Zárate, *Warachtighe historie* (Antwerp: Willem Silvius, 1563); and cf. *Ghenuechlijcke historie vanden . . . ridder Peeter van Provencien* (Antwerp: Jan van Waelberge, 1587), which bears on its title page an identical print of clashing, in this case, Provençal knights (and on Silvius, see note 105). McMahon points out that the 1563 Dutch edition of Zárate, translated by Rumoldus de Bacquere ("scrivner to the king"), actually suppressed materials from Book Five that Spanish censors found offensive: "Spanish and Foreign Editions." These editorial changes were not made to other (non-Dutch) editions, indicating just how conservatively the Dutch version of America followed the Spanish in the years preceding the Revolt.

56. For Pieter's letters "ad patres et fratres Provinciae Flandriae," see van Zierikzee, *Chronica compendiosissima*, fols. 124–7; and cf. Duncanus, *Vruchten der ecclesie Christie*. One or another of these sources came to the attention of Abraham Ortelius, who cites Pieter in his *Theatrum orbis terrarum* (1570). The manscript letters to the Spanish Crown are scattered in various modern editions. For a full bibliography, see Troeyer, *Bio-bibliographia*, 1:75–83, which also details the fascinating life of Pieter van Gent (aka Pedro de Gante). Note that the most severe of Pieter's comments to Charles appeared in a letter of 15 February 1552—coincident, that is, with the exceedingly critical, admonishing, and apocalyptic pleadings of Fray Bartolomé de Las Casas.

57. Though Cortés, too, was ultimately censored by the Crown (see note 52). For

an overview of Pieter's letters in their colonial context, see Everaert, "Conquest of the Indian soul," which cites (partially) the friar's exhortation to the emperor.

58. On Spain's imperial development, see Elliott, *Imperial Spain,* 135–81. Habsburg fiscal policy in the Netherlands is studied by Tracy, *Financial Revolution:* see 72 for the rebellion of Ghent.

59. The important exception to this rule was the international community of cod-fishers in the North Atlantic and the Valois-sponsored expeditions to Canada in 1524 and the mid-1540s. In neither case, though, did Spain or Portugal encounter *consistent* opposition to its control of the more desirable trade in the Caribbean or South America.

60. Staden, *Warhaftige historia und beschreibung eyner landtschafft der wilden, nacketen, grimmigen menschfresser leuthen, in . . . America.* The Dutch edition came out the following year with the somewhat less graphic title, *Warachtige historie ende beschrivinge eens lants in America ghelegen.* For further bibiographic details, see *EA,* vols. 1–2.

61. Staden, *True History,* esp. 69–72 (on the author's ordeal) and 27–8 (for Dryander's prefatory comments). See also the "Hymn," at the conclusion of the first book, in which Staden, in direct supplication to the Lord and in the best of Lutheran traditions, acknowledges "no power but thine own mighty hand . . . for I am indeed beyond the help of men." And further: "There is neither strength nor comfort, neither defense nor support save in God's name alone" (ibid., 124–5). Staden's patron, Johannes Dryander (aka Eichmann), was a professor of medicine and mathematics at the Protestant university of Marburg, where he later served as rector.

62. Christoffel Plantijn, "Die Boeckdrucker totten Leser," in Staden, *Warachtige historie,* n.p.

63. Thevet's *Singularitez* was published originally in Paris in 1557 and then in Antwerp the following year—two of seven editions that appeared within Thevet's lifetime (see *EA,* vol. 1). The success of the work—in addition to its author's not inconsiderable ambition—gained Thevet a series of prominent positions at the court: as *aumonier* to the queen, Catherine de' Medici, and later as royal cosmographer to Henri II, François II, Charles IX, and Henri III. On this most intriguing of Renaissance geographers, see Lestringant, *André Thevet;* and idem, *Atelier du cosmographe.* For Plantijn's timely endorsement of "Andreas Tevet," see Staden, *Warachtige historie,* n.p. ("Boeckdrucker totten Leser").

64. Julien, *Voyages de découverte,* provides an overview. For the fascinating *entrée* of Henri, see McGowan, *Entrée de Henri II,* which reproduces the most complete account of the event; and two more extensive studies: McGowan, "Form and Themes"; and Wintroub, "Civilizing the Savage." On "American" pageantry more generally, cf. Mullaney, "New World on Display."

65. Thevet, *Singularitez,* 54–5, sigs. 70v, 77v, 124r, 154r and *passim.* The story of *damoiselle* Marguerite—the narration of which in Marguerite de Navarre's fictional *Heptaméron* casts doubt on Thevet's subsequent, nonfiction version—can be found in the *Cosmographie universelle* (Paris, 1575), 1019–20.

66. As when the author compares the *sauvages Américains* encountered in Brazil and the proto-Frenchmen encountered in ancient France by "Hercules of Libya": Thevet, *Singularitez,* sig. 153v.

67. Thevet, *New found world,* 59 (and cf. idem., *Singularitez,* 116–17).

68. Léry, *Histoire d'un voyage.* For the role of America in the French Wars of Religion, see Lestringant, *Le huguenot et le sauvage.*

69. Thevet insisted he was a shoemaker, while Léry remained silent on the matter, stating only that his rank was above that of his detractor. For a brief review of their dispute and a superb introduction to Léry's life and work, see Whatley, "Introduction," in Léry, *History of a Voyage,* xv–xliii.

70. See Léry, *History of a Voyage,* 259–60, for bibliographic details. On the Dutch martyrology of van Haemstede: Lenger, *Bibiotheca Belgica,* 3:374–96 (H-170 *et seq.*); and Jelsma, *Van Haemstede.*

71. Léry, *History of a Voyage,* 220–4, 257–9. Note that the fourth and fifth French editions, of 1599–1600 and 1611 respectively, both contain dedications to the "Madame la Princesse d'Orange"—namely, Louise de Coligny, the widow of Willem the Silent and daughter of Gaspard de Coligny—suggesting the relevance that Léry, at least, saw his work having to political and religious events in the Netherlands. Léry's work was also taken up by that tireless Calvinist polemicist, Urbain Chauveton, who cited Léry profusely in Chauveton's translation of another New World classic: Benzoni's *Historia del mondo nuovo* (for which see the later discussion).

72. Léry, *History of a Voyage,* 46–7, 218. The author also details the *physical* cruelty inflicted by Villegagnon on the colonists. After brutally cudgeling one man "black and blue," Villegagnon snarls between blows (as quoted by Léry), "by the body of Saint James, lecher, turn the other side" (ibid., 46).

73. Ibid., 56, 147. Compare Léry's opinions of the natives with those of Villegagnon—as filtered by Léry—in the Preface to the work: "[T]here were wild and savage people, remote from courtesy and humanity, utterly different from us in their way of doing things and in their upbringing: without religion, nor any knowledge of honesty or virtue . . . so that it seemed to me that we had fallen among beasts bearing a human countenance" (ibid., xlix). On the ambiguities inherent in a "Calvinist" view of the Indians, see Gordon, "Léry, Laudonnière, et les Indiens."

74. Not that a Calvinist training precluded a humanist orientation: see Bouwsma, *John Calvin,* which explores the humanist currents in Calvin's theology.

75. Léry, *History of a Voyage,* 111, 56–7.

76. Ibid., 64, 76, 142, 145.

77. Mutual accusation of cannibalism became increasingly common during the French wars of religion, exploited by Catholics and Protestants alike. See Lestringant, "Calvinistes et Cannibales"; idem, "Catholiques et Cannibales"; and Whatley, "Révérence Réciproque."

78. Léry, *History of a Voyage,* 132–3.

79. Ibid., 198.

80. For Montaigne's use of Léry, see Weinberg, "Montaigne's Reading for 'Des

Cannibales'"; and on the local (French) context of the essay, see Quint, "Montaigne's 'Des Cannibales.'" The "noble savage" motif running through French literature of discovery is excellently studied by Dickason, *Myth of the Savage.*

81. See Lestringant, "Geneva and America."
82. Laudonnière, *Histoire notable.* The work appeared in five more editions: in English (in 1587, coincident with the campaign against Spain and the Armada), German, and, most famously, Latin (*Brevis narratio eorum quae in Florida Americae* [Frankfurt a. M., 1591]). Ribault's original account of Florida—written before the French and Spanish had clashed—appeared only in English: *The whole & true discoverye of Terra Florida* (London, [1563]).
83. Le Challeux, *True and perfect description,* 102, 106.
84. Ibid., 98–100, 104, 116.
85. Ibid., 106. A similar process of "Americanization"—of thematic transposition of New World themes to Old World settings—is analyzed by Mason with reference to witchcraft rites in rural Europe, described by certain elite observers in terms of "Indian savagery": "Seduction from Afar."
86. Parry, "Depicting a New World," 144.
87. Benzoni claimed that curiosity "to see the world" encouraged his journey, yet it is unlikely that he would have boarded the ship in Sanlúcar de Barrameda without a more clearly stated purpose or position in the crew. One of the few known documents of bibliographical significance refers to him as "a silversmith of Milan and a *vecino* of Honduras": see José Toribio Medina, *Bibliotheca Hispano-Americana,* 7 vols. (Santiago de Chile, 1898–1907), 2:115 (cited in Keen, "Vision of America", 108). Useful summaries of Benzoni's background can be found in Anders, "Girolamo Benzoni"; and Vig, "Prefazione."
88. Benzoni was largely responsible for the famous "egg" anecdote, which popularized the image of Columbus as a visionary hero in the employ of thankless Spanish patrons. (Columbus demonstrates to his Spanish hosts how to balance an egg; when they claim that his cunning method is obvious, the *Almirante* replies, "So is discovering a New World, once others show you the way.") See Benzoni, *New World,* 17.
89. Ibid., 83; cf. also 4, 75, 12, 27.
90. Ibid., 40.
91. The most important text to denigrate Spanish deeds in America, Bartholomé de las Casas's *Brevíssima relación de la destruyción de las Indias,* appeared in 1552 and may have exercised some influence, directly or indirectly, on Benzoni, whose text was composed sometime between 1555 and 1565. Las Casas's *relación,* however, would not have reached a wide audience at this point, since it remained untranslated (or even republished) until the Dutch printed and publicized the work in 1578.
92. Benzoni, *New World,* 6, 95, 143, 138, 180, 93–4. The last-cited passage refers, not without a degree of irony, to the "law of Baiona": the code of Spanish-Indian relations promulgated in Burgos in 1512–1513, sanctioning the use of

native labor in the *encomiendas*. Cf. Zárate, *Strange and delectable history*, 64 and *passim* for the heroic image of conquest "by fire and sword."

93. Benzoni, *New World*, 119, 108, 56, 111–12, 77–8. For a useful contrast between Benzoni and Martyr, cf. the far less pessimistic version of Hispaniola's demise, as rendered in the *Decades*: "[T]hese simple, naked natives were little accustomed to labour, and the immense fatigues they now suffer, labouring in the mines, is killing them in great numbers and reducing the others to such a state of despair that many kill themselves, or refuse to procreate their kind. It is alleged that the pregnant women take drugs to produce abortion, knowing that the children they bear will become the slaves of the Christians. Although a royal decree has declared all the islanders to be free, they are forced to work more than is fit for free men. The number of these unfortunate people diminishes in an extraordinary fashion. Many people claim that they formerly numbered more than twelve millions; how many there are today I will not venture to say, so much am I horrified. Let us finish with this sad subject and return to the charms of this admirable Hispaniola" (Anghiera, *Eight Decades*, 1:376). Benzoni's description plainly lacks the "charms" and sparkle of Martyr's humanist vision.

94. Benzoni, *New World*, 6, 8, 33, 147.

95. Ibid., 162, and see also 54 , where Benzoni despairs that even the Apostles would have failed in their mission, if they had been forced to follow in the wake of the Spanish *Conquista*.

96. Ibid., 118–19 (and see 254 for the ill-earned "praise" of the Spanish nation). The celebrated "egg" anecdote (see note 88) effectively conveys the same theme: of Spanish arrogance and—*nota bene*—the wit and talent native to Italy.

97. Vig explores the political context of Benzoni's anti-Spanish attitudes and the possible sources of the Sienna anecdote: "Prefazione," xvii–xix. One also discerns a measure of Christian indignation in Benzoni's narrative, which was dedicated to Pope Pius IV.

98. Francesco Guicciardini's *Istoria d'Italia* (Florence, 1561) was issued approximately thirty times in the sixteenth century alone. Guicciardini also discusses the discovery of America (bk. 6, cap. 9), which he describes as a state of nature (cannibalism notwithstanding) rudely disturbed by greedy and mercenary Spanish invaders, "now digging the gold . . . now purchasing it at ridiculous prices from the inhabitants, and now robbing them of what they had." Like Benzoni, he faults the Spanish equally severely for their failure to fulfill their Christian obligations. See Guicciardini, *History of Italy*, 179. Note, finally, the outbreak in 1563 of anti-Spanish protests in Milan—yet another provocation, in this case two years before Benzoni went to press.

99. Arnoldsson's classic study of the theme convincingly locates the cradle of the Black Legend in Italy, charting its movement northward over the course of the sixteenth century: *Leyenda Negra*. See also Gibson, *Black Legend*; Swart, "Black Legend" (particularly for the Dutch context); and the more extensive discussion of anti-Spanish propaganda in Chapter Two. For Léry's

speculative, if also strategic, invocation of Benzoni, see Whatley, "Révérence réciproque."

100. Seven German editions appeared by 1613, some as the third and fourth parts of de Bry's anthology. De Bry also included the work in his Latin anthologies as *Pars quarta, Pars quinta*, and *Pars sexta* (*EA* provides a complete bibliography). On the role played by Chauveton in popularizing the account, see Keen, "Vision of America." Note, too, that Chauveton appended to his 1579 edition of Benzoni (*Histoire nouvelle du Nouveau Monde*) "une petite histoire d'un massacre commis par les Hespagnols sur quelques François en la Floride"—that is, the very potent, propagandistic narrative of Le Challeux.

101. Benzoni, *Nieuwe weereld*. A second version, with a changed title page, was issued by Gillis Joosten Saeghman in the mid-seventeenth century as part of his travel anthology, *Verscheyde Oost Indische voyagien: Met beschrijvingen van Indien* (Amsterdam, [1663–1670?]).

102. The subject of Europe's earliest visual representations of America has been superbly explored in the agenda-setting studies of Honour: *European Vision; New Golden Land;* and "Science and Exoticism." See also Sturtevant, "First Visual Images"; Levenson, *Circa 1492;* and Vandenbroeck, *America* (the latter particularly relevant for the case of the Netherlands). The sluggish response of artists to the New World would accelerate dramatically in the final years of the sixteenth century, especially following the publication of de Bry's lavishly illustrated *Americae* (1590ff.).

103. Oviedo, *Historia general de las Indias* (1535), and Humboldt, *Ansichten von Natur* (1808) (both cited in Honour, *European Vision,* 1). The outstanding exception to this record of visual indifference—noted as such explicitly by Humboldt—is the production of the entourage of Johan Maurits, governor of Dutch Brazil, in the mid-seventeenth century. See the encyclopedic study of Whitehead and Boeseman, *Seventeenth-Century Brazil,* and the more extensive discussion of Johan Maurits in Chapter Five.

104. The German woodcuts illustrate Vespucci, *Diss büchlin*. See also Moffitt and Sebastián, *Brave New People,* which reproduces these and other of the earliest (and raciest) images of Native Americans; and Léry, *History of a Voyage,* which contains woodcuts from the 1580 edition (for "demons," see 137; for classicized Indians, see 63). Jean Cousin provided illustrations for Thevet's *Cosmographie universelle* and has therefore been credited with the stylized images of the *Singularitez* (there are other woodcuts in both volumes, from a less able hand). Along with the image of "Tobacco and Fire" reproduced here, Cousin would also have been responsible for the splendid representation of the "Maniere de guerroyer de Sauvages de Terre neuve," which shows a Roman-type military procession that could indeed have come from the hand of Mantegna, in whose monumental style it is done (*Singularitez,* 164; tobacco image on 101).

105. For Zárate, see *Warachtighe historie,* esp. 27, 29, 36, and 41; and cf. the identical images in *Ghenuechlijcke historie vanden . . . ridder Peeter van Provencien.* Zárate's Dutch text was printed by W. Silvius for J. Verwithagen. The for-

mer headed one of Antwerp's largest publishing houses and issued, just a few years later, the romance of chivalry, *Les aventures d'Amadis de Gaule*. The latter published a number of histories and cosmographies, including a tale of *oriental* chivalry, *Nieuwe tijdinghe van alle het ghene dat geschiet is tusschen de Christenen ende de ongeloovighe Turcken* (Antwerp, 1565). For de Bry's New World imagination, see Keazor, "De Bry's Images," which details the extensive process of borrowing pursued throughout the *Americae* project. The Deluge scene in question (not in fact discussed by Keazor) is engraved by Jan Sadeler after Maarten de Vos.

106. The woodcuts were part of a series illustrating the triumphal procession of the emperor, Maximilian I. Armitage has argued that the "Calicut" print may have served, if indirectly, as a model for the *Procession Portrait* of Queen Elizabeth I (Sherborne Castle, Dorset), thus complicating even further any traditional iconographic conclusions: "'Procession Portrait.'" For a further (and also Antwerp) example of this sort of iconographic multiculturalism, see the decorative title page of Juan Luis Vives, *De institutione feminae christianae* (Antwerp, 1525), which features a procession of putti, some of whom wear feathered "American" headdresses, leading a miniaturized African elephant.

107. Honour has suggested that the European clothing had been added to the Tupi visitor "to make him presentable in Church": *European Vision*, 27. In all events, the artist has affixed the accouterments of recently discovered "Indians" of the West (and the Portuguese encountered the Tupi of Brazil first in 1500) on this visitor from the East. Van Doesborch's convoluted Americana, based on a text by Balthasar Springer, appeared in an earlier Dutch version with a comparably chaotic illustration program, though a somewhat more accurate title: "The Voyage from Lisbon." This edition is reproduced in facsimile: Springer, *Reyse van Lissebone*. See also note 25.

108. Dürer cited in Panofsky, *Albrecht Dürer*, 1:209; and see Levenson, *Circa 1492*, 572, for the Weiditz drawings. In the sixteenth century, only John White would undertake a systematic program of drawings and watercolors of American images. These images, though, remained confined to a small circle of English colonialists and scholars until they fell into the hands of de Bry and his engravers, who stylized and classicized White's relatively "naturalistic" images. Again: it was de Bry more than anyone who was responsible for disseminating a visual language of the New World. See Hulten and Quinn, *Drawings of John White*; and Keazor, "De Bry's Images."

109. Weiss, "Neues Bild Jan Mostaerts"; Michel, "Tableau colonial." Michel's proposal was broadly accepted by art historians writing through the mid-twentieth century, including Friedländer (*Malerei*, 10:14) and Hoogewerff (*Schilderkunst*, 2:493).

110. Van Luttervelt, "Mostaert's West-Indisch landschap," which directs readers to the unlikely source of *Arizona Highways*. See also Snyder, "Mostaert's West Indies Landscape," which broadly follows van Luttervelt's case for Coronado while nuancing some of the more site-specific contentions pertaining to the American Southwest.

111. Larsen, "Mostaert's West Indian Landscape." Larsen's argument, conceived presumably while he was completing a monograph on Frans Post
and Dutch Brazil, contains a somewhat flawed series of assumptions of European knowledge of Brazil in the mid-sixteenth century. Though Staden
returned to Europe in 1555, his story appeared in print only in 1557, at least
a year after Mostaert's death, and obviously could not have influenced the
artist. Moreover, Brazil as such did not really enter the European imagination until well into the 1550s—when Portugal began to make profitable its
claims on the New World—and, more significantly, in the 1560s, when reports of French polemicists first publicized the Franco-Iberian clashes overseas. Brazil, in all events, hardly loomed as large in European letters as did
Mesoamerica and the Caribbean islands; none of the European-Indian encounters in Brazil got much press. Furthermore, even the most public display of Brazilians during this earlier period, the Rouen festival of 1550, featured *clothed* natives and not the "nude" Tupi that Larsen imagines as the
subject of Mostaert's work: see Denis, *Fête brésilienne,* which excellently reproduces a print of the spectacle. Finally, the parrot, taken by Larsen to be
a symbol specific to Brazil, appeared in fact on other prominent (and
prominently Dutch) publications as a symbol for America more generally:
on Aurelius's 1514 map (see note 13), and on the title page of the Dutch
Cortés (Antwerp, 1523), where the bird is perched, very much as in the
Mostaert panel, on a gnarled tree stump (see fig. 3).
112. Cuttler, "Errata." See also Mason, *Infelicities,* 26–39, which offers a point by
point rebuttal of Cuttler's case by way of demonstrating how American exotica from this period could very well include the ancient, the Asian, and
the generally eclectic sets of iconographies present in the Mostaert panel.
113. Van Mander, *Het leven,* 229, though van Mander (or his sources) possibly
exaggerated on this point. Mostaert came from a family of millers and entered the Haarlem guild of St. Luke around the same time that an upwardly
mobile marriage (to a wealthy widow) elevated his social standing. He
was, in all events, highly regarded by his peers and patrons, and seems to
have acquired a reputation for learning and gentility—what van Mander
considered a "noble" disposition. Biographical and archival data are collected in Thierry de Bye Dólleman, "Jan Jansz Mostaert."
114. The exact years of Mostaert's court period, as mentioned by van Mander,
are still obscure. Friedländer cites a 1521 document referring to a portrait
by "Jehan Masturd," executed sometime before 1504, that might have been
an official commission (*Malerei,* 10:12ff). Yet since Margaretha served from
1506–1529, this source only confuses matters. It is possible that Mostaert
maintained informal contacts with the court (Jacopo de' Barbari served the
regent between 1510 and 1515, and Bernaert van Orley served between
1518 and 1529, according to Friedländer), or with Margaretha's second husband, Philibert of Savoy, who was the subject of the aforementioned portrait. In any case, Mostaert had continual contact with Dutch patrons who,
according to van Mander, valued Mostaert's "refined" background and
payed him the highest respect.

115. The main reports came from Pedro Castañeda de Nájera, whose *relación* was written "twenty years after events" and published only in the eighteenth century. Sabin has an entry for a work by Coronado himself, *Relación del suceso de la jornada que Francisco Vázquez hizo en el descubrimiento de Civola* (1556), yet this volume would have come out after, or only months before, Mostaert's death (probably in 1555, though possibly in 1556). Moreover, since this work is known only from the copy in the Archive of the Indies in Seville, it seems more likely that it functioned as something of an "in-house" document for the use of the Spanish court and not a widely circulating text. See Sabin, *Bibliotheca Americana*, no. 98723.

116. Note that Mostaert's *Portrait of a Woman* also contains, aside from an *arco naturale*, a figure blowing on a horn in a manner similar to the "Indian" of the Haarlem composition (right side of panel). On the Flemish *Weltlandschaften*, see Gibson, *Mirror of the Earth*, which provides numerous samples of "exotic" landscapes within this genre.

117. Bruijn, *Omnium pene*, fig. 42 ("Tartaus gentis more armatus"). Since many early modern commentators considered the Americans descendants of "Tartars," or "Scythians," Mostaert's iconographic footnote here fits nicely, if subtly, into sixteenth-century ethnographic and etiological theory.

118. The visual representation of Arcadianism in the Renaissance is studied in a suggestive and gracefully argued essay of Panofsky, "Early History of Man." Cf. also the "primitivism" depicted in Cornelis van Dalem's *Dawn of Civilization* (Museum Boijmans Van Beuningen, Rotterdam), a painting that, with its prominent *arco naturale* and pastoral setting, hints at yet another iconographic context for Mostaert's "West Indies."

119. Van Mander, *Het Leven*, sig. 229v: "Daer is ook een Landtschap, wesende een West-Indien, met veel naeckt volck, met een bootstighe Clip, en vreemt ghebouw van huysen en hutten: doch is onvoldaen gelaten."

120. Karel van Mander, *Het leven der oude antijcke doorluchtighe schilders* (Alkmaar, 1603), and *Het leven der moderne, oft des-tijtsche doorluchtighe Italiaensche schilders* (Alkmaar, 1603), both of which were published, with the Dutch "Lives," under the collective title, *Het schilder-boeck*. Van Mander's literary translations were all made from Latin originals, with the exception of the *Iliad*, which he reworked from a French translation of the Greek. For complete titles and dates and the standard bibliography of van Mander, see Miedema, *Van Mander*. For van Mander's Italian trip, see Noë, *Van Mander en Italië*; and on the composition of the *Schilder-boeck*, see Melion, *Shaping of the Netherlandish Canon*.

121. This unidentified work is mentioned in the biography of van Mander appended to the *Schilder-boeck* (1618 edition) and composed, it is believed, by the artist's brother, Adam van Mander, or by G. A. Bredero. See *Geslacht*, sig. [Riiij]r. Van Mander also painted an *Arcadian Landscape* (1596) and *Massacre of the Innocents* (1600). Leesberg, "Van Mander as painter," provides a full catalogue of the known paintings.

122. Reznicek, "Van Mander as a Fresco Painter"; and idem, "Een en ander." The frescoes show *The Wounded Admiral Gaspard de Coligny, The Massacre of*

the Huguenots on St. Bartholomew's Eve, and *King Charles IX Sanctioning De Coligny's Assassination.*

123. *Geslacht,* sigs. [Riiij]v–Sr.

124. Van Mander, *Grondt,* 42v and 51v. See also van Mander's commentary on Ovid's *Metamorphosis,* where a discussion of Aeneas's rescue of Achaemenides (his former enemy) leads to ruminations on the noble character of the primitive "West Indians," who "lived among one another in greater harmony, equality, and peace, and with greater affection" than did the Europeans: idem, *Wtleggingh,* 110v. For the "Aureas Aetas" in its original form, see Ovid, *Metamorphosis* 1.89–112.

125. Karel van Mander, "Sonnetten van den Overseter," in Benzoni, *Nieuwe weereld:*

> Hard ijser wapen, daer te vooren noyt gesien
> Ter droever tijt, daer quam in wissel boven dien
> Den noyt gedwongen hals, swaer jock heeft moeten dulden:
> Saturnij eeuwe soet, voor eeuwich daer geplant
> Is dit ellendich volck, ghewisselt daer int lant
> Hard ijserich is den tijdt, die was te vooren gulden.

126. Passchier van Wesbusch, Dedication, in Benzoni, *Nieuwe weereld,* sig. Aij-v.

127. For the chronology of van Mander's literary activity, see Regteren Altena, "Carel van Mander"; and Miedema, *Van Mander.*

128. Las Casas, *Seer cort verhael,* and see *EA,* vols. 1–2, for further editions. Acosta's volume appeared in 1598, translated by Jan Huygen van Linschoten: *Historie naturael ende morael van de Westersche Indien* (Haarlem).

Chapter Two

1. Philip II to the duchess of Parma, 17 October 1565, in *Correspondance française,* 99–103. The letters also appear, excerpted and translated, in Kossmann and Mellink, *Texts,* 53–6. For the nobles' Request, see *Copye vande Requeste,* and cf. Kossmann, *Texts,* 62–5. On the significance of the developments of 1565–1566, see Israel, *Dutch Republic* (1995), 137–46 (which notes the "sensational effect" of the king's letters); Parker, *Dutch Revolt,* 68–70; and Geyl, *Revolt of the Netherlands,* 84–8. The political background of the Revolt more generally is reviewed in van Gelderen, *Political Thought;* and Kossmann, *Texts,* 1–51. The classic account of Motley, *Rise of the Dutch Republic,* still provides one of the more dramatic recitations of these events.

2. "Verbintenis van eenige Eedelen," in Water, *Historie van het verbond,* 4:61.

3. Lechner, "Dutch Humanists."

4. Zárate, *Warachtighe historie* (1563). A 1564 edition appeared likewise in Antwerp (with a preface identical to that of the 1563 edition), as did the Spanish original of 1555. All were published with royal privileges and, it should be added, in relatively accessible octavo.

5. Ibid., sigs. *2r–[*4]r. This sense of pride in Habsburg expansion is underscored by a map by Ioan Bellero (Jean Bellère) inserted after the first folio and decorated with a large, double-headed eagle and the Habsburg coat of arms.

The map's effect—and it was included only in Dutch editions of the six-teenth century—would seem to highlight rather than diminish the Habs-burg role in an epic *Conquista*. For a similar expression of Dutch pride in the progress of empire, see the discussion of America (and the escutcheoned map) in Aurelius, *Cronycke van Hollandt*, sigs. 15r and 279r.

6. Duncanus, *Vruchten der ecclesie Christi*, t.p.; and Ablijn, *Nieuwe weerelt*. Dun-canus (or Donk) was a Delft priest who sought to praise the achievements of the Catholic Church by pointing particularly to the evidence of Spanish America. Though the volume appeared in 1567 (in the, at that time, rela-tively sleepy town of Leiden), the text had been prepared for publication al-ready in 1566: see Noordeloos, *Maarten Donk*. On Ablijn, see the later dis-cussion.

7. On the convoluted bibliography of Ablijn's text, see Sabin, *Bibliotheca Amer-icana*, nos. 34100–107; and Alden and Landis, *European Americana*, 1:103. The contents of the compilation (for which Münster composed the original in-troduction) are discussed in Korinman, "Grynaeus et le 'Novus Orbis'"; and Johnson, "New Geographical Horizons."

8. Ablijn, *Nieuwe weerelt*, sig. *iiij-v and, more generally, sigs. *ii-v–[iiij]-r: "Al-soo moegen alle staeten der menschen, nuttelijc in desen boecke lesen, een yegelijck na sijnen verstande, ende alle int ghemeyne hen seer verwonderen ende danckbaer sijn. Dat Godt in desen lesten tijden, een sulcks groot getal der menschen, eerst bekent heeft laten worden . . . [D]aer af hen ende ons, groot proofiit comen mach. Hen, om dat sy waerachtich verstant van Godt ende Goddelijcke dingen vanden onsen leeren mogen. . . . Maer wy moghen voordaen tot grooter goet by hen comen, om goudt, peerlen, ende costelijck ghesteente, oock menigerley specerye, ende cruyden tot ghemeynen ghe-bruyck ende oock tot medecynen."

9. Heyns, *Spieghel der werelt*. Heyns, a schoolmaster in Antwerp, prominent member of the Chamber of Rhetoric in Berchem (near Antwerp), and friend of Ortelius, also composed a French version of the *Spieghel*, which appeared two years later (Antwerp, 1579), and an expanded edition of the Dutch work (Antwerp, 1583), which contained the elaborate introduction discussed in this chapter. These editions served as the basis for further French (1588, 1590, 1598) and Latin (1589, 1595) publications of what must be counted among the most widely dispersed atlases of the late sixteenth century. The maps for all editions were based on engravings by Philips Galle.

10. Heyns, *Spieghel der werelt*, sigs. **2v–**4v and passim.

11. On Silvius, see Blouw, "Silvius's remarkable start"; and Clair, "Willem Sil-vius." On Ablijn, see the *Biographie nationale*, 44 vols. (Brussels, 1866–1986), 1:4. Vosters, *Nederlandse literatuur*, discusses the idealized image of Spain in Netherlandish literature, both before and after the Revolt. Broader relations between the Low Countries and early Habsburg Spain are more meticu-lously studied in Fagel, *Hispano-Vlaamse wereld*.

12. The list of specifically and primarily Dutch-authored texts, published before the Revolt and mentioning America, is short. It includes, for example, a 1529 letter sent by the Franciscan missionary, Pieter van Gent (Pedro de Gante;

see Chapter One), which describes conditions in Mexico and is printed in van Zierikzee's *Chronica compendiosissima* (1534) and Duncanus's *Vruchten* (1567); the scattered comments of Gemma Frisius on the geographical and astrological ramifications of the discoveries that appear in his *Principiis astronomiae* (1530; and Frisius's Americana derived largely from the work of his teacher, the German mathematician Petrus Apianus, who condensed earlier descriptions of Spanish and Italian authors); and the botanical observations of Dodoens, including mention of tobacco, in his *Cruydeboeck* (1554).

13. *Vriendelicke vermaninghe*, sig. Aiv-r; *Vriendelijcke waerschouwinghe*, sig. Cvii-v; [Marnix], *Antwoorde op een cleyn boecxken*, 36 (printed by the renowned Christoffel Plantijn, who was appointed *prototypographus* by the duke of Alba and later *prototypographus regius* by Philip II).

14. *Beschriivinge van de gheschiedenissen*, 180–31; *Fidelle exhortation*, 13. On the ferocious war of words waged by the rebels, see van Nierop, "Censorship."

15. *Fidelle exhortation*, 13. On the rebels' propaganda, see the classic study of Geurts, *Nederlandse Opstand in de pamfletten;* the very useful (if underutilized) analysis by Van Ryn, "Patriotic Propaganda"; and Swart's provocative "Black Legend." The use of pamphlets in the Republic more generally is examined by Harline, *Pamphlets;* and see also van Gelderen, *Political Thought,* which offers a thorough review of the political and theoretical underpinnings of these materials.

16. The construction of a "national" identity among the Dutch rebels is analyzed, with an eye toward literary themes, by Spies, "Verbeeldingen van Vrijheid"; and Smits-Veldt, "Hollands zelfbewustzijn." For the dilemma of a national revolt in a prenational age, see Groenveld, "Natie en nationaal gevoel"; Rowen, "Dutch Revolt"; and, more generally, van Gelderen, *Political Thought.* On the endeavor of "writing a nation," see the suggestive studies (albeit in an early modern English context) of Helgerson, *Forms of Nationhood;* Knapp, *Empire Nowhere;* and Fuller, *Voyages in Print.*

17. Duke, "Salvation by Coercion"; and idem, "Legend in the Making." See also Truman and Kinder, "Pursuit of Spanish Heretics"; and Thomas, "Mythe van de Spaanse Inquisitie."

18. "Compromise," in Kossmann, *Texts,* 59–62. The reference to "foreigners" alludes most likely to Cardinal Granvelle who, though born in France, was no more foreign than the author of the (French-languaged) *Compromis,* Jean de Marnix, Lord of Toulouse. On the battle between Reformers and Inquisitors, see the excellent essays collected in *Ketters en papen.*

19. *Copye vande Requeste;* [Clercq], *Remonstrance,* sig. Aii-v and fols. 21r and 2r (and see 21v and 16r for a further discussion of the Inquisitor's habitual abuse of rights). The Request was published without royal privileges.

20. *Heylighe Spaensche inquisitie,* and see also the preface of the Norwich edition of the same year (with a slightly different title), sig. *ij-r; *Beschriivinge van de gheschiedenissen,* 180; "Waerschowinghe des Prince van Oraengien aen de ingheseten ende ondersaten van den Nederlanden," in Willem, *Geschriften van*

1568, 121 (and cf. Knuttel, *Pamfletten,* no. 168); *Fidelle exhortation,* 14–15. Willem's subtly colonialist complaint of "foreign invaders"—this despite the fact that the government derived largely from local populations—recurs throughout rebel literature and notably in the Pacification of Ghent, whose adherents swore "to drive and keep out of the provinces the Spanish soldiers and other foreigners" (Kossmann, *Texts,* 127).

21. [Clercq], *Remonstrance,* sig. Aii-v; "Verbintenis van eenige Eedelen," 61; [Saravia], "Een hertgrondighe begheerte vanden edelen, lanckmoedighen hoochgheboren Prince van Oraengien," in Willem, *Geschriften van 1568,* 139 (and cf. also 136); Mout, *Plakkaat van Verlatinge,* 105, and cf. Kossmann, *Texts,* 220, whose translation I have followed. Adrianus Saravia's rather interesting career—he went on to become a leading Calvinist theologian and a professor at Leiden before going into exile—is charted by Nijenhuis, *Adrianus Saravia.* Alba's comments ("Si V. M. mira bien lo que hay que hacer, verá que es plantar un mundo nuevo") appear in a letter to the king (6 January 1568) cited by Parker, "Francisco de Lixalde."

22. Marnix, *Vraye narration,* sigs. A6–A7, B1r; *Boecxken van de dry Pausen.* From internal evidence, it would appear that this second pamphlet was published originally in 1566 or 1567, though it is not a translation of *Les subtils moyens par le Cardinal de Granvelle,* as Swart surmised ("Black Legend," 40–1).

23. *Artijckelen ende besluyten;* and "Besluyt des Officiums teghen het volck van de Nederlanden," printed in ibid. The "Articles of the Inquisition" were apparently accepted as authentic until Royaards "exposed" them in the nineteenth century: "Nederlandsche volksgeest in de XVI [*sic*] eeuw." Belief in the veracity of the "Advice" was undermined only in the twentieth century: Blok, "Advies der Spaansche Inquisitie."

24. *Artijckelen ende besluyten,* sig. Av and passim; "Besluyt des Officiums," sig. Aij; Montanus, *Sanctae Inquisitionis.* Montanus's work was also published in Dutch (three times), German (twice), English (twice), and French, all in the years 1567–1569. On the identity of the author, see Vermaseren, "Reginaldus Gonsalvus Montanus."

25. *Boecxken van de dry Pausen,* sig. Biij-r; *Defense and true declaration,* sig. Av; "Warachtige waerschouwinghe teghens de absolute gratie ende generael pardoen by Don Loys de Requesens," in Fredericq, *Nedelandsche proza,* 63. The highly influential Emden *Defense* was published originally in Latin— *Libellus supplex Imperatoriae Maiestati* and *Apologeticon, et vera rerum in Belgicogermania nuper gestarum narratio*—promptly rendered into English, yet never translated into Dutch. A slighlty edited version appears in van Gelderen, *Dutch Revolt* (1993; hereafter cited as *Revolt*), 1–77. The pamphlet's authorship has traditionally been attributed to the Reformed minister Petrus Dathenus, yet recent research suggests Marnix as a possible candidate: Nauta, "Auteur van de Libellus Supplex." On the exile community in Emden, see Pettegree's fine study, *Emden and the Dutch Revolt.*

26. On the topos of the king's "evil-advisors," see Geurts, *Pamfletten,* 131–6; and Kossmann, *Texts,* 15. An early and classic expression of the theme appears

in Willem's "Waerschowinghe," which singles out for attack both Granvelle and Alba as men who took "unfair advantage of the faith and trust of the good Prince" (*Geschriften van 1568,* 121).

27. On the duke of Alba, see Maltby, *Alba,* esp. 110–261. Case studies of Alba's Council and fiscal policies include Verheyden, *Conseil des Troubles;* Dierickx, "Raad van beroertren"; and Grapperhuis, *Tiende Penning.* On the iron duke's army, see Parker, *Army of Flanders;* and for the massacres and mutinies of the mid-1570s, see idem, *Revolt,* 140–2.

28. See, for example, Janssens, "Alva's bestuur"; and Dierickx, "Nieuwe gegevens." It is worth noting that Alba had relatively little success in introducing, let alone collecting, his various and innovative taxes: Janssens, "Brabant in verzet"; and Craeybeckx, "Alva's tiende penning." On the other hand, Parker (*Revolt,* 298 n. 17) suggests that Alba's stern military policy did enjoy certain successes.

29. The terminology is Parker's (*Revolt,* 15 and passim), though his periodization has been implicitly followed by others—lately, for example, by van Gelderen (cf. *Political Thought,* 40–5).

30. "Remonstrance of William of Nassau, prince of Orange etc., redeemer of the freedom of the Netherlands, to the States and the people, 1572," in Kossmann, *Texts,* 94. Phalaris, who is also mentioned by Marnix in the *Oratio legatorum* (1578), was a tyrant of Acragas (ca. 550 B.C.E.) renowned for his cruelty and alleged habit of roasting his enemies in a hollow bronze bull. Sardanapalus was the last king of the Assyrian empire of Nineveh (ninth century B.C.E.) and gained a reputation for luxury and sloth—including the "effeminate" habit of crossdressing.

31. *Brieven van advertissemen,* 44; *Afgheworpene brieven,* sig. [A2]r; Parker, *Revolt,* 129–30; *Copie eens sendtbriefs,* sig. Biij-r. The mortar metaphor derives from medieval exegeses of Exodus 5:6–18. The more provincial "butter" trope served, ironically, as the basis for future Hollandophobia in the seventeenth-century English taunt that Hollanders were boorish "butter boxes": cf. Pincus, "Butterboxes to Wooden Shoes."

32. "Sendbrief in forme van Supplicatie aen die Con. Maj. van Spangien," in Fredericq, *Nederlandsche proza,* 51: "Ende, so het moghelic ware uwe Majesteyt voor ooghen te stellen, die onredelicheden, gewelden ende ongehoorde wreetheden, die alhier van den beginne zijns regiments ommegegaen zijn int plonderen, rooven ende ruyten, verjagen ende verwoesten, int vangen ende spannen, int bannen, verdrijven and goedern confisquieren, ja int bernen ende blaken, hangen, kappen, hacken, raybraken ende met afgrijselicke ende noyt gehoorde tormenten pijnigen ende vermoorden die ondersaten uwer Majesteyt so wel edelen als onedelen, armen als rijcken, jonck als out, weduwen ende weesen, mannen, vrouwen ende jonge maechden." The more succinct "savage wardogs of Spain" comes from the "Gentsche Vaderonze" (Paternoster of Ghent) cited in Motley, *Dutch Republic,* 3:508.

33. Brugmans, "Utrechtsche kroniek"; "Remonstrance of William of Nassau," 95. For a local study of reactions to the Spanish army, see van Deursen, "Holland's Experience of War."

34. *Vriendelicke vermaninghe,* sig. [Aiv]: "Dat sy ordre souden stellen op de ee-
terijen, plonderijen ende ander onghemacken door de welcke de arme Ondersaten ten platten lande grondtlick bedorven worden, en is van hen niet
te verwachten als de welcke meynen haer grootheyt ende verseeckertheyt
van heerschen ghelegen te wesen inde verderving ende armoede der Ghe-
meente. Het welck ons betuyghen mochte het Coninckrijck van Naples, Si-
cilien, Sardinien, en alle anderen Landen, in welcke sy de overhandt ghe-
creghen hebben. . . . Jae inde nieuwe ghevonden Landen, van de welcke sy
hem soo hooch beroemen, hebben sy de Inghebooren byna gheleelicken
ombrocht, op dat sy met weynich Spangiaerden . . . de reste te beter onder
hare bedwanck ende tyrannije mochte houden."

35. "Warachtige waerschouwinghe," 63; "Corte daer na is een aenslach
gebleken op den Pinxterdach, . . . Een nieu Liedeken," in Leendertz, *Geuzenliedboek,* 1:221 ("Sulcks als hy in Indien heeft ghedaen, / Ende meynt ons
oock soo te verraen, / Om Hollant en Zeelant te doen sterven / Ende gants
inden gront te bederven").

36. On Requesens, see Lovett, "New Governor"; and idem, "Don Luís de Requesens." For the propaganda campaign against Requesens: Geurts, *Pamfletten,* 48–55, 180–1; and Van Ryn, "Patriotic Propaganda," 92.

37. Parker, *Revolt,* 178; and more generally idem, *Army of Flanders.*

38. "Kort verhael van de rechte oorsaecken ende redenen, die de Generale
staten der Nederlanden gedwongen hebben, hen te versien tot hunder
beschermenisse, tegens den Heere Don Jehan van Oostenrijck," in Bor,
Byvoegsel, 1:161 (and cf. also Knuttel, *Pamfletten,* nos. 305 and 310). Requesens is cited in Parker, *Revolt,* 172.

39. Root, "Speaking Christian," addresses the "production of Morisco difference" in the Spanish context.

40. *Brieven van advertissement,* 21; Marnix, *Oratio legatorum;* Willem, *Apologie,* 52
(and on the *Apologie* and *Oratio,* see, nn. 42 and 77 resp.). For further examples of attacks on Don Juan, see those pamphlets cited in Knuttel, *Pamfletten,* nos. 343, 347, 354, and 379; for comparisons between the Spanish and
Carthaginians/Scythians, see ibid., nos. 361, 379, and 392. The Turkish topos
is discussed later.

41. On the composition of the Spanish army, see Parker, *Army of Flanders,* esp.
28, 271–2. Elsewhere Parker notes how rebel troops, from 1576, organized
their opposition under such rhetoricaly suggestive banners as *Pugno pro Patria* and *Pro Fide et Patria*—surely an effort to rally their forces to a unified
"Dutch" cause (*Revolt,* 15).

42. *Lettre contenant un avis,* in Kossmann, *Texts,* 153 (and cf. *Antwoorde van de
generale Staten,* in ibid., 151–52); Willem, *Apologie,* 53–4. Like many of the
rebel propagandists, Willem targeted a broad, international audience and
had the *Apologie,* written originally in French, immediately translated into
Dutch, German, Latin, and English. All citations come from the reprint of
the original English edition and have been crosschecked with the French
and Dutch versions.

43. Willem, *Apologie,* 53. As this and the quotations in the previous paragraph

well illustrate, Orange, or at least his ghostwriters, had a penchant for medical metaphors.

44. [Marnix], *Antwoorde op een cleyn boecxken,* 11, 14, 35: "De Spaignaert is zeer
hoveerdich, wraeckgierich ende tyrannich: ende meynen wy dat sy ons met
wapenen ghebrocht hebbende onder haerlieder subjectie, ons souden lief-
flijck ende vriendelijc tracteren? . . . wat moeten wy dan verwachten vande
ghene, dien hoverdye, opgheblasenheyt ende wreetheyt natuerlijcker is,
dan natuere selve? Laet ons voor ons stellen d'exempel vande Indianen,
ende ons voor oogen legghen dat ons naecomers ghetracteert sullen worden ghelijck als die."

45. *Clare vertoning,* sigs. Br, Cv, C4: "Om niet te verhalen die exempelen van
Naples, Milanen, Granaden, ende insonderheydt van Indyen, daer sy naer
haer eygene getuychgenisse over die twintich Millionen menschen sielen
moordadelick hebben omme gebracht, ende veele landen die grooter waren
als van Castilien tot Constantinopel ofte Jerusalem geheelyck ende wt den
gronde verwoestent ende gants eensaem hebben gemaect."

46. Cf., for example, Knuttel, *Pamfletten,* nos. 343, 354, 422, 440, 492, and 500,
all of which appeared in 1578–1579 and each of which mentions Spain in
America.

47. Blok, "Willem's 'Apologie'"; and more generally Swart, *Willem van Oranje.*

48. Willem, *Apologie,* 53, 55, 58–9.

49. Ibid., 59; *Plakkaat van Verlatinge,* 97, 99, 105, 117. Both of these documents, of
course, had a significant and widespread influence on public debate. See,
for example, the *Politicq onderwijs* (1582), published in the wake (and in support) of the Abjuration, which likewise makes reference to the histories of
the Indies, imploring its readers to "reread them often." The pamphlet is
reprinted in van Gelderen, *Revolt,* 163–226 (quotation on 209).

50. Koenigsberger, *Practice of Empire,* 48; Parker, "Francisco de Lixalde," 8;
Willem, *Apologie,* 58; *Plakkaat van Verlatinge,* 105. There exists one further,
and notably ironic, precedent that dates from 1520, when the Communeros
demanded of the new Habsburg monarch, Charles V, that he cease to treat
his Castilian subjects "as Indians." In this case, though, it was Spanish subjects complaining to "foreign" (read Habsburg) overlords of imperial, indeed colonial, rule. See Kamen, *Spain,* 78.

51. Parker, "Francisco de Lixalde," 8. On the *Geuzen,* see Cornelissen, *Waarom
zij Geuzen werden genoemd;* and van Nierop's semiotic study, "Beggars Banquet," which provides an extensive bibliography. The dismissal of the
Geuzen originated, of course, not with a Castilian as such, but a Dutch nobleman serving on Margaret's council—most likely the seigneur of Berlay-
mont, a Walloon of Namur—who, although certainly pro-Habsburg in his
politics, could only have registered as "Spanish" by the rebels' imaginative
calculus.

52. The pioneering study on the origins of the Black Legend is Arnoldsson,
Leyenda Negra. See also Keen's critique, "Black Legend Revisited"; and
Hanke's reply, "Modest Proposal." A useful anthology of sources and sen-

sible summary of the debate can be found in Gibson, *Black Legend.* For an updated overview of the historiography, see García Carcel, *Leyenda Negra.*

53. "Relazioni de Gasparo Contarini . . . a dì 16 Novembre 1525," in Alberi, *Relazioni,* 1st ser., 2:50, and cf. 2:51–4. On Contarini (who was friends with Peter Martyr, the probable source of his American information), see Gleason, *Gasparo Contarini.* For the Spanish military presence in Italy, see Elliott, *Imperial Spain,* 133–4. The Black Legend in Italy is examined by Arnoldsson, *Leyenda Negra,* 24–103, who notes the anti-Catalan tone that dominated anti-Spanish rhetoric until the late fifteenth century, targeting especially the medieval Aragonese conquerers of Sicily and Sardinia.

54. [Ponet], *Short treatise,* sig. [Fvii]; Loades, *Mary Tudor,* 213, 237, 229. Ponet (1514–1556) served as bishop of Winchester from March 1550/1. He fled England when Mary ascended the throne and ended up in the Protestant community of Strasbourg, where he composed the *Short treatise.* Many of his anti-Spanish themes, it should be stressed, were abandoned by English authors of the next quarter century—until, that is, Hakluyt and others revived them in the 1580s, and only *after* Dutch pamphleteers had codified them in the 1570s. See, by contrast, Richard Eden's emphatically *pro*-Spanish introduction to Martyr's *Decades,* published virtually simultaneously with Ponet's treatise—and discussed below.

55. On anti-Spanish sentiment in France, see Yardeni, *Conscience nationale;* Sutherland, *Massacre of St. Bartholomew;* Kelley, *Beginning of Ideology;* and Pollmann, "Natürliche Feindschaft." Pollmann follows Arnoldsson (*Leyenda Negra,* 104–33) in tracing the Black Legend to Germany, showing the possible influence that the German variant might have had on the Dutch. She cites, for example, Luther's opinion that the Spanish were naturally arrogant, cruel, and heathen (79). To this might be added the testimony of Luther's exact contemporary, Francisco Guicciardini, who was equally dismissive of the Spaniards, whom he characterized, in notably similar terms, as "small in stature and haughty by nature" (cited in Gibson, *Black Legend,* 32).

56. On Orange's internationalism, see Sutherland, "Orange and the Revolt." Another Franco-Dutch connection ran directly through a central piece of Calvinist Americana: the dedication "à Madame la Princesse d'Orange" in the fourth edition of Léry's *Histoire d'un voyage* (Geneva, 1599).

57. Jon, *Brief discours;* Duplessis-Mornay, *Discours.* On the authorship of the *Apologie,* see Blok, "Willem's 'Apologie.'"

58. Kelley, "Background of St. Bartholomew," 183–4. Kelley considers the leading figures of the Protestant community "something approaching a literary circle, a kind of Protestant pleiade of the exile circuit." In this regard he follows Koenigsberger, who describes "international Calvinism" in his important article, "Organization of Revolutionary Parties." See also Prestwich, *International Calvinism;* and Benedict et al., *Reformation, Revolt and Civil War.*

59. Crespin, *Livres des martyrs;* van Haemstede, *Martelaren.* The third edition of van Haemstede (1566) appeared after the author's death in 1562 and is of-

ten presumed to be the work of Crespin's friend, Guido de Bray. On Crespin, van Haemstede, and de Bray, see Pijper, *Martelaarsboeken;* and Jelsma, *Van Haemstede.* On the myths that arose following the St. Bartholomew's Day Massacre, see Kingdon, *Myths.* Gregory, *Salvation at Stake,* situates these sources in their early modern "martyrological" context.

There were plenty of non-Calvinist pamphleteers, of course, whose propaganda would naturally have avoided the Protestant tropes familiar to the Reformed writers. Still, as Van Ryn has shown ("Patriotic Propaganda"), Calvinists played a disproportionately large role among the propagandists, whatever the makeup of the rebel party more generally.

60. See Anghiera, *Decades of the newe worlde.* Eden, who obtained a position in the treasury under Prince Philip in 1554, dedicated his work of the following year, "Potentissimo al serenissimo Philippo." Also instructive is the preface, "Rycharde Eden to the reader" (sigs. a.i.r-[d.iii.]v), in which the kings of Spain are compared to the gods of antiquity for their role in bringing reason, culture, and (Christian) religion to New World (sig. a.i.v). In a passage that could hardly contrast more with the prose of Ponet, Eden notes "that the heroical feates of the Spaniardes of these days, deserve so great prayse that [the] authour of this booke (beinge no Spanyarde) doth woorthely extolle theyr doynge above the famous actes of Hercules and Saturnus and such other which for theyr glorious and vertuous enterpryses were accoumpted as goddes amonge men" (sig. a.ii.r).

61. See Pijper, *Martelaarsboeken,* 5–7, and cf. Léry, *History of a Voyage,* 218, which explains how Léry gave his manuscript personally "to the printer Jean Crespin who . . . inserted it into the *Book of Martyrs.*"

62. Verheiden, *Nootelijcke consideratien,* sigs. Cv, B3: "Indien men meyndt dat dit maer woorden zijn, leest t'ghene de Spaengaerden selve hebben gheschreven van hare Indische handelinghen, daer zy selve verhalen allen wt haren lust, oft omsichtelijck te maken, vele millioenen menschen vermoort te hebben die hen noyt vergrampt oft yet misdaen hadden, op dy welcke zy oock t'minste recht van heerschappije niet en hadden."

63. *Vriendelicke vermaninghe,* sig. Aiv-r; Marnix, *Bijencorf; Defense and true declaration,* Av (for which see van Gelderen, *Revolt,* 18, and note 25). Marnix cites Gómara in relating the famous story of Atahualpa, "King of Peru," and the Incan ruler's rejection of papal authority (*Bijencorf,* 134v). Note that, in the context of his diatribe against the Catholic Church, Marnix has nimbly transformed the Incan ruler into a proto-Protestant. On the sources used for the *Byencorf,* see Sterck, *Bronnen en samenstelling;* and cf. Brouwer, *Library of Philip Marnix.*

64. "Den lusthof van rhetorica," in van Vloten, *Nederlandsche geschiedzangen,* 1: 336 ("Merct wat een bisschop van de Spaenjaerts heeft geschreven, / Hoe sy d'Indiaensche heerlicke rijcken hebben verstoort"); Willem, *Apologie,* 59.

65. Accounts of the life and works of Las Casas include Hanke's standard biographies, *Life and Writing* and *Bookman, Scholar, and Propagandist;* Bataillon, *Las Casas;* and Giménez Fernández, *Las Casas.* A brief, though excellent, review of the *Brevíssima relación* within its historical context can be found in

Pagden's Introduction to Las Casas, *Short Account,* xiii–xli. See also Pagden's provocative essay on the "autoptic imagination" in *European Encounters,* 51–87.

66. Pagden notes just how self-conscious Las Casas's conversion was and how important it would have been to *represent* the experience to his readers in terms as Pauline as possible ("Introduction," xx–xxii).

67. On Las Casas's fortunes and on the reception of his ideas and published texts, see Friede and Keen, *Las Casas in History,* especially Keen's essay, "Approaches to Las Casas," 3–61. Las Casas's ideas attracted considerable attention in the debates on American policy that took place in mid-sixteenth-century Spain: see Pagden, *Fall of Natural Man.* Outside of Spain, however, the contents of these debates were less well-known, and the *Brevíssima relación* itself is scarcely quoted before 1578. Writing in the 1570s and 1580s, Montaigne would still cite Benzoni and Gómara—not Las Casas—in his famous critique of Spanish cruelties in the New World.

68. *Tyrannies et cruautez des Espagnols, perpetrees e's Indes Occidentales, qu'on dit Le Nouveau monde . . . . Pour servir d'exemple & advertissement aux XVII Provinces du païs bas. Heureux celuy qui devient sage en voyant d'autry le dommage* (Antwerp, 1579).

69. For the bibliography of the *Brevíssima relación,* see Hanke and Giménez Fernández, *Bibliografía crítica,* and Alden, *European Americana.* On the reception of the work in the Netherlands, see Lechner, "'Brevíssima relación'"; and more generally Afanasiev, "Literary Heritage." The French illustrated edition is studied by Conley, "De Bry's Las Casas."

70. A more complete discussion of the use made by Dutch authors of Las Casas is taken up in the following chapters.

71. *Vriendelicke vermaninghe; Defense and true declaration;* "Verbintenis van eenige Eedelen"; and *Historie van B. Cornelis Andriaensen,* 86, which satires events of 1566.

72. Touron, *Histoire générale,* 2:373, and cf. more generally 2:372–4. Keen cites Touron ("Black Legend," 712; I have altered his translation slightly) and reviews more broadly the reactions to Las Casas and the success of the *Brevíssima relación.* He suggests here and elsewhere ("Vision of America") that the Calvinist publicist, Urbain Chauveton, played a central role in bringing Las Casas to a wider audience. Chauveton, however, first mentions Las Casas in 1573—already *after* Dutch rebels had begun to develop their topos of Spanish tyranny in America—and without mentioning specifically the *Brevíssima relación,* which would appear in print only five years later.

73. *Trouhertighe vermaninghe.*

74. See, for example, Lynch, *Spain,* 95–105 and passim; Elliott, *Imperial Spain,* 164–81 and 247–77. On the perception of "universal monarchy" outside of the Netherlands, see Swart, "Black Legend"; and Pollmann, "Natürliche Feindschaft."

75. Though debates on a *monarchia universalis* did take place. See Pagden, *Lords of all the World,* 29–62 and passim; and Armitage, *Theories of Empire,* especially the essays by Headly and Bosbach.

76. *Boecxken van de dry Pausen,* sig. Biij-r; *Artijckelen ende besluyten* (1568); and cf. a similarly inspired pamphlet that appeared a few years later, *Avijs der ijnquizicie* (1571).

77. Marnix, *Oratio legatorum.* This pamphlet was translated into French (*Oraison des ambassadeurs du serenissime Prince Matthias* [Antwerp, 1578]) and later into Dutch by Bor: *Nederlantsche oorloghen,* 1:953–60 (esp. 958–9).

78. *Schriftelick bewijs,* 9–10; *Verhael op de questure,* sigs. A3r, A2r; *Pithie and most earnest exhortation,* 5–6, 19, 62–5; and cf. also the *Trouhertighe vermaninghe* (which, like the 1583 *Exhortation,* is attributed to Marnix).

79. See Holt, *Duke of Anjou;* Wilson, *Queen Elizabeth;* and Oosterhoff, *Leicester.*

80. Cited in de Vrankrijker, *Motiveering,* 120 n. 4: "al waer hij een Tartar, een Samaritaen, oft een Moscoviter, iae een Turcq, so verre als hy ons uyt den noot kan gehelpen ende onse privilegien, rechten, vrijheden ende Religie wilt bewaren ende onderhouden, wy moetent van Godes hant nemen, ten sy dat wij teghen Godt willen rebellich ende wederspannich sijn." Note how Christiani, the secretary in question, has equated the act of rebellion with religious orthodoxy and transformed complacency into heresy ("to act ... defiantly against God"). "Samaritan," one suspects, is a mistake for "Samoyeden," a member of a Uralic tribe associated with the Tartars.

81. The history of Dutch relations with the Ottomans is surveyed by de Groot, *Ottoman Empire.* On Dutch perceptions of the Turks in the sixteenth century particularly, see Mout, "Turken in het nieuws"; and cf. Mout's prior essay, focusing on the seventeenth century, "Calvinoturcisme." One important, non-Dutch initiative can also be cited: the Franco-Turkish alliance engineered in 1536 by an embattled François I "to erode the power of the Emperor"—in this case, Charles V. See Hale, *Civilization of Europe,* 38–43, which describes more broadly the ambivalence of Renaissance Europe toward its most important eastern neighbor.

82. Parker, "Spain, her Enemies and the Revolt of the Netherlands, 1559–1648," in *Spain and the Netherlands,* 29; Parker, *Revolt,* 165; van Gelder, "Bailleul, Bronkhorst, Brederode," in *Van Beeldenstorm tot Pacificatie,* 68–9.

83. Heyns, *Spieghel der werelt,* 52:

> Maer dat haer de Fortune licht laet bewegen,
> Blijckt hier oock: want het swaert van Zelimus bebloeyt
> Heeft de Kerstenen hier uut gedreven weer
> Doen wy door Spaengen deerlyck werden ontgoeyt:
> Die rooft, wordt ghemeynlyck tot roof ghegeven weer.

The term *Calvinoturcism* was coined by William Rainolds and William Gifford in a work printed, ironically, in Antwerp in 1597: *Calvino-turcismus, id est, Calvinisticae perfidiae cum Mahometana collatio et dilucida utriusque sectae confutatio.* As the title indicates, the term was meant as a one of abuse, not praise. See also Mout, "Calvinoturcisme," 577.

84. See Mout, "Calvinoturcisme," 579; and van Nierop, "Beggars' Banquet," 432. Note that the expression *Calvinoturcism* would have postdated the slogan "Liever Turxs dan Paus."

85. Van Gelder, "Bailleul," 62 ("se rendroit plus tost tributaire au Turcq de vivre contre sa conscience et estre traicté selon iceulx placcarts"); *Vray patriot,* sig. B3r; Motley, *Dutch Republic,* 2:563, which cites Fruytiers, *Corte beschrijvinghe.* For further examples of "Turkish tolerance," see van Schelven, "Politiek tolerantie"; and cf. Knuttel, *Pamfletten,* nos. 426 and 363.

86. Willem, *Apologie,* 90, 98. For futher examples of "Turkish violence," see Knuttel, *Pamfletten,* nos. 343, 355, 361, 379, 500, and 549. Cf. more generally Hale, *Civilization,* 40–1; and also Matar, *Islam in Britain,* for a (mostly) contrasting rhetorical response to the Ottomans.

87. *Vriendelicke vermaninghe,* sig. [Aiv]r; *Antwoorde op een cleyn boecxken,* 36; Willem, *Apologie,* 50, 55. For further samples of the rebels' "internationalism," see Knuttel, *Pamfletten,* nos. 160, 179b, 440, 492, 627, 766, and 1047. Note that Milan revolted in 1563 and Sicily followed in 1566.

88. *Vriendelijcke waerschouwinghe,* sigs. Cv-r, Biiij-v; *Wachtgheschrey,* sig. Aiij-r; and cf. Fredericq, *Nederlandsche proza,* 39. The reference to the "Italian mountains" alluded both to the Italian corridor through which the army of Flanders marched and the significant Italian component within that army. The Spanish road began in Genoa and normally traversed the Alps in Habsburg-controlled Lombardy and Piedmont: see Parker, *Army of Flanders.*

89. *Clare vertoning,* sigs. C3v–C4r; and cf. also *Rapport faict,* 10.

90. *Spaenschen ende Arragoenschen Spiegel.* The verse caption under the illustration reads: "Inde Spaenche Tiranij tot den deser spatie / Spiegelt hem te recht alle des Werelts natie" (The Spanish tyranny depicted in this space / Is accurately mirrored for all the world's nations).

91. This applies to the earliest propaganda of 1566 to ca. 1600. In the early seventeenth century, by which time the Dutch had expressed colonial aims of their own, the validity of Spanish colonization and of the Treaty of Tordesillas would come under attack by proponents of the Dutch West Indian Company.

92. Verheiden, *Oration,* 10. Virtually the same argument appears in the *Apologie,* where Willem speaks of "auncient priviledges and liberties" abused in America (55).

93. "Verbintenis van eenige Eedelen," 61; *Pithie and most earnest exhortation,* 64–5; *Antwoordt op het tweede refereyn,* sig. Ciiij-v; and cf. *Dialogue, ofte Tsamensprekinghe,* sig. Aij-v, which discusses the "embittered" Council of Spain's desire to govern in the Netherlands with the same autocratic methods—neglect of local law—that they had employed in the New World.

94. "Lusthof van rhetorica," 336; Verheiden, *Nootelijcke consideratien,* sig. B3; *Defense and true declaration,* sig. [Av] (and cf. van Gelderen, *Revolt,* 18).

95. *Defense and true declaration,* sigs. Giij, **v (and cf. van Gelderen, *Revolt,* 64–5).

96. *Discours d'un gentil-homme,* sig. B (and cf. Kossmann, *Texts,* 264–5, whose translation I have slightly modified).

97. Verheiden, *Nootelijcke consideratien,* sig. Cv.

98. *Antwoordt op het tweede refereyn,* sig. Cij-v ("ontschuldich en onnosel [sielen] syn versmoort; / Wie heeft oyt van schrickelijcker onmenschelijcker wreetheyt gehoort"). Van Mander's sonnets, cited in the previous chapter,

comment similarly on the Indians' innocence. Note that the expression "innocent blood" recurs in rebel descriptions of Spanish tyranny in the Netherlands—as in *Vriendelijcke waerschouwinghe* (sig. Cvii-v) and the *Geuzenlied* cited by Motley (*Dutch Republic*, 3:507), where "innocent blood" serves in fact as the song's refain.

99. *Trouhertighe vermaninghe*, sig. [Aiiij]r.

100. Verheiden, *Nootelijcke consideratien*, sig. Cv (emphasis added); and see Geurts, *Pamfletten*, 171–5, on the rebels' contention that Catholics would never treat Protestants fairly.

101. *Boecxken van de dry Pausen; Artijckelen ende besluyten*, sig. Ar; "Hertgrondighe begheerte," 139; Willem, *Apologie*, 58, 62; Marnix, *Vraye narration*, 46 (also cited in van Gelderen, *Political Thought*, 115); *Responce d'un bon patriot*, sig. A3v. The idea of naming a land after its discoverer or conqueror had, of course, only recently been put into practice in the naming of America after Amerigo Vespucci. Note too how Orange's dismissal of Philip II as a "Devourer of the People" finds a parallel in François Rabelais's critique of colonialism in *Pantagruel*, where Rabelais cites the original *Demovore* as the "wicked king" described by Homer: *The Histories of Gargantua and Pantagruel*, trans. J. M. Cohen (Harmondsworth, 1955), 290.

102. *Historie van B. Cornelis Andriaensen*, 86.

103. Horst, "Spotprenten op Alva," discusses a series of such prints and their iconography; and see further Tanis and Horst, *Images of Discord*, especially cat. nos. 17 ("The Plague of Alva's Tyranny in the Low Countries") and 12 ("The Throne of the Duke of Alva").

104. *Verhael op de questure*, sig. A3v; *Antwoorde op een cleyn boecxken*, 12, and cf. 14–15. Other examples can be found in *Clare vertoning*, sig. Br; Willem, *Apologie*, passim; *Spaenschen ende Arragoenschen Spiegel*; *Nederlandsche proza*, 35; and *Beclach der Spaenschen Naty*.

105. "Speech of Menin [Joost Menijn]," cited in Motley, *United Netherlands*, 1:318–19; *Vriendelijcke waerschouwinghe*, sig. Cvii-v.

106. Benedicti, *Rebus gestis illustrissimi principis Guilielmi*, lines 89–93 (for which see the modern edition, *Krijgsdaden van Willem*, 24–5); *Spaenschen ende Arragoenschen Spiegel*, t.p.; Las Casas, *Short Account*, 15. See also the engraving by Dirck Volckertsz Coornhert (after Adriaen de Weert), "Vervolging doodt Christum in sijn arme scapen," which appeared as the eleventh image in the series *The Decline of the Catholic Clergy, or, the Causes of the Dutch Revolt and the Iconoclastic Fury* (1604) and represents a flamboyant "Persecutio" skewering a similarly posed mother and child (reproduced in Tanis and Horst, *Images of Discord*, 72).

107. "Moort [Grouwelyckheyt] tot Oudewater," in *Spaensche tirannye in Nederlandt* (1620); Las Casas, *Short Account*, 15; and cf. also a similar passage in "Sendbrief in forme van Supplicatie aen die Con. Maj. van Spangien," in Fredericq, *Nederlandsche proza*, 51. The "Oudewater" verse reads:

> Niet en wert aldaer gespaert
> T'sy hoe Iongh of out beiaert

Moeders sonder te ontfarmen
Hinghen sy op aen haer armen
Sneden uyt haer tere vrucht
Met een boos en fel gerucht
Moorden dan die ionge spruyten
Hinghen Maechden aen haer tuyten

The passages of Las Casas on Hispaniola were "oft-cited" primarily because they appeared at the beginning of the *Brevíssima relación.* On "patriotic histories," see Schama, *Embarrassment of Riches,* 51–125, and Chapter Four below.

108. "Fire and sword" appear in virtually all Spanish accounts of the *Conquista*—including those of Córtes, Gómara, Las Casas, and Zárate—as well as countless Dutch polemics of the Revolt—including Orange's *Declaration,* le Clerq's *Remonstrance,* Marnix's *Cleyn boecxken,* and those works listed under Knuttel, *Pamfletten,* nos. 305, 440, and 500. See also *Brief discours sur la negotiation* (1579), which claims that Philip had "massacred and burned alive" his subjects in the Netherlands and the Indies alike (cited in van Gelderen, *Revolt,* 128).

109. See, for example, Las Casas, *Short Account,* 11, 96; *Clare vertoning,* sig. C4r; Verheiden, *Nootelijcke consideratien,* sig. Bv; *Antwoordt op het tweede refereyn,* sig. Cij-v; "Vermaninghe aen de gemeyne capiteynen ende krijchsknechten in Nederlandt," in *Nederlandsche proza,* 33–7; *Spaenschen ende Arragoenschen Spiegel.*

110. Las Casas, *Short Account,* 63, 125; "Waerschouwinghe aen de stadt van Ghent," in *Nederlandsche proza,* 393; and "Een cleyn claechliet," in ibid., 383:

Die lichamen . . .
Uwer knechten eerbaer
Den raven sy veurstelden;
Tvleesche uwer knechten goet
Wierpen sy met hoochmoet
Den dieren op den velden.

The American images originally appeared in Theodore de Bry's Latin translation of Las Casas—*Narratio regionum Indicarum quosdam devastarum verissima* (Frankfurt a. M., 1598)—and in most subsequent Dutch editions. The Dutch image of the Spanish Fury in Antwerp appears in *Spaensche tirannye* ("Antwerpen").

111. Pagden, "Introduction," xxv–xxvi.

112. Las Casas, *Short Account,* 11–12, 29–30, 45, 97.

113. "De verantwoordinge des Princen van Oraengien," in Willem, *Geschriften van 1568,* 40–1; Marnix, *Vraye narration; Brief discours sur la negotiation; Sentdbrieven van die van Gendt;* Willem, *Apologie,* 94–5; Bor, *Nederlantsche oorloghen,* 1:954.

114. *Antwoordt op het tweede refereyn,* sig. Cij-v.

115. See, for example, Gijsius, *Oorsprong en voortgang,* 302–7, 330, 356–9; *Antwoorde van de generale Staten;* Marnix, *Response a un libelle fameux.* On the ten-

dency of South Netherlandish authors especially to exaggerate their estimates, see Rogier, "Karakter en omvang." Geurts also discusses these and
other sources associated with the rebels' inflation of numbers: *Pamfletten*,
177–8.
116. Cf. Kingdon, *Myths;* Pollmann, "Natürliche Feindschaft."

Chapter Three
1. Jan Sadeler after Dirck Barendsz, *America* (1581), for which see Hollstein,
   Dutch and Flemish Etchings, 1:102; and Judson, *Dirck Barendsz.*, 151–2, whose
   translation I have altered slightly.
2. Poeschel, *Ikonographie der Erdteile*, offers an overview. Studies paying special attention to the particular place of America among the continents include Le Corbeiller, "America and her Sisters"; Honour, *New Golden Land*,
   84–91; and idem, *European Vision*, 112–30.
3. On continental pageantry, see (in addition to the works cited above) Hyde,
   "Parts of the World"; Williams and Jacquot, "Ommegangs anversois"; and
   Williams, "Ommegangs d'Anvers."
4. Münster's map and its vignettes (the latter attributed to Hans Holbein the
   Younger) are discussed in Harley, *Columbian Encounter*, 84–6. On the title
   page of the *Theatrum* (lately attributed to Philips Galle after Maarten de Vos),
   see Waterschoot, "Title page"; and van den Boogaart, "Empress Europe."
   Ortelius, it should be noted, paid relatively less attention to the New World
   in the *body* of his first atlases, which contain fewer maps of America (originally just one) than the other continents.
5. Van Mander, *Het leven*, 259; and cf. Judson, *Dirck Barendsz.*, 101–4. Van Mander also made much of Barendsz's Italian, noting the Amsterdammer's
   "proper" Venetian accent. Both Barendsz and van Mander spent appren-
   ticeships in Italy, and both (as will be suggested) seem to have brought
   Ovidian sensibilities to the task of comprehending the New World.
6. Judson, *Dirck Barendsz.*, 152, which cites the textual caption accompanying
   the print.
7. Waterschoot, "Title page," 53; and see also Feest, "Indian Artifacts," on the
   circulation of these objects in early modern Europe.
8. Theodor Galle after Jan van der Straet, *America* (ca. 1589), for which see Hollstein, *Dutch and Flemish Etchings*, 7:87; and McGinty, "Stradanus," passim.
   The Renaissance's engagement more generally with the "novelty" of America is treated by Grafton, *New Worlds*.
9. The inherent tension of this moment is suggestively discussed (for slightly
   other purposes) in Certeau, *Writing of History*, xxv–xxvi; and Montrose,
   "Discourse of Discovery," where Montrose engages with Certeau's reading.
10. The resemblance of the two figures is especially pronounced if one com-
    pares the Stradanus drawing with the Ortelius title page. The Galle print
    naturally reverses the original Stradanus design, so that the calf-bracelet of
    the former, for example, is now on America's left foot rather than right, as
    in the Ortelius title page.

11. Honour, *European Vision*, 114–15, reproduces the preparatory drawing (Metropolitan Museum of Art, New York) and transcribes much of the manuscript inscription on its verso. Stradanus cites Petrus Moffe's *Historiarum Indicarum* (Florence, 1588) as his source, though it is worth pointing out that Vespucci himself possessed a lively interest in America's *naturalia*, and this may have inspired Stradanus to surround the Florentine discoverer with the natural wonders of the New World. See Gerbi, *Nature in the New World*, 35–49.

12. Philips Galle after Marcus Gheeraerts, *America* (ca. 1590), for which see Hollstein, *Dutch and Flemish Etchings*, 7:102; Honour, *European Vision*, 118–19; and Vandenbroeck et al., *Bride of the Sun*, 301. On Gheeraerts, see Hodnett, *Marcus Gheeraerts*. The de Jode atlas (published originally in 1578 by Gerard de Jode, father of Cornelis) is available in facsimile: *Speculum orbis terrarum*, ed. R. A. Skelton (Amsterdam, 1965).

13. Adriaen Collaert after Maarten de Vos, *America* (ca. 1589); and see Hollstein, *Dutch and Flemish Etchings*, 4:205.

14. On de Vos, see Zweite, *Marten de Vos;* on the allegory itself, see Vandenbroeck, *Beeld van de Andere*, 22; and on the 1594 drawing, see Doutrepont, "Martin de Vos." Ripa's *Iconologia* appeared originally in Rome (1593), though it took a decade to devise the newest continent (Rome, 1603). A Dutch edition came out still a few decades later: *Iconologia, of uytbeeldingen des verstands* (Amsterdam, 1644), and see 605 for "America."

15. Waterschoot suggests de Vos as the author of the Ortelius "America," which helps to explain the similarity that figure bears to the de Vos model: "Title page," 45. Another possible connection is the engraver, Philips Galle, who may have worked on the Ortelius title page (see Delen, *Histoire de la gravure*, 157) and who produced a similarly weaponed allegory of America around this time (cf. Honour, *European Vision*, 118). The remarkable armadillo added to the de Vos allegory follows a tradition of linking the continents with animals, which has its origins in the myth of Europa's rape by Zeus in the form of a bull.

16. The model in this case might have been cartographic, as de Vos's scenes of cannibalism closely resemble those typically featured on contemporary maps of America and described in travel reports. See, for example, Münster's world map in Grynaeus, *Novus orbis* (cf. fig. 17 above).

17. Maarten de Vos, *America (Vier Werelddelen)* (ca. 1595): "Europa machte mich der Welt, Godt mir bekandt / Gold, das sonst Heeren macht, liess mich zur Sclavin werden / Ich ben bey Reichtum arm in meinem eigen Land / Weil meine Eide wird geführt auf andre Erden." Vandenbroeck, *Beeld van de Andere*, reproduces this (German) version of the print and discusses others (for example by the Galle atelier) that appeared in the late sixteenth century.

18. [Maarten de Vos?], *America* (ca. 1600), for which see *Architectural and Ornamental Drawings*, no. 5. Honour disputes the attribution to de Vos, though offers little further by way of explanation: *European Vision*, 117.

19. The Ann Arbor catalogue (*Architectural and Ornamental Drawings*, no. 5) sug-

gests that America has just *received* the gifts on her plate—an argument sustained by the position of the ship's stern. Still, America's own gesture would appear to be one of giving rather than receiving.

20. On the fundamental political, economic, and social shifts that occurred around the turn of the century, see especially Israel, *Dutch Republic* (1995), 241–360, along with Parker, *Dutch Revolt*, 225–40, and Geyl, *Revolt of the Netherlands*, 233–62. Prior to Israel's researches, surprisingly little had been written on this explosive period of Dutch development, which has traditionally fallen between historiographic cracks. Fruin's *Tien jaren* is still suggestive, as is a recent, more ambitious study, focusing on artistic developments: Luijten et al., *Dawn of the Golden Age.*

21. For economic developments, see above all de Vries and van der Woude, *First Modern Economy*, 279 ff. and 665–72. Israel, *Dutch Primacy*, 38–79, is particularly good on matters of commerce; and see also the first two chapters of idem, *Hispanic World*. Also useful are the appropriate sections in Blok, *Algemene Geschiedenis der Nederlanden* (esp. contributions by Noordegraaf, Klompmaker, Bruijn, and Boelmans Kranenburg, all in volume 7); and Noordegraaf, *Hollands welvaren*. Israel in particular has highlighted the magnitude of what he terms the "economic 'miracle'" of the late 1590s, describing a transitional moment that "was overwhelming, even unparalleled in history, in terms of the pace, and scope, of the socio-economic transformation, the galvanization of an urban civilization which followed in its wake" (*Dutch Republic* [1995], 307). Perhaps even more emphatically, de Vries and van der Woude discern in this period the foundation of the first "modern" economy.

22. Parker reviews the story of the Republic's expansion, while noting the continuation of this growth into the second quarter of the century: *Dutch Revolt*, 240–53. On the massive immigration to the northern provinces, see two essential monographs by Briels: *Zuidnederlandse immigratie* and *Zuidnederlanders in de Republiek.* The figures for Amsterdam's growth (which resulted from both internal and external migration: immigration, that is, within the North as well as from the South Netherlands) come from *Zuidnederlandse immigratie*, 26. In 1622, some 150,000 immigrants from the South are believed to have settled in the North, accounting for approximately ten percent of the Republic's total population.

23. Parker, *Dutch Revolt*, 250; Israel, *Dutch Primacy*, 12–79.

24. See Briels, *Zuidnederlandse boekdrukkers;* and Luijten, *Golden Age*, 167–99 ("Print Publishers in the Netherlands, 1580–1620").

25. Briels, *Zuidnederlandse immigratie*, 73, 148, and passim; idem, *Vlaamse Schilders.* On literary developments, see Knuvelder, *Handboek*, vol. 2; and for the visual arts, see Luijten, *Golden Age*, especially the essays of J. Bruyn ("A Turning-Point in the History of Dutch Art," 112–21) and H. Miedema ("The Appreciation of Paintings around 1600," 122–35), both of which express slightly revisionist views.

26. Philip II had always shown great reluctance to negotiate with "rebels" and became, if anything, more resolved toward the end of his life to win the war

against the Dutch "heretics." He gained greater leverage with his creditors following the Treaty of Vervins, negotiated with the French sovereign, Henri IV, in May 1598. Four months later, however, the king died in El Escorial, which left his lieutenant in the Netherlands, Albrecht, with greater leeway to negotiate with the Republic. Albrecht entered into talks without delay.

27. "Den lusthof van rhetorica," in van Vloten, *Nederlandsche geschiedzangen,* 2:335–6: "Besiet daer d'aengeboden pays, hoe die Spanjaerts houden woort, / Leest hoe sy int eylant Trinitá gingen haer gangen: / Hoewel sy met haer gemaect hadden vriendlijck accort, / Stadt en luyden zijn verbrant, veel tot slaven gevangen!"

28. *Spaenschen ende Arragoenschen Spiegel,* 3, 130. The pamphlet focuses on the Westphalian situation and recent Habsburg campaigns in neighboring Cleves.

29. *Aerdt ende eygenschappen.* French and German translations of this popular broadsheet are reproduced in Harms et al., *Herzog August Bibliothek,* 2:72–5. An English edition, "Translated out of Dutche" and dated 1599, is in the British Library and persuades Harms to date the Dutch original sometime in the earlier period of the Revolt (ca. 1571–1581). Kunzle suggests a later date of ca. 1600, which would seem justified on the basis of internal evidence: *Early Comic Strip,* 198.

30. Cf., for example, Bloomfield, *Seven Deadly Sins,* which surveys the "cardinal" and "deadly" sins of late medieval Europe.

31. "Lusthof van rhetorica." The song was composed by a poet from The Hague for a gathering of the Holland chambers, which took place in Leiden on 26 May 1596. It was published, together with other contributions to the festival, later that year: *Den lusthof van rhetorica* (Leiden, 1596). On such gatherings of chambers of rhetoric—civic corporations organized for the practice of literary culture—see Spies, *Rhetoric, Rhetoricians, and Poets;* and on the patriotic content of the 1596 gathering more particularly, see Smits-Veldt, "Hollands zelfbewustzijn."

32. *Antwoordt op het tweede refereyn;* and cf. Scribner, *Popular Propaganda,* for the broader, Protestant model.

33. *Antwoordt op het tweede refereyn,* sigs. Bij-v, Biij-r, Cij-v, Diij-v.

34. Benedicti, *Rebus gestis illustrissimi principis Guilielmi,* lines 89–93 (and cf. idem; *Krijgsdaden van Willem,* 24–5); Lipsius, *De constantia,* for which see the contemporary translation, *Two bookes of constancie* (London, 1594), 115. Van Houdt, "Amerika en de Oudheid," reviews other scattered Americana in Lipsius's oeuvre.

35. The poem was originally published in van der Noot's 1591 *Werken* and, is reproduced in facsimile: *Poetische Werken,* 2:367–70. Van der Noot's modern editor, W. Waterschoot, is disinclined to connect the reference to American "strife" with Spain's tyranny in the West Indies, citing the poet's standing and station and the timing of the ode itself. Yet precisely the opposite would appear to be the case: Van der Noot was a Calvinist with connections to the rebel party, and he composed the poem against a background of fierce polemical activity in the Netherlands. He saw himself, moreover, as some-

thing of a national poet with the task of promoting *patria*. The ode itself may derive from his ambitious "Europeiad," an unfinished epic: see Bostoen, "Vander Noot's 'Europeiad.'"

36. Prinsen, "Jan van Hout." A close friend of the geographer Petrus Bertius, van Hout makes reference to the recent voyage of Francis Drake, whom Steven reputedly accompanied to the West.

37. Fritz, *Christoffel Wagenaer,* 127–51. The original Dutch edition came out in Utrecht in 1597, based on a German version of 1593 (Prague?). The latter came on the heels of a German translation of Benzoni, which seems to have been the primary source for *Christoffel Wagenaer's* American passages.

38. Petty, *Beschryvinge* (1598). Three more Dutch editions appeared in 1617, 1623, and 1644, all based on the translation made by Emanuel van Meteren of a manuscript in the possession of Richard Hakluyt. Hakluyt issued an abbreviated version of Petty's report in 1589 (*Principall navigations,* 808–13), yet, once again, the Dutch had an edition (albeit abridged) already in circulation the year before: *Copye, overgeset wt de Engelsche taele . . . gheschreven aen Milore Tresorier. van Mr. Thomas Candishe* [sic](Amsterdam). The 1598 edition also includes accounts of voyages made by Francis Drake and John Hawkins undertaken in the mid-1590s.

39. Acosta, *Historie naturael ende morael,* sigs. aii-v, Ar. The Spanish original appeared in Seville in 1590.

40. Ralegh, *Waerachtighe ende grondighe beschryvinge* (1598), reissued in 1605, 1617, and 1644; and Kemys, *Tweede zeevaert* (1598), published together with Ralegh in 1605 and 1617, and on its own in 1648. Over the duration of the early modern period, both works proved more durable in Dutch than in any other language.

41. Ralegh, *Beschryvinge,* 6, 9, 26, 22, 3; and cf. Ralegh, *Discoverie* (London, 1596), 22–4, 33, 96, 81, 10. (Further Ralegh citations follow the original English edition of 1596 with cross-references to the Dutch edition of 1598.) Ralegh and the *Discoverie* have received a fair amount of recent attention: see Fuller, *Voyages in Print,* 53–84; Montrose, "Discourse of Discovery"; Nicholl, *Creature in the Map;* and Whitehead's excellent "Introduction," which provides a full bibliography.

42. Ralegh, *Discoverie,* 79 [*Beschryvinge,* 22]; Kemys, *Tweede zeevaert,* 41r. On another occassion, Ralegh tells of hearing daily and "lamentable complaints of [Spanish] cruelty" from the natives: *Discoverie,* 6 [*Beschryvinge,* 2].

43. Ralegh, *Discoverie,* 7 [*Beschryvinge,* 2v]; and Kemys, *Tweede zeevaert,* 38v, though Kemys does express certain doubt, at other points in the narrative, concerning native cooperation.

44. Ralegh, *Discoverie,* 62, 101 [*Beschryvinge,* 17r, 27v]. More generally, Ralegh shows exceptional skill in asserting his own personal deeds of heroism in Guiana—and then nimbly situating these individual acts of chivalry within the grander goals of Elizabethan empire. For Ralegh-as-courtier, see Greenblatt, *Walter Ralegh,* which places the Guiana adventure within the context of Ralegh's scandalous marriage to Elizabeth Throgmorton and the *chastened* courtier's precipitous fall from grace. Greenblatt further discusses the

Spenserian spirit of the mission, and it is worth noting in this regard Ralegh's "Cortésian" courage: He promises not merely to right the wrongs of the earlier conquistadors, but also—and perhaps paradoxically—to *outdo* the Spaniards (Cortés in particular) in feats of conquest and bravery.

45. Cf. Edmundson, "Trade on Rio Negro": "Nowhere, not even in England itself, did the narrative of Raleigh and his lieutenant excite so much interest and such general attention as in the United Provinces" (10). Harlow, *Last Voyage*, makes much the same emphatic point—"The narrative . . . was the direct cause of the Dutch intervention in Guiana" (2)—and reprints the manuscript "Account of a Journey to Guiana" by A. Cabeliau (128–32), which details initial Dutch reconnaissance of the region.

46. Kemys, *Tweede zeevaert*, 41v. On early Dutch economic hopes for Guiana and the Amazon region, see Edmundson, "Trade on Rio Negro"; idem, "Dutch on the Amazon"; and Goslinga, *Dutch in the Caribbean*, 56–8. Goslinga also transcribes the manuscript report of a Dutch sailor who actually followed Ralegh's inducements to explore Guiana, yet discovered it not quite all it was promised to be (ibid., 485–7). This sobering report was never published.

47. Kemys, *Tweede zeevaert*, 41r.

48. On early Dutch travel to America, see the overview in Goslinga, *Dutch in the Caribbean*, 20–88; and van den Boogaart, "Nederlandse expansie." The travel narratives themselves are available in the excellent series published by the Linschoten-Vereeniging, vols. 7, 15–16, 19, 21–2, 24, 28, and 49.

49. Van Gelder, Parmentier, and Roeper, *Souffrir pour parvenir;* Koeman, *Van Linschoten;* van der Moer, *Zestiende-eeuwse Hollander;* and Parr, *Van Linschoten.* See also Terpstra's excellent Introduction to Linschoten, *Itinerario* (1955), xxiii–lxxxiii; and ibid., 1, on van Linschoten's youthful wanderlust.

50. The *Itinerario* included two other accounts, published with separate title pages and pagination: *Reys-gheschrift van de navigatien der Portugaloysers in Orienten*, a navigational guide to the East, published originally in 1595; and *Beschryvinghe van de gantsche custe van Guinea, Manicongo, Angola, . . . volcht noch de beschryvinghe van West Indien* (1596), a descriptive account of Africa and America.

51. See Rouffaer and IJzerman, *Eerste schipvaart;* and Keuning, *Tweede schipvaart.* For an example of the effusive praise bestowed on van Linschoten, see the ode, Latin verse, and multiple sonnets that preface the *Itinerario.* Note, however, the derision that followed the failed (and costly) journeys undertaken by van Linschoten in search of a northeast passage to China.

52. Whatever Jan Huygen's policies while resident in the East, he was not above soliciting patronage from the Habsburgs' enemies—the States General— once back in the West. He had, at best, mixed results (see Parr, *Van Linschoten*, 273–80). Note, too, that the island of Terceira was engaged in a rebellion against Spain (ongoing since 1580) at the time of van Linschoten's stay there.

53. *Itinerario* (1596), 1, 10, 55, 68, and see the dedication, "Aende Hoogh ende Welgheborene . . . Generale Staten," for a description of the "sorrowful" trees of Mozambique. The letter of 1584, now in the Rijksarchief in The

Hague, is cited in the first modern edition: *Itinerario. Voyage ofte Schipvaert van Jan Huygen van Linschoten naer Oost ofte Portugaels Indiën, 1579–1592*, ed. H. Kern, Werken Uitgegeven door de Linschoten-Vereeniging, vol. 2 (The Hague, 1910), xvii–xviii. On the sources for the *Itinerario*, see note 64 below. The topic of travel and authenticity in early American narratives is studied in Pagden, *European Encounters*, 51–87.

54. "Aende Hoogh Welgheborene . . . Generale Staten," n.p.

55. On Paludanus's collection, see Bergvelt et al., *Wereld binnen handbereik* (exh. cat.), 28–32; and, more generally, ibid. (essays), especially the contribution of Roelof van Gelder, "Liefhebbers en geleerde luiden: Nederlandse kabinetten en hun bezoekers" (259–92).

56. De Marees, *Koninckrijck van Gunea*, 30, 150 (and note this volume's racy title-page illustration, showing the casual manner in which African women purportedly nourished their infants by throwing a breast over their shoulder); Warnsinck, *Joris van Spilbergen*, (2)-(4) (and see the translation of the Preface and "Ode" in Villiers, *East and West Indian Mirror*, 4 and 6); Ruiters, *Toortse der Zeevaert*, iv.

57. De Veer, *Waerachtige beschryvinge*, translated in Beynen, *Three voyages*, 15–16. Egmond, *Bekende Scheveninger*, describes Coenen's fascinating collection (and biography); and see the energetic reading of the "Visboeck" offered in Egmond and Mason, *Mammoth and the Mouse*, 23–33. On the display of Eskimos (more than a few of whom toured the late sixteenth-century Republic), see Sturtevant and Quinn, "This new prey"; and on Gheeraerts's print, see note 12 above. Dutch collecting more generally is studied in Bergvelt, *Wereld binnen handbereik*; and Egmond and Mason, "Armadillos in Unlikely Places."

58. Both the *Extract oft Kort verhael* (Rotterdam, 1601) and the longer *Beschryvinghe vande voyagie om den geheelen werelt cloot* (Rotterdam, 1602) are reprinted in IJzerman, *Olivier van Noort*, which reproduces the title-pages (27:1, 159) and introductory materials (27:i–viii, 158). On van Waesberghe, who served as *stadsdrukker* in his new hometown, see Briels, *Zuidnederlandse boekdrukkers*, 531–2.

59. IJzerman, *Journael* (and see vii for IJzerman's discussion of Ottsen's "platte zeemanstaal").

60. "We ever strive for what is forbidden, and ever covet what is denied." The quote comes from Ovid *Amores*, 3.4.17.

61. IJzerman, *Journael*, title-page and 62.

62. Van Linschoten, *Itinerario* (1596), "Prohemio ofte Voorreden totten leser," n.p. On the publication patterns of Claesz, see van Selm, *Menighte treffelijcke Boecken*, 174–319, and see 179 for the contract between Claesz and van Linschoten.

63. Van Linschoten, *Beschryvinghe* (1596), n.p.

64. Benzoni is cited explicitly in the *Beschryvinghe* on sigs. B4r and B6r, Martyr on sig. B4r, Oviedo on sig. B3v, and Léry throughout the section on Brazil (sigs. C6–E2). For a full review of van Linschoten's sources—including those used for Africa (Pigafetta), China (Mendoza), Japan (Maffei), and India

(Camões and Garcia de Orta)—see Parr, *Van Linschoten,* 204; and Lach, *Asia in the Making of Europe,* 1:197, 200–1.

65. For Léry, see the *Beschryvinghe,* sigs. Dr and D4r (and these sections were copied by van Linschoten, more or less word for word); for Martyr, sig. B3r; for Benzoni, sig. C2v (for which see the contemporary translation, *Discourse of voyages into the Easte & West Indies* [London, 1598], 234). The influence of the *Brevíssima relación* can be detected, for example, in the text's conspicuous number of Lascasian body counts.

66. The most prominent of these immigrants were Jodocus Hondius, who published the Mercator atlases in Amsterdam; Petrus Plancius, the leading colonial cartographer of his day; and Simon Stevin, advisor to the *stadhouder* on military cartography. See Zandvliet, *Groote waereld,* 37–43 ("Antwerpen en Amsterdam: Migratie"); and idem, *Mapping for money,* 33–53, which also discusses the internal migration of cartographers, from North Holland cities to Amsterdam.

67. Publication details can be traced in Koeman, *Atlantes Neerlandici,* 3: 25–83. Heyns's work is more extensively discussed in Chapter 2.

68. Koeman, *Abraham Ortelius,* reviews the reception of the atlas and the history of its publication. Karrow, *Mapmakers of the Sixteenth Century,* details the chronology of Ortelius's other publications, including his considerable work on antiquarian projects. The latter activity picked up conspicuously around the time that the political situation in Antwerp irrevocably worsened, a period during which—one might conjecture—Ortelius retreated in his research from the present to the past: witness the attention he paid to his historical atlas, *Parergon, sive veteris geographiae aliquot tabulae,* published in Antwerp in 1579. With numerous friends and relatives in the Calvinist camp, Ortelius conducted himself professionally with the utmost caution, abiding by the advice he offered his exiled nephew, Jacob Cool, "that a wise man must keep silent in these days" (cited in Koeman, *Ortelius,* 15). He certainly showed little desire in his published texts to recount the tyranny of his Spanish patrons.

69. Langenes, *Caert-thresoor,* "Aenden Leser" and "Ode," n.p.; and see Koeman, *Atlantes Neerlandici,* 2: 252–61, which lists the numerous later and derived editions.

70. For these and other atlases, tricky questions of quality or scholarship complicate easy generic categorizations. Koeman rates Langenes's atlas, its size and cost notwithstanding, "easily the best in this [six-volume] bibliography" and pays particularly high regard to Langenes's ability as a cartographer (*Atlantes Neerlandici,* 2:252). Langenes's text contained up-to-the-minute reports (of Dutch explorations in the Arctic, for example), which rendered the *Theatrum,* in many respects, relatively outmoded. Ortelius, for his part, had access to some of the best scholarship of Renaissance Europe, and his maps, by virtue of their size, could afford to be more detailed. The two genres, moreover, overlapped. The *Theatrum* was "reduced" by Ortelius's good friend, Heyns (who also wrote a dedicatory poem for the original *Theatrum*), while the *Caert-thresoor* was rendered into

Latin by Petrus Bertius (*Tabularum geographicum*), who reorganized Langenes's maps along Ptolemaic lines. Ultimately, though, language, and by extension audience, was the crucial indicator. Heyns's Dutch-language epitome, on the one hand, contained anti-Spanish passages that never would have made it into the *Theatrum* (Heyns, *nota bene,* worked on the *Spieghel* in 1576–1577, while Ortelius was out of the country). Bertius's Latin version of the *Caert-thresoor,* on the other hand, excised all of the polemical material from the vernacular original. The Dutch texts, then, made the case against Spanish tyranny, while the more broadly pitched Latin texts, whatever their format, took a more neutral stance on the political debates of the day.

71. Langenes, *Caert-thresoor,* "Ode," 3, 40, 152. For the Golden Age, Langenes casually cites "the poets," though later mentions Peter Martyr (152), his likely source.

72. [Viverius], *Hand-boeck,* 4r; and see Koeman, *Atlantes Neerlandici,* 2:257–8. Viverius's edition follows Langenes's original text of 1598, with additional materials borrowed from Bertius's *Tabularum geographicarum* and, naturally, Viverius's not inconsiderable poetic imagination.

73. [Viverius], *Hand-boeck,* 701–54, esp. 709–16 (Peruvian citation on 716: "Die dorst naer menschen bloed en wreed'lick willet woeden / Vaert wel een wyle voort also eenen Wolf verwoed / Doch eydlick moet hy 't land oock met zijn bloed bebloeden / Die bloed stort sonder schuld, vergiet zijn eyghen bloed"). Cf. the remakably similar poem by Pieter Heyns on Spanish tyrannies in Tunis, cited in Chapter Two.

74. Jacobus Viverius, *Spieghel,* sigs. A2r, A3v, B2v:

> Den Spangiaert soo seer brandt in het vier van begheeren,
> Dat hy nit is gherust de Schaepkens soet te scheeren
> De wolle van het lijf: he wilt vleysch, bloedt, en vacht:
> Dus hy naer Indi-landt ghenomen heeft de jacht.
>
> . . . .
> T'en is niet om 't Geloof dat men dit volk vermoort:
> Maer het is om het Goudt dat haer recht toebehoort.

75. Ibid., sig. A3v:

> Het aerme naeckte volck dat heeft hem eerbewesen
> Ghebrocht Goudts overvloedt en vruchten uytghelesen:
> Maer desen wreeden Wolf cost niet versadt zijn:
> Hy dede 't aerme volck Goudt graven met veel pijn.
> Och om het diere Goudt men men [sic] then dreef also dieren:
> Gheldt dorst ende ydel eer 't onnoosel volck schoofieren.

The American materials, which occupy the first half of the poem, preface a polemic against recent Habsburg campaigns in the Netherlands in general and Cleves in particular.

76. For a full bibliography and textual analysis of Dutch editions of Las Casas, see Veldhuyzen-Brouwer, "Nederlandse vertalingen"; and more generally EA vols. 1–2. The 1609 illustrated edition was based on a Latin edition of

1598, published by the South Netherlands émigré, Theodore de Bry, now settled in Frankfurt: see Conley, "De Bry's Las Casas."

77. Veldhuyzen-Brouwer, "Nederlandse vertalingen"; van Leuven-Zwart, "Comparación del texto."

78. [Van der Clyte], *Cort verhael,* sigs. aij-r, [aiij]r.

79. Las Casas, *Spieghel* (1609): "Der wreede Spangiaerts haer onmenschelijcke handel, / Haer woede rasery, haer goddeloose wandel, / . . . God sal in zijn gerecht dien grouwel niet vergeten."

80. Las Casas, *Spieghel* (1607), t.p.; [Van der Clyte], *Cort verhael,* sig. [aiij] r.

81. *Discours van Pieter en Pauwels,* sig. Ar.

82. *Tractaet paraeneticq,* 20v; *Oud schipper van Monickendam;* Massa, *Beschrijvinge,* and see Massa's manuscript "Letter to Maurits," 3.

83. *Catechismus,* sig. [Aiij] r: "Vraghe: Wat ambach doen sij? Antwoorde: Het sijn vleesch houwers. Vrag.: Waervan? Antw.: Van d'onnoosele sielen. . . . " For a children's version of Spanish tyrannies (with a good deal to say about America), see Allertsz, *Spieghel der jeught;* and Daalder, *Wormcruyt met suycker,* esp. 39.

84. [Van Middelgeest], *Testament; Vertoig der Zeeuscher nymphen; Discours van Pieter en Pauwels;* "Aende afgewekene Provintien van Hollandt, Zeelandt, . . . aenwysinghe opt vermaen vande verleyde ende overheerde Provintien van Nederlandt ghedaen aen de veeren," in Fredericq, *Nedelandsche proza,* 352.

85. *Catechismus,* sig. Aij-v; "Cort discours op de gheleghentheyt vanden ieghenwoordighen Nederlantschen Crijch," in Fredericq, *Nedelandsche proza,* 233: "Naer het jugement van alle luyden van verstande, wordt ghehouden voor een seker ende ghewisse saecke, dat d'oorloghe hier te lande niet en can cesseren noch gheeynt worden, so lange als de Coninck van Spaengien blijft paisibel posseseur van de conincrijcke van Portugael, met de Indien Orientael van deselve croone dependerende, eentsamentlijck van de Westersche Indien, waerdoor hy so machtich is van gelt ende goet, dat hy d'oorloge hier te lande sal blijven continueeren."

86. See *Secreet des conings van Spangien,* sig. Aij-r; *Schuyt-praetgens,* sig. Aij-r; and *Waerachtigh ende cort verhael,* sig. Av, each of which considers the riches of the Indies in connection with the oppression of the Netherlands. For the modern, somewhat revisionist, perspective of Spanish finances and the Indies, see Elliott, *The Old World and the New,* 54–78; and Israel, *Hispanic World,* 68–9, 293–5, and passim.

87. *Waerachtigh ende cort verhael,* sig. Av; *Echo ofte galm,* sig. A3.

88. *Oud schipper van Monickendam.* At least eight editions of this pamphlet appeared, chiefly in 1608–1609.

89. *Consideratien vande vrede,* sig. Aij-r. For similar discussions of the importance of the West Indian trade, see those pamphlets collected in *Nederlandtschen bye-korf* (1608), especially the *Buyr-praetjen* and *Schuyt-praetgens.*

90. [Migoen], *Proeve,* n.p., and see Burger, "Raadsel opgelost," on the question of authorship; and *Catechismus,* sig. Aij-v ("Vraghe: Dat zijn groote saecken ende van grooten consequentie voor hunlieden? Antwoorde: Ja groot ghe-

noech om de Spaensche Coop-lieden de misse van *Requiem* te doen singen").
Parker has argued that the Spanish king did in fact fear a Dutch presence in
the West Indies, so much so that he protracted the Eighty Years' War: "Why
Did the Dutch Revolt Last So Long?," in *Spain and the Netherlands*, 45–63.

91. [Migoen], *Proeve*, n.p.; Hakluyt, "Discourse of Western Planting," 249. On
the broader international scene, see Parker, "The Dutch Revolt and the Polarization of International Politics," in *Spain and the Netherlands*, 65–81.

92. Usselincx, *Vertoogh*, sig. A2v: "Soo is het dan seker Godt, den coophandel,
zeevaert als de verscheyden hantwerken . . . zijn de zenuwen van dit
lichaem, ende sonder de welcke dese landen niet en connen bestaen." Elizabeth's reference to "nervus belli" makes much the same point.

93. *Consideratien vande vrede*, sig. Ar: "Oorloge oock is geruster dan een twi-
jfelachtige ende twistige vrede." For the ditty on the West Indies—
"Westindjen kan sijn Nederlands groot gewin / Verkleynt 's vijands macht
brengt silver-platen in"—see the pamphlet, sometimes attributed to Usselincx, *Voortganck vande West-Indische Compagnie* (Amsterdam, 1623). The
ditty was republished in a number of contexts, including the title page of
the 1630 *Vryheden* (Amsterdam) of the WIC—following, that is, the capture
of bona fide "silver galore" by Piet Heyn in 1628.

94. *Buyr-praetjen*, sig. Biij-v ("ende het proffijt van dien [WIC] voor ons ende
onse Geallieerden openstaen daer toe de Inwoonders vande selve Landen,
onse mede soude helpen, als wy heur wt hare slavernije, ende der Spaen-
giaerts Tyrannie souden verlossen, ende vry stellen, . . . ende soude door dit
middel, niet alleen de gheheel Christenheyt, vande vreese vande onversadelijcke Spaensche Ambitie, ende Monarchie verlost, maer oock die Indianen ende andere van hare Tyrannie bevrijdt worden"); *Schuyt-praetgens*,
sig. Aij-v.

95. Usselincx, *Vertoogh*, t.p., sigs. Br, [B4]r; and note that this highly influential
pamphlet was published five times in 1608 alone. The poet in favor of
"God's dreadful wrath" is Simon van Middelgeest (*Testament*, sig. Bij-r:
"Gods schrickelicken toren / End rechtveerdich oordeel, welck hy oyt heeft
ghesworen / Over t'onnosel bloet onrechtelick ghestort").

96. The date of conception for the WIC is not entirely clear. Usselincx claims to
have been discussing the project from the early 1590s, and in a pamphlet of
1630 he notes (three times) that his efforts on behalf of the Company predated its foundation by thirty years—dating it, thus, from 1591. See his
Waerschouwinghe over den treves; and Jameson, *Usselinx*, 21–2 (nn. 18 and 22).

97. The biography of Usselincx is much in need of revision. The chief studies of
his life, composed at the turn of the twentieth century, are outdated: Jameson, *Usselinx* (1887); and Ligtenberg, *Usselinx* (1914). Jameson's biography,
written for one of the pioneer volumes of the American Historical Association, indicates the sort of enthusiasm that the Calvinist firebrand, Usselincx,
excited within the late nineteenth-century American historical establishment.

98. Jameson, *Usselinx*, 13–22, 41; Ligtenberg, *Usselinx*, 12–44. On the cargoes of
Seville, see the unpublished *Corte aenwysinge* (1620): "Wat de rijckdommen

bedragen, die jaerlijcx uyt America in Spaignen gebracht worden, weten diegene, die de ladinge sien van goederen, die de West-Indische vloten in Sivilla brengen" (cited in Ligtenberg, *Usselinx*, 15). On the circle of Plancius, the "preaching geographer," see Keuning, *Petrus Plancius.*

99. Briefly stated, Usselincx's plans emphasized the Company's colonial and evangelical mission, while the States General's gave priority to investors and traders. Usselincx also proposed a governing structure that would have been more democratic (favoring the subscribers) than the "patrician" one ultimately adopted (which favored the directors). The States finally granted Usselincx a pension of four thousand guilders per annum, yet refused to implement any of the changes for which he had lobbied. See Ligtenberg, *Usselinx*, 75–87.

100. The analogy perceived by Usselincx between his own life and that of Columbus is documented by Jameson (*Usselinx*, 80, 89, 151, 196), who further adds to the myth of Usselincx-as-neglected-prophet by suggesting a comparison between the father of the WIC and Helenus, the Trojan seer and son of Priam, who foresaw the founding of Rome by Aeneas—yet gained little credit in the aftermath.

101. Ligtenberg, *Usselinx*, 48, and 45–74 (passim); Jameson, *Usselinx*, 17 and passim; and see also Motley, *United Netherlands*, 4:298–300, which considers the ideological origins of the WIC. The Calvinist and military character of the Company's origins have been emphasized in the influential studies of van Hoboken ("Dutch West India Company") and Boxer (*Dutch in Brazil*).

102. See, most fundamentally, van Dillen, "West-Indische Compagnie." The high-profile study of van den Boogaart in the *Algemene Geschiedenis der Nederlanden* ("Nederlandse expansie") has followed van Dillen's lead on the economic origins of the WIC, as have the works of Israel (see *Dutch Republic* [1995], 325–6, where Usselincx is listed as an "economic writer"; and *Dutch Primacy*, 83–4). Other recent examinations of the Company, however, have tended to take a more balanced view of its economic as well as political origins: Emmer, "West India Company"; den Heijer, *Geschiedenis van de WIC*, esp. 21–3; Klooster, *Dutch in the Americas*, esp. 18–19; and Meijer, "Liefhebbers." None of these studies, though, takes seriously the "moral" legitimation of the Company as publicized by Usselincx himself.

103. The earliest published proposals for a WIC date from 1604—a now lost "*police*" recorded in van Meteren and discussed by Ligtenberg (*Usselinx*, 19–20)—though Usselincx claims to have explored the topic, if unofficially, from 1591 (see note 96). Hart, *Prehistory*, and van Winter, *Westindische Compagnie*, both discuss the early development of the Company.

104. Usselincx, *Naerder bedenckingen*, sigs. Er, Aij-r.

105. This elaborate metaphor of the burning Spanish empire is developed by Usselincx over a number of pamphlets, including *Naerder bedenckingen* (sig. Aij-r) and the anonymous *Levendich discours* (sig. B), generally attributed to Usselincx.

106. *Levendich discours*, sig. [C4]v; *Memorie vande ghewichtighe redenen*, sig. iij-r; *Onpartydich discours*, sig. Aij-r. Cf. also *Memorie*, sig. [ij]v, which appeals to

Dutch moral obligations to their Indian "friends" and warns that inaction could cause "irreparable" damage.

107. Usselincx, *Naerder bedenckingen,* sig. Ev. Cf. also the *"police"* of 1604 cited in Ligtenberg (*Usselinx,* 19–20 and 68), which touches on the subject of evangelization; and Usselincx, *Korte onderrichtinghe,* sig. Biij-v, which includes a discussion of the WIC's religious mission in America.

108. For the notion that the Dutch might civilize the Americans, see Usselincx, *Vertoogh,* sigs. Br and B3r; idem, *Korte onderrichtinghe,* sig. Cr; and the discussion in Ligtenberg, *Usselinx,* 63. Usselincx describes the Indians as "sighing and yearning" for the Dutch in *Korte onderrichtinghe,* sig. Biij-r.

109. An outline of Usselincx's early economic ideas can be found in his *Vertoogh, Naerder bedenckingen,* and *Grondich discours.* For two compelling, contemporary illustrations of the riches he had in mind (in both cases featuring Indians), see Joachim Wtewael's drawing, *Indian Homage* (ca. 1611, Albertina, Vienna); and Claes Jansz Visscher and Pieter Bast's engraving, *Profile of Amsterdam from the IJ (Allegory on the Prospensity of Amsterdam) (1611),* which is reproduced as fig. 24 above.

110. *Schuyt-praetgens,* sig. Aij-r (which, though probably not composed by Usselincx himself, was printed three times in the *Nederlandtschen bye-korf,* a publication closely associated with Usselincx and his circle); *Memorie,* sigs. [i]-iij; Usselincx, *Vertoogh,* sig. [A3]r.

111. *Levendich discours,* sig. [A4]r.

112. For Usselincx's confidence in competitive Dutch pricing, see *Levendich discours,* [B4]r. For the Indians as consumers, see Usselincx, *Vertoogh,* sig. Br; and *Memorie,* sig. [ij]v.

113. *Memorie,* sig. [ij]v, iij-r; and [Usselincx?], *Grondich discours,* sig. Bij-v. A few of the many examples of religious rhetoric used in the service of the WIC can be found in *Onpartydich discours,* sigs. A, Aiij-r; *Levendich discours,* sig. B3r; and Usselincx, *Vertoogh,* sig. A2v.

Chapter Four

1. The most thorough treatment of events leading up to the Truce appears in Jan den Tex's magisterial, *Oldenbarnevelt,* 2:550–677. For an updated synthesis, see Israel, *Dutch Republic* (1995), 399–410; idem, *Dutch Primacy,* 80–120 (especially useful on the commercial background of the negotiations); and idem, *Hispanic World,* 12–95. Geyl stresses the ties that bound the North and South in the period preceding the Truce: *Seventeenth Century,* 38–83. For an overview of the political, social, and economic state of the Republic circa 1609, see also Groenveld et al., *Kogel door de kerk?,* 182–238.

2. *Justificatie vande resolutie* (cited in Geyl, *Seventeenth Century,* 49, whose translation I have altered slightly). On the Truce and religious turbulence of the 1610s, see van Deursen, *Bavianen en slijkgeuzen;* den Tex, *Oldenbarnevelt,* vol. 3; and Groenveld and Leeuwenberg, *Bruid in de schuit,* 10–44.

3. Grotius would escape from Castle Loevestein two years later in an empty book chest arranged for by his wife, yet he would never reenter public life in

the Republic. A useful recitation of the political and religious narrative is found in Israel, *Dutch Republic* (1995), 421–49. Maurits's opinion of predestination is cited in H. Volmuller, *Geschiedenislexicon Nederland en België* (The Hague, 1981), 571 ("Twaalfjarig Bestand").

4. Typical examples of propaganda published around the expiry of the Truce are catalogued in Knuttel, *Pamfletten:* see nos. 3127–9, 3198–220, and especially the pamphlet ascribed to François van Aerssen, diplomat and advisor to the *stadhouder, Noodtwendigh ende levendigh discours* (no. 2610). On the economic dimensions of the *contra-Treviste* campaign, see Israel, who rightly contrasts the alacrity with which the Republic resumed economic warfare against Spain and the more hesitant return to the military battlefield: *Dutch Primacy,* 80–120, and *Hispanic World,* 86–95.

5. The suspect pamphlets had been collected in the *Nederlandtschen bye-korf* and published at least three times before most were banned by the States of Holland. All of these pamphlets (thirty to forty, depending on the edition) argued against the Truce; most encouraged the formation of a Dutch West India Company.

6. Usselincx, for example, continued to push for a settlement in Guiana (thus beyond the reach of Spanish sovereignty), a plan that gained the quiet support of Maurits: den Heijer, *Geschiedenis van de WIC,* 27–8. See more generally Goslinga, *Dutch in the Caribbean,* 67–88, which details colonial activity in South America during the Truce; and Hart, *Prehistory,* which discusses the earliest expeditions to North America. The historic voyage of Henry Hudson up the river that now bears his name (1609) went virtually unnoticed in contemporary Dutch letters; and no account dedicated to the voyage was printed in *any* language until Purchas published Robert Juet's journal (in English) in 1625. Although van Meteren did report the voyage in 1614, he buried it hundreds of pages into his history of the Revolt: *Historie,* fol. 629.

7. Las Casas, *Spiegel der Spaensche tyrannye* (1620), printed together with *Tweede deel van den Spiegel.* The publisher's warning comes from the similarly titled edition published by C. L. van der Plasse, sig. A2r. For the convoluted bibliography of the *Brevíssima relación,* see Hanke and Giménez Fernández, *Bibliografía crítica;* and EA. A helpful guide to Dutch-language editions can be found in Veldhuyzen-Brouwer, "Nederlandse vertalingen."

8. *Placcaet inghestelt,* sig. A2v; *Warachtighe beschrijvinghe,* 272–6; *Basuyne des oorloghs,* sig. A2v; Scott, *Belgick souldier,* title-page.

9. *Fin de la guerre:* "De West Indische *Interprinse* d'eenige ende beste middele is, niet alleenelijck om de Spangiaerden uyt den Nederlanden te jagen, en dese langdurige Oorloge t'eijndigen, de geheele Christenheyt te bevredighen: De ghepretendeerde Spaensche Monarchie ende hooghmoet te krencken, ende te dempen: Maer dat daer en boven noch *six cinq* op den Teerling loopt om de *West-Indien* voor een kans te strijcken. *Audaces Fortuna juvat timidosque repellit.*" The Latin tag, attributed to various Roman authors (Terence, *Phormio* 203, or more commonly Virgil, *Aeneid* 10.284), had been revived in the Re-

naissance by Machiavelli in his *Il Principe* and further popularized by the brash Cortés in the *Cartas de relación,* sent from the freshly subdued Mexico—an irony that was lost, one suspects, on the Dutch pamphleteer.

10. *Basuyne des oorloghs,* esp. sig. C3v; Moerbeeck, *Redenen waeromme,* 15; and cf. the formulation of these arguments for a neo-Latin reading audience in van Foreest, *Hispanus redux.*

11. The WIC charter, *Octroy, by de Hooge Mogende Heeren Staten Generael, verleent aende West-Indische Compagnie,* appeared in pamphlet form in 1621 and in subsequent, "amplified" versions in 1623 (three times) and 1624 (like the previous editions, from the official printer in The Hague). The full text, alongside an English translation (which I have followed with minor variations), can be found in van Laer, *Van Rensselaer Bowier Manuscripts* (hereafter *VRBM*), 86–135.

12. *Octroy,* passim. The rather bland discussion of "alliances," it is worth pointing out, derives from the VOC charter, the language of which is closely mimicked by the WIC. In the case of the East Indies, of course, alliances with indigenous governments were essential for commerce—and thus had no "moral" dimension to speak of.

13. "Ampliatie van't Octroy: Waer inne de zout-vaert op *Puncto del Rey* buyten de Compagnie verboden wert: Mede den tijdt van inleggen geprolongeert," *VRBM,* 116–21. Spain, as it turned out, had the last word anyway, by effectively barring Dutch traders from the salt pans.

14. "Ampliatie van't Octroy, in date den derthienden Februarij sestien-hondert drie-en-twintich," and "Accordt tusschen de Bewinthebberen ende Hooft-Participanten vande West-Indische Compagnie . . . In date den 21 Junij 1623," *VRBM,* 122–35.

15. On the WIC's difficulties in these years, see van Winter, *Westindische Compagnie,* 5–30; den Heijer, *Geschiedenis,* 28–34; Israel, *Hispanic World,* 122–9 (which points out the reluctance of the maritime provinces, especially Amsterdam, to invest in the WIC); idem, *Dutch Republic* (1995), 325–7 (which emphasizes the "failure" of the Company, even into the 1630s); and Bachman, *Peltries or Plantations,* 25–43.

16. An altogether different anxiety expressed the fear that the WIC would become a tool of the States General and forgo the purer pursuit of profit: "Some persons fear and pretend, but in secret, that an entirely political matter will be made of [the WIC], and excuse themselves in public with one or another frivolous excuse to avoid subscription," wrote one observer, in 1622, of the lackluster funding. See the "Advies tot aanbeveling van de verovering van Brazilië door de West-Indische Compagnie," *Kroniek van het Historisch Genootschap* 27 (1871), 231 (cited in Bachman, *Peltries or Plantations,* 32, whose translation I have modified slightly).

17. "Corte aenwysinge van de verovering van Brazilië door de West-Indische Compagnie [1622]," *Kroniek van het Historisch Genootschap* 27 (1871), 231 (cited in Bachman, *Peltries or Plantations,* 31–2, whose translation I have modified slightly). For Usselincx's low opinion of his more mercantile colleagues, see the "Corte aenwysinge van de voornaemste verschillen [. . .],"

which very interestingly spells out the distinctions Usselincx perceived between his own conception of the WIC and that by now (1620) before the
States. The document, which was submitted to the States General, is
reprinted in van Rees, *Geschiedenis der staathuishoudkunde,* 2: 424 (and cf. den
Heijer, *Geschiedenis,* 28).

18. Some of the WIC's foundational ambivalence is reflected in the modern historiography, which, taking its cue from early modern debates, offers a range
of explanations for the Company's original motives. The religious, or more
particularly Calvinist, background of Usselincx is stressed by some: see, for
example, Frijhoff, "West India Company" (which discerns "a distinctive
sign of religious concern" in the WIC's early policies); and Schama, *Embarrassment of Riches,* 194 and 252. Yet military and economic objectives have received greater attention in recent years. Emmer stresses the WIC's military
goals, emphasizes its Calvinist objectives, and faults the Company for its
economic failures: "Nederlandse handelaren," 15–17 (see also idem, *Atlantic
Economy*). Den Heijer maintains that the Company concerned itself "above
all with trade," though it functioned in the early years as a "war machine":
Geschiedenis, 25, 33–4. For van Goor, the Company's political objectives—
war against Spain—carried more weight than its economic goals: *Nederlandse Koloniën,* esp. 36–39. And Klooster (*Dutch in the Americas*) contends
that "the Company was a war instrument first and foremost" (20), which
may account for Usselincx's rapid disillusion. See also note 102 in Chapter
Three.

19. Sources for the Nassau Fleet are collected and excellently introduced in
Voorbeijtel Cannenburg, *Nassausche Vloot* (hereafter *NV*). Major expeditions
had left the Republic before the Truce, to be sure, yet without substantial
backing from the state. Fleets of salt ships carried out raids against the Spanish in Punta de Araya, for example, though without the official support of
the Republic or necessary aid of firepower. Of the 1637 personnel on the
Nassau Fleet, by contrast, a full six hundred were soldiers, making this the
most powerful force yet to enter the Pacific.

20. Spilbergen spent over half a year—May through November 1615—harassing enemy shipping and Spanish ports along the western coast of South
America. He scored his greatest victory just south of Lima, when he sank
the vice admiral of the (larger) Spanish fleet sent from Callao to challenge
him. Yet despite taking the lives of more than 400 Spaniards, he never managed to capture the precious cargo ships that sailed between Spanish America and the Philippines. Warnsinck, *Joris van Spilbergen,* provides the text of
the voyage's "Journaal," and see lxviii–lxxxii on the naval engagements off
the Peruvian coast.

21. *Journael vande Nassausche Vloot* (Amsterdam, 1631), in *NV,* 3.

22. See the contemporary descriptions of the fleet's departure in van Wassenaer,
Historisch verhael, 5:48; and Baudartius, *Memoryen,* 15:132–3.

23. *NV,* 3, and see xvii on the peerless status of the fleet (citing S. Prior, ed., *All
the Voyages Round the World* [London, 1820]).

24. Pieter van Dam, *Beschryvinge van de Oostindische Compagnie* (1693–1701),

cited in *NV,* xix. As van Dam observes, it was the directors of the VOC, in these pre-WIC days, who hatched a plan to contact (in this case) the "Chileans." Note that I have generally followed the nomenclature of my sources in describing these and other native peoples encountered—or imagined—by the Dutch.

25. See the "Instructie voor u, Jacques l'Hermite, vanwegen de Ho. Mo. Heeren, de Staten-Generaal" (esp. articles 11–13 and 29), signed by Maurits and reprinted in *NV,* 105–15; and cf. also the testimony of the deserters (recorded by their Spanish interrogators, it should be noted) as quoted in ibid., lvi. One of the articles of the "Instructie" does mention a supply of arms that the prince would provide the American allies, yet it then speaks of making the natives "understand" (presumably through persuasion) the Republic's good faith and the Habsburgs' malevolence. The "letters of liberation" are mentioned, too, in another Spanish source—the viceroy's report, as cited in Bradley, *Lure of Peru,* 70—indicating Spanish knowledge of, and concern with, these Dutch documents, which were understood by the viceroy to be drafted with native Americans *and* African slaves in mind.

26. Jacob Vegeer, "of Spanish parents," administered large doses of antimony to the patients in his care, causing their rapid and apparently dramatic deaths. Vegeer's motives were never adequately ascertained, though, after a failed attempt at suicide, he confessed to a pact with the devil and appropriately diabolic range of delusions. See *NV,* lxx; the report of van Wassenaer, *Historisch verhael,* 9:68; and the fascinating study of antimony's infamous past by McCallum, "Observations upon Antimony."

27. *Journael vande Nassausche Vloot,* in *NV,* 55, 68–71, 77–9, 92–3: "In het landen dachten wij mede te gebruycken den goeden dienst van eenighe Indianen in het barkjen op eergisteren bekomen. Dese toonden haer seer vyerig voor ons en versekerden ons van de toeval der Indianen ende revolte der Negros, so wij maer vaste plaetse aen lant kregen" (69). The details of the ambush are given in the unpublished journal of Witte Cornelisz de With, captain of the *Delft,* cited in *NV,* xciii–xciv (original manuscript in the Algemeen Rijksarchief in the Hague).

28. Herckmans, *Zee-vaert lof,* 194:

> Een ellef-kielde vloot, in Holland werd ghemant
> Die na de Zuyd-zee, en de Peruaensche strand,
> Door l'Hermijts beleyd, de Spanjaerds ende Mooren,
> Te water en te vyer, en swaerde ringhelooren.

29. *Waerachtigh verhael.* This pamphlet, ironically, was based on a Castilian report that describes the success of the much smaller *Spanish* fleet in defending the harbor against the Dutch.

30. Purchas, *Hakluytus Posthumus,* 1860 (pt. 2, bk. 10). The French pamphlet was published in Paris and alludes to a *"copie Flamande"* printed in Antwerp, yet no known copy of this edition exists.

31. *Journael vande Nassaussche vloot* (Amsterdam, 1626). Other editions appeared ca. 1630, 1631, 1643, 1644, 1648, and twice in the late 1660s.

32. Aventroot, *Sendt-brief aen die van Peru*. The original Spanish letter is dated 1627, as is the *Aliance* itself.

33. Aventroot, *Sendbrief van Joan Aventroot*.

34. See the thirteenth article of the "Instructie voor u, Jacques l'Hermite, vanwegen de Ho. Mo. Heeren, de Staten-Generaal" (*NV*, 108) and the "Instructie voor den Generael" (ibid., 115). Aventroot may himself have joined l'Hermite's crew on their voyage: the admiral's instructions refer explicitly to "Jan Aventroot, die onder u is." He may also have visited Peru in his capacity as a merchant in precious metals. For biographical details, see Elst, "Une dernière victime."

35. Aventroot, *Sendt-brief aen die van Peru*, 22, 14, and passim. Aventroot opens his work with a reference to Rev. 17 and maintains a decidedly apocalyptic tone throughout. He calculated the year of the American uprising by adding the days between his visions (105) plus the seven extra days it took him to realize his mistaken prediction (112), and then adding this figure to the year Charles V ascended to the Spanish throne (1516 + 112 = 1628). The reference to the purification of the temples derives from 1 Maccabees 4:36–61 and 2 Maccabees 10:1–9.

36. Aventroot, *Sendt-brief aen die van Peru*, 24–5 (and cf. also 26–8): "De conscientie des Conincx van Spaengien is alsoo versopen inde gierigheydt. . . . Niet toelatende dat ghy [Indianen] meught tracteren met vreemt volck, om te ghenieten den goeden koop van koopmanschappen ghelijck andere Natien: maer dat ghy die als slaven, alleenlijcken moet ontfangen uyt sijn geslooten handt van Spaengien."

37. Ibid., 28–9: "Ende aen desen uwen Koninck, beloven de Hooghe Moghende Heeren Staten hare assistentie, ende gheven in dese Aliance haer ghetrouwe Woordt, hem te assisteren soo vele moghelijck te water ende te lande, tot dat Godt u sal hebben ghestelt in uwe Christelijcke vryheydt. Ende desghelijcken beloven sy u oock eeuwighe correspondentie van koophandel, dat sy sullen soo uyt Oost-Indien als uyt dese hare Provintien, bevelen u te provideren van alle nootdruftighe Waren, beter ende ten pryse vele minder als ghy die nu uyt Spaengien moet betalen."

38. Peter Bradley refers to "the lure of Peru" in his account of Dutch and English forays into the South Sea, though most of the Republic's efforts (which preceded those English voyages studied by Bradley by three-quarters of a century) focus in fact on "Chile" in preference to "Peru": Bradley, *Lure of Peru*, and cf. also Bachman, *Peltries or Plantations*, 45–7. Note that, in the case of the "Chileans," the Dutch made bona fide contact with actual native peoples: most basically with the Araucanians (Araucano; see below); more specifically, with the Mapuche; and perhaps with the Huilliche.

39. IJzerman, *Olivier van Noort*, 1:69–79 and esp. 77–8. Van Noort (or his publisher) also represented the Chileans in rather flattering prints (e. g. facing 1:60 in the IJzerman edition and fol. 33v in the original), which render the natives as cheerful, Northern European-like, indeed almost Bruegelesque peasants.

40. Isaac le Maire, "Remonstrance to Oldenbarnevelt," as cited by Bachman,

Peltries or Plantations, 46 n. 7. When Oldenbarnevelt took no action, le Maire financed the voyage himself and sent his son, Jacques (together with Willem Schouten), to explore the region.

41. Baudartius, *Memoryen,* 174; and cf. Langenes, *Caert-thresoor,* 165, which contains a remarkably similar comment on the Chileans' "goede manieren."

42. De Laet, *Nieuwe wereldt,* 432 and bk. 11 passim. Much in de Laet's description of the Chilean uprising resembles contemporary Dutch representations of the ancient Batavians and *their* heroic resistance to Rome. The Batavians were led by their barbaric chieftain, Claudius Civilis (who, like the Araucanian leader, Caupolicano, had the use of only one eye) and were likewise believed to have gathered "conspiratorially" to swear an oath of resistance against imperial tyrants. For a remarkable visual illustration of this theme, see Rembrandt's monumental *Conspiracy of Claudius Civilis* (Nationalmuseum, Stockholm), painted for the Amsterdam Town Hall in 1661.

   Among the many other references to the "Chileans," their valor, and their resistance to Spain, see van Meteren, *Historie,* fol. 587v; *Warachtighe beschrijvinghe,* 277; [Geelkercken], *Reys-boeck,* sig. Br; and Usselincx, *Waerschouwinghe over den treves,* sig. Br. Special mention goes to Martinus Hamconius's verse history of Frisland (the northwestern province of the Netherlands), which advanced the theory that ancient Frisians had sailed to Chile and planted a cross there. Whether or not these intrepid Frisian explorers colonized, they did leave their cultural mark, according to Hamconius: the word "Chile" is Frisian for "severe cold," which would have been the ancient mariners' description of the land. See Hamconius, *Frisia,* 74–5.

43. Ercilla, *Historiale beschrijvinghe,* which was based on the Spanish edition printed in Antwerp: *Primera, segunda y tercera partes de la Arucana* (1597). The poem came out in three installments, which appeared originally in 1569, 1578, and 1589. A Spanish-language edition comprising the first two parts appeared in Antwerp already in 1586 at the address of "Pedro Bellero" (Petrus Bellère). Ercilla's critics have resisted calling the work an epic for a variety of technical and historical reasons. It is, in all events, a grand, heroic, and masterful poem, unhappily overlooked by most students of sixteenth-century literature and the history of the encounter. Notable exceptions include Pastor Bodmer, *Armature of Conquest,* esp. 207–76; and Quint, *Epic and Empire,* esp. 157–85.

44. Ercilla, *Araucaniad,* 37 (and cf. 33) and 163 (and cf. 128).

45. "Voor reden," in Ercilla, *Historiale beschrijvinghe,* sig. A. Note the irony of this Dutch appropriation of a work the Spanish original of which explicitly condemned the "godless States" of the Netherlands (Ercilla, *Araucaniad,* 179).

46. Brouwer's motives resembled those of Caupolicano remarkably: love of *patria* and liberty. This, at least, was the thesis forwarded in the published journal of the voyage, which notes that "just as birds were created to roam the skies and fish to swim the seas, so are the Netherlanders apparently born to defend their ancient freedoms": *Journael ende historis verhael,* 3. Ercilla could hardly have said it better.

47. Ibid., 29–32. The natives encountered were most likely Mapuches.

48. Ibid., 53–60. The Indians who crowded Brouwer's four ships and single yacht are reported to have brought their own provisions for the journey. They lacked, however, any navigational skill, and their poor advice caused the ships to be grounded in the sands approaching Valdivia.

49. Ibid., 69: " . . . over de gestalte der Schepen verwondert zijnde, doch waren seer diefachtigh ende begeerigh naer Yser-werck, alles wat sy saghen was haer gadinge, jae tot de Compassen toe, die sy uyt de nacht-huysen wegh namen."

50. Ibid., 70–4. However enthusiastic they might have been about the deal, the caciques pleaded ignorance when asked to *sign* an actual alliance. Though European writing, in theory, would not have meant all that much to them, they showed a wary reluctance, nonetheless, to stamp their approval on a Dutch deal.

51. Ibid., 75–6; and see 88–9, which discusses the richness of Chilean agriculture.

52. *Tydingh uyt Brasijl.*

53. Commelin, *Frederick Hendrick,* 2:150–1: "Dit alles behaeghde haer wel, maer soo haest men begon te segghen, dat men aldaer gekomen was, om met haer te handelen voor goudt ('t welcke het eenighste oogmerck van de West-Indische Compagnie was) begosten hare Casiques of Oversten sich te ontschuldigen, dat sy langhe jaeren geen goudt gehadt hadden, noch 't selve sochten." The esteemed humanist Caspar Barlaeus, writing around the same time as Commelin, similarly dismissed all but the most mercenary motives for the voyage. He saw Brouwer as an "ambitious man," autocratic and unpopular with his men. Herckmans, on the other hand, he considered a good man "and a poet." See Barlaeus, *Nederlandsch Brazilië,* 333.

54. Dutch plans for South America (and even "Chile") did in fact persist—if on less grandiose terms and with less official backing than during the first half of the century, when the Republic was actively at war with Spain. In the later 1650s, for example, the Dutch engaged a citizen of Cumana (Venezuela), who was interviewed in Amsterdam to determine if he might support an insurrection designed to seize the northern section of the continent (Venezuela to Brazil). Other plans called for attacks on the southern corner of the continent, too, and a Dutchman fluent in Spanish was dispatched to the region around the Rio Plata to make inquiries. He wandered some five hundred miles inland, drafted strategic maps, and made clandestine contacts—though ultimately failed to spark the much-anticipated American revolution. His efforts are dutifully reported in a letter to the Spanish ambassador to The Hague, 26 April 1662 (Archivo General de Simancas, Estado 8389, fol. 111).

55. For the Republic's political and military efforts in Brazil, see the classic account of Boxer, *Dutch in Brazil;* and cf. Cabral de Mello, *Olinda Restaurada.*

56. On the attack of Bahia, see the contemporary narrative of de Laet, *Iaerlyck verhael,* 1:14–30; and Boxer, *Dutch in Brazil,* 21–3.

57. [Geelkercken], *Reys-boeck,* sig. Aiij; *Consideratien ende redenen,* 10; Ruiters, *Toortse der Zeevaert,* 35. Ruiters's aside concerning the "Jews" is cited by

Boxer (*Dutch in Brazil,* 16) and Parker ("The Dutch Revolt and the Polarization of International Politics," in *Spain and the Netherlands,* 78), both of whom neglect to note Ruiters's own reservations. While he believed that the Portuguese ("of whom most are Jews") would rejoice to see Dutch arms free them from the Inquisition, Ruiters also warned that the Dutch would have to keep a close watch on that (to his mind) most untrustworthy race.

58. *Goede nieuwe tijdinghe;* Moerbeeck, *Redenen waeromme,* 3–4. On the Jews in Brazil more generally: Wiznitzer, *Jews in Colonial Brazil,* esp. 51–7, which deals with Bahia.

59. Dionysius Spranckhuysen, "Cort verhael vande voyage ghedaen door de vlote van de West-Indische Compagnye, onder het beleydt van den Heere Generael Pieter Pietersz. Heyn," in L'Honoré Naber and Wright, *Piet Heyn,* 1:177; and cf. van Wassenaer, *Historisch verhael,* 15:54, for a slightly less partisan account. De Laet tells a similar story about the attack of Dutch sailors on the island of Dominica: *Iaerlyck verhael,* 1:84.

60. Van Wassenaer, *Historisch verhael,* 7:48, 87, and cf. 7:40–6 for his report on Willekens.

61. Servaes Carpentier to the Heren XIX, 18 April 1634 (ARA / OWIC 50), cited in van den Boogaart, "Infernal Allies," 527 (and see also the letter of M. van Ceulen to the Heeren XIX, 18 April 1634, cited in ibid.). On the directors' disappointment with the Brazilian campaign, see Boxer, *Dutch in Brazil,* 45–6.

62. Herckmans, "Generale beschrijvinge"; de Laet, *Iaerlyck verhael,* 4:78; Soler, *Cort ende sonderlingh verhael,* 5–8. On Soler, see Gonsalves de Mello, "Vincent Joachim Soler." For another concerned report on the prospects of a Dutch-Tarairiu alliance, see the *Pertinent bericht.*

63. De Laet, *Nieuwe wereldt,* 106–7; van Wassenaer, *Historisch verhael,* 6:147 (and for both sources, cf. the translations in Jameson, *Narratives,* which I have altered slightly). For the early history of the colony, see Hart, *Prehistory;* and Rink, *Holland on the Hudson,* 69–93.

64. Michaëlius's letters are reprinted and translated in Eekhof, *Michaëlius,* 99–139, and see esp. 109–11, 132. The frigid weather is noted in both letters, as it is in virtually all other reports of the early colonists. See, for example, the "Memorie" of 1633, which notes, "Though these parts [New Netherland], according to climate ought to be as warm and suitable for fruit culture as the extreme limits of France adjoining Spain, . . . the same was found to be colder than these, yes, than more northerly countries" (cited in Bachman, *Peltries or Plantations,* 57). Such meteorological consternation was not unique: see Kupperman, "Puzzle of the American Climate."

65. *Wonderlicke avontuer,* and see also the excellent introduction to the modern edition by E. K. Grootes (Muiderberg, 1984). The reference to America as a "treasure chamber" comes from the *Discours, aengaende treves of vrede,* 26. Much the same visual message is conveyed in a drawing attributed to Joachim Wtewael, *Indian Homage* (Albertina, Vienna), part of a larger allegorical series on the history of the Republic. The drawing is believed to date from the early 1610s and to convey a hopeful message for American trade—represented by Wtewael in the form of superabundant riches. See McGrath,

"Netherlandish History," which contains an interesting discussion of the artist's politics and how they might pertain to the conception of the drawing.

66. The numerous pamphlets discussing the negotiations of 1629–1630 and the fate of the WIC include the *Consideratien ende redenen* (actually a position paper of the WIC); *Discours, aengaende treves of vrede; Klare aenwijsinge;* and *Redenen* (1630). A more extensive list can be found in Knuttel, *Pamfletten,* nos. 3909–25 and 4007–30 (which are concerned with the negotiations generally); and Asher, *Bibliographical and historical essay,* 124–8.

67. *Fin de la guerre,* 43 (and see 7–9 and 29 for similarly hawkish directives): "gaen ruyten ende rooven . . . ende luyden verwoesten, met branden ende blaken . . . ende van West-Indien een tonneel der ellendigheden maken, want de Spaensche natie sulckx wel verdient hebben, door de groote tyrannien by henlieden hier, ende oock daer te Lande ghepleecht." The "fighting words" are cited from Herckmans, *Zee-vaert lof,* 194–5; and *Discours, aengaende treves of vrede,* 29.

68. Ampzing, *West-Indische triumph-basuyne,* esp. 8–13; and on Ampzing, see van Nierop, "How to honour one's city," with an updated bibliography.

69. Van Waerdenburgh, *Copie vande missive,* sig. [A4]v; van Wassenaer, *Historisch verhael,* 18:89 (and note that this volume was completed by van Wassenaer's assistant, Barent Lampe); Herckmans, *Zee-vaert lof,* 195. Herckmans would develop an even sharper opinion (largely negative) of the native Tarairiu during his tour of Brazilian duty in the mid-1630s and early 1640s. See idem, "Generale beschrijvinge," esp. 361–2.

70. De Laet, *Nieuwe wereldt;* and cf. Lepore, *Name of War,* xvi, which discusses the Massachusetts Bay Colony's emblem featuring another Indian supplicant, this time citing Acts 16:9 ("Come over and help us"), and suggesting the difference between the more economically oriented attitudes of the Dutch and apocalyptic notions of the New Englanders—albeit half a century later. The engraved *Allegory of America* (n.d.) is ascribed to van den Hoeye by Honour (*New Golden Land,* 90), though the print itself (cropped in Honour) suggests Pieter Serwouters after Pieter Sibrantsz—an attribution that makes more sense when this American allegory is juxtaposed to Serwouter's Asian one reproduced in Hollstein, *Dutch and Flemish Etchings,* 26:243.

71. *Klare aenwijsinge,* sig. [H4]r; Teellinck, *Tweede wachter,* sig. C4r; Spranckhuysen, *Triumphe,* 22–3.

72. Baers, *Olinda; Fin de la guerre; Consideratien ende redenen.* References to the Bohemians include *Klare aenwijsinge,* sig. D; *Redenen* (1630), sig. Hiij-v; *Discours, aengaende treves,* 23; *Dialogus ofte t'samenspreekinge,* sigs. B4–C; *Missive inhoudende der aerdt vanden treves,* sig. Cij. Around this time, too, pamphleteers resuscitated the topos of universal monarchism, though they now situated the Bohemians, rather than Indians, among its central victims. See, for example, *Nederlandschen verre-kijcker,* 1–3; and Focanus, *Adoni-Beseck,* "Voorrede" (n.p.).

73. Teellinck, *Tweede wachter;* Ampzing, *West-Indische triumph-basuyne,* which

contains notably anti-Catholic prose in its opening passages. See also Wijnandts, *Lof-dicht,* which uses similar language to describe the blood spilled by the "Babylonian whore" in America.

74. This theme, of course, had originally been developed, in extraordinarily apocalyptic terms, outside of the Netherlands: by the Spanish cleric, Bartolomé de Las Casas, who preached the sermon of godly wrath most passionately in his *Brevíssima relación.* It is interesting to note how Dutch Calvinists, in this case, happily follow the Dominican's lead regarding divine justice, retribution, and grace. See Ampzing, *West-Indische triumph-basuyne,* "Voor-rede" (n.p.); and Focanus, *Adoni-Beseck,* 34–45, both of which cite Las Casas explicitly in this regard. On Lascasian hermeneutics, see Pagden, *European Encounters,* 69–83.

75. Focanus, *Adoni-Beseck,* 45 and passim; *Steyger-praetjen; Dialogus ofte t'samenspreekinge,* sig. [D4]r:

> 't Gewelt, en overdaet dat Spangien heeft bedreven,
> Aen d'Indien, en aen ons, daer van wert veel geschreven,
> Dat haer hanght over 't hooft een straf soo swaer als oyt
> Van yemandt is gehoort, jae 'tmoet heel uytgeroyt,
> En sijn aen haer getoont een sulcke Godes wraecke,
> Dat d'opganck van het vuyr de Werelt door sal blaecken.

76. Focanus, *Adoni-Beseck,* 100; *Fin de la guerre,* 16; Wijnandts, *Lof-dicht,* sigs. A2v–A3r ("Dat Landt is noch vol bloets, dat bloet dat roept noch wraecke / . . . Gheoctroyeert om 't bloet, int Landt weer op te dweylen / . . . Dit bloet roept Wraecke nu, en helpt ons in den strijdt, / Ten sal niet rusten voor, ghy uwen schat sijt quijt); and Herckmans, *Zee-vaert lof,* 202. For his less than orthodox vision of the transmigration of souls, Herckmans cites Pythagoras.

77. Souter, *Eben-ezer,* 109–11; and see also idem, *Sené-boher,* 334–7, which treats the capture of Olinda. Souterius's biblical allusion is to Exodus 12:35–6.

78. Ampzing, *West-Indische triumph-basuyne,* "Voor-rede," n.p. and 33:

> om dat Maraen dit land door quaede wegen,
> Door swaerd, en door geweld, en rooven heeft verkragt
> En daer so meenig mensch moorddadelijk geslacht:
> Wil God dien roof, die moord, op Spanjen gaen verhalen
> En dat onschuldig bloed hun op den kop betalen . . . ?

79. Teellinck, *Tweede wachter,* esp. sigs. F4v–Gv. Similar contentions can also be found in idem, *Derde wachter.* For the story of Äi, see Joshua 7:1–5, which relates how the Lord allowed the Israelites, upon their repentance, to smite the inhabitants of Äi to the last man. On Teellinck and the *Nadere Reformatie,* see Graham, *Later Calvinism,* particularly Fred Van Lieburg, "From Pure Church to Pious Culture" (409–30).

80. Joost van den Vondel, *Op het ontset van Piet Heyns buyt, Het West-Injes-huys spreeckt* (1629; published three times that year): "Ick docht, deus Geuzen bennen Spaens / Of is sint Pieter Harmians." Vondel implies that the

Geuzen—and by this term the poet meant to associate the WIC sailors with those lower-class followers of the more fiery, urban *predikanten*—attacked the West-Indies House as might greedy Spaniards, jealous of Dutch wealth, or as might orthodox Gomarists, intolerant of an Arminian ("Sint Pieter"). In another instance, the polemically playful Vondel went so far as to liken the Arminians to the oppressed natives of America, thus comparing the Gomarists, by extension, to marauding conquistadors. The modern, edited version of the poem is in Vondel, *Werken*, 3:259–60; and see Spies, "Verbeeldingen van Vrijheid," on Vondel's Arminian-as-Indian trope.

81. Usselincx, *Waerschouwinghe over den treves*, sigs. A2v–A3r and *passim* (and note the similar allegations—that a peace treaty favored the Arminians—in *Ghespreck van Langhe Piet met Keesje Maet*); van den Sande, *Nederlandtsche historie*, 111–57; van Wassenaer, *Historisch verhael*, 7:46 (and on van Wassenaer's orthodoxy, see Kannegieter, "Nicolaes Jansz. van Wassenaer"); Hommius, *Tweede vervolch*, 1064; van Buchell, *Diarium*, x (and see Pollmann, *Religious Choice*, for van Buchell's religious transformations); Ampzing, *West-Indische triumph-basuyne*, 6 ("Wien hoor ik van het volk hier tegens murmureren / Of wie ontkend hier in de rechte hand des Heren?").

82. Dionysius Spranckhuysen, "Tot den goetgunstigen leser," cited in L'Honoré Naber and Wright, *Piet Heyn*, 1: vii; and *Practiicke van den Spaenschen aes-sack*, n.p. The details of Heyn's adventure are superbly reviewed in L'Honoré Naber and Wright, *Piet Heyn* (see esp. 1: xi–clxxxvii), a volume that also collects the chief sources related to the event. See further de Laet, *Iaerlyck verhael*, 1:56–73; and the overview in Goslinga, *Dutch in the Caribbean*, 173–202. Note that, as Geyl put it, "what came off once never occurred again": Heyn's spectacular feat was never duplicated, despite persistent, and very costly, efforts (*Seventeenth Century*, 191).

83. Pels, *Lof-dicht* ("En self de jonge jeught al spelend' by der straaten, / Die wisten in hun Spel, voort van de vloot te praaten"); and cf. Heinsius, *Oratio panegyrica*. For a full bibliography of the tremendous contemporary reaction to Heyn, see L'Honoré Naber and Wright, *Piet Heyn*, 1: cxliv–clv; and Asher, *Bibliographical and historical essay*, 119–23. As Spranckhuysen himself pointed out, the poets were helped by the exceptionally euphonic, compact, and rhythmically adaptable name of their subject, "Piet Heyn": see L'Honoré Naber and Wright, *Piet Heyn*, 1: cliv.

84. "Een nieu liedeken, ter eeren van den Generael Pieter Pietersz Heyn, over den grooten schadt die hy op de zee bekomen heeft," in Leendertz, *Geuzenliedboek*, 2:268–71: "Den ed'len Generael / Eenen Zee-Heldt verkooren / Die gheen ghelijken heeft, / Van die oyt is ghebooren / Of teghenwoordich leeft."

85. Along with those sources cited above, see for example, *Rym-vieren op de jeghen-woordige victorie*; Lommelin, *Lof-dicht*; van Kennenburch, *Protest ofte scherp dreyghement*; and especially Spranckhuysen, *Triumphe*, and idem, "Tot den goetgunstigen leser," from which the final quotation comes. The fall of Jericho is described in Joshua 6, the story of Gideon in Judges 6–8.

86. Van Kennenburch, *Protest ofte scherp dreyghement,* sig. A3r:

> Oock dat dees jonghe maets met haer bepeckte broeck:
> Mijn wijff, mijn echte wijff, besoed'len haer doek;
> Haer hair, haer gout geel-hair, ontvlechten sy behendich
> Haer silveren blanck aenschijn, besmeuren sy oock schendich,
> Sy hebben eerst ontschaeckt mijn oude *Cocubijn* [sic],
> Nu willen sy van't wijff oock Heer en meester sijn.

Cf. Focanus, *Adoni-Beseck,* 98, which uses similar language to describe the combined conquest of the East and West Indies, comparing the latter, in somewhat less romantic terms, to the king's "favorite milch cow."

87. Eibergen, *Swymel-klacht,* 16; and cf. van Kennenburch, *Protest ofte scherp dreyghement;* Liefs, *Lof dicht;* idem, *Oost ende West-Indische Compagnye;* and *Tijdinge* (1628).

88. Liefs, *Lof dicht,* n. p. ("Om dese rijcke brudt met eerlust te beslapen / Ons kloecken Generael beschermt haer met sijn wapen"), and cf. idem, *Oost ende West-Indische Compagnye,* sigs. A4v–Bv; Ampzing, *West-Indische triumph-ba-suyne,* 4, 13–14, 24; and van Kennenburch, *Protest ofte scherp dreyghement,* sig. A3r. The allusion to David is in Spranckhuysen, *Triumphe,* 1.

89. Baudartius, *Morghen-wecker,* title-page. On patriotic history, see Schama, *Embarrassment of Riches,* 51–125 (esp. 69–93); and cf. also Parker, "History and National Identity."

90. *Practiicke van den Spaenschen aes-sack;* Spranckhuysen, *Tranen,* 17.

91. For a complete bibliography of these and other texts of early modern Dutch historiography, see Haitsma Mulier and van der Lem, *Repertorium.*

92. Valerius, *Nederlandsche gedenck-clanck,* 5–6 (emphasis added): "Historien . . . den aendachtigen ende vernuftigen leser voorstellen ende toebrenghen groote rycke stoffe, aenleydende tot wijsheyt, door de gedachtenisse dat geschiet is; tot vromigheyt, door de bedenckinge van't gene altyd behoort te geschieden; ende tot voorsichtigheyt, door de aenmerckinge van't gene noch geschieden kan." For the metaphor of history as a "treasury of time," see, for example, Merula, *Tijdt-threzoor;* and Twisck, *Onderganc der tijrannen . . . wesende een tydtthresoor.*

93. Gijsius, *Oorsprong en voortgang,* sigs. [ij]r–[iij]r; Focanus, *Adoni-Beseck,* Dedi-cation (n.p.).

94. Allertsz, *Spieghel der jeucht,* sig. Aij (emphasis added); and see Schama, *Embarrassment of Riches,* 82, which also distinguishes the Haggadah-like qual-ity of certain patriotic histories.

95. Valerius, *Gedenck-clanck,* 5–7.

96. Baudartius, *Morghen-wecker,* "Aen die . . . Staten Generael der Vrye Neder-landen" (n.p.), and see sig. Kij for Baudartius's explanation of the crane on the title-page.

97. Van Heemskerk, *Batavische arcadia,* sig. A2; Gijsius, *Oorsprong en voortgang,* sig. [iiij]v; and Allertsz, *Spieghel der jeucht,* sig. Av.

98. Allertsz, *Spieghel der jeucht,* sigs. Aiij–Aiiij.

99. Twisck, *Onderganc der tijrannen*, 1:898 (and cf. 1:893–9 for the principal materials relating to America's conquest): "Hoe wel beminde Leser, dat ick in Chronijcksche beschrijvinge niet geern veel in-reden ghebruycke, om de Historie daer door niet te verduysteren ofte al te seer te verlangen, . . . Soo en can ick het nochtans hier niet wel voor-by u een weynich te verhalen van dese saken die tot waerschouwinghe dienen, ende tot opmerckinghe verwercken, te weten: Dat u al-hier bysonder vanden Jare 1492. tot den Jare 1542. voorghedraghen, ende als in eenen Spiegel ontdeckt wordt, den aert, nature, listicheyt, bedroch, valscheyt, ontrou, eergiericheyt, wreetheyt, tyrannie, ende heerschappije der Spanjaerts . . . inde Nieuwe Werelt . . . bedreven: Ons dienende om altijdt inde memorie ende ghedachtenisse levendich ende naeckt voor onse ooghen te houden, ende nimmermeer in't huys der verghetelheydt te stellen, maer neerstich waken, vlijtich toe-sien, ende altijt op onse hoede te zijn . . . om niet weder te vallen onder de Spaensche heerschappije, tyrannie, ende ghewelt."

100. Cf. Baudartius, *Morghen-wecker*; Allertsz, *Spieghel der jeucht*; Gijsius, *Oorsprong en voortgang; Tweede deel;* and *Warachtighe beschrijvinghe*. Baudartius's text was distinguished as the outstanding *volkschrift* of the century by Tiele in the Bijlage to his *Bibliotheek van Nederlandsche pamfletten*, 1.

101. *Tweede deel,* 1. Of the other "popular" histories noted earlier, all mention the fate of the Indians, in some capacity, in their opening pages.

102. Gijsius, *Origio et historia* (Leiden 1619). The second edition came out in Amsterdam, 1641.

103. Van Meteren, *Historie*, fol. 418, and see the "Voor-rede" of the 1599 edition for a declaration of "impartiality"; Hooft, *Neederlandsche histoorien*, 333–4. On van Meteren, see Brummel, "Van Meteren als historicus," reprinted in an excellent collection that serves as the starting point for any study of Dutch historiography (with essays on both Bor and Hooft): Geurts and Janssen, *Geschiedschrijving in Nederland*.

104. Breen, "Gereformeerd populaire historiographie." The editors of the *Repertorium van geschiedschrijvers* (see note 91) name Johannes Bouillet as the author of the *Spieghel der jeught,* yet give no evidence to support a contention that flies in the face of the title-page. Breen himself suggests "J. Poulliet"; yet see the Bijlage to the first volume of Tiele's *Bibliotheek van Nederlandsche pamfletten*, which discusses the issue of authorship and explicitly designates "Herman Allertsz. Koster" for that role.

105. On Hommius (who was a chief antagonist of Arminius from the early 1600s), see Wijminga, *Festus Hommius;* and for de Laet's religious engagement, see his own *Commentarii de Pelagianis et Semi-Pelagianis* (Harderwijk, 1617). On van Meteren, see Brummel, "Van Meteren als historicus," and Verduyn, *Emanuel Van Meteren*. Hooft's role as historian is examined by Groenveld, *Hooft als historieschrijver;* and see also Haitsma Mulier, "History in the Dutch Republic." Bor is studied in two articles by Janssen, "Pieter Bor Christiaenszoon" and "'Trias historica.'" And on Twisck—a "vermaner" (exhorter) of the Mennonite community of Hoorn, who also wrote

a two-volume *Religions vryheyt* (1609)—see Penner, "Pieter Jansz. Twisck." A fine examination of "libertine" religious politics can be found in Kaplan, *Calvinists and Libertines.*

106. Valerius, *Gedenck-clanck,* esp. 11–13 (and cf. the song on 239, which invites the WIC to avenge the "hellish murders" of Spain in America); Hondius, *Moufe-schans,* esp. 409–29, which concentrates on the subject of history; van Heemskerk, *Batavische arcadia,* 173–5, and note the citation in the index (sig. [Rr12]r), "Spanjaerden soecken Nederlandt het uytghemoorden West Indien gelijk te maecken," listed under the letter *s.* Hondius and the country-house poem are treated in van Veen, *Soeticheydt des buyten-levens,* 19–23.

107. The print of the *pot,* engraved by Hessel Gerritsz, was intended as an advertisement. There were two other popular *doolhoven* in Amsterdam, both of which contained "memorials" to Alba's tyrannies. The first, the "Oude Doolhof" of Vincent Peylder, had a "panopticum" that showed important figures of Dutch and European history, including the iron duke. The second, the "Nieuwe Doolhof op de Roosegracht" owned by David Lingelbach, had statuary representing "the tyranny of the duke of Alba," together with a variety of other patriotic themes. See Meijer, "Het Oude Doolhof te Amsterdam"; and de Roever, "Het Nieuwe Doolhof." For a provocative exploration of the *modern* historical theme park, cf. Lowenthal, *Possessed by the Past.*

108. *Nederlandschen verre-kijcker,* sig. A2r.

109. Gijsius, *Oorsprong en voortgang,* "Aen alle vrome en oprechte Nederlanders, die den wel stand ende Vrijheydt hares lieven Vaderlands beminnen," sig. ij-r: "De onversadelijcke eergierigheyt, de onverdraechlijcke hoogmoet, ende de onmenschelijcke wreetheyt der Spaengiaerden, is in dese laetste hondert jaeren, na dat sy eenighe macht hebben beginnen te crijgen, door de geheele werelt, niet dan al te seer bekent geworden. De onnosele *Indianen* onder de *Heydenen* hebben de selve aldereerst moeten beproeven, ende daer na de vroome *Nederlanders* onder de *Christenen.*"

110. Ibid, 407 (which is lifted verbatim from Baudartius's *Morghen-wecker,* sig. Iiiij-r), and cf. the reference on the preceding page to Spanish attacks on French Huguenots in Florida; *Tweede deel,* 1; *Warachtighe beschrijvinghe,* 276–7.

111. *Tweede deel;* Hondius, *Moufe-schans,* 409–17 and 417–28.

112. Hooft, *Neederlandsche histoorien,* 333–34. Van Meteren uses a similar, if less dramatic, device to review the life of Philip II on the occasion of his death. He summarizes the essential hypocrisy of the king's religion with reference to "the millions of souls" slaughtered in the Indies "under the false pretext of religion": *Historie,* fol. 418.

113. Baudartius, *Morghen-wecker,* sig. A-v; *Warachtighe beschrijvinghe,* 154, 250 (and cf. the similar passage in the *Morghen-wecker,* sig. Dij-r, naming Alba one of the "voornaemste auteurs" of the *Conquista*). A striking, and strikingly precocious, version of such thematic exchange occurs in an early biography of Orange, which describes Alba preparing for battle against "the Indians" of the Netherlands, whom the duke hopes to slaughter in the

manner of a conqueror: see Benedicti, *Rebus gestis illustrissimi principis Guilielmi,* lines 89–93.

114. Cf. the specific atrocities described, on the one hand, in Hooft, *Neederland-sche histoorien,* 279, 424–25; Bor, *Nederlandsche oorlogen,* 1:418–19; Gijsius, *Oorsprong en voortgang,* 310, 351; *Warachtighe beschrijvinghe,* 249–50 (which pertains to Habsburg troops in Westphalia); and, on the other hand, the catalogue of tyrannies in Las Casas's *Spieghel de Spaensche tyrannye.* Particularly revealing is the comparison of those prints popularized in Las Casas's work with those in Gijsius's "Tweede deel" (*Spiegel der Spaensche tyrannye gheschiet in Nederlandt*).

115. Van Meteren, *Historie,* "Voor-reden aenden Leser," sig. *3r.

Chapter Five

1. Udemans, *Geestelyck roer;* and see also idem, *Geestelick compas,* which likewise contemplates commerce and conduct in the Indies. Udemans's title puns on the words "koopmanschap" (commerce) and "koopmans schip" (merchant's ship). It also suggests the metaphor of the merchant's vessel as a church at sea, guided (it was hoped) by a godly crew and "spiritual rudder." On Udemans (ca. 1580–1649), see Meertens, "Godefridus Cornelisz. Udemans"; and Fieret, *Udemans.*

2. Udemans, *Geestelyck roer,* Dedicatie (n.p.) and 92.

3. Ibid., 4, 102, and passim. On Dutch anxieties concerning the accumulation of commercial wealth in a godly republic, see Schama, *Embarrassment of Riches,* esp. 330–1, where Udemans's text is briefly discussed.

4. The very palpable sense of marvel was noted by contemporaries, both within and without the Republic: see Swart, *Miracle of the Dutch Republic;* and Davids and Lucassen, *Miracle Mirrored.*

5. Other Dutch colonies took root as well, if perhaps less deeply. Aside from settlements in Brazil and New Netherland, the WIC established trading posts on the Wild Coast (chiefly on the Essequibo and Berbice Rivers in Guiana) and in the Caribbean (including a presence on Curaçao from 1634 and St. Eustatius from 1636). None of these smaller settlements, however, had the same impact back in the Netherlands—economically, socially, culturally—as did the two larger colonies, and none received the same degree of press until later in the seventeenth century. See Goslinga, *Dutch in the Caribbean;* and Klooster, *Illicit Riches.*

6. For the history of New Netherland, the classic, nineteenth-century narratives may still be consulted with great profit: O'Callaghan, *History of New Netherland;* and Brodhead, *State of New York.* On matters of economy, see further Condon, *New York Beginnings;* Bachman, *Peltries or Plantations;* and Maika, "Commerce and Community," which covers the later years of the colony. An excellent study of church and religion can be found in Eekhof, *Hervormde Kerk;* though cf. the revisionist direction taken by Frijhoff, "West India Company." Social and cultural developments are surveyed by Raesly, *Portrait of New Netherland;* and see also Merwick, *Possessing Albany* and idem, *Death of a Notary,* which, though focused on the upper Hudson, are richly suggestive

for the entire colony. For an insightful overview of the state of research, see Rink, *Holland on the Hudson;* as well as Goodfriend, "Historiography," and Krewson, *New Netherland.* A relative flood of recent dissertations indicates the liveliness and diversity of current research on New Netherland: see (for example) Williams, "Cultural Mingling"; Maika, "Commerce and Community"; Van Zandt, "Negotiating Settlement"; and Jacobs, *Zegenrijk gewest.*

7. Dudley Carelton protested to the States General in 1622 regarding the encroachment of the "Hollanders" on English territory in Virginia and "certain quarters of Nova Anglica," though apparently with little effect. Somewhat earlier and even less consequential were the complaints of Samuel Argall, an adventurer and "governor" of the fledgling Virginia colony, who challenged Dutch sailors—this in 1614—and sent word to his superiors of their trespass upon "English" territory. Nothing came of it. In a typically more discreet manner, the French also laid claim to the region when they—or at least a consortium of French merchants—outfitted a certain David Pieters in 1624 to lead a fur-trading expedition to the region. In this case, WIC agents seized the ship, which was anchored in Hoorn, and prevented its departure. Rink, *Holland on the Hudson,* 69–72, discusses the Carelton and Pieters incidents and cites the original manuscript sources in the Algemeen Rijksarchief (The Hague). On Argall, see Schmidt, "Mapping an Empire" (note 33).

8. Van Laer, *Documents Relating to New Netherland,* 17, 39, 51–2, where the discussion pertains to "High," also known as "Verhulst," Island, near present-day Trenton, New Jersey. The 1625 Verhulst "Instructions" are exceedingly subtle. On the one hand, they make allowances even for less-than-solid claims staked by the natives—thus the generous phrasing, *"daerop pretenderen."* On the other hand, they go on to hint at a possible ulterior motive for dealing so contractually with the natives: "since such contracts upon other occasions may be very useful to the Company" (ibid., 52). The implication, however, that the Company wished to get the better of the Indians by legal maneuvers (and the perceived "usefulness" of contracts might relate to European rivals, of course, rather than Indian claimants) is dispelled by a set of "Further Instructions" to Verhulst, which vigorously discourage "craft or fraud" and explicitly state the reason for doing so: "lest we call down the wrath of God upon our unrighteous beginnings" (ibid., 106). At stake, ultimately, was godliness—on which see the discussion below.

9. Van Laer, *Van Rensselaer Bowier Manuscripts,* 150–1 (hereafter *VRBM*); and more generally, Trelease, *Indian Affairs,* 25–59, which contends that the Dutch "probably" purchased virtually all of the land they occupied.

American folk tradition, it is worth pointing out, has somewhat exaggerated Minuit's bargain. The celebrated sixty guilders, rendered since the mid-nineteenth century as twenty-four dollars, actually matched, in seventeenth-century terms, a half-year's wages for an ordinary seaman; and it may have exceeded the wages earned by a variety of skilled and unskilled laborers over the same period of time. Though this still would rank as a bargain in present markets, no contemporary references describe the purchase as anything remarkable. See Noordegraaf, *Hollands welvaren,* and de Vries and van der

Woude, *First Modern Economy,* which chart prices and wages in seventeenth-century Holland. For the considerable body of literature devoted to parsing Minuit's real estate savvy, see Weslager, "Manhattan Island"; Gehring, "Minuit's Purchase of Manhattan"; Francis, "Beads That Did *Not* Buy Manhattan"; and most recently (and lightheartedly), Burrows and Wallace, *Gotham,* xiv–xvi.

10. Though New Netherland's low population figures, when compared to those in the Republic, seem less minuscule—a point made by Emmer, "Nederlandse handelaren." See also Rink, "People of New Netherland," which provides migration data; and, on the notable heterogeneity of the colony, see Cohen, "How Dutch were the Dutch."

11. See the *Vryheden ende Exemptien,* reprinted with an English translation in *VRBM,* 136–53; and cf. Rink, *Holland on the Hudson,* 94–107, which provides an interesting discussion of the early drafts of this document. On the patroons more generally, see Nissenson, *Patroon's Domain;* and cf. Goslinga, *Dutch in the Caribbean,* 101–5, which describes a parallel set of patroonships in the Caribbean and on the Wild Coast.

12. See the "Proposed Articles for the Colonization and Trade of New Netherland" in Brodhead, *Documents,* 1:110–15.

13. For the history of Dutch Brazil, see Boxer's masterful *Dutch in Brazil,* in conjunction with Wätjen, *Holländische Kolonialreich,* the latter especially good on matters economic. The story is told from the other perspective by Cabral de Mello, *Olinda Restaurada,* and Gonsalves de Mello, *Tempos dos Flamengos.* See, too, the useful survey of Schulten, *Nederlandse Expansie.* The contemporary account of de Laet provides a wealth of archival detail: *Iaerlyck verhael.*

14. For a review of these events, see Boxer, *Dutch in Brazil,* 32–6, which makes excellent use of Spanish and Portuguese sources; and de Laet, *Iaerlyck verhael,* pts. 3–4, which provides the more triumphant, Company perspective. A presumably neutral French observer confirms the dire situation of the Dutch when he describes the unseasoned WIC troops as substantially emaciated, plagued by scurvy and worms, and generally "not cut out to be soldiers": Guelen, *Kort verhael* (cited in Klooster, *Dutch in the Americas,* 25–6).

15. On Johan Maurits's remarkable tenure in Brazil, see the outstanding narrative of Barlaeus, *Rerum per octennium in Brasilia,* translated as *Nederlandsch Brazilië* (and see 59 for the reference to "Augean stables"). See also Boxer, *Dutch in Brazil,* 67–158; and Bouman's biography, *Johan Maurits.*

16. Manuel Calado do Salvador, *O valeroso Lucideno e triumpho de liberdade* (Lisbon, 1648), 53 (cited in Boxer, *Dutch in Brazil,* 116).

17. The patronage of Johan Maurits, in Brazil as well as Europe, has been detailed in three excellent studies: van den Boogaart, *Johan Maurits;* idem, *Zo wijd de wereld strekt;* and de Werd, *Soweit der Erdkreis reicht.* The invaluable reference work for the artifacts produced in, or related to, Dutch Brazil (with an exhaustive bibliography) is Whitehead and Boeseman, *Seventeenth-Century Brazil.*

18. *Reglement byde West-Indische Compagnie.* The WIC continued to profit from

import and export duties levied on private traders and from the Company's own share in the trade itself. On the free-trade pamphlets and the polemics that accompanied them, see the more extensive discussion below.

19. The prince earned 1,500 florins per month as well as a percentage of all prizes won in Brazil—a hefty salary within the context of early American colonialism. The WIC also paid for three members of his entourage and contended with his constant demands for more cash, necessary, he claimed, for his building projects. More than likely, the prince also had enemies among the monopolist directors, who resented his politicking on behalf of free trade; and among hard-line Calvinists, who objected to his tolerance of "papists" and Jews. On his remarkable record with the latter, see Wiznitzer, *Jews in Colonial Brazil*, 63–91.

20. Boxer, *Dutch in Brazil*, 108, who makes a case for the high prospects of the WIC at this moment—this in contrast to the consensus among most Dutch historians that the project was doomed from the start. For the pessimistic persepective, see, for example, Geyl, *Seventeenth Century*, 193–7; and, more recently, van den Boogaart, "Nederlandse expansie." Sitting on the fence perhaps is den Heijer, who echoes Boxer in speaking of an expansive "South Atlantic imperium" not necessarily doomed to failure, yet characterizes this empire nonetheless as a wobbly "giant with feet of clay": *Geschiedenis van de WIC*, 48.

21. Baardt, *Friesche Triton;* Herckmans, *Zee-vaert lof*, 202–10; Bodecher Banning, *Epigrammata Americana;* de Lange, *Batavise Romeyn*, "Aen den Leser" (n.p.) and *passim.* De Lange's all-inclusive patriotism led him to adopt even Crestofle d'Artischau Arciszewski, the Polish soldier of fortune who served as a colonel for the WIC in the 1630s and was praised by Lange as a "Batavian" hero. On the wall map of Johan Maurits, see Zandvliet, "Cartography of Dutch Brazil." Other examples of the "epic" mood in contemporary Dutch Americana include Acronius van Buma, *Argo Belgica;* the relevant sections (on the Brazil campaign) of Orlers, *Wilhelm en Maurits;* and Commelin, *Frederick Hendrick*, which also managed to include sections on Dutch Brazil.

22. Joost van den Vondel, "Parnasloof," in Publius Vergilius Maro, *Wercken in Nederduitsch dicht vertaelt*, trans. Joost van den Vondel (Amsterdam, 1660), n.p.:

> daer vorst Maurits in Brezijl
> De leeusvaen planten, en een' burgerlijcken stijl
> Invoeren op de kust, daer andere starren schijnen,
> De mencheneeter dwaelt in wouden en woestijnen.

The "flag of the lion" refers to the arms of the United Provinces, which were emblazoned with a lion (*Leo Belgicus*); and the "coast where other stars shine" would be the coast of Brazil or, more generally, the Southern Hemisphere.

23. Plante, *Mauritiados*, lines 1–5. See also Eekhout, "'Mauritias,'" which summarizes the poem and draws attention to other sets of parallel, Virgilian passages: for example, Virgil's description of Aeolus's (god of the winds) efforts

to prevent Aeneas from landing in Italy (*Aeneid*, 1.81–107), and Plante's narration of Aeolus's like-minded labors to keep Willekens off the coast of Bahia (*Mauritias*, 2.8–26). Eekhout also cites a laudatory poem, written by Georg Raab and printed under the portrait of Plante, which commends the "Mantuan" flavor of the epic (Virgil came from Mantua) and the affinity of Plante's and Virgil's verse. Yet—such admiration notwithstanding—other of Plante's contemporaries had their doubts and took a less charitable view of the poetic qualities of the "Mauritias." Of the Virgilian pretensions of Plante's epic, Constantijn Huygens smartly quipped: "Aeneis en dit Boeck ['Mauritias'] zijn even lang gelesen / En dit is well soo lang, maar 't sal soo lang niet wesen" ("The Aeneid and this book take equally long to read / Sure, this one is quite lengthy, but it will not long succeed"; cited in Eekhout, "'Mauritias,'" n. 4; my translation). For Huygens's more admiring view of the Dutch-Brazilian adventure itself, see the discussion below.

24. The impressive list of poets and humanists contributing to Plante's volume attests to the high profile attained by the Brazilian project within the Dutch republic of letters. Constantijn Huygens, Daniël Heinsius, Caspar Barlaeus, Marcus Zuerius Boxhorn, and Dirck Graswinckel all composed laudatory verse for the occasion; and Antonius Thysius, professor of eloquence at Leiden, added an oration—like the poems, in Latin—celebrating the prince's safe return to Holland. The volume's engravings were largely the work of Frans Post.

25. The manner in which Plante entered the literary orbit of Johan Maurits is instructive. Plante sailed to Brazil as a preacher (court chaplain to Johan Maurits) rather than a poet, and he made his initial literary mark by celebrating the house of Nassau within its *European* setting: penning verses for Count Ernst Casimir, *stadhouder* of Friesland and Groningen; on Johan Maurits's 1645 siege of Hulst; for the beloved daughter of Frederik Hendrik, and so forth. He submitted his Brazilian poem in 1645 to Huygens *and* the prince, since both men's approval was deemed necessary to obtain further patronage and to assemble the necessary dedicatory poems from Huygens and his circle. See Eekhout, "'Mauritias,'" esp. 377–81.

26. Barlaeus, *Nederlandsch Brazilië*, 428, and see 421–32 for further publication details. L'Honoré Naber's editorial judgment should carry considerable weight. A member of the Royal Dutch Geographic Society, he edited or wrote some twenty volumes on travel, including very impressive works by van Linschoten and de Laet. For the place of Barlaeus's project within the broader context of Dutch culture—letters, art, trade—see also the accolades offered in Freedberg, "Science, Commerce, and Art," 389–92.

27. Details of Barlaeus's biography can be gleaned from Worp, "Casper Barlaeus." Barlaeus had been composing much-admired poetry for the Dutch court since at least the 1620s: the *Manes auriaci* appeared upon the death of Prince Maurits in 1625, and the *Auriacus triumphans* (1639) was one of many works by Barlaeus celebrating the deeds of Frederik Hendrik. He dabbled also, from a relatively early date, in Americana: in 1622 he adopted Antonio Herrera's history of the West Indies for a Latin audience (as the *Novus orbis*),

and he composed the *Argo Batava* (1629) upon Heyn's capture of the silver-fleet. For the literary and political background of Barlaeus's Brazilian masterpiece, see further Harmsen, "Barlaeus's Description."

28. Barlaeus, *Nederlandsch Brazilië,* 24. Barlaeus's pronouncement follows a discussion of Dutch clashes with the Spaniards and encounters with the Indians in the 1620s and 1630s, and the references are left deliberately ambiguous: "*immanitate & barbarie*" might refer to the Spanish enemy, the Indian natives, or perhaps both. For the Latin original, see *Rerum per octennium in Brasilia,* 19.

29. Barlaeus, *Nederlandsch Brazilië,* Dedication (IX–XVI), 200–10 (on the prince's building projects), and 229 (on military and naval exploits).

30. Ibid., Dedication, 16–20 (on the ancients' ignorance of the New World), 32 (on the progeny of Bato), and 278ff. (on the anabasis of Herckmans). For Brazil's happy embrace of the Chatti, see the poem, "Mauritius Redux," which Barlaeus appended to his original edition (*Rerum per octennium in Brasilia,* 334–40). Barlaeus further developed his Batavian theories in the ethnographic section of his history, where he drew a connection between the primitive Tarairiu (who were the closest native allies of the Dutch) and the ancient Batavians. He noted that the American and Teutonic races shared certain social habits and ceremonies—the vigilant protection of their virgins, for example (326–7)—and suggested a vague cultural affiliation. This implied kinship may have owed something to a tract by Barlaeus's humanist colleague and friend, Hugo de Groot, which spelled out more clearly the Batavian-American connection. Grotius argued that sea-faring Germanic peoples had migrated to North America, perhaps by way of Iceland, Frisland (a mythical island in the North Atlantic), and Greenland. He based his claims on presumed common customs and imagined linguistic affinities (positing, for example, that native American place names, such as Tenochtitlan or Ocotlan, were cognate with Germanic place names, such as Netherland and England). These arguments were challenged by Joannes de Laet in a famously arcane pamphlet war carried out in indignant neo-Latin. See de Groot, *Orginum gentium Americanarum;* de Laet's rebuttal, *Notae ad dissertationem Hugonis Grotii;* de Groot's patronizing counterattack, *Dissertatio altera;* and de Laet's final reply, every bit as scathing and disdainful as his opponent's, *Responsio.* The entire debate and its intellectual contexts are explored in Schmidt, "Space, Time, Travel." Note, finally, that a version of de Groot's argument found expression in Governor Kieft's comments, to the visiting Roger Williams, that local Algonquians (this in New Netherland) had descended from Icelandic navigators and that the Algonquian word *sachima* (sachem or chieftain) derived—so Kieft proposed—from an Icelandic word for prince: see Roger Williams, *A Key into the Language of America* (London, 1643) (cited in Raesly, *Portrait of New Netherland,* 75).

31. De Lange, *Batavise Romeyn,* 426; and see more generally, Weslager, *New Sweden,* which describes the international crowd that in fact inhabited the colony.

32. [Van der Donck?], *Vertoogh van Nieu Neder-land,* and see the translation,

"Representation of New Netherland," in Jameson, *Narratives* (hereafter "Representation"), 313; *Kort verhael,* 12, where the author also echoes van der Donck's comparison of the Delaware and Amazon Rivers.

33. Van der Donck, *Beschryvinge,* and see the translation in idem, *Description,* 9–10, 17–19, which I have followed with some modifications. Van Gastel has done well to expose the shortcomings of the nineteenth-century translation: "Van der Donck's Description." On the author more generally, see idem, "Adriaen van der Donck."

34. The vine native to northeastern America, *vitis labrusca,* produced what the Dutch called *speck-druyven,* or hog grapes. The alternative English name was fox grapes, a cultivated, well-known version of which is the Concord grape.

35. "Representation," 294–8, 318; van der Donck, *Description,* 19–23; Megapolensis, *Kort ontwerp,* in Jameson, *Narratives,* 168–9; *Kort verhael,* 3–4.

36. Jacob Steendam, "Prickel vaersen," in Murphy, *Anthology,* 68–9.

37. Steendam, '*t Lof van Nuw-Nederland* (Amsterdam, 1661), in Murphy, *Anthology,* 50–5, 64–5, and passim. The comparison of the Hudson's waters to fresh cow's milk comes from Megapolensis, *Kort ontwerp,* 170.

38. Nicasius de Sille to Maximiliaen van Beeckerke, 23 May 1653, in van Laer, "Letters," 101.

39. Steendam, *Lof,* 64–5 (and see Num. 17 for "Aaron's rod"). Steendam's exclamatory "Oh fortunate land!" echoes similar strains of rapture from Karel van Mander, who composed verse, over a half-century earlier, in celebration of the pastoralism of America: *Wtleggingh,* 110v. It also mimics, though in a very different vein, Donne's ravishing excitement and more intimate vision of the New World: "O my America! my new-found-land, / My kingdome, safeliest when with one man man'd" (*Elegie* XIX, "To his Mistress Going to Bed").

40. Jacobus Lydius, "Een gelt-hont," in *Vrolycke uren ofte der wijse vermaeck* (Dordrecht, 1650) (cited in Schama, *Embarrassment of Riches,* 331, and see more generally 323–43, on Calvinist ambivalence regarding commerce); Barlaeus, *Mercator sapiens,* 41–2 and passim.

41. Barlaeus, *Nederlandsch Brazilië,* 368, where the author cites the authority of Virgil. Barlaeus also offers subtle criticism of Herkmans's trip into the Brazilian interior (likewise in search of gold), though with none of the severity of his attack on the Chilean fiasco. Brouwer he considered a "vain" and "autocratic" commander and hopelessly greedy. Herckmans, in contrast, is admired as a courageous and resourceful leader and, most important, "a poet." See ibid., 278–89 and 350–68, for Herckmans's and Brouwer's stories, respectively. For the commentary on the Münster negotiations, see Philopatroön, *Nieuw-Keulsch,* 15, and see 39, which also refers to American gold and its corruptive powers.

42. On Brazil: *Ontdeckinghe van rijcke mijnen.* On New Netherland: van der Donck, *Description,* 34–7; *Kort verhael,* 6–7; "Journal of New Netherland, 1647," in Jameson, *Narratives,* 269. And on Guiana: Gerbier, *Waarachtige verklaringe,* sig. A2r, which is followed by Gerbier's own fantastic assertion of discovering seventy lasts (about 140 tons) of gold.

43. Jacob Cats, "Op den handel die met Indiaen of ander vergelegen volck gedreven wert," in *Invallende gedachten*, 79:

> Een veertje van een papegay,
> Is in haer oogen wonder fray.
> . . . .
> O wat een dwaesheyt! lieve Godt,
> Van ieder wert te zijn bespot
> . . . .
> En blijft niet aen het stof verpandt
> Den Hemel is uw' Vaderlandt.

44. Udemans, *Geestelyck roer*, 96–7, 101–5, 171, 122–3: "Ja van de Americanen wordt getuyght, datse het gout, silver, ende peerlen seer weynigh achten ende datse veel meer achten vogel-vederen. . . . Wat ist dan voor eenen oevel dat de Christenen soo rasen ende woelen naer *goudt* en *silver*, even als of al haer welvaren naer ziele ende lichaem daerinne gelegen ware."

45. Cf. Udemans [Poimenande], *Absaloms-hayr*, which provoked a learned response from Boxhorn (*Spiegeltjen*) and Borstius's fire-and-brimstone *Predikatie tegen lang hayr*. See also Schama, *Embarrassment of Riches*, 79, which briefly discusses the debate.

    And the length of the *Indians'* hair? Though it seems not to have bothered Udemans, the matter provoked the censure of other European observers, in rather telling ways. Thomas Hall, writing at the same time as Udemans though in the distinctly different context of (New) England, comprehended the Amerindians' long hair as a badge of cruelty and effeminacy; it rendered them "savages": *Comarum akosmia;* and see also Lepore, *Name of War*, 93, which describes the New England context of the work. To the Spanish, too, it was a mark of incivility. "Some regard long hair as bad," wrote a sixteenth-century official in Peru, whose exceptional opinion proves the rule. "Personally I see no objection, except perhaps on the grounds of cleanliness": Juan de Matienzo, *Gobierno de Perú* (1567) (cited by Elliott, *Britain and Spain*, 7). To Udemans, however, different cultures called for different coiffures. While the long-maned habits of his Dutch countrymen spelled vanity, the same style in America could denote uncomplicated virtue.

46. Udemans, *Geestelyck roer*, 110–27. Regarding New Netherland, van der Donck also noted the sobriety of the Algonquians, who were "in eating and drinking . . . not excessive, . . . cheerful and well satisfied. . . . It is not with them as it is here in Holland where the greatest, noblest, and richest live more luxuriously than a Calis, or a common man." In terms strikingly in line with Udemans's, he observed that the Indians are "not proud of their dress . . . they know not how to appear proud and foppish" (*Description*, 74–9). For a fine illustration of the foppish sort of youth that Udemans had in mind, see Frans Hals's wonderful portrait of *Jaspar Schade* (ca. 1645, National Gallery, Prague), discussed in Slive, *Frans Hals*, 306–8. On the whimsical idea to send Dutch youth to school in America, cf. the *Missive van twee Indi-*

aensche coninghen, which contains the appeal of two potentates from Amboina, requesting to send their sons to be educated in the Netherlands.

47. Barlaeus, *Nederlandsch Brazilië,* 87–90; Ortelius, *Theatre* (1573), fol. 2v; Jacob Cats, "Van suycker ende kruyt," in van Beverwijck, *Schat der gesontheyt,* 134 ("Hier is geen Suycker-riet dat in de dalen wast, / En noch wort hier de Ieught met suycker overlast."); van Beverwijck, *Inleydinge,* 4 and passim. On early sugar imports to the Republic, see Klooster, *Illicit Riches,* 35–7; and Israel, *Dutch Primacy,* 162–9.

48. Van Beverwijck, *Inleydinge,* 2–3; idem, *Schat der ongesontheit,* 191: "Dese *Oesters* werden met seer groote moeyten van de Indyanen gevischt, die om de selve te vinden ses, negen, jae somtijdts twaelf vademen onder 't water duycken, het welck aldaer zeer kout is, ende 't gene meerder benauwt is datse den adem qualick konnen halen, moetende aldaer een vierendeel, ofte half uyr blijven, ende dan de selvige, die gemeenlick vast liggen aen de steen-rotsen, met gewelt af-trecken." The Vondel citation comes from his *Bespiegelingen van Godt en godtsdienst* (Amsterdam, 1662), 102 (bk. 3, lines 570–80).

49. Van Meteren, *Historie,* fol. 396–97; and see the exhaustive study of the domestic Dutch industry by Roessingh, *Inlandse tabak.* Also useful are the relevant sections of Schama, *Embarrassment of Riches,* 193–216, and van Deursen, *Plain Lives,* 103–4.

50. Everard, *Herba panacea* (Antwerp, 1587; repr. Leiden, 1622, and Utrecht, 1644); Thorius, *Hymnus tabaci,* 1 and passim; van Beverwijck, *Schat der gesontheyt,* 177–8. Also pertinent are Neander, *Tabacologia,* which synthesizes most of the earlier writings on tobacco; Scriverius, *Saturnalia,* a humanist tract translated from the Latin by Samuel Ampzing; and a later text, Peima van Beintema's *Tabacologia,* which prescribes tobacco to all who would lengthen their lives, all who value fresh air (!), and, particularly, pregnant women— up to twenty pipes per day. The invaluable source for early modern tobacology is Brooks, *Tobacco,* a catalogue *cum* bibliography of the exceptional collection of the New York Public Library. For a broadly historical and cultural perspective, see Goodman, *Tobacco in History.*

51. Van Meteren, *Historie,* 397r; Udemans, *Geestelyck roer,* 49; and cf. van Deursen, *Plain Lives,* 103.

52. Visscher, *Sinnepoppen,* no. 10; Cats, *Emblemata,* no. 12.

53. See, on Brouwer, Knuttel, *Adriaen Brouwer;* on Buytewech, Haverkamp Begemann, *Willem Buytewech;* and on such genre scenes more generally, Sutton, *Dutch Genre Painting.* See also the discussion of smoking (and drinking) in Schama, *Embarrassment of Riches,* 211–18, which cites Psalms 102:3 ("my days are consumed like smoke") and the moralizing quote on the ephemerality of life; and Gaskell, "Tobacco."

54. Pers, *Wonder-wercken,* 67–70: "Dit wonderlijck kryd, van over zee gesonden, / In eensaemheyd geplant, van Apen eerst gevonden."

55. Ibid., 69. On the iconography of apes, see van Mander, *Schilder-boeck,* 128v ("Wtbeeldinge der figueren"); and Janson, *Apes and Ape Lore.*

56. Details of the Molenaer painting are provided in Sutton, *Dutch Genre Painting,* cat. 78. For an in-depth discussion of the "Lady World" theme—with further samples of paintings that likewise feature maps, expressly showing America, hanging above moralizing genre scenes—see de Jongh, "Vermommingen van Vrouw Wereld." De Jongh's strategy for reading genre paintings is considered in a collection devoted to Dutch pictorial "realism": Franits, *Seventeenth-Century Art.* For the Collier *Vanitas* and a similar *Vanitas with Globe* (1650) by Pieter de Ringh, see Haak, *Golden Age,* 437; and, more generally, *Ijdelheid der ijdelheden.*

57. Another presumed American import, syphilis, was also closely associated with sin, though chiefly connected with the Spanish—hence its Dutch name, *Spaanse pokken* (Spanish pox).

58. "Jonas Michaëlius to Joannes van Foreest, 8 August 1628," in Eekhof, *Michaëlius,* 111; Kieft cited in O'Callaghan, *History of New Netherland,* 1:189; van Rensselaer, *Waerschouwinge; idem, Redres van de abuysen,* and note that the *Redres* does list precisely seven causes for the ungodliness (and high debt) in the patroonship. Both of van Rensselaer's works are translated in *VRBM,* 682–97. See also the anonymous "Journal of New Netherland, 1647," in Jameson, *Narratives,* 273, which discusses the greed and other "abuses" rampant in the colony.

59. "Jonas Michaëlius to Joannes van Foreest, 13 September 1630," in Eekhof, *Michaëlius,* 68; van Laer, *Documents Relating to New Netherland,* 106.

60. De Vries, *Historiael ende journaels aenteyckeninge,* and cf. the translation in Jameson, *Narratives,* 187–91. Between van Twiller, who governed from 1633 to 1637, and Minuit (1626–1632), Sebastiaen Krol temporarily filled the governor's position.

61. "Representation," 325; *Breeden-raedt,* for which see Murphy, *Two Rare Tracts,* 144, and 138–60 more generally. Kieft still lacks a biographer. He was a descendant on his mother's side of the powerful Huydecoper clan, an Amsterdam family of regents; and, after a dismal career in commerce, his relatives secured him a position in New Netherland—where he hardly sparkled. Like many failed colonial administrators, though, Kieft showed genuine talent as a gentleman of leisure. He sketched, painted, read Latin (including Grotius's tract on the origins of the Indians; see note 30), and amassed a collection of curiosities including "very exact Maps; fully a hundred different samples of Minerals"—surely one of the first *Wunderkammern* in the American colonies. See Brodhead, *Documents,* 1:262, on his collection (ultimately lost in a shipwreck); and the updated biographical sketch in Garraty and Carnes, *American National Biography,* 12: 657–8.

62. *Breeden-raedt,* 161–9; "Representation," 328, 338, 342, 346–7 and passim.

63. "Representation," 324, 346–7; de Vries, *Historiael ende journaels aenteyckeninge,* 209; and *Breede-raedt,* 163–4.

64. De Vries, *Historiael ende journaels aenteyckeninge,* 212; "Representation," 326 (and see Jameson's note there, which suggests that van der Donck took deliberate liberties interpreting the church's inscription to make Kieft look bad); *Breeden-raedt,* 155–6.

65. For van Rensselaer, see the *Redres van de abuysen;* and see, more generally, Smith, *Religion and Trade,* as well as Oppenheim's classic *Jews in New York.* On van Tienhoven, see "Representation," 340–1; and *Breeden-raedt,* 179–80.

66. *Breeden-raedt,* 148–9 (with slight modifications of the nineteenth-century punctuation and diction). See also de Vries's nearly identical report, *Historiael ende journaels aenteyckeninge,* 228–9; as well as ibid., 226 (on Kieft's belligerent intentions), and 208–9 (on the attack against the Raritans; emphasis added). The anecdote describing the flaying of an Indian is in the *Breeden-raedt,* 152. On Kieft's Wars more generally, see Trelease, *Indian Affairs,* 60–84; Schulte Nordholt, "Oorlog van Kieft" (which pays special attention to literary representations of the war and the propaganda campaigns waged against the WIC); and Frijhoff, *Wegen van Evert Willemsz.,* 699–763 ("Oorlog").

67. "Representation," 343, 351, and see 322 for evidence of the restrictive commercial policies of the WIC.

68. Van Rensselaer, *Redres van de abuysen,* 688.

69. Nieuhof, *Brasiliaense zee- en lantreize,* 54. Nieuhof lived in Brazil from 1640 to 1649. His account, written shortly after his return to Europe, was published posthumously.

70. *Consideratie,* [3].

71. See, for example, *Vertoogh by een lief-hebber; Spel van Brazil; Ghepretendeerden overlast; Ontdeckinghe van rijke mijnen;* Guelen, *Kort verhael; Consideratie.*

72. *Consideratie,* 25; and cf. *Brasilsche breede-byl,* 23, which refers to "ten tijde van Duc d'Alba."

73. *Vervolgh op de t'samen-spraeck,* sig. A2v; *Brasilsche breede-byl,* 4, 22–3; *Brasilsche gelt-sack,* sig. A2; *Amsterdams dam-praetje* (and cf. the *Amsterdams vuur-praetje* and *Amsterdams tafel-praetje* of the same year); Guelen, *Kort verhael,* sigs. C2–C3; and *Brasyls schuyt-praetjen,* sig. Br. Note that, in a certain sense, the irony of the soldiers' comment may be double, since the dust-covered inmates laboring in the *Rasphuis* were sometimes compared to the "red-skin" Indians of America.

74. *Amsterdams dam-praetje,* sig. E3r. Details of the humiliating losses in this period—500 Dutch soldiers in the first battle of Guararapes, double that (including 100 officers) in the next—are related in Boxer, *Dutch in Brazil,* 184–203, 212–16.

75. *Brasyls schuyt-praetjen,* sigs. Cr, Bv, and passim; *Amsterdams dam-praetje,* sig. E3; *Breeden-raedt,* 134–6.

76. *Breeden-raedt,* 134; *Brasyls schuyt-praetjen,* sig. C.

77. *Breeden-raedt,* 130, 134; Moreau, *Waarachtige beschryving,* 30–1 (which includes a rather dramatic illustration of the Cunhau massacre); Potty, *Brasiliaensen brieff; Brasyls schuyt-praetjen,* sigs. Av, Cv. On Rabe and Dutch-Tarairiu relations, see van den Boogaart, "Infernal allies," 528–30. For the Canaan theme in a slightly different context, cf. Thomas Morton, *New English Canaan* (London, 1632).

78. Moreau, *Waarachtige beschryving,* 94; and cf. the early WIC "Instructions" cited in note 8, where the Company directors demonstrate the identical concern with "righteousness" in America.

79. *Zeeusche verre-kyker,* sig. [B4]r: "Naer dat wy 't selve Lant korten tijt hebben beseten, hebben wy de *Portegysen* in alle sonden verde te boven ghegaen, en in plaets van dat wy de Heydenen door een goedt leven souden bekeren, soo hebben onse Overheden, niet alleen Rijckdom, voor Godtsalicheyt gheprefereert, maer de gantsche menichte, heeft het Heyden leven, in plaets vant Christenen, nae ghevolcht, levende in alle wellusten hares herten, niet wetende hoe sy haer selven sullen versaden, soo dat het schijnt dat het Godt verdriet. . . . *Ter rechter tijt wort den straffer nu ghestraft van Godt.*"

80. *Brasyls schuyt-praetjen,* sig. [C4]r:

> Met recht mogen de Brasilische Portogysen seggen,
> Godt sal ons verlossen van 't Hollandsche Jock soo swaer,
> 'tWelcke ons heeft onder-druckt seer naer vijf en twintigh Jaer:
> Ghelijck Israël uyt Egipt is gheleyt door Godes kracht,
> Soo heeft ons Godt tot ons voorighe vryheyt ghebracht.
> Om dat d'Hollanders rijckdom voor haer God hebben ge-eert,
> Soo heeft Godt al haer werck tot niet ghekeert.

81. On the authorship of the anti-WIC literature, see note 88.

82. *Portogysen goeden buyrman; Vertoogh, over den toestant;* and especially *Kort, bondigh ende waerachtigh verhael,* which was published immediately following the forfeiture of the colony to Portugal. Two years later, ironically, there appeared two bona fide "remonstrances" from Brazil that did seek succor, in the name of the "Brazilian nation," from the "cruel and bloodthirsty Portuguese": Paräupába, *Twee verscheyden remonstrantien.* For the earlier period, before the war effort was abandoned as hopeless, see the *Kort discourse; Brasilsche oorloghs overwegingh;* and *Beneficien voor de soldaten,* a recruitment pamphlet that promised potential soldiers, *inter alia,* good-quality drinking water and excellent fishing conditions.

83. *Amsterdams dam-praetje,* sig. [D4]v; *Brasilsche gelt-sack,* sig. A2r; *Hollants wijve praetjen,* sig. [B2]. See also the *Amsterdamsche veerman,* which discusses the director's incompetence; and the *Accusatie ende conclusie,* which details the case against one WIC official accused of absconding with 250,000 florins earmarked for the war in Brazil.

84. On the abysmal management abilities of the *bewindhebberen,* see [de la Court], *Interest van Holland,* translated as *True interest,* 178. For WIC share prices, see Goslinga, *Dutch in the Caribbean,* 328–30, 509; and Israel, *Dutch Primacy,* 163. Owning stock in the Company on the Amsterdam Exchange remained profitable in 1640 (at 134); yet, by 1643, shares fell permanently below 100 (thus no longer profitable), and by 1645 they dropped to 46 and never recuperated from there. By contrast, share prices of the VOC shot up from just shy of 200 in 1630 to nearly 400 a decade later. They hovered, for most of the 1640s, in the 400s, peaking at 539 in 1648 (see Israel, *Dutch Primacy,* 186).

85. *Verheerlickte Nederland;* [de la Court], *True interest,* 26–8, 62, 72–3, 123, 177–8, 347. The WIC's second charter, granted in 1648, expired in 1672, at which point it was extended for two more years. In 1674, the States General dis-

solved the WIC to form an altogether new company. On the collapse of the WIC and failed plans to merge it with the fiscally healthy VOC (this in the 1640s and again in the 1670s, in both instances vigorously opposed by the VOC), see den Heijer, *Geschiedenis van de WIC*, 97–108.

86. Jan Six van Chandelier, "Op langdurigen regen" (cited in Schenkeveld-Van der Dussen, *Dutch Literature*, 105–6); Sousa-Leao, *Frans Post*, esp. cat. nos. 47, 66, 69, 74, 84, and 139, all of which show snakes consuming hares. The *zielkopers* are discussed in Moreau, *Waarachtige beschryving*, 86–7. De Pauw considered the degenerative nature of America in his *Recherches philosophiques sur les Américaines*.

87. *Verheerlickte Nederland*, 45.

88. The provenance of the rich, anti-WIC literature published in the mid-seventeenth century has induced much bibliographic speculation. Asher long ago advanced the argument that the *Breeden-raedt* and other libelous works appearing in 1649–50 (including the *Amsterdams dam-praetje, Amsterdams vuur-praetje, Amsterdams tafel-praetje, Amsterdamsche veerman, Haerlems schuyt-praetjen, Zeeuwsche verre-kycker,* and *Brasyls schuyt-praetjen*) came from "writers of the party of the King of Portugal," specifically polemicists in the circle of Sousa Coutinho: *Bibliographical and historical essay*, 183–200. All of these pamphlets, Asher contended, sought to shift the blame for the planters' revolt from the king of Portugal to the WIC. Asher originally made his case in opposition to an assertion by Brodhead (*History of New York*, 1:48, 509) that the *Breeden-raedt* was in fact the work of Cornelis Melijn, an ally of van der Donck on the council of Nine Men in New Amsterdam and an enemy of Stuyvesant and the WIC. Yet Asher disqualified Melijn as the potential author, since he refused to believe that a Dutchman could so excellently mimic, as does the author of these popular dialogues, the voices of a Frenchman, Englishman, Portuguese, et cetera. It might be suggested, however, that a *Portuguese* writer could only doubtfully pick up the cadences of Dutch propaganda as well as the author(s) of these pamphlets—the repetitive references to "wreedheden," "tyrannijen," "onnosele bloed," and so forth; the relentless moralizing; and the other distinctly Dutch patterns of these tracts. While perhaps some of these polemics were influenced by a "Portuguese party" in The Hague, it would seem that a Dutch hand, familiar with traditional topoi of vernacular propaganda, ultimately composed the bulk of these works. Raesly sensibly proposed van der Donck himself as author of the *Breeden-raedt* (*Portrait of New Netherland*, 88), an opinion recently echoed by Frijhoff (*Wegen van Evert Willemsz.*, 563; though note that Frijhoff has curiously chosen to skip over a century and a half of research in repositioning Melijn as the consensus author).

89. Bradley, *Lure of Peru*, 59, citing the Spanish reaction to Dutch misdeeds perpetrated, in this case, by the Nassau Fleet.

90. Three Dutch editions of Las Casas came out in the decade leading up to the Peace of Münster (1648), including one version "augmented" with tyrannies lately added: *Vermeerderden Spieghel* (1640). Note that, in this regard too, the English picked up the Republic's patterns of propaganda. The famous *Tears*

of the Indians edition of Las Casas appeared in 1656, just as Cromwell's regime sought to expand its dominion in the Spanish Caribbean—and, *nota bene,* just as English pamphleteers turned their pens, for altogether different reasons, against the original Dutch exporters of Lascasian literature.

91. For the Anglo-Dutch wars, see Wilson, *Profit and Power;* and Pincus, *Protestantism and Patriotism,* which emphasizes the ideological background of the wars, though only from the English perspective. Groenveld, *Verlopend getij,* gives the Dutch angle on events leading up to Cromwell's regime; and Geyl, *Orange and Stuart,* details the increasingly close ties that bound the royal families.

92. Wilson, *Profit and Power,* treats the political and naval history of the first two conflicts; while Roorda, *Rampjaar,* covers the prelude to the third war and the "year of disaster," 1672. See also Rowen, *John de Witt,* which examines the maneuvers of the de Witt regime.

93. Felltham, *Brief character,* 3–4 and passim; D. F., *Dutch-mens pedigree;* and cf. *Dutch deputies* (cited in Schama, *Embarrassment of Riches,* 263, which contains an excellent discussion of Hollandophobia more generally); and *Dutch boare dissected* (cited in Wilson, *Profit and Power,* 126).

94. Marvell, "Character of Holland," 112–16, which was written originally ca. 1653 and then republished in 1665 and 1672, for the occasions of the second and third Dutch wars. Pincus, *Protestantism and Patriotism,* usefully details the religious components of English propaganda; and see also idem, "Butterboxes to Wooden Shoes."

95. Felltham, *Brief character,* 27, 37–8; *Dutch-mens pedigree;* and cf. the Dutch war-party pamphlet, *Consideratien vande vrede,* which, as Felltham surmised, does convey a preference for war over peace.

96. See, for example, the early reports in *Newes out of East India* and *True relation* (1624), both of which express righteous indignation about the affair and rebuke the colonial governor (Herman van Speult) and his VOC superiors for their part—yet stop short of blaming the Dutch "nation" per se. Cf. also *True declaration of the news,* which was written from a Dutch perspective and partly rationalized the governor's actions based on his genuine (and conceivably legitimate) fear of conspiracy.

97. *True relation* (1665); and see also, *Memento for Holland,* 1, 44, and passim. Coolhaas, "Ambonschen moord," offers a more sober account of the narrative.

98. Dryden, *Amboyna,* 3:343–406, esp. 350 and 400. The Amboina "massacre" was rehashed again in the fourth Anglo-Dutch war (1780–84) and, remarkably, as late as the Boer War at the turn of the twentieth century.

99. *Memento for Holland,* 9; *Second part of the Tragedy,* 4. The *Second part* appeared, in fact, as New England colonists lobbied angrily for war, and it may have prompted Cromwell to dispatch a fleet to Boston in early 1654.

100. E. W., *Severall remarkable passages,* 8; and, on New Netherland, [Cliff], *Holland's deliverance,* 40. See also ibid., 45, for a curious comment that likens the Dutch exploitation of British Seas (for herring) to the Spanish exploitation of Indian mines (for silver). On Hudson's Englishness, see Wilson,

Profit and Power, 116; and Heylyn, *Cosmographie,* 111, which contends that the navigator explored North America originally under orders of the English Crown.

101. De Britaine, *Dutch usurpation,* 20, 24; and cf. de Britaine's other anti-Dutch pamphlet, published that same year, which attacks Dutch activities in North America: *Interest of England,* esp. 4–5.

102. Downing, *Discourse written by Sir George Downing,* 1–2, 4, 20, 26, 45; and cf. Downing's earlier work, commenting on New Netherland, *Discourse: vindicating His Royal Master,* 15–17. Felltham's remarks appear in *Brief character,* 36–7. Pirated editions of Felltham's work came out in 1648 (*Three moneths observations of the Low Countries*) and 1652 (*A true and exact character of the Low Countreyes*).

103. [Darell], *True and compendious narration,* 9, 35; Stubbes, *Further justification,* 9, 70; and cf. idem, *Justification of the present war,* 31. More generally, see Pincus, "Popery, Trade and Universal Monarchy."

104. See, for example, the *Amsterdams schutters-praatje,* which discusses the Irish campaign, and *Engleschen duyvel,* a fairly typical work, which opens on the issue of regicide. Most pamphlets adhered more closely to the benign controversy over fishing rights.

105. Van Valckenburgh, *Waerachtigh verhael;* and see also the broadsheet, *Brief van Johan van Valckenburgh,* and the lengthier account in Swinnas, *Krackeelen.* The Amboina affair is rationalized in the *Amsterdams schutters-praatje,* 23.

106. *Remonstratie vande bewinthebberen; Naerder klagh-vertoogh;* "Report on the Surrender of New Netherland, by Peter Stuyvesant, 1665," in Jameson, *Narratives,* 465; *Hollands venezoen,* sig. [A4]r:

> [Hollands] levering moet noch aan Engeland geschieden,
> Dan zal dien koning ons geweldiglijk gebieden;
> En voeren 'tslechte volk als Slaven uit het Land,
> Daar't voor den Engels-man Toebak bereid en plant.

107. *Nederlantsche absolutie,* sig. A2v, which is a direct response to the pro-France/anti-Pauw *Drukkers belydenisse.* The regents of Holland were the strongest supporters of peace with Spain, while the States of Zeeland and Utrecht, along with hard-line Calvinists, Orangists, and the military, generally opposed the settlement. See Israel, *Dutch Republic* (1995), 595–609, which neatly summarizes the political debates of the time and the ensuing turmoil.

108. See, for example, the guarded comments in *Brasilsche breede-byl,* 9; and the ambivalent conclusions in Nieuhof, *Brasiliaense zee- en lantreize,* 235–38. More plainly positive are the observations in [Keye], *Koude en warme landen,* Dedication (n. p.), sig. A3r, 86, and passim; and a work attributed to Jan or Pieter de la Court: D. L. C., *Politike discoursen,* 323–4.

109. *Achste maandags relaes,* esp. 74–6; *Negende maandags relaes* (which follows the "Achste relaes"); van der Sterre, *Aanmerkelijke reysen,* 18–19; [Zeiller], *Monarchia Hispanica.*

110. Exquemelin, *Americaensche zee-roovers*. On the work's popularity, see Sabin's monumental *Bibliotheca Americana*, no. 23468, which cites the great Dutch bibliographer, Frederick Muller, to a similar effect: "There is certainly no other book of that time which experienced a popularity similar to that of the 'Buccaniers of America.'" For possible runners-up, cf. Bontekoe, *Journael*, and *Begin, midden en eynde der see-roveryen*, both of which appeared in dozens of editions. For a bibliographic overview, see Gosse, "First Editions."

111. Ten Hoorn, a prolific bookseller and publisher of late seventeenth-century Amsterdam, certainly designed the volume's agenda-setting title-page (discussed below), its ten illustrations (at least two by H. Padt Brugge), and the two inserted maps. He most likely also had a hand in shaping the narrative itself, translating the text, and even composing some of the prose. See the excellent bibliographic essay of Fontaine Verwey, "Scheepsschirurgijn Exquemelin," where a convincing case is made that, whatever Exquemelin's origins, the *Americaensche zee-roovers* grew out of the milieu of Holland publishing.

112. These two very baroque texts further shared a concern with authenticity and veracity—hence both authors' emphasis on their status as eyewitnesses—and, perhaps not unrelatedly, a distinctive interest in the geography and *naturalia* of America. Note, too, that at least one Amsterdam publisher made clear the connection between the two genres of Lascasian and pirate literature by publishing a recent edition of the *Brevíssima relación* together with the narrative of the French *flibustier* Montauban: Las Casas, *Relation des voyages* (Amsterdam: Jean Louis de Lorme, 1698). A second edition of this text (which described Montauban's 1691 voyage) appeared in 1708.

113. Exquemelin, *Zee-roovers*, frontispiece (unsigned); Las Casas, *Spiegel* (Amsterdam: Jan Evertsz Cloppenburg, 1620), title-page ("DvB m," "DC fe").

114. Exquemelin, *Zee-roovers*, 7–8, offers sparse details of the author's life, though not enough to establish firmly his identity. Hoogewerff, who well knew the terrain of seventeenth-century naval narratives, proposed that Exquemelin was identical with Hendrik Smeeks, author of a contemporary work of utopian literature (*Krinke Kesmes*) and a Zwolle surgeon: "Hendrik Smeeks." This thesis proved untenable, however, when Vrijman discovered archival evidence establishing Exquemelin's background as a Huguenot, trained as a surgeon in Amsterdam: "Wie was Exquemelin?" Fontaine Verwey ("Scheepsschirurgijn Exquemelin") summarizes the literature deftly, filling in details of Exquemelin's eventful life. See also Camus, "Note critique," and the modern scholarly edition of Smeeks's *Mighty Kingdom*.

115. Exquemelin, *Zee-roovers*, 30–1: "sijn Meester maeckten hem aen een boom vast, ende sloegh hem tot dat het bloedt tappelings van sijn rugh af liep; daer na liet hy hem smeeren met een sause, toegemaeckt van Limoen-sap, Spaense Peper, en Sout, en liet hem alsoo aen de boom vierentwintigh uren

gebonden blijven staen, daer na sloegh hy hem weder op nieuw, tot dat hy onder sijn handen stierf. De laetste woorden, die hy sprack, waren dese: Godt geef, dat de Duyvel u mach quellen soo langh voor u doodt, als ghy my voor de mijne gequelt hebt." The parallel passage, written of the Spanish conquistadors, appears in Benzoni, *History of the New World,* 93–4.

116. Exquemelin, *Zee-roovers,* 61–2, 73, 88–9, and 93ff. for the lengthy section on Morgan.

117. Sir Henry Morgan was, in fact, Welsh, a distinction that does not seem to have bothered Exquemelin. The original Dutch edition refers to him as "John" Morgan and impugns his knightly status. Morgan sued the publisher of the first English translation for libel—the translator followed Exquemelin in assuming Morgan came to America as an indentured servant—and claimed for himself a proper yeoman's pedigree. Cf. Exquemelin, *Buccaneers of America,* 117–18. The original English translation—*Bucaniers of America*—appeared in 1684 at the address of the London printer William Crooke.

118. Klooster, *Illicit Riches,* 101–4, discusses the Dutch experience; and see also Barbour, "Privateers and Pirates." Cf. more generally Marley, *Pirates and Engineers;* and Cordingly, *Under the Black Flag.*

119. Exquemelin, *Zee-roovers,* 43, 47, 113.

120. Ibid., 10, 63–4, 110, 135–8.

Epilogue

1. Frans Post, *View of Serinhaém* (Musée du Louvre, Paris), for which see Sousa-Leão, *Frans Post,* no. 61; Larsen, *Frans Post,* no. 22; and Kellein and Frei, *Frans Post,* 98–9 (with an excellent color reproduction). The giant anteater in this case is a *tamandua-guaçu,* and the nine-banded armadillo a *tatuete*—both indigenous to the region. See Whitehead and Boeseman, *Seventeenth-Century Brazil,* 178–93, which provides rich detail on the flora and fauna of Post's oeuvre. Note that the European figure is taken to be Portuguese, since he rides in the "Moorish" fashion (higher stirrups and thus bent knees), which was the custom among the *moradores,* though not the Dutch.

2. Van den Sande, *Kort begrijp,* 191; and Joost van den Vondel, *Haec libertatis ergo* (1630), in *Werken van Vondel,* 3:332. Van den Sande, a former justice at the Synod of Dordrecht and a long-time advocate of Calvinist orthodoxy, neatly elided Spilbergen's American voyage and the religious discord of the late 1610s (this retrospectively, in 1650), suggesting that the former somehow induced the latter. Vondel made his comments apropos of the magistrates of Leiden, who stood accused of lording over the Arminians qua Americans in 1630.

Numerous further cases could be cited in which the American project was perceived in moralizing terms. See for example Wassenaer's warning—already in 1624!—that Dutch colonies in the New World must not succumb to the moral lapses of the Spanish: *Historisch verhael,* 7:17v–18. Tacking in the other direction is a pamphlet war from the 1650s (postdating, that is, the moral "lapses") in which a local official was attacked for behaving unethically and sinfully, like a "tyrannical" ruler in the West Indies: *Aen-wijsinge van de heyloose treken,* esp. sig. [A4]v.

3. Emmer speaks of the conclusion of a "heroic age" of colonialism ca. 1675, after which the Republic's American projects showed markedly less ambition and enjoyed less stature: "Nederlandse handelaren," 35–6, 76.

4. With this strategy—the depoliticization of American geography, essentially—the Dutch also moved in the opposite direction of other European powers. Compare the harshly polemical representations of Native Americans produced in England at this time and discussed in Lepore, *Name of War.* Just as the Dutch were getting out of the "innocence"/"tyranny" business, the English, who portrayed their Indian neighbors as indecently cruel and savagely violent, would appear to be getting in.

5. For examples of promotional/utopian literature, see Plockhoy, *Kort en klaer ontwerp; Verheerlickte Nederland;* [van den Enden?], *Vrye politijke stellingen;* and [Keye], *Koude en warme landen* (and note that, by the 1660s, efforts were made to sell the Guianese savanna as well). For natural histories, see Piso and Marcgraf, *Historia naturalis Brasiliae;* Piso, *Indiae utriusque;* and the many other "scientific" sources reviewed in Whitehead and Boeseman, *Seventeenth-Century Brazil.* Cartographic materials—especially the "major" atlases of Joan Blaeu, Johannes Janssonius, and Frederick de Wit—are catalogued in Koeman, *Atlantes Neerlandici;* and for the globes—especially of Blaeu, van Keulen, and Valk—see van der Krogt, *Globi Neerlandici.* For painting and other visual sources, see Sousa-Leão, *Frans Post;* Thomsen, *Albert Eckhout;* Whitehead and Boeseman, *Seventeenth-Century Brazil* (exhaustive on matters iconographic); and the superb essay of Joppien, "Dutch Vision of Brazil," which also traces the dispersal of Dutch visual materials throughout Baroque Europe (see 321–34 on Louis XIV). Patterns of Dutch collecting and forms of Dutch cabinets are studied in Bergvelt, *Wereld binnen handbereik;* and for literary ensembles, see Haitsma Mulier and van der Lem, *Repertorium van geschiedschrijvers,* which catalogues the extensive production of such *veelschrijvers* as van den Bosch, de Vries, and de Lange.

6. Montanus, *Nieuwe en onbekende weereld,* for which English and German editions quickly followed (prepared under the direction of the Amsterdam publisher and engraver, Jacob van Meurs, who also designed the frontispiece); and de Lange, *Wonderen des werelds.* Among the many massive Dutch geographies of this period, Simon de Vries's *Geheele weereld* (Amsterdam, 1686–94) surely takes the prize, weighing in at an astounding 3,762 pages.

7. De Lange, *Wonderen des werelds,* "Aen de Leser," sig. A2; de Vries, *Groote historische rariteit-kamer.* Cf. also idem, *Curieuse aenmerckingen, Groot historisch magazyn,* and *Wonderen,* which accuses the Spanish of being "gantsche niet nieuwsgierigh of nauwkeurigh . . . om iets t'ondersoecken" (266). De Vries ultimately does get around, in his vast compendia, to more typical "tyrannies" of Spain—though they appear consistently in the context of "marvels" rather than politics.

8. Bergvelt, *Wereld binnen handbereik,* cat. 83, which offers details on the (wooden) cabinet; and see also two relevant studies from the Bergvelt vol-

ume of essays: Jaap van der Veen, "'Dit klain Vertrek bevat een Weereld vol gewoel': Negentig Amsterdammers en hun kabinetten" (232–58); and Roelof van Gelder, "De wereld binnen handbereik: Nederlandse kunst- en rariteit-enverzamelingen, 1585–1735" (15–38), which notes the unique Dutch habit of selling collections to foreign buyers (this in the final decades of the century). For a rich essay on collecting, exotica, and the fluidity of meaning among these objects, see Kemp, "'Wrought by No Artist's Hand.'" More generally suggestive is Mason, *Infelicities.*

Bibliography

This study draws heavily on the immense body of Dutch pamphlet literature produced in the sixteenth and seventeenth centuries. Many of these materials are collected in the Royal Dutch Library in The Hague and are excellently catalogued in W. P. C. Knuttel's monumental *Catalogus van de pampletten-verzameling berustende in de Koninklijke Bibliotheek* (The Hague, 1889–1920). While individual pamphlets cited in the notes are listed only by their abbreviated title, the full citation in the Bibliography includes a number – bracketed and preceded by a *K* – that corresponds to the Knuttel catalogue number. All of these catalogued pamphlets are accessible, using this Knuttel number, on microfiche. Note, too, the use of the abbreviation *AGN* for articles published in D. P. Blok et al., eds., *Algemene Geschiedenis der Nederlanden*, 15 vols. (Haarlem, 1977–1983).

PRIMARY SOURCES

Ablijn, Cornelis, ed. and trans. *Die nieuwe weerelt der landtschappen ende eylanden, die tot hier toe allen ouden weerelt bescrijveren onbe[k]ent geweest sijn.* Antwerp, 1563.

Accusatie ende conclusie . . . op ende tegens den gewesenen Staet Generael Johan Schulenborch. Leeuwarden, [1662] [K8642].

Achste maandags relaes, . . . Mitsgaders een verhael van de zaken, betreffende het geschil der Spanjaarden met d'Engelschen in America. 1674 [K11160].

Acosta, José de. *Historie naturael ende morael van de Westersche Indien.* Haarlem, 1598.

Acronius van Buma, Johannes. *Argo Belgica.* Deventer, 1665.

Aen-wijsinge van de heyloose treken en gebreken, van Mr. Hendrik Thybout, voor desen grooten albeschik in Zeeland, en voornaamsten aan-rader van het belegeren van Amsterdam. Flushing, 1652 [K7318].

Aerdt ende eygenschappen van Seignor van Spangien. N.p., n. d.

Aerssen, François van. *Noodtwendigh ende levendigh discours van eenige getrouwe patriotten ende liefhebberen onses Vaderlandts; over onsen droevigen ende periculeusen staet.* 1618 [K2610].

Afgheworpene brieven vanden Cardinael van Granvelle ende vanden President Fonck, gheschreven aen sommige personagien vande malcontenten. Antwerp, 1580 [K536].

Alberi, Eugenio, ed. *Relazioni degli ambasciatori veneti al senato.* 15 vols. Florence, 1839–1863.

Allertsz, Herman. *Spieghel der jeught ofte korte kronijck der Nederlantsche geschiedenissen.* Amsterdam, 1614.

Ampzing, Samuel. *West-Indische triumph-basuyne, tot godes ere, ende roeme der Batavieren gesteken, van wegen der veroveringe der Spaensche silver-vlote van Nova Hispania inde Baij van Matanca door . . . Pieter Pieterszen Heyn.* Haarlem, 1629.

Amsterdams dam-praetje, van wat outs en wat nieuws en wat vreemts. Amsterdam, 1649 [K6477].

Amsterdams schutters-praatje, tusschen vier burgers, raeckende den teghenwoordighen tijdt, en de saecken van Engelandt. Amsterdam, 1652 [K7253].

Amsterdamsche veerman op Middelburgh. Flushing, 1650 [K6627].

Anghiera, Pietro Martire d'. *The decades of the newe worlde or west India, conteynyng the navigations and conquestes of the Spanyarde, with the particular description of the most rych and large landes and ilandes lately founde in the west Ocean perteynyng to the inheritaunce of the Kinges of Spayne.* Trans. Richard Eden. London, 1555.

    Descriptio terrae sancta exactissima . . . De novis insulis nuber repertis . . . per Petrum Martyr. Antwerp, 1536.

    De Orbe Novo. The Eight Decades of Peter Martyr d'Anghera. Trans. and ed. Francis Augustus MacNutt. 2 vols. New York, 1912.

    De orbe novo . . . decades. Alcalá de Henares, 1516.

Antwoorde van de generale Staten vande Nederlanden, op de propositie die henlieden is ghedaen van weghen der Keyserlijcke Maiesteyt. 1578 [K347].

Antwoordt op het tweede refereyn, by de overheerde Nederlantsche Provintien aen Hollant gheschreven: om haer met schoon-schijnende redenen, ongefondeerde dreygementen ende ongelijcke exempelen te bewegen, vrede te maken met den Spangiaert. 1598 [K1047].

Apologeticon, et vera rerum in Belgicogermania nuper gestarum narratio. [1570] [K179b].

De artijckelen ende besluyten der Inquisitie van Spaegnien om die van de Nederlanden te overvallen ende verhinderen. [1568?] [K157].

Aurelius, Cornelius. *De cronycke van Hollandt Zeelandt ende Vrieslant.* [Leiden, 1517].

Aventroot, Joan. *Sendbrief van Joan Aventroot tot den groot-machtichsten coninck van Spaengien.* Amsterdam, 1613 [K2035].

    Sendt-brief aen die van Peru, met een Aliance van de . . . Heeren Staten, der Vereenigder Provintien des Nederlands. Amsterdam, 1630 [K4001].

Het avijs der ijnquizicie van Spaengien bewijsinghe dat in alle de Nederlanden geen papist oft Catholijcke persoonen en sijn na het geluyt der selven ijnquizicie van Spaengien. 1571 [K192].

Baardt, Pieter. *Friesche Triton: Over t'geluckich veroveren van de stercke Stadt Olinda, met alle de forten in Fernambucq.* Leeuwarden, 1630.

Baers, Joannes. *Olinda, ghelegen int landt, inde capitania van Phernambuco, met mannelijcke dapperheyt ende groote couragie inghenomen, ende verovert op den 16. Februarij A. 1630.* Amsterdam, 1630 [K3997].

Barlaeus, Caspar. *Mercator sapiens.* Amsterdam, 1632.

    Nederlandsch Brazilië onder het bewind van Johan Maurits Grave van Nassau, 1637–1644. Trans. and ed. S. P. L'Honoré Naber. The Hague, 1923.

    Rerum per octennium in Brasilia et alibi nuper gestarum, sub praefectura. . . J. Mauriti. Amsterdam, 1647.

Basuyne des oorloghs, ofte waerschouwinghe aen de Vereenichde Nederlanden. 1625 [K3608].

Baudartius [Baudart], Willem. *Memoryen ofte Cort verhael der gedenck-weerdichste so kercklicke als wereltlicke gheschiedenissen . . . van den jaere 1603 tot in't jaer 1624.* 16 pts. Arnhem, 1624–1625.

    Morghen-wecker der vrye Nederlandse provintien, ofte, een cort verhael van de bloedighe vervolghinghen ende wreetheden door de Spaenjaerden ende haere adherenten in de Nederlanden, gheduerende dese veertich-jarighe troublen ende oorloghen. "Danswick," 1610.

Het Beclach der Spaenschen Naty. 1598 [K1019].

't Begin, midden en eynde der see-roveryen, van den alder-famieusten zee-roover, Claes G. Compaen van Oostsanen in Kennemerlant. 1659.

Benedicti, Georgius. *De krijgsdaden van Willem van Oranje.* Ed. and trans. EDEPOL. Leiden, 1990.

    De rebus gestis illustrissimi principis Guilielmi, comitis Nassouii libri II. Leiden, 1586.

Beneficien voor de soldaten gaende naer Brasil. The Hague, 1647.

Benzoni, Girolamo. *La historia del mondo nuovo.* Venice, 1565.

    De historie van de nieuwe weereld, te weten de beschrijvinghe van West Indien. Trans. Karel van Mander. Haarlem, 1610.

    History of the New World. Trans. and ed. W. H. Smyth. Works Issued by the Hakluyt Society, vol. 21. London, 1857.

Bertius, Petrus. *Tabularum geographicum.* Amsterdam, 1600.

De beschriivinge van de gheschiedenissen in der religien saken toeghedragen in den Nederlanden. 15[6]9 [K147].

Beverwijck, Johan van. *Inleydinge tot de Hollandsche geneesmiddelen.* Dordrecht, 1642. In *Alle de wercken.* Amsterdam, 1652.

    Schat der gesontheyt. Dordrecht, 1636. In *Wercken der genees-konste.* Amsterdam, 1664.

    Schat der ongesontheit, ofte Geneeskonste van de sieckten. Dordrecht, 1642.

Beynen, Koolemans, ed. and trans. *The three voyages of William Barentz to the Arctic regions.* Works issued by the Hakluyt Society, vol. 54. London, 1876.

Bodecher Banning, Johan. *Epigrammata Americana ad . . . Comitem I. Mauritium.* Leiden, 1639.

t'Boecxken van de dry Pausen, met een warachtighe verklaringe van de menichfuldighe loose practijcken zoo van d'Inquisitie als van het onderhouden der Placcaten ende anderssins. 1580 [K549].

Bontekoe, Willem Ysbrandtsz. *Journael ofte gedenckwaerdige beschrijvinge van de Oost-Indische reyse van Willem Ysbrandtsz. Bontekoe van Hoorn.* Hoorn, 1646.

Bor, Pieter Christiaensz. *Oorspronk, begin en vervolgh der Nederlantsche oorloghen, beroerten en borgerlijke oneenigheden.* 4 vols. Amsterdam, 1679–1684.

   comp. *Byvoegsel van authentyke stukken, die in de Historie van Pieter Bor Christiaensz, slechts sommierlijk en stuksgewijs of in't geheel niet gevonden worden.* 3 pts. Amsterdam, 1684.

Borstius, Jakob. *Predikatie tegen lang hayr.* Dordrecht, 1644.

Boxhorn, Marcus Zuerius. *Spiegeltjen, vertoonende 't lanck hayr ende hayrlocken, by de oude Hollanders ende Zeelanders gedragen.* Middelburg, 1644.

Brant, Sebastian. *Das Narrenschiff.* Faksimile der Esrstausgabe van 1494. Ed. Franz Schulz. Strassburg, 1913.

De Brasilsche breede-byl, ofte t'samen-spraek tusschen Kees Jansz. Schott, komende uyt Brasil, en Jan Maet, koopmansknecht, hebbende voor desen ook in Brasil geweest, over den verloop in Brasil. 1647 [K5546].

Brasilsche gelt-sack, waer in dat klaerlijck vertoont wort, waer dat de participanten van de West-Indische Compangie haer geldt ghebleven is. Recife [Amsterdam?], 1647 [K5547].

Brasilsche oorloghs overwegingh. Delft, 1648.

Brasyls schuyt-praetjen ghehouden tusschen een officier, een domine, en een coopman, nopende den staet van Brasyl. 1649 [K6482].

Breeden-raedt aende vereenichde Nederlantsche Provintien. Antwerp, 1649 [K6481].

Brief discours sur la negotation de la paix. 1579 [K492].

Brieven van advertissement oft waerschouwinge, geschreven aenden edeldom ende andere ghedeputeerde vande Generale Staten vande Nederlanden, by eenen dienaer van . . . Don Jan van Oostenrijck. 1578 [K350].

Britaine, William de. *The Dutch usurpation; or, A brief view of the behavior of the States General . . . towards the king of Great Britain.* London, 1672.

   The interest of England in the present war with Holland. London, 1672.

Brodhead, John Romeyn, comp., E. B. O'Callaghan and B. Fernow, eds. and trans. *Documents Relative to the Colonial History of the State of New York.* 15 vols. Albany, 1853–1887.

Brouwer, G. J., ed. *Catalogue of the Library of Philip Marnix van St. Aldegonde sold by auction (July 6th) Leiden, Christophorus Guyot, 1599.* Nieuwenkoop, 1964.

Bruijn, Abraham de. *Omnium pene Europae, Asiae, Aphricae atque Americae gentium habitus.* Antwerp, 1581.

Buchell, Arend van. *Diarium van Arend van Buchell.* Ed. G. Brom and L. A. van Langeraad. Werken Uitgegeven door het Historisch Genootschap, 3rd ser., no. 21. Amsterdam, 1907.

Buyr-praetjen: Ofte tsamensprekinge ende discours, op den brief vanden agent Aerssens uyt Vranckrijck, aende Eedele Moghende Heeren Staten Ghenerael geschreven. 1608 [K1525].

Cannenburg, W. Voorbeijtel, ed. *De reis om de wereld van de Nassausche Vloot 1623–1626.* Werken Uitgegeven door de Linschoten-Vereeniging, vol. 65. The Hague, 1964.

Catechismus, ofte, Tsamen-spreekinghe ghemaeckt op den vrede-handel. 1608 [K1414].

Cats, Jacob. *Emblemata, ofte minnelycke, zedlycke, ende stichtelycke sinnebeelden.* [1622?].

Invallende gedachten op voorvallenden gelegentheden. Amsterdam, 1655.

Clare vertoning ende bericht der articulen ende conditien nu onlancx tot Cuelen inde vrede-handel byden churfursten, fursten ende andere keyserlycke maiesteyts ghesanten, gheproponeert. 1579 [K500].

[Clercq, Gilles le.] *Remonstrance ofte vertoogh aen den grootmachtigen Coninck van Spaengen etc. op de Requeste byden Edeldom der Co. M. erfnederlanden den 5 April 1565. aen mijn Vrouwe de Hertoginne van Parme regente gepresenteert.* 1566 [K139b].

[Cliff, E.] *An abbreviate of Holland's deliverance by, and ingratitude to the Crown of England and the House of Nassau.* London, 1665.

[Clyte, Nicasius van der.] *Cort verhael der destructie van d'Indien.* Flushing, 1611 [K1837].

Columbus, Christopher. *Epistola . . . de insulis Indie supra Gangem nuper inventis.* Antwerp, 1493.

The Four Voyages of Columbus. Trans. and ed. Cecil Jane. 2 vols. 1930–33. Reprint. New York, 1988.

Commelin, Izaäk. *Frederick Hendrick van Nassauw prince van Orangien zijn leven en bedryf.* 2 vols. Amsterdam, 1651.

Consideratie over de tegenwoordige ghelegentheydt van Brasil. Amsterdam, 1644 [K5124].

Consideratien ende redenen der E. Heeren Bewind-hebberen vande Geoctrojeerde West-Indische Compagnie inde vergaederinghe vande . . . Staten Generael. Haarlem, 1629 [K3909].

Consideratien vande vrede in Nederlandt gheconcipieert. 1608 [K1447].

Copie eens sendtbriefs der Ridderschap, Edelen ende Steden van Hollandt . . . aen . . . die Staten vanden Lande van Herwaerts overe. 1573 [K210].

Copye, overgeset wt de Engelsche taele . . . gheschreven aen Milore Tresorier. van Mr. Thomas Candishe. Amsterdam, [1588] [K824].

Copye vande Requeste ghepresenteert aen de Hertoghinne van Parma etc., Regente, opten vijfsten dach van April, anno XVc. vijffentsestich voer Paesschen, bij diversche Edelmannen van Herwaertsovere, opt feyt van de Inquisitie ende executie vande Placcaten ende Catholijcke Religie. Brussels, 1566 [K137a].

Correspondance française de Marguerite d'Autriche duchesse de Parme avec Philippe II. Ed. J. S. Theissen. Utrecht, 1925.

Cortés, Hernán. *De contreyen vanden eylanden ende lantdouwen ghevonden ende gheconquesteert byden capiteyn vander alder doorluchtichsten aldermoghensten ende onverwinlijcsten Kaerle ghecoren Roomsch Keysere.* Antwerp, [1523].

Des marches ysles et pays trouvees et conquise par les captains du tres illustre Charles V. Antwerp, 1522.

Letters from Mexico. Trans. and ed. Anthony Pagden. 2d ed. New Haven, 1986.

[Court, Pieter de la]. *Interest van Holland.* Amsterdam, 1662.

The true interest and political maxims of the Republic of Holland. London, 1746.

Crespin, Jean. *Les livres des martyrs.* Geneva, 1554.

D. F. *The Dutch-mens pedigree, or a relation showing how they were first bred, and descended from horse-turd, which was enclosed in a butter-box.* London, 1653.

D. L. C. *Politike discoursen handelende in ses onderscheide boeken van steden, landen, oorlogen, kerken, regeeringen, en zeeden.* Amsterdam, 1662.

[Darell, John.] *A true and compendious narration; or (second part of Amboyney) of sundry notorious or remarkable injuries [. . .] in the East-Indies.* London, 1665.

A defense and true declaration of the thinges lately done in the lowe countrey. London, 1571.

Een dialogue, ofte Tsamensprekinghe tusschen de goetwillighe Ghemeynte ende die Edele . . . Hertoghe van Anjou, etc. onse gheduchtighe Heere. Antwerp, 1582 [K588].

Dialogus ofte t'samenspreekinge tusschen Jan Andersorgh end Govert Eygensin, over den huydendaeghschen handel van treves. 1630 [K4020].

Discours, aengaende treves of vrede, met de infante ofte koning van Hispanien, ende de Vereenighde Nederlanden. Haarlem, 1629 [K3919].

Discours d'un gentil-homme amateur de la patrie et du repos publicq, sur le fait de la paix et de la guerre en ces pays-bas. 1584 [K705].

Discours van Pieter en Pauwels op des handelinghe vanden Vrede. 1608 [K1456].

Dodoens, Rembert. *Cruydeboeck.* Antwerp, 1554.

Donck, Adriaen van der. *Beschryvinge van Nieuw-Nederlant.* Amsterdam, 1655.

   A Description of the New Netherlands. Ed. Thomas F. O'Donnell, trans. Jeremiah Johnson. Syracuse, New York, 1968.

[Donck, Adriaen van der?] *Vertoogh van Nieu Neder-land, weghens de gheleghen-theydt, vruchtbaerheydt, en soberen staet deszelfs.* The Hague, 1650.

Downing, George, Sir. *A discourse: vindicating His Royal Master from the insolen-cies of a scandalous libel.* London, 1664.

   A discourse written by Sir George Downing, the King of Great Britain's envoy ex-traordinary to the States of the United Provinces. London, 1672.

Des drukkers belydenisse. 1648 [K5765].

Dryden, John. *Amboyna: A Tragedy.* In *The Dramatic Works,* ed. Montague Sum-mers. 6 vols. London, 1931–1932.

Duncanus, Martinus [Maarten Donk]. *Die vruchten der ecclesie Christi. Van won-derlicke wonderheyden, dwelcken gevonden ende gedaen worden met met Godts gratie in veel ende groote landen van Indien, dwelcken nu in onsetijden eersten gevonden sijn.* Leiden, 1567.

Duplessis-Mornay, Philippe. *Discours sur la permission de liberté de religion, dicte Religions vrede, au Pais-Bas.* 1579 [K425].

The Dutch boare dissected. London, 1665.

The Dutch deputies. N.p., n.d.

E. W. *Severall remarkable passages concerning the Hollanders since the death of Queen Elizabeth until the 25. of December 1673.* 1673.

Echo ofte galm, dat is: Weder klinckende ghedicht van de teghenwoordighe vredehan-delinghe. 1607 [K1405].

Eibergen, Rutgerus. *Swymel-klacht des Spaenschen conincks Philippi Quarti, over het eerste verlies van sijn silver-vlote.* Amsterdam, 1629.

[Enden, Francois van den?]. *Vrye politijke stellingen en consideratien van staat, gedaen na der ware Christenen even gelijke vryheits gronden.* Amsterdam, 1665 [K9191].

Den Engelschen duyvel, ontdeckt door een botte schelm. [1652?] [K7301].

Erasmus, Desiderius. *The Correspondence of Erasmus.* Trans. and ed. R. A. B. Mynors et al. Toronto, 1974– .

Opera Omnia Des. Erasmi Roterodami. Ed. J. Leclercq. 10 vols. Leiden, 1703–1706.

Ercilla y Zúñiga, Alonso de. *The Araucaniad.* Trans. Charles Maxwell Lancaster and Paul Thomas Manchester. Nashville, 1945.

Historiale beschrijvinghe der goudtrijcke landen in Chile ende Arauco, ende andere provincien in Chili ghelegen. Rotterdam, 1619.

Primera, segunda y tercera partes de la Araucana. Antwerp, 1597.

Everard, Giles. *De herba panacea, quam alii tabacum.* Antwerp, 1587.

Exquemelin, Alexander Olivier. *De Americaensche zee-roovers. Behelsende een pertinente en waerachtige beschrijving van alle de voornaemste roveryen, en onmenschelijcke wreedheden, die de Engelse en Franse rovers, tegens de Spanjaerden in America gepleeght hebben.* Amsterdam, 1678.

The Buccaneers of America. Ed. William S. Stallybrass. London, [1935].

Felltham, Owen. *A brief character of the Low-Countries under the States.* London, 1652.

Fidelle exhortation aux inhabitants du pais bas, contre les vains et faux espoirs dont leurs oppresseurs les font amuser. 1568 [K171].

Fin de la guerre. Dialogus ofte t'samen-sprekinge P. Scipio Africanus raedt den Romeynen datmen naer Africam most trecken om Carthago te bekrygen ende bestryden so verre men Hannibal uyt Italien wilde jagen. Amsterdam [K3428].

Focanus, Jacobus. *Adoni-Beseck of Lex talionis, dat is rechtveerdighe straffe Godes over den tyrannen.* Delft, 1629 [K3922].

Foreest, Jan II van. *Hispanus redux. Sive exitus induciarum Belgicarum ad Foederatos Belgas.* Hoorn, 1622 [K3328].

Fracastoro, Girolamo. *Syphilis sive morbus gallicus.* Verona, 1530.

Fredericq, Paul, ed. *Nederlandsche proza in de zestiendeeuwsche pamfletten.* Brussel, 1907.

Fritz, Josef, ed. *Die Historie van Christoffel Wagenaer, discipel van D. Johannes Faustus.* Nederlandsche Volksboeken, vol. 12. Leiden, 1913.

Fruytiers, Jan. *Corte beschrijvinghe van der strenghe belegeringe en wonderbaerlijcke verlossing der stadt Leyden.* Delft, 1577.

G[eelkercken], N[icolaes]. *Reys-boeck van het rijcke Brasilien, Rio de la Plata, ende Magallanes.* 1624 [K3540].

Gelderen, Martin van, ed. and trans. *The Dutch Revolt.* Cambridge, 1993.

Gemma, Reinerus, Frisius. *De principiis astronomiae & cosmographiae.* Antwerp, 1530.

Gerbier, Balthazar. *Waarachtige verklaringe vanden Ridder Balthasar Gerbier, B: Douvilij; noopende sijn saecke van goude en silvere mynen.* 1657 [K7876].

't Geslacht, de geboort, plaets, tydt, leven, ende wercken van Karel van Mander, schilder, en poeet. Amsterdam, 1618.

De ghenuechlijcke historie vanden edelen ende vromen ridder Peeter van Provencien. Antwerp, 1587.

De ghepretendeerden overlast van eenighe ingeboorenen ende inghesetenen, door de Zeeuwen ende wtheemsche kamers haer in Brasil aengedaen. 1638 [K4584].

Ghespreck van Langhe Piet met Keesje Maet, belanghende den treves met den Spaigniaert. 1629 [K3924].

Gijsius, Joannes. *Oorsprong en voortgang der Neder-landtscher beroerten ende ellendicheden.* Leiden, 1616.

    Origio et historia Belgicorum tumultuum immanissimaeque crudelitatis per Cliviam et Westphaliam patratae. Fidelissime conscripta et tabellis aeneis repraesentata: accedit historia tragica de furoribus Gallicis. Leiden 1619.

Goede nieuwe tijdinghe ghecomen met het jacht de Vos gheneamt, afghesonden van den generael Jacob Wilckens uyt Bresilien, aen de Heeren Bewint-hebbers vande gheoctroyeerde West-Indische Compagnie. 1624.

Groot, Hugo de. *De origine gentium Americanarum dissertatio altera, adversus obtjectatorem.* Paris, 1643.

    De originum gentium Americanarum dissertatio. 1642.

Grynaeus, Simon, ed. *Novus orbis regionum ac insularum veteribus incognitarum.* Basel, 1532.

Guelen, Auguste de. *Kort verhael vanden staet van Fernanbuc.* Amsterdam, 1640 [K4689].

Guicciardini, Francesco. *The History of Italy.* Trans. Sidney Alexander. New York, 1969.

Guicciardini, Lodovico. *The description of the Low Countreys and of the Provinces thereof.* Trans. Thomas Danett. London, 1593.

Haemstede, Adriaan van. *De geschiedenisse ende den doodt der vromer martelaren.* 1559.

Hakluyt, Richard. "Discourse of Western Planting by Richard Hakluyt, 1584." In *The Original Writings & Correspondence of the Two Richard Hakluyts,* ed. E. G. R. Taylor. 2 vols. Works Issued by the Hakluyt Society, 2nd ser. vol. 76. London, 1935.

    The principall navigations, voiages and discoveries of the English nation, made by sea or over land, to the most remote and farthest distant quarters of the earth at any time within the the compasse of these 1500. yeeres. London, 1589.

Hall, Thomas. *Comarum akosmia. The loathsomnesse of long haire.* London, 1654.

Hamconius, Martinus [Maarten Hamckema]. *Frisia, seu De viris rebusque Frisiae illustribus libri duo.* Franeker, 1620.

Heemskerk, Johan van. *Inleydinghe tot het ontwerp van een Batavische arcadia.* Amsterdam, 1637.

Heinsius, Daniel. *Oratio panegyrica. De illustri victoria, quam amplissimi rerum Indiae Occidentalis administratores, ductu . . . Petri Henrici.* Leiden, 1629.

Herckmans, Elias. "Generale beschrijvinge vande Capitanie Paraiba." *Bijdragen en mededeelingen van het Historisch Genootschap gevestigd te Utrecht,* 2 (1879): 358–67.

    Der zee-vaert lof handelende vande gedenckwaerdighste zee-vaerden. Amsterdam, 1634.

Heylyn, Peter. *Cosmographie in four bookes.* London, 1652.

De heylighe Spaensche inquisitie, met haer loosheyt, valscheyt ende arghelisten ontdect, wtgestelt ende int licht gebracht. London, 1569.

Heyns, Peeter. *Spieghel der werelt ghestelt in ryme.* Antwerp, 1577.

Historie van B. Cornelis Andriaensen van Dordrecht, Minrebroeder binnen de stadt van Brugghe. [Bruges], 1569.

Hollands venezoen, in Englandt gebakken, en geopent voor de liefhebbers van 't Vaderlandt. 1672 [K10606–10].

Het Hollants wijve praetjen . . . noopende den tegenwoordighen staet der vrye Vereenichde Nederlanden, en het gepretendeerde Parlement van Engelandt. Haarlem, 1652 [K7233].

Hommius, Festius. *Tweede vervolch van het kort ende bondigh verhael van den standt der kercken, ende wereltlicke regieringhe.* Leiden, 1627.

Hondius, Petrus. *Dapes inemptae, of de Moufe-schans, dat is de soeticheydt des buyten-levens vergheselschapt met de boucken.* Leiden, 1621.

Hooft, Pieter Cornelisz. *Neederlandsche histoorien, sedert de ooverdracht der heerschappye van kaizer Karel den Vyfden op kooning Philips zynen zoon.* Amsterdam, 1642.

Humboldt, Alexander von. *Voyage de Humboldt et Bonpland. Premiere partie. Relation historique.* 3 vols. Paris, 1814.

IJzerman, J. W., ed. *Journael van de reis naar Zuid-Amerika door Hendrik Ottsen, 1598–1601.* Werken Uitgegeven door de Linschoten-Vereeniging, vol. 16. The Hague, 1918.

De reis om de wereld door Olivier van Noort, 1598–1601. Werken Uitgegeven door de Linschoten-Vereeniging, vols. 27–28. The Hague, 1926.

Jameson, J. Franklin. *Narratives of New Netherland 1609–1664.* New York, 1909.

Jode, Cornelis de, comp. *Speculum orbis terrarum.* Antwerp, 1593.

Jon, François du. *Brief discours envoyé au roy Philippe nostre sire et souverain Seigneur, pour le bien et profit de la Maiesté.* 1566.

Journael ende historis verhael van de reyse gedaen by oosten de Straet le Maire, naer de custen van Chili, onder het beleyt van den Heer Generael Hendrick Brouwer, in den jare 1643 voor gevallen. Amsterdam, 1646.

Journael vande Nassaussche vloot, ofte Beschryvingh vande voyagie om den gantsche aerdt-cloot ghedaen met elf schepen. Amsterdam, 1626.

Justificatie vande resolutie der H. M. Heeren de Staten van Hollandt ende West-Vrieslandt ghenomen den 4. Augusti 1617. 1618 [K2502].

Kemys, Lawrence. *Waerachtighe ende grondighe beschryvinghe vande tweede zeevaert der Engelschen nae Guiana.* Amsterdam, 1598.

Kennenburch, Hendrik van. *Protest ofte scherp dreyghement, 'twelck den coninck van Spagnen is doende d'Heeren Staten Generael . . . ter occasie van't veroveren vande Silver-vlote.* Middelburg, 1629 [K3861].

Keuning, J., ed. *De tweede schipvaart der Nederlanders naar Oost Indië onder Jacob Cornelisz van Neck en Wybrant Warwijck, 1598–1600.* 5 pts. Werken Uitgegeven door de Linschoten-Vereeniging, vols. 42, 44, 46, 48, and 50. The Hague, 1938–1947.

[Keye, Otto.] *Het waere onderscheyt tusschen koude en warme landen.* The Hague, [1659].

Klare aenwijsinge, dat de Vereenighde Nederlanden, gheen treves met de Vyandt dienen te maecken. The Hague, 1630 [K4014].

Kort, bondigh ende waerachtigh verhael van 't schandelijck overgeven ende verlaten vande voornaemste conquesten van Brasil. Middelburg, 1655 [K7655].

Kort discourse, ofte naerdere verklaringe over de onderstaende v. poincten. 1644 [K5122].

Kort verhael van Nieuw-Nederlants gelegentheit, deugden, natuerlijke voorrrechten, en byzondere bequaemheidt ter bevolkingh. 1662.

Laer, A. J. F. van, trans. and ed. *Documents Relating to New Netherland, 1624–1626, in the Henry E. Huntington Library.* San Marino, Calif., 1924.

Van Rensselaer Bowier Manuscripts. Albany, 1908.

Laet, Joannes de. *Iaerlyck verhael van de verrichtinghen der Geoctroyeerde West-Indische Compagnie.* Ed. S. P. L'Honoré Naber. 4 pts. Werken Uitgegeven door de Linschoten-Vereeniging, vols. 34–35, 37, 40. The Hague, 1924–36.

Nieuwe wereldt oft Beschrijvinghe van West Indien. Leiden, 1630.

Notae ad dissertationem Hugonis Grotii. Amsterdam, 1643.

Responsio ad dissertationem secundam Hugonis Grotii. Amsterdam, 1644.

Lange, Petrus de. *Batavise Romeyn.* Amsterdam, 1661.

Wonderen des werelds. Amsterdam, 1671.

Langenes, Barent. *Caert-thresoor.* Middelburg, 1598.

Las Casas, Bartolomé de. *Brevíssima relación de la destruyción de las Indias.* Seville, 1552.

Relation des voyages et des découvertes que les Espagnols ont fait dans les Indes Occidentales . . . Avec la relation . . . du sieur de Montauban. Amsterdam, 1698.

Seer cort verhael vande destructie van d'Indien. 1578.

A Short Account of the Destruction of the Indies. Ed. and trans. Nigel Griffen, introd. Anthony Pagden. London, 1992.

Den Spiegel der Spaensche tyrannye gheschiet in West Indien. Amsterdam: Jan Evertsz Cloppenburg, 1620.

Spieghel der Spaenscher tyrannye in West-Indien. Amsterdam, 1607.

Den spieghel vande Spaensche tyrannie beeldelijcken afgemaelt. Amsterdam, 1609.

Den vermeerderden Spieghel der Spaensche tierannije geschiet in Westindien. Amsterdam, 1640.

Laudonnière, René de. *L'histoire notable de la Floride.* Paris, 1586.

Le Challeux, Nicolas. *A true and perfect description of the last voyage . . . into Florida.* Trans. Thomas Hacket. In *The New World: The First Pictures of America . . . with Contemporary Narratives of the French Settlements in Florida, 1562–1565,* ed. Stefan Lorant. New York, 1965.

Leendertz, P., Jr., ed. *Het geuzenliedboek.* 2 vols. Zutphen, 1924–1925.

Léry, Jean de. *Histoire d'un voyage faict en la terre du Bresil autrement dite Amerique.* La Rochelle [Geneva?], 1578.

History of a Voyage to the Land of Brazil, Otherwise Called America. Trans. and ed. Janet Whatley. Berkeley, 1990.

Lettre contenant un avis de l'estat auquel sont les affaires des Pais Bas. Reims, 1578 [K358].

Levendich discours vant ghemeyne lants welvaert, voor desen de Oost, end nu de West-Indische generale compaignie aenghevanghen. 1622 [K3362].

L'Honoré Naber, S. P., and Irene A. Wright. *Piet Heyn en de Zilvervloot: Bescheiden uit Nederlandsche en Spaansche Archieven.* 2 pts. Werken Uitgegeven door het Historisch Genootschap, 3rd ser., no. 53. Utrecht, 1928.

Libellus supplex Imperatoriae Maiestati . . . nomine Belgarum ex inferiori Germania, evangelicae religionis causa per Albani Ducis tyrannidem eiectorum. 1570 [K179].

Liefs, Jacob. *Lof dicht over de wijt-vermaerde noyt gehoorde deser landen vreughden-rijcke victorie, by het veroveren vande schatriicke silver-vloot.* 1629.

Den lof van de geoctroyeerde Oost ende West-Indische Compagnye. Ende lof-rijcke zee-vaert, van dese vrye Vereenighde Nederlandtsche Provintien. Delft, 1630.

Linschoten, Jan Huygen van. *Itinerario, voyage ofte schipvaert.* Amsterdam, 1596.

Itinerario. Voyage ofte Schipvaert van Jan Huygen van Linschoten naer Oost ofte Portugaels Indiën, 1579–1592. Ed. H. Terpstra. Werken Uitgegeven door de Linschoten-Vereeniging, vol. 57. The Hague, 1955.

Lipsius, Justus. *De constantia libri duo.* Leiden, 1584.

Lommelin, D. *Lof-dicht ter eeren ende tot weerde fame, vanden . . . generael Pieter Pieterssz. Heyn.* 1629.

López de Gómara, Francisco. *La Istoria de las Indias.* Saragossa, 1552.

Den lusthof van rhetorica. Leiden, 1596.

Mander, Karel van. *Den grondt der vry edel schilder-const.* In Mander, *Het schilder-boeck.*

Het leven der doorluchtighe Nederlandtsche en Hoogduytsche schilders. Alkmaar, 1604. In Mander, *Het schilder-boeck.*

Het schilder-boeck. Haarlem, 1604.

Wtleggingh op den Metamorphosis Pub. Ovidij Nasonis. Haarlem, 1604.

Marees, Pieter de. *Beschryvinghe ende historische verhael van het gout Koninckrijck van Gunea.* Ed. S. P. L'Honoré Naber. Werken Uitgegeven door de Linschoten-Vereeniging, vol. 5. The Hague, 1912.

Marnix van St. Aldegonde, Philip van. *Oratio legatorum . . . Matthiae . . . Habita in Conventu Wormaciensi coram consiliariis à principibus electoribus, et reliquis S. R. Imperij Legtis.* 1578 [K354].

Response a un libelle fameux nagueres publié contre Monseigneur le Prince d'Orenges. Antwerp, 1579 [K468].

Vraye narration et apologie des choses passées au Pays-bas, touchant le fait de la religion, en l'an, MDLXVI. 1567 [K150].

[Isaac Rabbotenu, pseud.]. *De bijencorf der H. Roomsche Kercke.* Utrecht, 1574 (orig. 1569).

[Marnix van St. Aldegonde, Philip van.] *Antwoorde op een cleyn boecxken onlanxc wt ghegheven, ghenoemt de "Declaratie vande meyninge van Heer Don Jan van Oostenrijck."* Antwerp, 1578 [K343].

Marvell, Andrew. "The Character of Holland." In *The Complete Poems,* ed. Elizabeth Story Donno. Harmondsworth, England, 1972.

Massa, Isaac. *Beschrijvinge vander Samoyeden landt in Tatarien nieulijks onder 't ghebiet der Moscoviter gebracht.* Amsterdam, 1612.

"Letter to Maurits." In *A short history of the beginnings and origins of the present wars in Moscow under the reign of various sovereigns down to the year 1610,* trans. and ed. G. Edward Orchard. Toronto, 1982.

Megapolensis, Johannes. *Een kort ontwerp vande Mahakuase Indiaenen, haer landt, tale, statuere, dracht, godes-dienst ende magistrature.* Alkmaar, 1644.

A memento for Holland, or A true and exact history of the most villainous and barbarous cruelties used on the English merchants residing at Amboyna. London, 1653.

Memorie vande ghewichtighe redenen die de heeren Staten Generael behooren te beweghen, om gheensins te wijcken vande handelinghe ende vaert van Indien. 1608 [K1433].

Merula, Paullus. *Tijdt-threzoor. Ofte kort ende bondich verhael van den standt de kercken, ende de wereltlicke regieringe.* Leiden, 1614.

Meteren, Emanuel van. *Historie der Neder-landscher ende haerder na-buren oorlogen ende geschiedenissen.* The Hague, 1614.

[Middelgeest, Simon van.] *Het testament often wterste wille vande Nederlandsche Oorloghe.* 1609 [K1581].

[Migoen, Jacobus Willem.] *Proeve des nu onlangs uyt-ghegheven drooms off t'samenspraak den Coning van Hispanien ende den Paus van Roomen.* [K1401].

Missive inhoudende der aerdt vanden treves tusschen den koninck van Spaengien ende de Gheunieerde Provincien. 1630 [K4023].

Missive van twee Indiaensche coninghen . . . versoecken dat haere soonen, welcke sy mede overghesonden hebben, inde Christelijcke religie mochten opgetrocken worden. The Hague, 1621 [K3242].

Moerbeeck, Jan Andries. *Redenen waeromme de West-Indische Compagnie dient te trachten het landt van Brasilia den coninck van Spangien te ontmachtigen, en dat ten eersten.* Amsterdam, 1624 [K3541].

Montanus, Arnoldus. *De nieuwe en onbekende weereld: of Beschryving van America en 't Zuid-land.* Amsterdam, 1671.

Montanus, Reginaldus Gonsalvus. *Sanctae Inquisitionis Hispanicae artes aliquot detectae.* Heidelberg, 1567.

Moreau, Pierre. *Klare en waarachtige beschryving van de leste beroerten en afval der Portugezen in Brazil.* Amsterdam, 1652.

Mout, M. E. H. N., ed. *Plakkaat van Verlatinge 1581.* The Hague, 1979.

Murphy, H. C., ed. and trans. *Anthology of New Netheland.* New York, 1865.

——— ed. and trans. *"Vertoogh van Nieu Nederland" and "Breeden Raedt aende Vereenichde Nederlandsche Provintien." Two Rare Tracts, Printed in 1649–'50.* New York, 1854.

Naerder klagh-vertoogh aende Ho: Mo: Heeren Staten Generael, wegens de bewinthebberen vande generale geoctroyeerde West-Indische Compagnie, ter sake vande onwettelijke, ende grouwelijcke proceduren der Engelsche in Nieu Nederlant. 1664.

Neander, Johann. *Tabacologia. Hoc est Tabaci seu Nicotianae descriptio medico-cheirugico-pharmaceutica*. Leiden, 1622.

Nederlandschen verre-kijcker, om wt Hollandt te konnen sien tot in de cancellerije van Spaignien. The Hague, 1627 [K3743].

Den Nederlandtschen bye-korf. The Hague, 1608 [K1474].

Nederlantsche absolutie op de Fransche belydenis. Amsterdam, 1684 [1648] [K5770].

Negende maandags relaes, over een verhaal van de zaken betreffende het geschil der Spanjaarden met d'Engelschen in America. 1674 [K11161].

Newes out of East India of the cruell usage of our English merchants at Amboyna. [1624?].

Nieuhof, Johan. *Gedenkweerdige Brasiliaense zee- en lantreize*. Amsterdam, 1682.

Noot, Jan van der. *De Poetische Werken van Jonker Jan van der Noot*. Ed. W. Waterschoot. 3 vols. Ghent, 1975.

Octroy, by de Hooge Mogende Heeren Staten Generael, verleent aende West-Indische Compagnie, in date den derden, Junij 1621. The Hague, 1621.

Onpartydich discours opte handelinghe vande Indien. [K1436].

Ontdeckinghe van rijcke mijnen in Brasil. Amsterdam, 1639 [K4634].

Orlers, Jan Jansz. *Wilhelm en Maurits van Nassau*. Amsterdam, 1651.

Ortelius, Abraham. *Theatre oft Toonneel des aerdt-bodems*. Antwerp, [1573].

Een oud schipper van Monickendam, Daer ons den vromen held uyt quam, Die eerst den Spaengiaert de zee deed' ruymen, Sprack aldus naer scheeps coustuymen. [K1466].

Oviedo, Gonzalo Fernández de. *Libro del muy esforçado y invencible cavallero . . . don Claribalte*. Valencia, 1519.

De la natural hystoria de las Indias. Toledo, 1526.

La historia general de las Indias. Seville, 1535.

Paracelsus, Theophratus. *Een excellent tractaet leerende hoemen alle ghebreken der pocken sal moghen ghenesen*. Antwerp, 1557.

Von der frantzösischen Kranckheit. Nuremburg, 1530.

Paräupába, Antonio. *Twee verscheyden remonstrantien . . . overgegeven aen . . . de Heeren Staten Generael*. The Hague, 1657 [K7871].

Pauw, Cornelius de. *Recherches philosophiques sur les Américaines, ou, Mémoires intéressants pour servir à l'histoire de l'espèce humaine*. 2 vols. Berlin, 1768–69.

Peima van Beintema, I. I. W. *Tabacologia, ofte korte verhandelinge over de tabak, desselvs deugd, gebruyk, ende kennisse*. The Hague, 1690.

Pels, E. *Lof-dicht des vermaerde, wyt-beroemde, manhaftige zee-heldt Pieter Pietersen Heyn*. Amsterdam, 1629.

Pertinent bericht van alle particularteyten soo sich hebben toegedragen in West-Indien. The Hague, 1634 [K4347].

Pers, Dirck Pietersz. *Bacchus wonder-wercken*. Amsterdam, 1628.

Petty, Francis. *Beschryvinge van de overtreffelijcke ende wijdtvermaerde zeevaert vanden Edelen Heer ende Meester Thomas Candisch*. Amsterdam, 1598.

Philopatroön, Erasmum. *Nieuw-Keulsch of Spaensch bedrogh*. 1638 [K4575].

Piso, Willem et al. *De Indiae utriusque re naturali et medica libri quatuordecim*. Amsterdam, 1658.

Piso, Willem, and Georg Marcgraf. *Historia naturalis Brasiliae*. Leiden, 1648.

A pithie and most earnest exhortation, concerning the estate of Christiandome . . . Dedicated to all Christian Kings, Princes and Potentates. Antwerp [London?], 1583.

Placcaet inghestelt op den name van Philippus de II Coninck van Hispanien. Dordrecht, 1622 [K3327].

Plante, Franciscus. *Mauritiados Libri XII. Hoc est: Rerum ab illustrissimo heroe Ioanne Mauritio, comite Nassaviae &c. In Occidentali India gestarum descriptio poetica.* Leiden, 1647.

Plockhoy, Pieter Cornelisz. *Kort en klaer ontwerp dienende tot een onderling accoordt, om den arbeyd, onrust en moeyelijckheyt van alderley handwercx luyden te verlichten door een onderlinge compagnie . . . in Nieu-neder-land op te rechten.* Amsterdam, 1662 [K8668].

Politicq onderwijs. Mechelen, 1582 [K581].

[Ponet, John.] *A short treatise of politike power, and of the true obedience which subiectes owe to kynges and other civil governors, with an exhortation to all true naturall Englishe men.* [Strasbourg], 1556.

De Portogysen goeden buyrman, ghetrocken uyt de registers van sijn goet gebeurschap gehouden in Lisbona . . . Dienende tot antwoort op het ongefondeerde Brasylsschuyt-praetjen. Lisbon [The Hague?], 1649 [K6483].

Pot[t]y, Pieter. *Copye, van een Brasiliaensen brieff geschreven van Pieter Potty Brasiliaen . . . aen Camaron mede Brasiliaen.* Amstedam, 1646.

Practiicke van den Spaenschen aes-sack: Aen-gewesen op de veroveringe, en victorie van den loffelijcken, voorsienighen, manlijck-hertighen Heer Generael Pieter Pietersz. Heyn. The Hague, 1629 [K3862].

Purchas, Samuel. *Hakluytus Posthumus or Purchas his Pilgrimes.* London, 1625.

Rainolds, William, and William Gifford. *Calvino-turcismus, id est, Calvinisticae perfidiae cum Mahometana collatio et dilucida utriusque sectae confutatio.* Antwerp, 1597.

Ralegh, Walter, Sir. *The discoverie of the large, rich, and bewtiful Empyre of Guiana.* London, 1596.

   Waerachtighe ende grondighe beschryvinge van het groot ende goudt-rijck Coninck-rijck van Guiana. Amsterdam, 1598.

Rapport faict par le seigneur Guillaume vanden Hecke Tresorier, & maistre Cornille Aertssens Secretaire de la ville de Bruxelles, à Mesieurs du Magistrat d'icelle ville. Antwerp, 1579 [K440].

Raynal, Guillaume Thomas François, Abbé. *Histoire philosophique et politique des établissemens et du commerce des Européens dans les deux Indes.* 10 vols. Geneva, 1780.

Redenen, waeromme dat de Vereenighde Nederlanden, geensints eenighe vrede met de koningh van Spaignien konnen, mogen noch behooren te maecken. The Hague, 1630 [K4013].

Reglement byde West-Indische Compagnie . . . over het open-stellen vanden handel op Brasil. The Hague, 1638.

Remonstratie vande bewinthebberen der Nederlantsche West-Indische Compagnie, aende d'Heeren Staten Generael over verscheyde specien van tyrannye, ende gewelt, door de Englesche in Nieuw-Nederlant aende onderdanen van haer Hoogh-Mog: verrecht. Schiedam, 1663.

Rensselaer, Kiliaen van. *Redres van de abuysen ende faulten in de colonie van Rensselaers-wijck.* Amsterdam, 1643.

Waerschouwinge, verboth, ende toe-latinghe, weghens de colonie van Renselaerswyck. Amsterdam, 1643.

Responce d'un bon patriot et bourgeois de la ville Gand, au libelle fameux, intitulé "Avis d'un bourgeois de la ville de Gand, qui se ressent amerement des calamitez de sa ville." 1583 [K633].

Reys-boeck van het rijcke Brasilien, Rio de la Plata, ende Magallanes. 1624 [K3540].

Rouffaer, G. P., and J. W. IJzerman, ed. *De eerste schipvaart der Nederlanders naar Oost Indië onder Cornelis de Houtman, 1595–1597.* 3 pts. Werken Uitgegeven door de Linschoten-Vereeniging, vols. 7, 25, and 32. The Hague, 1915–1929.

Ruiters, Dierick. *Toortse der Zeevaert.* Ed. S. P. L'Honoré Naber. Werken Uitgegeven door de Linschoten-Vereeniging, vol. 6. The Hague, 1913.

Rym-vieren op de jeghen-woordige victorie, bekomen door den manhaften Generael Pieter Pietersz. Heyn. [The Hague, 1629] [K3862].

Sande, Johan van den. *Kort begrijp der Nederlandtsche historien, waer in 't begin, voortganck en eynde der selver beroerten en oneenigheden klaerlijck aengewesen wort.* Amsterdam, 1650.

Nederlandtsche historie, . . . diende voor continuatie vande historie van wijll. Everhard van Reyd. Leeuwarden, 1650.

[Ireneus Ammonius, pseud.]. *Trouhertighe vermaninghe aen het vereenichde Nederlandt.* 1605 [K1300].

Schriftelick bewijs des . . . Heeren Johan Casimiri, Palsgraven opden Rhijn, Hertogen in Beyeren, etc. 1578 [K361].

Schuyt-praetgens, op de vaert naer Amsterdam, tusschen een lantman, een hovelinck, een borger ende schipper. 1608 [K1450].

Scott, Thomas. *The Belgick souldier: warre is a blessing.* 1624.

Scriverius, Petrus. *Saturnalia ofte Poëtische vasten-avondspel.* Trans. Samuel Ampzing. Haarlem, 1630.

Second part of the Tragedy of Amboyna: or, A true relation of a most bloody, treacherous, and cruel design of the Dutch in New Netherlands in America. London, 1653.

Het secreet des conings van Spangien, Philippus den tweden, achter gelaten aen synen zoone, Philips de derde van dien name. 1599 [K1058].

Sentdbrieven van die van Gendt, aende Staten van Brabant, ende den steden Brussele ende Antwerpen. 1584 [K683].

Smeeks, Hendrik. *The Mighty Kingdom of Krinke Kesmes (1708).* Ed. David Fausett, trans. Robert H. Leek. Amsterdam, 1995.

Soler, Vincent Joachim. *Cort ende sonderlingh verhael van eenen brief van Monsieur Soler, bedienaer des H. Evangelij inde Ghereformeerde Kercke van Bresilien.* Amsterdam, 1639.

Souter, Daniel. *Eben-ezer, tot hier toe heeft ons de Heere gheholpen.* Haarlem, 1630.

Sené-boher. Brandende-bosche uyt welckers voncken, d'over-groote victorie vande stercke stadt s'Hertogen-bosch. Haarlem, 1630.

Den Spaenschen ende Arragoenschen Spiegel. Inde welcke men mach claerlick ende waerachtich sien tot wat eynde meeninge eygentlick het voornemen is streckende van 't Spaensche Crijchsvolck. 1599 [K1078].

Het spel van Brazil, vergheleken by een goedt verkeer spel. 1638 [K4582].

Spelen van sinne . . . 1561. Antwerp, 1562.

Spranckhuysen, Dionysius. *Tranen, over den doodt van . . . Pieter Pietersz. Heyn.* Delft, 1629 [K3867].

    Triumphe van weghen de gheluckighe ende over-rijcke victorie welcke de Heere onse God op den 8. en Septemberis des iaers 1628 verleent heeft aen de vloot vande West-Indische Compagnie onder . . . Pieter Pietersz. Heyn. Delft, 1629 [K3858].

Springer, Balthasar. *De reyse van Lissebone.* Trans. and ed. C. H. Coote. London, 1894.

Staden, Hans. *The True History of his Captivity, 1557.* Trans. and ed. Malcolm Letts. London, 1928.

    Warachtige historie ende beschrivinge eens lants in America ghelegen. Antwerp, 1558.

    Warhaftige historia und beschreibung eyner landtschafft der wilden, nacketen, grimmigen menschfresser leuthen, in . . . America. Marburg, 1557.

Steendam, Jacob. *'t Lof van Nuw-Nederland.* Amsterdam, 1661.

Sterre, D. van der. *Zeer aanmerkelijke reysen gedaen door Jan Erasmus Reining.* Amsterdam, 1691.

Steyger-praetjen tusschen Jan Batavier en Maetroos over het apprehenderen van den Gouverneur ende provinciael van gantsche Brasilien, met haer geselschap. Amsterdam, 1624 [K3539a].

[Stubbes, Henry.] *A further justification of the present war against the United Netherlands.* London, 1673.

    A justification of the present war against the United Provinces. London, 1673.

Swinnas, Willem. *Vermeerde, en verbeterde Engelse, Nederlandse en Munsterse krackeelen. Het eerste deel.* Amsterdam, 1666 [K9243a].

Teellinck, Ewout. *De derde wachter, brengende tijdinge vande nacht, dat is vande verstroying van onse vlote voor Duyn-kercken.* The Hague, 1625 [K3607a].

    [Ireneus Philalethius, pseud.]. *De tweede wachter, brenghende tijdinghe vande nacht, dat is, van het overgaan vande Bahia.* The Hague, 1625 [K3607].

Thevet, André. *The new found world, or Antarctike.* Trans. Thomas Hacket. London, 1568.

    Les singularitez de la France antarctique autrement nomée Amérique (Paris, 1557).

Thorius, Raphael. *Hymnus tabaci.* Leyden, 1625.

Tijdinge hoe dat den manhaftigen Heer Generael Pieter Pietersz. Heyn, ende den Vice Admirael Loncq, de vlote van Nova Spaengien inde Bahia Matanse hebben aenghetast, verovert ende verdestrueert, den 8. Septemb. 1628. Amsterdam, 1628 [K3796].

Touron, Antoine. *Histoire générale de l'Amérique depuis découverte.* 14 vols. Paris, 1768–70.

Tractaet paraeneticq, dat is te segghen; Onderwysinghe ofte vermaninghe. Amsterdam, 1598 [K1021].

Trouhertighe vermaninghe aende verheerde Nederlandsche provintien ende het alghe-meyne eynde ende voornemen des Spaengniaerds t'welck is d'oprechtinghe van een voorghenomene vijfde monarchie. Amsterdam, 1585 [K766].

A true declaration of the news that came out of the East Indies, with the pinace called "Hare," which arrived in Texel in June 1624. 1624.

A true relation of the unjust, cruel, and barbarous proceedings against the English at Amboyna in the East-Indies, by the Neatherlandish governour and councel there. London, 1624.

A true relation of the unjust, cruell, and barbarous proceedings against the English at Amboyna. London, 1665.

Tweede deel van den Spiegel der Spaensche tyrannye gheschiet in Nederlandt. Amsterdam, 1620.

Twisck, Pieter Jansz. *Chronijck van den onderganc der tijrannen: ofte jaerlycksche geschiedenissen in werltlycke ende kercklijcke saecken, van Christi geboorte af tot desen tyt toe. Wesende een tydtthresoor, wonderboeck en jaerrekening van de voornaemste geschiedenissen des gantsche aerdbodems.* 2 vols. Hoorn, 1619–1620.

Tydingh uyt Brasijl aende Heeren Bewinthebberen van de West-Indische Compagnie, van wegen den tocht by den Generael Brouwer nae de Zuyd-Zee gedaen. Amsterdam, 1644.

Udemans, Godefridus. *Geestelick compas, dat is nut ende nootwendigh bericht voor alle zee-varende.* Dordrecht, 1647.

't Geestelyck roer van 't coopmans schip, dat is: Trouw bericht, hoe dat een coopman, en coopvaerder, hem selven dragen moet in syne handelinge, in pays ende in oor-loge, voor Godt, ende de menschen, te water ende te lande, insonderheyt onder de heydenen in Oost- ende West-Indien. Gouda, 1638.

[Irenaeus Poimenande, pseud.]. *Absaloms-hayr off discours, daerinne ondersocht wordt, wat daer te houden zy vande wilde vliegende hayr-troffen.* Dordrecht, 1643.

Usselincx, Willem. *Korte onderrichtinghe ende vermaeninge aen alle liefhebbers des vaderlandts, om liberalijcken te teeckenen inde West-Indische Compagnie.* Leiden, 1622 [K3363].

Naerder bedenckingen, over de zee-vaerdt, coophandel ende neeringhe, alsmede de versekeringhe vanden staet deser vereenichde Landen, inde teghen woordighe Vrede-handelinghe met den Coninck van Spangnien ende de Aerts-hertoghen. 1608 [K1441].

Politiicq discours over den wel-standt van dese vereenichde Provincien, nu wederomme met haren vyandt ghetreden zijnde in openbare oorloghe. 1622 [K3358].

Vertoogh, hoe nootwendich, nut ende profijtelick het sy voor de Vereenighde Neder-landen te behouden de vryheyt van te handelen op West-Indien, inden vrede met-ten Coninck van Spaignen. [1608] [kn1442].

Waerschouwinghe over den treves met den coninck van Spaengien, aen alle goede Patriotten, gedaen met ghewichtige redenen. Flushing, 1630 [K4016].

[Usselincx, Willem?] *Grondich discours over desen aen-staenden vrede handel.* [K1440].

Valckenburgh, Johan van. *Brief van Johan van Valckenburgh.* The Hague, 1665 [K9046–7].

Waerachtigh verhael van de grouwelicke en barbarische moorderye, begaen door de Engelschen in Guinea aen onse Nederlandtsche natie. Middelburg, 1665 [K9048].

Valerius, Adriaen. *Nederlandsche gedenck-clanck.* Ed. and introd. P. J. Meertens et al. Amsterdam, 1947.

Veer, Gerrit de. *Waerachtige beschryvinge van drie seylagien.* Amsterdam, 1598.

Verhael op de questure van mijn heer den Prince van Oragnien. 1582 [K599].

't Verheerlickte Nederland door d'herstelde zee-vaert; klaerlijck voorgestelt, ontdeckt en aengewesen door manier van 'tsamen-sprekinge. 1659 [K8176].

Verheiden, Willem. *Nootelijcke consideratien die alle goede liefhebbers des Vaderlandts behooren rijpelick te overweghen opten voorgheslaghen Tractate van Peys met den Spaengiarden.* 1587 [K816].

An oration or speech appropriated unto the most mightie and illustrious princes of Christendom. 1624.

't Vertoig der Zeeuscher nymphen, aende onverwinnelicke Nasausche helden, voirstanderen der Nederlandsche vrijheyd ende Vaderen der Vaderlands. 1609 [K1573].

Vertoogh, over den toestant der West-Indische Compagnie, in haer begin, midden, ende eynde, met een remedie tot redres van deselve. Rotterdam, 1651 [K7002].

Vertoogh by een lief-hebber des vaderlants vertoont. Teghen het ongefondeerde ende schadelijcke sluyten der vryen handel in Brazil. [The Hague], 1637 [K4514].

't Vervolgh op de t'samen-spraeck, tusschen Teeuws ende Keesje Maet. Verhalende hoe dat sommige persoonen haer begeven hebben inden dienst vande West-Indische Compagnie na Brasil. [1647?] [K5600].

Vespucci, Amerigo. *Diss büchlin saget wie die zwen durch lüchtigsten herren her Fernandus K. zü Castilien und herr Emanuel K. zü Portugal haben das weyte mör ersüchet unnd funden vil Insulen unnd Nüwe welt von wilden nackenden Leüten, vormals unbekant.* Strassburg, 1509.

Lettere di Viaggio. Ed. Luciano Formisano. Milan, 1985.

Letters from a New World: Amerigo Vespucci's Discovery of America. Ed. Luciano Formisano; trans. David Jacobson. New York, 1992.

The Letters of Amerigo Vespucci. Trans. and ed. C. R. Markham. Works Issued by the Hakluyt Society, vol. 90. London, 1894.

Mundus novus. Antwerp, ca. 1505.

Vander nieuwer werelt oft landtscap. Antwerp, ca. 1506.

Villiers, J. A. J. de, ed. and trans. *East and West Indian mirror, being an account of Joris van Spilbergen's voyage around the world.* Works issued by the Hakluyt Society, 2d ser., vol. 18. London, 1906.

Visscher, Roemer. *Sinnepoppen.* Amsterdam, 1614.

[Viverius, Jacobus.] *Hand-boeck; of Cort begrijp der caerten ende beschrijvinghen van alle landen des werelds.* Amsterdam, 1609.

Den spieghel van Spaensche tyrannie. Amsterdam, 1601 [K1167].

Vives, Juan Luis. *De concordia et discordia in humano genere.* Antwerp, 1529.

De disciplinis libri xx. Antwerp, 1531.

De Europe dissidiis, & republica. Bruges, 1526.

Vloten, J. van, ed. *Nederlandsche geschiedzangen.* 2 vols. 2d ed. Amsterdam, 1864.

Vondel, Joost van den. *De werken van Vondel.* Ed. J. F. M. Sterck et al. 10 vols. Amsterdam, 1927–1940.

Le vray patriot aux bons patriot. 1578 [K392].

Vriendelicke vermaninghe aen de Heeren de Staten van Brabandt . . . op de supplicatie by hen aan Don Loys de Requesens. Delft, 1574 [K220].

Vriendelijcke waerschouwinghe aen de Staten van Artois, van Henegouwe, ende van Douay. 1579 [K422].

Vries, David de. *Korte historiael ende journaels aenteyckeninge van verscheyden voyagiens in de vier deelen des weereldts-ronde, als Europa, Africa, Asia, end America gedaen.* Hoorn, 1655.

Vries, Simon de. *Curieuse aenmerckingen der bysonderste Oost- en West Indische verwonderens-waerdige dingen.* 4 pts. Utrecht, 1682.

D'edelste tijdkortingh der weet-geerige verstanden: of De groote historische rariteit-kamer der sonderlinghste natuerlijcke en boven natuerlijcke saecken, geschiedenissen en voorvallen van allerley slagh. 3 vols. Amsterdam, 1682.

Groot historisch magazyn: Rijcklijck opgevuld met keur van aenmercklijcke stoffen, natuerwonderen, en sonderlinge geschiedenissen. Amsterdam, 1688.

Wonderen soo aen als in, en wonder-gevallen soo op als ontrent de zeeën, rivieren, meiren, poelen en fonteynen. Amsterdam, 1687.

Vryheden ende Exemptien voor de Patroonen. Amsterdam, 1631.

Wachtgheschrey. Allen liefhebbers der eeren Gods, des Vaderlandts, ende der privilegien ende vryheden des selven, tot waer schouwinghe ghestelt. 1578 [K379].

Waerachtigh ende cort verhael vande groote ambitie ende wreede tyrannye des conings van Hispaengien. 1608 [K1480].

Waerachtigh verhael, van het succes van het vlote, onder den Admirael Iaques L'Hermite, in de Zuyt-zee, op de custen van Peru, en de stadt Lima in Indien. 1625 [K3587].

Waerdenburgh, Dirk van. *Copie vande missive, gheschreven . . . aende Ho. Mo. Heeren Staten Generael, nopende de veroveringhe vande stadt Olinda de Fernabuco.* The Hague, 1630 [K3995].

Warachtighe beschrijvinghe ende levendighe afbeeldinghe van de meer dan onmenschelijcke ende barbarische tyrannije bedreven by de Spaengiaerden inde Nederlanden. 1621.

Warnsinck, J. C. M., ed. *De reis om de wereld van Joris van Spilbergen, 1614–1617.* Werken Uitgegeven door de Linschoten-Vereeniging, vol. 47. The Hague, 1943.

Wassenaer, Nicolaes Jansz. van. *Historisch verhael alder ghedenck-weerdichste geschiedenissen, die hier en daer . . . voorgevallen syn.* 17 pts. Amsterdam, 1622–1630.

Water, J. W. te. *Historie van het verbond en de smeekschriften der Nederlandsche edelen ter verkrijging van vrijheid in den godsdienst en burgerstaat in de jaren 1565–1567.* 4 vols. Middelburg, 1779–1796.

Wijnandts, Willem. *Lof-dicht, over de heerlijcke victorie, in het veroveren van de silver-vloot, in het Baey van Matanca, onder . . Pieter Pieterz. Heyn.* Middelburg, 1629.

Willem of Orange. *Geschriften van 1568.* Ed. M. G. Schenk. Amsterdam, 1933.

The Apologie of Prince William of Orange against the Proclamation of the King of Spaine.* Ed. H. Wansink. Leiden, 1969.

Wonderlicke avontuer van twee goelieven, de eene ghenaemt Sr. Waterbrandt ende de ander Joufvrouw Wintergroen. Leiden, 1624.

Zárate, Agustín de. *Historia del descubrimiento y conquista del Peru.* Antwerp, 1555.

The strange and delectable history of the discoverie and conquest of the provinces of Peru.* Trans. Thomas Nicholas. London, 1581. Reprint. London, 1933.

De wonderlijcke ende warachtighe historie vant coninckrijck van Peru geleghen in Indien. Antwerp, 1563.

De Zeeusche verre-kyker. Flushing, 1648 [K6484].

[Zeiller, Martin.] *Monarchia Hispanica ofte een Reys-beschryvinge aller koninckrijcken, vorstendommen, landen ende steden . . . onder der Spaenscher koningen.* Amsterdam, 1659.

Zierikzee, Amandus van. *Chronica compendiosissima ab exordio mundi usque ad annum domini millesimum, quingentesimum, trigesimum quartum.* Antwerp, 1534.

SECONDARY SOURCES

Adorno, Rolena. "Reconsidering Colonial Discourse for Sixteenth and Seventeenth-Century Spanish America." *Latin American Research Review* 28, no. 3 (1993): 135–45.

Afanasiev, V. "The Literary Heritage of Bartolomé de Las Casas." In Friede and Keen, *Las Casas in History.*

Alden, John, and Dennis Landis, eds. *European Americana: A Chronological Guide to Works Printed in Europe Relating to the Americas, 1493–1750.* 6 vols. New York, 1980–1997.

Anders, Ferdinand. "Girolamo Benzoni, Leben und Werk." In Girolamo Benzoni, *La historia del mondo nuovo.* Milan, 1572. Facs. rpt. Graz, 1962.

Anderson, Benedict. *Imagined Communities: Reflections on the Origin and Spread of Nationalism.* Rev. ed. London, 1991.

Andrien, Kenneth J., and Rolena Adorno. *Transatlantic Encounters: Europeans and Andeans in the Sixteenth Century.* Berkeley, 1991.

Architectural and Ornamental Drawings of the 16th to the early 19th Centuries in the Collection of the University of Michigan Museum of Art. Ann Arbor, 1965.

Armitage, David. "Making the Empire British: Scotland in the Atlantic World, 1542–1707." *Past and Present* 155 (May 1997): 34–63.

"The 'Procession Portrait' of Queen Elizabeth I: A Note on a Tradition." *Journal of the Warburg and Courtauld Institute* 53 (1990): 301–7.

ed. *Theories of Empire, 1450–1800.* Aldershot, 1998.

Arnoldsson, Sverker. *La Leyenda Negra. Estudios sobre sus orígenes.* Acta Universitatis Gothoburgensis, vol. 66, no. 3. Göteborg, 1960.

Asher, G. M. *A bibliographical and historical essay on the Dutch books and pamphlets relating to New Netherland and the Dutch West India Company.* Amsterdam, 1854–1867.

Atkinson, Geoffroy. *Les nouveaux horizons de la renaissance française.* Paris, 1935.

Axtell, James. "Columbian Encounters: Beyond 1992." *William and Mary Quarterly,* 3d ser., 49 (1992): 335–60.

The Invasion Within: The Contest of Cultures in Colonial North America. New York, 1985.

Bachman, Van Cleaf. *Peltries or Plantations: The Economic Policies of the Dutch West India Company in New Netherland, 1623–1639.* Baltimore, 1969.

Barbour, Violet. "Privateers and Pirates of the West Indies." *American Historical Review* 16 (1911): 529–66.

Bataillon, Marcel. *Études sur Bartolomé de Las Casas.* Paris, 1965.

Baudet, E. H. P. *Paradise on Earth: Some Thoughts on European Images of Non-European Man.* New Haven, 1965.

Bejczy, István. "Between Mandeville and Columbus: *Tvoyage* by Joos van Ghistele." In Martels, *Travel Fact and Travel Fiction.*

Benedict, Philip, et al., eds. *Reformation, Revolt and Civil War in France and the Netherlands, 1555–1585.* Amsterdam, 1999.

Bennett, J. W. *The Rediscovery of Sir John Mandeville.* New York, 1954.

Bergvelt, Ellinoor, et al. *De wereld binnen handbereik. Nederlandse kunst- en rariteitenverzamelingen, 1585–1735.* 2 vols. (Exhibition catalogue and essays.) Zwolle, 1992.

Blok, D. P., et al., eds. *Algemene Geschiedenis der Nederlanden.* 15 vols. Haarlem, 1977–1983.

Blok, P. J. "Het advies der Spaansche Inquisitie." *Bijdragen voor vaderlandsche geschiedenis en oudheidkunde.* 4th ser., 6 (1907): 241–57.

"Prins Willem's 'Apologie.'" *Bijdragen voor vaderlandsche geschiedenis en oudheidkunde.* 5th ser., 4 (1917): 259–86.

Bloomfield, Morton. *The Seven Deadly Sins.* East Lansing, Michigan, 1952.

Blouw, Paul Valkema. "Willem Silvius's remarkable start, 1559–62." *Quaerendo* 20 (1990): 167–206.

Boogaart, Ernst van den. "The Empress Europe and her three sisters: The symbolic representation of Europe's superiority claim in the Low Countries, 1570–1655." In Vandenbroeck, *America, bride of the sun.*

"Infernal Allies: The Dutch West India Company and the Tarairiu 1631–1654." In Boogaart, *Johan Maurits van Nassau Siegen.*

"De Nederlandse expansie in het Atlantisch gebied, 1590–1674." In *AGN* 7: 220–54.

ed. *Johan Maurits van Nassau Siegen: A humanist prince in Europe and Brazil.* The Hague, 1979.

ed. *Zo wijd de wereld strekt*. The Hague, 1979.

Bostoen, Karel. "Jan vander Noot's 'Europeiad': A Sixteenth-Century Masterpiece Shattered by Continental Discord." In *Standing Clear: A Festschrift for Reinder P. Meijer*, ed. Jane Fenoulhet and Theo Hermans. Series Crossways, vol. 1. London, 1991.

Bouman, D. J. *Johan Maurits van Nassau, de Braziliaan*. Utrecht, 1947.

Bouwsma, William J. *John Calvin: A Sixteenth-Century Portrait*. Oxford, 1988.

Boxer, C. R. *The Dutch in Brazil, 1624–54*. Oxford, 1957.

Bradley, Peter T. *The Lure of Peru: Maritime Intrusion into the South Sea, 1598–1701*. London, 1989.

Breen, J. C. "Gereformeerd populaire historiographie in de 17de and 18de eeuw." *Tijdschrift voor geschiedenis* 37 (1922): 254–73, 372–82.

Briels, J. G. C. A. *Vlaamse schilders in de Noordelijke Nederlanden in het begin van de Gouden Eeuw, 1585–1630*. Haarlem, 1987.

Zuidnederlanders in de Republiek 1572–1630: Een demografische en cultuurhistorische studie. Sint-Niklaas, 1985.

Zuidnederlandse boekdrukkers en boekverkopers in de Republiek der Verenigde Nederlanden omstreeks 1570–1630. Niewkoop, 1974.

De Zuidnederlandse immigratie in Amsterdam en Haarlem omstreeks 1572–1630. [Utrecht, 1976].

Brodhead, John Romeyn. *History of the State of New York*. 2 vols. New York, 1853–1871.

Brooks, Jerome E. *Tobacco: Its History Illustrated by the Books, Manuscripts and Engravings in the Library of George Arents, Jr.* 5 vols. New York, 1937–1952.

Brugmans, H. "Utrechtsche kroniek over 1566–1576." *Bijdragen en mededeelingen van het Historische Genootschap* 25 (1904): 1–258.

Brummel, L. "Van Meteren als historicus." In *Twee ballingen 's lands tijdens onze opstand tegen Spanje*. The Hague, 1972.

Burger, C. P. "Een raadsel opgelost." *Tijdschrift voor boek- en bibliotheekwesen* 4 (1906): 138.

Burke, Peter. "America and the Rewriting of World History." In Kupperman, *America in European Consciousness*.

"The Spread of Italian Humanism." In *The Impact of Humanism on Western Europe*, ed. A. Goodman and A. MacKay. London, 1990.

Burrows, Edwin G., and Mike Wallace. *Gotham: A History of New York City to 1898*. New York, 1999.

Cabral de Mello, Evaldo. *Olinda Restaurada: Guerra e Açúcar no Nordeste, 1630–1654*. Rio de Janeiro, 1975.

Campbell, Mary B. *The Witness and the Other World: Exotic European Travel Writing, 400–1600*. Ithaca, 1988.

Camus, Michel-Christian. "Une note critique a propos d'Exquemelin." *Revue francaise d'histoire d'outre-mer* 77, no. 286 (1990): 79–90.

Canny, Nicholas. *Elizabethan Conquest of Ireland: A Pattern Established*. New York, 1976.

Certeau, Michel de. *The Writing of History*. Trans. Tom Conley. New York, 1988.

Chatterjee, Partha. *Nationalist Thought and the Colonial World: A Derivative Discourse.* London, 1986.

Chiappelli, Fredi, ed. *First Images of America: The Impact of the New World on the Old.* 2 vols. Berkeley, 1976.

Chinard, Gabriel. *L'exotisme Américain dans la littérature Française au XVIe siècle.* Paris, 1911.

Clair, Colin. "Willem Silvius." *The Library,* 5th ser., 14 (Sept, 1959): 192–205.

Cohen, David Steven. "How Dutch were the Dutch of New Netherland?" *New York History* 62 (1981): 43–60.

Condon, Thomas J. *New York Beginnings: The Commercial Origins of New Netherland.* New York, 1968.

Conley, Tom. "De Bry's Las Casas." In *Amerindian Images and the Legacy of Columbus,* ed. René Jara and Nicholas Spadaccini. Hispanic Issues, vol. 9. Minneapolis, 1992.

Coolhaas, W. Ph. "Aanteekeningen en opmerkingen over den zogenaamden Ambonschen moord." *Bijdragen tot de taal-, land- en volkenkunde van Neërlandsch-Indië* 101 (1942): 49–93.

Cordingly, David. *Under the Black Flag: The Romance and the Reality of Life Among the Pirates.* New York, 1995.

Cornelissen, J. D. M. *Waarom zij Geuzen werden genoemd.* Tilburg, 1936.

Craeybeckx, J. "De moeizame definitieve afschaffing van Alva's tiende penning." In *Album aangeboden aan . . . Charles Verlinden.* [Ghent, 1975].

Cuttler, Charles. "Errata in Netherlandish Art: Jan Mostaert's 'New World' landscape." *Simiolus* 19, no. 3 (1989): 191–97.

Daalder, D. L. *Wormcruyt met suycker: Historisch-critisch overzicht van de Nederlandse kinderliteratuur.* Amsterdam, 1950.

Dandelet, Thomas. "Spanish Conquest and Colonization at the Center of the Old World: The Spanish Nation in Rome, 1555–1625." *Journal of Modern History* 69 (1997): 479–511.

Davids, Karel, and Jan Lucassen, eds. *A Miracle Mirrored: The Dutch Republic in a European Perspective.* Cambridge, 1995.

Debaene, L. "Nederlandse prozaromans en Spaanse Libros de Caballerias." In *Liber alumnorum E. Rombauts.* Leuven, 1968.

De Nederlandse volksboeken. Antwerp, 1951.

Delen, A. J. J. *Histoire de la gravure dans les anciens Pays-Bas.* Paris, 1969.

Denis, Ferdinand. *Une fête brésilienne, célébrée à Rouen en 1550.* Paris, 1850.

Deursen, A. Th. van. *Bavianen en slijkgeuzen: Kerk en kerkvolk ten tijde van Maurits en Oldenbarnevelt.* Assen, 1974.

"Holland's Experience of War during the Revolt of the Netherlands." In *War and Society,* ed. A. C. Duke and C. A. Tamse. Britain and the Netherlands, vol. 6. The Hague, 1977.

Plain Lives in a Golden Age: Popular Culture, Religion and Society in Seventeenth-Century Holland. Cambridge, 1991.

Dickason, Olive. *The Myth of the Savage and the Beginnings of French Colonialism in the Americas.* Edmonton, 1984.

Dierickx, M. "De lijst der veroordeelden door de Raad van beroertren." *Belgisch tijdshcrift voor filologie en geschiedenis* 40 (1962): 415–22.

"Nieuwe gegevens over het bestuur van de hertog van Alva in de Nederlanden." *Bijdragen voor de geschiedenis der Nederlanden* 18 (1963): 167–91.

Dillen, J. G. van. "De West-Indische Compagnie, het calvinisme, en de politiek." *Tijdschrift voor geschiedenis* 74 (1961): 145–71.

Doel, H. W. van den, P. C. Emmer, and H. Ph. Vogel. *Nederland en de Nieuwe Wereld.* Utrecht, 1992.

Doutrepont, Antoinette. "Martin de Vos et l'Entrée triomphale de l'Archiduc Ernest d'Autriche à Anvers en 1594." *Bulletin de l'Institut historique belge de Rome* 17 (1937): 152–55.

Duke, Alastair. "A Legend in the Making: News of the 'Spanish Inquisition' in the Low Countries in German Evangelical Pamphlets, 1546–1550." *Nederlands Archief voor Kerkgeschiedenis* 77 (1997): 125–44.

"Salvation by Coercion: The Controversy Surrounding the 'Inquisition' in the Low Countries on the Eve of the Revolt." In *Reformation Principle and Practice: Essays in Honour of A. G. Dickens,* ed. P. N. Brooks. London, 1980.

Duke, Alastair, and C. A. Tamse, eds. *Clio's Mirror: Historiography in Britain and the Netherlands.* Britain and the Netherlands, vol. 7. Zutphen, 1985.

Echeverria, Durand. *Mirage in the West: A History of the French Image of American Society to 1815.* Princeton, 1957.

Edmundson, George. "The Dutch on the Amazon and Negro in the Seventeenth Century." *English Historical Review* 18 (1903): 642–63.

"The Dutch Trade on Rio Negro in the Seventeenth Century." *English Historical Review* 19 (1904): 1–25.

Eekhof, Albert. *De Hervormde Kerk in Noord-Amerika, 1624–1664.* 2 vols. The Hague, 1913.

Jonas Michaëlius: Founder of the church in New Netherland. Leiden, 1929.

Eekhout, R. A. "The 'Mauritias': A neo-Latin epic by Franciscus Plante." In Boogaart, *Johan Maurits van Nassau Siegen.*

Egmond, Florike. *Een bekende Scheveninger: Adriaen Coenen en zijn Visboeck van 1578.* Scheveningen, 1997.

Egmond, Florike, and Peter Mason. "Armadillos in Unlikely Places: Some Unpublished Sixteenth-Century Sources for New World *Rezeptionsgeschichte* in Northern Europe." *Ibero-Amerikansches Archiv,* Neue Folge, Jahrgang 20 (1994): 3–52.

The Mammoth and the Mouse: Microhistory and Morphology. Baltimore, 1997.

Elliott, J. H. *Britain and Spain in America: Colonists and Colonized.* Stenton Lecture. Reading, 1994.

"Cortés, Velázquez and Charles V." In Cortés, *Letters from Mexico.*

"Final Reflections: The Old World and the New World Revisited." In Kupperman, *America in European Consciousness.*

Imperial Spain 1469–1716. 3rd ed. London, 1990.

The Old World and the New, 1492–1650. 1970. Reprint with new preface. Cambridge, 1992.

"Renaissance Europe and America: A Blunted Impact?" In Chiappelli, *First Images of America.*

Elst, C. van den. "Une dernière victime Belge du Saint-Office, 1632. J. B. Avontroot," *Revue Trimestrielle* 23 (1859): 3–21.

Emerson, Ralph Waldo. *English Traits*. Ed. Howard Mumford Jones. Cambridge, Mass., 1966.

Emmer, P. C. *The Dutch in the Atlantic Economy, 1580–1880*. Aldershot, 1998.

"Nederlandse handelaren, kolonisten en planters in de Nieuwe Wereld." In Doel, Emmer, and Vogel, *Nederland en de Nieuwe Wereld.*

"The West India Company, 1621–1791: Dutch or Atlantic?" In *Companies and Trade*, ed. L. Blussé and F. Gaastra. Comparative Studies in Overseas Trade, vol. 3. Leiden, 1981.

Everaert, John. "The conquest of the Indian soul: Missionaries from the Low Countries in Spanish America (1493–1767)." In Vandenbroeck, *America, bride of the sun.*

Fagel, Raymond. *De Hispano-Vlaamse wereld: De contacten tussen Spanjaarden en Nederlanders, 1496–1555*. Archives et bibliothèques de Belgique no. 52. Brussels, 1996.

Falkenburg, Reindert Leonard. *Joachim Patinir: Landscape as an Image of the Pilgrimage of Life*. 2 vols. Amsterdam, 1988.

Natuur en landschap in de Nederlandse kunst, 1500–1850. Nederlands kunsthistorisch jaarboek, vol. 48. Zwolle, 1998.

Feest, Christian F. "The Collecting of American Indian Artifacts in Europe, 1493–1750." In Kupperman, *America in European Consciousness.*

Fernández-Armesto, Felipe. *Before Columbus: Exploration and Colonization from the Mediterranean to the Atlantic, 1229–1492*. Philadelphia, 1987.

Fieret, W. *Udemans: Facetten uit zijn leven en werk*. Houten, 1985.

Flint, Valerie. *The Imaginative Landscape of Christopher Columbus*. Princeton, 1992.

Fontaine Verwey, H. de la. "De scheepsschirurgijn Exquemelin en zijn boek over de flibustiers." In *Drukkers, Liefhebbers en Piraten in de Zeventiende Eeuw*. Uit de wereld van het boek, vol. 2. Amsterdam, 1976.

Formisano, Luciano. *Amerigo Vespucci: La vita e i viaggi*. [Italy], 1991.

Francis, Peter, Jr. "The Beads That Did *Not* Buy Manhattan Island." *New York History* 67 (1986): 5–22.

Franits, Wayne, ed. *Looking at Seventeenth-Century Art: Realism Reconsidered*. Cambridge, 1997.

Freedberg, David. "Science, Commerce, and Art: Neglected Topics at the Junction of History and Art History." In *Art in History/History in Art: Studies in Seventeenth-Century Dutch Culture*, ed. David Freedberg and Jan de Vries. Chicago, 1991.

Friede, Juan, and Benjamin Keen, eds. *Bartolomé de Las Casas in History*. Dekalb, 1971.

Friedländer, Max J. *Die altniederländische Malerei*. 14 vols. Leiden, 1924–1937.

Frijhoff, Willem. *Wegen van Evert Willemsz.: Een Hollands weeskind op zoek naar zichzelf, 1607–1647.* Nijmegen, 1995.

"The West India Company and the Reformed Church: Neglect or Concern." *De Halve Maen* 70 (1997): 59–68.

Fruin, Robert. *Tien jaren uit den Tachtigjarigen Oorlog, 1588–1598.* Rev. 5th ed. The Hague, 1899.

Fuller, Mary C. "Ralegh's Fugitive Gold: Reference and Deferral in the 'Discoverie of Guiana.'" *Representations* 33 (1991): 42–64.

Voyages in Print: English Travel to America, 1576–1624. Cambridge, 1995.

García Carcel, Ricardo. *La Leyenda Negra: Historia y opinion.* Madrid, 1992.

Garraty, John A., and Mark C. Carnes, eds. *American National Biography.* 24 vols. New York, 1999.

Gaskell, Ivan. "Tobacco, Social Deviance, and Dutch Art in the Seventeenth Century." In Franits, *Looking at Seventeenth-Century Art.*

Gastel, Ada van. "Adriaen van der Donck, New Netherland, and America." Ph.D. diss., Pennsylvania State University, 1985.

"Van der Donck's Description of the Indians: Additions and Corrections." *William and Mary Quarterly,* 3d ser., vol. 47 (1990): 411–21.

Gehring, Charles. "Peter Minuit's Purchase of Manhattan Island – New Evidence." *De Halve Maen* 55 (1980): 6–7, 17.

Gelder, H. A. Enno van. *Van Beeldenstorm tot Pacificatie.* Amsterdam, 1964.

Gelder, Roelof van, Jan Parmentier, and V. D. Roeper. *Souffrir pour parvenir: De wereld van Jan Huygen van Linschoten.* Haarlem, 1998.

Gelderen, Martin van. *The Political Thought of the Dutch Revolt, 1555–1590.* Cambridge, 1992.

Gerbi, Antonello. *The Dispute of the New World.* 1955. Trans. Jeremy Moyle. Pittsburg, 1973.

Nature in the New World: From Christopher Columbus to Gonzalo Fernández de Oviedo. Trans. Jeremy Moyle. Pittsburg, 1985.

Geurts, P. A. M. *De Nederlandse Opstand in de pamfletten 1566–1584.* Nijmegen, 1956.

Geurts, P. A. M., and A. E. M. Janssen, eds. *Geschiedschrijving in Nederland.* 2 vols. The Hague, 1981.

Geyl, Pieter. *The Netherlands in the Seventeenth Century 1609–1648.* 1936. Reprint. London, 1989.

Orange and Stuart, 1641–72. London, 1969.

The Revolt of the Netherlands 1555–1609. 1932. Reprint. London, 1988.

Gibson, Charles, ed. *The Black Legend: Anti-Spanish Attitudes in the Old World and the New.* New York, 1971.

Gibson, Walter. *Mirror of the Earth: The World Landscape in Sixteenth-Century Flemish Painting.* Princeton, 1989.

Giménez Fernández, Manuel. *Bartolomé de las Casas.* 2 vols. Seville, 1953–1960. Reprint. Madrid, 1984.

Gleason, Elisabeth. *Gasparo Contarini: Venice, Rome, and Reform.* Berkeley, 1993.

Gonslaves de Mello, José Antônio. *Tempos dos Flamengos: Influência da ocupação holandesa na vida e na cultura do Norte do Brasil.* Rio de Janeiro, 1947.

"Vincent Joachim Soler in Dutch Brazil." In Boogaart, *Johan Maurits van Nassau Siegen.*

Goodfriend, Joyce D. "The Historiography of the Dutch in Colonial America." In *Colonial Dutch Studies: An Interdisciplinary Approach,* ed. Eric Nooter and Patricia U. Bonomi. New York, 1988.

Goodman, Jordan. *Tobacco in History: The Cultures of Dependence.* London, 1993.

Goor, J. van. *De Nederlandse Koloniën: Geschiedenis van de Nederlandse expansie, 1600–1975.* 2nd ed. [The Hague], 1997.

Gordon, Amy Glassner. "Léry, Laudonnière, et les Indiens d'Amérique." In *Voyager à la Renaissance. Actes du colloque de Tours, 30 juin-13 juillet 1983,* ed. J. Céard and J.-Cl. Margolin. Paris, 1987.

Goslinga, Cornelis. *The Dutch in the Caribbean and on the Wild Coast, 1580–1680.* Gainesville, 1971.

Gosse, Philip. "First Editions of the Most Famous Buccaneering Book." *Bookman* 6 (1922): 170–71.

Grafton, Anthony. *New Worlds, Ancient Texts: The Power of Tradition and the Shock of Discovery.* Cambridge, Mass., 1992.

"The Rest vs. the West." *New York Review of Books* 44, no. 6 (April 10, 1997): 57–64.

Graham, W. Fred, ed. *Later Calvinism: International Perspectives.* Kirksville, MO, 1994.

Grapperhuis, F. H. M. *Alva en de Tiende Penning.* Zutphen, 1982.

Greenblatt, Stephen J. *Marvelous Possessions: The Wonder of the New World.* Chicago, 1991.

Sir Walter Ralegh: The Renaissnace Man and his Role. New Haven, 1973.

ed. *New World Encounters.* Berkeley, 1993.

Gregory, Brad S. *Salvation at Stake: Christian Martyrdom in Early Modern Europe.* Cambridge, Mass., 1999.

Groenveld, Simon. *Hooft als historieschrijver. Twee Studies.* Weesp, 1981.

"Natie en nationaal gevoel in de zestiende-eeuwse Nederlanden." *Nederlands Archievenblad* 84 (1980): 61–83.

Verlopend getij: De Nederlandse Republiek en de Engelse Burgeroorlog, 1640–1646. Dieren, 1984.

et al. *De kogel door de kerk? De Opstand in de Nederlanden 1559–1609.* 2d ed. Zutphen, 1983.

Groenveld, Simon, and H. L. Ph. Leeuwenberg. *De Bruid in de schuit. De consolidatie van de Republiek 1609–1650.* Zutphen, 1985.

Groot, A. H. de. *The Ottoman Empire and the Dutch Republic: A History of the Earliest Diplomatic Relations 1610–1630.* Uitgave van het Nederlands Historisch-Archaeologisch Instituut, vol. 43. Leiden, 1978.

Gruzinsky, Serge. *The Conquest of Mexico: The Incorporation of Indian Societies into the Western World, 16th–18th Centuries.* Trans. Eileen Corrigan. Cambridge, 1993.

Haak, Bob. *The Golden Age: Dutch Painters of the Seventeenth Century*. New York, 1984.

Haak, Sikko Popta. *Paullus Merula, 1558–1607*. Zutphen, 1901.

Hadfield, Andrew. *Literature, Travel, and Colonial Writing in the English Renaissance 1545–1625*. Oxford, 1998.

Haitsma Mulier, E. O. G. "Grotius, Hooft and the writing of history in the Dutch Republic." In Duke and Tams, *Clio's Mirror*.

Haitsma Mulier, E. O. G., and G. A. C. van der Lem, comp. *Repertorium van geschiedschrijvers in Nederland 1500–1800*. Bibliografische reeks van het Nederlands Historisch Genootschap, vol. 7. The Hague, 1990.

Hale, John. *The Civilization of Europe in the Renaissance*. London, 1993.

Hanke, Lewis. *Bartolomé de las Casas. An Interpretation of his Life and Writing*. The Hague, 1951.

　Bartolomé de las Casas. Bookman, Scholar, and Propagandist. Philadelphia, 1952.

　"A Modest Proposal for a Moratorium on Grand Generalizations: Some Thoughts on the Black Legend." *Hispanic American Historical Review* 51 (1971): 112–27.

Hanke, Lewis, and Manuel Giménez Fernández. *Bartolomé de las Casas, 1474–1576: Bibliografía crítica*. Santiago de Chile, 1954.

Harley, J. B. *Maps and the Columbian Encounter*. Milwaukee, 1990.

Harline, Craig. *Pamphlets, Printing, and Political Culture in the Early Dutch Republic*. Dordrecht, 1987.

Harlow, V. T. *Ralegh's Last Voyage*. London, 1932.

Harms, Wolfgang, et al., comps. *Die Sammlung der Herzog August Bibliothek in Wolfenbüttel: Kommentierte Ausgabe*. Deutsche Illustrierte Flugblätter des 16. und 17. Jahrhunderts. 3 vols. Munich, 1980–1989.

Harmsen, A. J. E. "Barlaeus's Description of the Dutch Colony in Brazil." In Martels, *Travel Fact and Travel Fiction*.

Hart, Simon. *The prehistory of the New Netherland Company*. Amsterdam, 1959.

Hartog, François. *The Mirror of Herodotus: The Representation of the Other in the Writing of History*. Trans. Janet Lloyd. Berkeley, 1988.

Haverkamp Begemann, E. *Willem Buytewech 1591–1624*. Rotterdam, 1974.

Heijer, Henk den. *De geschiedenis van de WIC*. Zutphen, 1994.

Helgerson, Richard. *Forms of Nationhood: The Elizabethan Writing of England*. Chicago, 1992.

Hillgarth, J. N. *The Mirror of Spain, 1500–1700: The Formation of a Myth*. Michigan, 2000.

Hoboken, W. J. van. "The Dutch West India Company: The Political Background of its Rise and Fall." In *Britain and the Netherlands*, ed. J. S. Bromley and E. H. Kossmann. London, 1960.

Hodnett, Edward. *Marcus Gheeraerts the Elder of Bruges, London, and Antwerp*. Utrecht, 1971.

Hollstein, F. W. H. *Dutch and Flemish Etchings, Engravings and Woodcuts*. Amsterdam, 1949–.

Holt, Mack P. *The Duke of Anjou and the Politique Struggle during the Wars of Religion.* Cambridge, 1986.

Honour, Hugh. *The European Vision of America.* Cleveland, 1975.

The New Golden Land: European Images of America from the Discoveries to the Present Time. New York, 1975.

"Science and Exoticism: The European Artist and the Non-European World before Johan Maurits." In *Johan Maurits van Nassau Siegen.*

Hoogewerff, G. J. "Hendrik Smeeks, geschiedschrijver van de Boekaniers." *Tijdschrift voor geschiedenis* 45 (1930): 225–36.

De Noord-Nederlandsche Schilderkunst. 5 vols. The Hague, 1936–1947.

Horst, Daniël. "Spotprenten op Alva." Master's thesis, Univ. of Amsterdam, 1988.

Houdt, Toon van. "Amerika en de Oudheid: Een bechouwing van Lipsius." *Hermeneus* 64 (1992): 243–51.

Hulten, Paul, and David Beers Quinn. *The American Drawings of John White.* London, 1964.

Hyde, James H. "The Four Parts of the World as Represented in Old Time Pageants and Ballets." *Apollo* 4 (1926): 232–238 and 5 (1927): 20–26.

Ijdelheid der ijdelheden: Hollandse vanitasvoorstellingen uit de zeventiende eeuw. Leiden, 1970.

IJsewijn, Jozef. "Humanism in the Low Countries." In *Renaissance Humanism: Foundations, Forms, and Legacy,* ed. Albert Rabil. 3 vols. Philadelphia, 1988.

"De wereldlijke literatuur in het Latijn, 1384–1520." In *AGN* 4: 346–347.

Israel, Jonathan I. *Dutch Primacy in World Trade, 1585–1740.* Oxford, 1989.

The Dutch Republic and the Hispanic World, 1606–1661. Oxford, 1982.

The Dutch Republic: Its Rise, Greatness, and Fall, 1477–1806. Oxford, 1995.

Jacobs, Jaap. *Een zegenrijk gewest: Nieuw-Nederland in de zeventiende eeuw.* Amsterdam, 1999.

Jameson, J. Franklin. *Willem Usselinx. Founder of the Dutch and Swedish West India Companies.* Papers of the American Historical Association, vol. 2, no. 3. New York, 1887.

Janson, H. W. *Apes and Ape Lore in the Middle Ages and the Renaissance.* London, 1952.

Janssen, A. E. M. "Pieter Bor Christiaenszoon (1559–1635), geschiedschrijver van 'waerheyt ende onpartijschap.'" In Geurts and Janssen, *Geschiedschrijving in Nederland.*

"A 'trias historica' on the revolt of the Netherlands: Emanuel van Meteren, Pieter Bor and Everhard van Reyd as exponents of contemporary historiography." In Duke and Tamse, *Clio's Mirror.*

Janssens, G. "Brabant in verzet tegen Alva's tiende en twintigste penning." *Bijdragen en mededelingen betreffende de geschiedenis der Nederlanden* 89 (1974): 6–31.

"Het oordeeel van tijdgenoten en historici over Alva's bestuur in de Nederlanden." *Belgisch tijdschrift voor filologie en geschiedenis* 54 (1976): 472–88.

Jardine, Lisa. *Worldly Goods: A New History of the Renaissance.* London, 1996.

Jelsma, A. J. *Adriaan van Haemstede en zijn martelaarsboek.* The Hague, 1970.

Jennings, Francis. *The Invasion of America: Indians, Colonialism, and the Cant of Conquest.* Chapel Hill, 1975.

Johnson, Hildegard Binder. "New Geographical Horizons." In Chiappelli, *First Images of America.*

Jongh, E. de. "Vermommingen van Vrouw Wereld in de 17de eeuw." In *Album amicorum J. G. van Gelder,* ed J. Bruyn et al. The Hague, 1973.

Joppien, R. "The Dutch Vision of Brazil: Johan Maurits and his Artists." In Boogaart, *Johan Maurits van Nassau Siegen.*

Judson, J. Richard. *Dirck Barendsz. 1534–1592.* Amsterdam, 1970.

Julien, Charles-André. *Les Voyages de découverte et les premiers établissements (XVe-XVIe siècles).* Paris, 1948.

Kagan, Richard L. *Urban Images of the Hispanic World, 1493–1793.* New Haven, 2000.

Kamen, Henry. *Spain 1469–1714: A Society in Conflict.* 2nd ed. London, 1991.

Kannegieter, J. Z. "Dr. Nicolaes Jansz. van Wassenaer." *Jaarboek Amstelodamum* 56 (1964): 86–7.

Kaplan, Benjamin J. *Calvinists and Libertines: Confession and Community in Utrecht, 1578–1620.* Oxford, 1995.

Karrow, Robert, Jr. *Mapmakers of the Sixteenth Century and their Maps: Bio-Bibliography of the Cartographers of Abraham Ortelius, 1570.* Chicago, 1993.

Keazor, Henry. "Theodore de Bry's Images for 'America.'" *Print Quarterly* 15 (1998): 131–49.

Keen, Benjamin. "The Black Legend Revisited: Assumptions and Realities." *Hispanic American Historical Review* 49 (1969): 703–19.

"The Vision of America in the Writings of Urbain Chauveton." In Chiappelli, *First Images of America.*

Kellein, Thomas, and Urs-Beat Frei. *Frans Post, 1612–1680.* Basel, 1990.

Kelley, Donald. *The Beginning of Ideology: Consciousness and Society in the French Reformation.* Cambridge, 1981.

"Martyrs, Myths, and the Massacre: The Background of St. Bartholomew." In *The Massacre of St. Bartholomew: Reappraisals and Documents,* ed. Alfred Soman. The Hague, 1974.

Kemp, Martin. "'Wrought by No Artist's Hand': The Natural, the Artificial, the Exotic, and the Scientific in Some Artifacts from the Renaissance." In *Reframing the Renaissance: Visual Culture in Europe and Latin America, 1450–1650,* ed. Claire Farago. New Haven, 1995.

Ketters en papen onder Filips II. Utrecht, 1986.

Keuning, J. *Petrus Plancius, theoloog en geograaf, 1552–1622.* Amsterdam, 1946.

Kingdon, Robert M. *Myths about the St. Bartholomew's Day Massacres 1572–1576.* Cambridge, Mass., 1988.

Klooster, Wim. *The Dutch in the Americas, 1600–1800: A narrative history with the catalogue of an exhibition of rare prints, maps, and illustrated books from the John Carter Brown Library.* Providence, 1997.

Illicit Riches: Dutch Trade in the Caribbean, 1648–1795. KITLV Caribbean Series, vol. 18. Leiden, 1998.

Knapp, Jeffrey. *An Empire Nowhere: England, America, and Literature from "Utopia" to "The Tempest."* Berkeley, 1992.

Knuttel, G. *Adriaen Brouwer: The master and his work.* The Hague, 1962.

Knuttel, W. P. C. *Catalogus van de pamfletten-verzameling berustende in de Koninklijke Bibliotheek.* 9 pts. The Hague, 1889–1920.

Knuvelder, G. *Handboek tot de geschiedenis der Nederlandse letterkunde.* 5th ed. 4 vols. 's-Hertogenbosch, 1970–1976.

Koeman, Cornelis. *The History of Abraham Ortelius and his Theatrum Orbis Terrarum.* Lausanne, 1964.

———. *Jan Huygen van Linschoten.* Publication of the Centro de estudos de história e de cartografia antiga, no. 153. Lisbon, 1984.

———. comp. *Atlantes Neerlandici. Bibliography of terrestrial, maritime and celestial atlases and pilot books, published in the Netherlands up to 1880.* 6 vols. Amsterdam, 1967–1985.

Koenigsberger, H. G. "The Organization of Revolutionary Parties in France and the Netherlands during the Sixteenth Century." *Journal of Modern History* 27 (1955): 335–51.

———. *The Practice of Empire.* Rev. ed. Ithaca, 1969.

Korinman, Michel. "Symon Grynaeus et le 'Novus Orbis': Les pouvoirs d'une collection." In *Voyager à la Renaissance. Actes du colloque de Tours, 30 juin–13 juillet 1983,* ed. J. Céard and J.-Cl. Margolin. Paris, 1987.

Kossmann, E. H. and A. F. Mellink, eds. *Texts Concerning the Revolt of the Netherlands.* Cambridge, 1974.

Krewson, Margrit B. *New Netherland, 1609–1664: A Selective Bibliography.* Washington, 1995.

Krogt, P. C. J. van der. *Globi Neerlandici: De globeproduktie in de Nederlanden.* Utrecht, 1989.

Kunzle, David. *The Early Comic Strip: Narrative Strips and Picture Stories in the European Broadsheet from c. 1450–1825.* Berkeley, 1973.

Kupperman, Karen Ordahl. "The Beehive as a Model for Colonial Design." In Kupperman, *America in European Consiousness.*

———. "The Puzzle of the American Climate in the Early Colonial Period." *American Historical Review* 87 (1982): 1262–89.

———. *Settling with the Indians: The Meeting of English and Indian Cultures in America, 1580–1640.* Totowa, NJ, 1980.

———. ed. *America in European Consciousness, 1493–1750.* Chapel Hill, 1995.

Lach, Donald. *Asia in the Making of Europe.* 3 vols. Chicago, 1965–1993.

Laer, A. J. F. van. "Letters of Nicasius de Sille, 1654." *Quarterly Journal of the New York State Historical Association* 1 (April, 1920): 98–108.

Lankhorst, O. S., and Paul Hoftijzer. *Drukkers, boekverkopers en lezers in Nederland tijdens de Republiek.* The Hague, 1995.

Larner, John. "Foreword." *Renaissance Studies* 6 (1992): 247–8 (special issue "The Encounter of Two Worlds in the Renaissance").

Larsen, E. *Frans Post, interprète du Brésil.* Amsterdam, 1962.

———. "Once More Jan Mostaert's West Indian Landscape." In *Mélanges d'archéologie et d'histoire de l'art offerts au professeur Jacques Lavalleye.* Louvain, 1970.

Lawrance, N. H. "Humanism in the Iberian Penisula." In *The Impact of Humanism on Western Europe,* ed. A. Goodman and A. MacKay. London 1990.

Le Corbeiller, Clare. "Miss America and her Sisters: Personifications of the Four Parts of the World." *Metropolitain Museum of Art Bulletin,* n.s., 19 (1961): 209–23.

Lechner, J. "Dutch Humanists' Knowledge of America." *Itinerario* 16, no. 2 (1992): 101–13.

———. "En torno a la 'Brevíssima relación de la destruyción de las Indias' de Fray Bartolomé de las Casas." In *España, teatro y mujeres. Estudios dedicados a Henk Oostendorp,* ed. Martin Gosman and Hub. Hermans. Amsterdam, 1989.

Lechner, J., and H. Ph. Vogel, eds. *De Nieuwe Wereld en de Lage Landen: Onbekende aspecten van vijfhonderd jaar ontmoetingen tussen Latijns-Amerika en Nederland.* Amsterdam,1992.

Leesberg, Marjolein. "Karel van Mander as painter." *Simiolus* 22 (1993/1994): 5–57.

Lenger, Marie-Thèrése, ed. *Bibiotheca Belgica.* 7 vols. Brussels, 1964.

Lepore, Jill. *The Name of War: King Philip's War and the Origins of American Identity.* New York, 1998.

Lestringant, Frank. *André Thevet: Cosmographe des derniers Valois.* Geneva, 1991.

———. *L'atelier du cosmographe: ou l'image du monde à la Renaissance.* Paris, 1991. Trans. David Fausett, *Mapping the Renaissance World: The Geographical Imagination in the Age of Discovery.* Berkeley, 1994.

———. "Calvinistes et Cannibales: Les écrits protestants sur les Brésil français (1555–1560)." *Bulletin de la Société de l'histoire du protestantisme française* 1–2 (1980): 9–26, 167–92.

———. "Catholiques et Cannibales: Le théme du cannibalisme dans le discours protestant au temps des guerres de religion." In *Pratique et discours alimentaires à la Renaissance.,* ed. J.-Cl. Margolin and Robert Sauzet. Paris, 1982.

———. "Geneva and America in the Renaissance: The Dream of the Huguenot Refuge 1555–1600." *Sixteenth Century Journal* 26 (1995): 285–95.

———. *Le huguenot et le sauvage: l'Amérique et la controverse coloniale en France, au temps des guerres de religion (1555–1589).* Paris, 1990.

Leuven-Zwart, K. van. "Comparación del texto de la 'Brevíssima relación de la destruyción de las Indias': Colegida por el obispo Don Fray Bartolome de las Casas, o Casaus de la Orden de Sancto Domingo' con él de la traducción holandesa de 1578." Master's thesis, University of Amsterdam, n.d.

Levenson, Jay A., ed. *Circa 1492: Art in the Age of Exploration.* New Haven, 1991.

Levin, Harry. *The Myth of the Golden Age in the Renaissance.* Bloomington, 1969.

Liebersohn, Harry. *Aristocratic Encounters: European Travelers and North American Indians.* Cambridge, 1998.

Ligtenberg, C. *Willem Usselinx.* Utrecht, 1914.

Loades, D. M. *The Reign of Mary Tudor.* London, 1979.

Lovett, A. W. "The Governorship of Don Luís de Requesens, 1573–1576: A Spanish View." *European Studies Review* 2 (1972): 187–99.

——. "A New Governor for the Netherlands: The Appointment of Don Luís de Requesens, Comendador Mayor de Castilla." *European Studies Review* 1 (1971): 89–103.

Lowenthal, David. *Possessed by the Past: The Heritage Crusade and the Spoils of History.* New York, 1996.

Lowood, Henry. "The New World and the European Catalogue of Nature." In Kupperman, *America in European Consciousness.*

Luijten, Ger, et al., eds. *The Dawn of the Golden Age: Northern Netherlandish Art, 1580–1620.* Amsterdam, 1993.

Luttervelt, R. van. "Jan Mostaert's West-Indisch landschap." *Nederlands kunsthistorische jaarboek* 2 (1948/49): 107–17.

Lynch, John. *Spain, 1516–1598: From Nation State to World Empire.* Rev. ed. Oxford, 1992.

MacCormack, Sabine. *Religion in the Andes: Vision and Imagination in Early Colonial Peru.* Princeton, 1991.

Magnaghi, Alberto. *Amerigo Vespucci.* Rev. ed. 2 vols. Rome, 1926.

Maika, Dennis. "Commerce and Community: Manhattan Merchants in the Seventeenth Century." Ph.D. diss., New York University, 1995.

Maltby, W. S. *Alba: A Biography of Fernando Alvarez de Toledo, Third Duke of Alba 1507–1582.* Berkeley, 1983.

Marley, David F. *Pirates and Engineers: Dutch and Flemish Adventurers in New Spain (1607–1697).* Windsor, Ontario, 1992.

Marnef, Guido. *Antwerp in the Age of Reformation: Underground Protestantism in a Commercial Metropolis.* Trans. J. C. Grayson. Baltimore, 1996.

Martels, Zweder von, ed. *Travel Fact and Travel Fiction: Studies on Fiction, Literary Tradition, Scholarly Discovery and Observation in Travel Writing.* Leiden, 1994.

Mason, Peter. *Deconstructing America: Representations of the Other.* London, 1990.

——. *Infelicities: Representations of the Exotic.* Baltimore, 1998.

——. "Seduction from Afar: Europe's Inner Indians." *Anthropos* 82 (1987): 581–601.

Matar, Nabil. *Islam in Britain, 1558–1685.* Cambridge, 1998.

——. *Turks, Moors, and Englishmen in the Age of Discovery.* New York, 1999.

McCallum, R. I. "Observations upon Antimony." *Proceedings of the Royal Society of Medicine,* 70 (1977): 756–63.

McGinty, Alice B. "Stradanus (Jan van der Straet): His Role in the Visual Communication of Renaissance Discoveries, Technologies, and Values." Ph.D. diss., Tufts University, 1974.

McGowan, Margaret. "Form and Themes in Henri II's Entry into Rouen." *Renaissance Drama,* n.s., 1 (1968): 199–252.

——. ed. *L'Entrée de Henri II à Rouen 1550.* Amsterdam, n. d.

McGrath, Elizabeth. "A Netherlandish History by Joachim Wtewael." *Journal of the Warburg and Courtauld Institute* 38 (1975): 182–217.

McMahon, Dorothy. "Some Observations on the Spanish and Foreign Editions of Zárate's 'Historia de descubrimiento y conquista del Perú.'" *Proceedings of the Bibliographic Society of America* 49 (1955): 95–111.

McNeill, William H. "The Legacy of Columbus, or How by Crossing the Oceans He Shaped the Modern World." In *Encountering the New World, 1493–1800*, ed. Susan Danforth. Providence, 1991.

Meertens, P. J. "Godefridus Cornelisz. Udemans." *Nederlandsch archief voor kerkgeschiedenis*, n. s., 28 (1936): 65–106.

Meijer, A. C. "'Liefhebbers des vaderlandts ende beminders van de commercie': De plannen tot oprichting van een generale Westindische Compagnie gedurende de jaren 1606–1609." *Archief: Mededelingen van het Koninklijk Zeeuwsch Genootschap der Wetenschappen* (1986): 21–70.

Meijer, D. C. "Het Oude Doolhof te Amsterdam." *Oud Holland* 1 (1883): 30–36, 119–35.

Melion, Walter. *Shaping the Netherlandish Canon: Karel van Mander's "Schilderboeck."* Chicago, 1991.

Menkman, W. R. *De West-Indische Compagnie.* Amsterdam, 1947.

Merwick, Donna. *Death of a Notary: Conquest and Change in Colonial New York.* Ithaca, 1999.

   Possessing Albany, 1630–1710: The Dutch and English Experiences. Cambridge, 1990.

Michel, E. "Un Tableau colonial de Jan Mostaert." *Revue belge d'archéologie et d'histoire de l'art* 1 (1931): 133–41.

Miedema, H. *Karel van Mander (1548–1606): Het bio-bibliografisch materiaal.* Amsterdam, 1972.

Mignolo, Walter. *The Darker Side of the Renaissance: Literacy, Territoriality, and Colonization.* Ann Arbor, Michigan, 1995.

Moer, A. van der. *Een zestiende-eeuwse Hollander in het Verre Oosten en het Hoge Noorden. Leven, werken, reizen en avonturen van Jan Huygen van Linschoten.* The Hague, 1979.

Moffitt, John F., and Santiago Sebastián. *O Brave New People: The European Invention of the American Indian.* Albuquerque, 1996.

Montrose, Louis. "The Work of Gender in the Discourse of Discovery." *Representations* 33 (1991): 1–41.

Motley, John Lothrop. *History of the United Netherlands.* 4 vols. New York, 1860–1867.

   The Rise of the Dutch Republic. 3 vols. New York, 1855.

Mout, M. E. H. N. "Calvinoturcisme in de zeventiende eeuw: Comenius, Leidse oriëntalisten en de Turkse bijbel." *Tijdschrift voor geschiedenis* 91 (1978): 567–607.

   "Turken in het nieuws: Beeldvorming en publieke opinie in de zestiende-eeuwse Nederlanden." *Tijdschrift voor geschiedenis* 97 (1984): 362–81.

Mullaney, Steven. "The New World on Display." In *New World of Wonders: European Images of the Americas, 1492–1700*, ed. Rachel Doggett. Washington, 1992.

Muller, Frederik. *De Nederlandsche geschiedenis in platen: Beredeneerde beschrijving van Nederlandsche historieplaten, zinneprenten en historische kaarten.* 4 vols. Amsterdam, 1863–1882.

Nader, Helen. "The End of the Old World." *Renaissance Quarterly* 45 (1993): 791–807.

Nauta, D. "Marnix auteur van de Libellus Supplex aan de rijksdag van Spiers (1570)." *Nederlands Archief voor Kerkgeschiedenis* 55 (1975): 151–70.

Nicholas, David. *Medieval Flanders.* London, 1992.

Nicholl, Charles. *The Creature in the Map: A Journey to El Dorado.* London, 1995.

Nierop, Henk van. "A Beggars Banquet: The Compromise of the Nobility and the Politics of Inversion." *European History Quarterly* 21 (1991): 419–43.

   "Censorship, Illicit Printing and the Revolt of the Netherlands." In *Too Mighty to be Free: Censorship and the Press in Britain and the Netherlands,* ed. A. C. Duke and C. A. Tamse. Britain and the Netherlands, vol. 9. Zutphen, 1987.

   "How to honour one's city: Samuel Ampzing's vision of the history of Haarlem." *Theoretische geschiedenis* 20 (1993): 268–82.

   Het verraad van het Noorderkwartier: Oorlog, terreur en recht in de Nederlandse Opstand. Amsterdam, 1999.

Nijenhuis, W. *Adrianus Saravia (c. 1532–1613), Dutch Calvinist: First Reformed Defender of the English Episcopal Church on the Basis of the* Ius Divinum. Studies in the History of Christian Thought, vol. 21. Leiden, 1980.

Nissenson, S. G. *The Patroon's Domain.* New York, 1937.

Noë, Helen. *Carel van Mander en Italië.* The Hague, 1954.

Noordegraaf, L. *Hollands welvaren? Levensstandaard in Holland, 1450–1650.* Bergen, 1985.

Noordeloos, P. *Pastoor Maarten Donk.* 2 vols. Utrecht, 1948.

O'Callaghan, Edmund B. *The History of New Netherland: or, New York under the Dutch.* 2 vols. New York, 1845–1848.

O'Gorman, Edmundo. *The Invention of America: An Inquiry into the Historical Nature of the New World and the Meaning of its History.* Bloomington, 1961.

Obbema, P. F. J., and A. Derolez. "De produktie en verspreiding van het boek, 1300–1500." In *AGN* 4: 351–62.

Oosterhoff, F. G. *Leicester and the Netherlands, 1586–1587.* Utrecht, 1988.

Oppenheim, Samuel. *The Early History of the Jews in New York, 1654–1664.* New York, 1909.

Pagden, Anthony. *European Encounters with the New World: From Renaissance to Romanticism.* New Haven, 1993.

   The Fall of Natural Man: The American Indian and the Origins of Comparative Ethnology. Rev. ed. Cambridge, 1986.

   Lords of all the World: Ideologies of Empire in Spain, Britain and France c. 1500–c. 1800. New Haven, 1995.

Panofsky, Erwin. "The Early History of Man in Two Cycles of Paintings by Piero di Cosimo." In *Studies in Iconology.* New York, 1939.

   The Life and Art of Albrecht Dürer. 2 vols. Princeton, 1945.

Parker, Charles H. "To the Attentive, Nonpartisan Reader: The Appeal to History and National Identity in the Religious Disputes of the Seventeenth-Century Netherlands." *Sixteenth Century Journal* 28 (1997): 57–78.

Parker, Geoffrey. *The Army of Flanders and the Spanish Road 1567–1569*. Cambridge, 1972.

The Dutch Revolt. Rev. ed. London, 1985.

"Francisco de Lixalde and the Spanish Netherlands (1567–1577): Some new evidence." *Tijdschrift voor geschiedenis* 89 (1976): 1–9.

Spain and the Netherlands, 1559–1659. London, 1979.

Parr, Charles McKew. *Jan van Linschoten: The Dutch Marco Polo*. New York, 1964.

Parry, J. H. "Depicting a New World." In *The Early Illustrated Book: Essays in Honor of Lessing J. Rosenwald*, ed. Sandra Hindman. Washington, 1982.

Pastor Bodmer, Beatriz. *The Armature of Conquest*. Trans. Lydia Longstreth Hunt. Stanford, 1992.

Peeters-Fontainas, J. *Bibliographie des impressions espagnoles des Pays-Bas Méridionaux*. 2 vols. Nieuwkoop, 1965.

Penner, Archie. "Pieter Jansz. Twisck, Second Generation Anabaptist/Mennonite Churchman, Writer, and Polemicist." Ph.D. diss., University of Iowa, 1971.

Pettegree, Andrew. *Emden and the Dutch Revolt*. Oxford, 1992.

Pijper, F. *Martelaarsboeken*. The Hague, 1924.

Pincus, Steven C. A. "From Butterboxes to Wooden Shoes: The Shift in English Popular Sentiment from Anti-Dutch to Anti-French in the 1670s." *Historical Journal* 38 (1995): 333–62.

"Popery, Trade and Universal Monarchy: The Ideological Context of the Outbreak of the Second Anglo-Dutch War." *English Historical Review* 107 (1992): 1–29.

Protestantism and Patriotism: Ideologies and the Making of English Foreign Policy, 1650–1668. Cambridge, 1996.

Pleij, Herman. "Antwerp Described." In Stock, *Antwerp*.

"Literatuur en drukpers: De eerste vijftig jaar." In *Nederlandse literatuur van de late middeleeuwen*.

"Literatuur en natuurgenoot." In *Nederlandse literatuur van de late middeleeuwen*.

Nederlandse literatuur van de late middeleeuwen. Utrecht, 1990.

"The Rise of Urban Literature in the Low Countries." In *Medieval Dutch Literature in its European Context*, ed. Erik Kooper. Cambridge, 1994.

De sneeuwpoppen van 1511. Literatuur en stadscultuur tussen middeleeuwen en moderne tijd. Amsterdam, 1988.

De wereld volgens Thomas van der Noot. Muiderberg, 1982.

Poeschel, Sabine. *Studien zur Ikonographie der Erdteile in der Kunst des 16.-18. Jahrhunderts*. Munich, 1985.

Pollmann, Judith. "Eine natürliche Feindschaft: Ursprung und Funktion der Schwarzen Legende über Spanien in den Niederlanden, 1560–1581." In *Feindbilder. Die Darstellung der politischen Publizistik des Mittelalters und der Neuzeit*, ed. Franz Bosbach. Bayreuther Historische Kolloquien, vol. 6. Cologne, 1992.

Religious Choice in the Dutch Republic: The Reformation of Arnoldus Buchelius, 1565–1641. Manchester, 1999.

Prakash, Gyan. "Subaltern Studies as Postcolonial Criticism." *American Historical Review* 99 (1994): 1475–1490.

Pratt, Mary Louise. *Imperial Eyes: Travel Writing and Transculturation.* London, 1992.

Prestwich, Menna, ed. *International Calvinism, 1541–1715.* Oxford, 1985.

Prinsen, J. "Bronnen voor de kennis van leven en werken van Jan van Hout. II." *Tijdschrift voor Nederlandsche taal- en letterkunde,* n.s., 23 (1904): 193–256.

Quint, David. *Epic and Empire: Politics and Generic Form from Virgil to Milton.* Princeton, 1993.

"A Reconsideration of Montaigne's 'Des Cannibales.'" In Kupperman, *America in European Consciousness.*

Raesly, E. L. *Portrait of New Netherland.* New York, 1945.

Rees, Otto van. *Geschiedenis der staathuishoudkunde in Nederland tot het einde der achttiende eeuw.* 2 vols. Utrecht, 1865–1868.

Regteren Altena, I. Q. van. "Carel van Mander." *Elsevier's geïllustreerd maandschrift* 47 (1937): 153–69.

Reznicek, E. K. J. "Een en ander over Van Mander." *Oud Holland* 107 (1993): 75–83.

"Karel van Mander as a Fresco Painter." *The Hoogesteder Mercury* 10 (1989): 11–14.

Rink, Oliver. *Holland on the Hudson: An Economic and Social History of Dutch New York.* New York, 1986.

"The People of New Netherland: Notes on Non-English Immigration to New York in the Seventeenth Century." *New York History* 62 (1981): 61–82.

Robben, F. M. A. "Brandstichters en boekenkopers." In *Tussen twee culturen: De Nederlanden en de Iberische wereld, 1500–1800,* ed. P. J. A. N. Rietbergen et al. Nijmegen, 1988.

Robertson, William. *History of America.* 2 vols. London, 1777.

Roessingh, H. K. *Inlandse tabak: Expansie en contractie van een handelsgewas in de 17de en 18de eeuw in Nederland.* Zutphen, 1976.

Roever, N. de. "Het Nieuwe Doolhof, 'In de Oranje Pot' te Amsterdam." *Oud Holland* 6 (1888): 103–12.

Roey, Jan van. "De bevolking." In *Antwerpen in de XVIde eeuw.* Antwerp, 1975.

Rogier, L. J. "Over het karakter en omvang van de Nederlandse emigratie in de zestiende eeuw." *Historisch tijdschrift* 17 (1938): 5–27.

Roorda, D. J. *Het rampjaar 1672.* Bussum, 1971.

Root, Deborah. "Speaking Christian: Orthodoxy and Difference in Sixteenth-Century Spain." *Representations* 23 (1988): 118–34.

Rowen, Herbert H. "The Dutch Revolt: What Kind of Revolution." *Renaissance Quarterly* 43 (1990): 570–90.

John de Witt: Grand Pensionary of Holland. Princeton, 1978.

Royaards, H. J. "Bijdrage tot de geschiedenis van de Nederlandsche volksgeest in de XVI [sic] eeuw tegenover de Spaansche Inquisitie." *Archief voor kerkelijke geschiedenis* 1 (1829): 283–82.

Ryan, Michael. "Assimilating New Worlds in the Sixteenth and Seventeenth Centuries." *Comparative Studies in Society and History* 23 (1981): 519–38.

Sabin, Joseph, comp. *Bibliotheca Americana: A Dictionary of Books Relating to America, from its Discovery to the Present Time.* 29 vols. New York, 1868–1936.

Sayre, Gordon M. *Les Sauvages Américains: Representations of Native Americans in French and English Colonial Literature.* Chapel Hill, 1997.

Scammell, G. V. "The New World and Europe in the Sixteenth Century." *Historical Journal* 12 (1969): 389–412.

Scanlan, Thomas. *Colonial Writing and the New World, 1583–1671: Allegories of Desire.* Cambridge, 1999.

Schama, Simon. *The Embarrassment of Riches: An Interpretation of Dutch Culture in the Golden Age.* New York, 1987.

Schelven, A. A. van. "De opkomst van de idee der politieke tolerantie in de 15e eeuwsche Nederlanden." In *Uit den strijd der geesten.* Amsterdam, 1944.

Schenkeveld-Van der Dussen, Maria. *Dutch Literature in the Age of Rembrandt: Themes and Ideas.* Amsterdam, 1991.

Schmidt, Benjamin. "Mapping an Empire: Cartographic and Colonial Rivalry in Seventeenth-Century Dutch and English North America." *William and Mary Quarterly,* 3d ser., vol. 54 (1997): 549–78.

——— "Space, Time, Travel: Hugo de Groot, Johannes de Laet, and the Advancement of Geographic Learning." *Lias* 25, no. 2 (1998): 177–99.

Schulte Nordholt, J. W. "Nederlanders in Nieuw Nederland: De Oorlog van Kieft." *Bijdragen en Mededelingen van het Historisch Genootschap* 80 (1966): 38–94.

Schulten, C. M. *Nederlandse expansie in Latijns Amerika. Brazilië 1624–1654.* Bussum, 1968.

Schwartz, Stuart, ed. *Implicit Understanding: Observing, Reporting, and Reflecting on the Encounters Between Europeans and Other Peoples in the Early Modern Era.* Cambridge, 1994.

Scribner, Robert W. *For the Sake of Simple Folk: Popular Propaganda for the German Reformation.* Cambridge, 1981.

Seed, Patricia. *Ceremonies of Possession in Europe's Conquest of the New World, 1492–1640.* Cambridge, 1995.

——— "Colonial and Postcolonial Discourse." *Latin American Research Review* 26, no. 3 (1991): 181–200.

Selm, Bert van. *Inzichten en vergezichten: Zes beschouwingen over het onderzoek naar de geschiedenis van de Nederlandse boekhandel.* Ed. Hannie van Goinga and Paul Hoftijzer. Amsterdam, 1992.

——— *Een menighte treffelijcke boecken. Nederlandse boekhandelscatalogi in het begin van de zeventiende eeuw.* Utrecht, 1987.

Simmons, Richard C. "Americana in British Books, 1621–1760." In Kupperman, *America in European Consciousness.*

Skinner, Quentin. "Sir Thomas More's 'Utopia' and the Language of Renaissance Humanism." In *The Languages of Political Theory in Early-Modern Europe,* ed. Anthony Pagden. Cambridge, 1987.

Slive, Seymour, ed. *Frans Hals.* London, 1989.

Smail, Daniel Lord. *Imaginary Cartographies: Possession and Identity in Late Medieval Marseille.* Ithaca, 1999.

Smith, George. *Religion and Trade in New Netherland: Dutch Origins and American Development.* Ithaca, 1973.

Smits-Veldt, Mieke B. "'Waer in ons daden, boven de Romeynsche zijn te prijsen': Rederijkers dragen bij aan het Hollands zelfbewustzijn, Rotterdam 1598." *Spektator* 21 (1992): 83–100.

Snyder, James. "Jan Mostaert's West Indies Landscape." In Chiappelli, *First Images of America.*

Sousa-Leão, Joaquim de. *Frans Post, 1612–1680.* Amsterdam, 1973.

Spies, Marijke. *Rhetoric, Rhetoricians, and Poets: Studies in Renaissance Poetry and Poetics.* Ed. Henk Duits and Ton van Strien. Amsterdam, 1999.

"Verbeeldingen van Vrijheid: David en Mozes, Burgerhart en Bato, Brutus en Cato." *De zeventiende eeuw* 10 (1994): 141–58.

Spivak, Gayatri Chakravorty. "Subaltern Studies: Deconstructing Historiography." In *Selected Subaltern Studies,* ed. Ranajit Guha and Gayatri Chakravorty Spivak. Oxford, 1988.

Sterck, J. G. *Bronnen en samenstelling van Marnix' "Bienkorf der H. Roomsche Kercke."* Koninklijke Vlaamse Academie van Taal- en Letterkunde, 6th ser., no. 69. Leuven, 1952.

Stock, Jan van der, ed. *Antwerp: Story of a Metropolis.* Ghent, 1993.

Sturtevant, William C., and David Beers Quinn. "This New Prey: Eskimos in Europe in 1567, 1576 and 1577." In *Indians and Europe,* ed. Christian Feest. Aachen, 1987.

Sutherland, N. M. *The Massacre of St. Bartholomew and the European Conflict, 1559–1572.* New York, 1973.

"William of Orange and the Revolt of the Netherlands: A Missing Dimension." *Archiv für Reformationgeschichte* 74 (1983): 201–30.

Sutton, Peter C. *Masters of Seventeenth Century Dutch Genre Painting.* Philadelphia, 1984.

Swart, K. W. "The Black Legend During the Eighty Years War." In *Britain and the Netherlands,* ed. J. S. Bromley and E. H. Kossmann. Papers Delivered to the Anglo-Dutch Historical Conference, vol. 5. The Hague, 1975.

The Miracle of the Dutch Republic as Seen in the Seventeenth Century. London, 1969.

Willem van Oranje en de Nederlandse Opstand 1572–1584. Ed. R. P. Fagel, M. E. H. N. Mout, and H. F. K. van Nierop, introd. Alastair Duke and Jonathan I. Israel. The Hague, 1994.

Tanis, James, and Daniël Horst. *Images of Discord: A Graphic Interpretation of the Opening Decades of the Eighty Years' War.* Grand Rapids, Michigan, 1993.

Tex, Jan den. *Oldenbarnevelt.* 5 vols. Haarlem, 1960–1972.

Thierry de Bye Dólleman, M. "Jan Jansz Mostaert, schilder, een beroemd Haarlemmer (ca. 1473–ca.1555)." *Jaarboek van het Centraal Bureau voor Genealogie* 17 (1963): 123–36.

Thomas, Werner. "De Mythe van de Spaanse Inquisitie in de Nederlanden van de Zestiende Eeuw." *Bijdragen en mededelingen betreffende de geschiedenis der Nederlanden* 105 (1990): 325–53.

Thomsen, T. *Albert Eckhout, ein niederländischer Maler und sein Gönner Moritz der Brasilianer.* Copenhagen, 1938.

Tiele, P. A. *Bibliotheek van Nederlandsche pamfletten.* Amsterdam, 1858.

Tilmans, Karin. *Historiography and Humanism in Holland in the Age of Erasmus: Aurelius and the "Divisiekroniek" of 1517.* Nieuwkoop, 1992.

Tracy, James D. *A Financial Revolution in the Habsburg Netherlands: Renten and Renteniers in the County of Holland, 1515–1565.* Berkeley, 1985.

Trelease, Allen W. *Indian Affairs in Colonial New York: The Seventeenth Century.* Ithaca, 1960.

Troeyer, Benjamin de. *Bio-bibliographia franciscana neerlandica saeculi XVI.* 2 vols. Nieuwkoop, 1969–1970.

Truman, R. W., and A. Gordon Kinder. "The Pursuit of Spanish Heretics in the Low Countries: The Activities of Alonso del Canto." *Journal of Ecclesiastic History* 30 (1979): 65–93.

Turner, D. "Oviedo's 'Claribalte': The First American Novel." *Romance Notes* 6 (1964): 65–8.

Van Ryn, Elmer L. "Patriotic Propaganda and the Development of the Calvinist Party in the Netherlands, 1576–1581." Ph.D. diss., University of Michigan, 1955.

Van Zandt, Cynthia Jean. "Negotiating Settlement: Colonialism, Cultural Exchange, and Conflict in Early Colonial Atlantic North America, 1580–1660." Ph.D. diss., University of Connecticut, 1998.

Vandenbroeck, Paul. *Beeld van de andere, vertoog over het zelf. Over wilden en narren, boeren en bedelaars.* Antwerp, 1987.

et al. *America, bride of the sun: 500 years Latin America and the Low Countries.* Antwerp, 1992.

Veen, P. A. F. van. *De soeticheydt des buyten-levens, verghesselschapt met de boucken. Het hofdicht als tak van een Georgische litteratuur.* The Hague, 1960.

Veldhuyzen-Brouwer, A. J. "La Brevíssima relación de la destruyción de las Indias. Een vergelijkende studie van zeven Nederlandse vertalingen, 1578–1664." Master's thesis, University of Leiden, 1985.

Verduyn, W. D. *Emanuel van Meteren.* The Hague, 1926.

Verheyden, A. L. E. *Le Conseil des Troubles: List des condamnés.* Brussels, 1961.

Vermaseren, B. A. "Who was Reginaldus Gonsalvus Montanus?" *Bibliothèque d'Humanisme et Renaissance* 48 (1985): 47–77.

Vermeulen, Yves G. *'Tot profijt en genoegen': Motiveringen voor de produktie van Nederlandstalige gedrukte teksten, 1477–1540.* Groningen, 1986.

Vig, Alfredo. "Prefazione." In *La historia del mondo nuovo di Girolamo Benzoni Milanese,* ed. Alfredo Vig. Milan, 1965.

Visser, J. C. "Dichtheid van de bevolking in de laat-middeleeuwse stad." *Historisch Geografisch Tijdschrift* 3 (1985): 10–22.

Voet, Leon. *The Golden Compasses: A History and Evaluation of the Printing and Publishing Activities of the Officina Plantiniana at Antwerp.* 2 vols. Amsterdam, 1969–1973.

"De typografische bedrijvigheid te Antwerpen in de 16e eeuw." In *Antwerpen in de XVIde eeuw.* Antwerp, 1975.

Vosters, S. A. *Spanje in de Nederlandse literatuur.* Amsterdam, 1950.

Vrankrijker, A. C. J. de. *De motiveering van onzen Opstand.* Nijmegen, 1933.

Vries, Jan de. *European Urbanization, 1500–1800.* London, 1984.

Vries, Jan de, and A. M. van der Woude. *The First Modern Economy: Success, Failure, and Perseverance of the Dutch Economy, 1500–1815.* Cambridge, 1997.

Vrijman, L. C. "De kwestie, Wie was Exquemelin? volledig opgelost." *Tijdschrift voor geschiedenis* 47 (1932): 125–28.

Wagner, Henry R. "Peter Martyr and his Works." *Proceedings of the American Antiquarian Society* 56 (Oct. 1946): 239–88.

Watanabe, Hiroshi, comp. *Marco Polo Bibliography.* Tokyo, 1986.

Waterschoot, Werner. "The title page of Ortelius's *Theatrum Orbis Terrarum.*" *Quaerendo* 9 (1979): 43–68.

Wätjen, Hermann. *Das holländische Kolonialreich in Brasilien. Ein Kapitel aus der Kolonialgeschichte des 17. Jahrhunderts.* The Hague, 1921.

Wee, Herman van der. *The Growth of the Antwerp Market and the European Economy.* 3 vols. The Hague, 1963.

"Handel in de Zuidelijke Nederlanden." In *AGN* 6: 75–97.

Weinberg, Bernard. "Montaigne's Reading for 'Des Cannibales.'" In *Renaissance and Other Studies in Honor of William Leon Wiley.* Chapel Hill, 1968.

Weiss, E. "Ein neues Bild Jan Mostaerts." *Zeitschrift für Bildende Kunst,* n.s., 20 (1909/10): 215–17.

Werd, Guido de, ed. *Soweit der Erdkreis reicht: Johan Moritz von Nassau-Siegen, 1604–1679.* Kleve, 1979.

Weslager, C. A. "Did Minuit Buy Manhattan Island from the Indians?" *De Halve Maen* 43 (1968): 5–6.

New Sweden on the Delaware, 1638–1655. Wilmington, DE, 1988.

Westrem, Scott Douglas. "A Critical Edition of Johannes Witte de Hese's *Itinerarius,* the Middle Dutch Text, an English Translation, and Commentary, Together with an Introduction to European Accounts of Travel to the East (1240–1400). Ph.D. diss., Northwestern University, 1985.

Whatley, Janet. "Une Révérence Réciproque: Huguenot Writing on the New World." *University of Toronto Quarterly* 57 (1987/8): 270–89.

Whitehead, Neil L. "Introduction." In Walter Ralegh, *The Discoverie of the Large, Rich, and Bewtiful Empyre of Guiana,* ed. Neil L. Whitehead. The American Exploration and Travel Series, vol. 77. Norman, OK, 1997.

Whitehead, P. J. P., and M. Boeseman. *A Portrait of Dutch Seventeenth-Century Brazil: Animals, Plants and People by the Artists of John Maurits of Nassau.* Amsterdam, 1989.

Whitney, Charles. "The Naming of America as the Meaning of America: Vespucci, Publicity, Festivity, Modernity." *Clio* 22 (1993): 195–219.

Wijminga, P. J. *Festus Hommius.* Leiden, 1899.

Williams, James Homer. "Cultural Mingling and Religious Diversity Among Indians and Europeans in the Early Middle Colonies." Ph.D. diss., Vanderbilt University, 1993.

Williams, Sheila. "Les Ommegangs d'Anvers et les corteges du Lord-Maire de Londres." In *La Fêtes de la Renaissance,* ed. Jean Jacquot, 3 vols. (Paris, 1956–1975), 2:349–57.

Williams, Sheila, and Jean Jacquot. "Ommegangs anversois du temps de Bruegel et de Van Heemskerk." In *La Fêtes de la Renaissance,* ed. Jean Jacquot, 3 vols. (Paris, 1956–1975), 2:359–88.

Williamson, Arthur H. "Scots, Indians and Empire: The Scottish Politics of Civilization 1519–1609." *Past and Present* 150 (1996): 46–83.

Wilson, Charles. *Profit and Power: A Study of England and the Dutch Wars.* 2d ed. London, 1978.

Queen Elizabeth and the Revolt of the Netherlands. Berkeley, 1970.

Winichakul, Thongchai. *Siam Mapped: A History of the Geo-Body of a Nation.* Honolulu, 1994.

Winter, P. J. van. *De Westindische Compagnie ter kamer Stad en Lande.* The Hague, 1978.

Wintroub, Michael. "Civilizing the Savage and Making a King: The Royal Entry Festival of Henri II (Rouen, 1550)." *Sixteenth Century Journal* 29 (1998): 465–94.

Wiznitzer, Arnold. *The Jews in Colonial Brazil.* New York, 1960.

Worp, J. A. "Casper Barlaeus." *Oud Holland* 3 (1885): 241–65, 4 (1886): 24–40, 5 (1887): 93–125, 6 (1888): 87–102, 241–76, 7 (1889): 89–128.

Woude, A. M. van der. "De alphabetisering." In *AGN* 7: 257–64.

"Demografische ontwikkeling van de Noordelijke Nederlanden van 1500–1800." In *AGN* 5: 102–68.

Yardeni, Myriam. *La conscience nationale en France pendant les guerres de religion, 1559–1598.* Paris, 1971.

Zamora, Margarita. *Reading Columbus.* Berkeley, 1993.

Zandvliet, Kees. *De groote waereld in 't kleen geschildert: Nederlandse kartografie tussen de middeleeuwen en de industriële revolutie.* Alphen aan den Rijn, 1985.

"Johan Maurits and the cartography of Dutch Brazil." In Boogaart, *Johan Maurits van Nassau Siegen.*

Mapping for money: Maps, plans and topographical paintings and their role in Dutch overseas expansion during the sixteenth and seventeenth centuries. Amsterdam, 1998.

Zweite, Armin. *Marten de Vos als Maler: Eine Beitrag zur Geschichte der Antwerpener Malerei in der zweiten Hälfte des 16. Jahrhunderts.* Berlin, 1980.

Index